Enduring Legacies: Ancient and Medieval Cultures

Sixth Edition

Phillip C. Boardman

Custom Publishing
New York Boston San Fransisco
London Toronto Sydney Tokyo Singapore Madrid
Mexico City Munich Paris Cape Town Hong Kong Montreal

Cover Art: Courtesy of British Library.

Inside Cover: Physical map of Europe, by Tiber G. Roth, reprinted from *National Geographic Picture Atlas of Our World,* 1991. Copyright © 1991, 1990 by National Geographic Society, Washington, DC. All Rights Reserved.

Printed in the United States of America

20 19 18 17 16 15 14

2009300068

CY/LD

Pearson Custom Publishing is a division of

www.pearsonhighered.com

ISBN 10: 0-558-22850-X
ISBN 13: 978-0-558-22850-7

Copyright Acknowledgments

Grateful acknowledgment is made to the following sources for permission to reprint material copyrighted or controlled by them:

"Slide #1: Cosmographica for inside back cover," by Petrus Apianus (1545).

"The Story of the Flood," by translator N. K. Sandars, reprinted from *The Epic of Gilgamesh: An English Version with an Introduction by N. K. Sandars*, Revised Edition (1972), by permission of Penguin Books, Ltd.

"Selections from The Law Code," by Hammurabi, reprinted from *Babylonian and Assyrian Laws, Contracts and Letters* (1904).

"Minoan Snake Goddess from Knossos," courtesy of Erich Resource/Art Resource.

"Theogony," by Hesiod, reprinted from *Theogony*, translated by Norman O. Brown (1953), by permission of Prentice Hall, Inc.

"Poems #1–7," by Sappho, reprinted from *The Poems of Sappho* (1966).

"Olympian Ode XI," and "Pythian Ode VII," by Pindar, reprinted from *The Odes of Pindar*, translated by C. M. Bowra (1969), Penguin Books, Ltd.

"Introduction" and "The Story of Helen and Alexander (Paris)," by Herodotus, reprinted from *The Persian Wars*, translated by George Rawlinson (1942).

"The Story of Adrastus," by Herodotus, reprinted from *The History of Herodotus* Volume 1, translated by George Rawlinson (1875).

"Introduction," "Pericles' Funeral Oration," and "The Plague in Athens," by Thucydides, reprinted from *The Peloponnesian War*, translated by Benjamin Jowett (1942), by permission of Chrys Ingraham.

Excerpt from *Lysistrata*, by Aristophanes, edited by Sarah Ruden (2003), Hackett Publishing Company, Inc.

Excerpts from *The First Philosophers of Greece*, by Arthur Fairbanks (1898).

"The Oath," and "The Sacred Disease," by Hippocrates, reprinted from *Genuine Works of Hippocrates*, translated by Francis Adams (1849).

"Letter to Menoeceus," by Epicurus, reprinted from *Hellenistic Philosophy*, translated by Brad Inwood and L. P. Gerson (1988), by permission of Hackett Publishing Company, Inc.

"The Sand Reckoner," by Archimedes, reprinted from *The Works of Archimedes*, translated by T. L. Heath (1897).

Excerpts from *Discourses and Selected Writings*, by Epicteus, edited by Robert Dobbin (2008), Orion Publishing Group, Ltd.

Excerpt from *Almagest*, by Ptolemy, edited by G. J. Toomer (1984), by permission of Gerald Duckworth & Co., Ltd.

"Symposium," by Plato, reprinted from *The Dialogues of Plato Translated into English*, Volume 1, edited by Benjamin Jowett (1892), by permission of MacMillan.

"The Figure of the Cave," by Plato, reprinted from *The Republic*, translated by H. D. F. Lee (1955), Penguin Books, Ltd.

"The Story of Atlantis," by Plato, reprinted from *Timaeus*, translated by Benjamin Jowett (1892).

"Tragedy," by Aristotle, reprinted from *The Poetics of Aristotle*, translated by S. H. Butcher (1895).

"The Four Causes," by Plato, reprinted from *Physics*, translated by R. P. Hardie and R. K. Gaye (1930), Oxford University Press.

"The Pont du Gard in southern (Nimes) France, 19 BCE," courtesy of Giraudon/Art Resource.

"The Roman Republic Compared with Others," by Polybius, reprinted from *The Rise of the Roman Empire*, translated by Ian Scott-Kilvert (1979), by permission of Penguin Books, Ltd.

"Death Has No Sting" by Cicero, reprinted from *Selected Political Speeches of Cicero*, translated by Michael Grant (1969), by permission of Penguin Books, Ltd.

Excerpts from *Odi et Amo:The Complete Poetry of Catallus*, by Catallus, translated by Roy Arthur Swanson, (1959), by permission of Prentice Hall, Inc.

"The Fourth Eclogue," by Virgil, reprinted from *The Poems of Virgil, Translated into English Prose* (1872).

"The Landing Near Carthage" and "The Fall of Troy," by Virgil, reprinted from *The Aeneid of Virgil: A Verse Translation*, translated by Rolfe Humphries (1987), by permission of Simon & Schuster, Inc.

"Romulus and Remus," "The Abduction of the Sabine Women," "The Rape of Lucretia," "Horatius at the Bridge," "Cincinnatus Called from his Farm," by Livy, reprinted from *The Early History of Rome*, translated by Aubrey de Selincourt (1960), by permission of Penguin Books, Ltd.

"Creation and Flood" and "Arachne," by Ovid, reprinted from *The Metamorphoses of Ovid*, translated by Mary M. Innes (1955), by permission of Penguin Books, Ltd.

"Interior of Hagia Sophia in Istanbul, Turkey," courtesy of Giraudon/Art Resource.

"The Burning of Rome," by Tacitus, reprinted from *The Works of Tacitus: The Oxford Translation*, Revised Edition, Volume I (1903).

"The Jews," by Tacitus, reprinted from *The Works of Tacitus: The Oxford Translation*, Revised Edition, Volume II (1903).

"The Germans, from Germania," by Tacitus, reprinted from *The Complete Works of Tacitus*, translated by Alfred John Church and William Jackson Brodribb (1942), by permission of Random House, Inc.

Excerpts from *Meditations*, by Marcus Aurelius (1964), Penguin Books, Ltd.

"Correspondence between Pliny the Younger and Trajan," reprinted from *The Early Christian Persecutions*, Volume IV, translated by Dana Munro and Edith Bramball (1898).

"The Secret Gospel of Mark" and "The Infancy Gospel of Thomas, from Apocryphal Gospels," reprinted from *The Complete Gospels: Annotated Scholars Version*, edited by Robert J. Miller (1992), by permission of Polebridge Press.

"The Nicene Creed" and "The Apostles' Creed," reprinted from *Book of Common Prayer* (1549).

"The Gospel of Thomas," reprinted from *The Complete Gospels: Annotated Scholars Version*, Revised Edition, edited by Robert J. Miller (1994), by permission of Polebridge Press.

"Prescriptions Against the Heretics," by Tertullian, reprinted from *Early Latin Theology*, translated by Stanley Lawrence Greenslade (1956), by permission of Westminster John Knox Press.

"Plato and Christianity," by Saint Augustine, reprinted from *Concerning the City of God Against the Pagans*, translated by Henry Bettenson (1972), by permission of Penguin Books, Ltd.

"Excerpts from Books 2 & 3," by Saint Augustine, reprinted from *On Christian Doctrine*, translated by D. W. Robertson, Jr. (1958), by permission of Bobbs Merrill Co.

Excerpts from *The Consolation of Philosophy*, Revised Edition, by Boethius, translated by Victor Watts (1999), Penguin Books, Ltd.

"Selections from The Rule of Saint Benedict," by Saint Benedict, reprinted from *Benedict of Nursia*, translated by Cardinal Gasquet (1925), Chatto & Windus.

Excerpts from *The Koran*, translated with notes by N. J. Dawood (1999), Penguin Books, Ltd.

"The Night Journey to Jerusalem," by Ibn Ishaq reprinted from *The Life of Muhammad (Sirat Rasul Allah),* translated by Alfred Guillaume (1955), Oxford University Press.

"Painting of Boethius listening to the instruction of Philosophy while Fortune turns a wheel," courtesy of Wallace Collection/Bridgeman Art Library.

"Selections from Feudal Documents: Homage and Ordeal by Hot Iron," by Oliver J. Thatcher and Edgar H. McNeal, reprinted from *A Source Book for Medieval History* (1905).

"The Song of Roland," translated by Glyn Burgess (1990), Penguin Books, Ltd.

Excerpts from *A History of the Expedition to Jerusalem*, 1095-1127, by Fulcher of Chartres, edited by Frances Rita Ryan (1973), University of Tennessee Press.

"The University of Paris and Heloise" by Peter Abelard, reprinted from *The Story of My Misfortunes: The Autobiography of Peter Abelard* (1922).

"Letter I. Heloise to Abelard," by Heloise, reprinted from *The Letters of Abelard and Heloise*, edited by Betty Radice (1974), by permission of Penguin Books, Ltd.

"Protestificatio," by Hildegard Bingen, reprinted from *Scivias*, translated by Bruce Hozeski (1986), Bear and Company.

Excerpts from *The Book of Contemplation*, by Usama ibn Munqidh, edited by Paul M. Cobb (2008), Orion Publishing Group, Ltd.

"Letters to: Bernard of Clairvaux, Pope Anastasius IV, Monks of Zwiefalten, Elisabeth of Schonau, Wibert of Gembloux," by Hildegard Bingen, reprinted from *The Book of Divine Works, with Letters and Songs*, translated by Matthew Fox (1987), Bear and Company.

"Prologue" and "The Werewolf," by Marie France, reprinted from *French Medieval Romances from the Lays of Marie de France*, translated by Eugene Mason (1911).

"The Rules of Love," by Andreas Capellanus, reprinted from *The Art of Courtly Love*, translated by Phillip Boardman.

"The Town of Dire Adventures from The Knight with the Lion (Yvain)," by Chrétien de Troyes, reprinted from *Arthurian Romances*, translated by William Kibler (1991), by permission of Penguin Books, Ltd.

"Perceval in the Castle of the Fisher King from The Story of the Grail," by Chrétien de Troyes, reprinted from *Arthurian Romances*, edited by William Kibler (1991), Victor Boyer.

"Sigurd and the Dragon," reprinted from *The Saga of the Volsungs*, translated by Eriikr Magnusson and William Morris (1907).

"Magna Carta," reprinted from *Source Problems in English History*, edited by Albert Beebe White and Wallace Notestein (1915).

"Garden of Pleasure and Advice of Reason," by Guillaume de Lorris and Jean de Meun, reprinted from *The Romance of the Rose*, edited by Frances Horgan (1994), Oxford University Press.

"Statutes of Gregory IX for the University of Paris in 1231," reprinted from *University of Pennsylvania Translations and Reprints* (1897).

"On the Existence of God" and "Third Article: Whether God Exists," by Thomas Aquinas, reprinted from *Summa Theologica* (1947), by permission of Ave Maria Press.

"St. Mary Magdalene," "St. Dominic," and "The Eleven Thousand Virgins," by Jacobus de Voragine, reprinted from *The Golden Legend*, edited by Christopher Stace (1998), Orion Publishing Group, Ltd.

"Unam Sanctam," by Pope VIII, reprinted from *Basic Documents in Medieval History*, edited by Norton Downs (1959), by permission of Polynesian Society.

"O Fortuna" and "In Taberna," reprinted from *Selections from the Carmina Burana*, translated by Parlett, (1986), by permission of Penguin Books, Ltd.

"Ja nuls homs pris ne dira sa raison," by King I, reprinted from *Lyrics of the Middle Ages: An Anthology*, translated by James J. Wilhelm (1990), Taylor & Francis.

"A chantar m'er de so q'ieu no volria," by Contessa Dia, reprinted from *The Writings of Medieval Women: An Anthology* (1994), Taylor & Francis.

"Under der Linden," by Walther von der Vogelweide, reprinted from *Medieval Song: An Anthology of Hymns and Lyrics*, edited by James J. Wilhelm (1971), Penguin Putnam, Inc.

"Sonnet 10," "Sonnet 15," and "Sonnet 25," by Dante Alighieri, reprinted from *La Vita Nuova*, edited by Barbara Reynolds (1969), Penguin Classics.

"The Cremation of the Strasbourg Jewry, from Chronicle," by Jacob Konigshofen, reprinted from *The Jew in the Medieval World: A Source Book*, edited by Jacob R. Marcus, Union for Reform Judaism Press.

"Meditations on the Passions," by Richard Rolle, reprinted from *Yorkshire Writers: Richard Rolle*, Volume 1, translated by Phillip Boardman (1895).

"Selections from The Decameron," by Boccaccio, reprinted from *Tales from the Decameron of Giovanni Boccaccio*, translated by Richard Aldington Giovanni (1930), by permission of Rosica Colin Ltd.

"Wife of Bath's Prologue" and "Wife of Bath's Tale," by Geoffrey Chaucer, reprinted from *The Canterbury Tales in Modern English*, edited by Joseph Glaser, by permission of Hackett Publishing Company, Inc.

"The Book of Margery Kempe" translated by Phillip Boardman.

Contents

TIME LINES

Enduring Legacies

Introduction

Legacies, or inheritances, are mixed blessings. The treasures that are handed over to us may give us freedom, or they may bind and blind us. They may mean good fortune or bad luck. In the West our cultural legacies include influential perceptions of the nature of the divine; important habits of argument, critique, and self-examination; deep commitments to the ethical and moral grounding of human action; trust in the social efficacy of institutions; restless passion for exploration and discovery; recognition of the power of art to inspire, enslave, and subvert; and a striking faith in technological innovation. But they have also included slavery, exploitation of others, confusion of private interests and universal principles, and deeply held national and ethnic prejudices.

The pun in the title of this book lays this paradox open to view. For while the past may call up for some of us images of enduring monuments—the best of our music, art, literature, philosophy, and drama—it may also be felt as a burden to be endured (in a far deeper sense than the more obvious weight that students feel in the reading and writing assignments). The West, true to its habit of self-examination, developed myths to explore this paradox. The myth of progress values the power of education, enlightenment, and innovation to raise us above the limits and superstitions of a primitive past and promises hope for even higher achievements in the future. But the myth of the Golden Age finds in the past glimpses of lost worlds of peace, of harmony, of justice and equality, of reverence towards nature, of communion with the divine—all now gone because of a waywardness and depravity that subverts hope for the future.

The readings in this book have endured to become part of our legacy because they open up just such issues for serious reflection and discussion. My belief is that by understanding where we've been as humans, by seeing how we've changed for the better or for the worse, and by reflecting on what we mean by "better" or "worse," we will be equipped, as Henry David Thoreau said, to live deliberately, to know who we are and what we stand for.

* * *

This book contains selections chosen to supplement longer readings for a historically-organized text-based course in Western humanities. As such, I have avoided those works which are easily and cheaply available separately and are likely to be read in their entirety—*Odyssey,* Greek tragedies, books of the *Bible, Beowulf,* or the *Divine Comedy,* for instance. What does appear here is a modest selection of readings likely to be useful for discovering important points about historical change, political and social institutions, literary and philosophical influence, and which make sense in excerpts. Materials from the ancient Near East and from Islam are included because of their importance in the development of the West.

The guidance and suggestions of many people went into the making of this book, especially Dennis Cronan, David Fenimore, Craig Gibson, Cheryll Glotfelty, Frank Hartigan, Alison Harvey, Jen Hill, Horst Lange, James Mardock, Marc Oxoby, Eric Rasmussen, Valerie Reed, Bernard Schopen, and Kevin Stevens. As always, the many students who have used the book have been forthright and insightful in their comments and suggestions. I am also grateful for the support and encouragement of Jodie Helman, of Neal Ferguson, Director of Core Humanities at the University of Nevada, and of our series editor at Pearson, Jodelle Brosig Kibby.

From Megiddo, Israel, terracotta, fragment. Israel Museum (IDAM), Jerusalem, Israel. Courtesy of Erich Lessing/Art Resource.

The World of the Ancient Near East

Of the many inventions that came out of the Ancient Near East—a settled agriculture, the birth of cities, a calendar combining lunar months and solar year, a mathematics based on 60 that we still use to measure time and angles, the signs of the Zodiac, the study of astronomy, the use of the "Pythagorean" rule for right triangles, monumental architecture (the *zigurrats),* and many more—none may be more profound than the invention of writing. The first writing symbols were pictures scratched in clay. At first the symbol referred to the object (*sun,* for example), then to an idea associated with the object (*heat* or *light,* perhaps), then to the pronounced word ("sun"), and then perhaps to the syllable ("sun" or "son," as in rebus games or in texting shortcuts where the symbol 4 stands for the syllable "for"). A *logographic* writing system, with a symbol for each word (like Chinese), requires thousands of different symbols; a *syllabic* system, where the symbols represent the standard syllables used to pronounce words (like Japanese or Cherokee), might require around 75 to 100 symbols. The Phoenicians went the next step, using the symbols to represent the individual sounds customarily used in speaking a language. This *alphabetic* system (from Greek "alpha" and "beta") is very efficient because of the small number of symbols to be learned, but its dependence on pronunciation for relating symbols to words means that it is far more local and less universal than *pictographic* (picture-writing) or logographic systems (think about the signs in airports or along highways that are not tied to individual languages or pronunciations). In the ancient Near East a method of writing developed which proved flexible for all of these writing systems. Scribes very early found that pressing the end of a reed carved with a wedge shape (*cuneiform* writing) into clay was faster than drawing pictorial lines in the clay. The clusters of wedge-shapes, first based on pictures, came to stand for words, then syllables, then sounds, of a great variety of languages for almost 3,000 years. The baked clay, buried in destroyed libraries and archives, has lasted very well, but has usually been broken into small pieces. The tablet at left, for instance, shows the fragmentary nature of the text that scholars must often work with. This is a Middle Babylonian text of the *Epic of Gilgamesh,* the greatest literary work of ancient Mesopotamia. The fragment here describes the death of Gilgamesh's companion, Enkidu. It was found in Megiddo, Israel, and pre-dates the writing of the Hebrew Bible.

The Epic of Gilgamesh

The Epic of Gilgamesh *is among the oldest literary works to survive into the modern world. Its hero, Gilgamesh, was actually a king in the Sumerian city of Uruk around 2700 BCE, but the epic poem about him dates from centuries later and recounts events that are clearly legendary. The best text of the poem, on twelve fragmentary cuneiform tablets in the Akkadian language, survives from the great library in Nineveh of the Assyrian king Ashurbanipal (reigned 669–627 BCE). Versions of the poem have been found in other languages, as well.*

In the poem, the gods, troubled at the harsh rule of King Gilgamesh, create a wild man named Enkidu, who lives among animals in the forest. After being initiated into civilization by a prostitute, Enkidu enters the city of Uruk, where he is bested in a trial of strength with Gilgamesh. Afterwards, as companions, the two set out to kill Humbaba, the guardian of a cedar forest. After Gilgamesh refuses an offer of marriage from Ishtar, the goddess of love, he and Enkidu kill the sacred bull sent by Ishtar to destroy him. As punishment for slaying the bull, Enkidu falls ill, troubled by dreams telling him that the gods have decided he must die. After lamenting the death of his friend and organizing an elaborate state funeral for him, Gilgamesh sets out on a solitary quest for Utnapishtim, the only man reputed to have been granted immortality by the gods. In Tablet 11, translated here, Utnapishtim tells the story of a great flood, in which he and his wife were chosen to be the only survivors. Utnapishtim then tells Gilgamesh where to find a plant that will restore his youth. When Gilgamesh has the plant, it is stolen by a serpent, and the unhappy king returns, as a mortal who must die, to his home in Uruk.

The flood story was apparently an important part of Mesopotamian lore, and several similar stories survive in Babylonian texts, such as the Enuma Elish, *as well as in the book of Genesis in the Hebrew Bible. Genesis 11:31, in fact, says that Abraham migrated to Canaan from the Mesopotamian city of Ur, and therefore it is interesting to note parallels between the Genesis story of Noah's flood and the older account in the* Gilgamesh *epic. It*

Reprinted from *The Epic of Gilgamesh: An English Version with an Introduction*, Revised Edition, translated by N. K. Sandars (Penguin, 1972).

seems likely that the migrating Hebrew tribes carried with them the well-remembered story of the great flood which destroyed humankind. Also like the flood story in Genesis, Utnapishtim's story, especially in the speeches of the old god Ea, offers an insight into the nature of the gods and their care for humans.

THE STORY OF THE FLOOD

'You know the city Shurrupak, it stands on the banks of Euphrates? That city grew old and the gods that were in it were old. There was Anu, lord of the firmament, their father, and warrior Enlil their counsellor, Ninurta the helper, and Ennugi watcher over canals; and with them also was Ea. In those days the world teemed, the people multiplied, the world bellowed like a wild bull, and the great god was aroused by the clamour. Enlil heard the clamour and he said to the gods in council, "The uproar of mankind is intolerable and sleep is no longer possible by reason of the babel." So the gods agreed to exterminate mankind. Enlil did this, but Ea because of his oath warned me in a dream. He whispered their words to my house of reeds, "Reed-house, reed-house! Wall, O wall, hearken reed-house, wall reflect; O man of Shurrupak, son of Ubara-Tutu; tear down your house and build a boat, abandon possessions and look for life, despise worldly goods and save your soul alive. Tear down your house, I say, and build a boat. These are the measurements of the barque as you shall build her: let her beam equal her length, let her deck be roofed like the vault that covers the abyss; then take up into the boat the seed of all living creatures."

'When I had understood I said to my lord, "Behold, what you have commanded I will honour and perform, but how shall I answer the people, the city, the elders?" Then Ea opened his mouth and said to me, his servant, "Tell them this: I have learnt that Enlil is wrathful against me, I dare no longer walk in his land nor live in his city; I will go down to the Gulf to dwell with Ea my lord. But on you he will rain down abundance, rare fish and shy wild-fowl, a rich harvest-tide. In the evening the rider of the storm will bring you wheat in torrents."

'In the first light of dawn all my household gathered round me, the children brought pitch and the men whatever was necessary. On the fifth day I laid the keel and the ribs, then I made fast the planking. The ground-space was one acre, each side of the deck measured one hundred and twenty cubits, making a square. I built six decks below, seven in all, I divided them into nine sections with bulkheads between. I drove in wedges where needed, I saw to the punt-poles, and laid in supplies. The carriers brought oil in baskets, I poured pitch into the furnace and asphalt and oil; more oil was consumed in caulking, and more again the master of the boat took into his stores. I slaughtered bullocks for the people and every day I killed sheep. I gave the shipwrights wine to drink as though it were river water, raw wine and red wine and oil and white wine. There was feasting then as there is at the time of the New Year's festival; I myself anointed my head. On the seventh day the boat was complete.

'Then was the launching full of difficulty; there was shifting of ballast above and below till two thirds was submerged. I loaded into her all that I had of gold and of living things, my family, my kin, the beasts of the field both wild and tame, and all the craftsmen. I sent them on board, for the time that Shamash had ordained was already fulfilled when he said, "In the evening, when the rider of the storm sends down the destroying rain, enter the boat and batten her down." The time was fulfilled, the evening came, the rider of the storm sent down the rain. I looked out at the weather and it was terrible, so I too boarded the boat and battened her down. All was now complete, the battening and the caulking; so I handed the tiller to Puzur-Amurri the steersman, with the navigation and the care of the whole boat.

'With the first light of dawn a black cloud came from the horizon; it thundered within where Adad, lord of the storm was riding. In front over hill and plain Shullat and Hanish, heralds of the storm, led on. Then the gods of the abyss rose up; Nergal pulled out the dams of the nether waters, Ninurta the war-lord threw down the dykes, and the seven judges of hell, the Annunaki, raised their torches, lighting the land with their livid flame. A stupor of despair went up to heaven when the god of the storm turned daylight to darkness, when he smashed the land like a cup. One whole day the tempest raged, gathering fury as it went, it poured over the people like the tides of battle; a man could not see his brother nor the people be seen from heaven. Even the gods were terrified at the flood, they fled to the highest heaven, the firmament of Anu; they crouched against the walls, cowering like curs. Then Ishtar the sweet-voiced Queen of Heaven cried out like a woman in travail: "Alas the days of old are turned to dust because I commanded evil; why did I command this evil in the council of all the gods? I commanded wars to destroy the people, but are they not my people, for I brought them forth? Now like the spawn of fish they float in the ocean." The great gods of heaven and of hell wept, they covered their mouths.

'For six days and six nights the winds blew, torrent and tempest and flood overwhelmed the world, tempest and flood raged together like warring hosts. When the seventh day dawned the storm from the south subsided, the sea grew calm, the flood was stilled; I looked at the face of the world and there was silence, all mankind was turned to clay. The surface of the sea stretched as flat as a roof-top; I opened a hatch and the light fell on my face. Then I bowed low, I sat down and I wept, the tears streamed down my face, for on every side was the waste of water. I looked for land in vain, but fourteen leagues distant there appeared a mountain, and there the boat grounded; on the mountain of Nisir the boat held fast, she held fast and did not budge. One day she held, and a second day on the mountain of Nisir she held fast and did not budge. A third day, and a fourth day she held fast on the mountain and did not budge; a fifth day and a sixth day she held fast on the mountain. When the seventh day dawned I loosed a dove and let her go. She flew away, but finding no resting-place she returned. Then I loosed a swallow, and she flew away but finding no resting-place she returned. I loosed a raven, she saw that the waters had retreated, she ate, she flew around, she cawed, and she did not come back. Then I threw everything open to the four winds, I made a sacrifice and poured out a libation on the mountain top. Seven and again seven cauldrons I set up on their stands, I heaped up wood and cane and cedar and myrtle. When the gods smelled the sweet savour, they gathered like flies over the sacrifice. Then, at last, Ishtar also came, she lifted her necklace with the jewels of heaven that once Anu had made to please her. "O you gods here present, by the lapis lazuli round my neck I shall remember these days as I remember the jewels of my throat; these last days I shall not forget. Let all the gods gather round the sacrifice, except Enlil. He shall not approach this offering, for without reflection he brought the flood; he consigned my people to destruction."

'When Enlil had come, when he saw the boat, he was wrath and swelled with anger at the gods, the host of heaven, "Has any of these mortals escaped? Not one was to have survived the destruction." Then the god of the wells and canals Ninurta opened his mouth and said to the warrior Enlil, "Who is there of the gods that can devise without Ea? It is Ea alone who knows all things." Then Ea opened his mouth and spoke to warrior Enlil, "Wisest of gods, hero Enlil, how could you so senselessly bring down the flood?

> Lay upon the sinner his sin,
> Lay upon the transgressor his transgression,
> Punish him a little when he breaks loose,
> Do not drive him too hard or he perishes;
> Would that a lion had ravaged mankind
> Rather than the flood,
> Would that a wolf had ravaged mankind
> Rather than the flood,
> Would that famine had wasted the world
> Rather than the flood,
> Would that pestilence had wasted mankind
> Rather than the flood.

It was not I that revealed the secret of the gods; the wise man learned it in a dream. Now take your counsel what shall be done with him."

'Then Enlil went up into the boat, he took me by the hand and my wife and made us enter the boat and kneel down on either side, he standing between us. He touched our foreheads to bless us saying, "In time past Utnapishtim was a mortal man; henceforth he and his wife shall live in the distance at the mouth of the rivers." Thus it was that the gods took me and placed me here to live in the distance, at the mouth of the rivers.'

Hammurabi (1792–1750 BCE)

THE LAW CODE

The original text of Hammurabi's Law Code *is a cuneiform inscription on a stone monument, now in the Louvre Museum in Paris, discovered in Persia in 1901–1902. Under a relief carving of Hammurabi praying to the god of justice, some 282 paragraphs record royal pronouncements relating to punishments, persons (social stratification), families (marriage and patriarchal control), and compensation (property and contracts). Excerpts from Hammurabi's laws have been found all over the region from many cultures and periods, attesting to the importance of this formulation of a system of justice.*

Law codes always provide an interesting window into a culture. Hammurabi's laws do not, in fact, comprise a complete law code, for they assume a large body of well-known common law and custom. At first glance, Hammurabi's laws may not seem to be particularly fair or just. They enshrine the principle of lex talionis *("an eye for an eye"), as do ancient Hebrew laws. It is good first to imagine rule by arbitrary and absolute tyrants to conceive what is important about these laws: they are written down, in public, for all to see and know; they apply to all people; they prescribe, but also limit, the punishment for specified crimes; and they represent an attempt to realize ideals of justice and impartiality. Hammurabi's own writings speak of his desire "to cause justice to prevail in the land, to destroy the wicked and the evil, that the strong may not oppress the weak."*

Unlike the Ten Commandments given to Moses in the biblical book of Exodus, most of Hammurabi's laws take the form of case law: "If one does such-and-such, then this shall be done." The laws identify proper punishments for specific kinds of violations, attempting to match the penalty with the perceived severity of the crime. They carefully define relationships within the society according to an established hierarchy of rank and financial status. Intent and chance are also taken into account: one is usually not seriously liable for events that are accidental.

These excerpts from Hammurabi's law code are translated by C. H. W. Johns, *Babylonian and Assyrian Laws, Contracts and Letters* (New York: Scribner's, 1904). The numbering of the translation follows the traditional order.

[Selections]

1. If a man has accused another of laying a *nêrtu* (death spell?) upon him, but has not proved it, he shall be put to death.
2. If a man has accused another of laying a *kispu* (spell) upon him, but has not proved it, the accused shall go to the sacred river, he shall plunge into the sacred river, and if the sacred river shall conquer him, he that accused him shall take possession of his house. If the sacred river shall show his innocence and he is saved, his accuser shall be put to death. He that plunged into the sacred river shall appropriate the house of him that accused him.
3. If a man has borne false witness in a trial, or has not established the statement that he has made, if that case be a capital trial, that man shall be put to death.
8. If a patrician has stolen ox, sheep, ass, pig, or sheep, whether from a temple, or a house, he shall pay thirtyfold. If he be a plebeian, he shall return tenfold. If the thief cannot pay, he shall be put to death.
14. If a man has stolen a child, he shall be put to death.
15. If a man has induced either a male or female slave from the house of a patrician, or plebeian, to leave the city, he shall be put to death.
16. If a man has harbored in his house a male or female slave from a patrician's or plebeian's house, and has not caused the fugitive to leave on the demand of the officer over the slaves condemned to public forced labor, that householder shall be put to death.
17. If a man has caught either a male or female runaway slave in the open field and has brought him back to his owner, the owner of the slave shall give him two shekels of silver.
18. If such a slave will not name his owner, his captor shall bring him to the palace, where he shall be examined as to his past and returned to his owner.
19. If the captor has secreted that slave in his house and afterward that slave has been caught in his possession, he shall be put to death.
20. If the slave has fled from the hands of his captor, the latter shall swear to the owner of the slave and he shall be free from blame.
21. If a man has broken into a house he shall be killed before the breach and buried there.
22. If a man has committed highway robbery and has been caught, that man shall be put to death.
23. If the highwayman has not been caught, the man that has been robbed shall state on oath what he has lost and the city or district governor in whose territory or district the robbery took place shall restore to him what he has lost.
24. If a life [has been lost], the city or district governor shall pay one mina of silver to the deceased's relatives.
25. If a fire has broken out in a man's house and one who has come to put it out has coveted the property of the householder and appropriated any of it, that man shall be cast into the self-same fire.
44. If a man has taken a piece of virgin soil to open up, on a three years' lease, but has left it alone, has not opened up the land, in the fourth year he shall break it up, hoe it, and plough it, and shall return it to the owner of the field, and shall measure out ten GUR of corn for each *GAN* of land.

45. If a man has let his field to a farmer and has received his rent for the field but afterward the field has been flooded by rain, or a storm has carried off the crop, the loss shall be the farmer's.
46. If he has not received the rent of his field, whether he let it for a half, or for a third, of the crop, the farmer and the owner of the field shall share the corn that is left in the field, according to their agreement.
47. If a tenant farmer, because he did not start farming in the early part of the year, has sublet the field, the owner of the field shall not object; his field has been cultivated; at harvest-time he shall take rent, according to his agreement.
108. If the mistress of a beer-shop has not received corn as the price of beer or has demanded silver on an excessive scale, and has made the measure of beer less than the measure of corn, that beer-seller shall be prosecuted and drowned.
109. If the mistress of a beer-shop has assembled seditious slanderers in her house and those seditious persons have not been captured and have not been haled to the palace, that beer-seller shall be put to death.
110. If a votary, who is not living in the convent, open a beer-shop, or enter a beer-shop for drink, that woman shall be put to death.
111. If the mistress of a beer-shop has given sixty *KA* of *sakani* beer in the time of thirst, at harvest, she shall take fifty *KA* of corn.
126. If a man has said that something of his is lost, which is not, or has alleged a depreciation, though nothing of his is lost, he shall estimate the depreciation on oath, and he shall pay double whatever he has estimated.
127. If a man has caused the finger to be pointed at a votary, or a man's wife, and has not justified himself, that man shall be brought before the judges, and have his forehead branded.
128. If a man has taken a wife and has not executed a marriage-contract, that woman is not a wife.
129. If a man's wife be caught lying with another, they shall be strangled and cast into the water. If the wife's husband would save his wife, the king can save his servant.
130. If a man has ravished another's betrothed wife, who is a virgin, while still living in her father's house, and has been caught in the act, that man shall be put to death; the woman shall go free.
131. If a man's wife has been accused by her husband, and has not been caught lying with another, she shall swear her innocence, and return to her house.
132. If a man's wife has the finger pointed at her on account of another, but has not been caught lying with him, for her husband's sake she shall plunge into the sacred river.
133. If a man has been taken captive, and there was maintenance in his house, but his wife has left the house and entered into another man's house; because that woman has not preserved her body, and has entered into the house of another, that woman shall be prosecuted and shall be drowned.
134. If a man has been taken captive, but there was not maintenance in his house, and his wife has entered into the house of another, that woman has no blame.
135. If a man has been taken captive, but there was no maintenance in his house for his wife, and she has entered into the house of another, and has borne him children, if in the future her [first] husband shall return and regain his city, that

woman shall return to her first husband, but the children shall follow their own father.

136. If a man has left his city and fled, and, after he has gone, his wife has entered into the house of another; if the man return and seize his wife, the wife of the fugitive shall not return to her husband, because he hated his city and fled.
137. If a man has determined to divorce a concubine who has borne him children, or a votary who has granted him children, he shall return to that woman her marriage-portion, and shall give her the usufruct of field, garden, and goods, to bring up her children. After her children have grown up, out of whatever is given to her children, they shall give her one son's share, and the husband of her choice shall marry her.
138. If a man has divorced his wife, who has not borne him children, he shall pay over to her as much money as was given for her bride-price and the marriage-portion which she brought from her father's house, and so shall divorce her.
139. If there was no bride-price, he shall give her one mina of silver, as a price of divorce.
140. If he be a plebeian, he shall give her one-third of a mina of silver.
141. If a man's wife, living in her husband's house, has persisted in going out, has acted the fool, has wasted her house, has belittled her husband, he shall prosecute her. If her husband has said, "I divorce her," she shall go her way; he shall give her nothing as her price of divorce. If her husband has said, "I will not divorce her," he may take another woman to wife; the wife shall live as a slave in her husband's house.
142. If a woman has hated her husband and has said, "You shall not possess me," her past shall be inquired into as to what she lacks. If she has been discreet, and has no vice, and her husband has gone out, and has greatly belittled her, that woman has no blame, she shall take her marriage-portion and go off to her father's house.
143. If she has not been discreet, has gone out, ruined her house, belittled her husband, she shall be drowned.
152. From the time that woman entered into the man's house they together shall be liable for all debts subsequently incurred.
153. If a man's wife, for the sake of another, has caused her husband to be killed, that woman shall be impaled.
154. If a man has committed incest with his daughter, that man shall be banished from the city.
155. If a man has betrothed a maiden to his son and his son has known her, and afterward the man has lain in her bosom, and been caught, that man shall be strangled and she shall be cast into the water.
156. If a man has betrothed a maiden to his son, and his son has not known her, and that man has lain in her bosom, he shall pay her half a mina of silver, and shall pay over to her whatever she brought from her father's house, and the husband of her choice shall marry her.
157. If a man, after his father's death, be caught in the bosom of his mother, they shall both of them be burnt together.
158. If a man, after his father's death be caught in the bosom of his step-mother who has borne children, that man shall be cut off from his father's house.

159. If a man, who has presented a gift to the house of his prospective father-in-law and has given the bride-price, has afterward looked upon another woman and has said to his father-in-law, "I will not marry your daughter"; the father of the girl shall keep whatever he has brought as a present.
160. If a man has presented a gift to the house of his prospective father-in-law, and has given the bride-price, but his comrade has slandered him and his father-in-law has said to the suitor, "You shall not marry my daughter," [the father] shall return double all that was presented to him. Further, the comrade shall not marry the girl.
162. If a man has married a wife, and she has borne him children, and that woman has gone to her fate, her father shall lay no claim to her marriage-portion. Her marriage-portion is her children's only.
165. If a man has presented field, garden, or house to his son, the first in his eyes, and has written him a deed of gift; after the father has gone to his fate when the brothers share, he shall keep the present his father gave him, and over and above shall share equally with them in the goods of his father's estate.
166. If a man has taken wives for the other sons he had, but has not taken a wife for his young son, after the father has gone to his fate, when the brothers share, they shall set aside from the goods of their father's estate money, as a bride-price, for their young brother, who has not married a wife, over and above his share, and they shall cause him to take a wife.
167. If a man has taken a wife, and she has borne him children and that woman has gone to her fate, and he has taken a second wife, and she also has borne children; after the father has gone to his fate, the sons shall not share according to mothers, but each family shall take the marriage-portion of its mother, and all shall share the goods of their father's estate equally.
168. If a man has determined to disinherit his son and has declared before the judge, "I cut off my son," the judge shall inquire into the son's past, and, if the son has not committed a grave misdemeanor such as should cut him off from sonship, the father shall not disinherit his son.
169. If he has committed a grave crime against his father, which cuts off from sonship, for the first offence he shall pardon him. If he has committed a grave crime a second time, the father shall cut off his son from sonship.
170. If a man has had children borne to him by his wife, and also by a maid, if the father in his lifetime has said, "My sons," to the children whom his maid bore him, and has reckoned them with the sons of his wife; then after the father has gone to his fate, the children of the wife and of the maid shall share equally. The children of the wife shall apportion the shares and make their own selections.
175. If either a slave of a patrician, or of a plebeian, has married the daughter of a free man, and she has borne children, the owner of the slave shall have no claim for service on the children, of a free woman. And if a slave, either of a patrician or of a plebeian, has married a free woman and when he married her she entered the slave's house with a marriage-portion from her father's estate, be he slave of a patrician or of a plebeian, and from the time they started to keep house, they have acquired property; after the slave, whether of a patrician or of a plebeian, has gone to his fate, the free woman shall take her marriage-portion,

and whatever her husband and she acquired, since they started house-keeping. She shall divide it into two portions. The master of the slave shall take one half, the other half the free woman shall take for her children.

176. If the free woman had no marriage-portion, whatever her husband and she acquired since they started house-keeping he shall divide into two portions. The owner of the slave shall take one half, the other half the free woman shall take for her children.

177. If a widow, whose children are young, had determined to marry again, she shall not marry without consent of the judge. When she is allowed to remarry, the judge shall inquire as to what remains of the property of her former husband and shall intrust the property of her former husband to that woman and her second husband. He shall give them an inventory. They shall watch over the property, and bring up the children. Not a utensil shall they sell. A buyer of any utensil belonging to the widow's children shall lose his money and shall return the article to its owners.

181. If a father has vowed his daughter to a god, as a temple maid, or a virgin, and has given her no portion; after the father has gone to his fate, she shall share in the property of her father's estate, taking one-third of a child's share. She shall enjoy her share, as long as she lives. After her, it belongs to her brothers.

185. If a man had taken a young child, a natural son of his, to be his son, and has brought him up, no one shall make a claim against that foster child.

186. If a man has taken a young child to be his son, and after he has taken him, the child discover his own parents, he shall return to his father's house.

187. The son of a royal favorite, of one that stands in the palace, or the son of a votary shall not be reclaimed.

188, 189. If a craftsman has taken a child to bring up and has taught him his handicraft, he shall not be reclaimed. If he has not taught him his handicraft, that foster child shall return to his father's house.

192. If the son of a palace favorite or the son of a vowed woman has said to the father that brought him up, "You are not my father," or to the mother that brought him up, "You are not my mother," his tongue shall be cut out.

193. If the son of a palace favorite or the son of a vowed woman has come to know his father's house and has hated his father that brought him up, or his mother that brought him up, and shall go off to his father's house, his eyes shall be torn out.

194. If a man has given his son to a wet-nurse to suckle, and that son has died in the hands of the nurse, and the nurse, without consent of the child's father or mother, has nursed another child, they shall prosecute her; because she has nursed another child, without consent of the father or mother, her breasts shall be cut off.

195. If a son has struck his father, his hands shall be cut off.

Woman or Goddess with Snakes, from the palace complex, Knossos, Crete c. 1700–1550 BCE. Faience, height 11 5/8" (29.5 cm). Archeological Museum, Iraklion, Crete. Giraudon/Art Resource, NY.

The Greek World

In 1871, the wealthy German businessman Heinrich Schliemann began his life's work—the discovery of ancient Troy. Fascinated from his boyhood with the stories of Agamemnon, Odysseus, Priam, and Achilles, Schliemann set out to make a fortune to finance his quest. In the course of his business dealings, he learned nearly a dozen languages, became an American citizen, traveled around the world, and studied archeology. Attracted to a mound at Hissarlik, on the Turkish coast, he dug and discovered a cache of gold jewelry, which he called "Priam's treasure." Although he dug through what might have been Homer's Troy to a much older city beneath it, Schliemann's discovery effectively changed the way people thought about Homer's poems. Not simply imaginative fantasies, they now seemed to have a kernel of historical reality at their centers. This view was bolstered somewhat by Schliemann's next dig, at Mycenae in Greece. Once again digging to a level deeper and older than he sought, Schliemann found the graves of ancient Mycenian kings, along with gold funerary objects. Seeing a striking golden mask, Schliemann declared, "I have looked on the face of Agamemnon!" Schliemann also hoped to find the fabled palace of King Minos of Crete, central to the story of Theseus and the Minotaur. It was finally the British archeologist Sir Arthur Evans who located the great palace at Knossos in 1900. Evans found the impressive remains of an advanced civilization, called Minoan after the legendary king. The people lived in an unfortified palace so large and complex its name—*Labyrinth,* "Palace of the Double-Axes"—became the word for a maze. The discovery of many female figurines with snake motifs, like the so-called *snake goddess* shown here, has led to the suggestion that the Minoans of Crete were a peace-loving, goddess-worshipping people whose high culture, art, and literacy stood in tragic contrast with the male-centered, sky-god-worshipping Mycenians and then Dorian Greeks who succeeded them as powers in the Aegean.

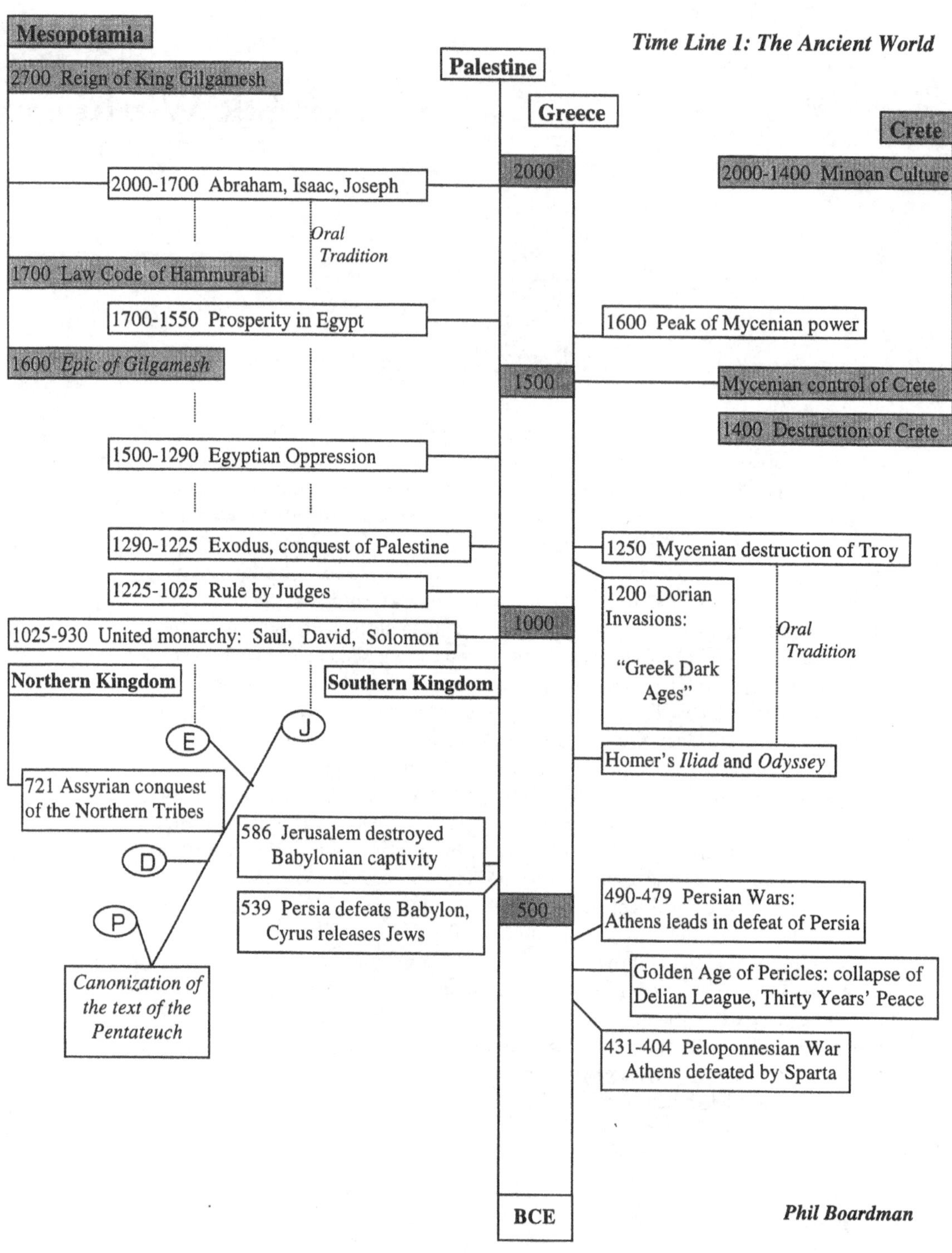
Time Line 1: The Ancient World
Mesopotamia
2700 Reign of King Gilgamesh
Palestine
Greece
Crete
2000
2000-1700 Abraham, Isaac, Joseph
2000-1400 Minoan Culture
Oral Tradition
1700 Law Code of Hammurabi
1700-1550 Prosperity in Egypt
1600 Peak of Mycenian power
1600 Epic of Gilgamesh
1500
Mycenian control of Crete
1400 Destruction of Crete
1500-1290 Egyptian Oppression
1290-1225 Exodus, conquest of Palestine
1250 Mycenian destruction of Troy
1225-1025 Rule by Judges
1200 Dorian Invasions: "Greek Dark Ages"
1000
1025-930 United monarchy: Saul, David, Solomon
Oral Tradition
Northern Kingdom
Southern Kingdom
E
J
Homer's Iliad and Odyssey
721 Assyrian conquest of the Northern Tribes
586 Jerusalem destroyed Babylonian captivity
D
539 Persia defeats Babylon, Cyrus releases Jews
500
490-479 Persian Wars: Athens leads in defeat of Persia
P
Golden Age of Pericles: collapse of Delian League, Thirty Years' Peace
Canonization of the text of the Pentateuch
431-404 Peloponnesian War Athens defeated by Sparta
BCE
Phil Boardman

Hesiod (8th century BCE*)*

THE THEOGONY [The Creation of the Gods]

We know very little of Hesiod other than what he tells us in his later epic, Works and Days, *a didactic poem based on his personal experiences as a farmer. In that poem he rails against his brother, who, according to Hesiod, stole his inheritance and bribed public officials for support. Hesiod, a shepherd who lived near Mt. Helicon in central Greece, began writing poems when he heard the Muses instructing him to "sing of the race of the blessed gods immortal." The song which he sang about these blessed gods is the* Theogony, *an account of the generations of the gods. Along with the epic poems of his near contemporary, Homer, Hesiod's poems came almost to have the status of religious texts to later Greeks.*

Theogony *is a difficult work because of the great procession of names and events identified but not elaborated in a work that seems to have no plot. In some ways it is this procession which is most important in the work, for it is the key to Hesiod's themes—the endless pattern of crime and rebellion and the supreme power of Zeus—and it provides an insight into the deeper ways of Greek myth. The poem shows us three generations of gods: the (1)* ***elemental generation*** *of Void* (Chaos), *Earth* (Gaea), *and Eros. After the birth of Darkness and Night, Earth herself gives birth to Sky (or Heaven,* Uranus*), who then breeds upon her the generation (2) of* ***Titans****, including gods representing Ocean, the Sun* (Hyperion), *Law, Memory, and Time* (Cronus). *These gods, whose very names evoke aspects of nature, lay in place the backdrop of natural forces against which humans construct their lives and with which they inevitably contend.*

The Titans seize power when Cronus, at the urging of Mother Earth, castrates his father Sky. Then he sleeps with his sister Rhea, who gives birth to the generation (3) of the ***Olympian gods****, so named because they eventually reside on Mount Olympus. A central episode of the* Theogony *is the so-called "Titanomachia," the battle by which the Olympians, led by the clever Zeus, defeat the Titans, who support Cronus. In the course of the battle we see yet another struggle emerging, this time between humans and the Olympians, who often show themselves to be fickle, petty, and dangerous. In* Theogony,

Reprinted from *Theogony*, translated by Norman O. Brown (Macmillan, 1953).

humans are treated to two models: the god Prometheus, who fights against Zeus on behalf of humans, and the first woman, later called Pandora, who is sent by Zeus as a curse to plague mankind.

[SELECTIONS]

Daughters of Zeus, I greet you; add passion to my song, and tell of the sacred race of gods who are forever, descended from Earth and starry Sky, from dark Night, and from salty Sea. Tell how in the beginning the gods and the earth came into being, as well as the rivers, the limitless sea with its raging surges, the shining stars, and the broad sky above—also how they divided the estate and distributed privileges among themselves, and how they first established themselves in the folds of Mount Olympus. Relate these things to me, Muses whose home is Olympus, from the beginning; tell me which of them first came into being.

II. First of all, the Void came into being, next broad-bosomed Earth, the solid and eternal home of all, and Eros [Desire], the most beautiful of the immortal gods, who in every man and every god softens the sinews and overpowers the prudent purpose of the mind. Out of Void came Darkness and black Night, and out of Night came Light and Day, her children conceived after union in love with Darkness. Earth first produced starry Sky, equal in size with herself, to cover her on all sides. Next she produced the tall mountains, the pleasant haunts of the gods, and also gave birth to the barren waters, sea with its raging surges—all this without the passion of love. Thereafter she lay with Sky and gave birth to Ocean with its deep current, Coeus and Crius and Hyperion and Iapetus; Thea and Rhea and Themis [Law] and Mnemosyne [Memory]; also golden-crowned Phoebe and lovely Tethys. After these came cunning Cronus, the youngest and boldest of her children; and he grew to hate the father who had begotten him.

Earth also gave birth to the violent Cyclopes—Thunderer, Lightner, and bold Flash—who made and gave to Zeus the thunder and the lightning-bolt. They were like the gods in all respects except that a single eye stood in the middle of their foreheads, and their strength and power and skill were in their hands.

There were also born to Earth and Sky three more children, big, strong, and horrible, Cottus and Briareus and Gyes. This unruly brood had a hundred monstrous hands sprouting from their shoulders, and fifty heads on top of their shoulders growing from their sturdy bodies. They had monstrous strength to match their huge size.

III. Of all the children born of Earth and Sky these were the boldest, and their father hated them from the beginning. As each of them was about to be born, Sky would not let them reach the light of day; instead he hid them all away in the bowels of Mother Earth. Sky took pleasure in doing this evil thing. In spite of her enormous size, Earth felt the strain within her and groaned. Finally she thought of an evil and cunning stratagem. She instantly produced a new metal, gray steel, and made a huge sickle. Then she laid the matter before her children; the anguish in her heart made her speak boldly: "My children, you have a savage father; if you will listen to me, we may be able to take vengeance for his evil outrage: he was the one who started using violence."

This was what she said; but all the children were gripped by fear, and not one of them spoke a word. Then great Cronus, the cunning trickster, took courage and answered his good mother with these words: "Mother, I am willing to undertake and carry through your plan. I have no respect for our infamous father, since he was the one who started using violence."

This was what he said, and enormous Earth was very pleased. She hid him in ambush and put in his hands the sickle with jagged teeth, and instructed him fully in her plot. Huge Sky came drawing night behind him and desiring to make love; he lay on top of Earth stretched all over her. Then from his ambush his son reached out with his left hand and with his right took the huge sickle with its long jagged teeth and quickly sheared the organs from his own father and threw them away, backward over his shoulder. But that was not the end of them. The drops of blood that spurted from them were all taken in by Mother Earth, and in the course of the revolving years she gave birth to the powerful Erinyes [Spirits of Vengeance] and the huge Giants with shining armor and long spears. As for the organs themselves, for a long time they drifted round the sea just as they were when Cronus cut them off with the steel edge and threw them from the land into the waves of the ocean; then white foam issued from the divine flesh, and in the foam a girl began to grow. First she came near to holy Cythera, then reached Cyprus, the land surrounded by sea. There she stepped out, a goddess, tender and beautiful, and round her slender feet the green grass shot up. She is called Aphrodite by gods and men, because she grew in the *froth*, and also Cytherea, because she came near to Cythera, and the Cyprian, because she was born in watery Cyprus. Eros [Desire] and beautiful Passion were her attendants both at her birth and at her first going to join the family of the gods. The rights and privileges assigned to her from the beginning and recognized by men and gods are these: to preside over the whispers and smiles and tricks which girls employ, and the sweet delight and tenderness of love.

Great Father Sky called his children the Titans, because of his feud with them: he said that they blindly had *tightened* the noose and had done a savage thing for which they would have to pay in time to come.

VIII. Rhea submitted to the embraces of Cronus and bore him children with a glorious destiny: Hestia, Demeter, and Hera, who walks on golden sandals; Hades, the powerful god whose home is underground and whose heart is pitiless; Poseidon, the god whose great blows make the earth quake; and Zeus the lord of wisdom, the father of gods and men, whose thunder makes the broad earth tremble. As each of these children came out of their mother's holy womb onto her knees, great Cronus swallowed them. His purpose was to prevent the kingship of the gods from passing to another one of the august descendants of Sky; he had been told by Earth and starry Sky that he was destined to be overcome by his own son. For that reason he kept a sleepless watch and waited for his own children to be born and then swallowed them. Rhea had no rest from grief; so, when she was about to give birth to Zeus, the father of gods and men, she begged her own dear parents, Earth and starry Sky, to help her contrive a plan whereby she might bear her child without Cronus' knowing it, and make amends to the vengeful spirits of her father Sky. Earth and Sky listened to their daughter and granted her request; they told her what was destined to happen to King Cronus and to his bold son. When she was about to give birth to great Zeus, her youngest child, they sent her to the rich Cretan town of Lyctus. Huge Mother Earth undertook to nurse and raise the infant in the broad land of Crete. Dark night was rushing on as Earth arrived there carrying him, and Lyctus was the first place where she stopped. She took him and hid him in an inaccessible cave, deep in the bowels of holy earth, in the dense woods of Mount Aegeum. Then she wrapped a huge stone in baby blankets and handed it to the royal son of Sky, who then was king of the gods. He took the stone and swallowed it into his belly—the fool! He did not know that a stone had replaced his son, who survived, unconquered and untroubled, and who was going to overcome him by force and drive him from his office and reign over the gods in his place.

The young prince grew quickly in strength and stature. After years had passed Cronus the great trickster fell victim to the cunning suggestions of Mother Earth and threw up his own children again. The first thing he vomited was the stone, the last thing he had swallowed; Zeus set it up on the highways of the earth in holy Pytho under the slopes of Parnassus, to be a sign and a wonder to mankind thereafter.

Zeus also set free his father's brothers from the cruel chains in which their father Sky had in foolish frenzy bound them. They gratefully remembered his kindness and gave him the thunder and the lightning-bolt and flash, which huge Earth had kept hidden till then. In these weapons Zeus trusts; they make him master over gods and men.

IX. Iapetus took Clymene, the shapely daughter of Ocean, as his wife and entered her bed. She gave birth to a violent-spirited son called Atlas; she also bore a proud-spirited Menoetius, and Prometheus the cunning trickster, and the half-wit Epimetheus, who brought bad luck on men who earn their bread by work: he first accepted the artificial woman sent by Zeus. Lawless Menoetius, because of his savage insolence and overbearing boldness, was struck by the smoking thunderbolt of Zeus and sent down to the lower darkness. Atlas was condemned to hold up the broad sky at the end of the earth, facing the place where the Hesperian nymphs raise their thrilling voices; there he stands and holds the sky up with head and hands that never tire. Such was the fate wise Zeus decreed for him. Cunning Prometheus he bound with unbreakable and painful chains and drove a stake through his middle.

And he turned on him a long-winged eagle, which ate his immortal liver; by night the liver grew as much again as the long-winged bird had eaten in the whole day. The bird was killed by shapely Alcmene's heroic son Heracles, who delivered the son of Iapetus from his evil plight and released him from his sufferings, with the consent of Olympian Zeus the heavenly king, who wanted to raise even higher than before the fame of Theban-born Heracles over all the populous earth. This was his purpose; he exalted his son with honor, and angry though he was he laid aside his former feud with Prometheus.

Such was Prometheus' punishment for having quarreled with the purposes of the all-powerful son of Cronus. For when gods and men came to Mecone to settle their dispute, Prometheus placed before them a huge ox, which he had carefully divided, intending to play a trick on Zeus. He served the men with meat and entrails rich in fat placed inside the skin and covered with the stomach of the ox, while he served Zeus with the bare bones of the ox dressed with a covering of white fat: this was his cunning trick. Zeus the father of gods and men spoke to him and said: "Son of Iapetus, second to none in this noble company, how unfairly you have divided the portions, my friend." With these words Zeus, full of immortal wisdom, rebuked him.

Cunning Prometheus had not forgotten his skill at trickery and replied, smiling slightly, "Zeus, noblest and greatest of the gods who are forever, choose whichever of these portions your heart prefers." He said this with intent to deceive: but Zeus, whose wisdom is invincible, saw and did not fail to see the deception; in his heart he was already planning bad luck for mankind, and his plan was about to be fulfilled. With both hands Zeus took up the white fat. Anger filled his mind and fury pierced his heart when he saw the white bones cunningly concealed underneath. (That is why the race of men on earth burn the white bones of animals as a savory offering on the altars of the gods.) But as for Prometheus, Zeus, the master of the clouds, indignantly addressed him saying, "Son of Iapetus, your mind was always the deepest, my friend, and it now appears that you have lost none of your cunning."

Zeus was angry, and his wisdom is invincible. He never forgot this trick, and in return for it he withheld from the race of men who live and die on earth the all-consuming power of fire. But the bold son of Iapetus tricked him again: he stole the radiant light of all-consuming fire in a hollow stalk. This bit deeper into the heart of Zeus the thunder-god: he was enraged when he saw mankind enjoying the radiant light of fire. In return for the theft of fire he instantly produced a curse to plague mankind. At the orders of the son of Cronus, the famous lame smith-god [Hephaestus] shaped some clay in the image of a tender girl. The bright-eyed goddess Athena dressed and decked her in silvery clothes. A marvelous embroidered veil fell from her head and was held in her hands. Round her head the goddess tied a golden diadem on which the smith-god himself had exercised his skill, to please his father Zeus. When Zeus had completed this beautiful curse to go with the blessing of fire, he displayed the girl in an assembly of the gods and men, all decked out in the finery supplied by the bright-eyed daughter of the lord of hosts. Gods and men were speechless when they say how deadly and how irresistible was the trick with which Zeus was going to catch mankind.

This was the origin of the damnable race of women—a plague which men must live with. They have no place where the curse of poverty is; they belong with luxury. Just as bees in their hollow hives support mischievous drones—the bees work busily all day till sunset making the white wax, while the drones sit at home in the shade of the hive and harvest into their bellies the fruits of another's labor—so Zeus the thunder-god made women mischievous in their ways and a curse for men: he dispensed a curse to go with a blessing.

Whoever seeks to avoid marriage and the troublesome ways of women, and therefore refuses to marry, finds old age a curse without anyone to tend his years; though he does not lack livelihood while he lives, on his death his kinsmen divide up his estate. As for the man fated to marry, even if he get a good wife well suited to his temper, evil is continually balanced with good in his life; if he should get pestilent children, the grief in his heart and soul is unremitting throughout life: this evil has no cure.

Thus it is not possible to deceive the mind of Zeus or escape his judgment. Even the trickster Prometheus, Iapetus' son, was not able to escape the heavy consequences of his anger. In spite of all his cleverness he lies helplessly bound by a great chain.

X. The Hundred-Arms—Briareus, Cottus, and Gyes—had been bound fast in chains by their father Sky when he turned against them in fear of their size and shape and overbearing boldness. He made them live underneath the highways of the earth.

For a long time they lay in their subterranean dungeon far away at the distant ends of the earth, suffering pain and anguish and grief. But now they were restored to the light by Zeus and the other gods born of the loves of Cronus and fair-haired Rhea. The gods were following the advice of Mother Earth, who revealed all the future to them, prophesying that with the aid of the Hundred-Arms they would win the glorious triumph which they prayed for. For there had been a long war with much suffering on both sides and many bloody battles between the Titan generation of gods and the children of Cronus. The mighty Titans fought from the top of Mount Othrys, while the Olympian gods, from whom all blessings flow, the children of Cronus and fair-haired Rhea, fought from Mount Olympus. For ten full years they had fought without ceasing, so bitterly did they hate each other: there was no truce in the hard-fought struggle, no decision for either side; the fortunes of war were equally balanced. Then the Olympians provided the Hundred-Arms with full equipment, with nectar and ambrosia, the gods' own food, and restored their fighting spirit. Zeus the father of gods and men chose this moment to address his new allies, saying: "You fine sons of Earth and Sky, listen while I tell you what is in my mind. For a long time now there has been warfare every day between the Titan generation of gods and the children of Cronus, to decide which shall be the victors and have the supreme power. Your duty is to employ the great strength of your invincible arms in the stress of battle on our side against the Titans; remember that we have been your good friends, and that you are indebted to our action for your release from the agony of imprisonment and for your return from the dark underworld to the light of day."

That was what Zeus said, and good Cottus replied to him saying: "Sir, you tell us nothing that we did not know. We know that you are first in wisdom, first in knowledge; and you have shown yourself able to save immortal beings from a chilling fate. Son of Cronus, you are our master. Thanks to your decision we have returned to this world from that forlorn dungeon in the dark underworld where we had abandoned all hope. For these reasons we will join the bloody battle against the Titans and strengthen your side in the fierce struggle with unflagging energy and loyal hearts."

When they had heard Cottus' speech, the Olympian gods, from whom all blessings flow, applauded. They became even more eager for war than before: so on that same day a dismal battle started in which all the gods, male and female, joined—the Titans on the one side and on the other the children of Cronus together with the terrible monsters with their enormous strength, whom Zeus had brought from the lower darkness to the light. Each of them had a hundred arms growing from their shoulders and fifty heads on top of their shoulders growing from their sturdy bodies. They grasped massive rocks in their sturdy hands and took their place in the bitter battle against the Titans.

On the other side the Titans prudently strengthened their ranks. Both sides employed all the strength in their hands. The limitless expanse of the sea echoed terribly; the earth rumbled loudly, and the broad area of the sky shook and groaned. Mount Olympus trembled from base to summit as the immortal beings clashed, and a heavy quaking penetrated to the gloomy depths of Tartarus—the sharp vibration of innumerable feet running and missiles thrown. While the weapons discharged at each other whistled through the air, both sides shouted loud battle cries as they came together, till the noise reached the starry sky.

Then Zeus decided to restrain his own power no longer. A sudden surge of energy filled his spirit, and he exerted all the strength he had. He advanced through the sky from Olympus sending flash upon flash of continuous lightning. The bolts of lightning and thunder flew thick and fast from his powerful arm, forming a solid roll of sacred fire. Fertile tracts of land all around crackled as they burned, and immense forests roared in the fire. The whole earth and the Ocean-streams and the barren sea began to boil. An immense flame shot up into the atmosphere, so that the hot air enveloped the Titans, while their eyes, powerful as they were, were blinded by the brilliant flash of the lightning-bolt. The prodigious heat filled the Void. The sight there was to see, and the noise there was to hear, made it seem as if Earth and vast Sky above were colliding. If Earth were being smashed and if Sky were smashing down upon her, the noise would be as great as the noise that arose when the gods met in battle. The winds added to the confusion, whirling dust around together with great Zeus' volleys of thunder and lightning-bolts, and carrying the battle cries and shouts from one side to the other, so that the uproar was deafening. It was a terrible conflict, which revealed the utmost power of the contestants. After many heavy engagements, in which both sides obstinately resisted each other, the battle was finally decided.

Throughout the bitter battle Cottus and Briareus and Gyes were in the forefront. They attacked relentlessly, throwing showers of three hundred stones one after another with all the force of their enormous hands, till they darkened the Titans with a cloud of missiles. Their brute force was stronger than all the valiant efforts of the Titans. They then conducted them under the highways of the earth as far below the ground as the ground is below the sky, and tied them with cruel chains. So far down below the ground is gloomy Tartarus: a bronze anvil falling from the sky would fall nine days and nights, and reach earth on the tenth; a bronze anvil falling from the earth would fall nine days and nights and reach Tartarus on the tenth. Tartarus is surrounded by a bronze moat; three thicknesses of night are spread round its bottleneck, above which the roots of earth and barren sea are planted. In that gloomy underground region the Titans were imprisoned by the decree of Zeus, the master of the clouds. The dismal place lies at the end of the monstrous earth. No exit is open to them: Poseidon made gates of bronze to secure the place; a wall runs all the way round; and the three strong brothers, Gyes, Cottus, and Briareus, now live there—guards on whose loyalty Zeus the lord of the aegis can rely.

Sappho (fl. c.600 BCE)

Poems

We know very little of Sappho's life, and even that little is encrusted with legend and fancy. Born in the mid- to late-seventh century, she grew up on the island of Lesbos. She possibly had a husband and a daughter. The poems suggest that she had responsibility for training young girls before their marriages. When they left her to get married, she composed bridal odes in their honor. Whatever her occupation, later references to her recognize her only as a poet and a singer of songs, and the vase paintings of her that survive usually show her playing a lyre. Because of her praise of Aphrodite and her references to rites, some think she was a priestess of that goddess.

Although widely known, Sappho's poetry survived only in quotations by others until papyruses of her poems were found in Egypt last century. Today nearly 200 of her poems have surfaced, only one of them surely complete (Poem #1, the "Hymn to Aphrodite"). The rest are fragments, several containing complete lines and stanzas, but most scattered phrases, and many only a few words. Many of her works have suffered mistranslation, either to give a false sense of greater completeness, or to hide the clear references to Sappho's passion for other women or girls. While there is little in the surviving poems to prove that her relationships with other women were sexual, the tradition that Sappho was a lesbian was current among the ancient Greeks who presumably were familiar with many more poems than we have. Her position as the first woman poet and as a passionate lyric voice in an age dominated by the Iliad *and the* Odyssey *have in recent years made her poetry the focus of much attention and praise.*

Sappho's poetry is notable especially for its energetic portrayal of feelings and passions, as in Poem #4. There the voyeur-poet who "must endure all this" suffers a startlingly physical reaction as part of her feelings of love or of jealousy. This strong emotion is heightened for the reader by the uncertainty about the object of those feelings: which of the two does she admire and which does she envy? Her poems also exploit a striking use of images. Poem #3, for instance, draws from Homer's world of horses, armor, chariots, and ships in order to use Helen as an example of the power of love.

The translations are by Suzy Q. Groden, in *The Poems of Sappho* (Indianapolis: Bobbs-Merrill, 1966). Because there are several competing ways of numbering the poems of Sappho, the seven poems included here are simply numbered in order.

[1]

Eternal Aphrodite, rainbow-throned,
you cunning, wily child of Zeus, I beg you,
do not break me, Lady,
with the pains and raging ills of love.
But come to me, if ever in the past
you heard my far-off cries
and heeding, came,
leaving the golden home of Zeus
in your bridled chariot.
Beautiful swift sparrows bore you,
eddying through the mid-air, their wings a-whirr,
from heaven to the dark earth,
and there they were. And you, blessed Lady,
smiling your immortal smile,
asked me what ailed me now,
and why I called again,
and what my mad heart most craved:

"Whom, Sappho,
shall I lead to be your love
this time?
Who wrongs you now?
Even if she flees you, soon she'll chase,
and if she scorns your gifts, why, she will offer hers.
And if she does not love you,
soon she'll love, although she does not want to."

Now come to me once again, and free me
from these aching sorrows. Do for my heart
what it desires, and be yourself my help and ally.

[2]

Come to me here, from Crete,
to this sacred temple of the lovely apple grove.
Your altars are fragrant here with offerings of frankincense,
and cool water rustles through the apple shoots.
All the place is shadowed with roses
and deep sleep slips down through the shimmering leaves.
In here is a meadow, with horses grazing, alive
with spring blossoms and breezes
that blow redolent.
And here may you, Cypris, pour,
with graceful charm,
your nectar, mixed with our own festive rites,
into these golden cups.

[3]

There are those who say
an array of horsemen,
and others of marching men,
and others of ships, is
the most beautiful thing on the dark earth.
But I say it is whatever one loves.

It is very easy
to show this to all:
for Helen,
by far the most beautiful of mortals,
left her husband
and sailed to Troy
giving no thought at all
to her child nor dear parents,
but was led . . .
[by her love alone.]

Now, far away, Anactoria
comes to my mind.
For I would rather watch her
moving in her lovely way,
and see her face, flashing radiant,
than all the force of Lydian chariots,
and their infantry in full display of arms.

[4]

An equal to the gods, he seems to me,
the man who, with his face toward yours,
sits close and listens to the whispers of
your sweet voice and enticing laugh.
To watch has made my heart a pounding hammer in my
breast.
For as I look at you, if only for an instant,
my voice no longer comes to me.
My silent tongue is broken,
and a quick and subtle flame
runs up beneath my skin.
I lose my sense of sight, hear only drumming in my ears.
I drip cold sweat,
and a trembling chases all through me.
I am greener than the pale grass
and it seems to me that I am close to death.
Still, I must endure all this.

[5]

To have beauty is to have only that,
but to have goodness
is to be beautiful
too.

[6]

Happy bridegroom!
Now your wedding has come true,
as you have prayed, and you have
the girl for whom you prayed.
You are a joy to look at,
with your gentle eyes,

and love showers down about
your handsome face . . .
Aphrodite has honored you
above all others . . .

[7]

These are the ashes of Timas
who died before she could wed,
whom the blue-dark room of Persephone
took in instead.
And when she was dead
every girl her own age
cut, with a fresh-sharpened blade,
a beautiful lock from her head
[to lay on the grave]

Pindar (518–438 BCE)

ODES

Pindar was an aristocrat from the city of Thebes. It is believed he wrote seventeen volumes of lyric poetry of virtually every kind during his lifetime, but only his epinicia, *choral odes in honor of the winners of the great athletic games, survive. The four volumes of* epinicia *that do survive were probably saved by being used in the second century CE as school textbooks. One volume was devoted to each of the most important of the ancient games: Olympian odes for the winners of the Olympic events held at Olympia every four years, Pythian odes for the winners of the games held at Delphi every four years, Nemean odes celebrating victories in the northeastern Peloponnese every two years, and the Isthmian odes for the games held near Corinth every two years. Pindar was the last and greatest master of the choral ode, a form that during his lifetime was being swallowed up into the immensely popular tragic drama. We thus have no idea how the odes were performed: Was the chorus static or did it move around? What was the range of voices used? What kind of music accompanied the poetry? What is clear is that Pindar was an innovative voice within a very formal poetic structure. No two of his odes have the same metrical form, and he uses these celebrations of athletic prowess to praise cities and families, to draw out deep religious connections with the past through stories from myth, to offer personal reflections, and to extol the enduring importance of leadership and competition—everything, in fact, but the grubby details of the competition itself. In place of the sweaty athlete, Pindar raised a vision of the hero as representative of his family, city, and aristocratic values.*

These values were apparently very important to Pindar, whose conservative attitudes seem to have changed very little in his eighty years. Although he must have traveled to many of the cities whose victorious athletes he celebrated in his poems, he remained loyal all his life to his home city of Thebes. He maintained this staunch patriotism even though Thebes was an ally of Persia in the Persian Wars, against the cities of Athens and Sparta that were giving the Greeks a proud new identity. Throughout this period of dangerous political turmoil, Pindar was admired for the quality and strength of his poetry. His voice gave powerful expression to the Greek admiration for physical beauty and competitive striving.

The two odes here have been translated from Greek into English verse by C. M. Bowra (Penguin, 1969).

Olympian XI

For Hagesidamos of Western Lokroi, winner in the boys' boxing

There is a time when men's strongest need
Is for the winds, and a time for the sky's water,
The clouds' showery children.
If anyone toils and succeeds,
Sweet voices of song
Are paid on account for words to come
And a faithful pledge to surpassing actions.

Beyond grudging, this praise
Is laid up for Olympian victors. Such themes
My tongue loves to tend,
But it is God who makes a man
To flower as his wise mind wishes.
Know now, son of Archestratos,
Hagesidamos, because of your boxing

I shall sing a sweet song
To be a jewel in your crown of golden olive,
And honour the Western Lokrians' race.
Join there in the revel! I shall give my word,
Muses, that he will not come
To a host that puts strangers to flight
Or knows not beautiful things;
They stand on wisdom's height and are soldiers.
—Its inborn ways neither the tawny fox
Shall change, nor loud-bellowing lions.

Pythian VII

For Megakles of Athens, winner in the chariot-race

Athens the mighty city!
For the strong house of the Alkmaionidai
This is the finest prelude
To lay as foundation-stone
Of my chariot-song.
For in what country, what clan, would you dwell
And have more magnificent renown
For Hellas to hear?

For in every city the story runs
Of the citizens of Erechtheus,
Who built in shining Pytho
Thy porch, Apollo, marvelous to behold.
There call to me also
Five victories at the Isthmos
And one paramount at God's Olympia
And two by Krisa,

Megakles, yours and your fathers'!
And in this last happy fortune
Some pleasure I have; but sorrow as well
At envy requiting your fine deeds.
—Thus always, they say,
Happiness, flowering and constant,
Brings after it
One thing with another.

Herodotus (c.484–c.430 BCE)

The Persian Wars

Herodotus (484–425 BCE) was exiled from his native Asia Minor (modern Turkey, then under Persian rule), traveled widely throughout Egypt and the Persian Empire, lived for a time in Athens, and settled in Italy before he began his groundbreaking Histories. *For Herodotus, "histories" meant, simply, "investigations." And investigations they were: through extensive travel, research, and interviews, Herodotus attempted to understand the truth of the events he wrote about. His writing is infused with an inquiring and skeptical attitude toward what happened. He works carefully to reconstruct events, using a historical method that we might call scientific, for he checks varying sources and interviews participants and observers. He speaks openly with the reader about problems with these sources, as in his "Introduction," where he says, "Which of these two accounts is true I shall not trouble to decide."*

The first part of his book is a review of the cultures and customs of the people inhabiting the Mediterranean world. The rest is devoted to his detailed account of the Persian Wars, which he saw as capping a great struggle between East and West. Though he clearly saw that the wars marked the rise of Greece as a power in the eastern Mediterranean, and the ascendancy of Athens (over Sparta) within Greece, he did not in his writings show a bias toward Athens or the Greeks. He emphasizes always the character of individual humans and discounts the intervention of the gods as agents in historical events. This approach brings to the fore the fundamental irony which became the magnetic center of the Greek view of history: the yawning gap between what humans intend or plan, on the one hand, and what their actions lead to, on the other.

The two selections here suggest interesting comparisons with other Greek stories. "Helen and Alexander" casts light on the differences in method between epic and history, for Herodotus offers an account of the events leading to the Trojan War which is different from Homer's. The Odyssey *suggests that Menelaus delayed his return from Troy for seven years because he was trading with the Egyptians, according to Nestor; Menelaus, for his part, attributes the delay to a god's anger at a failure in sacrifice. In Herodotus, Menelaus travels to Egypt after the war to redeem his wife, Helen, who actually resided there and not in Troy as the Greeks had thought. Leaving from Egypt, Menelaus sacrifices two Egyptian*

The translation used here is by George Rawlinson, first published 1858–60, and often reprinted.

children to gain favorable winds; in the Homeric tradition, Menelaus's brother Agamemnon sacrificed his own daughter Iphigenia on the way to Troy (a partial motive for Clytemnestra's slaughter of her husband). Herodotus's view is the rational one: "If Helen had been at Troy, the inhabitants would, I think, have given her up to the Greeks."

"The Story of Adrastus," for its part, can fruitfully be compared with Sophocles's tragedy of Oedipus. *In both stories we see men marked out for misfortune; oracles in both stories show that Oedipus and Adrastus are simply acting out the will of some god. Yet in spite of their moral innocence, each is repelled by the horror of what he has done and acts to remove himself from human society.*

[INTRODUCTION]

These are the researches of Herodotus of Halicarnassus, which he publishes, in the hope of thereby preserving from decay the remembrance of what men have done, and of preventing the great and wonderful actions of the Greeks and the Barbarians from losing their due meed of glory; and withal to put on record what were their grounds of feud.

1. According to the Persians best informed in history, the Phoenicians began the quarrel. This people, who had formerly dwelt on the shores of the Red Sea, having migrated to the Mediterranean and settled in the parts which they now inhabit, began at once, they say, to adventure on long voyages, freighting their vessels with the wares of Egypt and Assyria. They landed at many places on the coast, and among the rest at Argos, which was then pre-eminent above all the states included now under the common name of Hellas. Here they exposed their merchandise, and traded with the natives for five or six days; at the end of which time, when almost everything was sold, there came down to the beach a number of women, and among them the daughter of the king, who was, they say, agreeing in this with the Greeks, Io, the child of Inachus. The women were standing by the stern of the ship intent upon their purchases, when the Phoenicians, with a general shout, rushed upon them. The greater part made their escape, but some were seized and carried off. Io herself was among the captives. The Phoenicians put the women on board their vessel, and set sail for Egypt. Thus did Io pass into Egypt, according to the Persian story, which differs widely from the Phoenician: and thus commenced, according to their authors, the series of outrages.

2. At a later period, certain Greeks, with whose name they are unacquainted, but who would probably be the Cretans, made a landing at Tyre, on the Phoenician coast, and bore off the king's daughter, Europe. In this they only retaliated; but afterwards the Greeks, they say, were guilty of a second violence. They manned a ship of war, and sailed to Aea, a city of Colchis, on the river Phasis; from whence, after despatching the rest of the business on which they had come, they carried off Medea, the daughter of the king of the land. The monarch sent a herald into Greece to demand reparation of the wrong, and the restitution of his child; but the Greeks made answer, that having received no reparation of the wrong done them in the seizure of Io the Argive, they should give none in this instance.

3. In the next generation afterwards, according to the same authorities, Alexander the son of Priam, bearing these events in mind, resolved to procure himself a wife

out of Greece by violence, fully persuaded, that as the Greeks had not given satisfaction for their outrages, so neither would he be forced to make any for his. Accordingly he made prize of Helen; upon which the Greeks decided that, before resorting to other measures, they would send envoys to reclaim the princess and require reparation of the wrong. Their demands were met by a reference to the violence which had been offered to Medea, and they were asked with what face they could now require satisfaction, when they had formerly rejected all demands for either reparation or restitution addressed to them.

4. Hitherto the injuries on either side had been mere acts of common violence; but in what followed the Persians consider that the Greeks were greatly to blame, since before any attack had been made on Europe, they led an army into Asia. Now as for the carrying off of women, it is the deed, they say, of a rogue; but to make a stir about such as are carried off, argues a man a fool. Men of sense care nothing for such women, since it is plain that without their own consent they would never be forced away. The Asiatics, when the Greeks ran off with their women, never troubled themselves about the matter; but the Greeks, for the sake of a single Lacedaemonian girl, collected a vast armament, invaded Asia, and destroyed the kingdom of Priam. Henceforth they ever looked upon the Greeks as their open enemies. For Asia, with all the various tribes of barbarians that inhabit it, is regarded by the Persians as their own; but Europe and the Greek race they look on as distinct and separate.

5. Such is the account which the Persians give of these matters. They trace to the attack upon Troy their ancient enmity towards the Greeks. The Phoenicians, however, as regards Io, vary from the Persian statements. They deny that they used any violence to remove her into Egypt; she herself, they say, having formed an intimacy with the captain, while his vessel lay at Argos, and suspecting herself to be with child, of her own free will accompanied the Phoenicians on their leaving the shore, to escape the shame of detection and the reproaches of her parents. Which of these two accounts is true I shall not trouble to decide. I shall proceed at once to point out the person who first within my own knowledge commenced aggressions on the Greeks, after which I shall go forward with my history, describing equally the greater and the lesser cities. For the cities which were formerly great, have most of them become insignificant; and such as are at present powerful, were weak in the olden time. I shall therefore discourse equally of both, convinced that human happiness never continues long in one stay.

[The Story of Helen and Alexander (Paris)]

113. The priests, in answer to my inquiries on the subject of Helen, informed me of the following particulars. When Alexander had carried off Helen from Sparta, he took ship and sailed homewards. On his way across the Aegean a gale arose, which drove him from his course and took him down to the sea of Egypt; hence, as the wind did not abate, he was carried on to the coast, when he went ashore, landing at the Salt-Pans, in that mouth of the Nile which is now called the Canobic. At this place there stood upon the shore a temple, which still exists, dedicated to Heracles. If a slave runs away from his master, and taking sanctuary at this shrine gives himself up to the god, and receives certain sacred marks upon his person, whosoever his master may be, he cannot lay hand on him. This law still remained unchanged to my time.

Hearing, therefore, of the custom of the place, the attendants of Alexander deserted him, and fled to the temple where they sat as suppliants. While there, wishing to damage their master, they accused him to the Egyptians, narrating all the circumstances of the rape of Helen and the wrong done to Menelaus. These charges they brought, not only before the priests, but also before the warden of that mouth of the river, whose name was Thonis.

114. As soon as he received the intelligence, Thonis sent a message to Proteus, who was at Memphis, to this effect, "A stranger is arrived from Greece; he is by race a Teucrian, and has done a wicked deed in the country from which he is come. Having beguiled the wife of the man whose guest he was, he carried her away with him, and much treasure also. Compelled by stress of weather, he has now put in here. Are we to let him depart as he came, or shall we seize what he has brought?" Proteus replied, "Seize the man, be he who he may, that has dealt thus wickedly with his friend, and bring him before me, that I may hear what he will say for himself."

115. Thonis, on receiving these orders, arrested Alexander, and stopped the departure of his ships; then, taking with him Alexander, Helen, the treasures, and also the fugitive slaves, he went up to Memphis. When all were arrived, Proteus asked Alexander, "Who he was, and whence he had come?" Alexander replied by giving his descent, the name of his country, and a true account of his late voyage. Then Proteus questioned him as to how he got possession of Helen. In his reply Alexander became confused, and diverged from the truth, whereon the slaves interposed, confuted his statements, and told the whole history of the crime. Finally, Proteus delivered judgment as follows, "Did I not regard it as a matter of the utmost consequence that no stranger driven to my country by adverse winds should ever be put to death, I would certainly have avenged the Greek by slaying you, basest of men, after accepting hospitality, to do so wicked a deed! First, you did seduce the wife of your own host—then, not content therewith, you must violently excite her mind, and steal her away from her husband. Nay, even so you were not satisfied, but on leaving, you plundered the house in which you had been a guest. Now then, as I think it of the greatest importance to put no stranger to death, I suffer you to depart; but the woman and the treasures I shall not permit to be carried away. Here they must stay, till the Greek stranger comes in person and takes them back with him. For yourself and your companions, I command you to leave my land within the space of three days—and I warn you, that otherwise at the end of that time you will be treated as enemies."

116. Such was the tale told me by the priests concerning the arrival of Helen at the court of Proteus. It seems to me that Homer was acquainted with this story, and while discarding it, because he thought it less adapted for epic poetry than the version which he followed, showed that it was not unknown to him. This is evident from the travels which he assigns to Alexander in the *Iliad*—and let it be borne in mind that he has nowhere else contradicted himself—making him be carried out of his course on his return with Helen, and after divers wanderings come at last to Sidon in Phoenicia. The passage is in the Bravery of Diomede, and the words are as follows:

> There were the robes, many coloured, the work of Sidonian
> women:
> They from Sidon had come, what time god-shaped Alexander
> Over the broad sea brought, that way, the high-born Helen.

In the *Odyssey* also the same fact is alluded to, in these words:

> Such, so wisely prepared, were the drugs that her stores afforded,
> Excellent; gift which one Polydamna, partner of Thonis,
> Gave her in Egypt, where many the simples that grow in the meadows,
> Potent to cure in part, in part as potent to injure.

Menelaus too, in the same poem, thus addresses Telemachus:

> Much did I long to return, but the gods still kept me in Egypt—
> Angry because I had failed to pay them their hecatombs duly.

In these places Homer shows himself acquainted with the voyage of Alexander to Egypt, for Syria borders on Egypt, and the Phoenicians, to whom Sidon belongs, dwell in Syria.

117. From these various passages, and from that about Sidon especially, it is clear that Homer did not write the *Cypria*. For there it is said that Alexander arrived at Ilium with Helen on the third day after he left Sparta, the wind having been favourable, and the sea smooth; whereas in the *Iliad*, the poet makes him wander before he brings her home. Enough, however, for the present of Homer and the *Cypria*.

118. I made inquiry of the priests, whether the story which the Greeks tell about Ilium is a fable, or no. In reply they related the following particulars, of which they declared that Menelaus had himself informed them. After the rape of Helen, a vast army of Greeks, wishing to render help to Menelaus, set sail for the Teucrian territory; on their arrival they disembarked, and formed their camp, after which they sent ambassadors to Ilium, of whom Menelaus was one. The embassy was received within the walls, and demanded the restoration of Helen with the treasures which Alexander had carried off, and likewise required satisfaction for the wrong done. The Teucrians gave at once the answer in which they persisted ever afterwards, backing their assertions sometimes even with oaths, to wit, that neither Helen, nor the treasures claimed, were in their possession, both the one and the other had remained, they said, in Egypt; and it was not just to come upon them for what Proteus, king of Egypt, was detaining. The Greeks, imagining that the Teucrians were merely laughing at them, laid siege to the town, and never rested until they finally took it. As, however, no Helen was found, and they were still told the same story, they at length believed in its truth, and despatched Menelaus to the court of Proteus.

119. So Menelaus travelled to Egypt, and on his arrival sailed up the river as far as Memphis, and related all that had happened. He met with the utmost hospitality, received Helen back unharmed, and recovered all his treasures. After this friendly treatment Menelaus, they said, behaved most unjustly towards the Egyptians; for as it happened that at the time when he wanted to take his departure, he was detained by the wind being contrary, and as he found this obstruction continue, he had recourse to a most wicked expedient. He seized, they said, two children of the people of the country, and offered them up in sacrifice. When this became known, the indignation of the people was stirred, and they went in pursuit of Menelaus, who, however,

escaped with his ships to Libya, after which the Egyptians could not say whither he went. The rest they knew full well, partly by the inquiries which they had made, and partly from the circumstances having taken place in their own land, and therefore not admitting of doubt.

120. Such is the account given by the Egyptian priests, and I am myself inclined to regard as true all that they say of Helen from the following considerations: If Helen had been at Troy, the inhabitants would, I think, have given her up to the Greeks, whether Alexander consented to it or no. For surely neither Priam, nor his family, could have been so infatuated as to endanger their own persons, their children, and their city, merely that Alexander might possess Helen. At any rate, if they determined to refuse at first, yet afterwards when so many of the Trojans fell on every encounter with the Greeks, and Priam too in each battle lost a son, or sometimes two, or three, or even more, if we may credit the epic poets, I do not believe that even if Priam himself had been married to her he would have declined to deliver her up, with the view of bringing the series of calamities to a close. Nor was it as if Alexander had been heir to the crown, in which case he might have had the chief management of affairs, since Priam was already old. Hector, who was his elder brother, and a far braver man, stood before him, and was the heir to the kingdom on the death of their father Priam. And it could not be Hector's interest to uphold his brother in his wrong, when it brought such dire calamities upon himself and the other Trojans. But the fact was that they had no Helen to deliver, and so they told the Greeks, but the Greeks would not believe what they said—Divine Providence, as I think, so willing, that by their utter destruction it might be made evident to all men that when great wrongs are done, the gods will surely visit them with great punishments. Such, at least, is my view of the matter.

[The Story of Adrastus]

34. After Solon had gone away a dreadful vengeance, sent of God, came upon Croesus, to punish him, it is likely, for deeming himself the happiest of men. First he had a dream in the night, which foreshowed him truly the evils that were about to befall him in the person of his son. For Croesus had two sons, one blasted by a natural defect, being deaf and dumb; the other distinguished far above all his co-mates in every pursuit. The name of the last was Atys. It was this son concerning whom he dreamt a dream, that he would die by the blow of an iron weapon. When he woke, he considered earnestly with himself, and, greatly alarmed at the dream, instantly made his son take a wife, and whereas in former years the youth had been wont to command the Lydian forces in the field, he now would not suffer him to accompany them. All the spears and javelins, and weapons used in the wars, he removed out of the male apartments, and laid them in heaps in the chambers of the women, fearing lest perhaps one of the weapons that hung against the wall might fall and strike him.

35. Now it chanced that while he was making arrangements for the wedding, there came to Sardis a man under a misfortune who had upon him the stain of blood. He was by race a Phrygian, and belonged to the family of the king. Presenting himself at the palace of Croesus, he prayed to be admitted to purification according to the customs of the country. . . . Croesus granted the request, and went through all the customary rites, after which he asked the suppliant of his birth and country, address-

ing him as follows:—"Who are you, stranger, and from what part of Phrygia did you flee to take refuge at my hearth? And, whom, moreover, what man or what woman, have you slain?" "Oh! king," replied the Phrygian, "I am the son of Gordias, son of Midas. I am named Adrastus. The man I unintentionally slew was my own brother. For this my father drove me from the land, and I lost all. Then fled I here to you." "You are the offspring," Croesus rejoined, "of a house friendly to mine, and you have come to friends. You shall want for nothing so long as you abide in my dominions. Bear your misfortune as easily as you may, so will it go best with you." Thenceforth Adrastus lived in the palace of the king.

36. It chanced that at this very same time there was in the Mysian Olympus a huge monster of a boar, which went forth often from this mountain-country, and wasted the corn-fields of the Mysians. Many a time had the Mysians collected to hunt the beast, but instead of doing him any hurt, they came off always with some loss to themselves. At length they sent ambassadors to Croesus, who delivered their message to him in these words: "Oh! king, a mighty monster of a boar has appeared in our parts, and destroys the labour of our hands. We do our best to take him, but in vain. Now, therefore, we beseech you to let your son accompany us back, with some chosen youths and hounds, that we may rid our country of the animal." Such was the tenor of their prayer.

But Croesus thought about his dream, and answered, "Say no more of my son going with you; that may not be in any wise. He is but just joined in wedlock, and is busy enough with that. I will grant you a picked band of Lydians, and all my hunting army, and I will charge those whom I send to use all zeal in aiding you to rid your country of this brute."

37. With this reply the Mysians were content; but the king's son, hearing what the prayer of the Mysians was, came suddenly in, and on the refusal of Croesus to let him go with them, thus addressed his father: "Formerly, my father, it was deemed the noblest and most suitable thing for me to frequent the wars and hunting parties, and win myself glory in them; but now you keep me away from both, although you have never beheld in me either cowardice or lack of spirit. What face meanwhile must I wear as I walk to the forum or return from it? What must the citizens, what must my young bride think of me? What sort of man will she suppose her husband to be? Either, therefore, let me go to the chase of this boar, or give me a reason why it is best for me to do according to your wishes."

38. Then Croesus answered, "My son, it is not because I have seen in you either cowardice or aught else which has displeased me that I keep you back; but because a vision, which came before me in a dream as I slept, warned me that you were doomed to die young, pierced by an iron weapon. It was this which first led me to hasten on your wedding, and now it hinders me from sending you upon this enterprise. I would rather keep watch over you, if by any means I may cheat fate of you during my own lifetime. For you are the one and only son that I possess; the other, whose hearing is destroyed, I regard as if he were not."

39. "Ah! father," returned the youth, "I blame you not for keeping watch over me after a dream so terrible; but if you are mistaken, if you do not apprehend the dream aright, it is no blame for me to show you wherein you are wrong. Now the dream, you said yourself, foretold that I should die stricken by an iron weapon. But

what hands has a boar to strike with? What iron weapon does he wield? Yet, this is what you fear for me. Had the dream said that I should die pierced by a tusk, then you had done well to keep me away; but it said a weapon. Now here we do not combat men, but a wild animal. I pray you, therefore, let me go with them."

40. "There you have me, my son," said Croesus, "your interpretation is better than mine. I yield to it, and change my mind, and consent to let you go."

41. The king sent for Adrastus the Phrygian, and said to him, "Adrastus, when you were struck with the rod of affliction—no reproach, my friend—I purified you and have taken you to live with me in my palace, and have been at every charge. Now, therefore, it behoves you to repay the good offices which you have received at my hands by consenting to go with my son on this hunting-party, and to watch over him, if perchance you should be attacked upon the road by some band of daring robbers. Even apart from this, it were right for you to go where you may make yourself famous by noble deeds. They are the heritage of your family, and you too are so stalwart and strong."

42. Adrastus answered, "Except for your request, Oh! king, I would rather have kept away from this hunt, for I think it ill becomes a man under a misfortune such as mine to consort with his happier compeers, and besides, I have no heart for it. On many grounds I would rather stay behind, but, as you urge it, and I am bound to please you (for truly it does behove me to repay your good offices), I am content to do as you wish. For your son, whom you give into my charge, be sure you shall receive him back safe and sound, so far as depends upon a guardian's carefulness."

43. Thus assured, Croesus let them depart, accompanied by a band of picked youths, and well provided with dogs of chase. When they reached Olympus, they scattered in quest of the animal; he was soon found, and the hunters, drawing round him in a circle, hurled their weapons at him. Then the stranger, the man who had been purified of blood, whose name was Adrastus, he also hurled his spear at the boar, but missed his aim, and struck Atys. Thus was the son of Croesus slain by the point of an iron weapon, and the warning of the vision was fulfilled. Then one ran to Sardis to bear the tidings to the king, and he came and informed him of the combat, and of the fate that had befallen his son.

44. If it was a heavy blow to the father to learn that his child was dead, it yet more strongly affected him to think that the very man whom he himself once purified had done the deed. In the violence of his grief, he called aloud on Zeus, to be a witness of what he had suffered at the stranger's hand, . . . because he had unwittingly harboured in his house the man who had now slain his son; and because the stranger, who had been sent as his child's guardian, had turned out his most cruel enemy.

45. Presently the Lydians arrived, bearing the body of the youth, and behind them followed the murderer. He took his stand in front of the corpse, and, stretching forth his hands to Croesus, delivered himself into his power with earnest entreaties that he would sacrifice him upon the body of his son—"his former misfortune was burden enough; now that he had added to it a second, and had brought ruin on the man who purified him, he could not bear to live." Then Croesus, when he heard these words, was moved with pity towards Adrastus, notwithstanding the bitterness of his own calamity; and so he answered, "Enough, my friend; I have all the revenge that I require, since you give sentence of death against yourself. But in truth, it is not you who have injured me, except so far as you have unwittingly dealt the blow. Some

god is the author of my misfortune, and I was forewarned of it a long time ago." Croesus after this buried the body of his son, with such honours as befitted the occasion. Adrastus, son of Gordias, son of Midas, the destroyer of his brother in time past, the destroyer now of his purifier, regarding himself as the most unfortunate wretch whom he had ever known, so soon as all was quiet about the place, slew himself upon the tomb. Croesus, bereft of his son, gave himself up to mourning for two full years.

Thucydides (c.460–400 BCE)

THE PELOPONNESIAN WAR

Most of what we know about Thucydides comes from the history he wrote, a detailed account of the Peloponnesian War in which Athens and Sparta fought. During the first part of the war, as an Athenian citizen, he was directly involved in events. He was in Athens when the plague struck in 430 BCE, and he caught the disease himself, but recovered. In 424 he was named one of the ten strategoi *for the year and was put in command of the fleet responsible for defending Amphipolis. When the Spartans suddenly attacked and took the city, Thucydides was recalled in disgrace. A trial resulted in his exile, which ended only when Athens finally fell twenty years later. He took advantage of his exile to continue to do research on the Spartan side of the ongoing struggle, but when he died sometime shortly after the end of the war, his history was left incomplete.*

As a participant in events, Thucydides drew upon his great store of personal observation. But he was also very aware of the great bane of historians, that people recall and interpret events in very different ways. Thucydides is frank about weighing conflicting accounts in order to arrive at the most accurate historical picture possible. At the same time, it is a trademark of his method to utter, through the mouths of his subjects, great speeches of his own devising, always based on what he could first determine about the original speech. The funeral oration of Pericles is the best example of this practice and one of the most famous prose passages in Greek literature.

In this speech, Thucydides's Pericles both defines and models the ideal Athenian, in an exercise that provides a textbook study of rhetorical techniques. Over and over Pericles praises the virtues of freedom, excellence in body and mind, open discussion, versatility, and the pursuit of beauty and grace. But in spite of these ringing idealisms—perhaps because of them—the "Funeral Oration" is also a good place to find traces of deeper social customs in Greek society. Because men are writing the histories, for instance, it is hard to find solid evidence of the conditions of women in Greek society. In the "Funeral Oration," in fact, Pericles tells the women of Athens that their greatest glory would be to be least talked about by men. This makes a virtue of what we know to be the case with Greek women, that they lived in virtual seclusion, managing household duties and child-rearing,

This translation is a famous one by the Victorian professor of Greek at Oxford, Benjamin Jowett (1881).

while their husbands alone had recourse to the agora, *the public forum for politics, discussion, and exchange. It is therefore one of the motive forces of Greek literature to show women threatening these boundaries, as in* Antigone *by Sophocles or* Lysistrata *by Aristophanes.*

The plague, which broke out in Athens during the first year of the war and killed countless Athenians, provides a good example of the kind of irony that the Greeks saw as infesting human action and therefore historical narrative. Athens had prepared for war carefully by fortifying itself, even building long walls all the way to its port at the sea. After they retreated to the safety of the walled city, Athenians were made more vulnerable to disease by the crowded conditions and the difficulty of protecting their water supply. The loss of a third of the Athenian population in three years of plague, without significant victories over Sparta and her allies, was destructive of the Athenian spirit. Thucydides therefore exploits a double irony: the tremendous loss of life that resulted from the Athenian strategy of safe retreat, and the loss of heart among the Athenians almost before the noble echoes of the "Funeral Oration" have died down.

[Introduction]

1. Thucydides, an Athenian, wrote the history of the war in which the Peloponnesians and the Athenians fought against one another. He began to write when they first took up arms, believing that it would be great and memorable above any previous war. For he argued that both states were then at the full height of their military power, and he saw the rest of the Hellenes either siding or intending to side with one or other of them. No movement ever stirred Hellas more deeply than this; it was shared by many of the Barbarians, and might be said even to affect the world at large. The character of the events which preceded, whether immediately or in more remote antiquity, owing to the lapse of time cannot be made out with certainty. But, judging from the evidence which I am able to trust after most careful enquiry, I should imagine that former ages were not great either in their wars or in anything else.

2. The country which is now called Hellas was not regularly settled in ancient times. The people were migratory, and readily left their homes whenever they were overpowered by numbers. There was no commerce, and they could not safely hold intercourse with one another either by land or sea. The several tribes cultivated their own soil just enough to obtain a maintenance from it. But they had no accumulations of wealth, and did not plant the ground; for, being without walls, they were never sure that an invader might not come and despoil them. Living in this manner and knowing that they could anywhere obtain a bare subsistence, they were always ready to migrate; so that they had neither great cities nor any considerable resources. The richest districts were most constantly changing their inhabitants; for example, the countries which are now called Thessaly and Boeotia, the greater part of the Peloponnesus with the exception of Arcadia, and all the best parts of Hellas. For the productiveness of the land increased the power of individuals; this in turn was a source of quarrels by which communities were ruined, while at the same time they were more exposed to attacks from without. Certainly Attica, of which the soil was poor and thin, enjoyed a long freedom from civil strife, and therefore retained its original

inhabitants. And a striking confirmation of my argument is afforded by the fact that Attica through immigration increased in population more than any other region. For the leading men of Hellas, when driven out of their own country by war or revolution, sought an asylum at Athens; and from the very earliest times, being admitted to rights of citizenship, so greatly increased the number of inhabitants that Attica became incapable of containing them, and was at last obliged to send out colonies to Ionia.

3. The feebleness of antiquity is further proved to me by the circumstance that there appears to have been no common action in Hellas before the Trojan War. And I am inclined to think that the very name was not as yet given to the whole country, and in fact did not exist at all before the time of Hellen, the son of Deucalion; the different tribes, of which the Pelasgian was the most widely spread, gave their own names to different districts. But when Hellen and his sons became powerful in Phthiotis, their aid was invoked by other cities, and those who associated with them gradually began to be called Hellenes, though a long time elapsed before the name prevailed over the whole country. Of this Homer affords the best evidence; for he, although he lived long after the Trojan War, nowhere uses this name collectively, but confines it to the followers of Achilles from Phthiotis, who were the original Hellenes; when speaking of the entire host he calls them Danaans, or Argives, or Achaeans. Neither is there any mention of Barbarians in his poems, clearly because there were as yet no Hellenes opposed to them by a common distinctive name. Thus the several Hellenic tribes (and I mean by the term Hellenes those who, while forming separate communities, had a common language, and were afterwards called by a common name), owing to their weakness and isolation, were never united in any great enterprise before the Trojan War. And they only made the expedition against Troy after they had gained considerable experience of the sea.

[Pericles' Funeral Oration]

34. During the same winter, in accordance with an ancestral custom, the funeral of those who first fell in this war was celebrated by the Athenians at the public charge. The ceremony is as follows: Three days before the celebration they erect a tent in which the bones of the dead are laid out, and every one brings to his own dead any offering which he pleases. At the time of the funeral the bones are placed in chests of cypress wood, which are conveyed on waggons; there is one chest for each tribe. They also carry a single empty litter decked with a pall for all whose bodies are missing, and cannot be recovered after the battle. The procession is accompanied by any one who chooses, whether citizen or stranger, and the female relatives of the deceased are present at the place of interment and make lamentation. The public sepulchre is situated in the most beautiful spot outside the walls; there they always bury those who fall in war; only after the battle of Marathon the dead, in recognition of their pre-eminent valour, were interred on the field. When the remains have been laid in the earth, some man of known ability and high reputation, chosen by the city, delivers a suitable oration over them; after which the people depart. Such is the manner of interment; and the ceremony was repeated from time to time throughout the war. Over those who were the first buried Pericles was chosen to speak. At the fitting moment he advanced

from the sepulchre to a lofty platform, which had been erected in order that he might be heard as far as possible by the multitude, and spoke as follows:

35. "Most of those who have spoken here before me have commended the law-giver who added this oration to our other funeral customs; it seemed to them a worthy thing that such an honour should be given at their burial to the dead who have fallen on the field of battle. But I should have preferred that, when men's deeds have been brave, they should be honoured in deed only, and with such an honour as this public funeral, which you are now witnessing. Then the reputation of many would not have been imperilled on the eloquence or want of eloquence of one, and their virtues believed or not as he spoke well or ill. For it is difficult to say neither too little nor too much; and even moderation is apt not to give the impression of truthfulness. The friend of the dead who knows the facts is likely to think that the words of the speaker fall short of his knowledge and of his wishes; another who is not so well informed, when he hears of anything which surpasses his own powers, will be envious and will suspect exaggeration. Mankind are tolerant of the praises of others so long as each hearer thinks that he can do as well or nearly as well himself, but, when the deed is beyond him, jealousy is aroused and he begins to be incredulous. However, since our ancestors have set the seal of their approval upon the practice, I must obey, and to the utmost of my power shall endeavour to satisfy the wishes and beliefs of all who hear me.

36. "I will speak first of our ancestors, for it is right and becoming that now, when we are lamenting the dead, a tribute should be paid to their memory. There has never been a time when they did not inhabit this land, which by their valour they have handed down from generation to generation, and we have received from them a free state. But if they were worthy of praise, still more were our fathers, who added to their inheritance, and after many a struggle transmitted to us their sons this great empire. And we ourselves assembled here to-day, who are still most of us in the vigour of life, have chiefly done the work of improvement, and have richly endowed our city with all things, so that she is sufficient for herself both in peace and war. Of the military exploits by which our various possessions were acquired, or of the energy with which we or our fathers drove back the tide of war, Hellenic or barbarian, I will not speak; for the tale would be long and is familiar to you. But before I praise the dead, I should like to point out by what principles of action we rose to power, and under what institutions and through what manner of life our empire became great. For I conceive that such thoughts are not unsuited to the occasion, and that this numerous assembly of citizens and strangers may profitably listen to them.

37. "Our form of government does not enter into rivalry with the institutions of others. We do not copy our neighbours, but are an example to them. It is true that we are called a democracy, for the administration is in the hands of the many and not of the few. But while the law secures equal justice to all alike in their private disputes, the claim of excellence is also recognised; and when a citizen is in any way distinguished, he is preferred to the public service, not as a matter of privilege, but as the reward of merit. Neither is poverty a bar, but a man may benefit his country whatever be the obscurity of his condition. There is no exclusiveness in our public life, and in our private intercourse we are not suspicious of one another, nor angry with our neighbour if he does what he likes; we do not put on sour looks at him which, though

harmless, are not pleasant. While we are thus unconstrained in our private intercourse, a spirit of reverence pervades our public acts; we are prevented from doing wrong by respect for authority and for the laws, having an especial regard to those which are ordained for the protection of the injured as well as to those unwritten laws which bring upon the transgressor of them the reprobation of the general sentiment.

38. "And we have not forgotten to provide for our weary spirits many relaxations from toil; we have regular games and sacrifices throughout the year; at home the style of our life is refined; and the delight which we daily feel in all these things helps to banish melancholy. Because of the greatness of our city the fruits of the whole earth flow in upon us; so that we enjoy the goods of other countries as freely as our own.

39. "Then, again, our military training is in many respects superior to that of our adversaries. Our city is thrown open to the world, and we never expel a foreigner or prevent him from seeing or learning anything of which the secret if revealed to an enemy might profit him. We rely not upon management or trickery, but upon our own hearts and hands. And in the matter of education, whereas they from early youth are always undergoing laborious exercises which are to make them brave, we live at ease, and yet are equally ready to face the perils which they face. And here is the proof. The Lacedaemonians come into Attica not by themselves, but with their whole confederacy following; we go alone into a neighbour's country; and although our opponents are fighting for their homes and we on a foreign soil, we have seldom any difficulty in overcoming them. Our enemies have never yet felt our united strength; the care of a navy divides our attention, and on land we are obliged to send our own citizens everywhere. But they, if they meet and defeat a part of our army, are as proud as if they had routed us all, and when defeated they pretend to have been vanquished by us all.

"If then we prefer to meet danger with a light heart but without laborious training, and with a courage which is gained by habit and not enforced by law, are we not greatly the gainers? Since we do not anticipate the pain, although, when the hour comes, we can be as brave as those who never allow themselves to rest; and thus too our city is equally admirable in peace and in war.

40. "For we are lovers of the beautiful, yet with economy, and we cultivate the mind without the loss of manliness. Wealth we employ, not for talk and ostentation, but when there is a real use for it. To avow poverty with us is no disgrace; the true disgrace is in doing nothing to avoid it. An Athenian citizen does not neglect the state because he takes care of his own household; and even those of us who are engaged in business have a very fair idea of politics. We alone regard a man who takes no interest in public affairs, not as a harmless, but as a useless character; and if few of us are originators, we are all sound judges of a policy. The great impediment to action is, in our opinion, not discussion, but the want of that knowledge which is gained by discussion preparatory to action. For we have a peculiar power of thinking before we act and of acting too, whereas other men are courageous from ignorance but hesitate upon reflection. And they are surely to be esteemed the bravest spirits who, having the clearest sense both of the pains and pleasures of life, do not on that account shrink from danger. In doing good, again, we are unlike others; we make our friends by conferring, not by receiving favours. Now he who confers a favour is the firmer friend, because he would fain by kindness keep alive the memory of an obligation; but the

recipient is colder in his feelings, because he knows that in requiting another's generosity he will not be winning gratitude but only paying a debt. We alone do good to our neighbours not upon a calculation of interest, but in the confidence of freedom and in a frank and fearless spirit.

41. "To sum up: I say that Athens is the school of Hellas, and that the individual Athenian in his own person seems to have the power of adapting himself to the most varied forms of action with the utmost versatility and grace. This is no passing and idle word, but truth and fact; and the assertion is verified by the position to which these qualities have raised the state. For in the hour of trial Athens alone among her contemporaries is superior to the report of her. No enemy who comes against her is indignant at the reverses which he sustains at the hands of such a city; no subject complains that his masters are unworthy of him. And we shall assuredly not be without witnesses; there are mighty monuments of our power which will make us the wonder of this and of succeeding ages; we shall not need the praises of Homer or of any other panegyrist whose poetry may please for the moment, although his representation of the facts will not bear the light of day. For we have compelled every land and every sea to open a path for our valour, and have everywhere planted eternal memorials of our friendship and of our enmity. Such is the city for whose sake these men nobly fought and died; they could not bear the thought that she might be taken from them; and every one of us who survive should gladly toil on her behalf.

42. "I have dwelt upon the greatness of Athens because I want to show you that we are contending for a higher prize than those who enjoy none of these privileges, and to establish by manifest proof the merit of these men whom I am now commemorating. Their loftiest praise has been already spoken. For in magnifying the city I have magnified them, and men like them whose virtues made her glorious. And of how few Hellenes can it be said as of them, that their deeds when weighed in the balance have been found equal to their fame! It seems to me that a death such as theirs has been given the true measure of a man's worth; it may be the first revelation of his virtues, but is at any rate their final seal. For even those who come short in other ways may justly plead the valour with which they have fought for their country; they have blotted out the evil with the good, and have benefited the state more by their public services than they have injured her by their private actions. None of these men were enervated by wealth or hesitated to resign the pleasures of life; none of them put off the evil day in the hope, natural to poverty, that a man, though poor, may one day become rich. But, deeming that the punishment of their enemies was sweeter than any of these things, and that they could fall in no nobler cause, they determined at the hazard of their lives to be honourably avenged, and to leave the rest. They resigned to hope their unknown chance of happiness; but in the face of death they resolved to rely upon themselves alone. And when the moment came they were minded to resist and suffer, rather than to fly and save their lives; they ran away from the word of dishonour, but on the battle-field their feet stood fast, and in an instant, at the height of their fortune, they passed away from the scene, not of their fear, but of their glory.

43. "Such was the end of these men; they were worthy of Athens, and the living need not desire to have a more heroic spirit, although they may pray for a less fatal issue. The value of such a spirit is not to be expressed in words. Any one can discourse to you for ever about the advantages of a brave defence which you know already. But

instead of listening to him I would have you day by day fix your eyes upon the greatness of Athens, until you become filled with the love of her; and when you are impressed by the spectacle of her glory, reflect that this empire has been acquired by men who knew their duty and had the courage to do it, who in the hour of conflict had the fear of dishonour always present to them, and who, if ever they failed in an enterprize, would not allow their virtues to be lost to their country, but freely gave their lives to her as the fairest offering which they could present at her feast. The sacrifice which they collectively made was individually repaid to them; for they received again each one for himself a praise which grows not old, and the noblest of all sepulchres—I speak not of that in which their remains are laid, but of that in which their glory survives, and is proclaimed always and on every fitting occasion both in word and deed. For the whole earth is the sepulchre of famous men; not only are they commemorated by columns and inscriptions in their own country, but in foreign lands there dwells also an unwritten memorial of them, graven not on stone but in the hearts of men. Make them your examples, and esteeming courage to be freedom and freedom to be happiness, do not weigh too nicely the perils of war. The unfortunate who has no hope of a change for the better has less reason to throw away his life than the prosperous who, if he survive, is always liable to a change for the worse, and to whom any accidental fall makes the most serious difference. To a man of spirit, cowardice and disaster coming together are far more bitter than death striking him unperceived at a time when he is full of courage and animated by the general hope.

44. "Wherefore I do not now commiserate the parents of the dead who stand here; I would rather comfort them. You know that your life has been passed amid manifold vicissitudes; and that they may be deemed fortunate who have gained most honour, whether an honourable death like theirs, or an honourable sorrow like yours, and whose days have been so ordered that the term of their happiness is likewise the term of their life. I know how hard it is to make you feel this, when the good fortune of others will too often remind you of the gladness which once lightened your hearts. And sorrow is felt at the want of those blessings, not which a man never knew, but which were a part of his life before they were taken from him. Some of you are of an age at which they may hope to have other children, and they ought to bear their sorrow better; not only will the children who may hereafter be born make them forget their own lost ones, but the city will be doubly a gainer. She will not be left desolate, and she will be safer. For a man's counsel cannot have equal weight or worth, when he alone has no children to risk in the general danger. To those of you who have passed their prime, I say, 'Congratulate yourselves that you have been happy during the greater part of your days; remember that your life of sorrow will not last long, and be comforted by the glory of those who are gone. For the love of honour alone is ever young, and not riches, as some say, but honour is the delight of men when they are old and useless.'

45. "To you who are the sons and brothers of the departed, I see that the struggle to emulate them will be an arduous one. For all men praise the dead, and, however pre-eminent your virtue may be, hardly will you be thought, I do not say to equal, but even to approach them. The living have their rivals and detractors, but when a man is out of the way, the honour and good-will which he receives is unalloyed. And, if I am to speak of womanly virtues to those of you who will henceforth be widows, let me sum them up in one short admonition: To a woman not to show more weak-

ness than is natural to her sex is a great glory, and not to be talked about for good or for evil among men.

46. "I have paid the required tribute, in obedience to the law, making use of such fitting words as I had. The tribute of deeds has been paid in part; for the dead have been honourably interred, and it remains only that their children should be maintained at the public charge until they are grown up: this is the solid prize with which, as with a garland, Athens crowns her sons living and dead, after a struggle like theirs. For where the rewards of virtue are greatest, there the noblest of citizens are enlisted in the service of the state. And now, when you have duly lamented, every one his own dead, you may depart."

[The Plague in Athens]

47. Such was the order of the funeral celebrated in this winter, with the end of which ended the first year of the Peloponnesian War. As soon as summer returned, the Peloponnesian army, comprising as before two-thirds of the force of each confederate state, under the command of the Lacedaemonian king Archidamus, the son of Zeuxidamus, invaded Attica, where they established themselves and ravaged the country. They had not been there many days when the plague broke out at Athens for the first time. A similar disorder is said to have previously smitten many places, particularly Lemnos, but there is no record of such a pestilence occurring elsewhere, or of so great a destruction of human life. For a while physicians, in ignorance of the nature of the disease, sought to apply remedies; but it was in vain, and they themselves were among the first victims, because they oftenest came into contact with it. No human art was of any avail, and as to supplications in temples, enquiries of oracles, and the like, they were utterly useless, and at last men were overpowered by the calamity and gave them all up.

48. The disease is said to have begun south of Egypt in Aethiopia; thence it descended into Egypt and Libya, and after spreading over the greater part of the Persian empire, suddenly fell upon Athens. It first attacked the inhabitants of the Piraeus, and it was supposed that the Peloponnesians had poisoned the cisterns, no conduits having as yet been made there. It afterwards reached the upper city, and then the mortality became far greater. As to its probable origin or the causes which might or could have produced such a disturbance of nature, every man, whether a physician or not, will give his own opinion. But I shall describe its actual course, and the symptoms by which any one who knows them beforehand may recognise the disorder should it ever reappear. For I was myself attacked, and witnessed the sufferings of others.

49. The season was admitted to have been remarkably free from ordinary sickness; and if anybody was already ill of any other disease, it was absorbed in this. Many who were in perfect health, all in a moment, and without any apparent reason, were seized with violent heats in the head and with redness and inflammation of the eyes. Internally the throat and the tongue were quickly suffused with blood, and the breath became unnatural and fetid. There followed sneezing and hoarseness; in a short time the disorder, accompanied by a violent cough, reached the chest; then fastening lower down, it would move the stomach and bring on all the vomits of bile to which physicians have ever given names; and they were very distressing. An ineffectual retching

producing violent convulsions attacked most of the sufferers; some as soon as the previous symptoms had abated, others not until long afterwards. The body externally was not so very hot to the touch, nor yet pale; it was of a livid colour inclining to red, and breaking out in pustules and ulcers. But the internal fever was intense; the sufferers could not bear to have on them even the finest linen garment; they insisted on being naked, and there was nothing which they longed for more eagerly than to throw themselves into cold water. And many of those who had no one to look after them actually plunged into the cisterns, for they were tormented by unceasing thirst, which was not in the least assuaged whether they drank little or much. They could not sleep; a restlessness which was intolerable never left them. While the disease was at its height the body, instead of wasting away, held out amid these sufferings in a marvellous manner, and either they died on the seventh or ninth day, not of weakness, for their strength was not exhausted, but of internal fever, which was the end of most; or, if they survived, then the disease descended into the bowels and there produced violent ulceration; severe diarrhoea at the same time set in, and at a later stage caused exhaustion, which finally with few exceptions carried them off. For the disorder which had originally settled in the head passed gradually through the whole body, and, if a person got over the worst, would often seize the extremities and leave its mark, attacking the genitals and the fingers and the toes; and some escaped with the loss of these, some with the loss of their eyes. Some again had no sooner recovered than they were seized with a forgetfulness of all things and knew neither themselves nor their friends.

50. The malady took a form not to be described, and the fury with which it fastened upon each sufferer was too much for human nature to endure. There was one circumstance in particular which distinguished it from ordinary diseases. The birds and animals which feed on human flesh, although so many bodies were lying unburied, either never came near them, or died if they touched them. This was proved by a remarkable disappearance of the birds of prey, who were not to be seen either about the bodies or anywhere else; while in the case of the dogs the fact was even more obvious, because they live with man.

51. Such was the general nature of the disease; I omit many strange peculiarities which characterised individual cases. None of the ordinary sicknesses attacked any one while it lasted, or, if they did, they ended in the plague. Some of the sufferers died from want of care, others equally who were receiving the greatest attention. No single remedy could be deemed a specific; for that which did good to one did harm to another. No constitution was of itself strong enough to resist or weak enough to escape the attacks; the disease carried off all alike and defied every mode of treatment. Most appalling was the despondency which seized upon any one who felt himself sickening; for he instantly abandoned his mind to despair and, instead of holding out, absolutely threw away his chance of life. Appalling too was the rapidity with which men caught the infection; dying like sheep if they attended on one another; and this was the principal cause of mortality. When they were afraid to visit one another, the sufferers died in their solitude, so that many houses were empty because there had been no one left to take care of the sick; or if they ventured they perished, especially those who aspired to heroism. For they went to see their friends without thought of themselves and were ashamed to leave them, even at a time when the very relations of the dying were at last growing weary and ceased to make lamentations,

overwhelmed by the vastness of the calamity. But whatever instances there may have been of such devotion, more often the sick and the dying were tended by the pitying care of those who had recovered, because they knew the course of the disease and were themselves free from apprehension. For no one was ever attacked a second time, or not with a fatal result. All men congratulated them, and they themselves, in the excess of their joy at the moment, had an innocent fancy that they could not die of any other sickness.

52. The crowding of the people out of the country into the city aggravated the misery; and the newly arrived suffered most. For, having no houses of their own, but inhabiting in the height of summer stifling huts, the mortality among them was dreadful, and they perished in wild disorder. The dead lay as they had died, one upon another, while others hardly alive wallowed in the streets and crawled about every fountain craving for water. The temples in which they lodged were full of the corpses of those who died in them; for the violence of the calamity was such that man, not knowing where to turn, grew reckless of all law, human and divine. The customs which had hitherto been observed at funerals were universally violated, and they buried their dead each one as best he could. Many, having no proper appliances, because the deaths in their household had been so frequent, made no scruple of using the burial-place of others. When one man had raised a funeral pile, others would come, and throwing on their dead first, set fire to it; or when some other corpse was already burning, before they could be stopped would throw their own dead upon it and depart.

53. There were other and worse forms of lawlessness which the plague introduced at Athens. Men who had hitherto concealed their indulgence in pleasure now grew bolder. For, seeing the sudden change, how the rich died in a moment, and those who had nothing immediately inherited their property, they reflected that life and riches were alike transitory, and they resolved to enjoy themselves while they could, and to think only of pleasure. Who would be willing to sacrifice himself to the law of honour when he knew not whether he would ever live to be held in honour? The pleasure of the moment and any sort of thing which conduced to it took the place both of honour and of expediency. No fear of God or law of man deterred a criminal. Those who saw all perishing alike, thought that the worship or neglect of the gods made no difference. For offences against human law no punishment was to be feared; no one would live long enough to be called to account. Already a far heavier sentence had been passed and was hanging over a man's head; before that fell, why should he not take a little pleasure?

54. Such was the grievous calamity which now afflicted the Athenians; within the walls their people were dying, and without, their country was being ravaged. In their troubles they naturally called to mind a verse which the elder men among them declared to have been current long ago:

> A Dorian war will come and a plague with it.

There was a dispute about the precise expression; some saying that *limos*, a famine, and not *loimos*, a plague, was the original word. Nevertheless, as might have been expected, for men's memories reflected their sufferings, the argument in favour of *loimos* prevailed at the time. But if ever in future years another Dorian war arises which happens to be accompanied by a famine, they will probably repeat the verse in the other form. The answer of the oracle to the Lacedaemonians when the god was asked whether they should go to war or not, and he replied that if they fought with all their might, they would conquer, and that he himself would take their part, was not forgotten by those who had heard of it, and they quite imagined that they were witnessing the fulfilment of his words. The disease certainly did set in immediately after the invasion of the Peloponnesians, and did not spread into Peloponnesus in any degree worth speaking of, while Athens felt its ravages most severely, and next to Athens the places which were most populous. Such was the history of the plague.

Aristophanes (c.447–c.385 BCE)

LYSISTRATA

Lysistrata's *popular status as a great satirical anti-war play has ensured its continued popularity and relevance. That it also shows women scheming to overthrow the bumbling efforts of supposedly worthy warriors has given it an added punch with modern audiences. Its ultimate meaning for the original Greek audiences may have been a little more complicated, although its obscenity and sexual humor seem always to have encouraged private acclaim mixed with public disapproval. Aristophanes presented the play at Athens in 411 BCE, just more than a year after Athens's entire fleet of ships had been destroyed in a rash expedition to Sicily. It would not have seemed to Athenians in 411 that peace was possible in any way besides surrender, which was also out of the question. Besides that, from the time of his youth until his middle age, Aristophanes knew only the Peloponnesian War with its devastating rifts among the Greek city states.*

That an audience—especially an audience of more than 14,000—could laugh in these circumstances, and at *these circumstances, derives both from Aristophanes' comic gift and from the particulars of comic performance. Even during the war, there continued to be two festivals in honor of Dionysus in Athens each year, both involving dramatic competitions. At the City or Greater Dionysia in March, on each of three or four days there were five plays performed in succession: a trilogy of tragic dramas and a satirical satyr play, all by one playwright, and a comedy by another playwright. After an already rigorous selection process, the playwrights (technically the choruses of their plays) were competing for prizes and prestige. In January, when travel was more difficult, the Lenaia was also the occasion for plays, two tragedies each by two playwrights, and a single comedy by each of three playwrights. Aristophanes wrote as many as forty plays for these festivals (only eleven survive) and won a prize at least eight times. The audiences at these festivals, including nearly all the male citizens of the city, but women and children as well, were expert theatergoers who were accustomed to seeing dramatic—and challenging—representations of the city's highest values. Comedy as well as tragedy worked to reinforce the public good, even if its scurrilous satires and parodies (not sparing the audience or important individuals in the audience) at first seem to aim no higher than the belt.* Lysistrata, *for instance,*

This selection is taken from *Lysistrata,* translated by classicist and poet Sarah Ruden (Indianapolis: Hackett Publishing, 2003).

exposes the bullying and bluster of the men, but also indicts the self-concerned women as complicit in the endless and pointless war.

The passage below, the opening scene in the play, sets up the action nicely. Lysistrata must cajole her comrades—women from both sides in the war among the city states—into staging a sex strike to force the men to peace negotiations. The difficulty of this persuasion—late-arrivals, chatter about clothes and make-up, a formal oath over wine—exposes the stereotypical vices of women even before we see what passes for heroism among their husbands later in the play. And of course, the women are shown to be as enslaved to sexual desire as their men, although perhaps not quite so visibly so in most productions.

That sexual playfulness—no matter how serious the intent—is one of the play's chief attractions, and from ancient Greek times it has afforded directors opportunities for positively dirty stage business, from huge erections under the tunics to various degrees of nudity (remember, however, that all the actors in ancient Greek plays were male). And the language is another thing again.

Lysistrata *has always presented a problem to translators. The original Greek is colloquial, with puns and double meanings everywhere implied, but mixed too with outright obscenities. Furthermore, Aristophanes differentiates the dialects of some characters, so that Lampito of the Spartans and other characters speak in decidedly rustic or non-posh accents. But slang and vulgar language shift wildly from age to age and culture to culture. To translate the Greek literally, therefore, would convey none of the clever uses of language and probably be unintelligible to a modern audience. To treat the text with the formal sanctity accorded the elevated tragedies would miss the tremendous fun of the satire and be untrue to the sense of the play. Modern translators increasingly use current slang and vulgar terms to convey some of the impact of the original to an audience, and that is true of Sarah Ruden's translation, offered here.*

[Lysistrata Rallies the Women at the Acropolis]

Lysistrata:

Oh, Calonice, this just burns me up.
Women are slacking off, can't make the grade.
Our husbands say we're cunning to the point
Of—well—depravity.

Calonice:

Darn tootin' right!

Lysistrata:

But given word to meet me here today—
A vital matter needs our serious thought—
They're sleeping in.

Calonice:

But sweetie, soon they'll come.
Sometimes it's quite a challenge sneaking out.

The husband might require some straightening up,
The maid a screech to get her out of bed,
The kid a bath, a nibble, or a nap.

LYSISTRATA:
But what I have to say means more than that
To women.

CALONICE:
Precious, what *is* eating you?
Why summon us in this mysterious way?
What is it? Is it . . . big?

LYSISTRATA:
Of course.

CALONICE:
And hard?

LYSISTRATA:
Count on it.

CALONICE:
Then how could they not have *come?*

LYSISTRATA:
Oh, shut your mouth. They *would* have flocked for that.
No, this thing I've gone through exhaustively;
I've worked it over, chewed it late at night.

CALONICE:
Pathetic if it needed that much help.

LYSISTRATA:
It's this pathetic: in the women's hands
Is the salvation of the whole of Greece.

CALONICE:
In women's hands? It's hanging by a thread.

LYSISTRATA:
We hold within our grasp the city's plight.
The Peloponnesians may be wiped out—

CALONICE:
By Zeus, that's best, as far as we're concerned—

LYSISTRATA:
And the Boeotians with them, root and branch—

CALONICE:
All of them, fine, except those gorgeous eels.

Lysistrata:
I won't say Athens, since the omen's bad.
Imagine if I'd said it—shocking, huh?
If all the women come together here—
Boeotians, Peloponnesians, and the rest—
And us—together we can salvage Greece.

Calonice:
What thoughtful thing could women ever do?
What vivid venture? We just sit decked out
In saffron gowns, makeup about this thick,
Cimberian lingerie, and platform shoes.

Lysistrata:
It's those that I intend to save our race:
Those dresses, and perfume, and rouge, and shoes,
And little see-through numbers that we wear.

Calonice:
How's that?

Lysistrata:
The men surviving won't lift up
Their spears (against each other, anyway).

Calonice:
By the Two Gods, I've got a dress to dye!

Lysistrata:
Or shields—

Calonice:
I've got a negligée to try!

Lysistrata:
Or knives—

Calonice:
Ooh, ooh, and shoes! And shoes to buy!

Lysistrata:
So shouldn't all the other women come?

Calonice:
Well, YES! With wings to boost them, hours ago!

Lysistrata:
It's such a bitch assembling Attica.
You know they'd rather die than be on time.
Nobody even came here from the coast,
Or out of Salamis.

CALONICE:
I'm sure they got
Up on those mounts of theirs at break of day.

LYSISTRATA:
I thought it would be only logical
For the Acharnians to start the crowd,
But they're not here yet.

CALONICE:
Well, Theogenes' wife
Has raised her glass to us—any excuse.
No, wait. Look thataway: here come a few,

LYSISTRATA:
And now a couple more.

(Several women straggle in, among them Myrrhine, a young and beautiful matron.)

CALONICE:
Yuck, what a smell!
Where are they from?

LYSISTRATA:
The puke-bush swamp.

CALONICE:
By Zeus,
It must be quite a place to raise a stink.

MYRRHINE:
Ooh, Lysistrata, are we very late?
Too mad to say?

LYSISTRATA:
Why should I not be mad?
This is important! Why not come on time?

MYRRHINE:
Well, it was dark—I couldn't find my thing—
But say what's on your mind, now that we're here.

LYSISTRATA:
No, wait a little while. The other wives,
The Boeotians and the Peloponnesians,
Are on the way.

MYRRHINE:
All right, of course we'll wait.
Look over there, though—that's not Lampito?

(Enter Lampito, a strapping woman in a distinct, more revealing costume. Several others in various foreign dress accompany her, including a Boeotian and a Corinthian Woman.)

Lysistrata:
Darling Laconian, Lampito, hail!
How I admire your gleaming gorgeousness,
Your radiant skin, your body sleek and plump.
I bet that you could choke a bull.

Lampito:
I could.
I'm in such shape I kick my own sweet ass.

Calonice: *(Prodding curiously.)*
And what a brace of boobs. How bountiful!

Lampito:
What am I s'pposed to be? A pig for sale?

Lysistrata:
And what's this other young thing's origin?

Lampito:
Boeotia sent her as a delegate.
She's at your service.

Myrrhine: *(Peeking under woman's clothes.)*
Boeotian—sure enough:
Just look at what a broad and fertile plain.

Calonice: *(Peeking likewise.)*
She's even pulled the weeds. Now *that* is class.

Lysistrata:
And what's the other girl?

Lampito:
Corinthian.
Hell, ain't she fine?

Lysistrata:
Damn right she's fine . . . from here,
And get another angle on her—wow!

Lampito:
We're like a women's army. Who put out
The word to assemble?

Lysistrata:
That was me.

LAMPITO:

How come?
Tell us what's going on.

CALONICE:

Yeah, honey, what?
What all-important burr is up your butt?

LYSISTRATA:

The time has come. But first you answer me
One weensy little thing.

CALONICE:

Okay. Just ask.

LYSISTRATA:

I know you all have husbands far from home
On active service. Don't you miss the men,
The fathers of your children, all this time?

CALONICE:

My husband's been away five months in Thrace.
Somebody's gotta watch the general.

MYRRHINE:

Mine's been in Pylos seven freaking months.

LAMPITO:

Once in a while, mine's back, but then he's off.
It's like that shield's a friggin' pair of wings.

LYSISTRATA:

And since the Milesians deserted us
(Along with every scrap of lover here),
We've even lost those six-inch substitutes,
Those dinky dildos for emergencies.
If I could find a way to end this war,
Would you be willing partners?

CALONICE:

I sure would.
I'd sacrifice my nicest dress to buy
Some wine (and sacrifice the wine to me).

MYRRHINE:

I'd cut myself in two and donate half—
A flat slice like a bottom-feeding fish.

LAMPITO:

I'd hike clear up Mount Taygetus to see
If peace is flashin' somewhere way far off.

Lysistrata:
Fine. So. Here goes. You need to know the plan.
Yes, ladies. How we force the men to peace.
How are we going to do it? We must all
Hold off—

Calonice:
From *what?*

Lysistrata:
You're positive you will?

Calonice:
We'll do it! Even if it costs our lives.

Lysistrata:
From now on, no more penises for you.

(The women begin to disperse.)

Wait! You can't all just turn and walk away!
And what's this purse-lipped shaking of your heads?
You're turning pale—is that a tear I see?
Will you or not? You can't hold out on me!

Calonice:
No, I don't think so. Let the war go on.

Myrrhine:
Me? Not a chance in hell, so screw the war.

Lysistrata:
That's it, my piscine heroine? You said
Just now that you'd bisect yourself for peace.

Calonice:
ANYTHING else for me. I'd walk through fire,
But do without a dick? Be serious!
There's nothing, Lysistrata, like a dick.

Lysistrata: *(Turning to Woman #1.)*
And you?

Woman #1:
Me? Mmm, I'll take the fire, thanks.

Lysistrata:
Oh, gender fit for boning up the butt!
No wonder we're the stuff of tragedies:
Some guy, a bit of nookie, and a brat.

(To Lampito.)

But you, sweet foreigner, if you alone
Stand with me, then we still could save the day.
Give me your vote!

LAMPITO:
Shit, it's no easy thing
To lie in bed alone without no dong . . .
But count me in. Peace we just gotta have.

LYSISTRATA:
The only *woman* in this half-assed horde!

CALONICE:
Suppose we did—the thing you say we should—
Which gods forbid—what has that got to do
With peace?

LYSISTRATA:
A lot, I promise you. If we
Sit in our quarters, powdered daintily,
As good as nude in those imported slips,
And—just—slink by, with crotches nicely groomed,
The men will swell right up and want to boink,
But we won't let them near us, we'll refuse—
Trust me, they'll make a treaty at a dash.

LAMPITO:
You're right! You know how Menelaus saw
Helen's bazooms and threw his weapon down.

CALONICE:
But what if they just shrug and walk away?

LYSISTRATA:
For them, there's just one place a dildo fits.

CALONICE:
As if a fake is lots of fun for us.
Suppose they grab us, drag us into bed.
We'll have no choice.

LYSISTRATA:
Resist. Hang on the door.

CALONICE:
Suppose they beat us.

LYSISTRATA:
Yield a lousy lay.
They force a woman, and it's no more fun.
Plus, no more housework! They'll give up—you'll see
How fast. No husband's going to like to screw
Unless he knows his woman likes it too.

Calonice:
If that's the thing you're set on, fine—okay.

Lampito:
We'll force the Spartan husbands into peace:
No cheating, quibbling, squabbling any more.
But what about them lowlifes in your town?
What'll you do so they don't run amok?

Lysistrata:
We'll handle things on our side. Don't you fret.

Lampito:
I will. You know that god of yours has got
An expense account for sails and all the rest.

Lysistrata:
We've put aside that obstacle ourselves.
Today we occupy the citadel.
This is the mission of the senior squad.
While we confer here, they've gone up to fake
A sacrifice, and storm the Acropolis.

Lampito:
You *are* a clever thang. Fine all around!

Lysistrata:
Let's quickly swear an oath, my friend, and set
Our concord up unbendable as bronze.

Lampito:
Give us whatever oath you wanna give.

Lysistrata:
So where's the guard? (I'm talking to you! Wake up!)

(Enter Female Scythian Guard in an exotic uniform.)

Bring here your shield and set it upside down.

(She obeys. The women pause.)

Now where's the sacrifice?

Calonice:
What can we find
To swear on, Lysistrata?

Lysistrata:
Aeschylus
Had people drain the blood of slaughtered sheep
Into a shield.

CALONICE:
A shield? To swear for peace?
Excuse me, honey, but that can't be right.

LYSISTRATA:
What else, then?

CALONICE:
We could find a giant stud,
A pure white stallion, say, and hack him up.

LYSISTRATA:
What do you mean, a horse?

CALONICE:
We need to swear
On *something.*

LYSISTRATA:
Listen up! I know the way:
A big black drinking bowl laid on its back;
A jar of Thasian to sacrifice;
An oath to mix no water with the wine.

LAMPITO:
Shit sakes, I like that more than I can say.

LYSISTRATA:
Somebody bring a jar out, and a bowl.

(The items are brought.)

MYRRHINE:
Hey, sisters, that's some massive pottery!

CALONICE: *(Snatching.)*
Just fondling it, you'd start to feel real good.

LYSISTRATA:
Put the bowl down and help me hold the beast.

(Calonice relinquishes her hold. All the women join in lifting the jar.)

Holy Persuasion, and our Bowl for Pals,
Be gracious toward this women's sacrifice.

(Lysistrata opens the jar. The women pour.)

CALONICE:
Propitiously the gleaming blood spurts forth!

LAMPITO:
By Castor, and it smells real pretty too.

Myrrhine:
Girls, let me be the first to swear the oath.

Calonice:
No way, by Aphrodite. We'll draw lots.

Lysistrata:
Grip the bowl's rim, Lampito and the rest.

(They obey.)

One of you, speak for all, repeat my words,
Then everybody else confirm the oath.
Neither my boyfriend nor my wedded spouse—

Calonice:
Neither my boyfriend nor my wedded spouse—

Lysistrata:
Shall touch me when inflated. Say it, girl!

Calonice:
Shall touch me when inflated. Holy hell!
Knees—Lysistrata—wobbly. Gonna faint!

Lysistrata: *(Sternly, ignoring this distress.)*
I shall stay home unhumped both night and day,

Calonice:
I shall stay home unhumped both night and day,

Lysistrata:
While wearing makeup and a flashy dress,

Calonice:
While wearing makeup and a flashy dress,

Lysistrata:
That I may give my man the scorching hots,

Calonice:
That I may give my man the scorching hots,

Lysistrata:
But I will not consent to what he wants,

Calonice:
But I will not consent to what he wants,

Lysistrata:
And if he forces me, against my will,

Calonice:
And if he forces me, against my will,

LYSISTRATA:
Then I will sulk, I will not hump along;

CALONICE:
Then I will sulk, I will not hump along;

LYSISTRATA:
I will not point my slippers at the roof;

CALONICE:
I will not point my slippers at the roof;

LYSISTRATA:
Nor, like a lion knickknack, ass in air—

CALONICE:
Nor, like a lion knickknack, ass in air—

LYSISTRATA:
Abiding by these vows, may I drink wine;

CALONICE:
Abiding by these vows, may I drink wine;

LYSISTRATA:
If I transgress, let water fill the bowl.

CALONICE:
If I transgress, let water fill the bowl.

LYSISTRATA:
Now do you all consent?

ALL:
By Zeus, we do.

LYSISTRATA:
I dedicate this bowl. *(She drinks heartily.)*

CALONICE:
Just drink your share!
We've got to work together, starting now.

(All drink. A mass ululation is heard offstage.)

LAMPITO:
Somebody's shouting.

LYSISTRATA:
As I said before:
It's our contingent on the citadel.
They've taken it already. Lampito,
You go arrange things back in Sparta. These

(Indicates Spartan Women.)

Will need to stay with us as hostages.
We'll join the rest of the Athenians
And help them heave the bars behind the doors.

Calonice:
You think the men will find out right away
And all gang up on us?

Lysistrata:
The hell with them.
They can't make threats or fires fierce enough.
These doors stay shut. We only open them
On those exact conditions we've set down.

Calonice:
So Aphrodite help us, we'll stay put,
Or not deserve the cherished title "Bitch."

(All the women exit into stage building.)

(Enter a Chorus of twelve Old Men, carrying logs, unlit torches, and pots of burning charcoal.)

Greek Philosophy and Science

The first Greek thinkers were what we would call scientists. They examined the world around them and speculated about physical reality. Three kinds of investigation preoccupied them: terrestrial measurement, astronomy, and the analysis of physical matter. They developed a science that sought logical answers to questions that had previously been answered by mythic stories that were the basis of religious belief. Soon this logical inquiry into the things of the world embraced the human realm as well, and the famous motto of the Delphic Oracle—"Know Thyself"—became the central concern of thinkers like Heraclitus and Socrates.

Thales of Miletus (624–546 BCE)

Thales was the founder of the Milesian school of philosophy. Tradition has him traveling widely, introducing Egyptian geometry to Greece, working as an engineer and astronomer, meanwhile making a fortune in olive oil. He is popularly credited with determining the height of the pyramids by measuring their shadows at the time when his own shadow equaled his height. Although none of his writings survives, he was so widely admired by later generations that he was always placed among the Seven Sages and his ideas were repeated and challenged by later philosophers. Aristotle, for instance, credited him with four main ideas: that water is the first principle and basic ingredient of all things; that the earth, which is flat, floats upon water; that all things are full of gods; and that a magnetic stone has soul because it can cause iron to move.

Anaximander (fl. 560 BCE)
from *On Nature*

Anaximander, probably a student of Thales, did not agree that water was the basis of all things. Instead he sought the unity that lay behind the division of the natural world into

The translations come mainly from Arthur Fairbank's *The First Philosophers of Greece* (London: Kegan Paul, 1898). Xenophanes's poem is translated by Willis Barnstone (New York: Bantam, 1962). The works of Hippocrates are translated by Francis Adams (1849), Archimedes by T. L. Heath (London: Clay, 1897), and Ptolemy by G. J. Toomer (London: Duckworth, 1984). Epicurus is translated by Brad Inwood and L. P. Gerson, from *Hellenistic Philosophy* (Hackett, 1988).

properties like wet and dry, hot and cold. In his view, the essential substance of the natural world was what he called "the unlimited." He was the first western philosopher to write treatises, but only one sentence of his own writing survives: the principles he believed in were preserved by his followers and later writers. He was a geographer and astronomer. He made a map of the world, and introduced geometry into the mapping of the heavens. He invented the sundial and believed the earth was at rest in the center of the universe.

---

1. "Immortal and indestructible," surrounds all and directs all.
2. The first principle is older than water and is eternal motion; in this all things come into being, and all things perish.
3. The first principle and element of all things is infinite. . . . It is neither water nor any other one of the things called elements, but the infinite is something of a different nature, from which came all the heavens and the worlds in them; and from what source things arise, to that they return of necessity when they are destroyed.
4. There are no other causes besides the infinite (such as mind, or friendship), but . . . it itself is divine; for it is immortal and indestructible.
5. Things come into being [not] by change in the nature of the element, but by the separation of the opposites which the eternal motion causes.
6. Existing opposites are separated from the unity.
7. Motion is eternal, and as a result of it the heavens arise. The earth is a heavenly body, controlled by no other power, and keeping its position because it is the same distance from all things; the form of it is curved, cylindrical like a stone column; it has two faces, one of these is the ground beneath our feet, and the other is opposite to it. The stars are a circle of fire, separated from the fire about the world, and surrounded by air. There are certain breathing-holes like the holes of a flute through which we see the stars; so that when the holes are stopped up, there are eclipses. The moon is sometimes full and sometimes in other phases as these holes are stopped up or open. The circle of the sun is twenty-seven times that of the moon, and the sun is higher than the moon, but the circles of the fixed stars are lower.
8. Animals come into being through vapours raised by the sun. Man, however, came into being from another animal, namely the fish, for at first he was like a fish.
9. An infinite number of worlds have been generated and have perished again and returned to their source.

Anaximenes (fl. c.545 BCE)
from *Air*

Anaximenes, the pupil of Anaximander, was the third of the Milesian philosophers and he too sought the basic substance that informed all of nature. His observations led him to believe that air formed the underlying principle of creation, and that apparently different substances simply reflected different quantities of air. Invisible air condensed into visible mist, then water, then solid ice, earth, or stone. The constant movement of air meant that it was alive, and thus, in its divine form, the cause of the divine gods as well as the souls of humans. After two centuries, Anaximenes' works disappeared and were preserved only as quotations in other writers.

---

1. Air is the one, moveable, infinite, first principle of all things.

2. Air is the nearest to an immaterial thing; for since we are generated in the flow of air, it is necessary that it should be infinite and abundant, because it is never exhausted.

3. The earth was wet, and when it dried it broke apart, and . . . earthquakes are due to the breaking and falling of hills; accordingly earthquakes occur in droughts, and in rainy seasons also; they occur in drought, as has been said, because the earth dries and breaks apart, and it also crumbles when it is wet through with waters.

4. Air differs in rarity and in density as the nature of things is different; when very attenuated it becomes fire, when more condensed wind, and then cloud, and when still more condensed water and earth and stone, and all other things are composed of these. . . . Motion is eternal and by this changes are produced.

5. The form of air is as follows: When it is of very even consistency, it is imperceptible to vision, but it becomes evident as the result of cold or heat or moisture, or when it is moved. It is always in motion; for things would not change as they do unless it were in motion. It has a different appearance when it is made more dense or thinner; when it is expanded into a thinner state it becomes fire, and again winds are condensed air, and air becomes cloud by compression, and water when it is compressed farther, and earth and finally stones as it is more condensed. So that generation is controlled by the opposites, heat and cold.

6. The broad earth is supported on air; similarly the sun and the moon and all the rest of the stars, being fiery bodies, are supported on the air by their breadth.

7. The stars do not give forth heat because they are so far away. Winds are produced when the air that has been attenuated is set in motion; and when it comes together and is yet farther condensed, clouds are produced, and so it changes into water. And hail is formed when the water descending from the clouds is frozen; and snow, when these being yet more filled with moisture become frozen; and lightning, when clouds are separated by violence of the winds; for when they are separated, the flash is bright and like fire. And a rainbow is produced when the sun's rays fall on compressed air; and earthquakes are produced when the earth is changed yet more by heating and cooling.

8. Air is god, and . . . it is boundless and infinite and always in motion.

9. As our soul which is air holds us together, so wind [i.e., breath] and air encompass the whole world.

Xenophanes (c.570–c.455 BCE)

Xenophanes was less a natural philosopher than a poet, but in his poetry and other works he spoke of the unity he saw underlying everything. He was especially scornful of the popular religious views—based on Homer and Hesiod—that saw the gods as being like immoral humans in character and behavior. This is characteristic of his method, which is to examine popular beliefs from a rational viewpoint rather than to examine nature itself. In the poem included here, he makes fun of the notion of reincarnation popular among the followers of Pythagoras, the mystical philosopher who first used the word "cosmos" to describe the world and who saw the cosmos as generated from numbers and ordered mathematically.

"PYTHAGORAS AND THE TRANSMIGRATED SOUL"

One day a dog was being thrashed in the street,
and behold, Pythagoras, philosopher of spirits,
was walking by.
His heart was in his mouth
for the poor pup.
"Stop! Stop!" he cried.
"Don't beat him any more.
This is my dear friend's soul.
I recognize the voice when I hear him bark."

from *On Nature*

1. God is one, supreme among gods and men, and not like mortals in body or in mind.

2. The whole [of god] sees, the whole perceives, the whole hears.

3. But without effort he sets in motion all things by mind and thought.

4. It [i.e. being] always abides in the same place, not moved at all, nor is it fitting that it should move from one place to another.

5. But mortals suppose that the gods are born (as they themselves are), and that they wear man's clothing and have human voice and body.

6. But if cattle or lions had hands, so as to paint with their hands and produce works of art as men do, they would paint their gods and give them bodies in form like their own—horses like horses, cattle like cattle.

7. Homer and Hesiod attributed to the gods all things which are disreputable and worthy of blame when done by men; and they told of them many lawless deeds, stealing, adultery, and deception of each other.

8. For all things come from earth, and all things end by becoming earth.

9. All things that come into being and grow are earth and water.

10. This upper limit of earth at our feet is visible and touches the air, but below it reaches to infinity.

11. Accordingly there has not been a man, nor will there be, who knows distinctly what I say about the gods or in regard to all things, for even if one chances for the most part to say what is true, still he would not know; but every one thinks he knows.

12. In the beginning the gods did not at all reveal all things clearly to mortals, but by searching men in the course of time find them out better.

13. But if one wins a victory by swiftness of foot, or in the pentathlon, where the grove of Zeus lies by Pisas' stream at Olympia, or as a wrestler, or in painful boxing, or in that severe contest called the pancration, he would be more glorious in the eyes of the citizens, he would win a front seat at assemblies, and would be entertained by the city at the public table, and he would receive a gift which would be a keepsake for him. If he won by means of horses he would get all these things although he did not deserve them, as I deserve them, for our wisdom is better than the strength of men or of horses. This is indeed a very wrong custom, nor is it right to prefer strength to excellent wisdom. For if there should be in the city a man good at boxing, or in the

pentathlon, or in wrestling, or in swiftness of foot, which is honoured more than strength (among the contests men enter into at the games), the city would not on that account be any better governed. Small joy would it be to any city in this case if a citizen conquers at the games on the banks of the Pisas, for this does not fill with wealth its secret chambers.

HERACLITUS (fl. c.500 BCE)
from *On Nature*

Like most of the other early philosophers, Heraclitus exists for us in the record provided by other writers. His one book is lost, but the several fragments that survive show that he was controversial in his own time, and amazingly "modern" in anticipating ideas that have become central in our own time, like relativism, entropy, and the balance of opposing forces. Heraclitus saw that both stability and change were illusory, covering a huge system in which fire was the basic element and movement or flow the basic principle. Change is generated by the pull of opposites, by Strife, and the result is actually harmony and order. A river is for Heraclitus the perfect analogy: it is always the same, and yet it is forever moving and changing.

---

1. Not on my authority, but on that of truth, it is wise for you to accept the fact that all things are one.
2. Eyes and ears are bad witnesses for men, since their souls lack understanding.
3. Seekers for gold dig much earth, and find little gold.
4. Eyes are more exact witnesses than ears.
5. Wisdom is one thing: it is willing and it is unwilling to be called by the name Zeus.
6. This order, the same for all things, no one of gods or men has made, but it always was, and is, and ever shall be, an ever-living fire, kindling according to fixed measure, and extinguished according to fixed measure.
7. All things are exchanged for fire, and fire for all things; as wares are exchanged for gold, and gold for wares.
8. Hesiod is the teacher of most men; they suppose that his knowledge was very extensive, when in fact he did not know night and day, for they are one.
9. God is day and night, winter and summer, war and peace, satiety and hunger; but he assumes different forms, just as when incense is mingled with incense; every one gives him the name he pleases.
10. Cool things become warm, and warm grows cool; the wet dries, the parched becomes wet.
11. You could not step twice in the same rivers; for other and yet other waters are ever flowing on.
12. War is father of all and king of all; and some he made gods and some men, some slaves and some free.
13. Opposition unites. From what draws apart results the most beautiful harmony. All things take place by strife.
14. Good and bad are the same.
15. The limits of the soul you could not discover, though traversing every path.

16. Life and death, and waking and sleeping, and youth and old age, are the same; for the latter change and are the former, and the former change back to the latter.

17. Even a potion separates into its ingredients when it is not stirred.

18. Though reason is common, most people live as though they had an understanding peculiar to themselves.

19. It is hard to contend with passion; for whatever it desires to get it buys at the cost of soul.

20. It is better to conceal stupidity, but it is an effort in time of relaxation and over the wine.

21. There awaits men at death what they do not expect or think.

PARMENIDES (fl. 470 BCE)
from *On Nature*

Tradition has it that, at age 65, Parmenides visited Athens and discussed philosophy with Socrates. A student of Xenophanes, Parmenides also wrote poetry and brought philosophical inquiry to the study of metaphysics. He felt that change and multiplicity were appearances that masked the true reality, that of Being.

---

1. Come now I will tell you—and hear my word and heed it—what are the only ways of enquiry that lead to knowledge. The one way, assuming that being is and that it is impossible for it not to be, is the trustworthy path, for truth attends it. The other, that not-being is and that it necessarily is, I call a wholly incredible course, since you cannot recognize not-being (for this is impossible), nor could you speak of it, for thought and being are the same thing.

2. It is necessary both to say and to think that being is; for it is possible that being is, and it is impossible that not-being is; this is what I bid you ponder. I restrain you from this first course of investigation; and from that course also along which mortals knowing nothing wander aimlessly, since helplessness directs the roaming thought in their bosoms, and they are borne on deaf and likewise blind, amazed, headstrong races, they who consider being and not-being as the same and not the same; and that all things follow a back-turning course.

3. There is left but this single path to tell you of: namely, that being is. And on this path there are many proofs that being is without beginning and indestructible; it is universal, existing alone, immovable and without end; nor ever was it nor will it be, since it now is, all together, one, and continuous.... From what did it grow and how? I will not permit you to say or to think or to say that it came from non-being; for it is impossible to think or to say that not-being is.... So it is necessary that being either is absolute or is not. Nor will the force of the argument permit that anything spring from being except being itself.

4. Therefore thinking and that by reason of which thought exists are one and the same thing, for you will not find thinking without the being from which it receives its name. Nor is there nor will there be anything apart from being; for fate

has linked it together, so that it is a whole and immovable. Wherefore all these things will be but a name, all these things which mortals determined in the belief that they were true, namely, that things arise and perish, that they are and are not, that they change their position and vary in colour.

Anaxagoras (c.500–c.428 BCE) from *On Nature*

Born in what is today Turkey, Anaxagoras moved to Athens in 480 and brought with him the Ionian habits of scientific inquiry. During his time in Athens, he had Pericles as his principal supporter, even when he was tried for impiety for claiming that the sun was a fiery stone a bit larger than the Peloponnese. Besides discovering the cause of eclipses, Anaxagoras is remembered for two key ideas. He held, first, that everything was made up not of one or of four elements, but of an infinite number of different spermata *("seeds of things"); within each individual thing the seeds of all things are present, but the individual takes on the character of those elemental seeds which exist in greatest number. Second, and more importantly, Anaxagoras believed that the motive force of creation is* nous, *or "mind," which spins out material opposites and which, in each individual, directs its energies. Both Plato and Aristotle adopted Anaxagoras's concept of mind, developing it further by giving it an ethical motion: for them mind does not simply seek nourishment and satisfaction, but actively works toward the Good. After his trial for impiety, Anaxagoras left Athens and founded a school at Lampsacus.*

---

1. In all things there is a portion of everything except mind; and there are things in which there is mind also.

2. Other things include a portion of everything, but mind is infinite and self-powerful and mixed with nothing, but it exists alone itself by itself. For if it were not by itself, but were mixed with anything else, it would include parts of all things. . . . For it is the most rarified of all things and the purest, and it has all knowledge in regard to everything and the greatest power; over all that has life, both greater and less, mind rules. And mind ruled the rotation of the whole, so that it set it in rotation in the beginning. . . . And whatever things were to be, and whatever things were, as many as are now, and whatever things shall be, all these mind arranged in order; and it arranged that rotation, according to which now rotate stars and sun and moon and air and ether, now that they are separated.

3. And when mind began to set things in motion, there was separation from everything that was in motion, and however much mind set in motion, all this was made distinct. The rotation of the things that were moved and made distinct caused them to be yet more distinct.

4. Earth is condensed out of these things that are separated. For water is separated from the clouds, and earth from the water; and from the earth stones are condensed by cold; and these are separated farther from water.

5. But mind, as it always has been, especially now also is where all other things are, in the surrounding mass, and in the things that were separated, and in the things that are being separated.

6. For neither is there a least of what is small, but there is always a less. For being is not non-being. But there is always a greater than what is great. And it is equal to the small in number; but with reference to itself each thing is both small and great.

7. The Greeks do not rightly use the terms "coming into being" and "perishing." For nothing comes into being nor yet does anything perish, but there is mixture and separation of things that are. So they would do right in calling the coming into being "mixture," and the perishing "separation."

PROTAGORAS (C.485–C.415 BCE)

*Protagoras, unlike many of the other early philosophers, gave his attention to moral and political questions. In fact, he disliked science and mathematics and developed views of knowledge which emphasized subjectivity and relativity. He was the first professional sophist, and he made a fortune lecturing on grammar and rhetoric. He wrote books (*On Truth *and* On the Gods*) which were eventually lost, but he is well remembered through Plato's treating him as the Athenian rival of Socrates and through two fragments of his thought that do survive. "Man is the measure of all things," he said; "of things that are, that they are, and of things that are not, that they are not." While this sounds like the battle cry of Renaissance-style humanism, it is first a statement about subjectivity—that the world is filtered through human perceptions. The other fragment was equally upsetting of Athenian values: "Of the gods I know nothing, whether they exist or do not exist: nor what they are like in form." Because of his views about the gods, Protagoras was exiled from Athens and his books burnt.*

HIPPOCRATES (469–399 BCE)

Hippocrates has a great reputation, ancient and modern, but very little is known about him. Biographies written about him a few centuries after he lived contained lots of stories and legends, but little reliable information. The writings attributed to him constitute a medical library—about 70 works—and the books probably became part of the great library at Alexandria and were copied and re-copied. Thus Hippocrates' fate is very different from that of most Greek thinkers: about sixty of his works survive, and a version of his famous oath still is part of the initiation rite of physicians. Scholars believe that he did not write all of the works attributed to him (including the Oath itself), but the writings as a group show a willingness to look at the whole body as an organism and to treat diseases as having discoverable, physical causes. The treatise on epilepsy, for instance, argues that this "Sacred Disease" is like other diseases and can be treated as other diseases are. He then analyzes the functioning of the brain as part of the human body, a part with its own structure of strengths and weaknesses.

[The Oath]

I swear by Apollo the physician, and Aesculapius, and Health, and All-heal, and all the gods and goddesses, that, according to my ability and judgment, I will keep this Oath and this stipulation—to reckon him who taught me this Art equally dear to me as my parents, to share my substance with him, and relieve his necessities if required; to look upon his offspring in the same footing as my own brothers, and to teach them this art, if they shall wish to learn it, without fee or stipulation; and that by precept, lecture, and every other mode of instruction, I will impart a knowledge of the Art to my own sons, and those of my teachers, and to disciples bound by a stipulation and oath according to the law of medicine, but to none others. I will follow that system of regimen which, according to my ability and judgment, I consider for the benefit of my patients, and abstain from whatever is deleterious and mischievous. I will give no deadly medicine to any one if asked, nor suggest any such counsel; and in like manner I will not give to a woman a pessary to produce abortion. With purity and with holiness I will pass my life and practice my Art. I will not cut persons laboring under the stone, but will leave this to be done by men who are practitioners of this work. Into whatever houses I enter, I will go into them for the benefit of the sick, and will abstain from every voluntary act of mischief and corruption; and, further from the seduction of females or males, of freemen and slaves. Whatever, in connection with my professional practice or not, in connection with it, I see or hear, in the life of men, which ought not to be spoken of abroad, I will not divulge, as reckoning that all such should be kept secret. While I continue to keep this Oath unviolated, may it be granted to me to enjoy life and the practice of the art, respected by all men, in all times! But should I trespass and violate this Oath, may the reverse be my lot!

[The Sacred Disease]

It is thus with regard to the disease called Sacred: it appears to me to be nowise more divine nor more sacred than other diseases, but has a natural cause from the originates like other affections. Men regard its nature and cause as divine from ignorance and wonder, because it is not at all like to other diseases. And this notion of its divinity is kept up by their inability to comprehend it, and the simplicity of the mode by which it is cured, for men are freed from it by purifications and incantations. But if it is reckoned divine because it is wonderful, instead of one there are many diseases which would be sacred; for, as I will show, there are others no less wonderful and prodigious, which nobody imagines to be sacred. The quotidian, tertian, and quartan fevers, seem to me no less sacred and divine in their origin than this disease, although they are not reckoned so wonderful. And I see men become mad and demented from no manifest cause, and at the same time doing many things out of place; and I have known many persons in sleep groaning and crying out, some in a state of suffocation, some jumping up and fleeing out of doors, and deprived of their reason until they awaken, and afterward becoming well and rational as before, although they be pale and weak; and this will happen not once but frequently. And there are many and various things of the like kind, which it would be tedious to state particularly.

They who first referred this malady to the gods appear to me to have been just such persons as the conjurors, purificators, mountebanks, and charlatans now are, who give themselves out for being excessively religious, and as knowing more than other people. Such persons, then, using the divinity as a pretext and screen of their own inability to afford any assistance, have given out that the disease is sacred, adding suitable reasons for this opinion, and they have instituted a mode of treatment which is safe for themselves, namely, by applying purifications and incantations, and enforcing abstinence from baths and many articles of food which are unwholesome to men in diseases. . . . And they forbid to have a black robe, because black is expressive of death; and to sleep on a goat's skin, or to wear it, and to put one foot upon another, or one hand upon another; for all these things are held to be hindrances to the cure. All these they enjoin with reference to its divinity, as if possessed of more knowledge, and announcing beforehand other causes so that if the person should recover, theirs would be the honor and credit; and if he should die, they would have a certain defense, as if the gods, and not they, were to blame, seeing they had administered nothing either to eat or drink as medicines, nor had overheated him with baths, so as to prove the cause of what had happened. But I am of opinion that (if this were true) none of the Libyans, who live in the interior, would be free from this disease, since they all sleep on goats' skins, and live upon goats' flesh; neither have they couch, robe, nor shoe that is not made of goat's skin, for they have no other herds but goats and oxen. But if these things, when administered in food, aggravate the disease, and if it be cured by abstinence from them, godhead is not the cause at all; nor will purifications be of any avail, but it is the food which is beneficial and prejudicial, and the influence of the divinity vanishes.

Thus, they who try to cure these maladies in this way, appear to me neither to reckon them sacred nor divine. For when they are removed by such purifications, and this method of cure, what is to prevent them from being brought upon men and induced by other devices similar to these? So that the cause is no longer divine, but human. . . .

This disease seems to me to be no more divine than others; but it has its nature such as other diseases have, and a cause whence it originates, and its nature and cause are divine only just as much as all others are, and it is curable no less than the others, unless . . . it is confirmed, and has became stronger than the remedies applied. Its origin is hereditary, like that of other diseases. . . .

But the brain is the cause of this affection, as it is of other very great diseases, and in what manner and from what cause it is formed, I will now plainly declare. The brain of man, as in all other animals, is double, and a thin membrane divides it through the middle, and therefore the pain is not always in the same part of the head; for sometimes it is situated on either side, and sometimes the whole is affected; and veins run toward it from all parts of the body, many of which are small, but two are thick, the one from the liver, and the other from the spleen. . . .

Of little children who are seized with this disease, the greater part die, provided the defluxion be copious and humid, for the veins being slender cannot admit the phlegm, owing to its thickness and abundance; but the blood is cooled and congealed, and the child immediately dies. But if the phlegm be in small quantity, and make a defluxion into both the veins, or to those on either side, the children survive, but exhibit notable marks of the disorder; for either the mouth is drawn aside, or an eye, the neck, or a hand, wherever a vein being filled with phlegm loses its tone, and is attenuated, and the part of the body connected with this vein is necessarily rendered weaker and defective. . . .

To persons of a more advanced age, it neither proves fatal, nor produces distortions. For their veins are capacious and are filled with hot blood; and therefore the phlegm can neither prevail nor cool the blood, so as to coagulate it, but it is quickly overpowered and mixed with the blood, and thus the veins receive the air, and sensibility remains; and, owing to their strength, the aforesaid symptoms are less likely to seize them. But when this disease attacks very old people, it therefore proves fatal, or induces paraplegia, because the veins are empty, and the blood scanty, thin, and watery.

Men ought to know that from nothing else but the brain come joys, delights, laughter and sports, and sorrows, griefs, despondency, and lamentations. And by this, in an especial manner, we acquire wisdom and knowledge, and see and hear, and know what are foul and what are fair, what are bad and what are good, what are sweet, and what unsavory; some we discriminate by habit, and some we perceive by their utility. By this we distinguish objects of relish and disrelish, according to the seasons; and the same things do not always please us. And by the same organ we become mad and delirious, and fears and terrors assail us, some by night, and some by day, and dreams and untimely wanderings, and cares that are not suitable, and ignorance of present circumstances, desuetude, and unskillfulness. All these things we endure from the brain, when it is not healthy. . . .

And the disease called the Sacred arises from causes as the others, namely, those things which enter and quit the body, such as cold, the sun, and the winds, which are ever changing and are never at rest. And these things are divine, so that there is no necessity for making a distinction, and holding this disease to be more divine than the others, but all are divine, and all human. And each has its own peculiar nature and power, and none is of an ambiguous nature, or irremediable. And the most of them are curable by the same means as those by which any other thing is food to one, and injurious to another.

Epicurus (c.341–271 bce)

Epicurus, who was born on the Greek Island of Samos and died in Athens, is one of those philosophers whose name entered the language as the root of words that mostly misrepresent his ideas. "Epicure" and "epicurean" in English mostly attach to a life of sensual pleasure and a refined taste for wine and food. While it is true that Epicurus developed a moral philosophy based in seeking pleasure as the best route to a life of happiness, pleasure is primarily understood as a lack of pain. Thus Epicurus and his followers avoided extremes—even of pleasure—as likely to lead to pain, and urged a life of moderation. To be without hunger, thirst, and apprehension, and to feel sure these states will continue into the future, is secure pleasure to the epicurean. As an atomist who saw the gods and the human soul as "mortal," along with the body, Epicurus saw no reason to fear the gods or death: only the invisible, indivisible atoms would continue in perpetuity, and extravagant living and participating in the public world of politics could only perturb the order and equanimity of one's atomic makeup. Although reputed to have written immense amounts, Epicurus's writings did not fare well in the worlds of the austere Romans and early Christians, and only a few letters and two collections of maxims survive.

"Letter to Menoeceus"

Epicurus to Menoeceus, greetings:

Let no one delay the study of philosophy while young nor weary of it when old. For no one is either too young or too old for the health of the soul. He who says either that the time for philosophy has not yet come or that it has passed is like someone who says that the time for happiness has not yet come or that it has passed. Therefore, both young and old must philosophize, the latter so that although old he may stay young in good things owing to gratitude for what has occurred, the former so that although young he too may be like an old man owing to his lack of fear of what is to come. Therefore, one must practise the things which produce happiness, since if that is present we have everything and if it is absent we do everything in order to have it.

Do and practise what I constantly told you to do, believing these to be the elements of living well. First, believe that god is an indestructible and blessed animal, in accordance with the general conception of god commonly held, and do not ascribe to god anything foreign to his indestructibility or repugnant to his blessedness. Believe of him everything which is able to preserve his blessedness and indestructibility. For gods do exist, since we have clear knowledge of them. But they are not such as the many believe them to be. For they do not adhere to their own views about the gods. The man who denies the gods of the many is not impious, but rather he who ascribes to the gods the opinions of the many. For the pronouncements of the many about the gods are not basic grasps but false suppositions. Hence come the greatest harm from the gods to bad men and the greatest benefits [to the good]. For the gods always welcome men who are like themselves, being congenial to their own virtues and considering that whatever is not such is uncongenial.

Get used to believing that death is nothing to us. For all good and bad consists in sense-experience, and death is the privation of sense-experience. Hence, a correct knowledge of the fact that death is nothing to us makes the mortality of life a matter for contentment, not by adding a limitless time [to life] but by removing the longing for immortality. For there is nothing fearful in life for one who has grasped that there is nothing fearful in the absence of life. Thus, he is a fool who says that he fears death not because it will be painful when present but because it is painful when it is still to come. For that which while present causes no distress causes unnecessary pain when merely anticipated. So death, the most frightening of bad things, is nothing to us; since when we exist, death is not yet present, and when death is present, then we do not exist. Therefore, it is relevant neither to the living nor to the dead, since it does not affect the former, and the latter do not exist. But the many sometimes flee death as the greatest of bad things and sometimes choose it as a relief from the bad things of life. But the wise man neither rejects life nor fears death. For living does not offend him, nor does he believe not living to be something bad. And just as he does not unconditionally choose the largest amount of food but the most pleasant food, so he savours not the longest time but the most pleasant. He who advises the young man to live well and the old man to die well is simple-minded, not just because of the pleasing aspects of life but because the same kind of practice produces a good life and a good death. Much worse is he who says that it is good not to be born, "but when born to pass through the gates of Hades as quickly as possible." For if he really believes what he says, why doesn't he leave life? For it is easy for him to do, if he has firmly decided on it. But if he is joking, he is wasting his time among men who don't welcome it. We must remember that what will happen is neither unconditionally within our power nor unconditionally outside our power, so that we will not unconditionally expect that it will occur nor despair of it as unconditionally not going to occur.

One must reckon that of desires some are natural, some groundless; and of the natural desires some are necessary and some merely natural; and of the necessary, some are necessary for happiness and some for freeing the body from troubles and some for life itself. The unwavering contemplation of these enables one to refer every choice and avoidance to the health of the body and the freedom of the soul from disturbance, since this is the goal of a blessed life. For we do everything for the sake of being neither in pain nor in terror. As soon as we achieve this state every storm in the soul is dispelled, since the animal is not in a passion to go after some need nor to seek something else to complete the good of the body and the soul. For we are in need of pleasure only when we are in pain because of the absence of pleasure, and when we are not in pain, then we no longer need pleasure.

And this is why we say that pleasure is the starting-point and goal of living blessedly. For we recognized this as our first innate good, and this is our starting point for every choice and avoidance and we come to this by judging every good by the criterion of feeling. And it is just because this is the first innate good, that we do not choose every pleasure; but sometimes we pass up many pleasures when we get a larger amount of what is uncongenial from them. And we believe many pains to be better than pleasures when a greater pleasure follows for a long while if we endure the pains. So every pleasure is a good thing, since it has a nature congenial [to us], but not every one is to be chosen. Just as every pain too is a bad thing, but not every one is such as to be always avoided. It is, however, appropriate to make all these decisions by comparative measurement and an examination of the advantages and disadvantages. For at some times we treat the good things as bad and conversely, the bad things as good.

And we believe that self-sufficiency is a great good, not in order that we might make do with few things under all circumstances, but so that if we do not have a lot we can make do with few, being genuinely convinced that those who least need extravagance enjoy it most; and that everything natural is easy to obtain and whatever is groundless is hard to obtain; and that simple flavours provide a pleasure equal to that of an extravagant life-style when all pain from want is removed, and barley cakes and water provide the highest pleasure when someone in want takes them. Therefore, becoming accustomed to simple, not extravagant, ways of life makes one completely healthy, makes man unhesitant in the face of life's necessary duties, puts us in a better condition for the times of extravagance which occasionally come along, and makes us fearless in the face of chance. So when we say that pleasure is the goal we do not mean the pleasures of the profligate or the pleasures of consumption, as some believe, either from ignorance and disagreement or from deliberate misinterpretation, but rather the lack of pain in the body and disturbance in the soul. For it is not drinking bouts and continuous partying and enjoying boys and women, or consuming fish and the other dainties of an extravagant table, which produce the pleasant life, but sober calculation which searches out the reasons for every choice and avoidance and drives out the opinions which are the source of the greatest turmoil for men's souls.

Prudence is the principle of all these things and is the greatest good. That is why prudence is a more valuable thing than philosophy. For prudence is the source of all the other virtues, teaching that it is impossible to live pleasantly without living prudently, honourably, and justly, and impossible to live prudently, honourably, and justly without living pleasantly. For the virtues are natural adjuncts of the pleasant life and the pleasant life is inseparable from them.

For who do you believe is better than a man who has pious opinions about the gods, is always fearless about death, has reasoned out the natural goal of life and understands that the limit of good things is easy to achieve completely and easy to provide, and that the limit of bad things either has a short duration or causes little trouble?

As to [Fate], introduced by some as the mistress of all, (he is scornful, saying rather that some things happen of necessity,) others by chance and others by our own agency, and that he sees that necessity is not answerable [to anyone], that chance is unstable, while what occurs by our own agency is autonomous, and that it is to this that praise and blame are attached. For it would be better to follow the stories told about the gods than to be a slave to the fate of the natural philosophers. For the former suggests a hope of escaping bad things by honouring the gods, but the latter involves an inescapable and merciless necessity. And he [the wise man] believes that chance is not a god, as the many think, for nothing is done in a disorderly way by god; nor that it is an uncertain cause. For he does not think that anything good or bad with respect to living blessedly is given by chance to men, although it does provide the starting points of great good and bad things. And he thinks it better to be unlucky in a rational way than lucky in a senseless way; for it is better for a good decision not to turn out right in action than for a bad decision to turn out right because of chance.

Practise these and the related precepts day and night, by yourself and with a like-minded friend, and you will never be disturbed either when awake or in sleep, and you will live as a god among men. For a man who lives among immortal goods is in no respect like a mere mortal animal.

ARCHIMEDES (287–212 BCE)
from *The Sand Reckoner*

More is known about Archimedes than about any other ancient scientist, but many of the stories are popular anecdotes and perhaps fictions. During the Roman siege of Syracuse, where Archimedes spent most of his life, he is supposed to have set the Roman ships afire by placing large mirrors above the harbor. When he discovered how to determine the proportions of gold and silver in a wreath by weighing it in water, he is supposed to have leapt from his bath and run naked through the streets shouting "Eureka! I have found it!" Impressed by the mechanical power of pulleys and levers, he is supposed to have said, "Give me a place to stand and I can move the earth." Whether the appealing human part of these stories is true or not, the scientific part certainly is. Archimedes was a leading mathematician, with interests in mechanics, optics, and astronomy. Educated at Alexandria, Archimedes did not take much credit for his inventions, preferring instead to write theoretical treatises on mechanics, hydrostatics, spheres and cylinders, measurement of spirals, parabolas, and the circle (he calculated the value of π), centers of gravity, statics, and levers. His Sand-Reckoner *is fascinating for several reasons. He argues that the number of grains of sand in the universe is countable and then invents a place-value system for calculating large numbers to make up for weaknesses in the existing Greek notation. But he also describes and accounts for in his calculations, with an entirely open and searching mind, the system of the universe proposed by Aristarchus, with the sun at the center rather than the earth.*

There are some, king Gelon, who think that the number of the sand is infinite in multitude; and I mean by the sand not only that which exists about Syracuse and the rest of Sicily but also that which is found in every region whether inhabited or uninhabited. Again there are some who, without regarding it as infinite, yet think that no number has been named which is great enough to exceed its multitude. And it is clear that they who hold this view, if they imagined a mass made up of sand in other respects as large as the mass of the earth, including in it all the seas and the hollows of the earth filled up to a height equal to that of the highest of the mountains, would be many times further still from recognizing that any number could be expressed which exceeded the multitude of the sand so taken. But I will try to show you by means of geometrical proofs, which you will be able to follow, that, of the numbers named by me and given in the work which I sent to Zeuxippus, some exceed not only the number of the mass of sand equal in magnitude to the earth filled up in the way described, but also that of a mass equal in magnitude to the universe. Now you are aware that 'universe' is the name given by most astronomers to the sphere whose centre is the centre of the earth and whose radius is equal to the straight line between the centre of the sun and the centre of the earth. This is the common account . . . as you have heard from astronomers. But Aristarchus of Samos brought out a book consisting of some hypotheses, in which the premises lead to the result that the universe is many times greater than that now so called. His hypotheses are that the fixed stars and the sun remain unmoved, that the earth revolves about the sun in the circumference of a circle, the sun lying in the middle of the orbit, and that the sphere of the fixed stars situated about the same centre as the sun, is so great that the circle in which he supposes the earth to revolve bears such a proportion to the distance of the fixed stars as the centre of the sphere bears to its surface. Now it is easy to see that this is impossible; for, since the centre of the sphere has no magnitude, we cannot conceive it to bear any ratio whatever to the surface of the sphere. We must however take Aristarchus to mean this: since we conceive the earth to be, as it were, the centre of the universe, the ratio which the earth bears to what we describe as the "universe' is the same as the ratio which the sphere containing the circle in which he supposes the earth to revolve bears to the sphere of the fixed stars. For he adapts the proofs of his results to a hypothesis of this kind, and in particular he appears to suppose the magnitude of the sphere in which he represents the earth as moving to be equal to what we call the 'universe.'

I say then that, even if a sphere were made up of the sand, as great as Aristarchus supposes the sphere of the fixed stars to be, I shall still prove that, of the numbers named in the *Principles*, some exceed in multitude the number of the sand which is equal in magnitude to the sphere referred to, provided that the following assumptions be made.

1. *The perimeter of the earth is about 3,000,000 stadia and not greater. . . .*

2. *The diameter of the earth is greater than the diameter of the moon, and the diameter of the sun is greater than the diameter of the earth. . . .*

3. *The diameter of the sun is about 30 times the diameter of he moon and not greater. . . .*

Application to the number of the sand.

By Assumption 5

(diam. of poppy-seed) ≮ 1/40 (finger-breadth);

and, since spheres are to one another in the triplicate ratio of their diameters, it follows that

(sphere of diam. 1 finger-breadth ≮ 64,000 poppy-seeds
≯ 64,000 × 10,000
≯ 640,000,000
≯ 6 units of *second order* + 40,000,000 units of *first order*
(*a fortiori*) < 10 units of *second order* of numbers.
} grains of sand.

We now gradually increase the diameter of the supposed sphere, multiplying it by 100 each time. Thus, remembering that the sphere is thereby multiplied by 100^3 or 1,000,000, the number of grains of sand which would be contained in a sphere with each successive diameter may be arrived at as follows.

[Archimedes here goes through a series of multiplications that he prepared for earlier in the work by introducing and explaining a place-value system of notation for very large numbers. His calculations, figuring 1 stadium <10,000 finger-breadths, yield the number of grains of sand that would fill either an earth-centered or a sun-centered universe.]

Hence *the number of grains of sand which could be contained in a sphere of the size of our 'universe' is less than 1,000 units of the seventh order of numbers* [or 10^{51}].

From this we can prove further that *a sphere of the size attributed by Aristarchus to the sphere of the fixed stars would contain a number of grains of sand less than 10,000,000 units of the eighth order of numbers* [or $10^{56+7 = 10}63$].

For, by hypothesis,

(earth) : ('universe') = ('universe') : (sphere of fixed stars).

And

(diameter of 'universe') < 10,000 (diam. of earth);

whence

(diam. of sphere of fixed stars) < 10,000 (diam. of 'universe').

Therefore

(sphere of fixed stars) < $(10{,}000)^3$ ('universe').

It follows that the number of grains of sand which would be contained in a sphere equal to the sphere of the fixed stars

< $(10{,}000)^3$ × 1,000 units of *seventh order*
< (13th term of series) × (52nd term of series)
< 64th term of series [i.e. 10^{63}]
< [10^7 or] 10,000,000 units of *eighth order* of numbers.

Conclusion.

I conceive that these things, king Gelon, will appear incredible to the great majority of people who have not studied mathematics, but that to those who are conversant therewith and have given thought to the question of the distances and sizes of the earth the sun and moon and the whole universe the proof will carry conviction. And it was for this reason that I thought the subject would be not inappropriate for your consideration.

EPICTETUS (C.55–135 CE)
from *Enchiridion*

Epictetus, who was born in what is now Turkey, was an exemplar of the Greek philosophy of Stoicism. He believed that stoic principles were not merely theoretical ideals, but provided a practical guide to living a life of happiness. His starting point was to recognize what was in one's power to change, making that the sphere of concern and action, and then simply to accept all things that were out of one's control. His own life provides the textbook examples for testing this philosophy. Epictetus was a slave to one of Nero's freedmen in Rome during his early years. Even as a slave, he studied under a Roman stoic philosopher, eventually gaining his own freedom and beginning to teach philosophy in Rome. At some point, perhaps very early, he was crippled or lamed, and it is not surprising that this condition, as well as slavery, often provide examples for Epictetus of the necessities which are to be accepted as beyond one's control. Banishment as well: when the Emperor Domitian in 93 banned philosophers from Rome, Epictetus set up a school of philosophy in Greece, where he lived simply until his death.

As with earlier Greek philosophers, Epictetus did not write his own works. Rather, like Socrates with Plato, he had a devoted student named Arrian who collected his teachings and published them in two works, the Discourses *and the* Enchiridion *(= "Handbook"). As author of the* Campaigns of Alexander, *the chief historical source on Alexander the Great, Arrian was a serious writer on his own terms. But in his Preface he claims about the* Discourses*: "I have not 'composed' them at all. But whatever I used to hear him say I wrote down, word for word, as best I could, as a record for later use of his thought and frank expression." Whatever the role of Arrian, the teachings and the example of Epictetus remained important for later philosophy and for the tradition of Stoicism. In the next generation his teachings were influential, for instance, to the* Meditations *of the Roman Emperor Marcus Aurelius.*

CHAPTER 15

Remember to act always as if you were at a symposium. When the food or drink comes around, reach out and take some politely; if it passes you by don't try pulling it back. And if it has not reached you yet, don't let your desire run ahead of you, be patient until your turn comes. Adopt a similar attitude with regard to children, wife, wealth and status, and in time, you will be entitled to dine with the gods. Go further and decline these goods even when they are on offer and you will have a share in the gods' power as well as their company. That is how Diogenes, Heraclitus and philosophers like them came to be called, and considered, divine.

These Epictetus selections are taken from *Discourses and Selected Writings,* translated by Paul M. Cobb (London: Penguin Books, 2008).

CHAPTER 16

Whenever you see someone in tears, distraught because they are parted from a child, or have met with some material loss, be careful lest the impression move you to believe that their circumstances are truly bad. Have ready the reflection that they are not upset by what happened—because other people are not upset when the same thing happens to them—but by their own view of the matter. Nevertheless, you should not disdain to sympathize with them, at least with comforting words, or even to the extent of sharing outwardly in their grief. But do not commiserate with your whole heart and soul.

CHAPTER 17

Remember that you are an actor in a play, the nature of which is up to the director to decide. If he wants the play to be short, it will be short, if he wants it long, it will be long. And if he casts you as one of the poor, or as a cripple, as a king or as a commoner—whatever role is assigned, the accomplished actor will accept and perform it with impartial skill. But the assignment of roles belongs to another.

CHAPTER 18

If you hear a raven croak inauspiciously, do not be alarmed by the impression. Make a mental distinction at once, and say, 'These omens hold no significance for me; they only pertain to my body, property, family, or reputation. For *me* every sign is auspicious, if I want it to be, because, whatever happens, I can derive some benefit from it.'

CHAPTER 19

[I] You will never have to experience defeat if you avoid contests whose outcome is outside your control. [2] Don't let outward appearances mislead you into thinking that someone with more prestige, power or some other distinction must on that account be happy. If the essence of the good lies within us, then there is no place for jealousy or envy, and you will not care about being a general, a senator or a consul—only about being free. And the way to be free is to look down on externals.

CHAPTER 20

Remember, it is not enough to be hit or insulted to be harmed, you must believe that you are being harmed. If someone succeeds in provoking you, realize that your mind is complicit in the provocation. Which is why it is essential that we not respond impulsively to impressions; take a moment before reacting, and you will find it is easier to maintain control.

CHAPTER 21

Keep the prospect of death, exile and all such apparent tragedies before you every day—especially death—and you will never have an abject thought, or desire anything to excess.

CHAPTER 30

Duties are broadly defined by social roles. This man is your father: the relationship demands from you support, constant deference and tolerance for his verbal, even his physical, abuse.

'But he's a bad father.'

Look, nature has endeared you to a father, not necessarily a *good* one.

'My brother is unfair to me.'

Well then, keep up your side of the relationship; don't concern yourself with his behaviour, only with what *you* must do to keep your will in tune with nature. Another person will not hurt you without your cooperation; you are hurt the moment you believe yourself to be.

The titles of neighbour, citizen and general will likewise suggest to you what functions they entail, once you begin to give social relationships their due in your daily deliberations.

CHAPTER 33

[1] Settle on the type of person you want to be and stick to it, whether alone or in company.

[2] Let silence be your goal for the most part; say only what is necessary, and be brief about it. On the rare occasions when you're called upon to speak, then speak, but never about banalities like gladiators, horses, sports, food and drink—commonplace stuff. Above all don't gossip about people, praising, blaming or comparing them. [3] Try to influence your friends to speak appropriately by your example. If you find yourself in unfamiliar company, however, keep quiet.

[4] Keep laughter to a minimum; do not laugh too often or too loud.

[5] If possible, refuse altogether to take an oath; resist, in any case, as far as circumstances will permit.

[6] Avoid fraternizing with non-philosophers. If you must, though, be careful not to sink to their level; because, you know, if a companion is dirty, his friends cannot help but get a little dirty too, no matter how clean they started out.

[7] Where the body is concerned, take only what is strictly necessary in the way of food, drink, clothing, shelter and house-hold slaves. Cut out luxury and ostentation altogether.

[8] Concerning sex, stay as chaste as you can before marriage. If you do indulge, engage only in licit liaisons. Don't be harsh or judgemental towards others who have sex; if you are celibate yourself, don't advertise the fact.

[9] If you learn that someone is speaking ill of you, don't try to defend yourself against the rumours; respond instead with, 'Yes, and he doesn't know the half of it, because he could have said more.'

[10] There is no call to be a regular at the public games. But if the occasion should arise and you go, don't be seen siding with anyone except yourself; which is to say, hope only for what happens to happen, and for the actual winner to win; then you won't be unhappy. Yelling, jeering and excessive agitation should be avoided completely. Don't talk much about the event afterwards, or any more than is necessary to get it out of your system. Otherwise it becomes obvious that the experience captivated you.

[11] Don't too soon, or too lightly, attend other people's lectures; when you do go remain serious and reserved, without being disagreeable.

[12] When you are going to meet someone, especially someone deemed important, imagine to yourself what Socrates or Zeno would have done in the situation and you won't fail to get on, whatever happens. [13] When you are going to the house of someone influential, tell yourself that you won't find them in, that you will be locked out, that the door will be slammed in your face, that they won't give you the time of day. And, despite that, if it's the right thing to go, then go and face the consequences. Don't say to yourself later, 'It wasn't worth it.' That's the mark of a conventional person at odds with life.

[14] In your conversation, don't dwell at excessive length on your own deeds or adventures. Just because you enjoy recounting your exploits doesn't mean that others derive the same pleasure from hearing about them.

[15] And avoid trying to be funny. That way vulgarity lies, and at the same time it's likely to lower you in your friends' estimation.

[16] It is also not a good idea to venture on profanity. If it happens, and you aren't out of line, you may even criticize a person who indulges in it. Otherwise, signal your dislike of his language by falling silent, showing unease or giving him a sharp look.

Ptolemy (fl. 121–151 ce)
from *The Almagest*

Although we know practically nothing about his life, Claudius Ptolemaeus gained a reputation as a geographer and an astronomer. His treatise, The Mathematical Collection, *influential among medieval Arab thinkers, became known by its Arabic name and is still called by that today,* Almagest. *A study of the stars and planets, the* Almagest *became an encyclopedia for later astronomers, especially since it offered a catalog of 1,022 stars. He also argued passionately that the earth is round and that it lies at the center of the universe,*

Reprinted from *The Almagest*, translated by G. J. Toomer, Duckworth.

a view that leads us to call the belief in an earth-centered universe Ptolemaic, *as opposed to the sun-centered* Copernican *view that later won out. The Ptolemaic universe is depicted inside the back cover of this book.*

---

4. (THAT THE EARTH TOO, TAKEN AS A WHOLE, IS SENSIBLY SPHERICAL)

That the earth, too, taken as a whole, is sensibly spherical can best be grasped from the following considerations. We can see, again, that the sun, moon, and other stars do not rise and set simultaneously for everyone on earth, but do so earlier for those more toward the east, later for those toward the west. For we find that the phenomena at eclipses, especially lunar eclipses, which take place at the same time [for all observers], are nevertheless not recorded as occurring at the same hour (that is at an equal distance from noon) by all observers. Rather, the hour recorded by the more easterly observers is always later than that recorded by the more westerly. We find that the differences in the hour are proportional to the distances between the places [of observation]. Hence one can reasonably conclude that the earth's surface is spherical, because its evenly curving surface (for so it is when considered as a whole) cuts off [the heavenly bodies] for each set of observers in turn in a regular fashion.

If the earth's shape were any other, this would not happen, as one can see from the following arguments. If it were concave, the stars would be seen rising first by those more toward the west; if it were plane, they would rise and set simultaneously for everyone on earth; if it were triangular or square or any other polygonal shape, by a similar argument, they would rise and set simultaneously for all those living on the same plane surface. Yet it is apparent that nothing like this takes place. Nor could it be cylindrical, with the curved surface in the east-west direction, and the flat sides towards the poles of the universe, which some might suppose more plausible. This is clear from the following: For those living on the curved surface none of the stars would be ever-visible, but either all stars would rise and set for all observers, or the same stars, for an equal [celestial] distance from each of the poles, would always be invisible for all observers. In fact, the farther we travel toward the north, the more of the southern stars disappear and the more of the northern stars appear. Hence it is clear that here too the curvature of the earth cuts off [the heavenly bodies] in a regular fashion in a north-south direction, and proves the sphericity [of the earth] in all directions.

There is the further consideration that if we sail toward mountains or elevated places from and to any direction whatever, they are observed to increase gradually in size as if rising up from the sea itself in which they had previously been submerged: this is due to the curvature of the surface of the water.

5. (THAT THE EARTH IS IN THE MIDDLE OF THE HEAVENS)

Once one has grasped this, if one next considers the position of the earth, one will find that the phenomena associated with it could take place only if we assume that it is in the middle of the heavens, like the center of a sphere. . . .

To sum up, if the earth did not lie in the middle [of the universe], the whole order of things which we observe in the increase and decrease of the length of daylight would be fundamentally upset. Furthermore, eclipses of the moon would not be restricted to situations where the moon is diametrically opposite the sun (whatever part of the heaven [the luminaries are in]), since the earth would often come between them when they were not diametrically opposite, but at intervals of less than a semicircle.

6. (THAT THE EARTH HAS THE RATIO OF A POINT TO THE HEAVENS)

Moreover, the earth has, to the senses, the ratio of a point to the distance of the sphere of the so-called fixed stars. A strong indication of this is the fact that the sizes and distances of the stars, at any given time, appear equal and the same from all parts of the earth everywhere, as observations of the same [celestial] objects from different latitudes are found to have not the least discrepancy from each other. . . .

Another clear indication that this is so is that the planes drawn through the observer's lines of sight at any point [on earth], which we call "horizons," always bisect the whole heavenly sphere. This would not happen if the earth were of perceptible size in relation to the distance of the heavenly bodies; in that case only the plane drawn through the center of the earth could bisect the sphere, while a plane through any point on the surface of the earth would always make the section [of the heavens] below the earth greater than the section above it.

7. (THAT THE EARTH DOES NOT HAVE ANY MOTION FROM PLACE TO PLACE, EITHER)

One can show by the same arguments as the preceding that the earth cannot have any motion in the aforementioned directions, or indeed ever move at all from its position at the center. For the same phenomena would result as would if it had any position other than the central one. Hence I think it is idle to seek for causes for the motion of objects towards the center, once it has been so clearly established from the actual phenomena that the earth occupies the middle place in the universe, and that all heavy objects are carried toward the earth. The following fact alone would most readily lead one to this notion [that all objects fall towards the center]. In absolutely all parts of the earth, which, as we said, has been shown to be spherical and in the middle of the universe, the direction and path of the motion (I mean the proper, [natural] motion) of all bodies possessing weight is always and everywhere at right angles to the rigid plane drawn tangent to the point of impact. It is clear from this fact that, if [these falling objects] were not arrested by the surface of the earth, they would certainly reach the center of the earth itself, since the straight line to the center is also always at right angles to the plane tangent to the sphere at the point of intersection [of that radius] and the tangent.

Those who think it paradoxical that the earth, having such a great weight, is not supported by anything and yet does not move, seem to me to be making the mistake of judging on the basis of their own experience instead of taking into account the peculiar nature of the universe. They would not, I think, consider such a thing strange once they realized that this great bulk of the earth, when compared with the whole surrounding mass [of the universe], has the ratio of a point to it. For when one looks at it in that way, it will seem quite possible that that which is relatively smallest should be overpowered and pressed in equally from all directions to a position of equilibrium by that which is the greatest of all and of uniform nature. For there is no up and down in the universe with respect to itself, any more than one could imagine such a thing in a sphere; instead the proper and natural motion of the compound bodies in it is as follows: Light and rarefied bodies drift outward towards the circumference, but seem to move in the direction which is "up" for each observer, since the overhead direction for all of us, which is also called "up" points toward the surrounding surface; heavy and dense bodies, on the other hand, are carried toward the middle and the center, but seem to fall downward, because, again, the direction which is for all of us toward our feet, called "down," also points towards the center of the earth. These heavy bodies, as one would expect, settle about the center because of their mutual pressure and resistance, which is equal and uniform from all directions. Hence, too, one can see that it is plausible that the earth, since its total mass is so great compared with the bodies which fall toward it, can remain motionless under the impact of these very small weights (for they strike it from all sides), and receive, as it were, the objects falling on it. If the earth had a single motion in common with other heavy objects, it is obvious that it would be carried down faster than all of them because of its much greater size: Living things and individual heavy objects would be left behind, riding on the air, and the earth itself would very soon have fallen completely out of the heavens. But such things are utterly ridiculous merely to think of.

But certain people . . . think that there could be no evidence to oppose their view if, for instance, they supposed the heavens to remain motionless, and the earth to revolve from west to east about the same axis [as the heavens], making approximately one revolution each day. . . . They do not realize that, although there is perhaps nothing in the celestial phenomena which would count against that hypothesis, at least from simpler considerations, nevertheless from what would occur here on earth and in the air, one can see that such a notion is quite ridiculous. . . . Nevertheless, they would have to admit that the revolving motion of the earth must be the most violent of all motions associated with it, seeing that it makes one revolution in such a short time; the result would be that all objects not actually standing on the earth would appear to have the same motion, opposite to that of the earth: Neither clouds nor other flying or thrown objects would ever be seen moving toward the east, since the earth's motion toward the east would always outrun and overtake them, so that all other objects would seem to move in the direction of the west and the rear. But if they said that the air is carried around in the same direction and with the same speed as the earth, the compound objects in the air would nonetheless always seem to be left behind by the motion of both [earth and air]; or if those objects too were carried around, fused, as it were, to the air, then they would never appear to have any motion either in advance or rearwards: they would always appear still, neither wandering about nor changing position, whether they were flying or thrown objects. Yet we quite plainly see that they do undergo all these kinds of motion, in such a way that they are not even slowed down or speeded up at all by any motion of the earth. . . .

Plato (c.427–347 BCE)

Plato has the distinction of being perhaps the most influential philosopher in history and the attraction of being the most readable. This is due both to the form he developed to explore ideas, the dialogue, *and to the fascinating hero of most of the dialogues, his teacher Socrates. Plato may have wanted to become a playwright, and the dialogue form exploits his dramatic and rhetorical strengths. It also recreates the question-and-answer method associated with Socrates, whose ideas survive only in the writings of his students. Plato's school in Athens, the Academy, became known as the best in Greece and it survived for centuries. During the fourth century BCE, the most important mathematical discoveries (solid geometry, conic sections, the doctrine of proportion, the astronomical model of concentric spheres) were made by friends and students of Plato at his Academy. His most famous student, and later rival, was Aristotle.*

Plato's interests were very broad and his philosophical investigations into questions of the good life, proper education, the best form of the state, the nature of good, and the standards of judgment, draw on his knowledge of geometry, cosmology, science, and the law. His ideas became part of the fabric of Western thinking in later centuries, even during the Middle Ages when his writings could no longer be read because of the loss of Greek. Christianity, formed in the Hellenistic Greek milieu of first-century CE Palestine, is thoroughly Platonic in its perception of God as all goodness, truth, and love; the triumph of Christianity in Europe ensured the survival of the Platonic heritage until the Renaissance. Then the Platonic dialogues were "rediscovered" (they had been alive the whole time in the hands of Arabic scholars) and Plato became the rage: neo-Platonic academies were set up in Italy and France, and English poets wrote love poems steeped in Platonic ideas.

THE SYMPOSIUM

The Symposium *(=drinking party) is among Plato's most appealing dialogues, partly because its subject is love, and partly because, like any party, it unfolds as a small drama.*

This selection is taken from the classic version of *Plato* by Benjamin Jowett, the nineteenth-century classics scholar at Oxford University.

In this case the participants engage in a contest of speeches about the nature of love, only to have the party crashed by Socrates' former would-be-lover Alcibiades, who delivers a drunken tribute to Socrates. Socrates' own view of love, which he claims to have learned from the priestess or seer Diotima, is that love is the gateway in an ascent from earthly and bodily appearances to heavenly forms and knowledge of the divine. Along the way, the speeches of the characters, most of whom are well-known Athenians, have cataloged the variety of attitudes toward love.

The symposium is held at the house of Agathon, a tragic playwright. Among his guests is the comedian Aristophanes, who wrote Lysistrata *and who had made devastating fun of Socrates in his play* The Clouds *and elsewhere. Some of Socrates' followers may have felt that Aristophanes, through his caricatures of the philosopher, was partly responsible for his trial and death. Nevertheless, Plato in the* Symposium *assigns Aristophanes a speech which, while not in keeping with the Platonic direction of the dialogue, develops a delightful myth-like allegorical fable that resonates with many of our own popular notions about love: that there is a single person out there who will complete you or make you whole, in a marriage made in heaven!*

Eryximachus said: Beware, friend Aristophanes; although you are going to speak, you are making fun of me; and I shall have to watch your speech and see whether I cannot have a laugh at you, when you might speak in peace.

You are quite right, said Aristophanes, laughing. I will unsay my words; but do you please not to watch me, as I fear that in the speech which I am about to make, instead of others laughing with me, which is to the manner born of our muse and would be all the better, I shall only be laughed at by them.

Do you expect to shoot your bolt and escape, Aristophanes? Well, perhaps if you are very careful and bear in mind that you will be called to account, I may be induced to let you off.

Aristophanes professed to open another vein of discourse; he had a mind to praise Love in another way, unlike that either of Pausanias or Eryximachus. Mankind, he said, judging by their neglect of him, have never, as I think, at all understood the power of Love. For if they had understood him they would surely have built noble temples and altars, and offered solemn sacrifices in his honour; but this is not done, and most certainly ought to be done: since of all the gods he is the best friend of men, the helper and the healer of the ills which are the great impediment to the happiness of the race. I will try to describe his power to you, and you shall teach the rest of the world what I am teaching you. In the first place, let me treat of the nature of man and what has happened to it; for the original human nature was not like the present, but different. The sexes were not two as they are now, but originally three in number; there was man, woman, and the union of the two, having a name corresponding to this double nature, which had once a real existence, but is now lost, and the word "Androgynous" is only preserved as a term of reproach. In the second place, the primeval man was round, his back and sides forming a circle; and he had four hands and four feet, one head with two faces, looking opposite ways, set on a round neck and precisely alike; also four ears, two privy members, and the remainder to correspond. He could walk upright as men now do, backwards or forwards as he pleased, and he could also roll over and over at a great pace, turning on his four hands and four feet, eight in all, like tumblers going over and over with their legs in the air; this was when he wanted to run fast. Now the sexes were three, and such as I have described them; because the sun, moon, and earth are three; and the man was originally the child of the sun, the woman of the earth, and the man-woman of the moon, which is made up of sun and earth, and they were all round and moved round and round like their parents. Terrible was their might and strength, and the thoughts of their hearts were great, and they made an attack upon the gods; of them is told the tale of Otys and Ephialtes who, as Homer says, dared to scale heaven, and would have laid hands upon the gods. Doubt reigned in the celestial councils. Should they kill them and annihilate the race with thunderbolts, as they had done the giants, then there would be an end of the sacrifices and worship which men offered to them; but, on the other hand, the gods could not suffer their insolence to be unrestrained.

At last, after a good deal of reflection, Zeus discovered a way. He said: "Methinks I have a plan which will humble their pride and improve their manners; men shall continue to exist, but I will cut them in two and then they will be diminished in strength and increased in numbers; this will have the advantage of making them more profitable to us. They shall walk upright on two legs, and if they continue insolent and will not be quiet, I will split them again and they shall hop about on a single leg." He spoke and cut men in two, like a sorb-apple which is halved for pickling, or as you might divide an egg with a hair; and as he cut them one after another, he bade Apollo give the face and the half of the neck a turn in order that the man might contemplate the section of himself: he would thus learn a lesson of humility. Apollo was also bidden to heal their wounds and compose their forms. So he gave a turn to the face and pulled the skin from the sides all over that which in our language is called the belly, like the purses which draw in, and he made one mouth at the centre, which he fastened in a knot (the same which is called the navel); he also moulded the breast and took out most of the wrinkles, much as a shoemaker might smooth leather upon a last; he left a few, however, in the region of the belly and navel, as a memorial of the primeval state. After the division the two parts of man, each desiring his other half, came together, and throwing their arms about one another, entwined in mutual embraces, longing to grow into one, they were on the point of dying from hunger and self-neglect, because they did not like to do anything apart; and when one of the halves died and the other survived, the survivor sought another mate, man or woman as we call them,—being the sections of entire men or women,—and clung to that. They were being destroyed, when Zeus in pity of them invented a new plan: he turned the parts of generation round to the front, for this had not been always their position, and they sowed the seed no longer as hitherto like grasshoppers in the ground, but in one another; and after the transposition the male generated in the female in order that by the mutual embraces of man and woman they might breed, and the race might continue; or if man came to man they might be satisfied, and rest, and go their ways to the business of life: so ancient is the desire of one another which is implanted in us, reuniting our original nature, making one of two, and healing the state of man.

Each of us when separated, having one side only, like a flat fish, is but the indenture of a man, and he is always looking for his other half. Men who are a section of that double nature which was once called Androgynous are lovers of women; adulterers are generally of this breed, and also adulterous women who lust after men: the women who are a section of the woman do not care for men, but have female attachments; the female companions are of this sort. But they who are a section of the male follow the male, and while they are young, being slices of the original man, they hang about men and embrace them, and they are themselves the best of boys and youths, because they have the most manly nature. Some indeed assert that they are shameless, but this is not true; for they do not act thus from any want of shame, but because they are valiant and manly, and have a manly countenance, and they embrace that which is like them. And these when they grow up become our statesmen, and these only, which is a great proof of the truth of what I am saying. When they reach manhood they are lovers of youth, and are not naturally inclined to marry or beget children,—if at all, they do so only in obedience to the law; but they are satisfied if they may be allowed to live with one another unwedded; and such a nature is prone to love and ready to return love, always embracing that which is akin to him. And when one of them meets with his other half, the actual half of himself, whether he be a lover of youth or a lover of another sort, the pair are lost in an amazement of love and friendship and intimacy, and one will not be out of the other's sight, as I may say, even for a moment: these are the people who pass their whole lives together; yet they could not explain what they desire of one another. For the intense yearning which each of them has towards the other does not appear to be the desire of lover's intercourse, but of something else which the soul of either evidently desires and cannot tell, and of which she has only a dark and doubtful presentiment. Suppose Hephaestus, with his instruments, to come to the pair who are lying side by side and to say to them, "What do you two people want of one another?" they would be unable to explain. And suppose further, that when he saw their perplexity he said: "Do you desire to be wholly one; always day and night to be in one another's company? for if this is what you desire, I am ready to melt you into one and let you grow together, so that being two you shall become one, and while you live a common life as if you were a single man, and after your death in the world below still be one departed soul instead of two—I ask whether this is what you lovingly desire, and whether you are satisfied to attain this?"—there is not a man of them who when he heard the proposal would deny or would not acknowledge that this meeting and melting into one another, this becoming one instead of two, was the very expression of his ancient need. And the reason is that human nature was originally one and we were a whole, and the desire and pursuit of the whole is called love. There was a time, I say, when we were one, but now because of the wickedness of mankind God has dispersed us, as the Arcadians were dispersed into villages by the Lacedaemonians. And if we are not obedient to the gods, there is a danger that we shall be split up again and go about in basso-relievo, like the profile figures having only half a nose which are sculptured on monuments, and that we shall be like tallies.

Wherefore let us exhort all men to piety, that we may avoid evil, and obtain the good, of which Love is to us the lord and minister; and let no one oppose him—he is the enemy of the gods who oppose him. For if we are friends of the God and at peace with him we shall find our own true loves, which rarely happens in this world at present. I am serious, and therefore I must beg Eryximachus not to make fun or to find any allusion in what I am saying to Pausanias and Agathon, who, as I suspect, are both of the manly nature, and belong to the class which I have been describing. But my words have a wider application—they include men and women everywhere; and I believe that if our loves were perfectly accomplished, and each one returning to his primeval nature had his original true love, then our race would be happy. And if this would be best of all, the best in the next degree and under present circumstances must be the nearest approach to such an union; and that will be the attainment of a congenial love. Wherefore, if we would praise him who has given to us the benefit, we must praise the god Love, who is our greatest benefactor, both leading us in this life back to our own nature, and giving us high hopes for the future, for he promises that if we are pious, he will restore us to our original state, and heal us and make us happy and blessed. This, Eryximachus, is my discourse of love, which, although different to yours, I must beg you to leave unassailed by the shafts of your ridicule, in order that each may have his turn; each, or rather either, for Agathon and Socrates are the only ones left.

Indeed, I am not going to attack you, said Eryximachus, for I thought your speech charming. . . .

THE REPUBLIC

Plato is called an idealist, which means that he felt that the realm of ideas, of principles—the World of Forms—existed prior to and is more real than the material world we inhabit. He shows this in a figurative parable in the Republic, *Plato's evocation of the ideal state, ruled by a philosopher-king. Our life is likened to that of prisoners living in a cave whose knowledge of the outside world comes from reflected shadows on the wall. The world of the senses is darkness compared to the blazing sunlight of the knowledge apprehended by our souls in the* real *world we came from and to which we will return. One scholar suggests that students might think of a movie theater as an apt equivalent of the cave in Plato's figure.*

[THE FIGURE OF THE CAVE]

'I want you to go on to picture the enlightenment or ignorance of our human conditions somewhat as follows. Imagine an underground chamber, like a cave with an entrance open to the daylight and running a long way underground. In this chamber are men who have been prisoners there since they were children, their legs and necks being so fastened that they can only look straight ahead of them and cannot turn their heads. Behind them and above them a fire is burning, and between the fire and the prisoners runs a road, in front of which a curtain-wall has been built, like the screen at puppet shows between the operators and their audience, above which they show their puppets.'

'I see.'

Reprinted from *The Republic*, translated by H.D.F. Lee (Penguin, 1955).

'Imagine further that there are men carrying all sorts of gear along behind the curtain-wall, including figures of men and animals made of wood and stone and other materials, and that some of these men, as is natural, are talking and some not.'

'An odd picture and an odd sort of prisoner.'

'They are drawn from life,' I replied. 'For, tell me, do you think our prisoners could see anything of themselves or their fellows except the shadows thrown by the fire on the wall of the cave opposite them?'

'How could they see anything else if they were prevented from moving their heads all their lives?'

'And would they see anything more of the objects carried along the road?'

'Of course not.'

'Then if they were able to talk to each other, would they not assume that the shadows they saw were real things?'

'Inevitably.'

'And if the wall of their prison opposite them reflected sound, don't you think that they would suppose, whenever one of the passers-by on the road spoke, that the voice belonged to the shadow passing before them?'

'They would be bound to think so.'

'And so they would believe that the shadows of the objects we mentioned were in all respects real.'

'Yes, inevitably.'

'Then think what would naturally happen to them if they were released from their bonds and cured of their delusions. Suppose one of them were let loose, and suddenly compelled to stand up and turn his head and look and walk towards the fire; all these actions would be painful and he would be too dazzled to see properly the objects of which he used to see the shadows. So if he was told that what he used to see was mere illusion and that he was now nearer reality and seeing more correctly, because he was turned towards objects that were more real, and if on top of that he were compelled to say what each of the passing objects was when it was pointed out to him, don't you think he would be at a loss, and think that what he used to see was more real than the objects now being pointed out to him?'

'Much more real.'

'And if he were made to look directly at the light of the fire, it would hurt his eyes and he would turn back and take refuge in the things which he could see, which he would think really far clearer than the things being shown him.'

'Yes.'

'And if,' I went on, 'he were forcibly dragged up the steep and rocky ascent and not let go till he had been dragged out into the sunlight, the process would be a painful one, to which he would much object, and when he emerged into the light his eyes would be so overwhelmed by the brightness of it that he wouldn't be able to see a single one of the things he was now told were real.'

'Certainly not at first,' he agreed.

'Because he would need to grow accustomed to the light before he could see things in the world outside the cave. First he would find it easiest to look at shadows, next at the reflections of men and other objects in water, and later on at the objects themselves. After that he would find it easier to observe the heavenly bodies and the sky at night than by day, and to look at the light of the moon and stars, rather than at the sun and its light!'

'Of course!'

'The thing he would be able to do last would be to look directly at the sun, and observe its nature without using reflections in water or any other medium, but just as it is.'

'That must come last.'

'Later on he would come to the conclusion that it is the sun that produces the changing seasons and years and controls everything in the visible world, and is in a sense responsible for everything that he and his fellow-prisoners used to see.'

'That is the conclusion which he would obviously reach.'

'And when he thought of his first home and what passed for wisdom there, and of his fellow-prisoners, don't you think he would congratulate himself on his good fortune and be sorry for them?'

'Very much so.'

'There was probably a certain amount of honour and glory to be won among the prisoners, and prizes for keen-sightedness for anyone who could remember the order of sequence among the passing shadows and so be best able to predict their future appearances. Will our released prisoner hanker after these prizes or envy this power or honour? Won't he be more likely to feel, as Homer says, that he would far rather be "a serf in the house of some landless man" or indeed anything else in the world, than live and think as they do?'

'Yes,' he replied, 'he would prefer anything to a life like theirs!'

'Then what do you think would happen,' I asked, 'if he went back to sit in his old seat in the cave? Wouldn't his eyes be blinded by the darkness, because he had come in suddenly out of the daylight?'

'Certainly.'

'And if he had to discriminate between the shadows, in competition with the other prisoners, while he was still blinded and before his eyes got used to the darkness—a process that might take some time—wouldn't he be likely to make a fool of himself? And they would say that his visit to the upper world had ruined his sight, and that the ascent was not worth even attempting. And if anyone tried to release them and lead them up, they would kill him if they could lay hands on him.'

'They certainly would!

'Now, my dear Glaucon,' I went on, 'this simile must be connected, throughout, with what preceded it.' The visible realm corresponds to the prison, and the light of the fire in the prison to the power of the sun. And you won't go wrong if you connect the ascent into the upper world and the sight of the objects there with the upward progress of the mind into the intelligible realm—that's my guess, which is what you are anxious to hear. The truth of the matter is, after all, known only to God. But in my opinion, for what it is worth, the final thing to be perceived in the intelligible realm, and perceived only with difficulty, is the absolute form of Good; once seen, it is inferred to be responsible for everything right and good, producing in the visible realm light and the source of light, and being, in the intelligible realm itself, controlling source of reality and intelligence. And anyone who is going to act rationally either in public or private must perceive it.'

'I agree,' he said, 'so far as I am able to understand you.'

'Then you will perhaps also agree with me that it won't be surprising if those who get so far are unwilling to return to mundane affairs, and if their minds long to remain among higher things. That's what we should expect if our simile is to be trusted.'

'Yes, that's to be expected!'

'Nor will you think it strange that anyone who descends from contemplation of the divine to the imperfections of human life should blunder and make a fool of himself, if, while still blinded and unaccustomed to the surrounding darkness, he's forcibly put on trial in the law-courts or elsewhere about the images of justice or their shadows, and made to dispute about the conceptions of justice held by men who have never seen absolute justice.'

'There's nothing strange in that.'

'But anyone with any sense,' I said, 'will remember that the eyes may be unsighted in two ways, by a transition either from light to darkness or from darkness to light, and that the same distinction applies to the mind. So when he sees a mind confused and unable to see clearly he will not laugh without thinking, but will ask himself whether it has come from a clearer world and is confused by the unaccustomed darkness, or whether it is dazzled by the stronger light of the clearer world to which it has escaped from its previous ignorance. The first state is a reason for congratulation, the second for sympathy, though if one wants to laugh at it one can do so with less absurdity than at the mind that has descended from the daylight of the upper world.'

'You put it very reasonably.'

'If this is true,' I continued, 'we must reject the conception of education professed by those who say that they can put into the mind knowledge that was not there before—rather as if they could put sight into blind eyes.'

'It is a claim that is certainly made,' he said.

'But our argument indicates that this is a capacity which is innate in each man's mind, and that the faculty by which he learns is like an eye which cannot be turned from darkness to light unless the whole body is turned; in the same way the mind as a whole must be turned away from the world of change until its eye can bear to look straight at reality, and at the brightest of all realities which is what we call the Good. Isn't that so?'

'Yes.'

'Then this business of turning the mind round might be made a subject of professional skill, which would effect the conversion as easily and effectively as possible. It would not be concerned to implant sight, but to ensure that some one who had it already was turned in the right direction and looking the right way.'

'That may well be so.'

'The rest, therefore, of what are commonly called qualities of the mind perhaps resemble those of the body, in that they are not innate, but are implanted by training and practice; but the power of knowing, it seems, belongs to some diviner faculty, which never loses its power, but whose effects are good or bad according to the direction in which it is turned. Have you never noticed how shrewd is the glance of the type of men commonly called bad but clever? Their intelligence is limited, but their sight is sharp enough in matters that concern them; it's not that their sight is weak, but that they put it to bad use, so that the keener it is the worse its effects.'

'That's true.'

'But suppose,' I said, 'that such natures were cut loose, when they were still children, from the dead weight of worldliness, fastened on them by sensual indulgences like gluttony, which distorts their minds' vision to lower things, and suppose that when so freed they were turned towards the truth, then the same faculty in them would have as keen a vision of truth as it has of the objects on which it is at present turned.'

'Very likely.'

'And is it not also likely, and indeed a necessary consequence of that we have said, that society will never be properly governed either by the uneducated, who have no knowledge of the truth, or by those who are allowed to spend all their lives in purely intellectual pursuits? The uneducated have no single aim in life to which all their actions, public and private, are directed, the intellectuals will take no practical action of their own accord, fancying themselves to be no longer of this world.'

'True.'

'Then our job as Lawgivers is to compel the best minds to attain what we have called the highest form of knowledge, and to ascend to the vision of the Good as we have described, and when they have achieved this and seen enough, prevent them behaving as they now do.'

'What do you mean by that?'

'Remaining in the upper world, and refusing to return again to the prisoners in the cave below and share their labours and rewards, whether they are worth having or not.'

'But surely,' he protested, 'that will not be fair. We shall be compelling them to live a poorer life than they might live.'

'The object of our legislation,' I reminded him again, 'is not the welfare of any particular class, but of the whole community. It uses persuasion or force to unite all citizens and make them share together the benefits which each individually can confer on the community; and its purpose in fostering this attitude is not to enable everyone to please himself, but to make each man a link in the unity of the whole.'

'You are right; I had forgotten,' he said.

'You see, then, Glaucon,' I went on, 'we shan't be unfair to our philosophers, but shall be quite justified in compelling them to have some care and responsibility for others. We shall tell them that philosophers in other states can reasonably refuse to take part in the hard work of politics; for society produces them quite involuntarily and unintentionally, and it is only just that anything that grows up on its own should feel it has nothing to repay for an upbringing which it owes to no one. "But you," we shall say, "have been bred to rule to your own advantage and that of the whole community, like kingbees in a hive; you are better educated than the rest and better qualified to combine the practice of philosophy and politics. You must therefore each descend in turn and live with your fellows in the cave and get used to seeing in the dark; once you get used to it you will see a thousand times better than they do and will recognize the various shadows, and know what they are shadows of, because you have seen the truth about things right and just and good. And so our state and yours will be really awake, and not merely dreaming like most societies to-day, with their shadow battles and their struggles for political power, which they treat as some great prize. The truth is quite different: the state whose rulers come to their duties with least enthusiasm is bound to have the best and most tranquil government, and the state whose rulers are eager to rule the worst."

'I quite agree.'

'Then will our pupils, when they hear what we say, refuse to take their share of the hard work of government, though spending the greater part of their time together in the pure air of philosophy?'

'They cannot refuse, for we are making a just demand of just men. But of course, unlike present rulers, they will approach the business of government as an unavoidable necessity.'

'Yes, of course,' I agreed. 'The truth is that if you want a well-governed state you must find for your future rulers some career they like better than government; for only then will you have government by the truly rich, those, that is, whose riches consist not of money, but of the happiness of a right and rational life. If you get, in public affairs, men who are so morally impoverished that they have nothing they can contribute themselves, but who hope to snatch some compensation for their own inadequacy from a political career, there can never be good government. They start fighting for power, and the consequent internal and domestic conflicts ruin both them and society!

'True indeed.'

'Is there any other life except that of true philosophy which looks down on political power?'

'None that I know of.'

'And yet the only men to get power should be men who do not love it, otherwise we shall have rivals' quarrels.'

'That is certain.'

'Who else, then, are we to compel to undertake the responsibilities of ruling, if it is not to be those who know most about good government and who yet value other things more highly than politics and its rewards?

'There is no one else.'

Timaeus

The Timaeus, one of Plato's later dialogues, is not often read by students because its subject is science and cosmology, not metaphysics. In it, Plato introduces God as the intelligent cause of order and structure in a universe in the process of becoming. But the rule of reason is hemmed in and limited by the power of material necessity (ananke). *In this discussion of natural science, Plato introduces a myth that many people know and love but don't associate with Plato—the story of Atlantis, the lost continent for which the ocean is named.*

[THE STORY OF ATLANTIS]

Critias. Then listen, Socrates, to a tale which, though strange, is certainly true, having been attested by Solon, who was the wisest of the seven sages. He was a relative and a dear friend of my great-grandfather, Dropides, as he himself says in many passages of his poems, and he told the story to Critias, my grandfather, who remembered and repeated it to us. There were of old, he said, great and marvelous actions of the Athenian city, which have passed into oblivion through lapse of time and the destruction of mankind, and one in particular, greater than all the rest. . . .

Critias, at the time of telling it, was as he said, nearly ninety years of age, and I was about ten. Now the day was that day of the Apaturia which is called the Registration of Youth, at which, according to custom, our parents gave prizes for recitations, and the poems of several poets were recited by us boys, and many of us sang the poems of Solon, which at that time had not gone out of fashion. One of our tribe, either because he thought so or to please Critias, said that in his judgment Solon was not only the wisest of men, but also the noblest of poets. The old man, as I very well remember, brightened up at hearing this and said, smiling: Yes, Amynander, if Solon had only, like other poets, made poetry the business of his life, and had completed the tale which he brought with him from Egypt, and had not been compelled, by reason of the factions and troubles which he found stirring in his own country when he came home, to attend to other matters, in my opinion he would have been as famous as Homer or Hesiod, or any poet.

And what was the tale about, Critias? said Amynander.

About the greatest action which the Athenians ever did, and which ought to have been the most famous, but, through the lapse of time and the destruction of the actors, it has not come down to us.

Tell us, said the other, the whole story, and how and from whom Solon heard this veritable tradition.

He replied: In the Egyptian Delta, at the head of which the river Nile divides, there is a certain district which is called the district of Sais, and the great city of the district is also called Sais, and is the city from which King Amasis came. The citizens have a deity for their foundress; she is called in the Egyptian tongue Neith, and is asserted by them to be the same whom the Hellenes call Athene; they are great lovers of the Athenians, and say that they are in some way related to them. To this city came Solon, and was received there with great honour; he asked the priests who were most skilful in such matters, about antiquity, and made the discovery that neither he nor any other Hellene knew anything worth mentioning about the times of old. On one occasion, wishing to draw them on to speak of antiquity, he began to tell about the most ancient things in our part of the world—about Phoroneus, who is called "the first man," and about Niobe; and after the Deluge, of the survival of Deucalion and Pyrrha; and he traced the genealogy of their descendants, and reckoning up the dates, tried to compute how many years ago the events of which he was speaking happened. Thereupon one of the priests, who was of a very great age, said: O Solon, Solon, you Hellenes are never anything but children, and there is not an old man among you. Solon in return asked him what he meant. I mean to say, he replied, that in mind you

The translation is an old classic (1871) by Benjamin Jowett.

are all young; there is no old opinion handed down among you by ancient tradition, nor any science which is hoary with age. And I will tell you why. There have been, and will be again, many destructions of mankind arising out of many causes; the greatest have been brought about by the agencies of fire and water, and other lesser ones by innumerable other causes. There is a story, which even you have preserved, that once upon a time Phaethon, the son of Helios, having yoked the steeds in his father's chariot, because he was not able to drive them in the path of his father, burnt up all that was upon the earth, and was himself destroyed by a thunderbolt. Now this has the form of a myth but really signifies a declination of the bodies moving in the heavens around the earth, and a great conflagration of things upon the earth, which recurs after long intervals; at such times those who live upon the mountains and in dry and lofty places are more liable to destruction than those who dwell by rivers or on the seashore. And from this calamity the Nile, who is our never-failing saviour, delivers and preserves us. When, on the other hand, the gods purge the earth with a deluge of water, the survivors in your country are herdsmen and shepherds who dwell on the mountains, but those who, like you, live in cities are carried by the rivers into the sea. Whereas in this land, neither then nor at any other time, does the water come down from above on the fields, having always a tendency to come up from below; for which reason the traditions preserved here are the most ancient.

The fact is, that wherever the extremity of winter frost or of summer does not prevent, mankind exist, sometimes in greater, sometimes in lesser numbers. And whatever happened either in your country or in ours, or in any other region of which we are informed—if there were any actions noble or great or in any other way remarkable, they have all been written down by us of old, and are preserved in our temples. Whereas just when you and other nations are beginning to be provided with letters and the other requisites of civilized life, after the usual interval, the stream from heaven, like a pestilence, comes pouring down, and leaves only those of you who are destitute of letters and education; and so you have to begin all over again like children, and know nothing of what happened in ancient times, either among us or among yourselves. As for those genealogies of yours which you just now recounted to us, Solon, they are no better than the tales of children. In the first place you remember a single deluge only, but there were many previous ones; in the next place, you do not know that there formerly dwelt in your land the fairest and noblest race of men which ever lived, and that you and your whole city are descended from a small seed or remnant of them which survived. And this was unknown to you, because, for many generations, the survivors of that destruction died, leaving no written word. For there was a time, Solon, before the greatest deluge of all, when the city which now is Athens was first in war and in every way the best governed of all cities; it is said to have performed the noblest deeds and to have had the fairest constitution of any of which tradition tells, under the face of heaven.

Solon marvelled at his words and earnestly requested the priests to inform him exactly and in order about these former citizens. You are welcome to hear about them, Solon, said the priest, both for your own sake and for that of your city, and above all, for the sake of the goddess who is the common patron and parent and educator of both our cities. She founded your city a thousand years before ours, receiving from the Earth and Hephaestus the seed of your race, and afterwards she founded ours, of which the constitution is recorded in our sacred registers to be eight thousand years old. As touching your citizens of nine thousand years ago, I will briefly inform you of their laws and of their most famous action; the exact particulars of the whole we will hereafter go through at our leisure in the sacred registers themselves. If you compare these very laws with ours you will find that many of ours are the counterpart of yours as they were in the olden time. In the first place, there is the caste of priests, which is separated from all the others; next, there are the artificers, who ply their several crafts by themselves and do not intermix; and also there is the class of shepherds and of hunters, as well as that of husbandmen; and you will observe, too, that the warriors in Egypt are distinct from all the other classes, and are commanded by the law to devote themselves solely to military pursuits; moreover, the weapons which they carry are shields and spears, a style of equipment which the goddess taught of Asiatics first to us, as in your part of the world first to you. Then as to wisdom, do you observe how our law from the very first made a study of the whole order of things, extending even to prophecy and medicine which gives health, out of these divine elements deriving what was needful for human life, and adding every sort of knowledge which was akin to them. All this order and arrangement the goddess first imparted to you when establishing your city; and she chose the spot of earth in which you were born, because she saw that the happy temperament of the seasons in that land would produce the wisest of men. Wherefore the goddess, who was a lover both of war and of wisdom, selected and first of all settled that spot which was the most likely to produce men likest herself. And there you dwelt, having such laws as these and still better ones, and excelled all mankind in all virtue, as became the children and disciples of the gods.

Many great and wonderful deeds are recorded of your state in our histories. But one of them exceeds all the rest in greatness and valour. For these histories tell of a mighty power which unprovoked made an expedition against the whole of Europe and Asia, and to which your city put an end. This power came forth out of the Atlantic Ocean, for in those days the Atlantic was navigable; and there was an island situated in front of the straits which are by you called the Pillars of Heracles; the island was larger than Libya and Asia put together, and, was the way to other islands, and from these you might pass to the whole of the opposite continent which surrounded the true ocean; for this sea which is within the Straits of Heracles is only a harbour, having a narrow entrance, but that other is a real sea, and the surrounding land may be most truly called a boundless continent. Now in this island of Atlantis there was a great and wonderful empire which had rule over the whole island and several others, and over parts of the continent, and, furthermore, the men of Atlantis had subjected the parts of Libya within the columns of Heracles as far as Egypt, and of Europe as far as Tyrrhenia. This vast power, gathered into one, endeavoured to subdue at a blow our country and yours and the whole of the region within the straits; and then, Solon, your country shone forth, in the excellence of her virtue and strength, among all mankind. She was pre-eminent in courage and military skill, and was the leader of the Hellenes. And when the rest fell off from her, being compelled to stand alone, after having undergone the very extremity of danger, she defeated and triumphed over the invaders, and preserved from slavery those who were not yet subjugated, and generously liberated all the rest of us who dwell within the pillars. But afterwards there occurred violent earthquakes and floods; and in a single day and night of misfortune all your warlike men in a body sank into the earth, and the island of Atlantis in like manner disappeared in the depths of the sea. For which reason the sea in those parts is impassable and impenetrable, because there is a shoal of mud in the way; and this was caused by the subsidence of the island.

I have told you briefly, Socrates, what the aged Critias heard from Solon and related to us.

Aristotle (384–322 BCE)

If to Plato what is truly real lies outside the world of our senses, to Aristotle all knowledge is grounded in the things we perceive. Although he was perhaps Plato's greatest pupil, Aristotle finally rejected Plato's otherworldliness and wrote treatises examining almost every aspect of the world we know and live in. Everything, from rhetoric and ethics to physics and music, came under scrutiny in works which survive mainly in the form of lecture notes collected by his followers. His studies in biology helped him to see everything in terms of growth and movement from potentiality toward actuality. A great organizer, he saw the world arranged in categories and hierarchies, and he applied the same habits of thought to less tangible things, like tragedy, which he analyzes in his treatise on Poetics. *Even there, he starts from what is and not from what ought to be. Aristotle's most famous student was the son of King Philip of Macedon, Alexander, who later set out to conquer the world before his early death. Aristotle's notions of logic were central to the study of logic into our own century; his way of talking about God became part of Christianity in the medieval treatises of Thomas Aquinas, and his way of examining and classifying the world around him became the basis of our "modern" scientific method and our model of taxonomy.*

POETICS

It is hard to exaggerate the importance of Sophocles's play Oedipus the King, *since—besides being a powerful and terrifying play—it also suggested to Freud his "Oedipus Complex" and to Aristotle the outlines of a theory of tragedy. It is important to recognize, however, that this theory is as descriptive as it is prescriptive: when he characterizes tragedy, Aristotle is, in the main, describing the way* Oedipus *works, and not all tragedies. And even then it is possible to be misled by what he says. For centuries, literary critics have been looking for a tragic flaw in each of Shakespeare's tragic heroes, based on Aristotle's identification of the source of tragic action in the hero's* hamartia, *"error in judgment." While Shakespeare's heroes can sometimes be said to have moral flaws (Shakespeare, too,*

The selection here is from the translation by S. H. Butcher (London, 1895).

had misread his Aristotle!), Greek tragedies are quite varied in their evocation of a cause of the tragic action. In Antigone, *for instance, both Antigone and Creon hold staunchly to views that are right, although in conflict. Hamartia, then, might properly be thought of as "mistake," elevated in the plays by necessity, chance, and cosmic perversity into true catastrophe. The translation which follows may imply both views in the use of the words "error" and "frailty."*

The Poetics *contains discussions of both tragedy and epic. A companion work on comedy was lost early on. Some readers may remember that the appearance of a manuscript of Aristotle's supposedly lost* Comedy *in a French monastery in the fourteenth century motivates a series of murders in Umberto Eco's* The Name of the Rose, *a novel that became a popular movie with Sean Connery.*

[Tragedy]

IV. Poetry in general seems to have sprung from two causes, each of the them lying deep in our nature. First, the instinct of imitation is implanted in man from childhood, one difference between him and other animals being that he is the most imitative of living creatures; and through imitation he learns his earliest lessons; and no less universal is the pleasure felt in things imitated. We have evidence of this in the facts of experience. Objects which in themselves we view with pain, we delight to contemplate when reproduced with minute fidelity: such as the forms of the most ignoble animals and of dead bodies. The cause of this again is, that to learn gives the liveliest pleasure, not only to philosophers but to men in general; whose capacity, however, of learning is more limited. Thus the reason why men enjoy seeing a likeness is, that in contemplating it they find themselves learning or inferring, and saying perhaps, 'Ah, that is he.' For if you happen not to have seen the original, the pleasure will be due not to the imitation as such, but to the execution, the colouring, or some such other cause. . . .

Poetry now diverged in two directions, according to the individual character of the writers. The graver spirits imitated noble actions, and the actions of good men. The more trivial sort imitated the actions of meaner persons, at first composing satires, as the former did hymns to the gods and the praises of famous men. A poem of the satirical kind cannot indeed be put down to any author earlier than Homer; though many such writers probably there were. But from Homer onward, instances can be cited,—his own Margites, for example, and other similar compositions. The appropriate metre was also here introduced; hence the measure is still called the iambic or lampooning measure, being that in which people lampooned one another. Thus the older poets were distinguished as writers of heroic or of lampooning verse.

As, in the serious style, Homer is pre-eminent among poets, for he alone combined dramatic form with excellence of imitation, so he too first laid down the main lines of Comedy, by dramatising the ludicrous instead of writing personal satire. His Margites bears the same relation to Comedy that the Iliad and Odyssey do to Tragedy. But when Tragedy and Comedy came to light, the two classes of poets still followed their natural bent: the lampooners became writers of Comedy, and the Epic poets were succeeded by Tragedians, since the drama was a larger and higher form of art.

Whether Tragedy has as yet perfected its proper types or not; and whether it is to be judged in itself, or in relation also to the audience,—this raises another question. Be that as it may, Tragedy—as also Comedy—was at first mere improvisation. The one originated with the leaders of the Dithyramb, the other with those of the phallic songs, which are still in use in many of our cities. Tragedy advanced by slow degrees; each new element that showed itself was in turn developed. Having passed through many changes, it found its natural form, and there it stopped.

Aeschylus first introduced a second actor; he diminished the importance of the Chorus, and assigned the leading part to the dialogue. Sophocles raised the number of actors to three, and added scene-painting. Moreover, it was not till late that the short plot was discarded for one of greater compass, and the grotesque diction of the earlier satyric form for the stately manner of Tragedy. The iambic measure then replaced the trochaic tetrameter, which was originally employed when the poetry was of the satyric order, and had greater affinities with dancing. Once dialogue had come in, Nature herself discovered the appropriate measure. For the iambic is, of all measures, the most colloquial: we see it in the fact that conversational speech runs into iambic lines more frequently than into any other kind of verse; rarely into hexameters, and only when we drop the colloquial intonation. The additions to the number of 'episodes' or acts, and the other improvements of which tradition tells, must be taken as already described; for to discuss them in detail would, doubtless, be a large undertaking.

V. Comedy is, as we have said, an imitation of characters of a lower type,—not, however, in the full sense of the word bad, the Ludicrous being merely a subdivision of the ugly. It consists in some defect or ugliness which is not painful or destructive. To take an obvious example, the comic mask is ugly and distorted, but does not imply pain.

The successive changes through which Tragedy passed, and the authors of these changes, are well known, whereas Comedy has had no history, because it was not at first treated seriously. It was late before the Archon granted a comic chorus to a poet; the performers were till then voluntary. Comedy had already taken definite shape when comic poets, distinctively so called, are heard of. Who introduced masks, or prologues, or increased the number of actors,—these and other similar details remain unknown. As for the plot, it came originally from Sicily; but of Athenian writers Crates was the first who, abandoning the 'iambic' or lampooning form, generalised his themes and plots.

Epic poetry agrees with Tragedy in so far as it is an imitation in verse of characters of a higher type. They differ, in that Epic poetry admits but one kind of metre, and is narrative in form. They differ, again, in their length: for Tragedy endeavours, as far as possible, to confine itself to a single revolution of the sun, or but slightly to exceed this limit; whereas the Epic action has no limits of time. This, then, is a second point of difference; though at first the same freedom was admitted in Tragedy as in Epic poetry.

Of their constituent parts some are common to both, some peculiar to Tragedy. Whoever, therefore, knows what is good or bad Tragedy, knows also about Epic poetry: for all the elements of an Epic poem are found in Tragedy, but the elements of a Tragedy are not all found in the Epic poem.

VI. Of the poetry which imitates in hexameter verse, and of Comedy, we will speak hereafter. Let us now discuss Tragedy, resuming its formal definition, as resulting from what has been already said.

Tragedy, then, is an imitation of an action that is serious, complete, and of a certain magnitude; in language embellished with each kind of artistic ornament, the several kinds being found in separate parts of the play; in the form of action, not of narrative; through pity and fear effecting the proper purgation of these emotions. By 'language embellished,' I mean language into which rhythm, 'harmony,' and song enter. By 'the several kinds in separate parts,' I mean, that some parts are rendered through the medium of verse alone, others again with the aid of song. . . .

Again, Tragedy is the imitation of an action; and an action implies personal agents, who necessarily possess certain distinctive qualities both of character and thought; for it is by these that we qualify actions themselves, and these—thought and character—are the two natural causes from which actions spring, and on actions again all success or failure depends. Hence, the Plot is the imitation of the action:—for by plot I here mean the arrangement of the incidents. By Character I mean that in virtue of which we ascribe certain qualities to the agents. Thought is required wherever a statement is proved, or, it may be, a general truth enunciated. Every Tragedy, therefore, must have six parts, which parts determine its quality—namely, Plot, Character, Diction, Thought, Spectacle, Song. Two of the parts constitute the medium of imitation, one of the manner, and three the objects of imitation. And these complete the list. . . .

But most important of all is the structure of the incidents. For Tragedy is an imitation, not of men, but of an action and of life, and life consists in action, and its end is a mode of action, not a quality. Now character determines men's qualities, but it is by their actions that they are happy or the reverse. Dramatic action, therefore, is not with a view to the representation of character: character comes in as subsidiary to the actions. Hence the incidents and the plot are the end of a tragedy; and the end is the chief thing of all. Again, without action there cannot be a tragedy; there may be without character. The tragedies of most of our modern poets fail in the rendering of character; and of poets in general this is often true. . . . Again, if you string together a set of speeches expressive of character, and well finished in point of diction and thought, you will not produce the essential tragic effect nearly so well as with a play which, however deficient in these respects, yet has a plot and artistically constructed incidents. Besides which, the most powerful elements of emotional interest in Tragedy—Peripeteia or Reversal of the Situation, and Recognition scenes—are parts of the plot. A further proof is, that novices in the art attain to finish of diction and precision of portraiture before they can construct the plot. It is the same with almost all the early poets. . . .

VII. These principles being established, let us now discuss the proper structure of the Plot, since this is the first and most important part of Tragedy.

Now, according to our definition, Tragedy is an imitation of an action that is complete, and whole, and of a certain magnitude; for there may be a whole that is wanting in magnitude. A whole is that which has a beginning, a middle, and an end. A beginning is that which does not itself follow anything by causal necessity, but after which something naturally is or comes to be. An end, on the contrary, is that which itself naturally follows some other thing, either by necessity, or as a rule, but has nothing following it. A middle is that which follows something as some other thing follows it. A well constructed plot, therefore, must neither begin nor end at haphazard, but conform to these principles. . . .

VIII. Unity of plot does not, as some persons think, consist in the unity of the hero. For infinitely various are the incidents in one man's life which cannot be reduced to unity; and so, too, there are many actions of one man out of which we cannot make one action. Hence the error, as it appears, of all poets who have composed a Heracleid, a Theseid, or other poems of the kind. They imagine that as Heracles was one man, the story of Heracles must also be a unity. But Homer, as in all else he is of surpassing merit, here too—whether from art or natural genius—seems to have happily discerned the truth. In composing the Odyssey he did not include all the adventures of Odysseus—such as his wound on Parnassus, or his feigned madness at the mustering of the host—incidents between which there was no necessary or probable connexion: but he made the Odyssey, and likewise the Iliad, to centre round an action that in our sense of the word is one. As therefore, in the other imitative arts, the imitation is one when the object imitated is one, so the plot, being an imitation of an action, must imitate one action and that a whole, the structural union of the parts being such that, if any one of them is displaced or removed, the whole will be disjointed and disturbed. For a thing whose presence or absence makes no visible difference, is not an organic part of the whole.

IX. It is, moreover, evident from what has been said, that it is not the function of the poet to relate what has happened, but what may happen,—what is possible according to the law of probability or necessity. The poet and the historian differ not by writing in verse or in prose. The work of Herodotus might be put into verse, and it would still be a species of history, with metre no less than without it. The true difference is that one relates what has happened, the other what may happen. Poetry, therefore, is a more philosophical and a higher thing than history: for poetry tends to express the universal, history the particular. By the universal I mean how a person of a certain type will on occasion speak or act, according to the law of probability or necessity; and it is this universality at which poetry aims in the names she attaches to the personages. The particular is—for example—what Alcibiades did or suffered. In Comedy this is already apparent: for here the poet first constructs the plot on the lines of probability, and then inserts characteristic names;—unlike the lampooners who write about particular individuals. But tragedians still keep to real names, the reason being that what is possible is credible: what has not happened we do not at once feel sure to be possible: but what has happened is manifestly possible: otherwise it would not have happened. Still there are some tragedies in which there are only one or two well known names, the rest being fictitious. In others, none are well known,—as in Agathon's Antheus, where incidents and names alike are fictitious, and yet they give none the less pleasure. We must not, therefore, at all costs keep to the received legends, which are the usual subjects of Tragedy. Indeed, it would be absurd to attempt it; for even subjects that are known are known only to a few, and yet give pleasure to all. It clearly follows that the poet or 'maker' should be the maker of plots rather than of verses; since he is a poet because he imitates, and what he imitates are actions. And even if he chances to take an historical subject, he is none the less a poet;

for there is no reason why some events that have actually happened should not conform to the law of the probable and possible, and in virtue of that quality in them he is their poet or maker. . . .

But again, Tragedy is an imitation not only of a complete action, but of events terrible and pitiful. Such an effect is best produced when the events come on us by surprise; and the effect is heightened when, at the same time, they follow as cause and effect. The tragic wonder will then be greater than if they happened of themselves or by accident; for even coincidences are most striking when they have an air of design. We may instance the statue of Mitys at Argos, which fell upon his murderer while he was a spectator at a festival, and killed him. Such events seem not to be due to mere chance. Plots, therefore, constructed on these principles are necessarily the best.

X. Plots are either Simple or Complex, for the actions in real life, of which the plots are an imitation, obviously show a similar distinction. An action which is one and continuous in the sense above defined, I call Simple, when the change of fortune takes place without Reversal of the Situation and without Recognition.

A Complex action is one in which the change is accompanied by such Reversal, or by Recognition, or by both. These last should arise from the internal structure of the plot, so that what follows should be the necessary or probable result of the preceding action. It makes all the difference whether any given event is a case of *propter hoc* or *post hoc*.

XI. Reversal of the Situation is a change by which the action veers round to its opposite, subject always to our rule of probability or necessity. Thus in the Oedipus, the messenger comes to cheer Oedipus and free him from his alarms about his mother, but by revealing who he is, he produces the opposite effect. . . .

Recognition, as the name indicates, is a change from ignorance to knowledge, producing love or hate between the persons destined by the poet for good or bad fortune. The best form of recognition is coincident with a Reversal of the Situation, as in the Oedipus. There are indeed other forms. Even inanimate things of the most trivial kind may sometimes be objects of recognition. Again, we may recognise or discover whether a person has done a thing or not. But the recognition which is most intimately connected with the plot and action is, as we have said, the recognition of persons. This recognition, combined with Reversals, will produce either pity or fear; and actions producing these effects are those which, by our definition, Tragedy represents. Moreover, it is upon such situations that the issues of good or bad fortune will depend. . . .

Two parts, then, of the Plot—Reversal of the Situation and Recognition—turn upon surprises. A third part is the Tragic Incident. The Tragic Incident is a destructive or painful action, such as death on the stage, bodily agony, wounds and the like. . . .

XIII. As the sequel to what has already been said, we must proceed to consider what the poet should aim at, and what he should avoid, in constructing his plots; and by what means the specific effect of Tragedy will be produced.

A perfect tragedy should, as we have seen, be arranged not on the simple but on the complex plan. It should, moreover, imitate actions which excite pity and fear, this being the distinctive mark of tragic imitation. It follows plainly, in the first place, that the change of fortune presented must not be the spectacle of a virtuous man brought from prosperity to adversity: for this moves neither pity nor fear; it merely shocks us. Nor, again, that of a bad man passing from adversity to prosperity: for nothing can be more alien to the spirit of Tragedy; it possesses no single tragic quality; it neither satisfies the moral sense nor calls forth pity or fear. Nor, again, should the downfall of the utter villain be exhibited. A plot of this kind would, doubtless, satisfy the moral sense, but it would inspire neither pity nor fear; for pity is aroused by unmerited misfortune, fear by the misfortune of a man like ourselves. Such an event, therefore, will be neither pitiful nor terrible. There remains, then, the character between these two extremes,—that of a man who is not eminently good and just, yet whose misfortune is brought about not by vice or depravity, but by some error or frailty. He must be one who is highly renowned and prosperous,—a personage like Oedipus, Thyestes, or other illustrious men of such families.

A well constructed plot should, therefore, be single in its issue, rather than double as some maintain. The change of fortune should be not from bad to good, but, reversely, from good to bad. It should come about as the result not of vice, but of some great error or frailty, in a character either such as we have described, or better rather than worse. . . .

Physics

Among Aristotle's many structures and concepts, the notion of causation has a pre-eminent place. Because Aristotle saw the world in terms of potentiality and "becoming"—of movement, therefore—he also had to account for the fact and the direction of the movement. Causes, then, are the motive forces of Aristotle's world, denoting the material from which something is made (material cause), the shape it takes (formal cause), who makes it (efficient cause), and why it is made (final cause). Aristotle's best exposition of his model of causation can be found in the Physics, in the following passage.

[The Four Causes]

II.3. Now that we have established these distinctions, we must proceed to consider causes, their character and number. Knowledge is the object of our inquiry, and men do not think they know a thing till they have grasped the "why" of it (which is to grasp its primary cause). So clearly we too must do this as regards both coming to be and passing away and every kind of physical change, in order that, knowing their principles, we may try to refer to these principles each of our problems.

In one sense, then, (1) that out of which a thing comes to be and which persists, is called "cause," e.g. the bronze of the statue, the silver of the bowl, and the genera of which the bronze and the silver are species.

In another sense (2) the form or the archetype, i.e., the statement of the essence, and its genera, are called "causes" (e.g. of the octave the relation of 2:1, and generally number), and the parts in the definition.

Reprinted from *Physics*, translated by R.P. Hardie and R. K. Gaye, (1930).

Again (3) the primary source of the change or coming to rest; e.g. the man who gave advice is a cause, the father is cause of the child, and generally what makes of what is made and what causes change of what is changed.

Again (4) in the sense of end or "that for the sake of which" a thing is done, e.g. health is the cause of walking about. ("Why is he walking about?" we say. "To be healthy," and, having said that, we think we have assigned the cause.) The same is true also of all the intermediate steps which are brought about through the action of something else as means towards the end, e.g. reduction of flesh, urging, drugs, or surgical instruments are means towards health. All these things are "for the sake of" the end, though they differ from one another in that some are activities, others instruments.

This then perhaps exhausts the number of ways in which the term "cause" is used.

As the word has several senses, it follows that there are several causes of the same thing (not merely in virtue of a concomitant attribute), e.g. both the art of the sculptor and the bronze are causes of the statue. These are causes of the statue qua statue, not in virtue of anything else that it may be—only not in the same way, the one being the material cause, the other the cause whence the motion comes. Some things cause each other reciprocally, e.g. hard work causes fitness and vice versa, but again not in the same way, but the one as end, the other as the origin of change. Further the same thing is the cause of contrary results. For that which by its presence brings about one result is sometimes blamed for bringing about the contrary by its absence. Thus we ascribe the wreck of a ship to the absence of the pilot whose presence was the cause of its safety.

All the causes now mentioned fall into four familiar divisions. The letters are the causes of syllables, the material of artificial products, fire, &c., of bodies, the parts of the whole, and the premises of the conclusion, in the sense of "that from which." Of these pairs the one set are causes in the sense of substratum, e.g. the parts, the other set in the sense of essence—the whole and the combination and the form. But the seed and the doctor and the adviser, and generally the maker, are all sources whence the change or stationariness originates, while the others are causes in the sense of the end or the good of the rest; for "that for the sake of which" means what is best and the end of the things that lead up to it. (Whether we say the "good itself" or the "apparent good" makes no difference.) Such then is the number and nature of the kinds of cause.

Now the modes of causation are many, though when brought under heads they too can be reduced in number. For "cause" is used in many senses and even within the same kind one may be prior to another (e.g. the doctor and the expert are causes of health, the relation 2:1 and number of the octave), and always what is inclusive to what is particular. Another mode of causation is the incidental and its genera, e.g. in one way "Polyclitus," in another "sculptor" is the cause of a statue, because "being Polyclitus" and "sculptor" are incidentally conjoined. Also the classes in which the incidental attribute is included; thus "a man" could be said to be the cause of a statue or, generally, "a living creature." An incidental attribute too may be more or less remote, e.g. suppose that "a pale man" or "a musical man" were said to be the cause of the statue.

All causes, both proper and incidental, may be spoken of either as potential or as actual; e.g. the cause of a house being built is either "house-builder" or "house-builder building."

Similar distinctions can be made in the things of which the causes are cause, e.g. of "this statue" or of "statue" or of "image" generally, of "this bronze" or of "bronze" or of "material" generally. So too with the incidental attributes. Again we may use a complex expression for either and say, e.g. neither "Polyclitus" nor "sculptor" but "Polyclitus, sculptor."

All these various uses, however, come to six in number, under each of which again the usage is two-fold. Cause means either what is particular or a genus, or an incidental attribute or a genus of that, and these either as a complex or each by itself; and all six either as actual or as potential. The difference is this much, that causes which are actually at work and particular exist and cease to exist simultaneously with their effect, e.g. this healing person with this being-healed person and that house-building man with that being-built house; but this is not always true of potential causes—the house and the housebuilder do not pass away simultaneously.

In investigating the cause of each thing it is always necessary to seek what is most precise (as also in other things); thus man builds because he is a builder, and a builder builds in virtue of his art of building. This last cause then is prior: and so generally.

Further, generic effects should be assigned to generic causes, particular effects to particular causes, e.g. statue to sculptor, this statue to this sculptor; and powers are relative to possible effects, actually operating causes to things which are actually being effected.

This must suffice for our account of the number of causes and the modes of causation.

Roman aqueduct. 19 BCE. Pont du Gard, Nîmes, France. Giraudon/Art Resource, NY.

The World of Rome

Besides being effective soldiers, administrators, and empire-builders, the Romans were brilliant engineers. They pioneered the use of the arch and invented the architectural forms based on it: the barrel vault (an arch extended in space), the groin vault (two barrel vaults crossing each other), and the dome and half-dome (an arch rotated on its axis). The discovery of pozzuolana, volcanic ash that made a slow-drying concrete, allowed the creation of structures that were essentially welded together. The genius of Roman construction has left visible signs of its prowess on the landscape. The straightest, fastest roads in Britain were the Roman roads. The largest dome in the world for centuries was the great temple of the Pantheon, built during the reign of the Emperor Hadrian. The Colosseum, apparently an open sports arena, is a great fantasy of arches, barrel vaults, and groin vaults. But the Romans invested even simple structures with great virtuosity and beauty. The Pont du Gard near Nîmes in southern France is a good example. Built as an aqueduct late in the first century BCE, this beautiful structure was part of a system that carried water from the springs at Uzès to Nîmes thirty miles south. The span of 900 feet has a height of 180 feet above the Gard River. Designed as both a bridge and an aqueduct, it delivered 100 gallons of water per person every day to the town for centuries, and its use as a bridge for carts and pedestrians continues to this day.

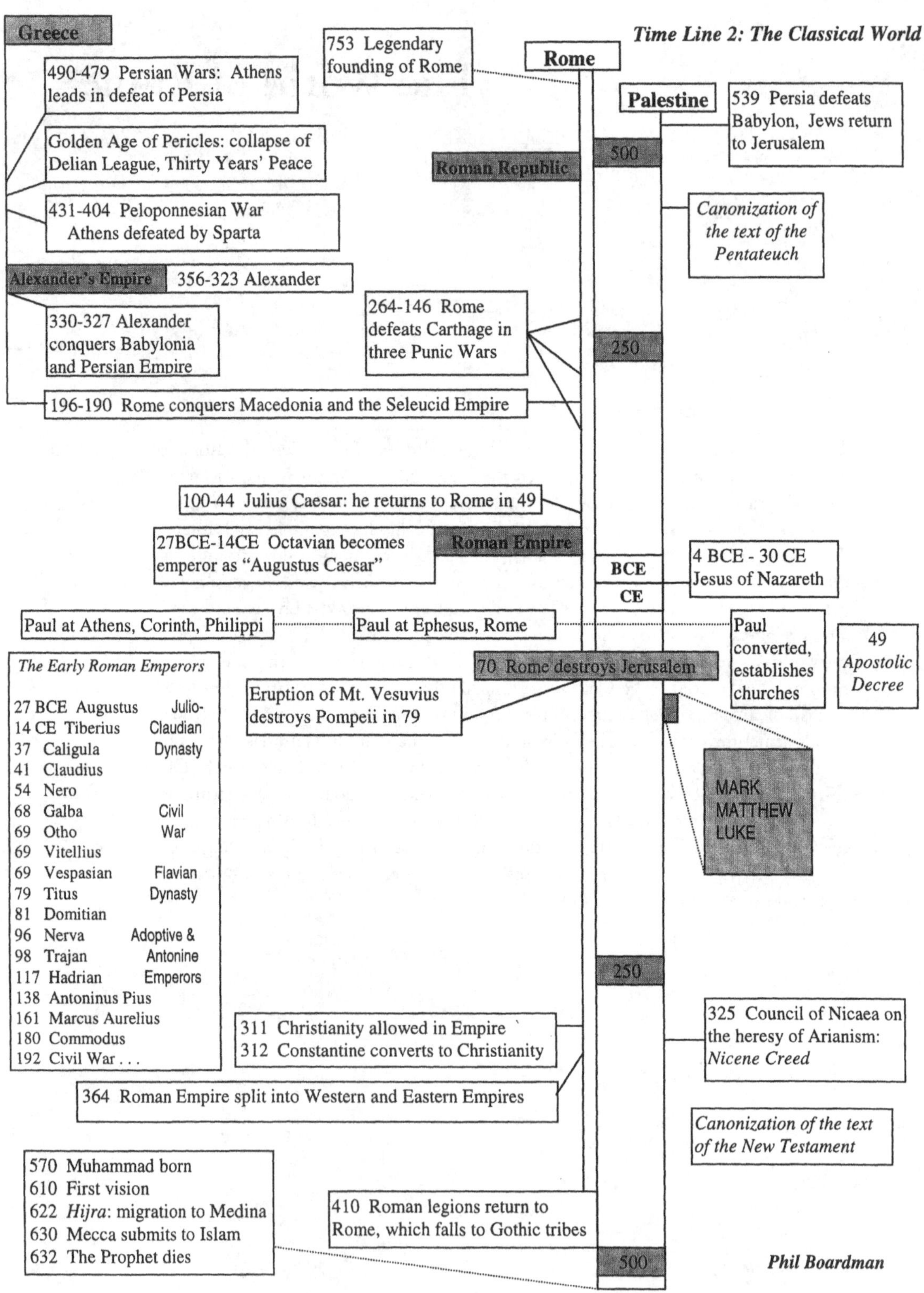
Time Line 2: The Classical World
Greece
753 Legendary founding of Rome
Rome
490-479 Persian Wars: Athens leads in defeat of Persia
Palestine
539 Persia defeats Babylon, Jews return to Jerusalem
Golden Age of Pericles: collapse of Delian League, Thirty Years' Peace
500
Roman Republic
431-404 Peloponnesian War Athens defeated by Sparta
Canonization of the text of the Pentateuch
Alexander's Empire
356-323 Alexander
264-146 Rome defeats Carthage in three Punic Wars
330-327 Alexander conquers Babylonia and Persian Empire
250
196-190 Rome conquers Macedonia and the Seleucid Empire
100-44 Julius Caesar: he returns to Rome in 49
27BCE-14CE Octavian becomes emperor as "Augustus Caesar"
Roman Empire
BCE
CE
4 BCE - 30 CE Jesus of Nazareth
Paul at Athens, Corinth, Philippi
Paul at Ephesus, Rome
Paul converted, establishes churches
49 Apostolic Decree
70 Rome destroys Jerusalem
The Early Roman Emperors
27 BCE Augustus
14 CE Tiberius
37 Caligula
41 Claudius
54 Nero
Julio-Claudian Dynasty
68 Galba
69 Otho
69 Vitellius
Civil War
69 Vespasian
79 Titus
81 Domitian
Flavian Dynasty
96 Nerva
98 Trajan
117 Hadrian
138 Antoninus Pius
161 Marcus Aurelius
180 Commodus
Adoptive & Antonine Emperors
192 Civil War . . .
Eruption of Mt. Vesuvius destroys Pompeii in 79
MARK
MATTHEW
LUKE
250
311 Christianity allowed in Empire
312 Constantine converts to Christianity
325 Council of Nicaea on the heresy of Arianism: Nicene Creed
364 Roman Empire split into Western and Eastern Empires
Canonization of the text of the New Testament
570 Muhammad born
610 First vision
622 Hijra: migration to Medina
630 Mecca submits to Islam
632 The Prophet dies
410 Roman legions return to Rome, which falls to Gothic tribes
500
Phil Boardman

Polybius (c.200–c.118 BCE)

UNIVERSAL HISTORY

Polybius, the historian who observed and described the rise of Rome during the age of the Punic Wars with Carthage, was not a Roman, but a Greek. He was sent by the Greeks as one of a thousand hostages to Rome after Macedonia fell in 168 BCE. In Rome he had the fortune to be made tutor to the two sons of a Roman general; the younger of these charges was taken into the Scipio family as adoptive grandson of Scipio Africanus the Elder, who had defeated Hannibal in north Africa in the decisive victory that ended the Second Punic War against Carthage. Being released after sixteen years to return to Greece with the 300 surviving exiles, Polybius was invited to join his former pupil, now known as Scipio Africanus the Younger, who was laying siege to Carthage at the beginning of the Third Punic War. Scipio lived up to the title he inherited from his famous grandfather by defeating Carthage and utterly destroying the city in 146 BCE, a campaign with Polybius as a participant. When war next broke out again between Rome and the Achaeans, the Greek Polybius helped negotiate terms favorable to the defeated Greeks.

The great work of Polybius's life was his Universal History, *an account of how Rome, during an intense period of conquest, from 220 to 167 BCE, supplanted Greece and Macedonia as the power in the Mediterranean. Only five of the work's forty books survive, but the general outlines are well known, and Polybius is explicit about his theme in the first paragraph of his Prologue: "There can surely be nobody so petty or so apathetic in his outlook that he has no desire to discover by what means and under what system of government the Romans succeeded in less than fifty-three years in bringing under their rule almost the whole of the inhabited world, an achievement which is without parallel in human history." Polybius recognized that the first war with Carthage (264–241 BCE) was fought locally, in the west. But the Second and Third Wars (218–202, 151–146 BCE) drew in all the Hellenistic world of the eastern Mediterranean, and in the end that world dissolved before the dominant virtues, skills, and values of the triumphant Romans. Aiming primarily at a Greek audience, and especially at future statesmen who might learn from his unique analysis of Roman success, he wrote history scientifically, largely without national prejudice, and from wide acquaintance with the people and places*

This selection is taken from *The Rise of the Roman Empire,* translated by Ian Scott-Kilvert (Penguin, 1990).

about which he wrote. The selection below shows his clear-headed interest in governmental and social institutions.

THE ROMAN REPUBLIC COMPARED WITH OTHERS

43. Almost all historians have commended to us the reputation for excellence of the constitutions of Sparta, Crete, Mantinea and Carthage, and several have also mentioned those of Athens and Thebes. I can agree with the praise of the first category, but I believe that little need be said of the systems of Athens and of Thebes. The rise of both of these states was abnormal; neither remained for long at the zenith of their power, and the decline which they suffered was on no modest scale. It was by a sudden stroke of chance that they obtained a spectacular predominance, but then, while still apparently flourishing and likely to remain so, they experienced a complete reverse of fortune. When they attacked the Lacedaemonians the Thebans were exploiting the senseless errors committed by their opponents, and the hatred which these had aroused among their allies; moreover, the reputation for superiority which they gained among the Greeks was due to the valour of one or at most two men who had observed these weaknesses. And indeed, Fortune soon proved that the successes which the Thebans gained at the time were due to the heroism of her leading men, not to the form of her constitution. It is well-known that the predominance of Thebes took its rise, attained its height and ceased with the lives of Pelopidas and Epaminondas, and we must conclude that the hegemony which she enjoyed at that time was the work of her citizens and not of her system of government.

44. Much the same verdict must be passed on the Athenian constitution. It is true that the Athenians enjoyed more frequent periods of success, but the most glorious of all was the one which coincided with the admirable leadership of Themistocles. Thereafter she experienced a complete reversal of fortune, which was due to the instability of the national character. For the Athenian populace is always more or less in the situation of a ship without a commander. So long as fear of the state of the sea or the occurrence of a storm obliges the sailors to behave sensibly and to obey the orders of the captain they do their duty admirably. But before long they become overconfident and begin to treat their superiors with contempt and to fall out with one another. Some are anxious to continue the voyage, while others urge the captain to bring the ship to anchor, some let out the sheets, while others hinder them and order the sails to be furled; and not only does the whole spectacle of their disunity and bickering appear disgraceful to any outside observer, but the situation is positively dangerous for all those who are taking part in the same voyage. The result which all too frequently follows is that after escaping the dangers of the wildest seas and the most violent storms, they succeed in wrecking the ship when it is within harbour and within reach of the shore.

This is precisely the fate which has more than once befallen the Athenian system of government. After warding off the greatest and most terrible dangers through the heroism of her people and their leaders, the state has passed into periods of unclouded tranquillity, and then quite gratuitously and senselessly suffered complete breakdown. For this reason I need say no more about this constitution or that of Thebes, since both are states in which the masses take all decisions according to their random impulses. In the case of Athens the populace is headstrong and spiteful; in that of Thebes it has been trained to grow up with habits of violence and ferocity.

45. When we turn to the constitution of Crete, there are two points which particularly call for attention. How could the most learned of the writers of earlier times, namely Ephorus, Xenophon, Callisthenes and Plato, claim in the first place that it resembled the constitution of Sparta, and secondly that it was worthy of admiration? I do not believe that either of these assertions is true, and I base my opinion on the following facts. Let me deal first with its dissimilarity to the Spartan constitution. We may name three distinguishing features of the latter. First of all, there are the land laws according to which no one citizen may own more land than another, but all are to possess an equal share of the public land. The second concerns the acquisition of money: since money is a commodity which was quite discredited among the Spartans, it follows that any rivalry which might arise from the possession of more or less of it is completely eliminated from the constitution. The third is the fact that of those officials by whom or with whose cooperation the whole administration is carried on, the kings hold a permanent office, while the members of the Senate are appointed for life.

46. Among the Cretans the practice in these matters is exactly the opposite. Their laws permit the citizen to acquire land without any restriction—the sky is the limit, as the saying is—and money is held in such high regard among them that the possession of it is regarded as not merely necessary, but also as most honourable. And indeed, avarice and greed are so much ingrained in the Cretan character that they are the only people in the world who consider no form of gain to be shameful. Again, their public offices are held on an annual tenure and through democratic election. In view of all this I have often felt at a loss to understand how the authors mentioned above can maintain that two constitutions which embody such diametrically opposed characteristics possess common features and are akin to one another. Besides overlooking such differences, these writers make lengthy comments into the bargain on the work of Lycurgus, claiming that he was the only legislator who grasped the essentials of the problem.

Now every state relies for its preservation on two fundamental qualities, namely bravery in the face of the enemy, and harmony among its citizens; and Lycurgus, by eliminating the desire for wealth, eliminated at the same time civil discord and strife. And so the Lacedaemonians, since they have been delivered from these evils, excel all the other Greeks both in the conduct of their internal affairs and in their spirit of unity. Having made this assertion, these writers observe at the same time that the Cretans, because of their ingrained craving for wealth, are involved in frequent seditions, public and private, murders, massacres and civil wars; yet this fact they consider immaterial, and still have the audacity to argue that the two political systems have much in common. Ephorus, indeed, apart from the names, uses the same terms to explain the political complexion of the two states, so that if one did not note the proper names, there would be no means of knowing which of the two he was describing.

The above are the points in which I believe these two political systems differ, and I shall now explain why I think the Cretan constitution should neither be praised nor imitated.

47. In my opinion there are two basic elements in every political system, by virtue of which its true form and quality are either desirable or the opposite. By these I mean its customs and its laws. The desirable ones are those which make men's private lives virtuous and well-disciplined and the public character of the state civilized and just; the undesirable are those which have the opposite effect. So when we see that the customs and laws of any given people are good, we can conclude with confidence that the citizens and their constitution will likewise be good; and on the same principle when we see a community in which private life is characterized by greed and avarice and public conduct by injustice, then clearly we have good reason to pronounce their laws, their particular customs and their constitution in general to be bad. Now with a few rare exceptions it would be impossible to find private conduct more deceitful nor public policy more unjust than that which prevails in Crete. Accordingly, since I cannot regard the Cretan constitution as being either similar to the Spartan or as in any way deserving praise or imitation in itself, I dismiss it from the comparison which I have proposed to make.

As for Plato's celebrated republic, which is highly praised by certain philosophers, I do not think it admissible that this should be brought into the argument about constitutions. For just as we do not allow artists or athletes who are not duly registered or have not been in training to take part in festivals or games, so we should not admit the Platonic constitution to this contest for the prize of merit, unless some example can be provided of it in action. Up to the present, at any rate, the idea of comparing it with the constitutions of Sparta, Rome or Carthage would be like bringing forward some statue and then comparing it with living and breathing men. For even if the statue were absolutely perfect in respect of its workmanship, the comparison of a lifeless object with a living being would strike the spectators as quite inadequate and incongruous.

48. I shall therefore omit constitutions of this kind, and continue with my account of that of Sparta. It seems to me that from the point of view of ensuring harmony among the citizens, keeping Spartan territory intact, and preserving the liberty of his country, Lycurgus' legislation and the foresight which he displayed were so admirable that one can only regard his wisdom as something divine rather than human. The equal division of landed property together with the simple diet and the practice of eating it communally which he instituted were well-calculated to create a temperate and disciplined private life, and to protect the community as a whole from dissensions and civil strife, as was his training in the endurance of hardships and dangers to produce a breed of noble and courageous men. Now when both these virtues, courage and self-discipline, are combined in one soul or one state, evil will not easily spring from such a soil, nor will such men easily be overcome by their neighbours. And so by constructing his constitution in this spirit and out of these elements, Lycurgus ensured the absolute safety of the whole territory of Sparta and bequeathed to the Spartans their freedom as a lasting inheritance. But as regards the annexation of neighbouring territories, or the assertion of their supremacy in Greece, or the pursuit of a wider policy of aggrandizement, he seems to have made no provision whatever, either in particular legislation or in the general constitution of the state. What he had still to do was to impose on his countrymen either some necessity or else an established principle whereby just as he had made them simple and contented in their private lives, so the spirit of the city should be rendered similarly moderate and

contented in its public policy. But as it was, while he made them into disinterested and sensible individuals in their private activities and their internal institutions, as regards their attitude to the rest of the Greeks he left them ambitious, eager for supremacy, and acquisitive in the highest degree.

49. It is notorious, for example, that the Spartans were among the first of the Greeks to cast a covetous eye upon the territory of their neighbours, and that they made war upon the Messenians out of greed and for the purpose of enslaving them. Besides this, all the historians are at one in recording how out of sheer obstinacy they bound themselves by an oath never to break off the siege of Messene until they had captured the place. And finally it is common knowledge that because of their craving for supremacy they were obliged to take orders from the very people whom they had conquered in battle. For when the Persians invaded Greece, the Spartans overcame them as champions of the freedom of Greece, yet after the invaders had retired and fled, the Spartans betrayed the Greek cities of Asia Minor to them through the Peace of Antalcidas, to obtain the money which would enable them to establish their supremacy over the rest of the Greeks. And it was then that an important defect in their constitution revealed itself.

So long as their ambitions extended only to ruling over their neighbours or the inhabitants of the Peloponnese, they found the supplies and resources which their own country could provide were sufficient, since all the provisions needed for their campaigns were at hand, and they could quickly return home to revictual or else send supplies to the army. But once they had begun to make expeditions by sea or to fight campaigns outside the Peloponnese, it became clear that neither their iron currency nor the exchange of their crops for the commodities they lacked could provide for their needs so long as they remained confined by Lycurgus' economic legislation, since these enterprises required a currency which was in universal circulation and a supply of goods from foreign sources. The result was that the Spartans were compelled to become petitioners to the Persians, to impose tribute on the Greek islanders, and to exact contributions from the rest of the Greeks. They were compelled to recognize that if they retained the Lycurgan system, it would be impossible to exert any important influence on affairs, let alone achieve the hegemony of Greece.

50. What then is the object of this digression? I wished to show in the light of historical fact that for the purpose of guarding a nation's territory securely and maintaining its liberty Lycurgus' constitution is perfectly adequate to its task. Thus from the point of view of those who hold that this is the supreme end of a constitution, we must admit that there is not and never was a preferable constitution or political system. But if a statesman aspires to larger ambitions than these, and finds greater prestige and honour in putting himself as the head of multitudes, becoming the ruler of vast areas and populations and causing the eyes of the whole world to be turned towards him, then we must admit that the Spartan constitution is deficient, and that the Roman is superior and certainly better devised for the attainment of power. The proof of this is that when the Lacedaemonians attempted to win supremacy in Greece it was not long before they were in danger of losing their own liberty, whereas the Romans, who had aimed in the first place merely at establishing their dominion over the Italians, went on in a very short time to bring the whole world under their rule, and in this achievement the abundance of supplies which they had at their disposal played no small part.

51. The constitution of Carthage seems to me to have been well-designed at the outset in its most important features. The Carthaginians had kings, the assembly of elders had the powers of an aristocracy, and the people were supreme in such matters as were appropriate, so that the general framework of the state was similar to that of Rome and Sparta. But at the time when the Hannibalic War began, the political state of Carthage was in decline, while that of Rome was growing better. Every organism, every state and every activity passes through a natural cycle, first of growth, then of maturity and finally of decay, and since the component parts are at their strongest when it reaches its zenith, it was for this reason that the difference between the two states displayed itself at this moment. The power and prosperity of Carthage had developed far earlier than that of Rome, and in proportion to this her strength had begun to decline, while that of Rome was at its height, at least so far as her system of government was concerned. Accordingly, at Carthage the influence of the people had already become predominant in the councils of state, while at Rome the Senate still had the decisive voice. This meant that in the one case the deliberations were conducted by the masses, and in the other by the most eminent men, with the result that the decisions on public policy made by the Romans proved superior; in other words, although they suffered several overwhelming disasters in the field, the wisdom of their counsels finally enabled them to overcome the Carthaginians in the war.

52. Let us now consider differences of detail, such as, in the first place, the conduct of the war. Here we find that in operations at sea the Carthaginians, as might be expected, were better trained and equipped, because seamanship had long been their national calling and they occupy themselves with the sea more than any other people; but in military campaigns the Romans train themselves to an altogether higher standard. In fact they devote their whole energies to this aspect of war, whereas the Carthaginians largely neglect their infantry, though they do show some degree of interest in their cavalry. The reason for this is that they employ foreign and mercenary troops, whereas those of the Romans are citizens and natives of their own country; so in this respect too we must judge the Roman political system to be superior to the Carthaginian. The Carthaginians depend at all times on the courage of mercenaries to safeguard their prospects of freedom, but the Romans rely on the bravery of their own citizens and the help of their allies. The result is that even if they happen to be defeated at the outset, the Romans carry on the war with all their resources, but this is impossible for the Carthaginians. For the Romans, knowing themselves to be fighting for their country and their children, can never weaken in the fury of their struggle, but continue to fight with all their heart and soul until the enemy is overcome. It follows that although the Romans are, as I have mentioned, much less skilled in the handling of their naval forces, they nevertheless prove successful in the end, because of the gallantry of their men; for although skill in seamanship is of great importance in naval battles, it is the courage of the marines which proves the decisive factor in winning a victory. The fact is that Italians in general have a natural advantage over Phoenicians and Africans both in physical strength and in personal courage, but at the same time their institutions contribute very powerfully towards fostering a spirit of bravery in their young men. I quote just one example to illustrate the pains taken by the Roman state to produce men who will endure anything to win a reputation for valour in their country.

53. Whenever one of their celebrated men dies, in the course of the funeral procession his body is carried with every kind of honour into the Forum to the so-called Rostra, sometimes in an upright position so as to be conspicuous, or else, more rarely, recumbent. The whole mass of the people stand round to watch, and his son, if he has left one of adult age who can be present, or if not some other relative, then mounts the Rostra and delivers an address which recounts the virtues and the successes achieved by the dead man during his lifetime. By these means the whole populace—not only those who played some part in these exploits, but those who did not—are involved in the ceremony, so that when the facts of the dead man's career are recalled to their minds and brought before their eyes, their sympathies are so deeply engaged that the loss seems not to be confined to the mourners but to be a public one which affects the whole people. Then after the burial of the body and the performance of the customary ceremonies, they place the image of the dead man in the most conspicuous position in the house, where it is enclosed in a wooden shrine. This image consists of a mask, which is fashioned with extraordinary fidelity both in its modelling and its complexion to represent the features of the dead man. On occasions when public sacrifices are offered, these masks are displayed and are decorated with great care. And when any distinguished member of the family dies, the masks are taken to the funeral, and are there worn by men who are considered to bear the closest resemblance to the original, both in height and in their general appearance and bearing. These substitutes are dressed according to the rank of the deceased: a toga with a purple border for a consul or praetor, a completely purple garment for a censor, and one embroidered with gold for a man who had celebrated a triumph or performed some similar exploit.

They all ride in chariots with the fasces, axes, and other insignia carried before them, according to the dignity of the offices of state which the dead man had held in his lifetime, and when they arrive at the Rostra they all seat themselves in a row upon chairs of ivory. It would be hard to imagine a more impressive scene for a young man who aspires to win fame and to practise virtue. For who could remain unmoved at the sight of the images of all these men who have won renown in their time, now gathered together as if alive and breathing? What spectacle could be more glorious than this?

54. Moreover, the speaker who pronounces the oration over the man who is about to be buried, when he has delivered his tribute, goes on to relate the successes and achievements of all the others whose images are displayed there, beginning with the oldest. By this constant renewal of the good report of brave men, the fame of those who have performed any noble deed is made immortal, and the renown of those who have served their country well becomes a matter of common knowledge and a heritage for posterity. But the most important consequence of the ceremony is that it inspires young men to endure the extremes of suffering for the common good in the hope of winning the glory that waits upon the brave. And what I have just said is attested by the facts. Many Romans have volunteered to engage in single combat so as to decide a whole battle, and not a few have chosen certain death, some in war to save the lives of their countrymen, others in times of peace to ensure the safety of the Republic. Besides this, there have been instances of men in office who have put their own sons to death, contrary to every law or custom, because they valued the interest of their country more dearly than their natural ties to their own flesh and blood.

Many stories of this kind can be told of many men in Roman history, but one in particular will serve as an example and a proof of my contention.

55. The story goes that while Horatius Cocles was engaged in combat with two of the enemy at the far end of the bridge over the Tiber which gives entrance to the city on the west, he saw a large body of reinforcements approaching. Fearing that they would succeed in forcing the passage and entering the city, he turned round and shouted to those behind him to retire at once and make haste to break down the bridge. His comrades obeyed, and all the time that they were demolishing it Horatius stood his ground. He suffered many wounds, but he held back the enemy's attack and astounded them not so much by his physical strength as by his endurance and courage. Once the bridge was cut the enemy's advance was halted, whereupon Cocles threw himself into the river still wearing his armour and weapons. He deliberately sacrificed himself because he valued the safety of his country and the glory which would later attach itself to his name more than his present existence and the years of life that remained to him. This is a typical example, it seems to me, of the spirit of emulation and the ambition to perform deeds of gallantry which the customs of the Romans help to implant in their young men.

56. Again, the Roman laws and customs which concern money transactions are superior to those of Carthage. In the latter country no activity which results in a profit is seen as a cause for reproach, but to the Romans nothing is more disgraceful than to receive bribes or to seek gain by improper means. Just as they wholeheartedly approve the acquisition of money if the methods are reputable, so they condemn it absolutely if the sources are forbidden. An illustration of this is the fact that among the Carthaginians bribery is openly practised by candidates for office, whereas at Rome it is a capital offence. And so, as the rewards offered to merit are precisely the opposite in the two countries, it is natural that the methods employed to obtain them should be equally dissimilar.

However, the sphere in which the Roman commonwealth seems to me to show its superiority most decisively is in that of religious belief. Here we find that the very phenomenon which among other peoples is regarded as a subject for reproach, namely superstition, is actually the element which holds the Roman state together. These matters are treated with such solemnity and introduced so frequently both into public and into private life that nothing could exceed them in importance. Many people may find this astonishing, but my own view is that the Romans have adopted these practices for the sake of the common people. This approach might not have been necessary had it ever been possible to form a state composed entirely of wise men. But as the masses are always fickle, filled with lawless desires, unreasoning anger and violent passions, they can only be restrained by mysterious terrors or other dramatizations of the subject. For this reason I believe that the ancients were by no means acting foolishly or haphazardly when they introduced to the people various notions concerning the gods and belief in the punishments of Hades, but rather that the moderns are foolish and take great risks in rejecting them. At any rate the result is that among the Greeks, apart from anything else, men who hold public office cannot be trusted with the safe-keeping of so much as a single talent, even if they have ten accountants and as many seals and twice as many witnesses, whereas among the Romans their magistrates handle large sums of money and scrupulously perform their duty because they have given their word on oath. Among other nations it is a rare phenomenon to find a man who keeps his hands off public funds and whose record is clean in this respect, while among the Romans it is quite the exception to find a man who has been detected in such conduct.

Conclusion

57. The fact, then, that all existing things are subject to decay is a proposition which scarcely requires proof, since the inexorable course of nature is sufficient to impose it on us. Every kind of state, we may say, is liable to decline from two sources, the one being external, and the other due to its own internal evolution. For the first we cannot lay down any fixed principle, but the second pursues a regular sequence. I have already indicated which kind of state is the first to evolve, which succeeds it, and how each is transformed into its successor, so that those who can connect the opening propositions of my argument with its conclusion will be able to make their own forecast concerning the future. This, in my opinion, is quite clear. When a state, after warding off many great perils, achieves supremacy and uncontested sovereignty, it is evident that under the influence of long-established prosperity life will become more luxurious, and among the citizens themselves rivalry for office and in other spheres of activity will become fiercer than it should. As these symptoms become more marked, the craving for office and the sense of humiliation which obscurity imposes, together with the spread of ostentation and extravagance, will usher in a period of general deterioration. The principal authors of this change will be the masses, who at some moments will believe that they have a grievance against the greed of other members of society, and at others are made conceited by the flattery of those who aspire to office. By this stage they will have been roused to fury and their deliberations will constantly be swayed by passion, so that they will no longer consent to obey or even to be the equals of their leaders, but will demand everything or by far the greatest share for themselves. When this happens, the constitution will change its *name* to the one which sounds the most imposing of all, that of freedom and democracy, but its *nature* to that which is the worst of all, that is the rule of the mob.

Now that I have described the formation of the Roman state, its rise, the attainment of its zenith, and its present condition, and likewise the differences for better or worse between it and the other constitutions, I will bring this study to an end.

58. I return, then, to the period which follows immediately after the date at which I began this digression, but first I propose to single out one episode for brief mention. My purpose in doing this is to give an illustration, not just in theory but in practice, of the perfection and the strength of the Roman constitution as it then existed, as though I were exhibiting one work as a specimen to reveal the skill of a fine artist.

After his victory at Cannae Hannibal captured the 8,000 Roman soldiers who had been left to guard their camp, but he then allowed them to send a deputation to Rome to discuss the matter of their ransom and release. The troops selected ten of their leaders, whom Hannibal sent off, after exacting an oath that they would return to him. One of these men, just as he was going beyond the palisade of the camp, said that he had forgotten something, and after collecting what he had left behind, once more set out, imagining that since he had returned he had kept his promise and released himself from his oath. On their arrival in Rome, the delegates begged and entreated the Senate not to grudge the prisoners their release, but to allow each to pay three *minae* and return to his people, for Hannibal, they said, had granted this concession. They pleaded further that the men deserved to be released, for they had not been guilty of cowardice in the fighting, nor had they done anything unworthy of Rome. They had been left behind to guard the camp, and after all the rest of the army had perished, they had been compelled by circumstances to surrender to the enemy. Yet although the Romans had suffered crushing reverses in the war, had lost virtually all their allies and expected from day to day that their city itself would be threatened, still, after listening to this plea they neither forgot their dignity under pressure of calamity nor allowed themselves to lose sight of what had to be done. They recognized that Hannibal's object was at once to lay his hands on some money and to sap the fighting spirit of the troops opposed to him by suggesting that even when they were beaten they still had a chance of safety. Therefore the Senate, so far from granting this request refused to allow either pity for their compatriots or any consideration of the service these men might render in future to prevail. They frustrated Hannibal's calculations and all the hopes he had built on these by declining to ransom the prisoners. At the same time they established the rule for their own men that they must either conquer or die on the field, since if they were beaten no hope of safety remained for them. After they had passed this resolution they dismissed the nine delegates, who then returned to Hannibal of their own free will, because they were bound by their oath. As for the man who had tried to free himself from his pledge by a trick, they put him in chains and sent him back to the enemy. In this way Hannibal experienced less joy from his victory than disappointment, when he saw with amazement the unshaken resolve and the lofty spirit which the Romans showed in their resolutions.

Marcus Tullius Cicero (c.106–43 BCE)

ON OLD AGE

A Newsweek *article about preparations for the 2004 presidential debates noted that the candidates, both "talented debaters," tried to lower expectations by playing down "their own skills while making the other out to be a latter-day Cicero" (9/27/04). Although Cicero is not read much any more, he continues to be known for the same skill that marked his meteoric reputation in the Roman Republic—a brilliant orator and stylist, whose skill at argument brought down many political and legal opponents. His reputation apparently reached as far as heaven: Saint Jerome, in the fourth century, noting his own great love of the pagan Latin classics, describes a frightening vision in a garden when the voice of God accused him of being, not a Christian, but "a Ciceronian!" For nearly two thousand years, while Latin held place as the central pillar of education in western schools, Cicero (along with Virgil) served as the epitome of classical style, and his essays, treatises, letters, and speeches were sourcebooks for moral education.*

Cicero was born to an aristocratic family who sent him to Rome early to gain a training in Greek, Latin, law, philosophy, and oratory. He studied with several philosophers, including an Epicurean, a Stoic, and a Platonist, then continued his study of Greek in Athens and rhetoric in Rhodes. By 70 BCE, back in Rome, he was already Rome's leading barrister and had embarked on a successful political career. Elected to several offices, he attached himself to Pompey, a man he believed strong enough to maintain the power of the Senate during times that were increasingly turbulent. When Catiline plotted to overthrow the government, Cicero delivered four orations that brought about a hasty execution, an execution that Julius Caesar thought violated the due process of law. Drawn into the conflicts between Pompey and Julius Caesar on Pompey's side, Cicero spent some time in exile. When Caesar was assassinated in the Senate, Cicero achieved a general amnesty by negotiating between Antony and the assassins Brutus and Cassius. When Antony left the city for Gaul, Cicero delivered his series of fourteen Philippics, mercilessly attacking Antony in the manner of Demosthenes's famous attacks on Philip II of Macedonia. At Cicero's urging, and hoping for a restoration of the Republic, the Senate sent a force against Antony on Brutus's behalf. But the leader of the forces, Octavian, instead allied with Antony and the

This translation, by the eminent historian of ancient Rome, Michael Grant, is taken from *Selected Works* (Penguin, 1969).

two drew up a list of enemies, topped by Cicero's name. During the fateful year 43 BCE, Cicero and hundreds of other senators were executed.

Cicero's works, because of their prestige and their importance in education, have survived in great number. He himself saw to the publication of his orations and treatises, and collections of nearly 900 letters (especially those to his wife and to Julius Caesar during his campaign in Gaul) became a window into his life and troubled times. His position was mainly that of a moderate and a humanist, and he wanted to be known as a philosopher rather than an orator. He believed in the gods, but perceived them as a divine spark in humans: "it is by helping others that man approaches closest to divinity." Among his greatest achievements was synthesizing, weighing, and encapsulating the Greek philosophical ideas with which he was so familiar, and handing them on to the Latin world of the West.

VII
DEATH HAS NO STING

Now we must consider the fourth objection to being old: one which might be thought well calculated to worry and distress a man of my years. I refer to the nearness of death. When a man is old, there can obviously be no doubt that it is near. Yet if, during his long life, he has failed to grasp that death is of no account he is unfortunate indeed. There are two alternatives: either death completely destroys human souls, in which case it is negligible; or it removes the soul to some place of eternal life—in which case its coming is greatly to be desired. There can be no third possibility. If, then, after death I shall either lack unhappiness or even be positively happy, I have nothing whatever to fear.

Besides, even the youngest of men would be rash to feel any confidence that he will still be alive this evening! Indeed, young people are actually more liable to accidental deaths than old: they fall ill more easily, their illnesses are more severe, and their convalescences are more painful. That is why few of them reach old age. If so many people did not die young, there would be more examples of decent and sensible living. For the people who have sense and prudence and judgment are the old. Had it not been for old men, no state would ever have existed!

But to return to the imminence of death. This is not a fault to blame on age, since you can see that youth may suffer from the same disability. The loss of my dear son, and of your two brothers, Scipio—both destined for brilliant careers—has underlined for both of us that death comes to all ages alike. Certainly you can argue that young men are entitled to hope for long lives, whereas old men are not. But such hopes are misguided, since it is unintelligent to mistake certainty for uncertainty, and untruth for truth.

The objector may go on to say that an old man has nothing even to hope for. Still, he is better off than his juniors, since what they are hoping for he has actually achieved: they want long lives, and he has had one.

And yet, for goodness' sake, what in the whole human condition lasts for any length of time? Think of the longest of all possible lives; let us imagine we shall attain the age of that king of Tartessus—I have been reading about Arganthonius of Gades who reigned for eighty years and lived for a hundred and twenty. Even so, I suggest that nothing can be called long if it has an end. For when that end comes, then all that is gone before has vanished. Only one thing remains—the credit you have gained by your good and right actions. Hours, days, months, and years go by; once they have passed they never come again. And what is to come in the future we cannot tell. So whatever life is allotted to us, we ought to be content.

An actor need not remain on the stage until the very end of the play: if he wins applause in those acts in which he appears, he will have done well enough. In life, too, a man can perform his part wisely without staying on the stage until the play is finished. However short your life may be, it will still be long enough to live honestly and decently. If, on the other hand, its duration is extended, there need be no more sorrow than a farmer feels when the pleasant springtime has passed, and summer and autumn have arrived. For spring, the season of youth, gives promise of fruits to come, but the later seasons are those that reap the harvests and gather them in. And the particular harvest of old age, I repeat, is its abundant recollection of blessings acquired in earlier years.

All things in keeping with nature must be classified as good; and nothing is so completely in keeping with nature than that the old should die. When the same fate sometimes attacks the young, nature rebels and resists: the death of a young person reminds me of a flame extinguished by a deluge. But the death of the old is like a fire sinking and going out of its own accord, without external impulsion. In the same way as apples, while green, can only be picked by force, but after ripening to maturity fall off by themselves, so death comes to the young with violence but to old people when the time is ripe. And the thought of this ripeness so greatly attracts me that as I approach death I feel like a man nearing harbour after a long voyage: I seem to be catching sight of land.

Yet old age has no fixed limit: as long as a man remains able to live up to his obligations and fulfil them, reckoning death of no account, he is entitled to live on. That gives age an actual advantage over youth in courage and toughness—a conclusion which is illustrated by the answer Solon once gave Pisistratus. When the king asked what support Solon relied upon in maintaining such stubborn opposition to his rule, Solon replied: 'Old age.'

The best end to life is with mind unclouded and faculties unimpaired, when nature herself dissolves what she has put together. The right person to take a ship or house to pieces is its builder; and by that analogy nature, which constructs human beings so skilfully, is also best at their demolition. But a new structure is always hard to destroy, whereas old buildings come down easily.

So the aged ought neither to cling too greedily to their small remnants of life nor, conversely, to abandon them before they need. Pythagoras forbids us desert life's sentry-post till God, our commander, has given the word. Wise Solon wrote a couplet expressing the hope that when he was dead his friends would grieve and mourn. His purpose, no doubt, was to show how much he valued their affection. But I am inclined to prefer Ennius's version: 'Let no one weep in my honour, or utter lamentations at my last rites.' Ennius finds death no cause for grief, seeing that what comes thereafter is immortality.

The act of dying, it is true, may be accompanied by certain sensations, but if so these only last a very short time, especially when one is old. After death, feelings are either non-existent or agreeable. From our youth upwards we should bear that in mind, since the thought will encourage us to regard death as of no account, and without such a conviction we can have no peace of mind. For we cannot avoid dying: perhaps this very day. Since, therefore, death is an imminent possibility from hour to hour, you must not let the prospect frighten you, or you will be in a state of perpetual anxiety.

There is no need to argue this point at any length. It is enough to remember Lucius Junius Brutus, who fell in the struggle for his country's freedom, and the two Decii, who rode full speed deliberately to their deaths. Or we may recall Marcus Atilius Regulus, who for the sake of keeping his faith with the enemy went back to be the victim of their tortures—and the two Scipios, Publius and Gnaeus Calvus, who blocked the advancing Carthaginians with their own dead bodies. And then, Scipio, there was your grandfather Lucius Aemilius Paullus, who amid Cannae's shameful rout gave his life to atone for his colleague's unwisdom; and Marcus Claudius Marcellus, who was conceded funeral honours even by a merciless foe. But let us pass these by, and rather consider our own Roman legionaries. I have written of them in my *Origins:* marching again and again, with indomitable enthusiasm, to destinations from which they never expected to return. So what those uneducated, rustic young soldiers think nothing of should surely not terrify men of advanced education and years.

One has had enough of life, in my opinion, when one has had enough of all its occupations. Boys have their characteristic pursuits, but adolescents do not hanker after them, since they have their own activities. Then these too, in their turn, cease to attract the grown-up and middle-aged, seeing that they also have their special interests—for which, however, when their time comes, old people feel no desire, since they again, finally, have interests peculiar to themselves. Then, like earlier occupations before them, these activities fall away; and when that happens a man has had enough of life and it is time for him to die.

Catullus (c.84–c.54 BCE)

Poems

Influenced by Greek lyric verse, Catullus wrote poems that were personal, informal, and emotional. Abandoning the pretentiousness of earlier Roman poetry, Catullus examined a wide range of subjects in language that is sometimes startlingly direct. Most successful were his poems addressed to his mistress, a married woman he calls Lesbia in the poems. The twenty-five poems to Lesbia are an encyclopedia of passionate love, showing in turns the emotions of infatuation, joy, passion, disappointment, despair, anger, and hatred—all that romantic love has come to mean in the modern West. His poems, written in the late republican Rome of Julius Caesar, Cicero, and Pompey, were influential with the next generation of poets under the new empire of Augustus. But while Latin poets like Virgil and Horace became part of the school curriculum and were on people's lips for centuries, Catullus suffered a very different fate. After the second century his poems disappeared from sight. A single manuscript surfaced around 1300, was copied twice, then was lost. One of those copies was copied twice and then it too was lost. Thus Catullus survives only in three manuscript copies dating from almost fourteen centuries after his death. It is fitting that this most modern of Roman poets should be known and admired now.

5

Vivamus, mea Lesbia, atque amemus
Lesbia, let's live and love
without one thought for gossip of
the boys grown old and stern.
Suns go down and can return,
but, once put out our own brief light,
we sleep through one eternal night.
Give me a thousand, a hundred kisses,
another thousand, a second hundred,

The translations, using standard numbering for the poems, are by Roy Arthur Swanson (New York: Liberal Arts Press, 1959).

a thousand complete, a hundred repeat;
and when we've many thousand more,
we'll scramble them, forget the score
so Malice cannot know how high
the count, and cast its evil eye.

8

Miser Catulle, desinas ineptire
Catullus, poor soul, stop playing the fool;
write off as loss what you see has been lost.
There used to be days full of sunshine for you,
when you followed the path laid out by your girl.
We loved her as no girl will ever be loved!
Those were the days when we had all the fun
which you dearly wanted and she didn't shun;
those were real days full of sunshine for you.
Now, though, she shuns it; so you, useless, don't
chase her and live a poor soul, as she runs:
instead, stick it out with a stubborn heart.
So long, girl; Catullus is sticking it out.
He won't look you up; he won't ask you out.
But you will be sorry when none asks you out.
What life—damn you, slut!—is left now for you?
Who'll come to you now or think you're a doll?
Whom now will you love or whose claim to be?
Whom will you kiss? Whose lips will you bite?
But you, then, Catullus, be stubborn; sit tight.

13

Cenabis bene, mi Fabulle, apud me
Fabullus, you will dine with me,
gods willing, in a day or three,
if you will bring the meal with you,
good and big, a bright girl too,
and wine and salt and lots of laughs.
If you bring this, my friend, why, look,
you will dine well: the pocketbook
of your Catullus is well filled
with cobwebs; but, in turn, you will
be unadulterably thrilled
by pleasure, taste—say what you will:
I'll have a perfume for you here,
which Love Gods proffered to my dear;
on smelling it, you will propose
that gods above make you all nose.

39

Egnatius, quod candidos habet dentes
Because Egnatius has white teeth, he smiles
without a stop. And should it come to trials
where lawyers move the court to tears, he smiles.
Suppose a mother mourns her only son,
he smiles. Whatever it is, whatever he's done,
wherever it is, he smiles. It's a disease,
not elegance, I think, nor does it please.

So, good Egnatius, I must give you warning,
were you a Roman, Sabine, Tiburtine,
or frugal Umbrian, or fat Etruscan,
or dark Lanuvian with big buck teeth,
or Transpadane—to bring my people in—
or one of any group which cleans its teeth
with water, constant smiles would still displease:
nothing's as far from tact as tactless grins.

But you're from Spain, and Spain's the spot
where teeth are scrubbed and red gums rubbed with what
is pissed the night before into a pot,
so that your tooth tells by its higher shine
how much you've drunk the dregs of bedroom wine.

58

Caeli, Lesbia nostra, Lesbia illa
Caelius, that Lesbia, my woman,
that—that Lesbia, whom once I, Catullus,
loved above himself and closest cronies,
now rubs up the grandsons of lordly Remus
on the corners and in the narrow alleys.

69

Noli admirari, quare tibi femina nulla
Don't wonder why no woman, Rufe, would want
to spread her tender thighs for you,
despite your gifts to her of high-class clothes
and charming bright translucent stones.
There's an ugly rumor that your underarms
are caves for a wild goat's stinking reek.
All are afraid of the goat; no wonder: no *bella*
puella would share her bed with a beast.
Dispose of this terrible plague to woman's nose,
or else don't wonder why she runs.

71

Si quoi iure bono sacer alarum obstitit hircus
If armpit odor ever rightly hurt
a guy, or gout cut down his speed,
that rival who cuts in on you has gained,
as he deserved, both maladies.
For, when he screws, he gives you your revenge:
the stink chokes her, the gout kills him.

72

Dicebas quondam solum te nosse Catullum
Catullus you once called your only love,
preferred to Jove, my Lesbia.
I loved you, not as men love mistresses,
but as a father loves his heirs.
I know you now: it makes my love more hot,
but you're more cheap, mere trash to me.
"How so?" you ask. Such dirt heaps up my love
but buries all my friendliness.

92

Lesbia mi dicit semper male nec tacet umquam
Lesbia loves to libel me, endlessly;
but she loves me I'm damned sure,
for I pay her back with dirty cracks, constantly,
and damned if I don't love her.

98

In te, si in quemquam, dici pote, putide Victi
Stinking Victius,
to you, if anyone, that can be said
which people say to loudmouthed louts:
that tongue of yours could wipe an ass or clean
a farmer's shoe, had you the chance.
Suppose you want to see us dead and gone:
to get your wish, just yawn, man, yawn.

101

Multas per gentes et multa per aequora vectus
I've sailed to many nations over many seas
and come now, brother, to this final rite,
these obsequies, to honor you in death and say
a word or two at unresponsive ash,
since fate, where I'm concerned, has been so rash
as uselessly to hasten you away.
So take this customary family mite—
our mourning duty, offerings like these:
they're moistened with your brother's many tears.
Goodbye for now: farewell for all the years.

Virgil (70–19 BCE)

Virgil's legacy to the west is enormous. Working from Homer's Iliad *and* Odyssey, *he transformed and preserved the epic conventions that inspired later works, like Spenser's* Faerie Queene, *Milton's* Paradise Lost, *James Joyce's* Ulysses, *even Ralph Ellison's* Invisible Man. *Useful for the study of poetry, of grammar, and of Latin, the* Aeneid *became the central text in European and American schools for nearly 1900 years, down to the end of the nineteenth century. Even the pattern of Virgil's career became the model for later poets. Virgil started by writing poems ("Eclogues") about shepherds based on the pastoral poems of the Greeks, and then wrote poems ("Georgics") about farming and farm life, before turning his hand to the great subject of his epic* The Aeneid. *Similarly, later poets felt that they should serve a poetic apprenticeship by writing pastoral poetry before they tackled the epic themes. Spenser, for instance, wrote the* Shepherd's Calendar *and Milton* Lycidas *before they composed their epics.*

Eclogues

The moral tone that tempers all of Virgil's poetry, including his great epic, the Aeneid, *was enough to bring Virgil the admiration of early Christians. But more compelling was a passage in the fourth of his pastoral poems, the Eclogues, in which he seemed to announce the coming of a baby boy who would usher in a reign of peace. Early Christians saw this as prophetic of the coming of Christ and recognized Virgil, who died only 15 years before Jesus was born, as a Christian prophet. Many Christians believed that had Virgil lived just a few years later, such a great and moral writer would have been among the most important of Christ's evangelists. So great was Virgil's reputation among literate Christians that early in the fifth century St. Augustine, in* On Christian Doctrine, *offered a defense of pagan writers like Virgil: "But we should not think that we ought not to learn literature because Mercury is said to be its inventor. . . . Rather, every good and true Christian should understand that wherever he may find truth, it is his Lord's." Similarly, when Dante wrote his great Christian epic, the* Divine Comedy, *in the early fourteenth century, he made Virgil, the greatest of the pre-Christian pagans, his guide through Hell.*

The translation of the *Fourth Eclogue* is by John Corrington Brown, published in London in 1872. It translates Virgil's Latin poem as English prose, and its language here has been somewhat modernized by the editor.

"The Fourth Eclogue"

Muses of Sicily, let us strike a somewhat louder chord. It is not for all that plantations have charms, or groundling tamarisks. If we are to sing of the woodland, let the woodland rise to a consul's dignity.

The last era of the song of Cuma has come at length; the grand file of the ages is being born anew; at length the virgin is returning, returning too the reign of Saturn; at length a new generation is descending from heaven on high. Smile your pure smile on the birth of the boy who shall at last bring the race of iron to an end, and bid the golden race spring up all the world over—you, Lucina—your own Apollo is at length on his throne. In your consulship it is—in yours, Pollio—that this glorious time shall come on, and the mighty months begin their march. Under your conduct, any remaining trace of our national guilt shall become void, and release the world from the thraldom of perpetual fear. He shall have the life of the gods conferred on him, and shall see gods and heroes mixing together, and shall himself be seen by them, and with his father's virtues shall govern a world at peace.

For you, sweet boy, the earth of her own unforced will shall pour forth a child's first presents—gadding ivy and foxglove everywhere, and Egyptian bean blending with the bright smiling acanthus. Of themselves, the goats shall carry home udders distended with milk; nor shall the herds fear huge lions in the way. Of itself, your grassy cradle shall pour out flowers to caress you. Death to the serpent, and to the treacherous plant of poisoned juice. Assyrian spices shall spring up by the wayside.

But soon as you shalt be of an age to read at length of the glories of heroes and your father's deeds, and to acquaint yourself with the nature of manly work, the yellow of the waving corn shall steal gradually over the plain, and from briers, that know nothing of culture, grapes shall hang in purple clusters, and the stubborn heart of oak shall exude dews of honey. Still, under all this show, some few traces shall remain of the sin and guile of old—such as may prompt men to defy the ocean goddess with their ships, to build towns with walls round them, to cleave furrows in the soil of earth. A second Tiphys shall there be in those days—a second Argo to convey the flower of chivalry; a second war of heroes, too, shall there be, and a second time shall Achilles be sent in his greatness to Troy.

Afterwards, when ripe years have at length made you a man, even the peaceful sailor shall leave the sea, nor shall the good ship of pine exchange merchandise—all lands shall produce all things; the ground shall not feel the harrow, nor the vineyard the pruning-hook; the sturdy ploughman, too, shall at length set his bulls free from the yoke; nor shall wool be taught to counterfeit varied hues, but of himself, as he feeds in the meadows, the ram shall transform his fleece, now into a lovely purple dye, now into saffron-yellow—of its own will, scarlet shall clothe the lambs as they graze. Ages like these, flow on!—so cried to their spindles the Fates, uttering in concert the fixed will of destiny.

Assume your august dignities—the time is at length at hand—you best-loved offspring of the gods, august scion of Jove! Look upon the world as it totters beneath the mass of its overhanging dome—earth and the expanse of sea and the deep of heaven—look how all are rejoicing in the age that is to be! O may my life's last days last long enough and breath be granted me enough to tell of your deeds! I will be overmatched in song by none—not by Orpheus of Thrace, nor by Linus, though that were backed by his mother, and this by his father—Orpheus by Calliope, Linus by Apollo in his beauty. Were Pan himself, with Arcady looking on, to enter the lists with me, Pan himself, with Arcady looking on, should own himself vanquished.

Begin, sweet child, with a smile, to take notice of your mother—that mother has had ten months of tedious sickness and loathing. Begin, sweet child—the babe on whom never parent smiled, never grew to deserve the table of a god or the bed of a goddess!

The Aeneid

Virgil's great masterpiece, the Aeneid, *is epic, public, and official; it celebrates the submission of the individual to the duties owed the gods and the state. In spite of Virgil's doubts about the tremendous power marshaled by the first emperor, Augustus, the poem also celebrates the triumph of Augustan peace, and Rome's potential to bring prosperity to the Western world.*

The Aeneid *tells the story of Aeneas, a Trojan who escaped from Troy when it fell to the Greek forces of Agamemnon. His destiny is to travel to Italy with his followers and found the colony from which later Romans will trace their ancestry. Like Odysseus among the Phaeacians, Aeneas lands in Carthage and during a respite he tells about his adventures, including an account of the fall of Troy (an event missing from Homer's two epics). Dido, the Queen of Carthage, falls in love with Aeneas, but reminded by the gods of his duty, Aeneas abandons her. Also like Odysseus, he journeys to the Underworld where he talks to the shade of Dido, who killed herself when he left her. He also confronts the shade of his father Anchises, who speaks prophetically about events that will lead to the founding of Rome. Later, in Italy, Aeneas fights to secure a safe abode for his followers but, like Moses, he does not live to see the city promised to his people.*

Aeneas's great virtue is piety, a devotion to the service of the gods and an awareness of his obligations to his family and his country. Aeneas is not a happy man; he suffers and comes to understand the suffering of others in the course of the epic. From Aeneas, Rome learns to temper its justice, dignity, and self-control with compassion. In the words offered to his son in the Underworld, Anchises spells out Rome's great destiny:

Others, no doubt, will better mould the bronze
To the semblance of soft breathing, draw, from marble,
The living countenance; and others plead
With greater eloquence, or learn to measure,
Better than we, the pathways of the heaven,
The risings of the stars: remember, Roman,
To rule the people under law, to establish
The way of peace, to battle down the haughty,
To spare the meek. Our fine arts, these, forever.

The translation of *Aeneid* used here is by Rolfe Humphries, a poet who taught high school Latin for years before returning to his *alma mater*, Amherst, to teach. His *Aeneid* (New York: Scribner's, 1951) is a companion to a verse translation of Ovid's *Metamorphoses*.

from Book I [The Landing Near Carthage]

Arms and the man I sing, the first who came,
Compelled by fate, an exile out of Troy,
To Italy and the Lavinian coast,
Much buffeted on land and on the deep
By violence of the gods, through that long rage,
That lasting hate, of Juno's. And he suffered
Much, also, in war, till he should build his town
And bring his gods to Latium, whence, in time,
The Latin race, the Alban fathers, rose
And the great walls of everlasting Rome.
Help me, O Muse, recall the reasons: why,
Why did the queen of heaven drive a man
So known for goodness, for devotion, through
So many toils and perils? Was there slight,
Affront, or outrage? Is vindictiveness
An attribute of the celestial mind?

There was an ancient city, Carthage, once
Founded by Tyrians, facing Italy
And Tiber's mouth, far-off, a wealthy town,
War-loving, and aggressive; and Juno held
Even her precious Samos in less regard.
Here were her arms, her chariot, and here,
Should fate at all permit, the goddess burned
To found the empire of the world forever.
But, she had heard, a Trojan race would come,
Some day, to overthrow the Tyrian towers,
A race would come, imperious people, proud
In war, with wide dominion, bringing doom
For Libya. Fate willed it so. And Juno
Feared, and remembered: there was the old war
She fought at Troy for her dear Greeks; her mind
Still fed on hurt and anger; deep in her heart
Paris' decision rankled, and the wrong
Offered her slighted beauty; and the hatred
Of the whole race; and Ganymede's honors—
All that was fuel to fire; she tossed and harried
All over the seas, wherever she could, those Trojans
Who had survived the Greeks and fierce Achilles,
And so they wandered over many an ocean,
Through many a year, fate-hounded. Such a struggle
It was to found the race of Rome!

They were happy
Spreading the sail, rushing the foam with bronze,
And Sicily hardly out of sight, when Juno,
Still nourishing the everlasting wound,
Raged to herself: "I am beaten, I suppose;
It seems I cannot keep this Trojan king
From Italy. The fates, no doubt, forbid me.
Pallas, of course, could burn the Argive ships,
Could drown the sailors, all for one man's guilt,
The crazy acts of Ajax. Her own hand
Hurled from the cloud Jove's thunderbolt, and shattered
Their ships all over the sea; she raised up storm
And tempest; she spiked Ajax on the rocks,
Whirled him in wind, blasted his heart with fire.
And I, who walk my way as queen of the gods,
Sister of Jove, and wife of Jove, keep warring
With one tribe through the long, long years. Who cares
For Juno's godhead? Who brings sacrifice
Devoutly to her altars?"

Brooding, burning,
She sought Aeolia, the storm-clouds' dwelling,
A land that sweeps and swarms with the winds' fury,
Whose monarch, Aeolus, in his deep cave rules
Imperious, weighing down with bolt and prison
Those boisterous struggling roarers, who go raging
Around their bars, under the moan of the mountain.
High over them their sceptered lord sits watching,
Soothing, restraining, their passionate proud spirit,
Lest, uncontrolled, they seize, in their wild keeping,
The land, the sea, the arch of sky, in ruin
Sweeping through space. This Jupiter feared; he hid them
Deep in dark caverns, with a mass of mountain
Piled over above them, and a king to give them
Most certain regulation, with a knowledge
When to hold in, when to let go. Him Juno
Approached in supplication:—"Aeolus,
Given by Jove the power to still the waters,
Or raise them with a gale, a tribe I hate
Is on its way to Italy, and they carry
Troy with them, and their household gods, once beaten.
Shake anger into those winds of yours, turn over
Their ships, and drown them; drive them in all directions,
Litter the sea with bodies! For such service
The loveliest nymph I have, Deiopea,
Shall be your bride forever, and you wilt father

Fair children on her fairness." Aeolus
Made answer: "Yours, O Queen, the task of seeking
Whatever it is you will; and mine the duty
To follow with performance. All my empire,
My sceptre, Jove's indulgence, are beholden
To Juno's favor, by whose blessing I
Attend the feasts of the gods and rule this storm-land."
His spear-butt struck the hollow mountain-side,
And the winds, wherever they could, came sweeping forth,
Whirled over the land, swooped down upon the ocean.
East, South, Southwest, they heave the billows, howl,
Storm, roll the giant combers toward the shore.
Men cry; the rigging creaks and strains; the clouds
Darken, and men see nothing; a weight of darkness
Broods over the deep; the heavy thunder rumbles
From pole to pole; the lightning rips and dazzles;
There is no way out but death. Aeneas shudders
In the chill shock, and lifts both hands to heaven:—
"O happy men, thrice happy, four times happy,
Who had the luck to die, with their fathers watching,
Below the walls of Troy! Ah, Diomedes,
Bravest of Greeks, why could I not have fallen,
Bleeding my life away on plains of Ilium
In our encounter there, where mighty Hector
Went down before Achilles' spear, and huge
Sarpedon lay in dust, and Simois river
Rolled to the sea so many noble heroes,
All drowned in all their armor?" And the gale
Howls from the north, striking the sail, head on;
The waves are lifted to the stars; the oars
Are broken, and the prow slews round; the ship
Lies broadside on; a wall of water, a mountain,
Looms up, comes pouring down; some ride the crest,
Some, in the trough, can see the boil of the sand.
The South wind hurls three ships on the hidden rocks,
That sea-reef which Italians call the Altars;
The West takes three, sweeping them from the deep
On shoal and quicksand; over the stern of one,
Before Aeneas' eyes, a great sea falls,
Washing the helmsman overboard; the ship
Whirls thrice in the suck of the water and goes down
In the devouring gulf; and here and there
A few survivors swim, the Lycian men
Whose captain was Orontes; now their arms,
Their Trojan treasures, float with the broken timbers
On the swing and slide of the waves. The storm, triumphant,

Rides down more boats, and more; there goes Achates;
Abas, Aletes, Ilioneus,
Receive the hostile water; the walls are broken;
The enemy pours in.

But meanwhile Neptune
Saw ocean in a welter of confusion,
The roar of storm, and deep and surface mingled.
Troublesome business, this; he rose, majestic,
From under the waves, and saw the Trojan vessels
Scattered all over the sea by the might of the waves
And the wreck of sky; he recognized the anger
And cunning of his sister, and he summoned
The winds by name:—"What arrogance is this,
What pride of birth, you winds, to meddle here
Without my sanction, raising all this trouble?
I'll—No, the waves come first: but listen to me,
You are going to pay for this! Get out of here!
Go tell your king the lordship of the ocean,
The trident, are not his, but mine. His realm
Reaches no further than the rocks and caverns
You brawlers dwell in; let him rule that palace,
Big as he pleases, shut you in, and stay there!"

This said, he calmed the swollen sea and cloud,
Brought back the sun; Cymothoe and Triton,
Heaving together, pulled the ships from the reef,
As Neptune used his trident for a lever,
Opened the quicksand, made the water smooth,
And the flying chariot skimmed the level surface.
Sometimes, in a great nation, there are riots
With the rabble out of hand, and firebrands fly
And cobblestones; whatever they lay their hands on
Is a weapon for their fury, but should they see
One man of noble presence, they fall silent,
Obedient dogs, with ears pricked up, and waiting,
Waiting his word, and he knows how to bring them
Back to good sense again. So ocean, roaring,
Subsided into stillness, as the sea-god
Looked forth upon the waters, and clear weather
Shone over him as he drove his flying horses.

Aeneas' weary children make for harbor,
Whichever lies most near, and the prows are turned
To Libya's coast-line. In a bay's deep curve
They find a haven, where the water lies
With never a ripple. A little island keeps

The sea-swell off, and the waves break on its sides
And slide back harmless. The great cliffs come down
Steep to deep water, and the background shimmers,
Darkens and shines, the tremulous aspen moving
And the dark fir pointing still. And there is a cave
Under the overhanging rocks, alive
With water running fresh, a home of the Nymphs,
With benches for them, cut from the living stone.
No anchor is needed here for weary ships,
No mooring-cable. Aeneas brings them in,
Seven weary vessels, and the men are glad
To be ashore again, to feel dry sand
Under the salt-stained limbs. Achates strikes
The spark from the flint, catches the fire on leaves,
Adds chips and kindling, blows and fans the flame,
And they bring out the soaked and salty corn,
The hand-mills, stone and mortar, and make ready,
As best they can, for bread.

Meanwhile Aeneas
Climbs to a look-out, for a view of the ocean,
Hoping for some good luck; the Phrygian galleys
Might meet his gaze, or Capys' boats, or a pennon
On a far-off mast-head flying. There is nothing,
Nothing to see out yonder, but near the water
Three stags are grazing, with a herd behind them,
A long line browsing through the peaceful valley.
He reaches for the bow and the swift arrows
Borne by Achates, and he shoots the leaders,
High-antlered, routs the common herd, and ceases
Only when seven are slain, a number equal
To the ships' tally, and then he seeks the harbor,
Divides the spoil, broaches the wine Acestes
Had stowed for them at Drepanum on their leaving,
A kingly present, and he calms their trouble,
Saying: "O comrades, we have been through evil
Together before this; we have been through worse,
Scylla, Charybdis, and the Cyclops' dwelling,
The sounding rocks. This, too, the god will end.
Call the nerve back; dismiss the fear, the sadness.
Some day, perhaps, remembering even this
Will be a pleasure. We are going on
Through whatsoever chance and change, until
We come to Latium, where the fates point out
A quiet dwelling-place, and Troy recovered.
Endure, and keep yourself for better days."
He kept to himself the sorrow in the heart,

Wearing, for them, a mask of hopefulness.
They were ready for the feasting. Part lay bare
The flesh from the torn hides, part cut the meat,
Impaling it, still quivering, on spits,
Setting the kettles, keeping the water boiling,
And strong with food again, sprawling stretched out
On comfortable grass, they take their fill
Of bread and wine and venison, till hunger
Is gone, and the board cleared. And then they talk
For a long time, of where their comrades are,
Are, or may be, hopeful and doubtful both.
Could they believe them living? or would a cry
Fall on deaf ears forever? All those captains,
Brave Gyas, brave Cloanthus, Amycus,
Lycus, Orontes,—in his secret heart
Aeneas mourns them.

Meanwhile, from the heaven
Jupiter watched the lands below, and the seas
With the white points of sails, and far-off people,
Turning his gaze toward Libya. And Venus
Came to him then, a little sadly, tears
Brimming in those bright eyes of hers. "Great father,"
She said, "Great ruler of the world
Of men and gods, great wielder of the lightning,
What has my poor Aeneas done? what outrage
Could Trojans perpetrate, so that the world
Rejects them everywhere, and many a death
Inflicted on them over Italy?
There was a promise once, that as the years
Rolled onward, they would father Rome and rulers
Of Roman stock, to hold dominion over
All sea and land. That was a promise, father;
What changed it? Once that promise was my comfort;
Troy fell; I weighed one fate against another
And found some consolation. But disaster
Keeps on; the same ill-fortune follows after.
What end of it all, great king? One man, Antenor,
Escaped the Greeks, came through Illyrian waters
Safe to Liburnian regions, where Timavus
Roars underground, comes up nine times, and reaches
The floodland near the seas. One man, Antenor,
Founded a city, Padua, a dwelling
For Trojan men, a resting-place from labor,
And shares their quietude. But we, your children,
To whom heaven's height is granted, we are betrayed,
We have lost our ships, we are kept from Italy,

Kept far away. One enemy—I tell you
This is a shameful thing! Do we deserve it?
Is this our rise to power?"

He smiled, in answer,
The kind of smile that clears the air, and kissed her.
"Fear not, my daughter; fate remains unmoved
For the Roman generations. You will witness
Lavinium's rise, her walls fulfill the promise;
You will bring to heaven lofty-souled Aeneas.
There has been no change in me whatever. Listen!
To ease this care, I will prophesy a little,
I will open the book of fate. Your son Aeneas
Will wage a mighty war in Italy,
Beat down proud nations, give his people laws,
Found them a city, a matter of three years
From victory to settlement. His son,
The boy Ascanius, named Ilius once,
When Troy was standing, and now called Iulus,
Shall reign for thirty years, and great in power
Forsake Lavinium, transfer the kingdom
To Alba Longa, new-built capital.
Here, for three hundred years, the line of Hector
Shall govern, till a royal priestess bears
Twin sons to Mars, and Romulus, rejoicing
In the brown wolf-skin of his foster-mother,
Takes up the tribe, and builds the martial walls
And calls the people, after himself, the Romans.
To these I set no bounds in space or time;
They shall rule forever. Even bitter Juno
Whose fear now harries earth and sea and heaven
Will change to better counsels, and will cherish
The race that wears the toga, Roman masters
Of all the world. It is decreed. The time
Will come, as holy years wheel on, when Troy
Will subjugate Mycenae, vanquish Phthia,
Be lord of Argos. And from this great line
Will come a Trojan, Caesar, to establish
The limit of his empire at the ocean,
His glory at the stars, a man called Julius
Whose name recalls Iulus. Welcome waits
For him in heaven; all the spoils of Asia
Will weigh him down, and prayer be made before him.
Then wars will cease, and a rough age grow gentler,
White Faith and Vesta, Romulus and Remus,
Give law to nations. War's grim gates will close,
Tight-shut with bars of iron, and inside them

The wickedness of war sit bound and silent,
The red mouth straining and the hands held tight
In fastenings of bronze, a hundred hundred."
With that, he sent down Mercury from heaven
That Carthage might be kindly, and her land
And new-built towers receive them with a welcome,
And their queen, Dido, knowing the will of fate,
Swing wide her doors. On the oarage of his wings
He flies through the wide sweep of air to Libya,
Where, at the will of the god, the folk make ready
In kindliness of heart, and their queen's purpose
Is gracious and gentle.

from BOOK II [THE FALL OF TROY]

They all were silent, watching. From his couch
Aeneas spoke: "A terrible grief, O Queen,
You bid me live again, how Troy went down
Before the Greeks, her wealth, her pitiful kingdom,
Sorrowful things I saw myself, wherein
I had my share and more. Even Ulysses,
Even his toughest soldiery might grieve
At such a story. And the hour is late
Already; night is sliding down the sky
And setting stars urge slumber. But if you long
To learn our downfall, to hear the final chapter
Of Troy no matter how I shrink, remembering,
And turn away in grief, let me begin it.

Broken in war, set back by fate, the leaders
Of the Greek host, as years went by, contrived,
With Pallas' help, a horse as big as a mountain,
They wove its sides with planks of fir, pretending
This was an offering for their safe return,
At least, so rumor had it. But inside
They packed, in secret, into the hollow sides
The fittest warriors; the belly's cavern,
Huge as it was, was filled with men in armor.
There is an island, Tenedos, well-known,
Rich in the days of Priam; now it is only
A bay, and not too good an anchorage
For any ship to trust. They sailed there, hid
On the deserted shore. We thought they had gone,
Bound for Mycenae, and Troy was very happy,
Shaking off grief, throwing the gates wide open.
It was a pleasure, for a change, to go
See the Greek camp, station and shore abandoned;

Why, this was where Achilles camped, his minions,
The Dolopes, were here; and the fleet just yonder,
And that was the plain where we used to meet in battle.
Some of us stared in wonder at the horse,
Astounded by its vastness, Minerva's gift,
Death from the virgin goddess, had we known it.
Thymoetes, whether in treachery, or because
The fates of Troy so ordered, was the first one
To urge us bring it in to the heart of the city,
But Capys, and some others, knowing better,
Suspicious of Greek plotting, said to throw it
Into the sea, to burn it up with fire,
To cut it open, see what there was inside it.
The wavering crowd could not make up its mind.

And, at that point, Laocoön came running,
With a great throng at his heels, down from the hilltop
As fast as ever he could, and before he reached us,
Cried in alarm: 'Are you crazy, wretched people?
Do you think they have gone, the foe? Do you think that any
Gifts of the Greeks lack treachery? Ulysses,—
What was his reputation? Let me tell you,
Either the Greeks are hiding in this monster,
Or it's some trick of war, a spy, or engine,
To come down on the city. Tricky business
Is hiding in it. Do not trust it, Trojans,
Do not believe this horse. Whatever it may be,
I fear the Greeks, even when bringing presents.'
With that, he hurled the great spear at the side
With all the strength he had. It fastened, trembling,
And the struck womb rang hollow, a moaning sound.
He had driven us, almost, to let the light in
With the point of the steel, to probe, to tear, but something
Got in his way, the gods, or fate, or counsel,
Ill-omened, in our hearts; or Troy would be standing
And Priam's lofty citadel unshaken.

Meanwhile, some Trojan shepherds, pulling and hauling,
Had a young fellow, with his hands behind him,
Tied up, and they were dragging him to Priam.
He had let himself be taken so, on purpose,
To open Troy to the Greeks, a stranger, ready
For death or shifty cunning, a cool intriguer,
Let come what may. They crowd around to see him,
Take turns in making fun of him, that captive.
Listen, and learn Greek trickiness; learn all
Their crimes from one.

He stopped in the middle, frightened and defenseless,
Looked at the Trojan ranks,—'What land, what waters,
Can take me now?' he cried, 'There is nothing, nothing
Left for me any more, no place with the Greeks,
And here are the Trojans howling for my blood!'
Our mood was changed. We pitied him, poor fellow,
Sobbing his heart out. We bade him tell his story,
His lineage, his news: what can he count on,
The captive that he is? His fear had gone
As he began: 'O King, whatever happens,
I will tell the truth, tell all of it; to start with,
I own I am a Greek. Sinon is wretched,
Fortune has made him so, but she will never
Make him a liar. You may perhaps have heard
Rumors of Palamedes, son of Belus,
A man of glorious fame. But the Greeks killed him,—
He was against the war, and so they killed him,
An innocent man, by perjury and lying
False witness. Now that he is dead they mourn him.
My father, his poor relative, had sent me
To soldier in his company; I was then
Scarcely beyond my boyhood. Palamedes
Held, for some time, some influence and standing
In royal councils, and we shared his glory,
But, and all men know this, Ulysses' hatred,
His cunning malice, pulled him down; thereafter
I lived in darkness, dragging out a lifetime
In sorrow for my innocent lord, and anger,
And in my anger I was very foolish,
I talked; I vowed, if I got home to Argos,
I would have vengeance: so I roused Ulysses
To hate me in his turn, and that began it,
Downfall and evil, Ulysses always trying
To frighten me with hint and accusation,
With rumors planted where the crowd would listen;
Oh yes, Ulysses knew what he was doing,
He never stopped, until with Calchas working
Hand in glove with him—why am I telling this,
And what's the use? I am stalling. All the Greeks,
You think, are all alike; what more do you want?
Inflict the punishment. That would be something
Ulysses would rejoice in, and some others
Pay handsome money for!'
But we were all on fire to hear him further.
Pelasgian craft meant nothing to our folly.
Trembling and nervous, he resumed his lying:
'The Greeks were tired of the long war; they often

Wanted to sail from Troy for home. Oh, would
That they had only done it! But a storm
Would cut them off, or the wrong wind terrify them.
Especially, just after the horse was finished,
With the joined planks of maple, all the heaven
Roared loud with storm-clouds. In suspense and terror
We sent Eurypylus to ask Apollo
What could be done; the oracle was gloomy,
Foreboding: "Blood, O Greeks, and a slain virgin
appeased the winds when first you came here; blood
Must pay for your return, a life be given,
An Argive life." The word came to our ears
With terror in it, our blood ran cold in our veins,
For whom was fate preparing? who would be
The victim of Apollo? Then Ulysses
Dragged Calchas into our midst, with a great uproar,
Trying his best to make the prophet tell us
What the gods wanted. And there were many then
Who told me what was coming, or kept silent
Because they saw, and all too well, the scheme
Ulysses had in mind. For ten days Calchas
Said nothing at all, hid in his tent, refusing
To have a word of his pronounce the sentence,
And all the time Ulysses kept on shouting,
Till Calchas broke, and doomed me to the altar.
And all assented; what each man had feared
In his own case, he bore with great composure
When turned another way.
The terrible day was almost on me; fillets
Were ready for my temples, the salted meal
Prepared, the altars standing. But I fled,
I tore myself away from death, I admit it,
I hid all night in sedge and muddy water
At the edge of the lake, hoping, forever hoping,
They might set sail. And now I hope no longer
To see my home, my parents, or my children,
Poor things, whom they will kill because I fled them,
Whom they will murder for my sacrilege.
But oh, by the gods above, by any power
That values truth, by any uncorrupted
Remnant of faith in all the world, have pity,
Have pity on a soul that bears such sorrow,
More than I ever deserved.'
He had no need to ask us. Priam said,
Untie him, and we did so with a promise
To spare his life. Our king, with friendly words,
Addressed him, saying, 'Whoever you are, forget

The Greeks, from now on. You are ours; but tell me
Why they have built this monstrous horse? who made it,
Who thought of it? What is it, war-machine,
Religious offering?' And he, instructed
In every trick and artifice, made answer,
Lifting his hands, now free: 'Eternal fires,
Inviolable godhead, be my witness,
You altars, you accursed swords, you fillets
Which I as victim wore, I had the right
To break those solemn bonds, I had the right
To hate those men, to bring whatever they hide
Into the light and air; I am bound no longer
To any country, any laws, but, Trojans,
Keep to the promise, if I tell the truth,
If I pay back with interest.
All the Greek hope, since first the war began,
Rested in Pallas, always. But Ulysses,
The crime-contriver, and the son of Tydeus
Attacked Minerva's temple, stole her image
Out of the holy shrine, and slew the guards,
And laid their bloody hands upon the goddess,
And from that time the Danaan hopes were broken,
Faltered and failed. It was no doubtful anger
Pallas revealed; she gave them signs and portents.
From her image in the camp the upraised eyes
Shot fire, and sweat ran salty down the limbs,
Thrice from the ground she seemed to flash and leap
With vibrant spear and clashing shield. The priest,
Calchas, made prophecy: they must take to flight
Over the sea, and Troy could not be taken
Without new omens; they must go to Argos,
Bring back the goddess again, whom they have taken
In curved ships over the sea. And if they have gone,
They are bound for home, Mycenae, for new arms,
New gods, new soldiers; they will be here again
When least expected. Calchas' message warned them,
And so they built this image, to replace
The one they had stolen, a gigantic offering
For a tremendous sacrilege. It was Calchas,
Again, who bade them build a mass so mighty
It almost reached the stars, too big to enter
Through any gate, or be brought inside the walls.
For if your hands should damage it, destruction,
(May God avert it) would come upon the city,
But if your hands helped bring it home, then Asia
Would be invading Greece, and doom await
Our children's children.'

We believed him, we
Whom neither Diomede nor great Achilles
Had taken, nor ten years, nor that armada,
A thousand ships of war. But Sinon did it
By perjury and guile.

Then something else,
Much greater and more terrible, was forced
Upon us, troubling our unseeing spirits.
Laocoön, allotted priest of Neptune,
Was slaying a great bull beside the altars,
When suddenly, over the tranquil deep
From Tenedos,—I shudder even now,
Recalling it—there came a pair of serpents
With monstrous coils, breasting the sea, and aiming
Together for the shore. Their heads and shoulders
Rose over the waves, upright, with bloody crests,
The rest of them trailing along the water,
Looping in giant spirals; the foaming sea
Hissed under their motion. And they reached the land,
Their burning eyes suffused with blood and fire,
Their darting tongues licking the hissing mouths.
Pale at the sight, we fled. But they went on
Straight toward Laocoön, and first each serpent
Seized in its coils his two young sons, and fastened
The fangs in those poor bodies. And the priest
Struggled to help them, weapons in his hand.
They seized him, bound him with their mighty coils,
Twice round his waist, twice round his neck, they squeezed
With scaly pressure, and still towered above him.
Straining his hands to tear the knots apart,
His chaplets stained with blood and the black poison,
He uttered horrible cries, not even human,
More like the bellowing of a bull when, wounded,
It flees the altar, shaking from the shoulder
The ill-aimed axe. And on the pair went gliding
To the highest shrine, the citadel of Pallas,
And vanished underneath the feet of the goddess
And the circle of her shield.

The people trembled
Again; they said Laocoön deserved it,
Having, with spear, profaned the sacred image.
It must be brought to its place, they cried, the goddess
Must be appeased. We broke the walls, exposing
The city's battlements, and all were busy
Helping the work, with rollers underfoot

And ropes around the neck. It climbed our walls,
The deadly engine. Boys, unwedded girls
Sang alleluias round it, all rejoicing
To have a hand on the tow-rope. It came nearer,
Threatening, gliding, into the very city.
O motherland! O Ilium, home of gods,
O walls of Troy! Four times it stopped, four times
The sound of arms came from it, and we pressed on,
Unheedful, blind in madness, till we set it,
Ill-omened thing, on the citadel we worshipped.
And even when Cassandra gave us warning,
We never believed her; so a god had ordered.
That day, our last, poor wretches, we were happy,
Garlanding the temples of the gods
All through the town.

And the sky turned, and darkness
Came from the ocean, the great shade covering earth
And heaven, and the trickery of the Greeks.
Sprawling along the walls, the Trojans slumbered,
Sleep holding their weary limbs, and the Greek armada,
From Tenedos, under the friendly silence
Of a still moon, came surely on. The flagship
Blazed at the masthead with a sudden signal,
And Sinon, guarded by the fates, the hostile
Will of the gods, swung loose the bolts; the Greeks
Came out of the wooden womb. The air received them,
The happy captains, Sthenelus, Ulysses,
Thessandrus, Acamas, Achilles' son
Called Neoptolemus, Thoas, Machaon,
Epeos, who designed the thing,—they all
Came sliding down the rope, and Menelaus
Was with them in the storming of a city
Buried in sleep and wine. The watch was murdered,
The open doors welcome the rush of comrades,
They marshal the determined ranks for battle.
It was the time when the first sleep begins
For weary mortals, heaven's most welcome gift.
In sleep, before my eyes, I seemed to see
Hector, most sorrowful, black with bloody dust,
Torn, as he had been, by Achilles' car,
The thong-marks on his swollen feet. How changed
He was from that great Hector who came, once,
Triumphant in Achilles' spoil, from hurling
Fire at the Grecian ships. With ragged beard,
Hair matted with his blood, wearing the wounds
He earned around the walls of Troy, he stood there.

It seemed that I spoke first:—'O light of Troy,
Our surest hope, we have long been waiting for you,
What shores have kept you from us? Many deaths,
Much suffering, have visited our city,
And we are tired. Why do I see these wounds?
What shame has caused them?' Those were foolish questions;
He made no answer but a sigh or a groan,
And then: 'Alas, O goddess-born! Take flight,
Escape these flames! The enemy has the walls,
Troy topples from her lofty height; enough
Has been paid out to Priam and to country.
Could any hand have saved them, Hector's would have.
Troy trusts to you her household gods, commending
Her holy things to you; take them, companions
Of destiny; seek walls for them, and a city
To be established, a long sea-wandering over.
From the inner shrine he carried Vesta's chaplets
In his own hands, and her undying fire.

Livy (59 BCE–17 CE)

THE HISTORY OF ROME

Rome, always aware of its greatness, had no shortage of chroniclers, record keepers, letter writers, and historians. But only Livy was what we would call a professional historian, a person who sets as his life work the writing of a great history and does only that, without other occupation or preoccupation. In 142 books, Livy wrote the history of Rome down to his own time. His lack of connections to the military or to the Roman senate gave him a view of events that belonged to an outsider (as opposed, say, to Julius Caesar's insider's account of his conquest of Gaul). Livy saw the study of history as morally profitable, as he says in his preface, because "in history you have a record of the infinite variety of human experience plainly set out for all to see, and in that record you can find for yourself and your country both examples and warnings; fine things to take as models, base things, rotten through and through, to avoid." Of the 142 books that Livy completed, only books 1–10 and 21–45 survive.

[ROMULUS AND REMUS]

But (I must believe) it was already written in the book of fate that this great city of ours should arise, and the first steps be taken to the founding of the mightiest empire the world has known—next to God's. The Vestal Virgin was raped and gave birth to twin boys. Mars, she declared, was their father—perhaps she believed it, perhaps she was merely hoping by the pretence to palliate her guilt. Whatever the truth of the matter, neither gods nor men could save her or her babes from the savage hands of the king. The mother was bound and flung into prison; the boys, by the king's order, were condemned to be drowned in the river. Destiny, however, intervened; the Tiber had overflowed its banks; because of the flooded ground it was impossible to get to the actual river, and the men entrusted to do the deed thought that the flood-water, sluggish though it was, would serve their purpose. Accordingly they made shift to carry out the king's orders by leaving the infants on the edge of the first flood-water they came to, at the spot where

Reprinted from *The Early History of Rome*, translated by Aubrey de Selincourt (Penguin, 1960).

now stands the Ruminal fig-tree—said to have once been known as the fig-tree of Romulus. In those days the country thereabouts was all wild and uncultivated, and the story goes that when the basket in which the infants had been exposed was left high and dry by the receding water, a she-wolf, coming down from the neighboring hills to quench her thirst, heard the children crying and made her way to where they were. She offered them her teats to suck and treated them with such gentleness that Faustulus, the king's herdsman, found her licking them with her tongue. Faustulus took them to his hut and gave them to his wife Larentia to nurse. Some think that the origin of this fable was the fact that Larentia was a common whore and was called Wolf by the shepherds.

Such, then, was the birth and upbringing of the twins. By the time they were grown boys, they employed themselves actively on the farm and with the flocks and began to go hunting in the woods; their strength grew with their resolution, until not content only with the chase they took to attacking robbers and sharing their stolen goods with their friends the shepherds. Other young fellows joined them, and they and the shepherds would fleet the time together, now in serious talk, now in jollity.

Even in that remote age the Palatine hill (which got its name from the Arcadian settlement Pallanteum) is supposed to have been the scene of the gay festival of the Lupercalia. The Arcadian Evander, who many years before held that region, is said to have instituted there the old Arcadian practice of holding an annual festival in honor of Lycean Pan (afterwards called Inuus by the Romans), in which young men ran about naked and disported themselves in various pranks and fooleries. The day of the festival was common knowledge, and on one occasion when it was in full swing some brigands, incensed at the loss of their ill-gotten gains, laid a trap for Romulus and Remus. Romulus successfully defended himself, but Remus was caught and handed over to Amulius. The brigands laid a complaint against their prisoner, the main charge being that he and his brother were in the habit of raiding Numitor's land with an organized gang of ruffians and stealing the cattle. Thereupon Remus was handed over for punishment to Numitor.

Now Faustulus had suspected all along that the boys he was bringing up were of royal blood. He knew that two infants had been exposed by the king's orders, and the rescue of his own two fitted perfectly in point of time. Hitherto, however, he had been unwilling to declare what he knew, until either a suitable opportunity occurred or circumstances compelled him. Now the truth could no longer be concealed, so in his alarm he told Romulus the whole story; Numitor, too, when he had Remus in custody and was told that the brothers were twins, was set thinking about his grandsons; the young men's age and character, so different from the lowly born, confirmed his suspicions; and further inquiries led him to the same conclusion, until he was on the point of acknowledging Remus. The net was closing in, and Romulus acted. He was not strong enough for open hostilities, so he instructed a number of the herdsmen to meet at the king's house by different routes at a preordained time; this was done, and with the help of Remus, at the head of another body of men, the king was surprised and killed. Before the first blows were struck, Numitor gave it out that an enemy had broken into the town and attacked the palace; he then drew off all the men of military age to garrison the inner fortress, and, as soon as he saw Romulus and Remus, their purpose accomplished, coming to congratulate him, he summoned a meeting of the people and laid the facts before it: Amulius's crime against himself, the birth of his grandsons, and the circumstances attending it, how they were brought up and ultimately recognized, and, finally, the murder of the king for which he himself assumed responsibility. The two brothers marched through the crowd at the head of their men and saluted their grandfather as king, and by a shout of unanimous consent his royal title was confirmed.

Romulus and Remus, after the control of Alba had passed to Numitor in the way I have described, were suddenly seized by an urge to found a new settlement on the spot where they had been left to drown as infants and had been subsequently brought up. There was, in point of fact, already an excess of population at Alba, what with the Albans themselves, the Latins, and the addition of the herdsmen: enough, indeed, to justify the hope that Alba and Lavinium would one day be small places compared with the proposed new settlement. Unhappily the brothers' plans for the future were marred by the same source which had divided their grandfather and Amulius—jealousy and ambition. A disgraceful quarrel arose from a matter in itself trivial. As the brothers were twins and all question of seniority was thereby precluded, they determined to ask the tutelary gods of the countryside to declare by augury which of them should govern the new town once it was founded, and give his name to it. For this purpose Romulus took the Palatine hill and Remus the Aventine as their respective stations from which to observe the auspices. Remus, the story goes, was the first to receive a sign—six vultures; and no sooner was this made known to the people than double the number of birds appeared to Romulus. The followers of each promptly saluted their master as king, one side basing its claim upon priority, the other upon number. Angry words ensued, followed all too soon by blows, and in the course of the affray Remus was killed. There is another story, a commoner one, according to which Remus, by way of jeering at his brother, jumped over the half-built walls of the new settlement; whereupon Romulus killed him in a fit of rage, adding the threat, 'So perish whoever else shall overleap my battlements.'

This, then, was how Romulus obtained the sole power. The newly built city was called by its founder's name.

[The Abduction of the Sabine Women]

Rome was now strong enough to challenge any of her neighbors; but, great though she was, her greatness seemed likely to last only for a single generation. There were not enough women, and that, added to the fact that there was no intermarriage with neighboring communities, ruled out any hope of maintaining the level of population. Romulus accordingly, on the advice of his senators, sent representatives to the various peoples across his borders to negotiate alliances and the right of intermarriage for the newly established state. The envoys were instructed to point out that cities, like everything else, have to begin small; in course of time, helped by their own worth and the favor of heaven, some, at least, grow rich and famous, and of these Rome would assuredly be one: Gods had blessed her birth, and the valor of her people would not fail in the days to come. The Romans were men, as they were; why, then, be reluctant to intermarry with them?

Romulus's overtures were nowhere favorably received; it was clear that everyone despised the new community, and at the same time feared, both for themselves and for posterity, the growth of this new power in their midst. More often than not his envoys were dismissed with the question of whether Rome had thrown open her doors to female, as well as to male, runaways and vagabonds, as that would evidently be the most suitable way for Romans to get wives. The young Romans naturally resented this jibe, and a clash seemed inevitable. Romulus, seeing it must come, set the scene for it with elaborate care. Deliberately hiding his resentment, he prepared to celebrate the Consualia, a solemn festival in honor of Neptune, patron of the horse, and sent notice of his intention all over the neighboring countryside. The better to advertise it, his people lavished upon their preparations for the spectacle all the resources—such as they were in those days—at their command. On the appointed day crowds flocked to Rome, partly, no doubt, out of sheer curiosity to see the new town. The majority were from the neighboring settlements of Caenina, Crustumium, and Antemnae, but all the Sabines were there too, with their wives and children. Many houses offered hospitable entertainment to the visitors; they were invited to inspect the fortifications, layout, and numerous buildings of the town, and expressed their surprise at the rapidity of its growth. Then the great moment came; the show began, and nobody had eyes or thoughts for anything else. This was the Romans' opportunity: at a given signal all the able-bodied men burst through the crowd and seized the young women. Most of the girls were the prize of whoever got hold of them first, but a few conspicuously handsome ones had been previously marked down for leading senators, and these were brought to their houses by special gangs. There was one young woman of much greater beauty than the rest; and the story goes that she was seized by a party of men belonging to the household of someone called Thalassius, and in reply to the many questions about whose house they were taking her to, they, to prevent anyone else laying hands upon her, kept shouting, 'Thalassius, Thalassius!' This was the origin of the use of this word at weddings.

By this act of violence the fun of the festival broke up in panic. The girls' unfortunate parents made good their escape, not without bitter comments on the treachery of their hosts and heartfelt prayers to the God to whose festival they had come in all good faith in the solemnity of the occasion, only to be grossly deceived. The young women were no less indignant and as full of foreboding for the future.

Romulus, however, reassured them. Going from one to another he declared that their own parents were really to blame, in that they had been too proud to allow intermarriage with their neighbors; nevertheless, they need not fear; as married women they would share all the fortunes of Rome, all the privileges of the community, and they would be bound to their husbands by the dearest bond of all, their children. He urged them to forget their wrath and give their hearts to those to whom chance had given their bodies. Often, he said, a sense of injury yields in the end to affection, and their husbands would treat them all the more kindly in that they would try, each one of them, not only to fulfil their own part of the bargain but also to make up to their wives for the homes and parents they had lost. The men, too, played their part: they spoke honeyed words and vowed that it was passionate love which had prompted their offence. No plea can better touch a woman's heart.

[The Rape of Lucretia]

The young princes were drinking one day in the quarters of Sextus Tarquinius—Collatinus, son of Egerius, was also present—when someone chanced to mention the subject of wives. Each of them, of course, extravagantly praised his own; and the rivalry got hotter and hotter, until Collatinus suddenly cried: 'Stop! What need is there of words, when in a few hours we can prove beyond doubt the incomparable superiority of my Lucretia? We are all young and strong: why shouldn't we ride to Rome and see with our own eyes what kind of women our wives are? There is no better evidence, I assure you, than what a man finds when he enters his wife's room unexpectedly.'

They had all drunk a good deal, and the proposal appealed to them; so they mounted their horses and galloped off to Rome. They reached the city as dusk was falling; and there the wives of the royal princes were found enjoying themselves with a group of young friends at a dinner-party, in the greatest luxury. The riders then went on to Collatia, where they found Lucretia very differently employed: it was already late at night, but there, in the hall of her house, surrounded by her busy maid-servants, she was still hard at work by lamplight upon her spinning. Which wife had won the contest in womanly virtue was no longer in doubt.

With all courtesy Lucretia rose to bid her husband and the princes welcome, and Collatinus, pleased with his success, invited his friends to sup with him. It was at that fatal supper that Lucretia's beauty, and proven chastity, kindled in Sextus Tarquinias the flame of lust, and determined him to debauch her.

Nothing further occurred that night. The little jaunt was over, and the young men rode back to camp.

A few days later Sextus, without Collatinus's knowledge, returned with one companion to Collatia, where he was hospitably welcomed in Lucretia's house, and, after supper, escorted, like the honored visitor he was thought to be, to the guest-chamber. Here he waited till the house was asleep, and then, when all was quiet, he drew his sword and made his way to Lucretia's room determined to rape her. She was asleep. Laying his left hand on her breast, 'Lucretia,' he whispered, 'not a sound! I am Sextus Tarquinius. I am armed—if you utter a word, I will kill you.' Lucretia opened her eyes in terror; death was imminent, no help at hand. Sextus urged his love, begged her to submit, pleaded, threatened, used every weapon that might conquer a woman's heart. But all in vain; not even the fear of death could bend her will. 'If death will not move you,' Sextus cried, 'dishonor shall. I will kill you first, then cut the throat of a slave and lay his naked body by your side. Will they not believe that you have been caught in adultery with a servant—and paid the price?' Even the most resolute chastity could not have stood against this dreadful threat.

Lucretia yielded. Sextus enjoyed her, and rode away, proud of his success.

The unhappy girl wrote to her father in Rome and to her husband in Ardea, urging them both to come at once with a trusted friend and quickly, for a frightful thing had happened. Her father came with Valerius, Volesus's son, her husband with Brutus, with whom he was returning to Rome when he was met by the messenger. They found Lucretia sitting in her room, in deep distress. Tears rose to her eyes as they entered, and to her husband's question, 'Is it well with you?' she answered, 'No. What can be well with a woman who has lost her honor? In your bed, Collatinus, is the impress of another man. My body only has been violated. My heart is innocent, and death will be my witness. Give me your solemn promise that the adulterer shall be punished—he is Sextus Tarquinius. He it is who last night came as my enemy disguised as my guest, and took his pleasure of me. That pleasure will be my death—and his, too, if you are men.'

The promise was given. One after another they tried to comfort her. They told her she was helpless, and therefore innocent; that he alone was guilty. It was the mind, they said, that sinned, not the body: without intention there could never be guilt.

'What is due to him,' Lucretia said, 'is for you to decide. As for me I am innocent of fault, but I will take my punishment. Never shall Lucretia provide a precedent for unchaste women to escape what they deserve.' With these words she drew a knife from under her robe, drove it into her heart, and fell forward, dead.

Her father and husband were overwhelmed with grief. While they stood weeping helplessly, Brutus drew the bloody knife from Lucretia's body, and holding it before him cried: 'By this girl's blood—none more chaste till a tyrant wronged her—and by the gods, I swear that with sword and fire, and whatever else can lend strength to my arm, I will pursue Lucius Tarquinius the Proud, his wicked wife, and all his children, and never again will I let them or any other man be King in Rome.'

He put the knife into Collatinus's hands, then passed it to Lucretius, then to Valerius. All looked at him in astonishment: a miracle had happened—he was a changed man. Obedient to his command, they swore their oath. Grief was forgotten in the sudden surge of anger, and when Brutus called upon them to make war, from that instant, upon the tyrant's throne, they took him for their leader.

Lucretia's body was carried from the house into the public square. Crowds gathered, as crowds will, to gape and wonder—and the sight was unexpected enough, and horrible enough, to attract them. Anger at the criminal brutality of the king's son and sympathy with the father's grief stirred every heart; and when Brutus cried out that it was time for deeds not tears, and urged them, like true Romans, to take up arms against the tyrants who had dared to treat them as a vanquished enemy, not a man amongst them could resist the call.

. . . When news of the rebellion reached Ardea, the king immediately started for Rome, to restore order. Brutus got wind of his approach, and changed his route to avoid meeting him, finally reaching Ardea almost at the same moment as Tarquin arrived at Rome. Tarquin found the city gates shut against him and his exile decreed. Brutus the Liberator was enthusiastically welcomed by the troops, and Tarquin's sons were expelled from the camp. Two of them followed their father into exile at Caere in Etruria. Sextus Tarquinius went to Gabii—his own territory, as he doubtless hoped; but his previous record there of robbery and violence had made him many enemies, who now took their revenge and assassinated him.

[Horatius at the Bridge]

The Tarquins, meanwhile, had taken refuge at the court of Lars Porsena, the king of Clusium. By every means in their power they tried to win his support, now begging him not to allow fellow Etruscans, men of the same blood as himself, to continue living in penniless exile, now warning him of the dangerous consequences of letting republicanism go unavenged. The expulsion of kings, they urged, once it had begun, might well become common practice; liberty was an attractive idea, and unless reigning monarchs defended their thrones as vigorously as states now seemed to be trying to destroy them, all order and subordination would collapse; nothing would be left in any country but flat equality; greatness and eminence would be gone for ever. Monarchy, the noblest thing in heaven or on earth, was nearing its end. Porsena, who felt that his own security would be increased by restoring the monarchy in Rome, and also that Etruscan prestige would be enhanced if the king were of Etruscan blood, was convinced by these arguments and lost no time in invading Roman territory.

Never before had there been such consternation in the Senate, so powerful was Clusium at that time and so great the fame of Porsena. Nor was the menace of Porsena the only cause for alarm: the Roman populace itself was hardly less to be feared, for they might well be scared into admitting the Tarquins into the city and buying peace even at the price of servitude. To secure their support, therefore, the Senate granted them a number of favours, especially in the matter of food supplies. Missions were sent to Cumae and the Volscians to purchase grain; the monopoly in salt, the price of which was high, was taken from private individuals and transferred wholly to state control; the commons were exempted from tolls and taxes, the loss of revenue being made up by the rich, who could afford it; the poor, it was said, made contribution enough if they reared children. These concessions proved wonderfully effective, for during the misery and privation of the subsequent blockade the city remained united—so closely, indeed, that the poorest in Rome hated the very name of 'king' as bitterly as did the great. Wise government in this crisis gave the Senate greater popularity, in the true sense of the word, than was ever won by a demagogue in after years.

On the approach of the Etruscan army, the Romans abandoned their farmsteads and moved into the city. Garrisons were posted. In some sections the city walls seemed sufficient protection, in others the barrier of the Tiber. The most vulnerable point was the wooden bridge, and the Etruscans would have crossed it and forced an entrance into the city, had it not been for the courage of one man, Horatius Cocles—that great soldier whom the fortune of Rome gave to be her shield on that day of peril. Horatius was on guard at the bridge when the Janiculum was captured by a sudden attack. The enemy forces came pouring down the hill, while the Roman troops, throwing away their weapons, were behaving more like an undisciplined rabble than a fighting force. Horatius acted promptly: as his routed comrades approached the bridge, he stopped as many as he could catch and compelled them to listen to him. 'By God,' he cried, 'can't you see that if you desert your post escape is hopeless? If you leave the bridge open in your rear, there will soon be more of them in the Palatine and the Capitol than on the Janiculum.' Urging them with all the power at his command to destroy the bridge by fire or steel or any means they could muster, he offered to hold up the Etruscan advance, so far as was possible, alone. Proudly he took his stand at the outer end of the bridge; conspicuous amongst the rout of fugitives, sword and shield ready for action, he prepared himself for close combat, one man against an army. The advancing enemy paused in sheer astonishment at such reckless courage. Two other men, Spurius Lartius and Titus Herminius, both aristocrats with a fine military record, were ashamed to leave Horatius alone, and with their support he won through the first few minutes of desperate danger. Soon, however, he forced them to save themselves and leave him; for little was now left of the bridge, and the demolition squads were calling them back before it was too late. Once more Horatius stood alone; with defiance in his eyes he confronted the Etruscan chivalry, challenging one after another to single combat, and mocking them all as tyrants' slaves who, careless of their own liberty, were coming to destroy the liberty of others. For a while they hung back, each waiting for his neighbour to make the first move, until shame at the unequal battle drove them to action, and with a fierce cry they hurled their spears at the solitary figure which barred their way. Horatius caught the missiles on his shield and, resolute as ever, straddled the bridge and held his ground. The Etruscans moved forward, and would have thrust him aside by the sheer weight of numbers, but their advance was suddenly checked by the crash of the falling bridge and the simultaneous shout of triumph from the Roman soldiers who had done their work in time. The Etruscans could only stare in bewilderment as Horatius, with a prayer to Father Tiber to bless him and his sword, plunged fully armed into the water and swam, through the missiles which fell thick about him, safely to the other side where his friends were waiting to receive him. It was a noble piece of work—legendary, maybe, but destined to be celebrated in story through the years to come.

[Cincinnatus Called from His Farm]

The Senate, on the envoys' return, instructed one consul to proceed against Gracchus and the other to direct an invasion of Aequian territory. The tribunes proved true to form by trying to obstruct the raising of troops—and might, indeed, have succeeded, had not a fresh cause for alarm presented itself in an unexpected move by the Sabines. A large force of these people penetrated nearly to the walls of Rome; crops in the countryside were ruined and everyone in the City felt his safety seriously threatened. In these circumstances the commons were willing enough to enlist and despite the tribunes' protests two large armies were enrolled, one of which, under Nautius's command, took the field against the Sabines. Nautius fortified a position at Eretum and proceeded to send out a series of raiding-parties, usually under cover of darkness, into enemy territory; these parties, none of which was numerically strong, did so much damage that the Sabine raids on Roman territory seemed to have been comparatively harmless. Minucius, on the other hand, whether by ill luck or lack of enterprise, was less successful than his colleague; for after an unsuccessful, but quite minor, engagement he refused to take any further risks and stayed within the fortifications of his camp, not far from the enemy lines. Such timidity, naturally enough, was a fillip to the enemy's confidence, and they boldly attacked Minucius's camp during the night. The attack failed, but next day they set to work to wall him in with earthworks; before these were completed and every exit barred, five men were ordered out to ride through the enemy posts and carry to Rome the news that the consul and his army were under siege. Nothing could have been more unexpected. The city was thrown into a state of turmoil, and the general alarm was as great as if Rome herself were surrounded. Nautius was sent for, but it was quickly decided that he was not the man to inspire full confidence; the situation evidently called for a dictator, and, with no dissentient voice, Lucius Quinctius Cincinnatus was named for the post.

Now I would solicit the particular attention of those numerous people who imagine that money is everything in this world, and that rank and ability are inseparable from wealth: let them observe that Cincinnatus, the one man in whom Rome reposed all her hope of survival, was at that moment working a little three-acre farm (now known as the Quinctian meadows) west of the Tiber, just opposite the spot where the shipyards are today. A mission from the city found him at work on his land—digging a ditch, maybe, or ploughing. Greetings were exchanged, and he was asked—with a prayer for God's blessing on himself and his country—to put on his toga and hear the Senate's instructions. This naturally surprised him, and, asking if all were well, he told his wife Racilia to run to their cottage and fetch his toga. The toga was brought, and wiping the grimy sweat from his hands and face he put it on; at once the envoys from the city saluted him, with congratulations, as Dictator, invited him to enter Rome, and informed him of the terrible danger of Minucius's army. A state vessel was waiting for him on the river, and on the city bank he was welcomed by his three sons who had come to meet him, then by other kinsmen and friends, and finally by nearly the whole body of senators. Closely attended by all these people and preceded by his lictors he was then escorted to his residence through streets lined with great crowds of common folk who, be it said, were by no means so pleased to see the new Dictator, as they thought his power excessive and dreaded the way in which he was likely to use it.

Next day, after a quiet night in which nothing was done beyond keeping careful watch, the Dictator was in the Forum before dawn. He appointed as his Master of Horse a patrician named Lucius Tarquitius—a man who had the reputation of being the best soldier in Rome, in spite of the fact that he was too poor to keep a horse and had served, in consequence, as an infantryman. Accompanied by Tarquitius, the Dictator then appeared before the assembled people, to issue his instructions: legal business was to be suspended, all shops closed and no private business of any kind transacted; all men of military age were to parade before sunset in the Campus Martius with their equipment, each man bringing with him a five days' bread ration and twelve stakes. All men over military age were to prepare the food for their younger neighbours, who would employ themselves meanwhile in looking over their equipment and collecting their stakes.

The Dictator's orders were promptly executed: stakes were hunted out by the soldiers and taken from wherever they were found, nobody objecting to their removal; every man presented himself punctually. Then column of march was formed, all prepared, should need arise, for instant action, and moved off with Cincinnatus at the head of the infantry and Tarquitius in command of the mounted troops.

In each division, infantry and cavalry, could be heard such words of command or encouragement as the occasion demanded: the men were urged to step out, reminded of the need for haste, in order to reach the scene of action that night, pressed to remember that a Roman army with its commander had already been three days under siege; no one could tell what the next day or the next night might bring, and events of tremendous import often hung upon a single moment of time. The men themselves, too, to show their spirit and gratify their officers, exhorted each other to every effort, shouting to the standard-bearer to move faster and to their companions to follow him.

At midnight the army reached Algidus and halted not far from the enemy's position. The Dictator rode round it on his horse, to inform himself, so far as he could in the darkness, of the extent and lay-out of their camp, and then ordered his officers to instruct their men to pile their baggage in a selected spot and return to their ranks with only their weapons and the stakes which each was carrying. Then, in the same formation as on the march from Rome—a long column, that is—he so manoeuvred them as to form a complete ring round the enemy's position. Their orders then were to raise the war-cry on a given signal, and then to begin digging, each man at the spot where he stood, and to fix his stakes, so as to form a continuous trench and palisade. The signal soon came and the work began. The shout which rose from the Romans' throats told the enemy that they were surrounded, and carried beyond their lines into the beleaguered camp of Minucius, bringing alarm to the one and joy to the other. Minucius's men knew it was the voice of friends; with satisfaction and relief they told each other that help had come, and their sentries and outposts began to assume the offensive. Minucius himself, aware that instant action was vital, urged that the welcome cry meant not only that their friends had come but that they were already engaged, and had almost certainly started an assault on the outer ring of the enemy's position. So he ordered his men to draw their swords and follow him.

It was still dark when the fight began, and the relieving troops of Cincinnatus knew by the war-cry of their beleaguered friends that they, too, were in action at last.

The Aequians were preparing to resist the work of circumvallation, when Minucius started his offensive. To prevent his troops from forcing a way right through their lines, they were compelled to turn inward to face them, thus withdrawing their attention from the troops of the Dictator, who were, in consequence, left free to continue all night the construction of their trench and palisade. The battle with Minucius lasted till dawn; by that time the circumvallation was completed, and Minucius's men were beginning to get the upper hand. For the Aequians the moment was critical: the Dictator's troops, their work finished, promptly began an assault on the outer defences, thus forcing the Aequians to fight on a second front while still heavily engaged on the first. Caught as it were between the two fires, they soon gave up the struggle and begged both Cincinnatus and Minucius not to proceed to a general massacre but to disarm them and let them go with their lives. Minucius referred them to the Dictator, who accepted their surrender, but on humiliating terms: their commander Gracchus, with other leading men, was to be brought before him in chains; the town of Corbio was to be evacuated; the Aequian soldiers were to be allowed to go with their lives, but, to force a final confession of absolute defeat, they were to pass 'under the yoke'. A 'yoke' was made from three spears, two fixed upright in the ground and the third tied across them, and the Aequian soldiers were made to pass under it.

As the Aequians had been stripped before their dismissal, their camp, when it fell into the Dictator's hands, was found to contain much valuable property. All this Cincinnatus turned over to his own men exclusively; Minucius's men, and Minucius himself, got nothing. 'You,' the Dictator remarked severely, 'shall have no share of the plunder taken from an enemy who nearly took *you*.' Then, turning to Minucius, he added: 'Until, Lucius Minucius, you learn to behave like a consul and commander, you will act as my lieutenant and take your instructions from me.'

Minucius resigned the consulship and remained with his troops as second in command; his men were quick to appreciate the military qualities of the Dictator, and gave him implicit obedience; they forgot their disgrace in the memory of the service he had done them, and voted him a gold circlet of a pound in weight, and when he left them saluted him as their protector.

In Rome the Senate was convened by Quintus Fabius the City Prefect, and a decree was passed inviting Cincinnatus to enter in triumph with his troops. The chariot he rode in was preceded by the enemy commanders and the military standards, and followed by his army loaded with its spoils. We read in accounts of this great day that there was not a house in Rome but had a table spread with food before its door, for the entertainment of the soldiers who regaled themselves as they followed the triumphal chariot, singing and joking as befitted the occasion, like men out to enjoy themselves. The same day Mamilius of Tusculum by universal consent was granted Roman citizenship.

Only the impending trial of Volscius for perjury prevented Cincinnatus from resigning immediately. The tribunes who were thoroughly in awe of him made no attempt to interfere with the proceedings, and Volscius was found guilty and went into exile at Lanuvium. Cincinnatus finally resigned after holding office for fifteen days, having originally accepted it for a period of six months.

Ovid (43 BCE–c. 17 CE)

METAMORPHOSES

Unlike Virgil, who was rescued from an early exile by Augustus and who during his career enjoyed the patronage of a wealthy friend of the emperor, Ovid was a brilliant poet who lost Augustus's favor and ended his life in bitter exile on the Black Sea. We are not sure what brought about the break in his relations with the emperor; he himself says the cause was "his poetry and his mistake," and his punishment was heightened by the removal of his books from libraries in Rome.

In spite of his bad end, Ovid became one of the most popular and influential poets during the centuries to follow, partly because of his brilliant and witty treatment of love in poems like the Art of Love, *a handbook of seduction. But his greatest poem is* Metamorphoses, *a compendium of Greek and Roman mythical stories, cleverly woven together around the central theme of change. Because the Greek (and Roman) myths show so many humans and gods changed into plants, birds, animals, trees, and stars, Ovid's theme allows him to retell a huge number of stories. In fact, his poem became a kind of encyclopedia of myth, the sourcebook for later writers and artists in the West who were seduced by Ovid's versions of the stories.*

But Ovid's style is very much unlike an encyclopedia: he draws from the stories all their emotion, sentiment, and irony. With great insight, Ovid searches the stories for deeper strains of passion, of terror, of fate. So successful is his enterprise that many of his stories, barely known in earlier versions, have become emblems for us of human psychology: the self-love of Narcissus, Pygmalion's possessive love for the image of the woman he crafted, Icarus's death in the sea after he fails to heed his father's warning about flying too close to the sun, Orpheus's winning his wife out of hell only to lose her again. And Arachne, in the story included here, who challenges to a weaving contest the very goddess who gave her her skill. Although she weaves a tapestry depicting the treachery of the gods toward humans, she fails to learn her own lesson and, in besting Minerva (Athena), invites the goddess's resentment and revenge.

Reprinted from *Metamorphoses*, translated by Mary M. Innes (Penguin, 1955).

[Creation and Flood]

My purpose is to tell of bodies which have been transformed into shapes of a different kind. You heavenly powers, since you were responsible for those changes, as for all else, look favourably on my attempts, and spin an unbroken thread of verse, from the earliest beginnings of the world, down to my own times.

Before there was any earth or sea, before the canopy of heaven stretched overhead, Nature presented the same aspect the world over, that to which men have given the name of Chaos. This was a shapeless uncoordinated mass, nothing but a weight of lifeless matter, whose ill-assorted elements were indiscriminately heaped together in one place. There was no sun, in those days, to provide the world with light, no crescent moon ever filling out her horns: the earth was not poised in the enveloping air, balanced there by its own weight, nor did the sea stretch out its arms along the margins of the shores. Although the elements of land and air and sea were there, the earth had no firmness, the water no fluidity, there was no brightness in the sky. Nothing had any lasting shape, but everything got in the way of everything else; for, within that one body, cold warred with hot, moist with dry, soft with hard, and light with heavy.

This strife was finally resolved by a god, a natural force of a higher kind, who separated the earth from heaven, and the water from the earth, and set the clear air apart from the cloudy atmosphere. When he had freed these elements, sorting them out from the heap where they had lain, indistinguishable from one another, he bound them fast, each in its separate place, forming a harmonious union. The fiery aether, which has no weight, formed the vault of heaven, flashing upwards to take its place in the highest sphere. The air, next to it in lightness, occupied the neighbouring regions. Earth, heavier than these, attracted to itself the grosser elements, and sank down under its own weight, while the encircling sea took possession of the last place of all, and held the solid earth in its embrace. In this way the god, whichever of the gods it was, set the chaotic mass in order, and, after dividing it up, arranged it in its constituent parts.

When this was done, his first care was to shape the earth into a great ball, so that it might be the same in all directions. After that, he commanded the seas to spread out this way and that, to swell into waves under the influence of the rushing winds, and to pour themselves around earth's shores. Springs, too, he created, and great pools and lakes, and confined between sloping banks the rivers which flow down from the hills and continue, each in its own channel, until they are either swallowed up by the earth itself, or reach the sea and enter its expanse of wider waters, there to wash against shores instead of banks. Then the god further ordained that earth's plains should unroll, its valleys sink down, the woods be clothed with leaves, and rocky mountain peaks rise up.

As the sky is divided into two zones on the right hand, and two on the left, with a fifth in between, hotter than any of the rest, so the world which the sky encloses was marked off in the same way thanks to the providence of the god: he imposed the same number of zones on earth as there are in the heavens. The central zone is so hot as to be uninhabitable, while two others are covered in deep snow: but between these extremes he set two zones to which he gave a temperate climate, compounded of heat and cold.

Over all these regions hangs the air, as much heavier than the fiery aether as it is lighter than earth or water. To the air the god assigned mists and clouds, and thunder that was destined to cause human hearts to tremble: here too he placed the thunderbolts, and winds that strike out lightnings from the clouds. Nor did the builder of the world allow the winds, any more than the rest, to roam at will throughout the air—they can scarcely be prevented from tearing the world apart, even as it is, although each blows in a different direction: so violent is the strife between brothers. The East wind withdrew to the lands of the dawn, to the kingdoms of Arabia and Persia, and to the mountain ridges that lie close to the sun's morning rays. The West, and the shores which are warmed by the setting sun, are subject to Zephyr. Boreas, who makes men shudder with his chill breath, invaded Scythia and the North, while the lands opposite to those are continually drenched with rain and clouds, brought by the South wind.

Above all these, the god set the clear aether that has no weight, and is untainted by any earthly particles.

No sooner were all things separated in this way, and confined within definite limits, than the stars which had long been buried in darkness and obscurity began to blaze forth all through the sky. So that every region should have its appropriate inhabitants, stars and divine forms occupied the heavens, the waters afforded a home to gleaming fishes, earth harboured wild beasts, and the yielding air welcomed the birds.

There was as yet no animal which was more akin to the gods than these, none more capable of intelligence, none that could be master over all the rest. It was at this point that man was born: either the Creator, who was responsible for this better world, made him from divine seed, or else Prometheus, son of Iapetus, took the new-made earth which, only recently separated from the lofty aether, still retained some elements related to those of heaven and, mixing it with rainwater, fashioned it into the image of the all-governing gods. Whereas other animals hang their heads and look at the ground, he made man stand erect, bidding him look up to heaven, and lift his head to the stars. So the earth, which had been rough and formless, was moulded into the shape of man, a creature till then unknown.

In the beginning was the Golden Age, when men of their own accord, without threat of punishment, without laws, maintained good faith and did what was right. There were no penalties to be afraid of, no bronze tablets were erected, carrying threats of legal action, no crowd of wrong-doers, anxious for mercy, trembled before the face of their judge: indeed, there were no judges, men lived securely without them. Never yet had any pine tree, cut down from its home on the mountains, been launched on ocean's waves, to visit foreign lands: men knew only their own shores. Their cities were not yet surrounded by sheer moats, they had no straight brass trumpets, no coiling brass horns, no helmets and no swords. The peoples of the world, untroubled by any fears, enjoyed a leisurely and peaceful existence, and had no use for soldiers. The earth itself, without compulsion, untouched by the hoe, unfurrowed by any share, produced all things spontaneously, and men were content with foods that grew without cultivation. They gathered arbute berries and mountain strawberries, wild cherries and blackberries that cling to thorny bramble bushes: or acorns, fallen from Jupiter's spreading oak. It was a season of everlasting spring, when peaceful zephyrs, with their warm breath, caressed the flowers that sprang up without having been planted. In time the earth, though untilled, produced corn too, and fields that never lay fallow whitened with heavy ears of grain. Then there flowed rivers of milk and rivers of nectar, and golden honey dripped from the green holm-oak.

When Saturn was consigned to the darkness of Tartarus, and the world passed under the rule of Jove, the age of silver replaced that of gold, inferior to it, but superior to the age of tawny bronze. Jupiter shortened the springtime which had prevailed of old, and instituted a cycle of four seasons in the year, winter, summer, changeable autumn, and a brief spring. Then, for the first time, the air became parched and arid, and glowed with white heat, then hanging icicles formed under the chilling blasts of the wind. It was in those days that men first sought covered dwelling places: they made their homes in caves and thick shrubberies, or bound branches together with bark. The corn, the gift of Ceres, first began to be sown in long furrows, and straining bullocks groaned beneath the yoke.

After that came the third age, the age of bronze, when men were of a fiercer character, more ready to turn to cruel warfare, but still free from any taint of wickedness.

Last of all arose the age of hard iron: immediately, in this period which took its name from a baser ore, all manner of crime broke out; modesty, truth, and loyalty fled. Treachery and trickery took their place, deceit and violence and criminal greed. Now sailors spread their canvas to the winds, though they had as yet but little knowledge of these, and trees which had once clothed the high mountains were fashioned into ships, and tossed upon the ocean waves, far removed from their own element. The land, which had previously been common to all, like the sunlight and the breezes, was now divided up far and wide by boundaries, set by cautious surveyors. Nor was it only corn and their due nourishment that men demanded of the rich earth: they explored its very bowels, and dug out the wealth which it had hidden away, close to the Stygian shades; and this wealth was a further incitement to wickedness. By this time iron had been discovered, to the hurt of mankind, and gold, more hurtful still than iron. War made its appearance, using both those metals in its conflict, and shaking clashing weapons in bloodstained hands. Men lived on what they could plunder: friend was not safe from friend, nor father-in-law from son-in-law, and even between brothers affection was rare. Husbands waited eagerly for the death of their wives, and wives for that of their husbands. Ruthless stepmothers mixed brews of deadly aconite, and sons pried into their fathers' horoscopes, impatient for them to die. All proper affection lay vanquished and, last of the immortals, the maiden Justice left the blood-soaked earth.

The heights of heaven were no safer than the earth; for the giants, so runs the story, assailed the kingdom of the gods and, piling mountains together, built them up to the stars above. Then the almighty father hurled his thunderbolt, smashed through Olympus, and flung down Pelion from where it had been piled on top of Ossa. The terrible bodies of the giants lay crushed beneath their own massive structures, and the earth was drenched and soaked with torrents of blood from her sons. Then, they say, she breathed life into this warm blood and, so that her offspring might not be completely forgotten, changed it into the shape of men. But the men thus born, no less than the giants, were contemptuous of the gods, violent and cruel, with a lust to kill: it was obvious that they were the children of blood.

When the father of the gods, the son of Saturn, looked down from his high citadel, and saw what was going on, he groaned aloud. He recalled the horrid banquet of Lycaon which had not yet become common knowledge, so recent was the deed, and his heart swelled with dreadful wrath, worthy of Jupiter. He called together his council, and they did not delay when they heard his summons.

There is a track across the heavens, plain to see in the clear sky. It is called the Milky Way, and is famous for its brightness. It is by this road that the gods come to the palace of the mighty Thunderer, and to his royal home. On the right hand and on the left stand the houses of distinguished gods, filled with crowds that throng their open doors. The ordinary inhabitants of heaven live elsewhere, in different places. Here the powerful and noble divinities have made their homes. This is the spot which, were I allowed to speak boldly, I would not hesitate to call the Palatine district of high heaven.

So the gods took their seats in the marble council chamber, and their lord sat, throned high above them, leaning on his ivory sceptre. Three times, four times, he shook those awe-inspiring locks and with them moved the earth, the sea, the stars. Then he opened his lips, and spoke these indignant words: 'Never was I more anxious concerning the sovereignty of the universe, no, not even at that time when each of the snaky-footed giants was preparing to throw his hundred arms round the sky and take it captive. For then the attack was made by one small group of enemies and, although they were fierce ones, still the trouble originated from one source. Now the entire human race must be destroyed, throughout all the lands which Nereus surrounds with his roaring waters. I swear by the rivers of the underworld that flow through the Stygian grove beneath the earth: all other remedies have already been tried. This cancer is incurable, and must be cut out by the knife, in case the healthy part become infected. We have the demigods to care for, the spirits of the countryside, nymphs and fauns, satyrs and silvani, who roam the hills. Since we have not, as yet, considered them worthy of the honour of a place in heaven, let us at least ensure that they can live on the earth which we have given them. For can you believe, you gods, that they will go unmolested when Lycaon, a man notorious for his savagery, has laid plots against me, the lord and master of the thunderbolt, aye, and your king and master too?'

All the gods muttered uneasily, and eagerly demanded the punishment of the man who had dared to do such a deed. Their dismay was such as was felt by the human race, when a wicked band of fanatics tried to extinguish the Roman name by shedding Caesar's blood: all men were seized by panic fear of instant destruction, and the whole world shuddered. Just as the loyal devotion of your subjects pleases you, Augustus, so did that of the gods please Jupiter. He checked their murmurs with a word, and as he raised his hand, all fell silent. When the uproar had subsided, hushed by the authority of the king of heaven, Jupiter again broke the silence with these words: "As far as he is concerned, he has paid the penalty. Have no fear on that score. But I shall tell you what his crime was, and what his punishment."

"Scandalous rumours concerning the state of the times had reached my ears. Hoping to find them false, I descended from the heights of Olympus, and walked the earth, a god in human form. It would take long to tell what wickedness I found on every side. Even the scandalous rumours were less than the truth. I had crossed over the ridge of Maenalus, a place bristling with the lairs of wild beasts, over Cyllene, and through the pinewoods of chill Lycaeus. From there, when the last shades of twilight were heralding the night, I entered the inhospitable home of the Arcadian tyrant. I revealed myself as a god, and the people began to do me homage. Lycaon, however, first laughed at their pious prayers, and then exclaimed: 'I shall find out, by an infallible test, whether he be god or mortal: there will be no doubt about the truth.' His plan was to take me unawares, as I lay sound asleep at night, and kill me. This was the test of truth on which he was resolved. Not content with that, he took a hostage sent him by the Molossian people, slit the man's throat with his sharp blade, and cooked his limbs, still warm with life, boiling some and roasting others over the fire. Then he set this banquet on the table. No sooner had he done so, than I with my avenging flames brought the house crashing down upon its household gods, gods worthy of such a master. Lycaon fled, terrified, until he reached the safety of the silent countryside. There he uttered howling noises, and his attempts to speak were all in vain. His clothes changed into bristling hairs, his arms to legs, and he became a wolf. His own savage nature showed in his rabid jaws, and he now directed against the flocks his innate lust for killing. He had a mania, even yet, for shedding blood. But, though he was a wolf, he retained some traces of his original shape. The greyness of his hair was the same, his face showed the same violence, his eyes gleamed as before, and he presented the same picture of ferocity."

"One house has fallen, but far more than one have deserved to perish. To the ends of the earth, the dread Fury holds sway. You would think men had sworn allegiance to crime! They shall all be punished, forthwith, as they deserve. Such is my resolve."

Some of the gods shouted their approval of Jove's words, and sought to increase his indignation: others played the part of silent supporters. Yet all were grieved at the thought of the destruction of the human race, and wondered what the earth would be like, in future, when it had been cleared of mortal inhabitants. They inquired who would bring offerings of incense to their altars, whether Jove meant to abandon the world to the plundering of wild beasts. In answer to their questions, the kin of the gods assured them that they need not be anxious, for he himself would attend to everything. He promised them a new stock of men, unlike the former ones, a race of miraculous origin.

Now he was on the point of launching his thunderbolts against every part of the earth, when he felt a sudden dread lest he should set light to the pure upper air by so many fiery bolts, and send the whole vault of heaven up in flames. He remembered, too, one of fate's decrees, that a time would come when sea and earth and the dome of the sky would blaze up, and the massive structure of the universe collapse in ruins. So he laid aside the weapons forged by the hands of the Cyclopes, and resolved on a different punishment, namely to send rain pouring down from every quarter of the sky, and so destroy mankind beneath the waters.

He wasted no time, but imprisoned the North wind in Aeolus' cave, together with all the gusts which dispel the gathering clouds; and he let loose the South wind. On dripping wings the South wind flew, his terrible features shrouded in pitchy darkness. His beard was heavy with rain, water streamed from his hoary locks, mists wreathed his brow, his robes and feathers dripped with moisture. When he crushed the hanging clouds in his broad hand, there was a crash; thereafter sheets of rain poured down from heaven. Juno's messenger Iris, clad in rainbow hues, drew up water and supplied nourishment to the clouds. The corn was laid low, and the crops the farmer had prayed for now lay flattened and sadly mourned, the long year's toil was wasted and gone for nothing.

Nor was Jupiter's anger satisfied with the resources of his own realm of heaven: his brother Neptune, the god of the sea, lent him the assistance of his waves. He sent forth a summons to the rivers, and when they entered their king's home: "No time now for long exhortations!" he cried. "Exert your strength to the utmost: that is what we need. Fling wide your homes, withdraw all barriers, and give free course to your waters." These were his orders. The rivers returned to their homes and, opening up the mouths of their springs, went rushing to the sea in frenzied torrents.

Neptune himself struck the earth with his trident; it trembled, and by its movement threw open channels for the waters. Across the wide plains the rivers raced, overflowing their banks, sweeping away in one torrential flood crops and orchards, cattle and men, houses and temples, sacred images and all. Any building which did manage to survive this terrible disaster unshaken and remain standing, was in the end submerged when some wave yet higher than the rest covered its roof, and its gables lay drowned beneath the waters. Now sea and earth could no longer be distinguished: all was sea, and a sea that had no shores.

Some tried to escape by climbing to the hilltops, others, sitting in the curved boats, plied the oars where lately they had been ploughing; some sailed over cornlands, over the submerged roofs of their homes, while some found fish in the topmost branches of the elms. At times it happened that they dropped anchor in green meadows, sometimes the curved keels grazed vineyards that lay beneath them. Where lately sinewy goats cropped the grass, now ugly seals disported themselves. The Nereids wondered to see groves and towns and houses under the water; dolphins took possession of the woods, and dashed against high branches, shaking the oak trees as they knocked against them. Wolves swam among the flocks, and the waves supported tawny lions, and tigers too. The lightning stroke of his strong tusk was of no use, then, to the wild boar, nor his swift legs to the stag—both alike were swept away. Wandering birds searched long for some land where they might rest, till their wings grew weary and they fell into the sea. The ocean, all restrains removed, overwhelmed the hills, and waves were washing the mountain peaks, a sight never seen before. The greater part of the human race was swallowed up by the waters: those whom the sea spared died from lack of food, overcome by long-continued famine.

There is a land, Phocis, which separates the fields of Boeotia from those of Oeta. It was a fertile spot while it was land, but now had become part of the sea, a broad stretch of waters, suddenly formed. In that region a high mountain, called Parnassus, raises twin summits to the stars, and its ridges pierce the clouds. When the waters had covered all the rest of the earth, the little boat which carried Deucalion and his wife ran aground here. Of all the men who ever lived, Deucalion was the best and the most upright, no woman ever showed more reverence for the gods than Pyrrha, his wife. Their first action was to offer prayers to the Corycian nymphs, to the deities of the mountain, and to Themis, the goddess who foretold the future from its oracular shrine.

Now Jupiter saw the earth all covered with standing waters. He perceived that one alone survived of so many thousand men, one only of so many thousand women, and he knew that both were guiltless, both true worshippers of god. So, with the help of the North wind he drove away the storm clouds and, scattering the veils of mist, displayed heaven to earth and earth to heaven. The sea was no longer angry, for the ruler of ocean soothed the waves, laying aside his trident. Then he called to the sea-god Triton, who rose from the deep, his shoulders covered with clustering shellfish. Neptune bade him blow on his echoing conch shell, and recall waves and rivers by his signal. He lifted his hollow trumpet, a coiling instrument which broadens out in circling spirals from its base. When he blows upon it in mid-ocean, its notes fill the furthest shores of east and west. So now, too, the god put it to his lips, which were all damp from his dripping beard, and blew it, sending forth the signal for retreat as he had been bidden. The sound was heard by all the waters that covered earth and sea, and all the waves which heard it were checked in their course. The sea had shores once more, the swollen rivers were contained within their own channels, the floods sank down, and hills were seen to emerge. Earth rose up, its lands advancing as the waves retreated, and after a long interval the woods displayed their treetops uncovered, the mud left behind still clinging to their leaves.

The world was restored: but when Deucalion saw its emptiness, the desolate lands all deeply silent, tears started to his eyes, and he said to Pyrrha: "My cousin, my wife, the only woman left alive, related to me first by birth and blood, then joined to me in marriage—now, Pyrrha, our very dangers unite us. We two are the sole inhabitants of all the lands which east and west behold. The sea has taken the rest. Indeed, even yet, I feel no certainty that we shall survive; even now the clouds strike terror to my heart. What would your feelings be now, my poor wife, had fate snatched you to safety, without saving me? How could you have endured your fears, had you been left all alone? Who would have comforted you in your grief? For believe me, if the sea had taken you with the rest, I should follow you, my dear one, and the sea would have me too. If only I could create the nations anew, by my father's skill! If only I could mould the earth and give it breath: now the human race depends upon us two. It is god's will: we have been left as samples of mankind." So he spoke, and they wept together.

Then they decided to pray to the god in heaven, and to seek help from the holy oracle. Without delay, they went side by side to the waters of Cephisus which, though not yet clear, were already flowing in their accustomed channel. When they had sprinkled their heads and garments with water drawn from the river they turned their steps to the shrine of the holy goddess. The gables of the temple were discoloured with foul moss, and its altars stood unlit. At the temple steps they both fell forward, prone upon the ground, and timidly kissed the chill rock, saying: "If the gods may be touched and softened by the prayers of the righteous, if divine anger may be thus turned aside, tell us, O Themis, how we may repair the destruction that has overtaken our race. Most gentle goddess, assist us in our distress."

The goddess pitied them, and uttered this oracle. "Depart from my temple, veil your heads, loosen the girdles of your garments and throw behind you the bones of your great mother." For long they stood in speechless wonder at this reply. Pyrrha was the first to break the silence, by declaring that she would not obey the commands of the goddess. With trembling lips she prayed to be excused: for she was afraid to injure her mother's ghost by disturbing her bones. But meanwhile they considered again the words of the oracle, so puzzling and obscure, and pondered them deeply: till after a time the son of Prometheus soothed the fears of Epimetheus' daughter with these comforting words: "Oracles are righteous, and never advise guilty action; so, unless my intuition deceives me, our great mother is the earth, and by her bones I think the oracle means the stones in the body of the earth. It is those we are instructed to throw behind our backs." The Titan's daughter was impressed by her husband's surmise; but she did not trust her hopes, for neither of them had any confidence in heaven's counsel. Still, there could be no harm in putting the matter to the test.

They went down the hillside, veiled their heads, loosened their tunics, and threw the stones behind them, as they had been bidden. Who would believe what followed, did not ancient tradition bear witness to it? The stones began to lose their hardness and rigidity, and after a little, grew soft. Then, once softened, they acquired a definite shape. When they had grown in size, and developed a tenderer nature, a certain likeness to a human form could be seen, though it was still not clear: they were like marble images, begun but not yet properly chiselled out, or like unfinished statues. The damp earthy parts, containing some moisture, were adapted to make the body: that which was solid and inflexible became bone. What was lately a vein in the rock kept the same name, and in a brief space of time, thanks to the divine will of the gods, the stones thrown from male hands took on the appearance of men, while from those the woman threw, women were recreated. So it comes about that we are a hardy race, well accustomed to toil, giving evidence of the origin from which we sprang.

Other animals of different kinds were produced by the earth, of its own accord, when the long-lingering moisture was warmed through by the rays of the sun. Then the mud and soggy marshes swelled under the heat, and fertile seeds, nourished in the life-giving earth as in a mother's womb, grew and in the fullness of time acquired a definite shape. This is what happens when the Nile, the river with seven mouths, recedes from the flooded fields and returns its streams to their original bed. The new mud becomes burning hot under the sun's rays, and the farmers, as they turn over the sods of earth, come upon many animals. Among these creatures they see some just begun, but already on the point of coming alive, others unfinished, lacking their full complement of limbs; and often in one and the same body one part is alive, while another is still only raw earth. Indeed, when heat and moisture have reached the proper balance, they bring forth life, and all things are born from these two elements. Although fire and water are always opposites, none the less moist heat is the source of everything, and this discordant harmony is suited to creation.

So when the earth, all muddied by the recent flood, grew warm again, under the kindly radiance of the sun in heaven, she brought forth countless forms of life. In some cases she reproduced shapes which had been previously known, others were new and strange.

[ARACHNE]

When Minerva had listened to such stories, she expressed her approval of the Muses' song, and of their righteous indignation. Then she said to herself: "It is not enough to praise other people: what I want is to be praised myself, and not to have others scorn my divine powers with impunity." As she spoke, her thoughts turned to the fortunes of Arachne, a young woman of Maeonia, whose skill in spinning, so the goddess had heard, was earning no less admiration than that of Minerva herself. Arachne was not of high rank, or noble family, but her talent had made her famous. Her father was a native of Colophon, called Idmon, who earned his living by dying absorbent wool with Phocaean purple. Her mother was dead, but she also had been of humble origin, no better than her husband. Their daughter, however, although she had been born in a cottage and still lived in the small village of Hypaepae, had gained a reputation throughout all Lydia by reason of her skill. Often the nymphs used to leave the vine-clad slopes of their beloved Tmolus to admire her work, and the river nymphs came from the waters of Pactolus. They enjoyed seeing the cloths, not only when they were completed, but even while they were still being woven. There was such grace in Arachne's skilful movements, whether she was winding the coarse yarn into balls in the first stages of her task, or working the stuff with her fingers, drawing out the fleecy cloud of wool, with constant handling, into one long soft thread, or whether she was twirling the slender spindle with deft thumb, or embroidering the finished material.

It was easy to see that she had been taught by Pallas: but the girl herself denied this. Offended at the suggestion that she had had any teacher, no matter how distinguished, "Let Pallas come and compete with me!" she cried. "If I am defeated, she can do what she likes with me!" Pallas made herself up as an old woman, put false streaks of grey in the hair at her temples, and took a stick to support her tottering steps. Then she began to speak to Arachne, saying: "Not all the things that old age brings in its train are to be shunned: with advancing years, we gain experience. Pay heed, then, to my advice; seek recognition as the best of all mortal spinners, but admit the supremacy of the goddess, and humbly ask her pardon for your hot-headed words. She will forgive you, if you ask her." Arachne left the piece of weaving which she had begun. She eyed the old woman sullenly, and could scarcely keep herself from striking her. Anger showed plainly on her face, as she answered Pallas, whom, of course, she did not recognize. "You have lived too long," she said, "that is what is wrong with you. You are worn out with old age, and your mind is feeble too. If you have any daughters or daughters-in-law, let them listen to what you have to say. I can look after myself. Don't imagine that your warnings have had any effect on me; I am still of the same opinion. Why does Pallas not come in person? Why does she avoid my challenge?" "She has come!" cried the goddess and, throwing off the disguise of an old woman, she revealed that she was indeed Pallas.

The nymphs and women of Mygdonia reverently humbled themselves before the goddess. They were all terrified, except Arachne, and even she leaped to her feet, and a sudden flush swept over her unwilling cheeks, and receded again, just as the sky crimsons when Aurora first stirs, but in a little while shines white with the light of sunrise. She persisted in going on with her plan and, in her eagerness for a victory which she foolishly thought she could win, rushed upon her fate. Jove's daughter uttered no more warnings; she accepted the challenge, and postponed the competition no further. Without wasting any time, she and Arachne took their stance in different parts of the room, and each stretched the slender threads on her loom. Then they bound their frames to the crossbeams, separated the threads of the warp with the heddle and, with flying fingers wove the crossthreads in between, by means of the sharp-tipped shuttles. As these threads were drawn through the warp, a blow from the comb with its notched teeth beat them into place. With their garments tucked up beneath their breasts, out of the way, the goddess and the girl worked with all speed, their hands moving skilfully over the looms. In their eagerness, they were not conscious of the labour involved. Into the cloth they wove threads dyed purple in Tyrian coppers, shades of colour differing so slightly that they could scarcely be distinguished: so, after a shower, when the sunlit rainbow paints heaven's vault with its long arc, though a thousand different colours shine there, the transition from one to another is so gradual that the eye of the beholder cannot perceive it. Where they met, the colours look the same, yet their outer bands are completely different. Pliant gold thread, too, was interwoven, as old stories were pictured on the looms.

Pallas' tapestry showed the rock of Mars, on the acropolis of Cecrops' city, and the ancient contest that took place there, to determine what name the land should have. Twelve gods, in all their glorious majesty, were seated on lofty thrones, with Jupiter in their midst. Each of the gods was recognized by his own particular features: the figure of Jove was one of royal dignity, while Neptune was standing up, striking the rugged rocks with his long trident. From the cleft, the sea gushed out, and by this token he claimed the city. To herself, Pallas gave a shield and a sharp-tipped spear. On her head she wore her helmet, and her breast was protected by the aegis. Then she showed the earth putting forth a hoary olive tree, complete with berries, where she had struck the ground with her spear. The gods were gazing in awe at this miracle, and the figure of Victory completed the picture.

Then, to give her rival illustrations of the reward she might expect for her insane audacity, the goddess added four scenes, depicting contests, one in each corner, all brilliantly coloured, though shown in miniature. One corner held Haemon and Thracian Rhodope, now icy mountains but once human beings, who dared to give themselves the names of the greatest of the gods. A second corner showed the unhappy fate of the queen of the Pygmies. Juno, after defeating her in a contest, had ordained that she become a crane, and declare war on her own people. The goddess portrayed Antigone too, who once dared to compete with the consort of almighty Jupiter: royal Juno changed her into a bird. Neither the city of Troy nor her father, Laomedon, could save her then. She grew wings and, as a shining white stork, still applauds herself with clattering beak. The remaining corner showed Cinyras after his bereavement, embracing the temple steps which had once been his daughters' limbs, and weeping as he lay on the stone. Then Pallas embroidered the edges with olives, the symbol of peace. This was the end of her task: she finished her weaving with her own tree.

Arachne wove a picture of Europa, deceived by Jupiter when he presented himself in the shape of a bull. You would have thought that the bull was a live one, and that the waves were real waves. Europa herself was seen, looking back at the shore she had left behind, crying to her companions, and timidly drawing up her feet, shrinking from the touch of the surging waters. The tapestry showed Asterie too, held fast by the struggling eagle, and Leda reclining under the swan's wings. Then the girl added further pictures of Jupiter in disguise, showing how he turned himself into a satyr to bestow twins on fair Antiope, and assumed the likeness of Amphitryon when he embraced the lady of Tiryns: how he tricked Danae by changing into a shower of gold, deceived Asopus' daughter as a flame, Mnemosyne as a shepherd, and Demeter's daughter, Proserpine, as a spotted snake.

She showed Neptune, too, changed into a fierce bull for his affair with Aeolus' daughter. Disguised as the river god Enipeus, he was making love to Aloeus' wife, who later bore him twin sons, and he was deceiving Bisaltis as a ram. The golden-haired mother of the corn crops, gentlest of goddesses, knew him in the shape of a horse, Melantho as a dolphin, and to the snaky-haired princess, who was the mother of the winged steed, he appeared as a bird. All these incidents were correctly depicted, people and places had their authentic features.

Phoebus was there, in peasant garb, and other scenes showed how he dressed himself, at one time in a hawk's plumage, at another in a lion's skin, and how he disguised himself as a shepherd to deceive Macareus' daughter, Isse. There was also a picture of Bacchus, tricking Erigone with the semblance of a bunch of grapes, and one of Saturn, in the shape of a horse, creating the centaur Chiron, half horse, half man. The outer edge of the cloth, bordered by a fine hem, was gay with flowers, intertwined with clustering ivy.

Neither Pallas nor even Jealousy personified could find any flaw in the work. The golden-haired goddess, wild with indignation at her rival's success, tore to pieces the tapestry which displayed the crimes committed by the gods. Then, with the shuttle of Cytorian boxwood which she held in her hand, three times, four times, she struck Idmon's daughter on the forehead. Arachne found her plight beyond endurance: with a fine show of spirit, she fastened a noose round her neck, to hang herself. But Pallas pitied her, as she hung there; lifting her up, the goddess said: "You may go on living, you wicked girl, but you must be suspended in the air like this, all the time. Do not hope for any respite in the future—this same condition is imposed on your race, to your remote descendants." Then, as she departed, she sprinkled Arachne with the juice of Hecate's herb. Immediately, at the touch of this baneful potion, the girl's hair dropped out, her nostrils and her ears went too, and her head shrank almost to nothing. Her whole body, likewise, became tiny. Her slender fingers were fastened to her sides, to serve as legs, and all the rest of her was belly; from that belly, she yet spins her thread, and as a spider is busy with her web as of old.

Interior View. Hagia Sophia, Istanbul, Turkey. Courtesy of Giraudon/Art Resource, NY.

The World Beyond Rome

The Church of *Hagia Sophia* ("Holy Wisdom") is a great work of architecture and also a perfect emblem for "the world beyond Rome." It is located on a promontory in Istanbul, the old city of Byzantium that the Emperor Constantine made the capital—Constantinople—of the Roman Empire early in the fourth century. Hagia Sophia was built under the direction of the Emperor Justinian; his architects, Anthemius of Tralles and Isidore of Miletus, saw to its completion in 537 after less than six years of construction. Its complex plan makes extravagant use of the triumphs of Roman engineering, the arch and the dome. It is, furthermore, a combination of the square Greek Cross common in eastern basilicas, with the longer Roman basilica common in the western church: the half-domes on opposite ends give the illusion of great length, while a triple aisle along the other two sides make for a square outline on the ground. The church also brilliantly uses the innovative pendentive, the curved triangle that joins the large supporting arches with the base of the dome. The pendentives and other open surfaces were covered with the mosaics (now lost or damaged) that glorified Byzantine churches. But Hagia Sophia shows signs of the other sea change in the post-Roman world. In 1453 the Ottoman (Turkish) emperor Mehmed II defeated Constantinople. When he entered the city, he is said to have marched straight to Hagia Sophia, the city's chief emblem of Byzantine Christianity, and converted it to an Islamic mosque. In the photograph at left the large medallions with Arabic calligraphy can be seen. On the walls the representational art of Byzantine Christianity has been replaced by the abstract arabesque of Islam.

Tacitus (c.55–c.117)

The great historian of the early Roman Empire, Tacitus, gives us a strong sense of the reach of the Roman Empire, both in territory and into peoples' lives. Tacitus was a senator who turned to the writing of history during the reigns of the "good emperors" in the second century, when it was again possible to write freely and critically of the empire. Writing about the great period of colonial expansion, Tacitus studied closely the enemies of Rome. Because he was intent on exposing the corruption of emperors like Nero, he was willing to look at the cultures and practices of the Jews or of the German tribes and praise their integrity where he found it, especially in contrast to Roman failures.

The groups that Tacitus described—the Jews, the Christians, the Germans—developed in important ways during the period of the empire and after. Other readings in this section show some of those developments. The Germans, who eventually would be the conquerors of the Romans, always threatened the outposts of the empire. Christianity rode with travelers, Roman soldiers, and other converts to all parts of the empire, becoming at the same time a convenient scapegoat for emperors like Nero. Yet when Rome collapsed, a skeleton of Roman Christianity was left standing. Judaism responded to Roman attempts to destroy its heart in Jerusalem by strengthening the preservation of its learning and tradition through rabbis at the periphery.

The Annals [The Burning of Rome]

38. There followed a dreadful disaster; whether fortuitously, or by the wicked contrivance of the prince, is not determined, for both are asserted by historians: but of all the calamities which ever befell this city from the rage of fire, this was the most terrible and severe. It broke out in that part of the Circus which is contiguous to mounts Palatine and Cœlius; where, by reason of shops in which were kept such goods as minister

The versions used here are from *The Oxford Translation, Revised* (London: Bell, 1903), except for *Germania,* which is translated by Alfred John Church and William Jackson Brodribb, reprinted in Random House's Modern Library in 1942.

aliment to fire, the moment it commenced it acquired strength, and being accelerated by the wind, it spread at once through the whole extent of the Circus: for neither were the houses secured by enclosures, nor the temples environed with walls, nor was there any other obstacle to intercept its progress; but the flame, spreading every way impetuously, invaded first the lower regions of the city, then mounted to the higher; then again ravaging the lower, it baffled every effort to extinguish it, by the rapidity of its destructive course, and from the liability of the city to conflagration, in consequence of the narrow and intricate alleys, and the irregularity of the streets in ancient Rome. Add to this, the wailings of terrified women, the infirm condition of the aged, and the helplessness of childhood: such as strove to provide for themselves and those who laboured to assist others; these dragging the feeble, those waiting for them; some hurrying, others lingering; altogether created a scene of universal confusion and embarrassment: and while they looked back upon the danger in their rear, they often found themselves beset before, and on their sides: or if they had escaped into the quarters adjoining, these too were already seized by the devouring flames; even the parts which they believed remote and exempt, were found to be in the same distress. At last, not knowing what to shun, or where to seek sanctuary, they crowded the streets, and lay along in the open fields. Some, from the loss of their whole substance, even the means of their daily sustenance, others, from affection for their relations, whom they had not been able to snatch from the flames, suffered themselves to perish in them, though they had opportunity to escape. Neither dared any man offer to check the fire: so repeated were the menaces of many who forbade to extinguish it; and because others openly threw firebrands, with loud declarations "that they had one who authorized them;" whether they did it that they might plunder with the less restraint, or in consequence of orders given.

39. Nero, who was at that juncture sojourning at Antium, did not return to the city till the fire approached that quarter of his house which connected the palace with the gardens of Mæcenas; nor could it, however, be prevented from devouring the house and palace, and everything around. But for the relief of the people, thus destitute, and driven from their dwellings, he opened the field of Mars and the monumental edifices erected by Agrippa, and even his own gardens. He likewise reared temporary houses for the reception of the forlorn multitude: and from Ostia and the neighbouring cities, were brought, up the river, household necessaries; and the price of grain was reduced to three sesterces the measure. All which proceedings, though of a popular character, were thrown away, because a rumour had become universally current, "that at the very time the city was in flames, Nero, going on the stage of his private theatre, sang 'The Destruction of Troy,' assimilating the present disaster to that catastrophe of ancient times."

40. At length, on the sixth day, the conflagration was stayed at the foot of Esquiliæ, by pulling down an immense quantity of buildings, so that an open space, and, as it were, void air, might check the raging element by breaking the continuity. But ere the consternation had subsided, the fire broke out afresh, with no little violence, but in regions more spacious, and therefore with less destruction of human life: but more extensive havoc was made of the temples, and the porticoes dedicated to amusement. This conflagration, too, was the subject of more censorious remark, as it arose in the Æmilian possessions of Tigellinus: and Nero seemed to aim at the glory of building a new city, and calling it by his own name: for, of the fourteen sections into which Rome is divided, four were still standing entire, three were levelled with

the ground, and in the seven others there remained only here and there a few remnants of houses, shattered and half consumed.

41. It were no very easy task to recount the number of tenements and temples which were lost: but the following, most venerable for antiquity and sanctity, were consumed: that dedicated by Servius Tullius to the Moon; the temple and great altar consecrated by Evander the Arcadian to Hercules while present; the chapel vowed by Romulus to Jupiter Stator; the palace of Numa, with the temple of Vesta, and in it the tutelar gods of Rome. Moreover, the treasures accumulated by so many victories, the beautiful productions of Greek artists, ancient writings of authors celebrated for genius, and till then preserved entire, were consumed: and though great was the beauty of the city, in its renovated form, the older inhabitants remembered many decorations of the ancient which could not be replaced in the modern city. There were some who remarked that the commencement of the fire showed itself on the fourteenth before the calends of July, the day on which the Senones set fire to the captured city. Others carried their investigation so far as to determine that an equal number of years, months, and days intervened between the two fires.

42. To proceed: Nero appropriated to his own purposes the ruins of his country, and founded upon them a palace; in which the old-fashioned, and, in those luxurious times, common ornaments of gold and precious stones, were not so much the objects of attraction as lands and lakes; in one part, woods like vast deserts; in another part, open spaces and expansive prospects. The projectors and superintendents of this plan were Severus and Celer, men of such ingenuity and daring enterprise as to attempt to conquer by art the obstacles of nature, and fool away the treasures of the prince: they had even undertaken to sink a navigable canal from the lake Avernus to the mouth of the Tiber, over an arid shore, or through opposing mountains: nor indeed does there occur anything of a humid nature for supplying water, except the Pomptine marshes; the rest is either craggy rock or a parched soil: and had it even been possible to break through these obstructions, the toil had been intolerable, and disproportioned to the object. Nero, however, who longed to achieve things that exceeded credibility, exerted all his might to perforate the mountains adjoining to Avernus: and to this day there remain traces of his abortive project.

43. But the rest of the old site not occupied by his palace was laid out, not as after the Gallic fire, without discrimination and regularity, but with the lines of streets measured out, broad spaces left for transit, the height of the buildings limited, open areas left, and porticoes added to protect the front of the clustered dwellings: these porticoes Nero engaged to rear at his own expense, and then to deliver to each proprietor the areas about them cleared. He moreover proposed rewards proportioned to every man's rank and private substance, and fixed a day within which, if their houses, single or clustered, were finished, they should receive them: he appointed the marshes of Ostia for a receptacle of the rubbish, and that the vessels which had conveyed the grain up the Tiber should return laden with rubbish; that the buildings themselves should be raised to a certain portion of their height without beams, and arched with stone from the quarries of Gabii or Alba, that stone being proof against fire: that over the water springs, which had been improperly intercepted by private individuals, overseers should be placed, to provide for their flowing in greater abundance, and in a greater number of places, for the supply of the public: that every housekeeper should have in his yard means for extinguishing fire; neither should there be party-walls, but

every house should be enclosed by its own walls. These regulations, which were favourably received, in consideration of their utility, were also a source of beauty to the new city: yet some there were who believed that the ancient form was more conducive to health, as from the narrowness of the streets and the height of the buildings the rays of the sun were more excluded; whereas now, the spacious breadth of the streets, without any shade to protect it, was more intensely heated in warm weather.

44. Such were the provisions made by human counsels. The gods were next addressed with expiations; and recourse had to the Sibyl's books. By admonition from them to Vulcan, Ceres, and Proserpina, supplicatory sacrifices were made, and Juno propitiated by the matrons, first in the Capitol, then upon the nearest shore, where, by water drawn from the sea, the temple and image of the goddess were besprinkled; and the ceremony of placing the goddess in her sacred chair, and her vigil, were celebrated by ladies who had husbands. But not all the relief that could come from man, not all the bounties that the prince could bestow, nor all the atonements which could be presented to the gods, availed to relieve Nero of the infamy of being believed to have ordered the conflagration. Hence, to suppress the rumour, he falsely charged with the guilt, and punished with the most exquisite tortures, the persons commonly called Christians, who were hated for their enormities. Christus, the founder of that name, was put to death as a criminal by Pontius Pilate, procurator of Judea, in the reign of Tiberius: but the pernicious superstition, repressed for a time, broke out again, not only through Judea, where the mischief originated, but through the city of Rome also, whither all things horrible and disgraceful flow, from all quarters, as to a common receptacle, and where they are encouraged. Accordingly, first those were seized who confessed they were Christians: next, on their information, a vast multitude were convicted, not so much on the charge of burning the city, as of hating the human race. And in their deaths they were also made the subjects of sport, for they were covered with the hides of wild beasts, and worried to death by dogs, or nailed to crosses, or set fire to, and when day declined, burnt to serve for nocturnal lights. Nero offered his own gardens for that spectacle, and exhibited a Circensian game, indiscriminately mingling with the common people in the habit of a charioteer, or else standing in his chariot. Whence a feeling of compassion arose towards the sufferers, though guilty and deserving to be made examples of by capital punishment, because they seemed not to be cut off for the public good, but victims to the ferocity of one man.

The History [The Jews]

1. In the beginning of the same year, Titus, who was appointed by his father to complete the subjugation of Judaea, and who, when both were no higher than subjects, had gained a reputation for military talents, now exercised a more extended influence, and shone with augmented lustre; the provinces and armies emulating each other in their zeal and attachment to him. Titus, on his part, that he might be thought deserving of still higher distinctions, appeared in all the splendour of external embellishments, and showed himself a prompt and resolute soldier, challenging respect by courtesy and affability; mixing with the common soldiers when engaged in the works and on their march, without impairing the dignity of the general. He succeeded to the command of three legions in Judaea, the fifth, the tenth, and the fifteenth; who had long served under Vespasian. To these he added the twelfth, from

Syria, and the third and twenty-second, withdrawn from Alexandria. He was attended, besides, by twenty cohorts of the allies, and eight squadrons of horse, with the two kings Agrippa and Sohemus, and auxiliaries from Antiochus. He had also a band of Arabs, formidable in themselves, and harbouring towards the Jews the bitter animosity usually subsisting between neighbouring nations. Many persons had come from Rome and Italy, each impelled by the hopes he had of preoccupying the favour of a prince who had not yet chosen his friends. With this force Titus, advancing into the enemy's country in order of battle, by his scouts diligently exploring the motions of the enemy, and prepared for action, formed a camp a short distance from Jerusalem.

2. Being now about to relate the catastrophe of that celebrated city, it seems fitting that I should unfold the particulars of its origin. The Jews, we are told, escaping from the island of Crete, at the time when Saturn was driven from his throne by the violence of Jupiter, settled in the extreme parts of Libya. Their name is adduced as a proof. Ida, it is alleged, is a well-known mountain in Crete: the neighbouring Idaeans, by an addition to the name to adapt it to the language of barbarians, are ordinarily called Judaeans. Some say that the population, overflowing throughout Egypt, in the reign of Isis, was relieved by emigration into the neighbouring countries, under the conduct of Hierosolymus and Juda. Many state that they are the progeny of the Aethiopians, who were impelled by fear and detestation to change their abode in the reign of king Cepheus. There are those who report that they are a heterogeneous band from Assyria, a people who, being destitute of a country, made themselves masters of a portion of Egypt, and subsequently settled in cities of their own in the Hebrew territories, and the parts bordering on Syria. Others, ascribing to the Jews an illustrious origin, say that the Solymi, a nation celebrated in the poetry of Homer, called the city which they built Hierosolyma from their own name.

3. Very many authors agree in recording that a pestilential disease, which disfigured the body in a loathsome manner, spreading over Egypt, Bocchoris, at that time king, repairing to the oracle of Jupiter Hammon, in quest of a remedy, was directed to purify his kingdom, and exterminate that race of men as being detested by the gods: that a mass of people thus searched out and collected together were in a wild and barren desert abandoned to their misery, when, all the rest being bathed in tears and torpid with despair, Moses, one of the exiles, admonished them not to look for any aid from gods or men, being deserted of both, but to trust themselves to him as a heaven-commissioned guide, by whose aid already they had warded off the miseries that beset them. They assented, and commenced a venturous journey, not knowing whither they went. But nothing distressed them so much as want of water; and now they lay stretched through all the plains, ready to expire, when a herd of wild asses, returning from pasture, went up a rock shaded with a grove. Moses followed them, and forming his conjecture by the herbage that grew upon the ground, opened copious springs of water. This was a relief; and pursuing their journey for six days without intermission, on the seventh, having expelled the natives, they took possession of a country where they built their city, and dedicated their temple.

4. In order to bind the people to him for the time to come, Moses prescribed to them a new form of worship, and opposed to those of all the world beside. Whatever is held sacred by the Romans, with the Jews is profane: and what in other nations is unlawful and impure, with them is permitted. The figure of the animal through

whose guidance they slaked their thirst, and were enabled to terminate their wanderings, is consecrated in the sanctuary in their temple; while in contempt of Jupiter Hammon, they sacrifice a ram. The ox, worshipped in Egypt for the god Apis, is slain as a victim by the Jews. They abstain from the flesh of swine, from the recollection of the loathsome affliction which they had formerly suffered from leprosy, to which that animal is subject. The famine, with which they were for a long time distressed, is still commemorated by frequent fastings; and the Jewish bread, made without leaven, is a standing evidence of their seizure of corn. They say that they instituted a rest on the seventh day because that day brought them rest from their toils; but afterwards, charmed with the pleasures of idleness, the seventh year also was devoted to sloth. Others allege that this is an honour rendered to Saturn, either because their religious institutes were handed down by the Idaeans, who, we are informed, were expelled from their country with Saturn, and were the founders of the nation; or else because, of the seven stars by which men are governed, the star of Saturn moves in the highest orbit, and exercises the greatest influence; and most of the heavenly bodies complete their effects and course by the number seven.

5. These rites and ceremonies, howsoever introduced, have the support of antiquity. Their other institutions, which have been extensively adopted, are tainted with execrable knavery; for the scum and refuse of other nations, renouncing the religion of their country, were in the habit of bringing gifts and offerings to Jerusalem,—hence the wealth and grandeur of the state; and also because faith is inviolably observed, and compassion is cheerfully shown towards each other, while the bitterest animosity is harboured against all others. They eat and lodge with one another only; and though a people of unbridled lust, they admit no intercourse with women from other nations. Among themselves no restraints are imposed. That they may be known by a distinctive mark, they have established the practice of circumcision. All who embrace their faith submit to the same operation. The first thing instilled into their proselytes is to despise the gods, to abjure their country, to set at nought parents, children, brothers. They show concern, however, for the increase of their population, for it is forbidden to put any of their brethren to death; and the souls of such as die in battle, or by the hand of the executioner, are thought to be immortal. Hence their desire of procreation, and contempt of death. The bodies of the deceased they choose rather to bury than burn, following in this the Egyptian custom; with whom they also agree in their attention to the dead, and their persuasion as to the regions below, but are opposed to them in their notions about celestial things. The Egyptians worship various animals and images, the work of men's hands; the Jews acknowledge one God only, and conceive of him by the mind alone, condemning, as impious, all who, with perishable materials, wrought into the human shape, form representations of the Deity. That Being, they say, is above all, and everlasting, neither susceptible of likeness nor subject to decay. In consequence they allow no resemblance of him in their city, much less in their temples. In this way they do not flatter their kings, nor show their respect for the Caesars. But because their priests performed in concert with the pipe and timbrels, were crowned with ivy, and a golden vine was found in the temple, some have supposed that Bacchus, the conqueror of the East, was the object of their adoration; but the Jewish institutions have no conformity whatever to the rites of Bacchus. For Bacchus has ordained festive and jocund rites, while the usages of the Jews are dull and repulsive. . . .

9. Pompey was the first Roman that subdued the Jews, and by right of conquest entered their temple. Thenceforward it became generally known that the habitation was empty, and the sanctuary unoccupied, no representation of the Deity being found within it. The walls of the city were levelled to the ground; the Temple remained. In the civil wars that afterwards shook the empire, when the eastern provinces fell to the lot of Mark Antony, Pacorus, the Parthian king, made himself master of Judaea; but was, in a short time after, put to death by Ventidius, and his forces retired beyond the Euphrates. Caius Sosius once more reduced the Jews to obedience. Herod was placed on the throne by Mark Antony, and Augustus enlarged his privileges. On the death of Herod, a man of the name of Simon, without waiting for the authority of the emperor, seized the sovereignty. He, however, was punished for his ambition by Quinctilius Varus, the governor of Syria; and the nation, reduced to submission, was divided in three portions between the sons of Herod. During the reign of Tiberius things remained in a state of tranquillity. Afterwards, being ordered by Caligula to place his statue in the Temple, the Jews, rather than submit, had recourse to arms. This commotion the death of Caligula extinguished. Claudius, the Jewish kings being either dead, or the dominion reduced to narrow limits, committed the province of Judaea to Roman knights, or his freedmen. One of these, Antonius Felix, exercised the prerogatives of a king with the spirit of a slave, rioting in cruelty and licentiousness. He married Drusilla, the granddaughter of Antony and Cleopatra, that he might be grandson-in-law of Mark Antony, who was the grandfather of Claudius.

10. The patience, however, of the Jews held out to the time of Cassius Florus, the procurator. Under him a war broke out. Cestius Gallus, the governor of Syria, endeavoured to crush the revolt. He fought some obstinate battles, most of them unsuccessfully. After his death, which happened either by destiny or from disappointment and vexation, Vespasian, who was sent by Nero, succeeded to the command. By his character, the good fortune that attended his arms, and with the advantage of excellent officers, in two summer campaigns he overran the whole country, and made himself master of all the cities except Jerusalem. The following year, which was devoted to civil war, passed in tranquillity so far as concerned the Jews. The peace of Italy restored, the care of foreign affairs returned. It inflamed his resentment that the Jews were the only nation that had not submitted. At the same time it was deemed politic for Titus to remain at the head of the armies, with a view to any events or casualties that might arise under the new reign. Accordingly the prince, as already mentioned, encamped under the walls of Jerusalem, and displayed his legions in the face of the enemy.

11. The Jews formed in order of battle under the very walls, determined, if successful, to push forward; and, if obliged to give ground, secure of a retreat. The cavalry, with the light-armed cohorts, sent against them, fought with doubtful success. Soon the enemy gave way, and on the following days engaged in frequent skirmishes before the gates, till at length, after a series of losses, they were forced to retire within the walls. The Romans resolved now to carry the place by storm. To linger before it till famine compelled a surrender, appeared indeed unworthy of them, and the soldiers demanded the post of danger, some from courage, many from hardihood and the hope of gaining rewards. Rome, her splendours and her pleasures, kept flitting before the eyes of Titus himself; and if Jerusalem did not fall at once, he looked upon

it as obstructing his enjoyments. But Jerusalem, standing upon an eminence, naturally difficult of approach, was rendered still more impregnable by redoubts and bulwarks by which even places on a level plain would have been competently fortified. Two hills that rose to a prodigious height were enclosed by walls constructed so as in some places to project in angles, in others to curve inwards. In consequence the flanks of the besiegers were exposed to the enemy's weapons. The extremities of the rock were abrupt and craggy; and the towers were built, upon the mountain, sixty feet high; in the low ground, a hundred and twenty feet. These works presented a spectacle altogether astonishing. To the distant eye they seemed to be an equal elevation. Within the city there were other fortifications enclosing the palace of the kings, and the tower of Antonia, with its conspicuous pinnacles, so called by Herod, in honour of Mark Antony.

12. The Temple itself was in the nature of a citadel, enclosed in walls of its own, and more elaborate and massy than the rest. The very porticoes that surrounded it were a capital defence. A perennial spring supplied the place with water. Subterraneous caverns were scooped out in the mountains, and there were basins and tanks as reservoirs of rain-water. It was foreseen by the founders of the city, that the manners and institutions of the nation, so repugnant to the rest of mankind, would be productive of frequent wars; hence every kind of provision against a siege, howsoever protracted; and exposed as they had been to the successful assault of Pompey, their fears and experience had taught them many expedients. On the other hand, having purchased the privilege of raising fortifications through the venality of the Claudian times, they constructed such walls in a period of peace as showed they had an eye to war; while their numbers were augmented by a conflux of people from every quarter, and from the overthrow of other cities; for all the most indomitable spirits took refuge with them and by consequence they lived in a state of greater dissension. They had three armies, and as many generals. The outward walls, which were of the widest extent, were defended by Simon: John, otherwise called Bargioras, guarded the middle precinct; and Eleazar the Temple. The two former were strong in the number of men; the latter in situation. But battles, plots, and burnings occurred among themselves, and a large quantity of grain was consumed by fire. After a short time, John, sending a band of assassins under colour of performing a sacrifice, to cut off Eleazar and his party, gained possession of the Temple. From that time the citizens separated into two factions; and in this state they continued till, the Romans approaching, an enemy without produced unanimity within.

13. Prodigies had occurred which that race, enslaved to superstition, but opposed to religion, held it unlawful, either by vows or victims, to expiate. Embattled armies were seen rushing to the encounter, with burnished arms, and the whole Temple appeared to blaze with fire that flashed from the clouds. Suddenly the portals of the sanctuary were flung wide open, and a voice, in more than mortal accents, was heard to announce that the gods were going forth; at the same time, a prodigious bustle, as of persons taking their departure: occurrences which few interpreted as indicative of impending woe: the majority were deeply impressed with a persuasion that it was contained in the ancient writings of the priests, that it would come to pass at that very time, that the East would renew its strength, and they that should go forth from Judaea should be rulers of the world. Mysterious words, which foreshowed Vespasian and Titus: but the people, according to the usual course of human fondness, inter-

preting this consummation of destiny as referring to themselves, were not induced to abandon their error even by affliction. We learn that the number of the besieged of every age, male and female, was six hundred thousand; all that were capable bore arms, and more than could be expected out of that number had the fortitude to do so. The devotion of the women was equal to that of the men; and if they must needs move their seat, and quit the habitation of their fathers, they dreaded to live more than to die. Such was the city, such the nation, against which Titus Caesar determined to act by means of mounds and mantelets, since the nature of the locality was adverse to assault and sudden attacks. The legions had each their several duties assigned them, and there was a cessation of fighting until all the engines and appliances for reducing cities, invented by ancient or modern genius, were prepared. . . .

Germania [The Germans]

4. For my own part, I agree with those who think that the tribes of Germany are free from all taint of inter-marriages with foreign nations, and that they appear as a distinct, unmixed race, like none but themselves. Hence, too, the same physical peculiarities throughout so vast a population. All have fierce blue eyes, red hair, huge frames, fit only for a sudden exertion. They are less able to bear laborious work. Heat and thirst they cannot in the least endure; to cold and hunger their climate and their soil inure them.

7. They choose their kings by birth, their generals for merit. These kings have not unlimited or arbitrary power, and the generals do more by example than by authority. If they are energetic, if they are conspicuous, if they fight in the front, they lead because they are admired. But to reprimand, to imprison, even to flog, is permitted to the priests alone, and that not as a punishment, or at the general's bidding, but, as it were, by the mandate of the god whom they believe to inspire the warrior. They also carry with them into battle certain figures and images taken from their sacred groves. And what most stimulates their courage is, that their squadrons or battalions, instead of being formed by chance or by a fortuitous gathering, are composed of families and clans. Close by them, too, are those dearest to them, so that they hear the shrieks of women, the cries of infants. They are to every man the most sacred witnesses of his bravery—they are his most generous applauders. The soldier brings his wounds to mother and wife, who shrink not from counting or even demanding them and who administer both food and encouragement to the combatants.

8. Tradition says that armies already wavering and giving way have been rallied by women who, with earnest entreaties and bosoms laid bare, have vividly represented the horrors of captivity, which the Germans fear with such extreme dread on behalf of their women, that the strongest tie by which a state can be bound is the being required to give, among the number of hostages, maidens of noble birth. They even believe that the sex has a certain sanctity and prescience, and they do not despise their counsels, or make light of their answers. In Vespasian's days we saw Veleda, long regarded by many as a divinity. In former times, too, they venerated Aurinia, and many other women, but not with servile flatteries, or with sham deification.

11. About minor matters the chiefs deliberate, about the more important the whole tribe. Yet even when the final decision rests with the people, the affair is always thoroughly discussed by the chiefs. They assemble, except in the case of a sudden

emergency, on certain fixed days, either at new or at full moon; for this they consider the most auspicious season for the transaction of business. Instead of reckoning by days as we do, they reckon by nights, and in this manner fix both their ordinary and their legal appointments. Night they regard as bringing on day. Their freedom has this disadvantage, that they do not meet simultaneously or as they are bidden, but two or three days are wasted in the delays of assembling. When the multitude think proper, they sit down armed. Silence is proclaimed by the priests, who have on these occasions the right of keeping order. Then the king or the chief, according to age, birth, distinction in war, or eloquence, is heard, more because he has influence to persuade than because he has power to command. If his sentiments displease them, they reject them with murmurs; if they are satisfied, they brandish their spears. The most complimentary form of assent is to express approbation with their weapons.

12. In their councils an accusation may be preferred or a capital crime prosecuted. Penalties are distinguished according to the offence. Traitors and deserters are hanged on trees; the coward, the unwarlike, the man stained with abominable vices, is plunged into the mire of the morass, with a hurdle put over him. This distinction in punishment means that crime, they think, ought, in being punished, to be exposed, while infamy ought to be buried out of sight. Lighter offences, too, have penalties proportioned to them; he who is convicted, is fined in a certain number of horses or of cattle. Half of the fine is paid to the king or to the state, half to the person whose wrongs are avenged and to his relatives. In these same councils they also elect the chief magistrates, who administer law in the cantons and the towns. Each of these has a hundred associates chosen from the people, who support him with their advice and influence.

13. They transact no public or private business without being armed. It is not, however, usual for anyone to wear arms till the state has recognised his power to use them. Then in the presence of the council one of the chiefs, or the young man's father, or some kinsman, equips him with a shield and a spear. These arms are what the "toga" is with us, the first honour with which youth is invested. Up to this time he is regarded as a member of a household, afterwards as a member of the commonwealth. Very noble birth or great services rendered by the father secure for lads the rank of a chief; such lads attach themselves to men of mature strength and of long approved valour. It is no shame to be seen among a chief's followers. Even in his escort there are gradations of rank, dependent on the choice of the man to whom they are attached. These followers vie keenly with each other as to who shall rank first with his chief, the chiefs as to who shall have the most numerous and the bravest followers. It is an honour as well as a source of strength to be thus always surrounded by a large body of picked youths; it is an ornament in peace and a defence in war. And not only in his own tribe but also in the neighbouring states it is the renown and glory of a chief to be distinguished for the number and valour of his followers, for such a man is courted by embassies, is honoured with presents, and the very prestige of his name often settles a war.

14. When they go into battle, it is a disgrace for the chief to be surpassed in valour, a disgrace for his followers not to equal the valour of the chief. And it is an infamy and a reproach for life to have survived the chief, and returned from the field. To defend, to protect him, to ascribe one's own brave deeds to his renown, is the height of loyalty. The chief fights for victory; his vassals fight for their chief. If their native state sinks into the sloth of prolonged peace and repose, many of its noble

youths voluntarily seek those tribes which are waging some war, both because inaction is odious to their race, and because they win renown more readily in the midst of peril, and cannot maintain a numerous following except by violence and war. Indeed, men look to the liberality of their chief for their war-horse and their blood-stained and victorious lance. Feasts and entertainments, which, though inelegant, are plentifully furnished, are their only pay. The means of this bounty come from war and rapine. Nor are they as easily persuaded to plough the earth and to wait for the year's produce as to challenge an enemy and earn the honour of wounds. Nay, they actually think it tame and stupid to acquire by the sweat of toil what they might win by their blood.

15. Whenever they are not fighting, they pass much of their time in the chase, and still more in idleness, giving themselves up to sleep and to feasting, the bravest and the most warlike doing nothing, and surrendering the management of the household, of the home, and of the land, to the women, the old men, and all the weakest members of the family. They themselves lie buried in sloth, a strange combination in their nature that the same men should be so fond of idleness, so averse to peace. It is the custom of the states to bestow by voluntary and individual contribution on the chiefs a present of cattle or of grain, which, while accepted as a compliment, supplies their wants. They are particularly delighted by gifts from neighboring tribes, which are sent not only by individuals but also by the state, such as choice steeds, heavy armour, trappings, and neckchains. We have now taught them to accept money also.

18. Their marriage code, however, is strict, and indeed no part of their manners is more praiseworthy. Almost alone among barbarians they are content with one wife, except a very few among them, and these not from sensuality, but because their noble birth procures for them many offers of alliance. The wife does not bring a dower to the husband, but the husband to the wife. The parents and relatives are present, and pass judgment on the marriage-gifts, gifts not meant to suit a woman's taste, nor such as a bride would deck herself with, but oxen, a caparisoned steed, a shield, a lance, and a sword. With these presents the wife is espoused, and she herself in her turn brings her husband a gift of arms. This they count their strongest bond of union, these their sacred mysteries, these their gods of marriage. Lest the woman should think herself to stand apart from aspirations after noble deeds and from the perils of war, she is reminded by the ceremony which inaugurates marriage that she is her husband's partner in toil and danger, destined to suffer and to dare with him alike both in peace and in war. The yoked oxen, the harnessed steed, the gift of arms, proclaim this fact. She must live and die with the feeling that she is receiving what she must hand down to her children neither tarnished nor depreciated, what future daughters-in-law may receive, and may be so passed on to her grand-children.

19. Thus with their virtue protected they live uncorrupted by the allurements of public shows or the stimulant of feastings. Clandestine correspondence is equally unknown to men and women. Very rare for so numerous a population is adultery, the punishment for which is prompt, and in the husband's power. Having cut off the hair of the adulteress and stripped her naked, he expels her from the house in the presence of her kinsfolk, and then flogs her through the whole village. The loss of chastity meets with no indulgence; neither beauty, youth, nor wealth will procure the culprit a husband. No one in Germany laughs at vice, nor do they call it the fashion to corrupt and to be corrupted. Still better is the condition of those states in which only maidens

are given in marriage, and where the hopes and expectations of a bride are then finally terminated. They receive one husband, as having one body and one life, that they may have no thoughts beyond, no further-reaching desires, that they may love not so much the husband as the married state. To limit the number of their children or to destroy any of their subsequent offspring is accounted infamous, and good habits are here more effectual than good laws elsewhere.

20. In every household the children, naked and filthy, grow up with those stout frames and limbs which we so much admire. Every mother suckles her own offspring, and never entrusts it to servants and nurses. The master is not distinguished from the slave by being brought up with greater delicacy. Both live amid the same flocks and lie on the same ground till the freeborn are distinguished by age and recognised by merit. The young men marry late, and their vigour is thus unimpaired. Nor are the maidens hurried into marriage: the same age and a similar stature is required; well-matched and vigorous they wed, and the offspring reproduce the strength of the parents. Sister's sons are held in as much esteem by their uncles as by their fathers; indeed, some regard the relation as even more sacred and binding, and prefer it in receiving hostages, thinking thus to secure a stronger hold on the affections and a wider bond for the family. But every man's own children are his heirs and successors, and there are no wills. Should there be no issue, the next in succession to the property are his brothers and his uncles on either side. The more relatives he has, the more numerous his connections, the more honoured is his old age; nor are there any advantages in childlessness.

21. It is a duty among them to adopt the feuds as well as the friendships of a father or a kinsman. These feuds are not implacable; even homicide is expiated by the payment of a certain number of cattle and of sheep, and the satisfaction is accepted by the entire family, greatly to the advantage of the state, since feuds are dangerous in proportion to a people's freedom.

No nation indulges more profusely in entertainments and hospitality. To exclude any human being from their roof is thought impious; every German, according to his means, receives his guest with a well-furnished table. When his supplies are exhausted, he who was but now the host becomes the guide and companion to further hospitality, and without invitation they go to the next house. It matters not; they are entertained with like cordiality. No one distinguishes between an acquaintance and a stranger, as regards the rights of hospitality. It is usual to give the departing guest whatever he may ask for, and a present in return is asked with as little hesitation.

27. In their funerals there is no pomp; they simply observe the custom of burning the bodies of illustrious men with certain kinds of wood. They do not heap garments or spices on the funeral pile. The arms of the dead man and in some cases his horse are consigned to the fire. A turf mound forms the tomb. Monuments with their lofty elaborate splendour they reject as oppressive to the dead. Tears and lamentations they soon dismiss; grief and sorrow but slowly. It is thought becoming for women to bewail, for men to remember, the dead.

Such on the whole is the account which I have received of the origin and manners of the entire German people.

Marcus Aurelius (121–180)

Meditations

Marcus Annius Verus was born during the reign of the Emperor Hadrian to noble parents, who died when he was young. Marcus was raised by his grandfather, who provided him with excellent tutors devoted to the stoic philosophy. When Marcus was seventeen, Hadrian died and was succeeded by Aurelius Antoninus. Antoninus was married to Faustina, who was Marcus's aunt. The childless emperor adopted Marcus, placed him in the succession as Marcus Aurelius Antoninus, and married him to his daughter Faustina. For the next 23 years, Marcus studied in preparation to become emperor. When Antoninus died in 161, Marcus took as co-emperor the other adopted son of Antoninus, Lucius Verus, who only reigned until his death in 169. The long-lasting Roman Peace finally yielded to turmoil during the reign of Marcus Aurelius. An epidemic of plague, followed by floods and famine, ravaged the empire, and barbarians began to push at the eastern borders. Marcus had to travel to Asia to put down a rebellion by the leader of his troops; his wife died during this campaign. Otherwise he spent most of his time with his legions along the Danube, attempting to quell invasions by marauding tribes. Until his death of disease in 180, he was camped on the borderlands of empire, occupying his mind by recording in a journal or commonplace book his musings about how to live the perfect life. His Meditations *are simply a collection of reflections that give voice to the stoic philosophy in which he had been trained and which presumably gave him the strength to face years of military campaigns.*

I

1. Courtesy and serenity of temper I first learnt to know from my grandfather Verus.

2. Manliness without ostentation I learnt from what I have heard and remember of my father.

Reprinted from *Meditations*, translated by Maxwell Staniforth (Penguin, 1964).

3. My mother set me an example of piety and generosity, avoidance of all uncharitableness—not in actions only, but in thought as well—and a simplicity of life quite unlike the usual habits of the rich.

4. To my great-grandfather I owed the advice to dispense with the education of the schools and have good masters at home instead—and to realize that no expense should be grudged for this purpose.

5. It was my tutor who dissuaded me from patronizing Green or Blue at the races, or Light or Heavy in the ring; and encouraged me not to be afraid of work, to be sparing in my wants, attend to my own needs, mind my own business, and never listen to gossip.

6. Thanks to Diognetus I learnt not to be absorbed in trivial pursuits; to be sceptical of wizards and wonder-workers with their tales of spells, exorcisms, and the like; to eschew cockfighting and other such distractions; not to resent outspokenness; to familiarize myself with philosophy, beginning with Bacchius and going on to Tandasis and Marcian; to write compositions in my early years; and to be ardent for the plank-and-skin pallet and other rigours of the Greek discipline.

7. From Rusticus I derived the notion that my character needed training and care, and that I must not allow myself to be led astray into a sophist's enthusiasm for concocting speculative treatises, edifying homilies, or imaginary sketches of The Ascetic or The Altruist. He also taught me to avoid rhetoric, poetry, and verbal conceits, affectations of dress at home, and other such lapses of taste, and to imitate the easy epistolary style of his own letter written at Sinuessa to my mother. If anyone, after falling out with me in a moment of temper, showed signs of wanting to make peace again, I was to be ready at once to meet them half-way. Also I was to be accurate in my reading, and not content with a mere general idea of the meaning; and not to let myself be too quickly convinced by a glib tongue. Through him, too, I came to know Epictetus's *Dissertations*, of which he gave me a copy from his library.

8. Apollonius impressed on me the need to make decisions for myself instead of depending on the hazards of chance, and never for a moment to leave reason out of sight. He also schooled me to meet spasms of acute pain, the loss of my son, and the tedium of a chronic ailment with the same unaltered composure. He himself was a living proof that the fieriest energy is not incompatible with the ability to relax. His expositions were always a model of clarity; yet he was evidently one who rated practical experience and an aptitude for teaching philosophy as the least of his accomplishments. It was he, moreover, who taught me how to accept the pretended favours of friends without either lowering my own self-respect or giving the impression of an unfeeling indifference.

9. My debts to Sextus include kindliness, how to rule a household with paternal authority, the real meaning of the Natural Life, an unselfconscious dignity, an intuitive concern for the interests of one's friends, and a good-natured patience with amateurs and visionaries. The aptness of his courtesy to each individual lent a charm to his society more potent than any flattery, yet at the same time it exacted the complete respect of all present. His manner, too, of determining and systematizing the essential rules of life was as comprehensive as it was methodical. Never displaying a sign of anger nor any kind of emotion, he was at once entirely imperturbable and yet full of kindly affection. His approval was always quietly and undemonstratively expressed, and he never paraded his encyclopaedic learning.

10. It was the critic Alexander who put me on my guard against unnecessary fault-finding. People should not be sharply corrected for bad grammar, provincialisms, or mispronunciation; it is better to suggest the proper expression by tactfully introducing it oneself in, say, one's reply to a question or one's acquiescence in their sentiments, or into a friendly discussion of the topic itself (not of the diction), or by some other suitable form of reminder. . . .

III

6. If mortal life can offer you anything better than justice and truth, self-control and courage—that is, peace of mind in the evident conformity of your actions to the laws of reason, and peace of mind under the visitations of a destiny you cannot control—if, I say, you can discern any higher ideal, why, turn to it with your whole soul, and rejoice in the prize you have found. But if nothing seems to you better than the deity which dwells within you, directing each impulse, weighing each impression, abjuring (in the Socratic phrase) the temptations of the flesh, and avowing allegiance to the gods and compassion for mankind; if you find all else to be mean and worthless in comparison, then leave yourself no room for any rival pursuits. For if you once falter and turn aside, you will no longer be able to give unswerving loyalty to this ideal you have chosen for your own. No ambitions of a different nature can contest the title to goodness which belongs to reason and civic duty; not the world's applause, nor power, nor wealth, nor the enjoyment of pleasure. For a while there may seem to be no incongruity in these things, but very quickly they get the upper hand and sweep a man off his balance. Do you then, I would say, simply and spontaneously make your choice of the highest, and cleave to that. 'But what is best for myself is the highest,' you say? If it is best for you as a reasonable being, hold fast to it; but if as an animal merely, then say so outright, and maintain your view with becoming humility—only be very sure that you have probed the matter aright. . . .

10. Letting go all else, cling to the following few truths. Remember that man lives only in the present, in this fleeting instant: all the rest of his life is either past and gone, or not yet revealed. This mortal life is a little thing, lived in a little corner of the earth; and little, too, is the longest fame to come—dependent as it is on a succession of fast-perishing little men who have no knowledge even of their own selves, much less of one long dead and gone.

11. To these maxims add yet another. When an object presents itself to your perception, make a mental definition or at least an outline of it, so as to discern its essential character, to pierce beyond its separate attributes to a distinct view of the naked whole, and to identify for yourself both the object itself and the elements of which it is composed, and into which it will again be resolved. Nothing so enlarges the mind as this ability to examine methodically and accurately every one of life's experiences, with an eye to determining its classification, the ends it serves, its worth to the universe, and its worth to men as the members of that supreme City in which all other cities are as households. . . .

IV

3. Men seek for seclusion in the wilderness, by the seashore, or in the mountains—a dream you have cherished only too fondly yourself. But such fancies are wholly unworthy of a philosopher, since at any moment you choose you can retire within yourself. Nowhere can man find a quieter or more untroubled retreat than in his own soul; above all, he who possesses resources in himself, which he need only contemplate to secure immediate ease of mind—the ease that is but another word for a well-ordered spirit. Avail yourself often, then, of this retirement, and so continually renew yourself. Make your rules of life brief, yet so as to embrace the fundamentals; recurrence to them will then suffice to remove all vexation, and send you back without fretting to the duties to which you must return.

After all, what is it that frets you? The vices of humanity? Remember the doctrine that all rational beings are created for one another; that toleration is a part of justice; and that men are not intentional evildoers. Think of the myriad enmities, suspicions, animosities, and conflicts that are now vanished with the dust and ashes of the men who knew them; and fret no more.

Or is it your allotted portion in the universe that chafes you? Recall once again the dilemma, 'if not a wise Providence, then a mere jumble of atoms', and consider the profusion of evidence that this world is as it were a city. Do the ills of the body afflict you? Reflect that the mind has but to detach itself and apprehend its own powers, to be no longer involved with the movements of the breath, whether they be smooth or rough. In short, recollect all you have learnt and accepted regarding pain and pleasure.

Or does the bubble reputation distract you? Keep before your eyes the swift onset of oblivion, and the abysses of eternity before us and behind; mark how hollow are the echoes of applause, how fickle and undiscerning the judgements of professed admirers, and how puny the arena of human fame. For the entire earth is but a point, and the place of our own habitation but a minute corner in it; and how many are therein who will praise you, and what sort of men are they?

Remember then to withdraw into the little field of self. Above all, never struggle or strain; but be master of yourself, and view life as a man, as a human being, as a citizen, and as a mortal. Among the truths you will do well to contemplate most frequently are these two: first, that things can never touch the soul, but stand inert outside it, so that disquiet can arise only from fancies within; and secondly, that all visible objects change in a moment, and will be no more. Think of the countless changes in which you yourself have had a part. The whole universe is change, and life itself is but what you deem it.

4. If the power of thought is universal among mankind, so likewise is the possession of reason, making us rational creatures. It follows, therefore, that this reason speaks no less universally to us all with its 'thou shalt' or 'thou shalt not'. So then there is a world-law; which in turn means that we are all fellow-citizens and share a common citizenship, and that the world is a single city. Is there any other common citizenship that can be claimed by all humanity? And it is from this world-polity that mind, reason, and law themselves derive. If not, whence else? As the earthy portion of me has its origin from earth, the watery from a different element, my breath from one source and my hot and fiery parts from another of their own elsewhere (for nothing

comes from nothing, or can return to nothing), so too there must be an origin for the mind.

5. Death, like birth, is one of Nature's secrets; the same elements that have been combined are then dispersed. Nothing about it need give cause for shame. For beings endowed with mind it is no anomaly, nor in any way inconsistent with the plan of their creation. . . .

48. Remind yourself constantly of all the physicians, now dead, who used to knit their brows over their ailing patients; of all the astrologers who so solemnly predicted their clients' doom; the philosophers who expatiated so endlessly on death or immortality; the great commanders who slew their thousands; the despots who wielded powers of life and death with such terrible arrogance, as if themselves were gods who could never die; the whole cities which have perished completely, Helice, Pompeii, Herculaneum, and others without number. After that, recall one by one each of your own acquaintances; how one buried another, only to be laid low himself and buried in turn by a third, and all in so brief a space of time. Observe, in short, how transient and trivial is all mortal life; yesterday a drop of semen, tomorrow a handful of spice or ashes. Spend, therefore, these fleeting moments on earth as Nature would have you spend them, and then go to your rest with a good grace, as an olive falls in its season, with a blessing for the earth that bore it and a thanksgiving to the tree that gave it life.

49. Be like the headland against which the waves break and break: it stands firm, until presently the watery tumult around it subsides once more to rest. 'How unlucky I am, that this should have happened to me!' By no means; say rather, 'How lucky I am, that it has left me with no bitterness; unshaken by the present, and undismayed by the future.' The thing could have happened to anyone, but not everyone would have emerged unembittered. So why put the one down to misfortune, rather than the other to good fortune? Can a man call anything at all a misfortune, if it is not a contravention of his nature; and can it be a contravention of his nature if it is not against that nature's will? Well, then: you have learnt to know that will. Does this thing which has happened hinder you from being just, magnanimous, temperate, judicious, discreet, truthful, self-respecting, independent, and all else by which a man's nature comes to its fulfillment? So here is a rule to remember in future, when anything tempts you to feel bitter: not, 'This is a misfortune,' but 'To bear this worthily is good fortune.' . . .

VI

13. When meat and other dainties are before you, you reflect: This is dead fish, or fowl, or pig; or: This Falernian is some of the juice from a bunch of grapes; my purple robe is sheep's wool stained with a little gore from a shellfish; copulation is friction of the members and an ejaculatory discharge. Reflections of this kind go to the bottom of things, penetrating into them and exposing their real nature. The same process should be applied to the whole of life. When a thing's credentials look most plausible, lay it bare, observe its triviality, and strip it of the cloak of verbiage that dignifies it. Pretentiousness is the arch deceiver, and never more delusive than when you imagine your work is most meritorious. Note what Crates has to say about Xenocrates himself. . . .

15. One thing hastens into being, another hastens out of it. Even while a thing is in the act of coming into existence, some part of it has already ceased to be. Flux and change are for ever renewing the fabric of the universe, just as the ceaseless sweep of time is for ever renewing the face of eternity. In such a running river, where there is no firm foothold, what is there for a man to value among all the many things that are racing past him? It would be like setting the affections on some sparrow flitting by, which in the selfsame moment is lost to sight. A man's life is no more than an inhalation from the air and an exhalation from the blood; and there is no true difference between drawing in a single breath, only to emit it again, as we do every instant, and receiving the power to breathe at all, as you did but yesterday at your birth, only to yield it back one day to the source from which you drew it. . . .

21. If anyone can show me, and prove to me, that I am wrong in thought or deed, I will gladly change. I seek the truth, which never yet hurt anybody. It is only persistence in self-delusion and ignorance which does harm. . . .

24. In death, Alexander of Macedon's end differed no whit from his stable-boy's. Either both were received into the same generative principle of the universe, or both alike were dispersed into atoms. . . .

42. All of us are working together for the same end; some of us knowingly and purposefully, others unconsciously (as Heraclitus, I think, has remarked that 'even in their sleep men are at work' and contributing their share to the cosmic process). To one man falls this share of the task, to another that; indeed, no small part is performed by that very malcontent who does all he can to hinder and undo the course of events. The universe has need even of such as he. It remains for you, then, to consider with whom you will range yourself; for in any case he who directs all things will find some good use to make of you, and give you your place among his helpmates and fellow-labourers. Only, have a care that yours is not that sorry function which, according to Chrysippus, is performed by the clown's part on the stage. . . .

44. If the gods took counsel together about myself, and what should befall me, then their counsel was good. For it were hard to conceive of divinity counselling unwisely. After all, what incentive would they have to work my hurt? Where would be the gain, either to themselves, or to the universe which is their chief care? Even if they took no special thought for myself, at least they took thought for the universe; and I ought to welcome and feel kindly disposed towards anything that happens as a result. If, of course, they took no thought for anything at all—an impious thing to believe—why then, let us make an end of sacrifice and prayer and vow, and all other actions whereby we acknowledge the presence of living gods in our midst. Yet even so, and even if it is true that they care nothing for our mortal concerns, I am still able to take care of myself and to look to my own interests; and the interest of every creature lies in conformity with its own constitution and nature. My own nature is a rational and civic one; I have a city, and I have a country; as Marcus I have Rome, and as a human being I have the universe; and consequently, what is beneficial to these communities is the sole good for me. . . .

VIII

50. Is your cucumber bitter? Throw it away. Are there briars in your path? Turn aside. That is enough. Do not go on to say, 'Why were things of this sort ever brought

into the world?' The student of nature will only laugh at you; just as a carpenter or a shoemaker would laugh, if you found fault with the shavings and scraps from their work which you saw in the shop. Yet they, at least, have somewhere to throw their litter; whereas Nature has no such out-place. That is the miracle of her workmanship: that in spite of this self-limitation, she nevertheless transmutes into herself everything that seems worn-out or old or useless, and re-fashions it into new creations, so as never to need either fresh supplies from without, or a place to discard her refuse. Her own space, her own materials and her own skill are sufficient for her. . . .

IX

30. Look down from above on the numberless herds of mankind, with their mysterious ceremonies, their divers voyagings in storm and calm, and all the chequered pattern of their comings and gatherings and goings. Go on to consider the life of bygone generations; and then the life of all those who are yet to come; and even at the present day, the life of the hordes of far-off savages. In short, reflect what multitudes there are who are ignorant of your very name; how many more will have speedily forgotten it; how many, perhaps praising you now, who will soon enough be abusing you; and that therefore remembrance, glory, and all else together are things of no worth. . . .

Christian Documents

Christianity grew out of the first flowerings of rabbinic culture, but, as the book of Acts in the New Testament makes clear, it quickly defined itself over against Judaism. This is somewhat ironic, for Jesus's teachings fell within the tenor of the teachings of Hillel and other liberal rabbis. And Paul, in the book of Acts, claimed to be a student of the rabbi Gamaliel. But the intellectual move away from, first, Judaic law, and then Judaic practice, along with the definitive movement toward the western reaches of the Roman Empire, meant that Christianity was kept from dissolving back into Judaism, like so many other sects started by roving messiahs.

Correspondence between Pliny the Younger and Trajan

After his father died, Pliny (61 or 62–c.113) was adopted by his famous uncle Pliny the Elder, a Roman lawyer specializing in property law. During his lifetime in public administration he collected and published his private letters in ten volumes. These letters, following a fashion among wealthy Romans, were litterae curiosius scriptae *("letters written with special care"), and Pliny came to be admired as a master of this rhetorical art. The letters, which focus on details of life and politics at the turn of the second century, are a treasure trove for historians. Volume 10, devoted entirely to letters to the Emperor Trajan, contains the letter reproduced here; it includes an important account of early Christianity.*

It is my custom, my Lord, to refer to you all things concerning which I am in doubt. For who can better guide my indecision or enlighten my ignorance?

I have never taken part in the trials of Christians: hence I do not know for what crime nor to what extent it is customary to punish or investigate. I have been in no little doubt as to whether any discrimination is made for age, or whether the treatment of the weakest does not differ from that of the stronger; whether pardon is granted in case of repentance, or whether he who has ever been a Christian gains nothing by having ceased

The translation is by Dana Munro and Edith Bramhall (Philadelphia: University of Pennsylvania Press, 1898).

to be one; whether the *name* itself without the proof of crimes, or the crimes, inseparably connected with the *name,* are punished. Meanwhile, I have followed this procedure in the case of those who have been brought before me as Christians. I asked them whether they were Christians a second and a third time and with threats of punishment; I questioned those who confessed; I ordered those who were obstinate to be executed. For I did not doubt that, whatever it was that they confessed, their stubbornness and inflexible obstinacy ought certainly to be punished. There were others of similar madness, who because they were Roman citizens, I have noted for sending to the City. Soon, the crime spreading, as is usual when attention is called to it, more cases arose. An anonymous accusation containing many names was presented. Those who denied that they were or had been Christians, ought, I thought, to be dismissed since they repeated after me a prayer to the gods and made supplication with incense and wine to your image, which I had ordered to be brought for the purpose together with the statues of the gods, and since besides they cursed Christ, not one of which things they say, those who are really Christians can be compelled to do. Others, accused by the informer, said that they were Christians and afterwards denied it; in fact they had been but had ceased to be, some many years ago, some even twenty years before. All both worshipped your image and the statues of the gods, and cursed Christ. They continued to maintain that this was the amount of their fault or error, that on a fixed day they were accustomed to come together before daylight and to sing by turns a hymn to Christ as a god, and that they bound themselves by oath, not for some crime but that they would not commit robbery, theft, or adultery, that they would not betray a trust nor deny a deposit when called upon. After this it was their custom to disperse and to come together again to partake of food, of an ordinary and harmless kind, however; even this they had ceased to do after the publication of my edict in which according to your command I had forbidden associations. Hence I believed it the more necessary to examine two female slaves, who were called deaconesses, in order to find out what was true, and to do it by torture. I found nothing but a vicious, extravagant superstition. Consequently I have postponed the examination and make haste to consult you. For it seemed to me that the subject would justify consultation, especially on account of the number of those in peril. For many of all ages, of every rank, and even of both sexes are and will be called into danger. The infection of this superstition has not only spread to the cities but even to the villages and country districts. It seems possible to stay it and bring about a reform. It is plain enough that the temples, which had been almost deserted, have begun to be frequented again, that the sacred rites, which had been neglected for a long time, have begun to be restored, and that fodder for victims, for which till now there was scarcely a purchaser, is sold. From which one may readily judge what a number of men can be reclaimed if repentance is permitted.

Trajan's Reply:

You have followed the correct procedure, my Secundus, in conducting the cases of those who were accused before you as Christians, for no general rule can be laid down as a set form. They ought not to be sought out; if they are brought before you and convicted they ought to be punished; provided that he who denies that he is a Christian, and proves this by making supplication to our gods, however much he may have been under suspicion in the past, shall secure pardon on repentance. In the case of no crime should attention be paid to anonymous charges, for they afford a bad precedent and are not worthy of our age.

APOCRYPHAL GOSPELS

The collection of Christian scriptures, the New Testament, like the writings in the Hebrew Bible, gives the appearance of completeness. The three gospel examples offered here serve as a reminder of the process of selection that went into the making of the canonical scriptures. Recent discoveries of whole libraries of ancient texts, like the Dead Sea Scrolls and the Nag Hammadi Library, have added to our store of gospels, letters, and apocalypses that were not considered authoritative enough to make it into the finished collection of the New Testament. The New Testament as we know it took on its present shape in the third and fourth centuries and included only those texts that seemed to bear the ancient weight of authority. The "books" that didn't make it in sometimes survived in a separate existence, often contributing to Christian legends and doctrines that sound biblical but are nowhere to be found in the Bible. For instance, the reader will look in vain in the Bible for an account of the "Harrowing of Hell," when Jesus descended into hell and released the souls of all the beloved Old Testament figures that Christians admired; that story is told in the Gospel of Nicodemus, which was not accepted into the New Testament canon.

[THE GOSPEL OF THOMAS]

Perhaps the best known event in biblical archeology in this century was the discovery of the Dead Sea Scrolls in caves at Qumran near the Dead Sea in 1947. The scrolls, dating from the time of Jesus, include documents from a group, perhaps of Essenes, who had withdrawn into the wilderness in reaction against perceived abuses by the powers within Judaism. The scrolls included texts and fragments of books of the Hebrew Bible in Hebrew—the oldest such texts to survive. Less well known was a discovery of ancient religious texts near the Egyptian town of Nag Hammadi in 1945. Among the texts is the complete Gospel of Thomas in the common Egyptian language Coptic, probably translated from Greek. Although the existence of Thomas in early Christian times had been known, scholars believed that no actual text had survived. Thomas is remarkable because, unlike the four gospels collected in the New Testament, it is a sayings gospel, without stories, biography, or narrative order. It is therefore much more like the sayings of Greek philosophers or like Jewish wisdom literature (Proverbs in the Bible) than like the gospel accounts that became central in Christian literature. Thomas is important to many scholars because they had already judged that the writers of Matthew and Luke, while they were writing their gospels, had before them both Mark and some other collection of sayings of Jesus. Scholars have reconstructed this other source, calling it "Q" (German Quelle, *"source") and including in it sayings found in the same order in both Matthew and Luke, but not in Mark. The main argument against some such text as* Q *was that the known gospels were narratives, not collections of sayings. The existence of the Gospel of Thomas therefore allowed the possibility of a source like* Q. *Thomas also suggested, in its portrait of Jesus, that some in the earliest Christian communities viewed Jesus as a teacher of wisdom rather than as a healer or miracle worker. Scholars date Thomas to the same period as the synoptic gospels (70–100 CE), and believe it originated in Greek in the region in Syria most associated with traditions of the disciple Thomas. Students who have seen the recent film* Stigmata *(1999) will remember that the plot hinges on the suppression of a secret text that has Jesus saying, "The Kingdom of God is inside you and all around you, not in buildings of wood and stone. Split a piece of wood and I*

The three gospel texts here are translated by members of the Jesus Seminar and included in *The Complete Gospels: Annotated Scholars Version*, first published by the Polebridge Press in San Francisco, 1992.

am there; lift a stone and you will find me." These sayings are to be found in Thomas 3 and 77, and the opening lines of Thomas are also quoted in the film. A postscript to the film mentions the discovery of the Nag Hammadi Library and announces, probably erroneously, that the Catholic Church judges the Gospel of Thomas to be heretical. Most conservatives who want to downplay the importance of Thomas will argue that it is a much later text, like some of the other non-canonical gospels.

More recently, the best-selling novel by Dan Brown, The Da Vinci Code *(2003), has drawn considerable attention to Gnostic gospels, like those in the Nag Hammadi Library, because of their suggestion of a special role for Mary Magdalene among the earliest followers of Jesus. The fragmentary Gospel of Philip, for instance, says "And the companion of the [. . .] Mary Magdalene. [. . .] loved her more than all the disciples, and used to kiss her often on her mouth" (Nag Hammadi Library, ed. James Robinson [Harper & Row, 1981], p. 138). More tellingly, the Gospel of Mary [Magdalene] shows an argument breaking out among the disciples after Mary Magdalene, at their request, tells them of some secret teachings she received from Jesus in a vision. After Andrew says that he doesn't believe her, Peter says, "Has the Sa[vior] spoken secretly to a wo[m]an and [not] openly so that [we] would all hear? [Surely] he did [not wish to indicate] that [she] is more worthy than we are" (Mary 9:3-4* [The Complete Gospels, 1992]*). The Gospel of Thomas, which Brown doesn't cite in his novel, cuts both ways, for 114 (below), the last saying in the book, reaffirms Mary's importance, along with Peter's jealousy. But it also mysteriously has Jesus turn Brown's claim about the Gnostics' quest for the "divine feminine" on its head.*

Gnostic beliefs hold that the divine soul is trapped in an evil body and longs to escape to the spiritual realm of pure knowledge, akin to the One or Plato's world of Forms. In 2006 the National Geographic Society presented a television special on the Gnostic Gospel of Judas, *a fragmentary Coptic text that had surfaced in the 1970s and had recently been studied, translated, and interpreted. The unique manuscript dates from the third or fourth century but was possibly translated from earlier versions. As presented on the program, Judas Iscariot, in turning Jesus over to Roman authorities, was not "betraying" Jesus (as the gospels in the New Testament assert) but was instead acting under Jesus's orders, to aid him in his return to the Godhead. Doubters say that* this *interpretation is itself wrong and it is more likely that Judas was duped into believing that he was acting on Jesus's behalf. These texts and debates, in any event, show us that early Christian communities were not unified in their understanding of Jesus and his message; they listened to wildly varying gospels and developed interpretations of them that were as widely scattered theologically as the communities were geographically.*

These are the secret sayings that the living Jesus spoke and Didymos Judas Thomas recorded.

1 And he said, "Whoever discovers the interpretation of these sayings will not taste death."

2 Jesus said, "Those who seek should not stop seeking until they find. [2]When they find, they will be disturbed. [3]When they are disturbed, they will marvel, and will rule over all."

3 Jesus said, If your leaders say to you, 'Look, the (Father's) imperial rule is in the sky,' then the birds of the sky will precede you. [2]If they say to you, 'It is in the sea,' then the fish will precede you. [3]Rather, the (Father's) imperial rule is inside you and

outside you. [4]When you know yourselves, then you will be known, and you will understand that you are children of the living Father. [5]But if you do not know yourselves, then you live in poverty, and you are the poverty."

12 The disciples said to Jesus, "We know that you are going to leave us. Who will be our leader?"

[2]Jesus said to them, "No matter where you are, you are to go to James the Just, for whose sake heaven and earth came into being."

13 Jesus said to his disciples, "Compare me to something and tell me what I am like."

[2]Simon Peter said to him, "You are like a just angel."

[3]Matthew said to him, "You are like a wise philosopher."

[4]Thomas said to him, "Teacher, my mouth is utterly unable to say what you are like."

[5]Jesus said, "I am not your teacher. Because you have drunk, you have become intoxicated from the bubbling spring that I have tended."

[6]And he took him, and withdrew, and spoke three sayings to him.

[7]When Thomas came back to his friends, they asked him, "What did Jesus say to you?"

[8]Thomas said to them, "If I tell you one of the sayings he spoke to me, you will pick up rocks and stone me, and fire will come from the rocks and devour you."

15 Jesus said, "When you see one who was not born of woman, fall on your faces and worship. That one is your Father."

16 Jesus said, "Perhaps people think that I have come to cast peace upon the world. [2]They do not know that I have come to cast conflicts upon the earth: fire, sword, war. [3]For there will be five in a house: there'll be three against two and two against three, father against son and son against father, [4]and they will stand alone."

17 Jesus said, "I will give you what no eye has seen, what no ear has heard, what no hand has touched, what has not arisen in the human heart."

18 The disciples said to Jesus, "Tell us, how will our end come?" [2]Jesus said, "Have you found the beginning, then, that you are looking for the end? You see, the end will be where the beginning is. [3]Congratulations to the one who stands at the beginning: that one will know the end and will not taste death."

24 His disciples said, "Show us the place where you are, for we must seek it."

[2]He said to them, "Anyone here with two ears had better listen!

[3]There is light within a person of light, and it shines on the whole world. If it does not shine, it is dark."

25 Jesus said, "Love your friends like your own soul, [2]protect them like the pupil of your eye."

28 Jesus said, "I took my stand in the midst of the world, and in flesh I appeared to them. [2]I found them all drunk, and I did not find any of them thirsty. [3]My soul ached for the children of humanity, because they are blind in their hearts and do not see, for they came into the world empty, and they also seek to depart from the world empty. [4]But meanwhile they are drunk. When they shake off their wine, then they will change their ways."

31 Jesus said, "No prophet is welcome on his home turf; [2]doctors don't cure those who know them."

34 Jesus said, "If a blind person leads a blind person, both of them will fall into a hole."

35 Jesus said, "One can't enter a strong man's house and take it by force without tying his hands. [2]Then one can loot his house."

36 Jesus said, "Don't fret, from morning to evening and from evening to morning, about what you're going to wear."

37 His disciples said, "When will you appear to us, and when will we see you?"

[2]Jesus said, "When you strip without being ashamed, and you take your clothes and put them under your feet like little children and trample them, [3]then [you] will see the son of the living one and you will not be afraid."

38 Jesus said, "Often you have desired to hear these sayings that I am speaking to you, and you have no one else from whom to hear them. [2]There will be days when you will seek me and you will not find me."

44 Jesus said, "Whoever blasphemes against the Father will be forgiven, [2]and whoever blasphemes against the son will be forgiven, [3]but whoever blasphemes against the holy spirit will not be forgiven, either on earth or in heaven."

62 Jesus said, "I disclose my mysteries to those [who are worthy] of [my] mysteries. [2]Do not let your left hand know what your right hand is doing."

63 Jesus said,

There was a rich man who had a great deal of money. [2]He said, "I shall invest my money so that I may sow, reap, plant, and fill my storehouses with produce, that I may lack nothing." [3]These were the things he was thinking in his heart, but that very night he died. [4]Anyone here with two ears had better listen!

74 He said, "Lord, there are many around the drinking trough, but there is nothing in the well."

75 Jesus said, "There are many standing at the door, but those who are alone will enter the bridal suite."

76 Jesus said,

The Father's imperial rule is like a merchant who had a supply of merchandise and then found a pearl. [2]That merchant was prudent; he sold the merchandise and bought the single pearl for himself.

[3]"So also with you, seek his treasure that is unfailing, that is enduring, where no moth comes to eat and no worm destroys."

77 Jesus said, "I am the light that is over all things. I am all: from me all came forth, and to me all attained. [2]Split a piece of wood; I am there. [3]Lift up the stone, and you will find me there."

89 Jesus said, "Why do you wash the outside of the cup? [2]Don't you understand that the one who made the inside is also the one who made the outside?"

90 Jesus said, "Come to me, for my yoke is comfortable and my lordship is gentle, [2]and you will find rest for yourselves."

113 His disciples said to him, "When will the (Father's) imperial rule come?"

[2]"It will not come by watching for it. 'It will not be said, 'Look, here!' or 'Look, there!' 'Rather, the Father's imperial rule is spread out upon the earth, and people don't see it."

114 Simon Peter said to them, "Make Mary leave us, for females don't deserve life."

[2]Jesus said, "Look, I will guide her to make her male, so that she too may become a living spirit resembling you males. [3]For every female who makes herself male will enter the domain of Heaven."

[The Secret Gospel of Mark]

The existence of the Secret Gospel of Mark *was only revealed in the discovery of a copy of an ancient letter in a Judean monastery in 1958. The letter was written by Clement of Alexandria (c.150–c.211), an Athenian leading the Christian school in Alexandria. Clement was an opponent of gnostic dualists who believed in salvation through esoteric knowledge that revealed to Christians their spiritual origins, identities, and destinies. The letter, written to a certain Theodore, attacks the authenticity of a version of Mark used by a gnostic sect, and then says that there are only two authentic versions of the gospel, one for the general public and the second, "a more spiritual gospel for the use of those being perfected." According to Clement, when Mark died he left this second version in the care of the Church at Alexandria, "where it even now is very carefully guarded, being read only to those being initiated into the great mysteries." Clement then cites the two short passages that are in the* Secret Gospel *but not in the public version. Whether the initiation hinted at in the* Secret Gospel *is sexual in nature is unclear, and it is, naturally, the subject of heated debate.*

The existence of a separate insider's text simply carries a step further one of the themes found in the gospel of Mark as it appears in the New Testament. In Mark, knowledge and understanding are reserved for a special group of insiders and Jesus tells his disciples that they are initiated into a wisdom that most will be unable to understand. Jesus even suggests that the parables are designed to be difficult so that not everyone can understand them. Over and over, in fact, the gospel shows that even the disciples can barely make sense of what Jesus is trying to get them to see. The two passages in the Secret Gospel *also parallel the story of the raising of Lazarus and the references to the "Beloved Disciple" in the gospel of John.*

Fragment 1: To be located between Mark 10:34 and 10:35.
Clement to Theodore, Folio 1, verso, line 23–Folio 2, recto, line 11.

1. And they come into Bethany, and this woman was there whose brother had died. She knelt down in front of Jesus and says to him, "Son of David, have mercy on me." But the disciples rebuked her. And Jesus got angry and went with her into the garden where the tomb was. Just then a loud voice was heard from inside the tomb. Then Jesus went up and rolled the stone away from the entrance to the tomb. He went right in where the young man was, stuck out his hand, grabbed him by the hand, and raised him up. The young man looked at Jesus, loved him, and began to beg him to be with him. Then they left the tomb and went into the young man's house. (Incidentally, he was rich.) Six days later Jesus gave him an order; and when evening had come, the young man went to him, dressed only in a linen cloth. He spent that night with him, because Jesus taught him the mystery of God's domain. From there [Jesus] got up and returned to the other side of the Jordan.

Fragment 2: To be located between 10:46a ("Then they came to Jericho") and 10:46b ("As he was leaving Jericho . . ."). Clement to Theodore, Folio 2, recto, lines 14–16

2. The sister of the young man whom Jesus loved was there, along with his mother and Salome, but Jesus refused to see them.

[The Infancy Gospel of Thomas]

The many rejected biblical texts arose partly because there was often disagreement about what the core beliefs of Christianity were to be, even, as we see in the Infancy Gospel of Thomas, *about what the essential nature of Jesus was meant to be. This strange text shows us Jesus as a child, barely in control of the tremendous power he wields and behaving toward his fellow humans with insolence. The trouble his parents face is similar to that shown in the single infancy story that made it into the canonical gospels, when Jesus debates with rabbis and then talks back to his mother in the gospel of Luke. This text was apparently very popular among early Christians, for it survives in many versions in thirteen different languages. As a written text, it may date from the second century (probably in Syria), but it contains popular folk stories that would have been handed down orally from the time that Jesus's followers began to be curious about his youthful years.*

Boyhood deeds of our Lord Jesus Christ.

1. ***I, Thomas*** the Israelite, am reporting to you, all my non-Jewish brothers and sisters, to make known the extraordinary childhood deeds of our Lord Jesus Christ—what he did after his birth in my region. This is how it all started:

2. ***When this boy, Jesus,*** was five years old, he was playing at the ford of a rushing stream. He was collecting the flowing water into ponds and made the water instantly pure. He did this with a single command. He then made soft clay and shaped it into twelve sparrows. He did this on the sabbath day, and many other boys were playing with him.

But when a Jew saw what Jesus was doing while playing on the sabbath day, he immediately went off and told Joseph, Jesus' father: "See here, your boy is at the ford and has taken mud and fashioned twelve birds with it, and so has violated the sabbath."

So Joseph went there, and as soon as he spotted him he shouted, "Why are you doing what's not permitted on the sabbath?"

But Jesus simply clapped his hands and shouted to the sparrows: "Be off, fly away, and remember me, you who are now alive!" And the sparrows took off and flew away noisily.

The Jews watched with amazement, then left the scene to report to their leaders what they had seen Jesus doing.

3. ***The son of Annas the scholar,*** standing there with Jesus, took a willow branch and drained the water Jesus had collected. Jesus, however, saw what had happened and became angry, saying to him, "Damn you, you irreverent fool! What harm did the ponds of water do to you? From this moment you, too, will dry up like a tree, and you'll never produce leaves or root or bear fruit."

In an instant the boy had completely withered away. Then Jesus departed and left for the house of Joseph. The parents of the boy who had withered away picked him up and were carrying him out, sad because he was so young. And they came to Joseph and accused him: "It's your fault—your boy did all this."

4. ***Later he was going*** through the village again when a boy ran by and bumped him on the shoulder. Jesus got angry and said to him, "You won't continue your journey." And all of a sudden he fell down and died.

Some people saw what had happened and said, "Where has this boy come from? Everything he says happens instantly!"

The parents of the dead boy came to Joseph and blamed him, saying, "Because you have such a boy, you can't live with us in the village, or else teach him to bless and not curse. He's killing our children!"

5. So Joseph summoned his child and admonished him in private, saying, "Why are you doing all this? These people are suffering and so they hate and harass us." Jesus said, "I know that the words I spoke are not my words. Still, I'll keep quiet for your sake. But those people must take their punishment." There and then his accusers became blind.

Those who saw this became very fearful and at a loss. All they could say was, "Every word he says, whether good or bad, has became a deed—a miracle, even!" When Joseph saw that Jesus had done such a thing, he got angry and grabbed his ear and pulled very hard. The boy became infuriated with him and replied, "It's one thing for you to seek and not find; it's quite another for you to act this unwisely. Don't you know that I don't really belong to you? Don't make me upset."

TWO CHRISTIAN CREEDS

Paul's letters in the New Testament show a constant struggle to keep far-flung groups of converts from very different backgrounds focused on a single set of accepted beliefs and practices. Christianity's response to the strain of opposed orthodoxies and differences in interpretation was very different from that of Judaism. The Talmud essentially collects and places in direct juxtaposition the accumulated and often contradictory teachings of the sages. It does not often choose winners or pick sides. Instead, wisdom was found to lie in the accumulation, in the conflict itself, and in the magnificence of its expressions.

The teachings of Jesus, similar to those of other rabbis, were open to many interpretations and uses. But as Christianity spread, faced with alternations of official support and persecution, many sought decisive resolution of doctrinal disputes. Where beliefs clashed, it seemed wise to determine a winner. Councils were held to debate doctrinal issues, and the losing views were declared heresies. The arguments over some beliefs lasted centuries and sometimes resulted in open warfare. One such controversy can be perceived in the two creeds in common liturgical use in the Christian church over the centuries. The Apostle's Creed is a well-known and concise statement of Christian belief, elaborating the central mystery of the Trinity—Father, Son, and Holy Spirit—and mentioning the church, baptism, resurrection, and the afterlife as important articles of Christian faith. This creed probably developed out of a question-and-answer baptism ritual in the early church, reached its present form in the seventh century, and became the church's official creed about 1200. Through its name, it pretends to greater antiquity and authority than it really had, however, for many of the doctrines it enshrines would have been unknown to the original followers of Jesus.

The Nicene Creed, while structurally similar to the Apostle's Creed, is actually intended to stamp out a particularly stubborn heresy. Arius, the bishop in Alexandria, Egypt, after the year 300, proposed that if God was absolutely one (as Plato believed),

Christ had to be a created being, subject to the kind of growth and change some readers see in the gospels. Because this seemed to deny full Godhead to Christ and therefore to undercut the doctrine of the Trinity, Arius's teachings aroused a controversy so great that the Emperor Constantine convened a Council at Nicaea in 325 to discuss the issue. The Council declared the Arian doctrine a heresy and issued a declaration that clarified the church's official position. The liturgical version of that declaration, the Nicene Creed, with its decisive phrases, "of one substance with the Father" and "begotten not made," is thus a banner of victory in a war over a theological argument. That victory was not immediate or continuous, however, for Arianism reigned in the empire and among the German tribes who succeeded to power in the empire for several centuries after Constantine's council. The continuing power of these doctrinal disputes can be seen in the Nicene Creed's touchstone phrase filioque *applied to the Holy Spirit ("Who procedeth from the Father* and the Son*"): for more than a thousand years church councils have been unable to come to agreement on the doctrine represented by that phrase, and it remains today one of the key points of contention separating the Western (Roman Catholic) and Eastern (Orthodox) churches.*

Apostles' Creed

I believe in God the Father Almighty, Maker of Heaven and Earth:

And in Jesus Christ his only Son our Lord; Who was conceived by the Holy Ghost, Born of the Virgin Mary, Suffered under Pontius Pilate, Was crucified, dead, and buried: He descended into hell; The third day he rose again from the dead; He ascended into Heaven, And sitteth on the right hand of God, the Father Almighty; From thence he shall come to judge the quick and the dead.

I believe in the Holy Ghost; The Holy Catholic Church, the Communion of Saints; The Forgiveness of sins; The Resurrection of the body, And the Life everlasting. Amen.

Nicene Creed

I believe in one God, the Father Almighty, Maker of heaven and earth, And of all things visible and invisible.

And in one Lord Jesus Christ, the only begotten Son of God, Begotten of his Father before all worlds, God of God, Light of Light, Very God of very God, Begotten, not made, Being of one substance with the Father, By whom all things were made: Who for us men, and for our salvation, came down from heaven, And was incarnate by the Holy Ghost of the Virgin Mary, And was made man; And was crucified also for us under Pontius Pilate. He suffered and was buried; And the third day he rose again according to the Scriptures, And ascended into heaven, And sitteth at the right hand of the Father. And he shall come again with glory to judge both the quick and the dead: Whose kingdom shall have no end.

And I believe in the Holy Ghost, the Lord and Giver of Life, Who procedeth from the Father and the Son, Who with the Father and the Son together is worshipped and glorified, Who spake by the Prophets. And I believe one Holy Catholic and Apostolic Church. I acknowledge one Baptism for the remission of sins. And I look for the Resurrection of the dead, And the Life of the World to come. Amen.

THE MASS

In the tradition of Christian liturgy, the mass is the musical setting, either polyphonic or in plainchant, of the service of the Eucharist (Communion). In the Roman Catholic church, a well-established ordering of texts in Latin was in place from about the 4th century to 1966, when vernacular languages were required in place of Latin. The mass is made up of two parts: the Ordinary, *those texts that remain the same for every mass; and the* Proper, *the liturgical and scriptural texts that change daily throughout the seasons of the church calendar. The parts of the Ordinary, sung by the choir and occasionally by the celebrant, are the Kyrie, Gloria, Credo, Sanctus (sometimes divided into Sanctus and Benedictus), and Agnus Dei. The Proper texts, sung by the choir with the participation of soloists, are the Introit, Gradual, Alleluia or Tract, Sequence, Offertory, and Communion. The standard order of service followed this pattern:*

Chants		
Proper	*Ordinary*	*Prayers and lessons*
I. INTRODUCTORY RITES		
Introit		
	Kyrie Gloria	
		Collect (opening prayer)
II. LITURGY OF THE WORD		
		Epistle
Gradual Alleluia/tract Sequence (rare)		
		Gospel Homily (sermon)
	Credo	
		(general intercessions)
III. LITURGY OF THE EUCHARIST		
Offertory		
		Preface
	Sanctus	
		Te igitur, etc. to the conclusion of the Eucharistic Prayer, which began with Preface, Sanctus
		Pater noster (Lord's Prayer)
	Agnus Dei	
Communion		Post-Communion prayer
	Ite missa est (dismissal)	

The standardized texts of the Ordinary proved to be one of the greatest impulses to creativity in Western music, for from the ninth century on, through the addition of tropes (additional texts), through settings in plainchant, then through polyphonic settings, musicians and composers offered praise to God in specially composed masses. Most of the composers of the late Middle Ages whose names come down to us were best known for their settings of the mass texts. The great classical composers, like Haydn, Mozart, and Beethoven, wrote mass settings for chorus, soloists, and orchestra, in a tradition that continues with modern and contemporary composers.

KYRIE (GREEK)

Kyrie eleison. (three times)	Lord have mercy.
Christe eleison. (three times)	Christ have mercy.
Kyrie eleison. (three times)	Lord have mercy.

GLORIA

Gloria in excelsis Deo.	Glory to God on high.
Et in terra pax hominibus	And on earth peace to men
bonae voluntatis.	of good will.
Laudamus te.	We praise you.
Benedicimus te.	We bless you.
Adoramus te.	We adore you.
Glorificamus te.	We glorify you.
Gratias agimus te	We give thanks to you
propter magnam gloriam tuam.	for your great glory.
Domine Deus, Rex caelestis,	O Lord God, heavenly King,
Deus Pater omnipotens.	God the Father almighty.
Domine fili unigenite,	O Lord the only-begotten son,
Jesu Christe.	Jesus Christ.
Domine Deus,	O Lord God,
Agnus Dei,	Lamb of God,
Filius Patris,	Son of the Father,
Qui tollis peccata mundi,	who takes away the sins of the world,
miserere nobis,	have mercy upon us,
suscipe deprecationem nostram,	receive our prayer,
Qui sedes ad dexteram Patris,	you who sit at the right hand of the Father,
miserere nobis.	have mercy on us.
Suscipe deprecationem nostram,	Receive our prayer,
Qui sedes ad dexteram Patris,	you who sit at the right hand of the Father,
miserere nobis.	have mercy on us.
Quoniam tu solus sanctus.	For you alone are holy.
Tu solus Dominus.	You alone are the Lord.
Tu solus altissimus,	You alone are the most high,
Jesu Christe.	Jesus Christ.
Cum Sancto Spiritu,	With the Holy Spirit,
in gloria Dei Patris. Amen.	in the glory of God the Father. Amen.

CREDO

The text of the Credo is the Nicene Creed, the English translation of which is given earlier in this section.

SANCTUS (WITH BENEDICTUS)

Sanctus, Dominus Deus Sabaoth. Pleni sunt caeli et terra gloria tua.	Holy, holy, holy, Lord God of Hosts. Heaven and earth are full of your glory.
Osanna, Osanna in excelsis.	Hosanna in the highest.
Benedictus qui venit	Blessed is he who comes
in nomine Domini.	in the name of the Lord.
Osanna, Osanna in excelsis.	Hosanna in the highest.

AGNUS DEI

Agnus Dei, qui tollis peccata mundi, miserere nobis. Agnus Dei, qui tollis peccata mundi, miserere nobis. Agnus Dei, qui tollis peccata mundi, dona nobis pacem.	Lamb of God, who takes away the sins of the world, have mercy on us, grant us peace.

THE "QUEM QUAERITIS" TROPE

A trope is an addition to the existing liturgy, either by adding new words to existing melodic lines, or by inserting new words and music into an existing liturgical section. Because the Alleluia of the mass ended with florid musical passages on the last syllable of "Alleluia," tropes called Sequences *were commonly added between the Alleluia and the Gospel, using the existing chanted melodies and new texts appropriate to the season. These sequences became popular creative additions to the liturgy that in their turn influenced secular dances and songs. Among the best known sequences is the "Dies irae" (see below) added to the Mass for the Dead. Among the most influential of tropes may have been one added to the Introit for the Easter morning service during the tenth century: the voices were alternated so that a small scene could be enacted in which the angel at the now empty tomb of Jesus asks the three Marys as they approach: "Quem quaeritis in sepulchro?" ("Whom do you seek in the tomb?"). As liturgical scenes like this became popular, they came to be acted on the church steps and eventually grew into full scale dramatic cycles portraying biblical stories. Because knowledge of Greek and Roman drama had effectively disappeared during the early Middle*

This version of "Quem quaeritis" is translated by the editor for this collection.

Ages, many scholars believe that the enactment of these liturgical scenes was the first step in a reinvention of drama in Western Europe. The simplest of these tropes, which spread widely and elaborately in the middle of the tenth century, dates from about 950 from the monastery in St. Gall (St. Gall Stiftsbibliothek MS 484).

Quem quaeritis in sepulchro, Christicolae?	Whom do you seek in the tomb, O followers of Christ?
Jesum Nazarenum crucifixum, o caelicolae. Non est hic, surrexit sicut praedixerat; ite, nuntiate quia surrexit de sepulchro.	Jesus of Nazareth, the crucified, O heaven-dwellers He is not here, he has risen as he foretold; go, announce that he has risen from the tomb.
Resurrexi.	I have risen . . . (the first word of the Introit of the Easter Mass to which the trope has been added as an Introduction)

THE *REQUIEM* MASS

One of the best known of the specialized masses is the Mass for the Dead, *called the* Requiem *from the opening words of its Introit, "Requiem aeternam dona eis Domine" ("Give them eternal rest, O Lord"). Its musical setting contains the Kyrie, the Sanctus, and the Agnus Dei from the Ordinary, the Introit and Gradual from the Proper, a tract and the special sequence "Dies irae" ("Day of wrath"). The "Dies irae," because of its dramatic evocation of the terrors of the Last Judgment, became a special focus of attention in musical settings of the Requiem. Many great composers have written settings of the Requiem Mass for orchestra, soloists, and chorus, including Mozart, Dvorák, Verdi, Fauré, and Durufle. Brahms'* German Requiem *uses German scriptural passages instead of the usual Latin texts. The* War Requiem *of Benjamin Britten intersperses the traditional Latin text with anti-war poems of the British poet Wilfred Owen.*

"DIES IRAE"

Dies irae, dies illa, Solvet saeclum in favilla Teste David cum Sibylla.	Day of wrath, that day when the world will be reduced to ashes, as David prophesied with the Sibyl.
Quantus tremor est futurus, Quando judex est venturus, Cuncta stricte discussurus.	What trembling will there be when the judge ventures forth to thresh all out strictly.

Translated by the editor for this collection.

Tuba, mirum spargens sonum Per sepulchra regionum, Coget omnes ante thronum.	The trumpet, scattering a wondrous sound through the tombs of all lands, shall drive all before the throne.
Mors stupebit et natura Cum resurget creatura Judicanti responsura. Liber scriptus proferetur In quo totum continetur Unde mundus judicetur.	Death and nature will be astounded when every creature arises to answer the judge. A written book will be brought forth in which all is contained by which the world will be judged.
Judex ergo cum sedebit, Quidquid latet apparebit: Nil inultum remanebit.	Therefore when the judge shall sit, whatever was hidden will be revealed, And nothing will remain unpunished.
Quid sum miser tunc dicturus, Quem patronum rogaturus, Cum vix justus sit securus?	What shall I say in misery? Whom shall I seek as patron, when even the just are not secure?
Rex tremendae majestatis, Qui salvandos salvas gratis, Salva me, fons pietatis.	King of tremendous majesty, who freely saves the saved, save me, fount of mercy.
. . . .	. . . .
Lacrimosa dies illa Qua resurget ex favilla Judicandus homo reus.	Full of tears will be that day when from the ashes will arise the guilty man to be judged.
Huic ergo parce, Deus, Pie Jesu Domine: Dona eis requiem. Amen.	Then spare this one, O God, merciful Lord Jesus. Grant them rest. Amen.

Tertullian (c.160–c.220)

Prescriptions Against Heretics

Among the so-called "Fathers of the Church," Tertullian was influential both for being first to formulate key ideas that became doctrine and for bridging the Greek and Roman worlds. Born in Carthage as the son of a Roman centurion, he was highly educated, and took up the practice of law in Rome. Sometime around 190 or 195 he converted to Christianity, by tradition in admiration for young slaves who faced martyrdom with great courage. He became aligned with the Montanists, a sect of Christianity who believed in a continuing tradition of prophecy, in a rigidly ascetic form of life, and in martyrdom as a positive ideal. Montanism, which started in Asia Minor, had been declared heretical in 177, but had a continuing presence in Carthage. Although he wrote in both Greek and Latin, his Greek works have not survived. The thirty-one Latin works extant are, however, the first significant body of Christian writing in Latin.

Tertullian was a spirited, unrelenting, sometimes angry voice in defense of Christianity and against what he considered heresy. He argued vociferously that the Church had the right to determine what constituted heresy, and he closely analyzed church belief and practice. He coined the phrase "original sin," which Saint Augustine later elaborated into the influential doctrine about fallen human nature. He developed the idea of the bodily resurrection of the flesh. He translated the Greek musterion *("mystery") with the Latin* sacramentum *("sacrament"), and he maintained the Montanist position against remarriage. The strongly world-rejecting bent of his belief became even more harsh as time went on, and he rejected the pleasures that pagan literature had brought him in his pre-conversion days. Even more troubling for modern readers, he used his barbed sarcasm to define views of marriage and of women that shaped centuries of ecclesiastical and social practice: "And do you know that you are an Eve? God's sentence hangs over all your sex and His punishment weighs down upon you. You are the devil's gateway; it was you who first violated the forbidden tree and broke God's law . . . You should always go in mourning and rags." Nevertheless, Tertullian was a decisive voice in shaping the theological and doctrinal practice of the early church in the critical period when persecution was declining and a centralized orthodoxy was developing.*

This translation is taken from *Early Latin Theology,* edited by S. L. Greenslade (Louisville: Westminster Press, 1956).

["WHAT HAS JERUSALEM TO DO WITH ATHENS?"]

5. Again, when he blames party strife and schism, which are unquestionably evils, he at once adds heresy. What he links with evils, he is of course proclaiming to be itself an evil. Indeed in saying that he had believed in their schisms and parties just because he knew that heresies must come, he makes heresy the greater evil, showing that it was in view of the greater evil that he readily believed in the lesser ones. He cannot have meant that he believed in the evil things because heresy is good. He was warning them not to be surprised at temptations of an even worse character, which were intended, he said, to "make manifest those who are approved," that is, those whom heresy failed to corrupt. In short, as the whole passage aims at the preservation of unity and the restraint of faction, while heresy is just as destructive of unity as schism and party strife, it must be that he is setting heresy in the same reprehensible category as schism and party. So he is not approving those who have turned aside to heresy. On the contrary, he urges us with strong words to turn aside from them, and teaches us all to speak and think alike. That is what heresy will not allow.

6. I need say no more on that point, for it is the same Paul who elsewhere, when writing to the Galatians, classes heresy among the sins of the flesh, and who counsels Titus to shun a heretic after the first reproof because such a man is perverted and sinful, standing self-condemned. Besides, he censures heresy in almost every letter when he presses the duty of avoiding false doctrine, which is in fact the product of heresy. This is a Greek word meaning choice, the choice which anyone exercises when he teaches heresy or adopts it. That is why he calls a heretic self-condemned; he chooses for himself the cause of his condemnation. We Christians are forbidden to introduce anything on our own authority or to choose what someone else introduces on his own authority. Our authorities are the Lord's apostles, and they in turn chose to introduce nothing on their own authority. They faithfully passed on to the nations the teaching which they had received from Christ. So we should anathematize even an angel from heaven if he were to preach a different gospel. The Holy Ghost had already at that time foreseen that an angel of deceit would come in a virgin called Philumene, transforming himself into an angel of light, by whose miracles and tricks Apelles was deceived into introducing a new heresy.

7. These are human and demonic doctrines, engendered for itching ears by the ingenuity of that worldly wisdom which the Lord called foolishness, choosing the foolish things of the world to put philosophy to shame. For worldly wisdom culminates in philosophy with its rash interpretation of God's nature and purpose. It is philosophy that supplies the heresies with their equipment. From philosophy come the aeons and those infinite forms—whatever they are—and Valentinus's human trinity. He had been a Platonist. From philosophy came Marcion's God, the better for his inactivity. He had come from the Stoics. The idea of a mortal soul was picked up from the Epicureans, and the denial of the restitution of the flesh was taken over from the common tradition of the philosophical schools. Zeno taught them to equate God and matter, and Heracleitus comes on the scene when anything is being laid down about a god of fire. Heretics and philosophers perpend the same themes and are caught up in the same discussions. What is the origin of evil, and why? The origin of man, and how? And—Valentinus's latest subject—what is the origin of God? No

doubt in Desire and Abortion! A plague on Aristotle, who taught them dialectic, the art which destroys as much as it builds, which changes its opinions like a coat, forces its conjectures, is stubborn in argument, works hard at being contentious and is a burden even to itself. For it reconsiders every point to make sure it never finishes a discussion.

From philosophy come those fables and endless genealogies and fruitless questionings, those "words that creep like as doth a canker." To hold us back from such things, the Apostle testifies expressly in his letter to the Colossians that we should beware of philosophy. "Take heed lest any man circumvent you through philosophy or vain deceit, after the tradition of men," against the providence of the Holy Ghost. He had been at Athens where he had come to grips with the human wisdom which attacks and perverts truth, being itself divided up into its own swarm of heresies by the variety of its mutually antagonistic sects. What has Jerusalem to do with Athens, the Church with the Academy, the Christian with the heretic? Our principles come from the Porch of Solomon, who had himself taught that the Lord is to be sought in simplicity of heart. I have no use for a Stoic or a Platonic or a dialectic Christianity. After Jesus Christ we have no need of speculation, after the Gospel no need of research. When we come to believe, we have no desire to believe anything else; for we begin by believing that there is nothing else which we have to believe.

8. I come then to the point which members of the Church adduce to justify speculation and which heretics press in order to import scruple and hesitation. It is written, they say: "Seek, and ye shall find." But we must not forget *when* the Lord said these words. It was surely at the very beginning of his teaching when everyone was still doubtful whether he was the Christ. Peter had not yet pronounced him to be the Son of God, and even John had lost his conviction about him. It was right to say: "Seek, and ye shall find," at the time when, being still unrecognized, he had still to be sought. Besides, it applied only to the Jews. Every word in that criticism was pointed at those who had the means of seeking Christ. "They have Moses and Elijah," it says; that is, the law and the prophets which preach Christ. Similarly he says elsewhere, and plainly: "Search the Scriptures, in which ye hope for salvation, for they speak of me." That will be what he meant by "Seek, and ye shall find."

The following words, "Knock, and it shall be opened unto you," obviously apply to the Jews. At one time inside the house of God, the Jews found themselves outside when they were thrown out because of their sins. The Gentiles, however, were never in God's house. They were but a drop from the bucket, dust from the threshing-floor, always outside. How can anyone who has always been outside knock where he has never been? How can he recognize the door if he has never been taken in or thrown out by it? Surely it is the man who knows that he was once inside and was turned out, who recognizes the door and knocks? Again, the words, "Ask, and ye shall receive," fit those who know whom to ask and by whom something has been promised, namely the God of Abraham, of Isaac, and of Jacob, of whose person and promises the Gentiles were equally ignorant. Accordingly he said to Israel: "I am not sent but unto the lost sheep of the house of Israel." He had not yet begun to cast the children's bread to the dogs nor yet told the apostles to go into the way of the Gentiles. If at the end he ordered them to go and teach and baptize the Gentiles, it was only because they were soon to receive the Holy Spirit, the Paraclete, who would guide them into all truth. This also supports our conclusion. If the apostles, the appointed teachers of the

Gentiles, were themselves to receive the Paraclete as their teacher, then the words, "Seek, and ye shall find," were much less applicable to us than to the Jews. For we were to be taught by the apostles without any effort of our own, as they were taught by the Holy Spirit. All the Lord's sayings, I admit, were set down for all men. They have come through the ears of the Jews to us Christians. Still, many were aimed at particular people and constitute for us an example rather than a command immediately applicable to ourselves.

9. However, I shall now make you a present of that point. Suppose that "Seek, and ye shall find" was said to us all. Even then it would be wrong to determine the sense without reference to the guiding principles of exegesis. No word of God is so unqualified or so unrestricted in application that the mere words can be pleaded without respect to their underlying meaning.

My first principle is this. Christ laid down one definite system of truth which the world must believe without qualification, and which we must seek precisely in order to believe it when we find it. Now you cannot search indefinitely for a single definite truth. You must seek until you find, and when you find, you must believe. Then you have simply to keep what you have come to believe, since you also believe that there is nothing else to believe, and therefore nothing else to seek, once you have found and believed what he taught who bids you seek nothing beyond what he taught. If you feel any doubt as to what this truth is, I undertake to establish that Christ's teaching is to be found with us. For the moment, my confidence in my proof allows me to anticipate it, and I warn certain people not to seek for anything beyond what they came to believe, for that was all they needed to seek for. They must not interpret, "Seek, and ye shall find," without regard to reasonable methods of exegesis.

10. The reasonable exegesis of this saying turns on three points: matter, time, and limitation. As to matter, you are to consider what is to be sought; as to time, when; and as to limitation, how far. What you must seek is what Christ taught, and precisely as long as you are not finding it, precisely until you do find it. And you did find it when you came to believe. You would not have believed if you had not found, just as you would not have sought except in order to find. Since finding was the object of your search and belief of your finding, your acceptance of the faith debars any prolongation of seeking and finding. The very success of your seeking has set up this limitation for you. Your boundary has been marked out by him who would not have you believe, and so would not have you seek, outside the limits of his teaching.

But if we are bound to go on seeking as long as there is any possibility of finding, simply because so much has been taught by others as well, we shall be always seeking and never believing. What end will there be to seeking? What point of rest for belief? Where the fruition of finding? With Marcion? But Valentinus also propounds: "Seek, and ye shall find." With Valentinus? But Apelles also will knock at my door with the same pronouncement, and Ebion and Simon and the whole row of them can find no other way to ingratiate themselves with me and bring me over to their side. There will be no end, as long as I meet everywhere with, "Seek and ye shall find," and I shall wish I had never begun to seek, if I never grasp what Christ taught, what should be sought, what must be believed.

St. Augustine (354–430)

There was no more vociferous debater in arguments about heresy than Augustine, the bishop of Hippo in North Africa. Although he is best known for his autobiographical account of his belated conversion, the Confessions, *his greatest achievement lay in his providing a coherent philosophical and theological ground for developing Christian doctrines. All of this important work occurred after the events he describes in the* Confessions. *His account of his early life displays his shifting adherence to a number of leading philosophies, including Manichaeism and Platonism. Augustine's early commitment to philosophy actually gave him the foundation for his expositions of Christian doctrine, and the deeply infused Platonism in Christianity is largely his creation. In the* City of God *he says that the Platonists represent "the closest approximation to our Christian position."*

While some Christians, moved by the impulses given voice in Tertullian, were willing simply to banish the classics, Augustine worked for a humanist accommodation, allowing that where Virgil seemed to speak truth, that truth came from God. On the other hand, Augustine also argued in On Christian Doctrine *that the Bible contained everything a Christian needed to know to recognize what to avoid and what to embrace: "Scripture teaches nothing but charity, nor condemns anything except cupidity." These great opposites,* caritas *and* cupiditas, *are dimensions of the human will, as Augustine goes on to argue.*

Augustine's Confessions *is the first autobiography, but the book is more than memoir: it is a celebration of God's power over human intransigence, and it is deeply colored by the perspective of the writer, a bishop looking back on events that reached a climax twelve years before, in 386. By the time of his conversion, Augustine could recognize God as the* One *he had met in Platonism, but was unable to abandon a life of cupidity in order to believe whole-heartedly in the faith of his pious mother. In the climactic scene, a model for thousands of conversions through the ages, Augustine is "kicked over the edge" (as C. S. Lewis says of his own conversion) by reading a random scripture passage in which God seems to speak directly to him.*

The excerpt from Augustine's *Confessions* is translated for this collection by the editor. The selection from *City of God* is translated by Henry Bettenson and published by Penguin (1972). *On Christian Doctrine* (Bobbs Merrill/Liberal Arts Press, 1958) was translated by the late Chaucerian scholar, D. W. Robertson, Jr.

[Conversion to Christianity]
from *The Confessions*

VIII. 11. Thus I was soul-sick and tormented, accusing myself much more severely than usual, rolling and turning in my chain, awaiting the time that chain would be wholly broken in which I now was only barely held, but held nevertheless. And you, O Lord, pressed upon me—in my soul—with a severe mercy, redoubling the lashes of fear and shame, so that I should not again give way, and rather than bursting that last weak bit of chain, should find it instead stronger and more binding than ever. For I said to myself, "Let it be done now; let it be done now." And as I spoke, I all but accomplished it: I almost did it, but not quite. Yet I didn't sink back to my former state, but kept my stand near by, and caught my breath. And I tried again, and fell somewhat less short of it, and somewhat less, and all but touched and laid hold of it—and yet I didn't come close enough to touch or lay hold of it. Still I hesitated to die to death and to live to life: and the bad things I was used to carried more weight with me than the good things which were new to me. As the very moment in which I was to become a new person drew nearer, the more horror it struck into me. Still, it didn't strike me back or turn me away; it held me in suspense.

Mere toys of toys, and vanities of vanities—my ancient mistresses, as it were—still held me; they plucked at my garment of flesh and whispered softly: "Do you cast us off?" and "From this moment shall we no longer be with you forever?" and "From now on will this or that no longer be lawful for you?" And what was it which they meant in what I just wrote—"this" or "that?" What were they suggesting, O my God? Let your mercy keep it away from the soul of your servant! What defilements did they suggest! What shame! And now I only partly heard them; they no longer openly showed themselves to contradict me, but muttered as it were behind my back, pulling at me as I was leaving to get me to look back on them. Yet they did hold me back, for I hesitated to burst free and shake them off, and to leap in the direction I was called. Violent habits warned me, "Do you think you can live without them?"

But now it spoke very faintly. For in the direction toward which I had turned my face, even though I still trembled to go there, I could see the chaste dignity of Continence: she was serene and self-possessed, friendly but not wanton, beckoning honestly for me to come without fear or doubt. She stretched forth her holy hands to receive and embrace me, full of multitudes of good examples. There were so many boys and girls here, a multitude of youth and every age, grave widows and aged virgins; and Continence herself in all of them, not barren, but a fruitful mother of children—of joys—by you her husband, O Lord. And she smiled on me with a pleasant persuasiveness, as if she were saying, "Can't you do what these men and women are doing? Can they even do it by themselves, without the help of the Lord their God? The Lord their God gave me to them. Why do you try to stand by yourself, and therefore not at all? Let him support you as well. Don't be afraid. He won't pull away and let you fall. Cast yourself fearlessly upon him, for he will receive you; he will heal you." And I blushed in shame, for I still heard the voices of those vanities, and I hung back, hesitating. And then she seemed to say, "Stop your ears against those unclean members of yours, so that they may be mortified. They tell you of delights, but those delights can't compare with delight in the law of the Lord your God." This controversy took place in my heart, self warring against self. . . .

VIII. 12. . . . There rose within me a mighty storm, bringing with it a shower of tears. . . . I somehow cast myself down under a fig-tree, giving full vent to my tears; and the floods of my eyes gushed out an acceptable sacrifice to you. And then I spoke to you words to this effect: "And you, O Lord, how long? How long, Lord? Will you be angry for ever? Remember not our former iniquities"—for I felt that my sins were still holding me back. I raised my voice in sorrow: "How long, how long, this 'tomorrow, and tomorrow?' Why not now? Why not end my uncleanness this very hour?"

So I was speaking and weeping in the bitter contrition of my heart. Suddenly I heard from a neighboring house a chanting voice, like that of a boy or a girl (I couldn't tell which), repeating, "Take up and read. Take up and read." My face changed at once, and I began to think most intently whether children ever sang such words in their games, but I couldn't remember ever hearing words like that before. So I stopped the flow of my tears and rose to go, certain that this sign could only be a command from God to open the book, and read the first passage I should find. For indeed I had heard that Antony, coming in during the reading of the Gospel, had received the admonition, as if what was being read was spoken directly to him: "Go, sell all that you have, and give to the poor, and you shall have treasure in heaven, and come and follow me." And by such an oracle he had been immediately converted to you.

So I returned eagerly to the place where Alypius was sitting, for I had left there the volume of the Apostle. I seized the book, opened it, and read in silence that passage on which my eyes first fell: "Not in rioting and drunkenness, not in chambering and wantonness, not in strife and envying; but put on the Lord Jesus Christ, and make not provision for the flesh, in concupiscence." I had no wish to read further; there was no need to. For at the end of this sentence, instantly a light of serenity infused my heart, and all the shadows of my former doubt vanished.

Then putting my finger or some other marker between the pages to mark my place, I shut the book, and with a calm countenance made known to Alypius what had happened. . . .

Next we go in to my mother. We tell her, and she rejoices. We describe for her how it all took place, and in triumph she leaps for joy. She blessed you, "Who are able to do above that which we ask or think"; for she perceived that you had given her more with regard to me than she used to ask for in her pitiful and sorrowful groanings. For you converted me to you in such a way that I no longer sought a wife nor any other worldly hope. I was now standing in that rule of faith where you had shown me to her in a vision so many years before. And so you changed her mourning into joy, a joy more plentiful than she had imagined, and in a purer and more precious way than she had earlier sought when she desired grandchildren of my body.

[Plato and Christianity] from *City of God*

Thus there are philosophers who have conceived of God, the supreme and true God, as the author of all created things, the light of knowledge, the Final Good of all activity, and who have recognized him as being for us the origin of existence, the truth of doctrine and the blessedness of life. They may be called, most suitably, Platonists; or they may give some other title to their school. It may be that it was only the leading members of the Ionian school who held the same opinions as Plato, and who understood him thoroughly; on the other hand, the same concepts may have been held also by Italian philosophers, because of Pythagoras and the Pythagoreans, and perhaps by some others of the same way of thinking and from the same part of the world. There may be others to be found who perceived and taught this truth among those who were esteemed as sages or philosophers in other nations: Libyans of Atlas, Egyptians, Indians, Persians, Chaldeans, Scythians, Gauls, Spaniards. Whoever they may have been, we rank such thinkers above all others and acknowledge them as representing the closest approximation to our Christian position.

A Christian whose education has been confined to the study of the Church's literature may be quite unfamiliar with the name of Platonist, and may not know of the existence of two types of Greek-speaking philosophy, the Ionian and the Italian. For all that, he is not so out of touch with life in general as to be unaware that philosophers profess the pursuit of wisdom, or even the possession of it. But he is wary of those whose philosophy is 'based on the elements of this world', and not on God, the world's creator. That is because he is put on his guard by the Apostle's injunction, and gives an attentive hearing to those words: 'Take care that no one leads you astray by philosophy and useless misleading teaching, based on the elements of the world.' However, he is prevented from regarding all thinkers as belonging to this class, when he listens to the Apostle's remarks about some of them. 'What can be known of God has been revealed among them. God in fact has revealed it to them. For his invisible realities, from the foundation of the world, have been made visible to the intelligence through his created works, as well as his eternal power and divinity.' And in his speech to the Athenians, after uttering that great saying about God, a saying which only a few can understand, 'It is in him that we have our life, our movement, and our being,' Paul goes on to say, 'as some of your own writers have also said.' The Christian knows, to be sure, that he must be on his guard against their errors. For while the Apostle says that through his created works God has revealed to them his invisible qualities by making them visible to the intelligence, he says at the same time that they have not offered the right sort of worship to God himself, because they have transferred the divine honours, due to God alone, to other objects, which have no right to them.

> Though having some acquaintance with God, they have not glorified him as God, nor have they given thanks to him; but they have dwindled into futility in their thinking and their stupid heart is shrouded in darkness. In claiming to be wise they have become fools and have exchanged the glory of the incorruptible God for images representing corruptible man, or birds, beasts or snakes.

In this passage Paul intends us to understand a reference to the Romans, the Greeks and the Egyptians, who were proud of their reputation for wisdom. We shall later on engage in argument with them on this subject. But they agree with us in the conception of one God, who is the author of this whole universe, who is not only above all material things, as immaterial, but also, as incorruptible, above all souls, who is, in fact, our source, our light, our good; and in respect of this we rank them above all the others.

A Christian may be unacquainted with the writings of the philosophers; he may not employ in debate words which he has never learnt; he may not apply the Latin term 'natural' or the Greek term 'physical' to the division of philosophy which deals with the study of nature, or the term 'rational', or 'logical', to the division which discusses how we can reach the truth; or 'moral' or 'ethical' to the part which treats of morality, of the good ends which are to be pursued and the evil ends to be avoided. It does not follow that he fails to realize that we derive from the one true God of all goodness the nature with which we were created in his image. It does not mean that he is ignorant of the teaching thanks to which we acquire knowledge of God and of ourselves, nor that he is ignorant of the grace through which we are united to him and thus attain our happiness.

This is why we rate the Platonists above the rest of the philosophers. The others have employed their talents and concentrated their interests on the investigation of the causes of things, of the method of acquiring knowledge, and the rules of the moral life, while the Platonists, coming to a knowledge of God, have found the cause of the organized universe, the light by which truth is perceived, and the spring which offers the drink of felicity. All philosophers who have this conception of God are in agreement with our idea of him, whether they are Platonists or philosophers of any other kind, of any nation. The reason why I have decided to concentrate on the Platonists is that their writings are more generally known. For one thing, the Greeks, whose language enjoys a pre-eminent position internationally, have given the Platonists the widest publicity; for another, the Latins, struck by their excellence, or by their renown, have studied their writings in preference to others, and by translating them into our language have made them better known and more highly regarded.

VI
from *On Christian Doctrine*

7. But many and varied obscurities and ambiguities deceive those who read casually, understanding one thing instead of another; indeed, in certain places they do not find anything to interpret erroneously, so obscurely are certain sayings covered with a most dense mist. I do not doubt that this situation was provided by God to conquer pride by work and to combat disdain in our minds, to which those things which are easily discovered seem frequently to become worthless. For example, it may be said that there are holy and perfect men with whose lives and customs as an exemplar the Church of Christ is able to destroy all sorts of superstitions in those who come to it and to incorporate them into itself, men of good faith, true servants of God, who, putting aside the burden of the world, come to the holy laver of baptism and, ascending thence, conceive through the Holy Spirit and produce the fruit of a twofold love of God and their neighbor. But why is it, I ask, that if anyone says this he delights his hearers less than if he had said the same thing in expounding that place in the Canticle of Canticles where it is said of the Church, as she is being praised as a beautiful woman, "Thy teeth are as flocks of sheep, that are shorn, which come up from the washing, all with twins, and there is none barren among them"? Does one learn anything else besides that which he learns when he hears the same thought expressed in plain words without this similitude? Nevertheless, in a strange way, I contemplate the saints more pleasantly when I envisage them as the teeth of the Church cutting off men from their errors and transferring them to her body after their hardness has been softened as if by being bitten and chewed. I recognize them most pleasantly as shorn sheep having put aside the burdens of the world like so much fleece, and as ascending from the washing, which is baptism, all to create twins, which are the two precepts of love, and I see no one of them sterile of this holy fruit.

8. But why it seems sweeter to me than if no such similitude were offered in the divine books, since the thing perceived is the same, is difficult to say and is a problem for another discussion. For the present, however, no one doubts that things are perceived more readily through similitudes and that what is sought with difficulty is discovered with more pleasure. Those who do not find what they seek directly stated labor in hunger; those who do not seek because they have what they wish at once frequently become indolent in disdain. In either of these situations indifference is an evil. Thus the Holy Spirit has magnificently and wholesomely modulated the Holy Scriptures so that the more open places present themselves to hunger and the more obscure places may deter a disdainful attitude. Hardly anything may be found in these obscure places which is not found plainly said elsewhere.

XVIII

28. . . . But we should not think that we ought not to learn literature because Mercury is said to be its inventor, nor that because the pagans dedicated temples to Justice and Virtue and adored in stones what should be performed in the heart, we should therefore avoid justice and virtue. Rather, every good and true Christian should understand that wherever he may find truth, it is his Lord's.

XLII

63. To the extent that the wealth of gold and silver and clothing which that people took with them from Egypt was less than that they afterwards acquired at Jerusalem, especially during the reign of King Solomon, the knowledge collected from the books of the pagans, although some of it is useful, is also little as compared with that derived from the Holy Scriptures. For whatever a man has learned elsewhere is censured there if it is harmful; if it is useful, it is found there. And although anyone may find everything which he has usefully learned elsewhere there, he will also find very abundantly things which are found nowhere else at all except as they are taught with the wonderful nobility and remarkable humility of the Holy Scriptures.

X

16. I call "charity" the motion of the soul toward the enjoyment of God for His own sake, and the enjoyment of one's self and of one's neighbor for the sake of God; but "cupidity" is a motion of the soul toward the enjoyment of one's self, one's neighbor, or any corporal thing for the sake of something other than God. That which uncontrolled cupidity does to corrupt the soul and its body is called a "vice"; what it does in such a way that someone else is harmed is called a "crime." And these are the two classes of all sins, but vices occur first. When vices have emptied the soul and led it to a kind of extreme hunger, it leaps into crimes by means of which impediments to the vices may be removed or the vices themselves sustained. On the other hand, what charity does to the charitable person is called "utility"; what it does to benefit one's neighbor is called "beneficence." And here utility occurs first, for no one may benefit another with that which he does not have himself. The more the reign of cupidity is destroyed, the more charity is increased.

Boethius (c.480–524)

THE CONSOLATION OF PHILOSOPHY

If any writer of philosophy between St. Augustine and Thomas Aquinas can command the attention and interest of modern readers it is Boethius. Students who read the Consolation of Philosophy *often feel that Boethius gives expression to sentiments about the world, about mortality, and about the value of contemporary pursuits, that match their own. This is partly because Boethius is laying out that generalized stoic point of view that passes for what we popularly call* philosophical, *as in "She's taking the bad news philosophically." It is also because Boethius, a disciple of Plato, wrote in the dramatic* consolatio *form that was similar to Plato's dialogues, with the added variety of alternating prose and verse sections borrowed from the form of* Menippean satire. *So important was the* Consolation of Philosophy *in the Middle Ages that it became a best-seller, and manuscripts even survive that are small and wrapped in leather with an attached leather ball that could be slipped under the belt for traveling—a medieval pocket book. It was translated into Old English by King Alfred the Great, into Middle English by Geoffrey Chaucer, and into early Modern English by Queen Elizabeth I.*

Anicius Boethius came from a wealthy and aristocratic Roman family that claimed consuls, a Pope, and two emperors as ancestors. From his youth he proved a gifted scholar—one of the last in the Western Empire to master Greek—and he set as his life's task the translating of all of Plato and Aristotle into Latin, as well as demonstrating that their philosophies were in agreement, and not at odds as was generally thought. In actual fact, he managed to translate only Aristotle's treatises on logic, and these became the basis of the meager knowledge of Aristotle's writings in the West until the rest were acquired from Muslim scholars in Spain in the twelfth century.

Boethius didn't complete this project because he became involved in politics, with personally disastrous results. At the end of the fifth century, the Ostrogothic king, Theodoric, became king over the Romans in Italy on behalf of the Emperor in Constantinople. A powerful monarch, he enlisted Boethius and other brilliant Romans to serve in his capital in Ravenna. Boethius was impelled, he says in the Consolation, *by Plato's belief "that the reason why it was necessary for philosophers to take part in government was to prevent the reins of government falling into the hands of wicked and unprincipled men to the ruin*

Reprinted from *The Consolation of Philosophy,* Revised Edition, translated by Victor Watts (Penguin, 1999).

and destruction of the good" (I.4). In a political conflict between Theodoric, the Pope, and the Emperor, Boethius was accused (falsely, he says in the Consolation*) of treason and sentenced by Theodoric to exile in Pavia until he could be tortured and executed.*

From prison, during the year before his execution, Boethius wrote the Consolation of Philosophy, *a dream vision in which his old teacher, Philosophy, appears to him to recall him from his feelings of anger and betrayal and to nurse him back to intellectual health. Using the striking image of the Wheel of Fortune, Philosophy forces him to recognize again what he already knew—that the wealth, power, position, and fame that were his and that are now lost were of no real value. Happiness can be found only through the evident self-sufficiency of the mind. To be happy is to turn away from the darkness of the world, and, like the cave-dweller in Plato's "Figure of the Cave" (earlier in this collection), to ascend into the light by apprehending the higher truth of God's providential order.*

II.1. After this she fell silent for a while and the very forbearance of her silence made me turn my attention to her. At this she began to speak again.

"If I have fully diagnosed the cause and nature of your condition, you are wasting away in pining and longing for your former good fortune. It is the loss of this which, as your imagination works upon you, has so corrupted your mind. I know the many disguises of that monster, Fortune, and the extent to which she seduces with friendship the very people she is striving to cheat, until she overwhelms them with unbearable grief at the suddenness of her desertion. If you can recall to mind her character, her methods, and the kind of favour she proffers, you will see that in her you did not have and did not lose anything of value. But I am sure it will require no hard work on my part to bring all this back to your memory. It used to be your way whenever she came near with her flattery to attack her with manly arguments and hound her with pronouncements taken from the oracle of my shrine. However, no sudden change of circumstances ever occurs without some upheaval in the mind; and that is why you, too, have deserted for a while your usual calm. . . .

"What is it then O mortal man, that has thrown you down into the slough of grief and despondency? You must have seen something strange and unexpected. But you are wrong if you think Fortune has changed towards you. Change is her normal behaviour, her true nature. In the very act of changing she has preserved her own particular kind of constancy towards you. She was exactly the same when she was flattering you and luring you on with enticements of a false kind of happiness. You have discovered the changing faces of the random goddess. To others she still veils herself, but to you she has revealed herself to the full. If you are satisfied with her ways, you must accept them and not complain. But if you shudder to think of her unreliability, you must turn away and have nothing more to do with her dangerous games. She has caused you untold sorrow when she ought to have been a source of peace. For she has left you, she in whose constancy no man can ever trust. Do you really hold dear that kind of happiness which is destined to pass away? Do you really value the presence of Fortune when you cannot trust her to stay and when her departure will plunge you in sorrow? And if it is impossible to keep her at will and if her flight exposes men to ruin, what else is such a fleeting thing except a warning of coming disaster? It will never be sufficient just to notice what is under one's nose: prudence calculates what the outcome of things will be. Either way Fortune's very mutability deprives her threats of their terror and her enticements of their allure. And last of all, once you have bowed your neck beneath her yoke, you ought to bear with equanimity whatever happens on Fortune's playground. If after freely choosing her as the mistress to rule your life you want to draw up a law to control her coming and going, you will be acting without any justification and your very impatience will only worsen a lot which you cannot alter. Commit your boat to the winds and you must sail whichever way they blow, not just where you want. If you were a farmer who entrusts his seed to the fields, you would balance the bad years against the good. So now you have committed yourself to the rule of Fortune, you must acquiesce in her ways. If you are trying to stop her wheel from turning,[1] you are of all men the most obtuse. For if it once begins to stop, it will no longer be the wheel of chance.

"With domineering hand she moves the turning wheel,
Like currents in a treacherous bay swept to and fro:
Her ruthless will has just deposed once fearful kings
While trustless still, from low she lifts a conquered head;
No cries of misery she hears, no tears she heeds,
But steely hearted laughs at groans her deeds have wrung.
Such is the game she plays, and so she tests her strength;
Of mighty power she makes parade when one short hour
Sees happiness from utter desolation grow."

II.2. "I would like to continue our discussion a while by using Fortune's own arguments, and I would like you to consider whether her demands are just. 'Why do you burden me each day, mortal man,' she asks, 'with your querulous accusations? What harm have I done you? What possessions of yours have I stolen? Choose any judge you like and sue me for possession of wealth and rank, and if you can show that any part of these belongs by right to any mortal man, I will willingly concede that what you are seeking to regain really did belong to you. When nature brought you forth from your mother's womb I received you naked and devoid of everything and fed you from my own resources. I was inclined to favour you, and I brought you up—and this is what makes you lose patience with me—with a measure of indulgence, surrounding you with all the splendour and affluence at my command. Now I have decided to withdraw my hand. You have been receiving a favour as one who has had the use of another's possessions, and you have no right to complain as if what you have lost was fully your own. You have no cause to begin groaning at me: I have done you no violence. Wealth, honours and the like are all under my jurisdiction. They are my servants and know their mistress. When I come, they come with me, and when

1. Though not original—the wheel of Fortune was a favourite expression of Cicero for instance—this is one of the most striking images in the *Consolation* and is the source of the many medieval allusions to Fortune and her wheel. [Editor's note: an illustration of Fortune's wheel from a manuscript of Boethius can be found on page 258.]

I go, they leave as well. I can say with confidence that if the things whose loss you are bemoaning were really yours, you could never have lost them. . . .'"

II.4. "All that you say is true," I agreed. "You truly are mother of all virtues, and I cannot deny the speed with which I rose to prosperity. It is the very thing, in fact, which makes me burn with grief as I remember it. In all adversity of fortune, the most wretched kind is once to have been happy."

"But you are suffering because of your misguided belief, and you can't blame events for that," she replied. "If you are really so moved by the empty name of chance happiness, you can reckon up with me now the number of the very great blessings you still enjoy. And if you find that you still possess that which among all the gifts of Fortune was most precious to you and find it through God's power unharmed and still untouched, you will hardly be able to talk about misfortune with any justice while you still possess outstanding blessings.

"Take your father-in-law, Symmachus, one of the most precious ornaments of the human race; he is still full of vigour and—something you would willingly pay for with your life—a man wholly composed of wisdom and virtue, who disregards his own sufferings and weeps for yours. Your wife, too, is alive, a lady unsurpassed in nobility and modesty of character; to sum up all her qualities in a word, I would say she is the mirror of her father. She is, as I say, still alive and in her disgust with this life draws every breath for you alone. She longs for you and is consumed with tears and suffering, one thing in which I would concede that your happiness is diminished. I don't know what more to add about your consular sons. Now, as when they were boys, they reflect the example of their father's and grandfather's character. You are a happy man, then, if you know where your true happiness lies, since when the chief concern of mortal men is to keep their hold on life, you even now possess blessings which no one can doubt are more precious than life itself. So dry your tears. Fortune has not yet turned her hatred against all your blessings. The storm has not yet broken upon you with too much violence. Your anchors are holding firm and they permit you both comfort in the present, and hope in the future."

"And I pray that they will hold," I said. "So long as they do, we will ride the storm out. But look how far events have gone since the time of my glory."

"If you are no longer dissatisfied with the whole of your fortune, we have made a little progress," she said. "But I can't put up with your dilly-dallying and the dramatization of your care-worn grief-stricken complaints that something is lacking from your happiness. No man is so completely happy that something somewhere does not clash with his condition. It is the nature of human affairs to be fraught with anxiety; they never prosper perfectly and they never remain constant. In one man's case you will find riches offset by the shame of a humble birth and in another's noble birth offset by unwelcome publicity on account of the crippling poverty of his family fortunes. Some men are blessed with both wealth and noble birth, but are unhappy because they have no wife. Some are happily married but without children, and husband their money for an heir of alien blood. Some again have been blessed with children only to weep over their misdeeds. No one finds it easy to accept the lot Fortune has sent him. There is something in the case of each of us that escapes the notice of the man who has not experienced it, but causes horror to the man who has. Remember, too, that all the most happy men are over-sensitive. They have never experienced adversity and so unless everything obeys their slightest whim they are prostrated by every minor upset, so trifling are the things that can detract from the complete happiness of a man at the summit of fortune. How many men do you think would believe themselves almost in heaven if they possessed even the smallest part of the luck you still enjoy? This very place which is banishment to you is home to those who live here. So nothing is miserable except when you think it so, and vice versa, all luck is good luck to the man who bears it with equanimity. No one is so happy that he would not want to change his lot if he gives in to impatience. Such is the bitter-sweetness of human happiness. To him that enjoys it, it may seem full of delight, but he cannot prevent it slipping away when it will. It is evident, therefore, how miserable the happiness of human life is; it does not remain long with those who are patient, and doesn't satisfy those who are troubled.

"Why then do you mortal men seek after happiness outside yourselves, when it lies within you? . . ."

II.5. . . . "From all this it is obvious that not one of those things which you count among your blessings is in fact any blessing of your own at all. And if, then, they don't contain a spark of beauty worth seeking, why weep over their loss or rejoice at their preservation? If Nature gives them their beauty, how does it involve you? They would still have been pleasing by themselves, even if separated from your possessions. It isn't because they are part of your wealth that they are precious, but because you thought them precious that you wanted to add them to the sum of your riches.

"What in fact is it that you are looking for in all this outcry against Fortune? To put poverty to flight with plenty? If so, it has turned out the very opposite. The more varied your precious possessions, the more help you need to protect them, and the old saying is proved correct, he who hath much, wants much. And the contrary is true as well, he needs least who measures wealth according to the needs of nature, and not the excesses of ostentation.

"It seems as if you feel a lack of any blessing of your own inside you, which is driving you to seek your blessings in things separate and external. And so when a being endowed with a godlike quality in virtue of his rational nature thinks that his only splendour lies in the possession of inanimate goods, it is the overthrow of the natural order. Other creatures are content with what is their own, but you, whose mind is made in the image of God, seek to adorn your superior nature with inferior objects, oblivious of the great wrong you do your Creator. . . ."

III.2. She stood gazing at the ground for a while, as if she had retreated into the recesses of thought, and then began to speak again.

"In all the care with which they toil at countless enterprises, mortal men travel by different paths, though all are striving to reach one and the same goal, namely, happiness, beatitude, which is a good which once obtained leaves nothing more to be desired. It is the perfection of all good things and contains in itself all that is good; and if anything were missing from it, it couldn't be perfect, because something would remain outside it, which could still be wished for. It is clear, therefore, that happiness is a state made perfect by the presence of everything that is good, a state, which, as we said, all mortal men are striving to reach though by different paths. For the desire for true good is planted by nature in the minds of men, only error leads them astray towards false good.

"Some men believe that perfect good consists in having no wants, and so they toil in order to end up rolling in wealth. Some think that the true good is that which is most worthy of respect, and so struggle for position in order to be held in respect by their fellow citizens. Some decide that it lies in the highest power, and either want to be rulers themselves, or try to attach themselves to those in power. Others think that the best thing is fame and busy themselves to make a name in the arts of war or peace. But most people measure the possession of the good by the amount of enjoyment and delight it brings, convinced that being abandoned to pleasure is the highest form of happiness. Others again confuse ends and means with regard to these things, such as people who desire riches for the sake of power and pleasure, or those who want power for the sake of money or fame. So it is in these and other such objectives that the aim of human activity and desire is to be found, in fame and popularity which appear to confer a kind of renown, or in a wife and children which men desire for the sake of the pleasure they give. And as for friendship, the purest kind is counted as a mark not of good fortune, but of moral worth, but all other friendship is cultivated for the sake of power or pleasure.

"Now, it is clear that physical endowments are aspects of higher blessings: for clearly bodily strength and size give a man might; beauty and speed give him renown; and health gives him pleasure. And through all of this it is clear that the only thing men desire is happiness. Each man considers whatever he desires above all else to be the supreme good. We have already defined the supreme good as happiness; so that the state which each man desires above all others is judged by him to be one of happiness. So you have before you the general pattern of human happiness—wealth, position, power, fame, pleasure. Taking only these into consideration, Epicurus with perfect consistency stated that pleasure was the highest good, because all the others bring the mind enjoyment. . . .

"These, then, are the things which people long to obtain. And they want riches, position, estates, glory and pleasures, because it is their conviction that through them they will achieve self-sufficiency, respect, power, celebrity and happiness. This is the good that men are looking for in such a variety of pursuits."

III.8. "There is no doubt, then, that these roads to happiness are side-tracks and cannot bring us to the destination they promise. The evils with which they are beset are great, as I will briefly show you. If you try to hoard money, you will have to take it by force. If you want to be resplendent in the dignities of high office, you will have to grovel before the man who bestows it: in your desire to outdo others in high honour you will have to cheapen and humiliate yourself by begging. If you want power, you will have to expose yourself to the plots of your subjects and run dangerous risks. If fame is what you seek, you will find yourself on a hard road, drawn this way and that until you are worn with care. Decide to lead a life of pleasure, and there will be no one who will not reject you with scorn as the slave of that most worthless and brittle master, the human body. . . ."

III.9. . . . "O Thou who dost by everlasting reason rule,
Creator of the planets and the sky, who time
From timelessness dost bring, unchanging Mover,
No cause drove Thee to mould unstable matter, but
The form benign of highest good within Thee set.

All things Thou bringest forth from Thy high archetype:
Thou, height of beauty, in Thy mind the beauteous world
Dost bear, and in that ideal likeness shaping it,
Dost order perfect parts a perfect whole to frame.
The elements by harmony Thou dost constrain,
That hot to cold and wet to dry are equal made,
That fire grow not too light, or earth too fraught with weight.
The bridge of threefold nature mad'st Thou soul, which spreads
Through nature's limbs harmonious and all things moves.
The soul once cut, in circles two its motion joins,
Goes round and to itself returns encircling mind,
And turns in pattern similar the firmament.
From causes like Thou bringst forth souls and lesser lives,
Which from above in chariots swift Thou dost disperse
Through sky and earth, and by Thy law benign they turn
And back to Thee they come through fire that brings them home.
Grant, Father, that our minds Thy august seat may scan,
Grant us the sight of true good's source, and grant us light
That we may fix on Thee our mind's unblinded eye.
Disperse the clouds of earthly matter's cloying weight;
Shine out in all Thy glory; for Thou art rest and peace
To those who worship Thee; to see Thee is our end,
Who art our source and maker, lord and path and goal."

IV.6. . . . "The generation of all things, the whole progress of things subject to change and whatever moves in any way, receive their causes, their due order and their form from the unchanging mind of God. In the high citadel of its oneness, the mind of God has set up a plan for the multitude of events. When this plan is thought of as in the purity of God's understanding, it is called Providence, and when it is thought of with reference to all things, whose motion and order it controls, it is called by the name the ancients gave it, Fate. If anyone will examine their meaning, it will soon be clear to him that these two aspects are different. Providence is the divine reason itself. It is set at the head of all things and disposes all things. Fate, on the other hand, is the planned order inherent in things subject to change through the medium of which Providence binds everything in its own allotted place. Providence includes all things at the same time, however diverse or infinite, while Fate controls the motion of different individual things in different places and in different times. So this unfolding of the plan in time when brought together as a unified whole in the foresight of God's mind is Providence; and the same unified whole when dissolved and unfolded in the course of time is Fate.

"They are different, but the one depends on the other. The order of Fate is derived from the simplicity of Providence. . . ."

Benedict of Nursia (480–542)

The Rule of St. Benedict

Benedict, from a good family and educated in good Roman schools, had a temperament well-suited to the monastic movement which was spreading during his lifetime. His response to the growing corruption and decay in Rome was to retreat to a cave outside the city to live a life of contemplation. He lived alone there, wearing borrowed monastic garb, for three years. His reputation for sanctity led to his being named abbot of a nearby monastery and soon the number of his followers led him to found a large order at Monte Cassino, between Rome and Naples.

While he admired the life of the solitary hermit, Benedict realized that most Christians dedicated to a life of absolute devotion would thrive better in a community, and he developed his Rule *as a guide for that working and praying community. The* Rule *takes notice of all aspects of monastic life, from the times of religious observances, to the duties of every level of worker and monk. More impressive is Benedict's care for spiritual growth and for human concerns, and his careful provision of sufficient food, clothing, and sleep to balance the routines of work, prayer, and study. Young men entering orders would take vows that acknowledged the permanence of the arrangement. One typical vow recorded in the early church ran like this:*

> I, brother Gerald, in the presence of abbot Gerald and the other brothers, promise steadfastness in this monastery according to the rule of St. Benedict and the precepts of Sts. Peter and Paul; and I hereby surrender all my possessions to this monastery, built in the honor of St. Peter and governed by the abbot Gerald.

A more detailed vow announced the kind of life that lay ahead:

> I hereby renounce my parents, my brothers and relatives, my friends, my possessions and my property, and the vain and empty glory and pleasure of this world. I also renounce my own will, for the will of God. I accept all the hardships of the monastic life,

Reprinted from *Benedict of Nursia*, translated by Cardinal Gasquet (Chatto and Windus, 1925).

> and take the vows of purity, chastity, and poverty, in the hope of heaven; and I promise to remain a monk in this monastery all the days of my life.

The Rule *remained the chief guide to the monastic life for monks of many orders for more than fifteen centuries. The order founded by Benedict is known as the Benedictine order. In 1964, because of the civilizing work of Benedictine monks in Europe during the Middle Ages, Pope Paul VI proclaimed Benedict the patron saint of Europe. Benedict's famous abbey at Monte Cassino, the parent house of European monasticism, was not so peaceful a place as Benedict's* Rule *would dictate. It was taken by Lombards in 589, by Saracens in 884, and by Normans in 1030. During the Black Death an earthquake damaged the buildings, which were rebuilt in the sixteenth and seventeenth centuries. In 1944, falsely believing the monastery to be a German stronghold, the Allies bombed the building to rubble, then rebuilt it to its original plans after the war.*

What the Abbot Should Be

An abbot to be fit to rule a monastery should ever remember what he is called, and in his acts illustrate his high calling. For in a monastery he is considered to take the place of Christ, since he is called by His name as the apostle saith, *Ye have received the spirit of the adoption of sons, whereby we cry, Abba, Father.* Therefore the abbot should neither teach, ordain, nor require anything against the command of our Lord (God forbid!), but in the minds of his disciples let his orders and teaching be mingled with the leaven of divine justice.

The abbot should ever be mindful that at the dread judgment of God there will be inquiry both as to his teaching and as to the obedience of his disciples. Let the abbot know that any lack of goodness, which the master of the family shall find in his flock, will be accounted the shepherd's fault. On the other hand, he shall be acquitted in so far as he shall have shown all the watchfulness of a shepherd over a restless and disobedient flock: and if as their pastor he shall have employed every care to cure their corrupt manners, he shall be declared guiltless in the Lord's judgment, and he may say with the prophet, *I have not hidden Thy justice in my heart; I have told Thy truth and Thy salvation; but they contemned and despised me.* And then in the end shall death be inflicted as a meet punishment upon the sheep which have not responded to his care. When, therefore, any one shall receive the name of abbot, he ought to rule his disciples with a twofold teaching: that is, he should first show them in deeds rather than words all that is good and holy. To such as are understanding, indeed, he may expound the Lord's behests by words; but to the hard-hearted and to the simple-minded he must manifest the divine precepts in his life. Thus, what he has taught his disciples to be contrary to God's law, let him show in his own deeds that such things are not be done, lest preaching to others *he himself become a castaway,* and God say unto him thus sinning, *why dost thou declare My justices, and take My testament in thy mouth? Thou hast hated discipline, and cast My speeches behind thee.* And *Thou, who didst see the mote in thy brother's eye, hast thou not seen the beam that is in thine own?*

Let him make no distinction of persons in the monastery. Let not one be loved more than another, save such as be found to excel in obedience or good works. Let not the free-born be put before the serf-born in religion, unless there be other reasonable cause for it. If upon due consideration the abbot shall see such cause he may place him where he pleases; otherwise let all keep their own places, because *whether bond or free we are all one in Christ,* and bear an equal burden of service under one Lord: *for with God there is no accepting of persons.* For one thing only are we preferred by Him, if we are found better than others in good works and more humble. Let the abbot therefore have equal love for all, and let all, according to their deserts, be under the same discipline.

The abbot in his teaching should always observe that apostolic rule which saith, Reprove, entreat, rebuke. That is to say, as occasions require he ought to mingle encouragement with reproofs. Let him manifest the sternness of a master and the loving affection of a father. He must reprove the undisciplined and restless severely, but he should exhort such as are obedient, quiet and patient, for their better profit. We charge him, however, to reprove and punish the stubborn and negligent. Let him not shut his eyes to the sins of offenders; but, directly they begin to show themselves and to grow, he must use every means to root them up utterly. . . .

To the more virtuous and apprehensive, indeed, he may for the first or second time use words of warning; but in dealing with the stubborn, the hard-headed, the proud and the disobedient, even at the very beginning of their sin, let him chastise them with stripes and with bodily punishments; knowing that it is written, *The fool is not corrected with words.* And again, *strike thy son with a rod and thou shalt deliver his soul from death.*

The abbot ought ever to bear in mind what he is and what he is called; he ought to know that to whom more is entrusted, from him more is exacted. Let him recognize how difficult and how hard a task he has undertaken, to rule souls and to make himself a servant to the humours of many. One, forsooth, must be led by gentle words, another by sharp reprehension, another by persuasion; and thus shall he so shape and adapt himself to the character and intelligence of each, that he not only suffer no loss in the flock entrusted to his care, but may even rejoice in its good growth. Above all things let him not slight nor make little of the souls committed to his care, heeding more fleeting, worldly and frivolous things; but let him remember always that he has undertaken the government of souls, of which he shall also have to give an account. And that he may not complain of the want of temporal means, let him remember that it is written, *Seek first the kingdom of God, and His justice, and all things shall be given to you.* And again, *Nothing is wanting to such as fear Him.*

He should know that whoever undertakes the government of souls must prepare himself to account for them. And however great the number of the brethren under him may be, let him understand for certain that at the Day of Judgment he will have to give to our Lord an account of all their souls as well as of his own. In this way, by fearing the inquiry concerning his flock which the Shepherd will hold, he is solicitous on account of others' souls as well as of his own, and thus whilst reclaiming other men by his corrections, he frees himself also from all vice.

ON TAKING COUNSEL OF THE BRETHREN

Whenever any weighty matters have to be transacted in the monastery let the abbot call together all the community and himself propose the matter for discussion. After hearing the advice of the brethren let him consider it in his own mind, and then do what he shall judge most expedient. We ordain that all must be called to council, because the Lord often reveals to younger members what is best. And let the brethren give their advice with all humble subjection, and presume not stiffly to defend their own opinion. Let them rather leave the matter to the abbot's discretion, so that all submit to what he shall deem best. As it becometh disciples to obey their master, so doth it behoove the master to dispose of all things with forethought and justice. . . .

The Instruments of Good Works

First of all, to love the Lord God with all our heart, with all our soul, with all our strength.

Then, to love our neighbor as ourselves.
Then, not to kill.
Not to commit adultery.
Not to steal.
Not to be covetous.
Not to bear false witness.
To respect all men.
Not to do to another what one would not have done to oneself.
To deny oneself in order to follow Christ.
To chastise the body.
Not to be fond of pleasures.
To love fasting.
To give refreshment to the poor.
To clothe the naked.
To visit the sick.
To bury the dead.
To come to the help of those in trouble.
To comfort those in sadness. . . .
Not to wish to be called holy before one is so; but to be holy first so as to be called such with truth.
Daily in one's acts to keep God's commandments.
To love chastity.
To hate no man.
Not to be jealous or envious.
Not to love wrangling.
To show no arrogant spirit.
To reverence the old.
To love the young.
To pray for one's enemies for the love of Christ.
To make peace with an adversary before the sun sets.
And, never to despair of God's mercy.

Behold these are the tools of our spiritual craft; when we shall have made use of them constantly day and night, and shall have proved them at the day of judgment, that reward shall be given us by our Lord, which He has promised, *Which eye hath not seen, nor ear heard, nor hath it entered into the heart of man to conceive what God hath prepared for those that love Him.* Steadfastly abiding in the community, the workshop where all these instruments are made use of is the cloister of the monastery.

How Young Children Are to Be Corrected

Every age and state of intelligence ought to be governed in the way suitable to it. Thus the faults of those who are children or youths, or who cannot understand the seriousness of the penalty of excommunication, shall be punished by rigorous fasting or corrected by sharp stripes.

Ought Monks to Have Anything of Their Own

Above all others, let this vice be extirpated in the monastery. No one, without leave of the abbot, shall presume to give, or receive, or keep as his own, anything whatever: neither book, nor tablets, nor pen: nothing at all. For monks are men who can claim no dominion even over their own bodies or wills. All that is necessary, however, they may hope from the Father of the monastery; but they shall keep nothing which the abbot has not given or allowed. All things are to be common to all, as it is written, *Neither did any one say or think that aught was his own.* Hence if any one shall be found given to this most wicked vice let him be admonished once or twice, and if he do not amend let him be subjected to correction.

Whether All Ought to Receive Necessary Things Uniformly

It is written, *Distribution was made to every one, according as he had need.* By this we do not mean that there is to be a personal preference (which God forbid), but a consideration for infirmities. In this wise let him who needs less thank God and be not distressed, and let him who requires more be humiliated because of his infirmity, and not puffed up by the mercy that is shown him: so all the members shall be in peace. Above all things let not the pest of murmuring, for whatever cause, by any word or sign, be manifested. If any one shall be found faulty in this let him be subjected to the most severe punishment.

Of the Weekly Servers in the Kitchen

The brethren are so to serve each other that no one be excused from work of the kitchen unless on the score of health, or because he is occupied in some matter of great utility, for thence great reward is obtained and charity is exercised. Let the weaker brethren, however, have help that they may not do their work in sadness; and let all generally be helped according to the circumstances of the community or the position of the place (i.e. kitchen). If the community be large the cellarer may be eased from the service of the kitchen, and any others who (as we have said) are engaged in matters of greater utility. Let the rest serve one another in charity. On Saturday, he who ends his weekly service must clean up everything. He must wash the towels with which the brethren wipe their hands and feet; and he who finishes his service, and he who enters on it, are to wash the feet of all. He shall give back to the cellarer all the vessels used in his ministry, cleaned and unbroken, and the cellarer shall hand them to the one entering on his office, that he may know what he gives and what he receives. . . .

The Weekly Reader

There ought always to be reading whilst the brethren eat at table. Yet no one shall presume to read there from any book taken up at haphazard; but whoever is appointed to read for the whole week is to enter on his office on the Sunday. Let the brother when beginning his service after Mass and Communion ask all to pray for him, that God may preserve him from the spirit of pride. And let the following verse be thrice repeated by all in the oratory, he, the reader, first beginning: *O Lord, Thou wilt open my lips, and my mouth shall declare Thy praise,* then, having received a blessing, let the reader enter upon his office. The greatest silence shall be kept, so that no whispering, nor noise, save the voice of the reader alone, be heard there.

Whatever is required for eating and drinking the brethren shall minister to each other so that no one need ask for anything. Yet should anything be wanted it ought to be demanded by sign rather than by word. Let no one ask any question there about what is being read or about anything else, lest occasion be given to the evil one; unless, perhaps, the prior shall wish to say something briefly for the purpose of edification. The brother who is reader for the week may take a mess of pottage before beginning to read, on account of Holy Communion, and lest perchance it may be too long for him to fast. He shall eat afterwards with the weekly servers and kitchen helpers. The brethren, however, are not all to read or sing in course, but only such as may edify the hearers.

Of the Amount of Food

We believe that it is enough to satisfy just requirement if in the daily meals, at both the sixth and ninth hours, there be at all seasons of the year two cooked dishes, so that he who cannot eat of the one may make his meal of the other. Therefore two dishes of cooked food must suffice for all the brethren, and if there be any fruit or young vegetables these may be added to the meal as a third dish. Let a pound weight of bread suffice for each day, whether there be one meal or two, that is, for both dinner and supper. If there is to be supper a third of the pound is to be kept back by the cellarer and given to the brethren at that meal.

If however, the community has been occupied in any great labor it shall be at the will, and in the power of the abbot, if he think fit, to increase the allowance, so long as every care be taken to guard against excess, and that no monk be incapacitated by surfeiting. For nothing is more contrary to the Christian spirit than gluttony, as our Lord declares, *Take heed to yourselves lest perhaps your hearts be overcharged with surfeiting.* And the same quantity shall not be given to young children, but a lesser amount than those older; frugality being maintained in everything. All, save the very weak and sick, are to abstain wholly from eating the flesh of quadrupeds [animals with four feet].

Of the Measure of Drinks

Every one hath his proper gift from God, one thus, another thus. For this reason the amount of other people's food cannot be determined without some misgiving. Still, having regard to the weak state of the sick, we think that a pint of wine a day is sufficient for any one. But let those whom God gives the gift of abstinence know that they shall receive their proper reward. If either local circumstances, the amount of labour, or the heat of the summer require more, it can be allowed at the will of the prior, care being taken in all things that gluttony and drunkenness creep not in.

Although we read that "wine is not the drink of monks at all," yet, since in our days they cannot be persuaded of this, let us at least agree not to drink to satiety, but sparingly, *Because wine maketh even the wise to fall away.*

THE KORAN

The Koran is the holy book of Islam, one of the three great monotheistic religions of the West. The Koran is actually a collection of the prophetic utterances of Muhammad, as they were given to him in visions by messengers of God. Recognized as the same God worshipped in their own ways by Jews and by Christians, the God of Islam is starkly alone, all-powerful, and deeply concerned with humans. Islam means submission, and the proper stance of the Muslim is undisputing obedience. Acknowledging the importance of the stories and traditions of both Jews and Christians, Islam gives special place to Abraham, who submitted to God in his willingness to sacrifice his son Isaac at God's command, and who was the father of Ishmael.

The founder of Islam, Muhammad, was born into the Quraysh, the tribe who controlled the city of Mecca and its sacred shrine, the Kaaba. The Kaaba was a structure which held a sacred black stone traditionally believed to have been carried by Adam as he left Eden. Before Muhammad's time, the Kaaba was a holy place to many Arabian tribes, each recognizing it as a shrine. Thus, as keepers of the shrine, the Quraysh managed a lucrative pilgrimage trade in Mecca.

His father died just before Muhammad was born in 570 CE, and his mother died when he was young. Raised first by his grandfather and then by an uncle, Muhammad early sought a living in trade, and didn't learn to read or write. When he was about 25, he began running the caravans of the wealthy widow, Kadijah, who asked him to marry her, though she was 15 years older than he.

In 610, during the month of Ramadan, when Muhammad had retreated to a cave outside of Mecca for meditation and reflection, a powerful voice ordered him to read or to recite "in the name of your Lord, who created humankind from a clot of blood!" When Muhammad returned home, Kadijah recognized that he had had a revelation and she became the first convert to Islam, which sees Muhammad as the last in a line of prophets that includes Adam, Noah, Abraham, Moses, and Jesus.

Attempts to convert other Meccans were not entirely successful: submission to God was one thing, but when Muhammad began to claim that the Kaaba was the shrine of Allah alone, he became a threat to the economy of the city. Finally in 622, having gathered very few followers in twelve years, he was forced, under cover of night, to flee the city and journey

Reprinted from *The Koran*, translated by N.J. Dawood (Penguin, 1999).

to the city later called Medina. This journey, about 300 miles, is called the hijra *(or "hegira"), and marks the beginning date of the Islamic calendar. After the hijra, Muhammad moved actively to strengthen Islam by becoming an administrator and political leader as well as a prophet. He expelled Jewish and pagan groups in Medina who failed to respond to his announcements of God's commands, and increasingly his visions dealt in the legal and ethical details of running a community.*

Throughout his years in Medina, Muhammad continued his conflict with his former tribe in Mecca, who were routed in several skirmishes and saw their trade dwindle. Finally in 629, Muhammad led a force against the city, which surrendered without bloodshed, leaving Muhammad in control of both city and sacred shrine. After the prophet's death three years later, Mecca became the center of Islam, with a pilgrimage to Mecca (hajj) *required of Muslims who are able to undertake the journey.*

The revelations to Muhammad were collected by his friends and followers into a book called the Koran (Qu'ran). *It is strikingly different from both the Hebrew Bible and the Christian New Testament. The chapters (or* surahs*) are arranged simply in order of length, longest first; because the earlier revelations tended to be shorter and simpler, they fall near the end of the book. The traditional titles of the Surahs do not announce a theme for the whole chapter; instead, they are simply a striking word or phrase that occurs early in the chapter. There is almost no narrative or story-telling in the Koran; instead the collection has the quality of almost random pronouncements, with much repetition. Throughout there are demands of submission to God's absolute will, colored by continual reminders of God's great mercy and kindness. The language of the Koran, a written dialect of Arabic, is considered sacred and perfect, the language of God himself.*

The Muslim religion is based centrally on the Koran, with peripheral importance attached to customs, sayings, and traditions associated with Muhammad. But Muhammad insisted that he not be viewed as divine or extraordinary: he was simply the messenger who carried the Koran to the people. The emphasis, then, is upon acting in accordance with God's will, beginning with five practices so important they have come to be called the Pillars of Islam. First, the Muslim must make a profession of faith. To say "There is no God but God, and Muhammad is his prophet" with sincerity is all that is required to become a Muslim. This simple statement, in striking contrast with the Christian creeds earlier in this section, captures the key doctrines of Islam, that God is one and that his last messenger was Muhammad.

The second pillar is prayer. Five times a day, at set times, the Muslim must bow down toward Mecca and pray in Arabic. This prayer can be done with others at a mosque, but the worship of God is primarily a private act and the relationship with God does not depend on intercessors or intermediaries.

The third pillar is giving, both charitable giving to the poor and needy, and the giving of a levied amount to support the religious and political policies of the government in certain Islamic countries. The fourth pillar is fasting, required every year during the month of Ramadan, the time of Muhammad's first vision. Food and drink are prohibited during daylight hours. Because Muslims follow a lunar calendar, Ramadan moves from season to season, which means that in some years the fasting occurs during long days in hot summer weather and in other years in cooler winter.

The fifth pillar is pilgrimage. Every Muslim who is able and can afford it is supposed to make the pilgrimage (hajj) *to Mecca once during his or her lifetime. Because the pilgrimage most properly happens at a given time each year, tens of thousands of pilgrims from all over the world converge on Mecca at the same time, living in huge tent cities.*

The hajj *is a personal experience that makes manifest the notion that Islam creates a new brotherhood of faith that transcends the rivalries of tribes, nations, and races. In actual practice, of course, Islam itself split within a few generations of the death of Muhammad into a number of sects based on differences in belief. The chief split came about over the question of whether the leaders* (caliphs) *of Islam had to be direct descendants of Muhammad through his daughter Fatima. That division, alive today, separates the conservative* shiites *(based in Iran) from the sunnis, based in Saudi Arabia. With perhaps 700 million believers worldwide, Islam is still rapidly gaining converts, and is reported to be the fastest growing religion in the United States.*

---

2. The Cow

2:125 We made the House [Kaaba] a resort and a sanctuary for mankind, saying: 'Make the place where Abraham stood a house of worship.' We enjoined Abraham and Ishmael to cleanse Our House for those who walk round it, who meditate in it, and who kneel and prostrate themselves.

'Lord,' said Abraham, 'make this a secure land and bestow plenty upon its people, those of them that believe in God and the Last Day.'

'As for those that do not,' He answered, 'I shall let them live awhile, and then shall drag them to the scourge of the Fire: an evil fate.'

2:127 Abraham and Ishmael built the House and dedicated it, saying: 'Accept this from us, Lord. You are the One that hears all and knows all. Lord, make us submissive to You; make of our descendants a community that will submit to You. Teach us our rites of worship and turn to us with mercy; You are the Forgiving One the Merciful. Lord, send forth to them an apostle of their own who shall declare to them Your revelations, and shall instruct them in the Book and in wisdom, and shall purify them of sin. You are the Mighty, the Wise One.'

Who but a foolish man, would renounce the faith of Abraham? We
chose him in this world, and in the world to come he shall abide among the
2:131 righteous. When his Lord said to him: 'Submit,' he answered: 'I have submitted to the Lord of the Universe.'

2:132 Abraham enjoined the faith on his children, and so did Jacob, saying: 'My children, God has chosen for you the true faith. Do not depart this life except in full submission.'

Were you present when death came to Jacob? He said to his children: 'What will you worship when I am gone?' They replied: 'We will worship your God and the God of your forefathers Abraham and Ishmael and Isaac: the One God. To Him we will submit.'

That community has passed away. Theirs is what they did and yours what you have done. You shall not be questioned about their actions.

They say: 'Accept the Jewish or the Christian faith and you shall be rightly guided.'

Say: 'By no means! We believe in the faith of Abraham, the upright one. He was no idolater.'

3. The 'Imrams

3:15 God is watching His servants, those who say: 'Lord, we believe in You: forgive us our sins and keep us from the torment of the Fire'; who are steadfast, sincere, obedient, and charitable; and who implore forgiveness at break of day.

God bears witness that there is no god but Him, and so do the angels and the sages. He is the Executor of Justice, the Only God, the Mighty, the Wise One.

3:19 The only true faith in God's sight is Islām. Those to whom the Scriptures were given disagreed among themselves, through insolence, only after knowledge had been vouchsafed them. He that denies God's revelations should know that swift is God's reckoning.

If they argue with you, say: 'I have submitted to God and so have those that follow me.'

To those who were given the Scriptures and to the Gentiles say: 'Will you submit to God? If they become Muslims they shall be rightly guided; if they pay no heed, then your only duty is to warn them. God is watching all His servants.

Those that deny God's revelations and slay the prophets unjustly and kill the men who preach fair dealing—warn them of a woeful scourge. Their works shall come to nothing in this world and in the world to come, and there shall be none to help them.

Do but consider those who have received a portion of the Scriptures. When they are called on to accept the judgement of God's Book, some turn their backs and pay no heed. For they declare: 'We shall endure the Fire for a few days only.' In their religion they are deceived by their own lies.

3:25 What will they do when We gather them all together upon a day which is sure to come, when every soul will be given what it has earned with no injustice?

3:26 Say: 'Lord, Sovereign of all sovereignty, You bestow sovereignty on whom You will and take it away from whom You please; You exalt whomever You will and abase whomever You please. In Your hand lies all that is good; You have power over all things. You cause the night to pass into the day, and the day to pass into the night; You bring forth the living from the dead and You bring forth the dead from the living. You give without stint to whom You will.'

4. Women

4:27 God wishes to forgive you, but those who follow their own appetites wish to see you stray grievously into error. God wishes to lighten your burdens, for man was created weak.

Believers, do not consume your wealth among yourselves in vanity, but rather trade with it by mutual consent.

Do not kill yourselves. God is merciful to you, but he that does that through wickedness and injustice shall be burned in fire. That is easy enough for God.

If you avoid the enormities you are forbidden, We shall pardon your
misdeeds and usher you in with all honour. Do not covet the favours by
which God has exalted some among you above others. Men shall be
rewarded according to their deeds, and women shall be rewarded according
to their deeds. Rather implore God to bestow on you His gifts. Surely God
has knowledge of all things.

To every parent and kinsman We have appointed heirs who will inherit
from them. As for those with whom you have entered into agreements, let
them, too, have their share. Surely God bears witness to all things.

4:34 Men have authority over women because God has made the one superior to the other, and because they spend their wealth to maintain them.
Good women are obedient. They guard their unseen parts because God has
guarded them. As for those from whom you fear disobedience, admonish
them, forsake them in beds apart, and beat them. Then if they obey you,
take no further action against them. Surely God is high, supreme.

If you fear a breach between a man and his wife, appoint an arbiter
from his people and another from hers. If they wish to be reconciled, God
will bring them together again. Surely God is all-knowing and wise.

4:36 Serve God and associate none with Him. Show kindness to parents and
kindred, to orphans and to the destitute, to near and distant neighbours, to
those that keep company with you, to the traveller in need, and to the slaves
you own. God does not love arrogant and boastful men, who are themselves
4:37 tight-fisted and enjoin others to be tight-fisted; who conceal the riches
which God of His bounty has bestowed upon them (We have prepared a
shameful punishment for the unbelievers); and who spend their wealth for
the sake of ostentation, believing neither in God nor in the Last Day. He
that chooses Satan for his friend, an evil friend has he. . . .

4:74 Let those who would exchange the life of this world for the hereafter,
fight for the cause of God [jihad]; whoever fights for the cause of God,
whether he dies or triumphs, on him We shall bestow a rich recompense.

4:75 And how should you not fight for the cause of God, and for the helpless old men, women, and children who say: 'Deliver us, Lord, from this
city of wrongdoers; send forth to us a guardian from Your presence; send to
us from Your presence one that will help us'?

The true believers fight for the cause of God, but the infidels fight for
the devil. Fight then against the friends of Satan. Satan's cunning is weak
indeed. . . .

4:92 It is unlawful for a believer to kill another believer, accidents excepted.
He that accidentally kills a believer must free one Muslim slave and pay
blood-money to the family of the victim, unless they choose to give it away
in alms. If the victim be a Muslim from a hostile tribe, the penalty is the
freeing of one Muslim slave. But if the victim be a member of an allied tribe,
then blood-money must be paid to his family and a Muslim slave set free.
He that lacks the means must fast two consecutive months. Such is the
penance imposed by God: God is all-knowing and wise.

4:93 He that kills a believer by design shall burn in Hell for ever. He shall incur the wrath of God, who will lay His curse on him and prepare for him a mighty scourge.

Believers, show discernment when you go to fight for the cause of God, and do not say to those that offer you peace: 'You are not believers,'—seeking the chance booty of this world; for with God there are abundant gains. Such was your custom in days gone by, but now God has bestowed on you His grace. Therefore show discernment; God is cognizant of all your actions.

The believers who stay at home—apart from those that suffer from a grave disability—are not the equals of those who fight for the cause of God with their goods and their persons. God has exalted the men who fight with their goods and their persons above those who stay at home. God has promised all a good reward; but far richer is the recompense of those who fight for Him: ranks of His own bestowal, forgiveness, and mercy. Surely God is forgiving and merciful.

7. THE HEIGHTS

7:4 How many cities have We destroyed! In the night Our scourge fell upon them, or at midday, when they were drowsing.

And when Our scourge fell upon them, their only cry was: 'We have indeed been wicked men.'

We will surely question those to whom the messengers were sent, and We will question the messengers themselves. With knowledge We will recount to them what they have done, for We were never away from them.

On that day all shall be weighed with justice. Those whose good deeds weigh heavy in the scales shall triumph, but those whose deeds are light shall lose their souls, because they have denied Our revelations.

We have given you power in the land and provided you with a livelihood: yet you are seldom thankful.

7:11 We created you and gave you form. Then We said to the angels: 'Prostrate yourselves before Adam.' They all prostrated themselves except Satan, who refused to prostrate himself.

'Why did you not prostrate yourself when I commanded you?' He asked.

'I am nobler than he,' he replied. 'You created me from fire, but You created him from clay.'

He said: 'Get you down hence! This is no place for your contemptuous pride. Away with you! Humble shall you henceforth be.'

He replied: 'Reprieve me till the Day of Resurrection.'

'You are reprieved,' said He.

'Because You have led me into sin,' he declared, 'I will waylay Your servants as they walk on Your straight path, then spring upon them from the
7:17 front and from the rear, from their right and from their left. Then You will
find the greater part of them ungrateful.'

7:18 'Begone!' He said. 'A despicable outcast you shall henceforth be. As for those that follow you, I shall fill Hell with you all.'

To Adam He said: 'Dwell with your wife in Paradise, and eat of any fruit you please; but never approach this tree or you shall both become transgressors.'

But Satan tempted them, so that he might reveal to them their shameful parts, which they had never seen before. He said: 'Your Lord has forbidden you to approach this tree only to prevent you from becoming angels or immortals.' Then he swore to them that he would give them friendly counsel.

Thus did he cunningly seduce them. And when they had eaten of the tree, their shame became visible to them, and they both covered themselves with the leaves of the garden.

Their Lord called out to them, saying: 'Did I not forbid you to approach that tree, and did I not say to you that Satan was your inveterate foe?'

They replied: 'Lord, we have wronged our souls. Pardon us and have mercy on us, or we shall surely be among the lost.'

7:24 He said: 'Get you down hence, and may your descendants be enemies
to each other. The earth will for a while provide your dwelling and your
comforts. There you shall live and there shall you die, and thence shall you
be raised to life.'

Children of Adam! We have given you clothes to cover your shameful parts, and garments pleasing to the eye; but the finest of all these is the robe of piety.

That is one of God's revelations. Perchance they will take heed.

Children of Adam! Let not Satan tempt you, as he seduced your parents out of Paradise. He stripped them of their garments to reveal to them their shameful parts. He and his minions see you whence you cannot see them. We have made the devils guardians over the unbelievers.

11. Hūd

11:12 You may chance to omit a part of what is revealed to you and be distressed because they say: 'Why has no treasure been sent down to him? Why
has no angel come with him?'

But you are only to give warning. God is the guardian of all things. If they say: 'He has invented it [the Koran] himself,' say to them: 'Produce ten invented chapters like it.' Call on whom you will among your idols, if what you say be true. But if they fail you, know that it is revealed with God's knowledge, and that there is no god but Him. Will you then accept Islām?'

11:15 Those that desire the life of this world with all its finery shall be
rewarded for their deeds in their own lifetime: they shall not be given less.
They are those who in the world to come shall have earned nothing but the
Fire. Fruitless are their deeds, and vain are all their works.

Are they to be compared to those that have received a revelation from their Lord, recited by a witness from Him and heralded by the Book of Moses, a guide and a blessing? These have faith in it, but the factions who deny it shall be consigned to the Fire. Therefore do not doubt it. It is the truth from your Lord: yet most men have no faith.

And who is more wicked than the man who invents a falsehood about God? Such men shall be brought before their Lord, and witnesses will say: 'These are they who lied about their Lord.'

17. THE NIGHT JOURNEY

17:13 The fate of each man We have bound about his neck. On the Day of Resurrection We shall confront him with a book spread wide open, saying: 'Here is your book: read it. Enough for you this day that your own soul should call you to account.'

He that seeks guidance shall be guided to his advantage, but he that errs shall err at his peril. No soul shall bear another's burden. Nor do We punish until We have sent forth a messenger.

17:16 When We resolve to raze a city, We first give warning to those of its people who live in comfort. If they persist in sin, judgement is irrevocably passed, and We destroy it utterly.

How many generations have We cut down since Noah's time! Suffice it that your Lord is well aware of His servants' sins and observes them all.

He that desires this fleeting life shall soon receive in it whatever We will for whomever We please. But then We have prepared Hell for him, where he will burn despised and rejected.

As for him that desires the life to come and strives for it as he ought to, being a true believer, his endeavours shall be recompensed by God.

On all—on these and those—We bestow the bounty of your Lord: none shall be denied the bounty of your Lord.

See how We have exalted some above others. Yet the life to come has greater honours and is more exalted.

Serve no other deity besides God, lest you incur disgrace and ruin. Your
17:23 Lord has enjoined you to worship none but Him, and to show kindness to
your parents. If either or both of them attain old age in your dwelling, show
them no sign of impatience, nor rebuke them; but speak to them kind
17:24 words. Treat them with humility and tenderness and say: 'Lord, be merciful
to them. They nursed me when I was an infant.'

Your Lord best knows what is in your hearts; He knows if you are good. He will surely forgive those that turn to Him.

Give to the near of kin their due, and also to the destitute and to the traveller in need. Do not squander your substance wastefully, for the wasteful are Satan's brothers; and Satan is ever ungrateful to his Lord. But if, while waiting for your Lord's bounty, you lack the means to assist them, then at least speak to them kindly.

Be neither miserly nor prodigal, for then you should either earn reproach or be reduced to penury.

Your Lord gives abundantly to whom He will and sparingly to whom He pleases. He knows and observes His servants.

17:31 You shall not kill your children for fear of want. We will provide for them and for you. To kill them is a grievous sin.

You shall not commit adultery, for it is lewd and evil.

You shall not kill any man whom God has forbidden you to kill, except for a just cause. If a man is slain unjustly, his heir shall be entitled to satisfaction. But let him not carry his vengeance to excess, for his victim is sure to be assisted and avenged.

Do not approach the property of orphans except with the best of motives, until they reach maturity. Keep your promises; you are accountable for all that you promise.

Give full measure, when you measure, and weigh with even scales. That is better and fairer in the end.

Do not follow what you know not. Man's eyes, ears, and heart—each of his senses shall be closely questioned.

17:37 Do not walk proudly on the earth. You cannot split the earth, nor can you rival the mountains in stature.

19. Mary

19:16 And you shall recount in the Book the story of Mary: how she left her people and betook herself to a solitary place to the east.

We sent to her Our spirit in the semblance of a full-grown man. And when she saw him she said: 'May the Merciful defend me from you! If you fear the Lord, [leave me and go your way].'

'I am but your Lord's emissary,' he replied, 'and have come to give you a holy son.'

'How shall I bear a child,' she answered, 'when I have neither been touched by any man nor ever been unchaste?'

'Thus did your Lord speak,' he replied. '"That is easy enough for Me. He shall be a sign to mankind and a blessing from Ourself. Our decree shall come to pass."'

19:22 Thereupon she conceived him, and retired to a far-off place. And when she felt the throes of childbirth she lay down by the trunk of a palm-tree, crying: 'Oh, would that I had died before this and passed into oblivion!'

But a voice from below cried out to her: 'Do not despair. Your Lord has provided a brook that runs at your feet, and if you shake the trunk of the palm-tree it will drop fresh ripe dates in your lap. Therefore eat and drink and rejoice; and should you meet any mortal say to him: "I have vowed a fast to the Merciful and will not speak with any man today."'

Carrying the child, she came to her people, who said to her: 'Mary, this
19:28 is indeed a strange thing! Sister of Aaron, your father was never a whore-
monger, nor was your mother a harlot.'

19:29 She made a sign to them, pointing to the child. But they replied: 'How can we speak with a babe in the cradle?'

Whereupon he spoke and said: 'I am the servant of God. He has given me the Book and ordained me a prophet. His blessing is upon me wherever I go, and He has exhorted me to be steadfast in prayer and to give alms as long as I shall live. He has exhorted me to honour my mother and has purged me of vanity and wickedness. Blessed was I on the day I was born, and blessed I shall be on the day of my death and on the day I shall be raised to life.'

Such was Jesus son of Mary. That is the whole truth, which they still doubt. God forbid that He Himself should beget a son! When He decrees a thing He need only say: 'Be,' and it is.

God is my Lord and your Lord: therefore serve Him. That is a straight path.

22. PILGRIMAGE

22:16 When We prepared for Abraham the site of the Sacred Mosque We said: 'Worship none besides Me. Keep My House clean for those who walk around it, and those who stand upright or kneel in worship.'

Exhort all men to make the pilgrimage. They will come to you on foot and on the backs of swift camels from every distant quarter; they will come to avail themselves of many a benefit, and to pronounce on the appointed days the name of God over the cattle which He has given them for food. Eat of their flesh, and feed the poor and the unfortunate.

Then let the pilgrims tidy themselves, make their vows, and circle the Ancient House. Such is God's commandment. He that reveres the sacred rites of God shall fare better in the sight of his Lord.

25. AL-FURQĀN

25:4 The unbelievers say: 'This is but a forgery of his own invention, in which others have helped him.' Unjust is what they say and false.

And they say: 'Fables of the ancients he has written: they are dictated to him morning and evening.'

Say: 'It is revealed by Him who knows the secrets of the heavens and the earth. He is surely forgiving and merciful.'

They also say: 'How is it that this apostle eats and walks about the market-squares? Why has no angel been sent down with him to give warning? Why has no treasure been given him, no garden to provide his sustenance?'

And the wrongdoers say: 'The man you follow is surely bewitched.'

25:9 See what epithets they bestow upon you! Surely they have gone astray and cannot return to the true path.

Blessed be He who, if He wills, can give you better things than these; gardens watered by running streams, and palaces too.

47. MUḤAMMAD

47:4 When you meet the unbelievers in the battlefield strike off their heads and, when you have laid them low, bind your captives firmly. Then grant them their freedom or take a ransom from them, until War shall lay down her burdens.

Thus shall you do. Had God willed, He could Himself have punished them; [but He has ordained it thus] that He may test you, the one by the other.

As for those who are slain in the cause of God, He will not allow their works to perish. He will vouchsafe them guidance and ennoble their state; He will admit them to the Paradise He has made known to them.

Believers, if you help God, God will help you and make you strong. But the unbelievers shall be consigned to perdition. He will bring their deeds to nothing. Because they have abhorred His revelations, He will frustrate their works.

47:10 Have they never journeyed through the land and seen what was the end of those who have gone before them? God destroyed them utterly. A similar fate awaits the unbelievers, because God is the protector of the faithful: because the unbelievers have no protector.

God will admit those who embrace the true Faith and do good works to gardens watered by running streams. The unbelievers take their fill of pleasure and eat as cattle eat: but the Fire shall be their home.

56. That Which is Coming

In the Name of God, the Compassionate, the Merciful

56:1 When that which is coming comes—and no soul shall then deny its coming—some shall be abased and others exalted.

When the earth shakes and quivers, and the mountains crumble away
56:6 and scatter abroad into fine dust, you shall be divided into three multitudes:
those on the right (blessed shall be those on the right); those on the left (damned shall be those on the left); and those to the fore (foremost shall be those). Such are they that shall be brought near to their Lord in the gardens of delight: a whole multitude from the men of old, but only a few from the latter generations.

They shall recline on jewelled couches face to face, and there shall wait on them immortal youths with bowls and ewers and a cup of purest wine (that will neither pain their heads nor take away their reason); with fruits of their own choice and flesh of fowls that they relish. And theirs shall be the dark-eyed houris, chaste as virgin pearls: a guerdon for their deeds.

There they shall hear no idle talk, no sinful speech, but only the greeting, 'Peace! Peace!'

56:27 Those on the right hand—happy shall be those on the right hand! They shall recline on couches raised on high in the shade of thornless sidrs and clusters of talh; amidst gushing waters and abundant fruits, unforbidden, never-ending.

We created the houris and made them virgins, loving companions for those on the right hand: a multitude from the men of old, and a multitude from the latter generations.

As for those on the left hand (wretched shall be those on the left hand!) they shall dwell amidst scorching winds and seething water: in the shade of pitch-black smoke, neither cool nor refreshing. For they have lived in comfort and persisted in the heinous sin; saying: 'When we are once dead and turned to dust and bones, shall we be raised to life? And our forefathers, too?'

Say: 'Those of old, and those of the present age, shall be brought
together on an appointed day. As for you sinners who deny the truth, you
shall eat the fruit of the Zaqqūm tree and fill your bellies with it. You shall
56:55 drink scalding water: yet you shall drink it as the thirsty camel drinks.'

61. Battle Array

In the Name of God, the Compassionate, the Merciful

61:1 All that is in the heavens and the earth gives glory to God. He is the Mighty, the Wise One.

Believers, why do you profess what you never do? It is most odious in God's sight that you should say one thing and do another.

God loves those who fight for His cause in ranks as firm as a mighty edifice.

Tell of Moses, who said to his people: 'Why do you seek to harm me, my people, when you know that I am sent to you by God?' And when they went astray, God led their very hearts astray. God does not guide the evil-doers.

And of Jesus son of Mary, who said to the Israelites: 'I am sent forth to you from God to confirm the Torah already revealed, and to give news of an apostle that will come after me whose name is Ahmad [Muhammad].' Yet when he brought them conspicuous signs, they said: 'This is plain sorcery.'

And who is more wicked than the man who invents a falsehood about God when called upon to submit to Him? God does not guide the wrongdoers.

62. Friday

62:9 Believers, when you are summoned to Friday prayers hasten to the remembrance of God and cease your trading. That would be best for you, if you but knew it. Then, when the prayers are ended, disperse and go your ways in quest of God's bounty. Remember God always, so that you may prosper.

96. Clots of Blood

In the Name of God, the Compassionate, the Merciful

96:1 Recite in the name of your Lord who created—created man from clots of blood.

Recite! Your Lord is the Most Bountiful One, who by the pen taught man what he did not know.

Indeed, man transgresses in thinking himself his own master: for to your Lord all things return.

Observe the man who rebukes Our servant when he prays. Think: does he follow the right guidance or enjoin true piety?

96:13 Think: if he denies the Truth and pays no heed, does he not realize that God observes all?

No. Let him desist, or We will drag him by the forelock, his lying, sinful forelock.

Then let him call his helpmates. We will call the guards of Hell.

96:19 No, never obey him! Prostrate yourself and come nearer.

Ibn Ishaq (c.85–151 AH*)*

The Life of Muhammad

Muhammad Ibn Ishaq was born in Medina, the grandson of a slave freed upon conversion to Islam, and the son of a gatherer of historical traditions about the life of the Prophet. Ibn Ishaq continued his father's task, basing his biography of Muhammad on a variety of writings and oral stories that circulated during the first century of Islam. As the first comprehensive life of the Prophet, the book captured events and sayings that became central to Islam as the Hadith, *the traditions of the Prophet. At some point during his work in Medina, Ibn Ishaq raised the ire of rivals, and he moved eastward, to Baghdad, and it was there that he died.*

Editors often relieve the wordiness of the extraordinarily long biography by cutting the many introductory phrases that describe the route by which a story or incident has come to Ishaq. In this selection these phrases have been left in, for they show both the way in which Ishaq pieces together his narrative from different sources and his own reservations about the absolute truth of the traditions he recounts. Nowhere is this more true in the biography than in the fabulous account of Muhammad's night journey to the holy city of Jerusalem and his miraculous ascent into heaven. This incident strained the credulity even of some of Muhammad's followers, and it led to an intense debate over whether the journey occurred bodily, whether it somehow involved only the Prophet's spirit while his body remained in Mecca, or whether it was—no miracle at all—simply a dream vision.

The Night Journey and the Ascent to Heaven

Ziyad b. 'Abdullah al-Bakkā'i from Muhammad b. Ishāq told me the following: Then the apostle was carried by night from the mosque at Mecca to the Masjid al-Aqsā, which is the temple of Aelia, when Islam had spread in Mecca among the Quraysh and all the tribes.

The following account reached me from 'Abdullah b. Mas'ūd and Abū Sa'īd al-Khudrī, and 'Ā'isha the prophet's wife, and Mu'āwiya b. Abū Sufyān, and al-Hasan b.

This selection from the *Life of Muhammad* is translated by Alfred Guillaume (Lahore, Pakistan: Oxford University Press, 1955).

Abū'l-Hasan al-Basrī, and Ibn Shihāb al-Zuhrī and Qatāda and other traditionists, and Umm Hāni' d. of Abū Tālib. It is pieced together in the story that follows, each one contributing something of what he was told about what happened when he was taken on the night journey. The matter of the place of the journey and what is said about it is a searching test and a matter of God's power and authority wherein is a lesson for the intelligent; and guidance and mercy and strengthening to those who believe. It was certainly an act of God by which He took him by night in what way He pleased to show him His signs which He willed him to see so that he witnessed His mighty sovereignty and power by which He does what He wills to do.

According to what I have heard 'Abdullah b. Mas'ūd used to say: Burāq, the animal whose every stride carried it as far as its eye could reach on which the prophets before him used to ride was brought to the apostle and he was mounted on it. His companion (Gabriel) went with him to see the wonders between heaven and earth, until he came to Jerusalem's temple. There he found Abraham the friend of God, Moses, and Jesus assembled with a company of the prophets, and he prayed with them. Then he was brought three vessels containing milk, wine, and water respectively. The apostle said: 'I heard a voice saying when these were offered to me: If he takes the water he will be drowned and his people also; if he takes the wine he will go astray and his people also; and if he takes the milk he will be rightly guided and his people also. So I took the vessel containing milk and drank it. Gabriel said to me, You have been rightly guided and so will your people be, Muhammad.'

I was told that al-Hasan said that the apostle said: 'While I was sleeping in the Hījr Gabriel came and stirred me with his foot. I sat up but saw nothing and lay down again. He came a second time and stirred me with his foot. I sat up but saw nothing and lay down again. He came to me the third time and stirred me with his foot. I sat up and he took hold of my arm and I stood beside him and he brought me out to the door of the mosque and there was a white animal, half mule, half donkey, with wings on its sides with which it propelled its feet, putting down each forefoot at the limit of its sight and he mounted me on it. Then he went out with me keeping close to me.

I was told that Qatāda said that he was told that the apostle said: 'When I came up to mount him he shied. Gabriel placed his hand on its mane and said, Are you not ashamed, O Burāq, to behave in this way? By God, none more honourable before God than Muhammad has ever ridden you before. The animal was so ashamed that he broke out into a sweat and stood still so that I could mount him.'

In his story al-Hasan said: 'The apostle and Gabriel went their way until they arrived at the temple at Jerusalem. There he found Abraham, Moses, and Jesus among a company of the prophets. The apostle acted as their imam in prayer. Then he was brought two vessels, one containing wine and the other milk. The apostle took the milk and drank it, leaving the wine. Gabriel said: "You have been rightly guided to the way of nature and so will your people be, Muhammad. Wine is forbidden you." Then the apostle returned to Mecca and in the morning he told Quraysh what had happened. Most of them said, "By God, this is a plain absurdity! A caravan takes a month to go to Syria and a month to return and can Muhammad do the return journey in one night?" Many Muslims gave up their faith; some went to Abū Bakr and said, "What do you think of your friend now, Abū Bakr? He alleges that he went to Jerusalem last night and prayed there and came back to Mecca." He replied that they were lying about the apostle; but they said that he was in the mosque at that very moment telling the people about it. Abū Bakr said, "If he says so then it is true. And what is so surprising in that? He tells me that communications from God from heaven to earth come to him in an hour of a day or night and I believe him, and that is more extraordinary than that at which you boggle!" He then went to the apostle and asked him if these reports were true, and when he said they were, he asked him to describe Jerusalem to him.' Al-Hasan said that he was lifted up so that he could see the apostle speaking as he told Abū Bakr what Jerusalem was like. Whenever he described a part of it he said, 'That's true. I testify that you are the apostle of God' until he had completed the description, and then the apostle said, 'And you, Abū Bakr, are the *Siddīq.'* This was the occasion on which he got this honorific.

Al-Hasan continued: God sent down concerning those who left Islam for this reason: 'We made the vision which we showed thee only for a test to men and the accursed tree in the Quran. We put them in fear, but it only adds to their heinous error.' Such is al-Hasan's story with additions from Qatāda.

One of Abū Bakr's family told me that 'Ā'isha the prophet's wife used to say: 'The Apostle's body remained where it was but God removed his spirit by night.'

Ya'qūb b. 'Utba b. al-Mughīra b. al-Akhnas told me that Mu'āwiya b. Abū Sufyān when he was asked about the apostle's night journey said, 'It was a true vision from God.' What these two latter said does not contradict what al-Hasan said, seeing that God Himself said, 'We made the vision which we showed thee only for a test to men;' nor does it contradict what God said in the story of Abraham when he said to his son, 'O my son, verily I saw in a dream that I must sacrifice thee,' and he acted accordingly. Thus, as I see it, revelation from God comes to the prophets waking or sleeping.

I have heard that the apostle used to say, 'My eyes sleep while my heart is awake.' Only God knows how revelation came and he saw what he saw. But whether he was asleep or awake, it was all true and actually happened.

Al-Zuhrī alleged as from Sa'id b. al-Musayyab that the apostle described to his companions Abraham, Moses, and Jesus, as he saw them that night, saying: 'I have never seen a man more like myself than Abraham. Moses was a ruddy faced man, tall, thinly fleshed, curly haired with a hooked nose as though he were of the Shanu'a. Jesus, Son of Mary, was a reddish man of medium height with lank hair with many freckles on his face as though he had just come from a bath. One would suppose that his head was dripping with water, though there was no water on it. The man most like him among you is 'Urwa b. Mas'ūd al-Thaqafī.'

The following report has reached me from Umm Hāni' d. of Abū Tālib, whose name was Hind, concerning the apostle's night journey. She said: 'The apostle went on no night journey except while he was in my house. He slept that night in my house. He prayed the final night prayer, then he slept and we slept. A little before dawn the apostle woke us, and when we had prayed the dawn prayer he said, "O Umm Hāni', I prayed with you the last evening prayer in this valley as you saw. Then I went to Jerusalem and prayed there. Then I have just prayed the morning prayer with you as you see." He got up to go out and I took hold of his robe and laid bare his belly as though it were a folded Egyptian garment. I said, "O prophet of God, don't talk to the people about it for they will give you the lie and insult you." He said, "By God, I certainly will tell them." I said to a negress, a slave of mine, Follow the apostle and listen to what he says to the people, and what they say to him. He did tell them and they were amazed and asked what proof he had. He replied that he had passed the caravan of so-and-so in such-and-such a valley and the animal he bestrode scared them and a camel bolted, "and I showed them where it was as I was on the way to Syria. I carried on until in Dajanān I passed by a caravan of the Banū so-and-so. I found the people asleep. They had a jar of water covered with something. I took the covering off and drank the water replacing the cover. The proof of that is that their caravan is this moment coming down from al-Baidā' by the pass of al-Tan'īm led by a dusky camel loaded with two sacks one black and the other multihued". The people hurried to the pass and the first camel they met was as he had described. They asked the men about the vessel and they told them that they had left it full of water and covered it and that when they woke it was covered but empty. They asked the others too who were in Mecca and they said that it was quite right: they had been scared and a camel had bolted, and they had heard a man calling them to it so that they were able to recover it.'

The Ascent to Heaven

One whom I have no reason to doubt told me on the authority of Abu¯ Sa‘ı¯d al-Khudrı¯: I heard the apostle say, 'After the completion of my business in Jerusalem a ladder was brought to me finer than any I have ever seen. It was that to which the dying man looks when death approaches. My companion mounted it with me until we came to one of the gates of heaven called the Gate of the Watchers. An angel called Isma¯‘ı¯l was in charge of it, and under his command were twelve thousand angels each of them having twelve thousand angels under his command.' As he told this story the apostle used to say, 'and none knows the armies of God but He.' When Gabriel brought me in, Isma¯‘ı¯l asked who I was, and when he was told that I was Muhammad he asked if I had been given a mission, and on being assured of this he wished me well.

A traditionist who had got it from one who had heard it from the apostle told me that the latter said: 'All the angels who met me when I entered the lowest heaven smiled in welcome and wished me well except one who said the same things but did not smile or show that joyful expression which the others had. And when I asked Gabriel the reason he told me that if he had ever smiled on anyone before or would smile on anyone hereafter he would have smiled on me; but he does not smile because he is Mālik, the Keeper of Hell. I said to Gabriel, he holding the position with regard to God which he has described to you "obeyed there, trustworthy", "Will you not order him to show me hell?" And he said, "Certainly! O Mālik, show Muhammad Hell." Thereupon he removed its covering and the flames blazed high into the air until I thought that they would consume everything. So I asked Gabriel to order him to send them back to their place which he did. I can only compare the effect of their withdrawal to the falling of a shadow, until when the flames retreated whence they had come, Mālik placed their cover on them.'

In his tradition Abū Sa'īd al-Khudrī said that the apostle said: 'When I entered the lowest heaven I saw a man sitting there with the spirits of men passing before him. To one he would speak well and rejoice in him saying: "A good spirit from a good body" and of another he would say "Faugh!" and frown, saying: "An evil spirit from an evil body." In answer to my question Gabriel told me that this was our father

Adam reviewing the spirits of his offspring; the spirit of a believer excited his pleasure, and the spirit of an infidel excited his disgust so that he said the words just quoted.

'Then I saw men with lips like camels; in their hands were pieces of fire like stones which they used to thrust into their mouths and they would come out of their posteriors. I was told that these were those who sinfully devoured the wealth of orphans.

'Then I saw men in the way of the family of Pharaoh, with such bellies as I have never seen; there were passing over them as it were camels maddened by thirst when they were cast into hell, treading them down, they being unable to move out of the way. These were the usurers.

'Then I saw men with good fat meat before them side by side with lean stinking meat, eating of the latter and leaving the former. These are those who forsake the women which God has permitted and go after those he has forbidden.

'Then I saw women hanging by their breasts. These were those who had fathered bastards on their husbands.'

Ja'far b. 'Amr told me from al-Qāsim b. Muhammad that the apostle said: 'Great is God's anger against a woman who brings a bastard into her family. He deprives the true sons of their portion and learns the secrets of the *harim*.'

To continue the tradition of Sa'īd al-Khudrī: 'Then I was taken up to the second heaven and there were the two maternal cousins Jesus, Son of Mary, and John, son of Zakariah. Then to the third heaven and there was a man whose face was as the moon at the full. This was my brother Joseph, son of Jacob. Then to the fourth heaven and there was a man called Idrīs. "And we have exalted him to a lofty place." Then to the fifth heaven and there was a man with white hair and a long beard, never have I seen a more handsome man than he. This was the beloved among his people Aaron son of 'Imrān. Then to the sixth heaven, and there was a dark man with a hooked nose like the Shanū'a. This was my brother Moses, son of 'Imrān. Then to the seventh heaven and there was a man sitting on a throne at the gate of the immortal mansion. Every day seventy thousand angels went in not to come back until the resurrection day. Never have I seen a man more like myself. This was my father Abraham. Then he took me into Paradise and there I saw a damsel with dark red lips and I asked her to whom she belonged, for she pleased me much when I saw her, and she told me "Zayd b. Hāritha". The apostle gave Zayd the good news about her.'

From a tradition of 'Abdullah b. Mas'ūd from the prophet there has reached me the following: When Gabriel took him up to each of the heavens and asked permission to enter he had to say whom he had brought and whether he had received a mission and they would say 'God grant him life, brother and friend!' until they reached the seventh heaven and his Lord. There the duty of fifty prayers a day was laid upon him.

ARTHURIAN SOURCE DOCUMENTS

The small collection of excerpts collected here provide an example of the kinds of materials historians have to work with when they make decisions about sometimes compelling questions. In this case, the question is one that occurs to almost every reader acquainted with the Arthurian legends: Did King Arthur really exist? The documentary evidence below is surprisingly slim, and it is cast in such a way as to defeat a decisive answer to that question. The documents point to a real certainty, that if Arthur existed, he lived in that time after 410 when the Roman legions had pulled out of Britain and left the native Britons (a Celtic people) to fend for themselves. To ward off invading Pictish tribes in the north, the Britons hired Germanic settlers as mercenaries to fight for them. Within a few years, as the Germans themselves tell us in the Anglo-Saxon Chronicle, *the payments stopped and the German tribes themselves became the enemy, settling in the fertile land to the south and inviting over more of their people, the Angles, Saxons, and Jutes. Two chronicles written by the monks Gildas and Nennius tell this story from the side of the British. Nennius identifies as crucial a battle that occurred at Mount Badon and names Arthur as the winning war-leader. But Nennius is writing in 800, nearly 300 years after the key battle.*

As it happens, there is an earlier, almost contemporary, mention of the Battle of Mount Badon. The Welsh monk Gildas, in an attack upon his countrymen for their spinelessness in the face of the treacherous Germans, also calls the Battle of Mount Badon decisive. He says that it occurred in the very year of his birth, within living memory of friends or relatives. But Gildas doesn't mention Arthur!

These chronicles are in Latin. It is interesting to note that the Welsh themselves mention Arthur in works that are decidedly more imaginative. But only one poem might bear on the historical question because it has such an early date. The Welsh poem, the Gododdin, *is an account of a battle in which only the poet, Aneirin, is reputed to have escaped alive. In a portion of the poem that dates from around the year 600, the poet says, in praise of a warrior named Gwawddur, that he was brave and generous, "but he was no Arthur."*

The Anglo-Saxon Chronicle, originally written in Old English, is taken from the translation of G. N. Garmonsway (London: J. M. Dent, 1953). The other documents, all originally in Latin, have been translated for this anthology by the editor.

What are we to make of this evidence? A strict historian might have to agree with the view put forward by J. N. L. Myres in The English Settlements *(Oxford History of England, 1986):*

"What is certainly more significant is that Gildas, in writing the only contemporary narrative of these momentous events, has no mention whatever of Arthur. His silence is decisive in determining the historical insignificance of this enigmatic figure. It is inconceivable that Gildas, with his intense interest in the outcome of a struggle that he believed had been decisively settled in the year of his own birth, should not have mentioned Arthur's part in it had that part been of any political consequence. The fact is that there is no contemporary or near-contemporary evidence for Arthur playing any decisive part in these events at all. No figure on the borderline of history and mythology has wasted more of the historian's time. There are just enough casual references in later Welsh legend, one or two of which may go back to the seventh century, to suggest that a man with this late Roman name Artorius *may have won repute at some ill-defined point of time and place during the struggle. But if we add anything to the bare statement that Arthur may have lived and fought the Saxons, we pass at once from history to romance."*

But that is certainly not the view of history itself, for it has embraced this enigmatic figure, made him a medieval king and showered him with stories of love, adventure, treachery, incest, violence, and spiritual longing. More than 7,000 works based on the Arthurian legends exist in English alone, including novels, plays, poems, movies, comic books, and computer games. And from these slim beginnings!

The Anglo-Saxon Chronicles: *Laud Chronicle*, Early 12th Century

443. In this year the Britons sent overseas to Rome and asked them for troops against the Picts, but they had none there because they were at war with Attila, king of the Huns; and then they sent to the Angles and made the same request to the princes of the Angles.

449. . . . In this year Marcian and Valentinian obtained the kingdom and reigned seven years. In their days Vortigern invited the Angles hither, and they then came hither to Britain3 in three ships at a place *Hoepwinesfleot* [Ebbsfleet, K]. King Vortigern gave them land to the south-east of this land on condition that they fought against the Picts. They then fought against the Picts and had victory wherever they came. Then they sent to Angel; ordered (them) to send more aid and to be told of the worthlessness of the Britons and of the excellence of the land. They then at once sent hither a larger force to help the others. These men came from three nations of Germany: from the Old Saxons, from the Angles, from the Jutes. From the Jutes came the people of Kent and the people of the Isle of Wight, that is the race which now dwells in the Isle of Wight, and the race among the West Saxons which is still called the race of the Jutes. From the Old Saxons came the East Saxons and South Saxons and West Saxons. From Angel, which has stood waste ever since between the Jutes and the Saxons, came the East Angles, Middle Angles, Mercians and all the Northumbrians. Their leaders were two brothers, Hengest and Horsa; they were sons of Wihtgils. Wihtgils was the son of Witta, the son of Weeta, the son of Woden; from

this Woden sprang all our royal family and that of the peoples dwelling south of the Humber.

455. In this year Hengest and Horsa fought against king Vortigern at a place which is called *Ægelesthrep [Aylesford, K]*, and his brother Horsa was slain. And after that Hengest succeeded to the kingdom and Æsc, his son.

456. In this year Hengest and Æsc fought against the Britons at a place which is called *Crecganford [Crayford, K]*, and there slew four companies; and the Britons then forsook Kent and fled to London in great terror.

GILDAS: *DE EXCIDIO ET CONQUESTU BRITANNIAE* (C.550)

Then some time passed, and the cruel invaders returned to their homes. . . . The survivors collected their strength under their leader, Ambrosius Aurelianus, a moderate man, who by chance alone of the Roman people had survived the catastrophe in which his parents, who had undoubtedly once worn the royal purple toga, had been killed, and whose present-day descendants have greatly degenerated from their former virtue. He and his men challenged their previous conquerors to battle, and by God's favor, victory was theirs. . . . From that time, now our countrymen and now the enemy have triumphed . . . up to the year of the siege of Mount Badon, when the last but certainly not the least slaughter of these scoundrels took place, which, I know, makes forty-four years and one month, and which was also the year of my birth.

NENNIUS: *HISTORIA BRITTONUM* (C.800)

At that time the Saxons thrived in multitudes and increased in Britain. With Hengist dead, his son Octha crossed over from the left side of Britain to the realm of the Kentish people, and from him are descended the kings of the Kentish people. Then Arthur fought against them in those days along with the kings of the Britons, and he was himself the leader in their battles. His first battle was at the mouth of the river which is called Glein. The second, third, fourth, and fifth were upon another river, which is called Dubglas and is in the region of Linnuis. The sixth battle was upon the river which is called Bassas. The seventh battle was in the Wood of Celidon, that is Cat Coit Celidon. The eighth was at Castle Guinnion, in which Arthur carried an image of St. Mary, the Perpetual Virgin, on his shoulders, and the pagans were put to flight on that day, and there was a great slaughter of them by the virtue of Our Lord Jesus Christ and by the virtue of Saint Mary the Virgin his mother. The ninth battle was fought in the City of the Legion. The tenth was fought on the banks of the river which is called Tribruit. The eleventh battle occurred on the mountain which is called Agned. The twelfth battle was on Mount Badon, in which nine hundred and sixty men fell from a single attack of Arthur, and nobody overthrew them but he alone, and in all of the battles he emerged as victor. But although the others were overcome in the battle, they sent for help from Germany, and their forces were ceaselessly reinforced. The Saxons brought over leaders from Germany to rule the Britons. . . .

There is another wonder in the region which is called Ercing. It is a tomb near a fountain that is called Licat Anir, and the name of the man who is buried there was called Anir. He was the son of Arthur the soldier, who himself killed and buried him in that place. Men come to measure the mound, which is sometimes six, sometimes nine, sometimes twelve, or sometimes fifteen feet in length. However you measure it again and again, you will never get the same figure—and I have tested this myself.

Annales Cambriae (c.960)

An. 72 [c.518]. The battle of Badon, in which Arthur carried the cross of our Lord Jesus Christ for three days and three nights on his shoulders, and the Britons were victorious.

An. 93 [c.539]. The battle of Camlann, in which Arthur and Medraut fell, and there was death in Britain and in Ireland.

William of Malmesbury: *De Rebus Gestis Regum Anglorum* (c.1125)

But with Vortimer [son of Vortigern] dead, the vigor of the Britons faded, and their diminishing hopes flowed away, and indeed would have vanished entirely if Ambrosius, the lone survivor of the Romans who after Vortigern was monarch of the realm, had not checked the proud barbarians with the exemplary assistance of the warlike Arthur. This is that Arthur who is raved about even today in the trifles of the Bretons—a man who is surely worthy of being described in true histories rather than dreamed about in fallacious myths—for he truly sustained his tottering homeland for a long time and aroused the broken spirits of his fellow citizens to battle. Finally at the siege of Mount Badon, relying on the image of the mother of the Lord, which he had sewn on his armor, rising up alone, he routed nine hundred of the enemy in an incredible slaughter. . . .

But the tomb of Arthur is nowhere to be seen, so ancient dirges fable that he is still to come.

Boethius listening to the instruction of Philosophy while Fortune turns a wheel, illumination from a French translation of *De Consolatione Philosophiae*, c. 1460–70, in the Wallace Collection, London (photo: Bridgeman Art Library).

The Medieval World

Literature in the Middle Ages circulated primarily in manuscript, and had to be copied by hand, at great expense of time and money. As a result, many works have been lost, and many others exist only in single copies that have somehow managed to survive (*Beowulf* and *Sir Gawain and the Green Knight,* for instance). Other works that exist in numerous versions (like Chaucer's *Canterbury Tales*) vary widely because of the carelessness of scribes or because of changes deliberately introduced in copying. Furthermore, because paper did not come into wide use until late in the Middle Ages, manuscripts, made of animal skins, were very expensive, reserved for wealthy patrons, collectors, and church libraries. The growth of administrative bureaucracies stimulated a demand for literate scribes who specialized in legal and government documents. But the best-known of the scribes were the monks, many of whom worked in monasteries that specialized in producing prayer books, liturgies, religious texts, and sometimes secular texts. The most expensive and elaborate of these were illuminated with paintings and marginal decorations, even sometimes highlighted with gold leaf.

The picture at left is a manuscript illumination from a fifteenth-century French translation of *The Consolation of Philosophy,* by the sixth-century philosopher Boethius. Sentenced to death for treason, Boethius, an aristocratic high official in the service of King Theodoric, spent the last year of his life writing this philosophical synthesis of stoic and Platonic ideas as a way of coming to terms with his terrible reversal of fortune. In the panel at the left, a distraught Boethius is visited by the visionary figure of his mentor, Philosophy, who will restore him to mental health by reminding him of what he knows to be the truth. She begins by calling up a poetic vision of the Wheel of Fortune to show that his downfall came as the predictable result of his seeking happiness in worldly things—wealth, power, position, fame, pleasure. True happiness that can't be taken away, she explains, can only be found when the mind seeks the one true good, in God. Although the figure of the Wheel of Fortune was already commonplace by the time Boethius consoled himself with it, his *Consolation* became the most important statement of popular philosophical ideas in the Middle Ages, deeply influencing such writers as Dante and Chaucer.

The manuscript illumination on the cover of this book shows a scene from the *Roman de la Rose,* by Guillaume de Lorris (the text is included in this section). The Lover, in his dream, has just discovered a delightful enclosed garden, owned by Pleasure. The locked gate is tended by the porter, named Idleness, who admits the Lover to the garden (he is seen a second time, entering). Inside he sees handsome young men and women dancing and enjoying themselves. In the middle of the garden is a fountain, the Spring of Narcissus, in which the Lover will see reflected a beautiful rosebush whose blossom he will desire to pluck. This allegorical romance was the most popular secular work of the Middle Ages, and this manuscript (Harley 4425 in the British Library) is representative of its continued popularity. It was executed by an unknown Flemish artist in about 1490, after the introduction of printing. The text of the manuscript is based on a printed version of the romance, but a wealthy patron has commissioned this richly illustrated private copy.

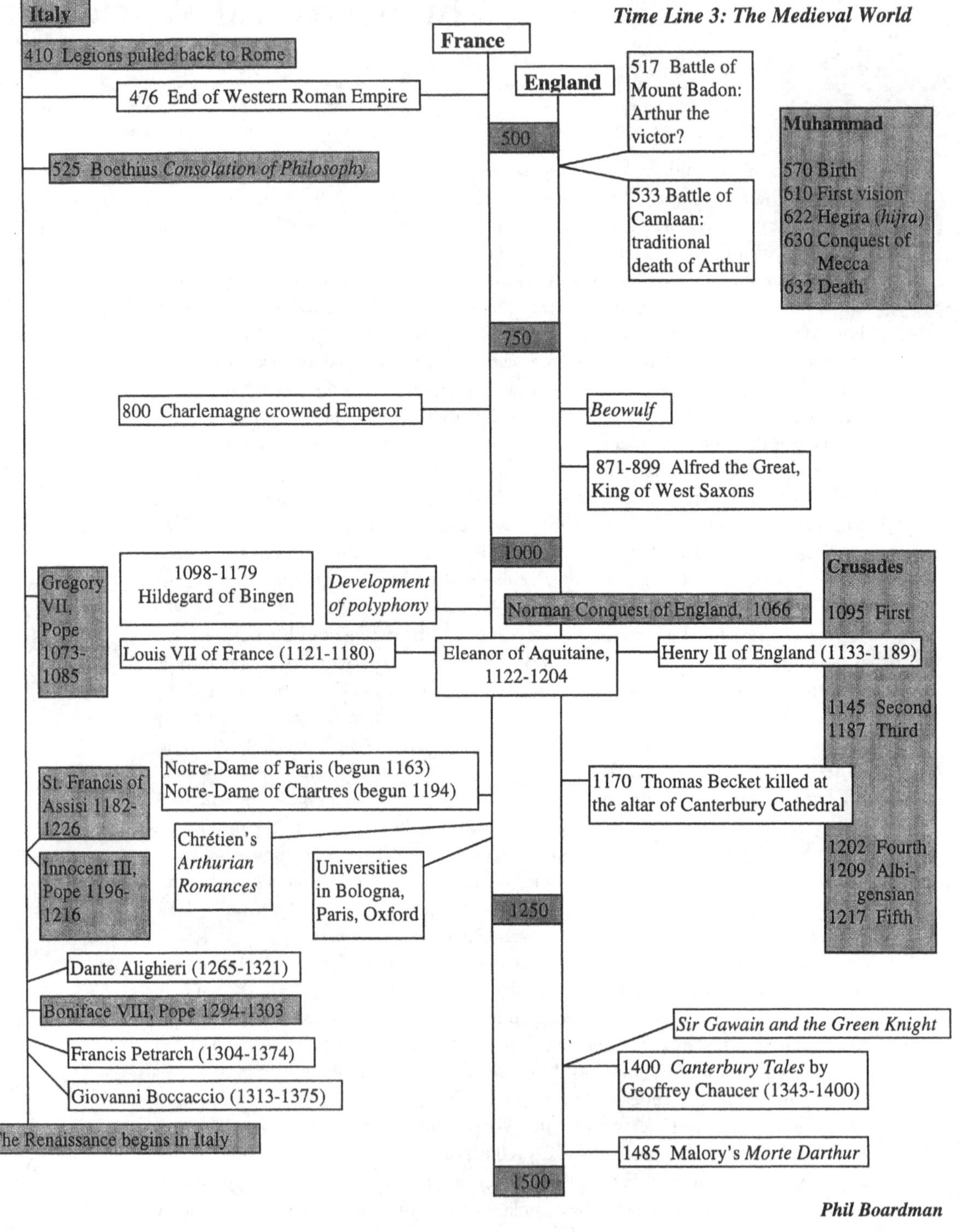
Time Line 3: The Medieval World
Italy
France
England
410 Legions pulled back to Rome
476 End of Western Roman Empire
517 Battle of Mount Badon: Arthur the victor?
500
525 Boethius Consolation of Philosophy
533 Battle of Camlaan: traditional death of Arthur
Muhammad
570 Birth
610 First vision
622 Hegira (hijra)
630 Conquest of Mecca
632 Death
750
800 Charlemagne crowned Emperor
Beowulf
871-899 Alfred the Great, King of West Saxons
1000
Gregory VII, Pope 1073-1085
1098-1179 Hildegard of Bingen
Development of polyphony
Norman Conquest of England, 1066
Crusades
1095 First
1145 Second
1187 Third
1202 Fourth
1209 Albigensian
1217 Fifth
Louis VII of France (1121-1180)
Eleanor of Aquitaine, 1122-1204
Henry II of England (1133-1189)
St. Francis of Assisi 1182-1226
Notre-Dame of Paris (begun 1163)
Notre-Dame of Chartres (begun 1194)
1170 Thomas Becket killed at the altar of Canterbury Cathedral
Innocent III, Pope 1196-1216
Chrétien's Arthurian Romances
Universities in Bologna, Paris, Oxford
1250
Dante Alighieri (1265-1321)
Boniface VIII, Pope 1294-1303
Sir Gawain and the Green Knight
Francis Petrarch (1304-1374)
1400 Canterbury Tales by Geoffrey Chaucer (1343-1400)
Giovanni Boccaccio (1313-1375)
The Renaissance begins in Italy
1485 Malory's Morte Darthur
1500
Phil Boardman

FEUDAL DOCUMENTS

Feudalism was a system of rights and duties that drew its power from land ownership and was common in Western Europe from the ninth to the fourteenth centuries. Land was held "in fief" (as a source of income) in return for specified services, like military service. The hierarchies built into medieval society—kings, nobles, knights, peasants, common serfs—ensured that people were entangled in a web of loyalties and obligations. The king might grant land to a noble in return for military service or the provision of troops in time of war. A vassal *was anyone who held land (a fief) in return for service to an overlord. In a feudal contract, the lord was obligated to provide the fief to the vassal, to protect him, and to offer justice in his court. In return, the lord had the right to demand the services attached to the fief, and these services might be military, but they might also be judicial, administrative, or religious. The two homages below are actual feudal contracts. The second one, through its escape clauses, shows the loyalties demanded of a vassal might often be in conflict. In fact the chivalric literature that grew out of the tempering of late feudalism with doctrines of love and social grace often has as its main theme the problem of conflicting loyalties, such as Lancelot's duties both to Guinevere and to King Arthur in the Arthurian legends.*

[HOMAGE, SOMME RURALE]

The man should put his hands together as a sign of humility, and place them between the two hands of his lord as a token that he vows everything to him and promises

These documents are taken from the *Source Book for Mediæval History*, edited by Oliver J. Thatcher and Edgar H. McNeal (New York: Scribner's, 1905).

faith to him; and the lord should receive him and promise to keep faith with him. Then the man should say: "Sir, I enter your homage and faith and become your man by mouth and hands [i.e., by taking the oath and placing his hands between those of the lord], and I swear and promise to keep faith and loyalty to you against all others, and to guard your rights with all my strength."

[HOMAGE OF JOHN OF TOUL]

I, John of Toul, make known that I am the liege man of the lady Beatrice, countess of Troyes, and of her son, Theobald, count of Champagne, against every creature, living or dead, saving my allegiance to lord Enjorand of Coucy, lord John of Arcis, and the count of Grandpré. If it should happen that the count of Grandpré should be at war with the countess and count of Champagne on his own quarrel, I will aid the count of Grandpré in my own person, and will send to the count and the countess of Champagne the knights whose service I owe to them for the fief which I hold of them.

But if the count of Grandpré shall make war on the countess and the count of Champagne on behalf of his friends and not in his own quarrel, I will aid in my own person the countess and count of Champagne, and will send one knight to the count of Grandpré for the service which I owe him for the fief which I hold of him, but I will not go myself into the territory of the count of Grandpré to make war on him.

[FORMULA FOR THE ORDEAL BY HOT IRON]

The ordeal is popularly seen as an example of the strange idiosyncrasies of medieval notions of justice. Ordeals were tests which allowed (or forced) God to step in and decide whether a defendant was guilty or not. Most ordeals were tortures in which God had to protect his righteous servants as a matter of judicial practice, saving them from being burned or drowned or killed in combat if they were innocent. Because of this, the formula for the ordeal has strong echoes of religious liturgies.

---

(1) First the priest says the prescribed mass; then he has the fire lighted, and blesses the water and sprinkles it over the fire, over the spectators, and over the place where the ordeal is to be held; then he says this prayer:

(2) O Lord, our God, the omnipotent Father, the unfailing Light, hear us, for thou art the maker of all lights. Bless, O God, the fire which we have sanctified and blessed in thy name, thou who hast illumined the whole world, that we may receive

from it the light of thy glory. As thou didst illumine Moses with the fire, so illumine our hearts and minds that we may win eternal life.

(3) Then he shall say the litany....

(4) The prayers....

(5) Then the priest approaches the fire and blesses the pieces of iron, saying: O God, the just judge, who art the author of peace and judgest with equity, we humbly beseech thee so to bless this iron, which is to be used for the trial of this case, that if this man is innocent of the charge he may take the iron in his hand, or walk upon it, without receiving harm or injury; and if he is guilty this may be made manifest upon him by thy righteous power; that iniquity may not prevail over justice, nor falsehood over truth.

(6) O Lord, the holy Father, we beseech thee by the invocation of thy most holy name, by the advent of thy Son, our Lord Jesus Christ, and by the gift of the Holy Spirit, the Comforter, to bless these pieces of iron to the manifestation of thy righteous judgment, that they may be so sanctified and dedicated that thy truth may be made known to thy faithful subjects in this trial. In the name of our Lord Jesus Christ, etc.

(7) Omnipotent God, we humbly beseech thee that in the trial which we are about to make, iniquity may not prevail over justice, nor falsehood over truth. And if anyone shall attempt to circumvent this trial by witchcraft or dealing with herbs, may it be prevented by thy power.

(8) May the blessing of God the Father, Son, and Holy Spirit descend upon these pieces of iron, that the judgment of God may be manifest in them.

(9) Then this psalm shall be said on behalf of the accused: Hear my prayer, O Lord, and give ear unto my cry....

(10) Prayer: Hear, we beseech thee, O Lord, the prayer of thy suppliants, and pardon those that confess their sins, and give us pardon and peace.

(11) Then those who are to be tried shall be adjured as follows: I adjure you (name), by omnipotent God who made heaven and earth, the sea, and all that in them is, by Jesus Christ his Son, who was born and suffered for us, by the Holy Spirit, by the holy Mary, the Mother of God, and by all the holy angels, apostles, martyrs, confessors, and virgins, that you do not yield to the persuasions of the devil and presume to take the iron in your hand, if you are guilty of the crime of which you are accused, or if you know the guilty person. If you are guilty and are rash enough to take the test, may you be put to confusion and condemned, by the virtue of our Lord Jesus Christ, and by the sign of his holy cross. But if you are innocent of the crime, in the name of our Lord Jesus Christ and by the sign of his holy cross, may you have faith to take this iron in your hand; and may God, the just Judge, keep you from harm, even as he saved the three children from the fiery furnace and freed Susanna from the false accusation; may you go through the ordeal safe and secure, and may the power of our Lord be made manifest in you this day.

(12) Then he who is about to be tried shall say: In this ordeal which I am about to undergo, I put my trust rather in the power of God the omnipotent Father to show

his justice and truth in this trial, than in the power of the devil or of witchcraft to circumvent the justice and the truth of God.

(13) Then the man who is accused takes the sacrament and carries the iron to the designated place. After that the deacon shall bind up his hand and place the seal upon it. And until the hand is unwrapped [*i.e.,* at the end of three days] the man should put salt and holy water in all his food and drink.

The Song of Roland (c.1100)

The Song of Roland *is a* chanson de geste, *a heroic song of deeds, and the oldest surviving epic poem in French. This links it to the tradition of the* Epic of Gilgamesh, *the* Iliad, *the* Odyssey, *and* Beowulf*—all heroic songs that were sung by expert bards and passed on orally for centuries before finally being written down for an audience of readers. Like many such heroic songs, there is a grain of historical truth around which the pearl of the finished work has formed. In the case of* Roland, *the historical event was Charlemagne's campaign in Spain in 778 to settle a dispute between two Muslim warlords. While he was laying siege to Saragossa, Charles received word of a Saxon uprising in his own kingdom. While returning to France, he destroyed the Basque town of Pamplona, only to have his own rear guard attacked and destroyed in the mountain pass at Roncesvalles. According to Charlemagne's biographer, Einhard, who wrote a mere fifty years or so after these events, the attackers in the pass were Basques, and after the attack they simply scattered and blended into the surrounding countryside. Among the leaders killed in the ambush, according to Einhard, was Roland, Count of the Breton Marches.*

The Song of Roland *provides a textbook case of the influence of audience and current events on old stories. The poem as we have it written down is in Anglo-Norman (the French spoken in England after the Norman Conquest in 1066) and, although we don't know the author, there are signs that the manuscript dates from around 1100. This would place the poem at the time of the First Crusade, the attempt to take back the Holy Land from the Muslim forces that had seized it in 638, just six years after the death of the Prophet. The First Crusade was proclaimed in 1095, and in 1099 the army, made up mainly of French knights, seized Jerusalem and established a Latin Kingdom there. It is not surprising that, under the spell of the Christian Holy War, Charlemagne's campaign in the* Song of Roland *has become a cosmic struggle against the pagan forces of the Muslim King Marsile, with God and his angels deeply involved on behalf of Charlemagne. But the outcome of the central event, the slaughter of the rear guard, remains unchanged, for heroic poems relish the exploration of brave deeds in a tragically lost cause. This poet, like so many epic poets, looks rather unblinkingly at his heroes, for he shows that the fatal*

Reprinted from *The Song of Roland*, translated by Glyn Burgess (Penguin, 1990).

ambush is at least partly bolstered by Roland's rash refusal to blow his horn to recall Charlemagne's large force to the scene. The poet further complicates issues by balancing against brave Roland the wise Oliver, and by indicting Roland's own stepfather, Ganelon, as the traitor who betrays Roland and his force to the Muslim army.

79

The pagans arm themselves with Saracen hauberks,
Most of which are triple linked.
They lace on their fine helmets from Saragossa
And gird themselves with swords of steel from Viana.
They have shields which are fair and spears from Valence,
And pennons which are white, blue and red.
Leaving their mules and all their palfreys
They mount their war-horses and ride in close array.
The day was fine and the sun bright;
They have no equipment which does not gleam in the light.
They sound a thousand trumpets to enhance the effect.
The noise is great and the Franks heard it.
Oliver said: 'Lord companion, I think
We may have a battle with the Saracens.'
Roland replies: 'And may God grant it to us.
It is our duty to be here for our king:
For his lord a vassal must suffer hardships
And endure great heat and great cold;
And he must lose both hair and hide.
Now let each man take care to strike great blows,
So that no one can sing a shameful song about us.
The pagans are wrong and the Christians are right.
No dishonourable tale will ever be told about me.' AOI.

80

Oliver is on a lofty hilltop.
He looks down to the right over a grassy vale
And he sees the approach of the pagan army.
He called to Roland, his companion:
'Over towards Spain I can see the glint of burnished steel,
So many shining hauberks and gleaming helmets.
These men will cause our Franks great sorrow;
Ganelon was aware of this, the felon, the traitor,
He who appointed us before the emperor.'
'Be silent, Oliver,' replies Count Roland,
'He is my stepfather; I want no word said about him.'

81

Oliver has climbed a hill.
Now he has a clear view of the kingdom of Spain
And of the Saracens assembled in such numbers.
Their hauberks, studded with gold and gems, gleam
Like their shields and saffron helmets
And their spears with pennons fixed.
On his own he cannot count the divisions;
They are too numerous for him to measure their extent.
And he himself is greatly disturbed;
With all speed he came down the hill,
Approached the Franks and told them everything.

82

Oliver said: 'I have seen pagans;
Never has any man on earth seen more.
A hundred thousand men with shields make up the van,
With helmets laced and clad in gleaming hauberks,
Their lances erect and burnished spears aglow.
You will have a battle, never has there been one such.
Frankish lords, may God grant you strength;
Stand firm, lest we should be defeated.'
The Franks say: 'A curse on him who flees.
No one of us will fail you for fear of death.' AOI.

83

Oliver said: 'There is a huge army of pagans,
But mighty few of our Franks, it seems to me.
Companion Roland, blow your horn;
Charles will hear it and the army will turn back.'
Roland replies: 'That would be an act of folly;
Throughout the fair land of France I should lose my good name.
Straightway I shall strike great blows with Durendal;
Right up to its golden hilt the blade will run with blood.
These treacherous pagans will rue the day they came to this pass.
I swear to you, they are all condemned to death.' AOI.

84

'Companion Roland, blow your horn;
Charles will hear it and turn the army round.
With his barons the king will come to our aid.'
Roland replies: 'God forbid that
My kinsmen should incur reproach because of me

Or that the fair land of France should fall into disrepute.
No, I shall strike many a blow with Durendal,
My good sword, which is girt about me;
You will see the entire blade all smeared with blood.
These treacherous pagans will rue the day they gathered here.
I swear to you, all are doomed to die.' AOI.

85

'Companion Roland, blow your horn;
Charles will hear it, as he rides through the pass.
I swear to you, the Franks will soon return.'
'God forbid,' replies Roland to him,
'That any man alive should say that
Pagans made me blow the horn;
My kinsmen will never have to bear that reproach.
When I enter into the thick of the battle,
I shall strike one thousand and seven hundred blows;
You will see the steel blade of Durendal covered in blood.
The Franks are brave men, they will strike courageously;
For those from Spain there will be no escape from death.'

86

Oliver said: 'I see no blame in this.
I have seen the Saracens from Spain;
The valleys and the mountains are covered with them,
The hillsides and all the plains.
Vast is the army of this foreign race;
But we have a tiny company of men.'
Roland replies: 'My desire becomes all the greater;
May it never please the Lord God and his angels
That France should ever lose its fame because of me.
I prefer to die than to suffer such shame;
For the fine blows we strike the emperor loves us all the more.'

87

Roland is brave and Oliver is wise;
Both are marvellous vassals.
Now that they are armed and mounted on their horses,
Neither will avoid the fray for fear of death.
The counts are brave and their words lofty;
The treacherous pagans ride on in great fury.
Oliver said: 'Roland, just see all this;
The enemy is near us, Charles is so far away.
You did not deign to blow your horn;

If the king were here, we should suffer no harm.
Look up towards the Spanish pass;
The rearguard, as you see, is in a sorry plight.
Those who are part of this one will never form another.'
Roland replies: 'Do not speak of such outrage;
A curse on the heart which cowers in the breast!
We shall stand firm and hold our ground;
It is we who shall deal the blows and hack men down.' AOI.

88

When Roland sees that battle will begin,
He becomes fiercer than a lion or a leopard.
He hails the Franks and calls to Oliver:
'Lord companion, friend, such words should not be spoken;
The emperor who left the Franks with us
Allotted us twenty thousand men,
And to his knowledge there was not a coward amongst them.
For his lord a vassal must suffer great hardship
And endure both great heat and great cold;
He must also part with flesh and blood.
Strike with your lance and I with Durendal,
My good sword, which was a gift from the king.
If I die here, the man who owns it next can say
That it belonged to a noble vassal.'

89

Archbishop Turpin, some way across the field,
Spurs on his horse and gallops up a hill.
With these solemn words he calls upon the Franks:
'Lord barons, Charles has left us here;
For our king we must be prepared to die.
Help us now to sustain the Christian faith.
You will have to engage in battle, as you well know;
For you see the Saracens with your own eyes.
Confess your sins, pray for the grace of God;
To save your souls I shall absolve you all.
If you die, you will be blessed martyrs
And take your place in paradise on high.'
The Franks dismount and kneel upon the ground;
In God's name the archbishop blessed them.
As penance he orders them to strike.

90

The Franks rise and get to their feet;
They are fully absolved and freed of their sins
And the archbishop in God's name has blessed them.
Then they mounted their swift war-horses,
Armed in knightly fashion
And all well equipped for battle.
Count Roland summons Oliver:
'Lord companion, you realized full well
That Ganelon has betrayed us all.
He has accepted gold, riches and money;
It is the emperor's duty to avenge us.
King Marsile has struck a bargain for our lives;
But he will have to pay for it with the sword.' AOI.

91

Roland has made his way to the Spanish pass,
Riding Veillantif, his good, swift horse.
The arms he bears become him well.
But he brandishes his spear,
And turns its point towards the sky,
A pure white pennon fixed upon its tip,
And its golden streamers fluttering down upon his hands.
His body is noble, his face fair and smiling;
His companion follows close behind
And the Franks hail him as their protector.
Towards the Saracens he looks fiercely
And humbly and tenderly towards the Franks.
And he addressed them in courtly fashion:
'My lord barons, gently, not too fast!
These pagans are heading for great slaughter;
Today our spoils will be fine and noble.
No king of France has ever had such wealth.'
At these words the armies come together. AOI.

92

Oliver said: 'I have no desire to speak.
You did not deign to sound your oliphant
So you receive no help at all from Charles.
He knows nothing of this and shares no guilt;
Those who remain with him are not to blame.
Now ride for all you are worth;
My lord barons, hold your ground in the field.
In God's name, I beg you, let it be your resolve

To strike blows, to give and to receive;
We must not forget Charles's battle-cry.'
At these words the Franks cried out.
Anyone who heard the call of 'Monjoie'
Would have been reminded of true courage.
Then they ride, O God, with such great zest;
They spur on their horses with vigour to speed upon their way.
And they go to strike; what else were they to do?
But the Saracens had no dread of them;
See now, Franks and pagans joined in battle.

93

Marsile's nephew, whose name is Aelroth,
Is first to ride out before the host.
He hurls insulting words at our Franks:
'Treacherous Franks, you will join battle with us today;
He who should have protected you has betrayed you;
The king is a fool to have left you in the pass.
Today the fair land of France will lose its fame
And Charlemagne the right hand from his body.'
When Roland hears these words, O God, what anger!
He spurs on his horse, lets it race ahead;
The count rides on to strike him with all his might.
He breaks his shield and tears his hauberk open;
He splits his breast and shatters all his bones,
Severing from his back his entire spine.
With his spear he casts forth his soul,
And, giving him a firm push, makes his body topple.
With a free blow of his lance he flings him dead from his horse;
He has broken his neck in two.
He will not forgo, he says, the chance to rail at him:
'You utter wretch, Charles is no fool
And never a man to care for treachery.
He acted properly in leaving us in the pass;
Today the fair land of France will not lose its fame.
Strike, Franks, the first blow is ours!
We are right, but these wretches are wrong.' AOI.

94

A duke is there, his name is Falsaron;
He was brother to King Marsile.
He held the land of Dathan and Abiram;
No more foul traitor exists upon this earth.
Between his eyes his brow was spread so broad
Its measure was a good half-foot.

His grief is great to see his nephew slain;
He breaks out from the throng, intent upon a fight,
And shouts the pagan battle-cry.
Towards the Franks he hurls these mocking words:
'This day the fair land of France will lose its honour.'
Oliver hears him and is greatly enraged.
He urges on his horse with his golden spurs
And goes to strike him in courageous fashion.
He breaks his shield and rends his hauberk,
Ramming the tails of his pennon right into his body.
With a free blow of his lance he flings him dead from his saddle.
Looking down, he sees the wretch lying there
And addressed him in ferocious terms:
'I am not hindered, villain, by your threats;
Strike, Franks, for we shall vanquish them with ease.'
He shouts 'Monjoie', the battle-cry of Charles. AOI.

. . . .

104

The battle is terrible and now joined by all.
Count Roland is no laggard;
He strikes with his spear, while the shaft still lasts.
With fifteen blows he has broken and destroyed it;
He draws forth Durendal, his fine, naked sword,
And spurs on his horse to strike at Chernubles.
He breaks his helmet with its gleaming carbuncles,
Slices off his coif and his scalp,
As well as slicing through his eyes and his face,
His shining hauberk with its close-meshed mail
His whole body right down to his crotch,
And right into his saddle which is of beaten gold;
His sword came to rest in the horse itself.
He slices through its spine, seeking no joint,
And flinging them both dead in the meadow on the lush grass.
Then he said to him: 'Villain, you set out to meet your doom;
You will receive no help from Muhammad.
A wretch like you will not win today's battle.'

. . . .

116

The Franks see that there are so many pagans;
On all sides the fields are covered with them.
Time and again they call upon Oliver and Roland
And the twelve peers to act as their protectors.

And the archbishop told them what was on his mind:
'Lord barons, do not indulge in base thoughts;
In God's name I beg you not to flee,
So that no man of worth can sing a shameful song.
It is far better for us to die fighting.
We are promised this: soon we shall meet our end;
Beyond this day we shall cease to be alive.
But in one thing I can act as guarantor:
Holy paradise is open to you;
You will take your seat amongst the Innocents.'
At these words the Franks rejoice;
No one fails to call out 'Monjoie'. AOI.

. . . .

128

Count Roland sees the heavy losses of his men;
He calls to his companion Oliver:
'Fair lord, dear companion, in God's name, what is your view of this?
You see so many fine knights lying on the ground.
We cannot but lament for the fair, sweet land of France;
Of how many men it now stands bereft!
O king, friend, if only you were here.
Oliver, brother, how should we now act?
In what way shall we send him news?'
Oliver said: 'I do not know how to reach him;
I should rather die than have us suffer shame.' AOI.

129

Roland said: 'I shall sound the oliphant
And Charles, who is going through the pass, will hear it.
I pledge to you, the Franks will soon return.'
Oliver said: 'That would be most shameful
And all your kinsmen would then be blamed;
Such shame would endure as long as they live.
When I spoke to you of this, you did nothing.
But you will not now act so on my advice.
If you sound the horn, there will be no valour in it.
Both your arms are now smeared with blood.'
The count replies: 'I have struck most noble blows.' AOI.

130

Roland says: 'Our battle is fierce;
I shall sound the horn and King Charles will hear it.'
Oliver said: 'That would not be a courageous act;
When I spoke of this, companion, you did not deign to do it;
If the king had been here, we should have come to no harm.
Those who are there with him deserve no blame.'
Oliver said: 'By this beard of mine;
If ever I see my noble sister Aude,
You will not lie in her arms.' AOI.

131

Roland said: 'Why do you bear a grudge?'
And he replies: 'Companion, you have been the cause of it.
For a true vassal's act, in its wisdom, avoids folly;
Caution is better than great zeal.
Franks are dead because of your recklessness;
Charles will never again receive our service.
If you had heeded me, my lord would now be here;
We should have fought this battle and won it.
King Marsile would have been captured or killed.
Roland, we can only rue your prowess;
Charlemagne will have no aid from us.
There will be none like him until the Day of Judgement;
You will die here and France will be shamed by it.
Today our loyal comradeship is at its end;
Before evening there will be a sorrowful farewell.' AOI.

132

The archbishop hears their quarrel.
Urging on his horse, with his spurs of pure gold,
He rode up to them and began to rebuke them:
'Lord Roland and Lord Oliver,
In God's name, I beg you, do not argue.
To blow the horn would be to no avail;
But nevertheless it is now for the best.
Let the king come, then he can avenge our deaths;
The men of Spain must never leave here joyful.
Our Franks will dismount here;
They will find us dead and hacked to pieces
And will raise us on to pack-horses in coffins.
They will shed tears of sorrow and pity for us
And bury us in a church's hallowed ground.
No wolf or pig or dog will devour us.'
Roland replies: 'Lord, you speak well.' AOI.

133

Roland set the oliphant to his lips.
He takes a firm grip of it and blows with all his might;
The hills are high and the sound travels far.
A full thirty leagues they heard it echo;
Charles heard it and all his companions.
The king said: 'Our men are doing battle.'
But Ganelon made this retort:
'From anyone else, this would have seemed a great untruth.' AOI.

134

Count Roland with pain and distress
Sounds his oliphant in great agony.
The clear blood gushes forth from his mouth
And in his skull the temple bursts.
The sound of the horn which he holds carries far;
Charles hears it, as he makes his way through the pass.
Duke Naimes heard it and the Franks listen to it.
The king said: 'I can hear Roland's horn;
He would never have blown it, if he were not in a fight.'
Ganelon replies: 'There is no battle;
You are old, hoary and white-haired.
Such words make you seem like a child;
You are well aware of Roland's great pride.
It is a wonder that God has stood for it so long.
Once he captured Noples without your orders;
The Saracens poured out from within it
And attacked the good vassal Roland.
Later he cleansed the blood from the meadows with water,
So that no one would see what he had done.
For a mere hare he would blow his horn all day.
Now he is just boasting before his peers;
There is no army on earth who would have dared attack him.
Keep riding; why do you delay?
The great land of France is very far ahead.' AOI.

135

Count Roland is bleeding from the mouth;
In his skull the temple is burst.
He blows the oliphant with pain and anguish;
Charles heard it and so did the Franks.
The king said: 'The sound of the horn is long drawn out.'
Duke Naimes replies: 'A true vassal makes the effort;
In my estimation there is a battle.

He who wants you to be faint-hearted has betrayed him.
Arm yourself and shout out your battle-cry
And ride to the aid of your noble household.
You can hear clearly the distress cry which Roland sends.'

. . . .

174

Roland feels that death is upon him;
It is moving down from his head to his heart.
He ran over to a pine and beneath it
And lay face down on the green grass.
He places his sword and the oliphant beneath him;
Towards the pagan host he turned his head,
Because it was his earnest wish that
Charles and all his men should say
That he, the noble count, had died victoriously.
He confesses his sins over and over again;
For his sins he proffered his glove to God. AOI.

175

Roland feels that his time has come;
He is on a steep hill facing Spain.
With one hand he beat his breast:
'O God, the Almighty, I confess
My sins, both great and small,
Which I have committed since the time I was born,
Until this day on which I have been overtaken.'
He held out his right glove to God;
Angels come down to him from Heaven. AOI.

176

Count Roland lay down beneath a pine tree;
He has turned his face towards Spain.
Many things began to pass through his mind:
All the lands which he conquered as a warrior,
The fair land of France, the men of his lineage,
Charlemagne, his lord, who raised him.
He cannot help weeping and heaving great sighs;
But he does not wish to be unmindful of himself.
He confesses his sins and prays for the grace of God:
'True Father, who has never lied,
You who brought back Lazarus from the dead
And rescued Daniel from the lions,
Protect my soul from every peril

And from the sins which I have committed in my life.'
He proffered his right glove to God;
Saint Gabriel took it from his hand.
Roland laid his head down over his arm;
With his hands joined he went to his end.
God sent down his angel Cherubin
And with him Saint Michael of the Peril.
With them both came Saint Gabriel.
They bear the count's soul to paradise.

Fulcher of Chartres (c.1059–1127?)

A History of the Expedition to Jerusalem, 1095–1127

Within only a few years of the Prophet Muhammad's death in 632, Muslim forces moved rapidly to conquer Christian territories in North Africa, Spain, and, by 638, Jerusalem and the surrounding "Holy Land," a festering reminder to Christians of their lack of resolve. In many places there were accommodations and treaties that nurtured a mixing of cultural traditions. For instance, in Jerusalem, a city sacred to Jews, Christians, and Muslims, Christian holy sites were preserved (until Muslims destroyed the Church of the Holy Sepulchre in 1009). In Spain, a bit later, the famous convivencia *flourished, a rich blending of Muslim, Jewish, and Christian ideas, traditions, and cultures, traces of which can be seen in Toledo even today. Meanwhile, violence within Western Christianity increased to intolerable levels.*

The toll of this violence on the social fabric, and successful incursions by Muslim Seljuk Turks into Byzantine territories (in present-day Turkey), reached a crisis point in 1095. When Alexius I, the Byzantine emperor, asked for help against the Muslims from the head of the Western Church, Pope Urban II, Urban seized the opportunity to rally Christians to renewed religious zeal. On November 27, 1095, at a council held in Clermont, France, Pope Urban delivered a sermon in which he called for reform of practices in the Church that had become corrupt (like the sale of Church offices) and for the reinstatement of the Peace of God (to deflect from local violence those Christians who "wantonly wage private warfare against the faithful"). And then Urban turned the attention of the assembled clergy and nobles to the Muslim threat to the Eastern Orthodox Church. He called Christians to a Holy War, a campaign which offered a remission of previous sins and the sure reward of Heaven for warriors who died in the endeavor.

Across Europe peasants and nobles responded enthusiastically, many out of genuine religious zeal, and the First Crusade was launched. By 1099 the front lines of the Turks had been engaged, and the victorious Christians had gone on to seize Antioch and Jerusalem, and to establish several "Crusader states," tended by Christian forces under Christian "kings." In the long run, of course, Christian control was not to last, and further crusades, over nearly two centuries, poured resources and lives into the conflicts with opponents and supposed opponents of Christianity. And the crusading zeal itself could lead the

This translation of Fulcher's Latin is by Francis Rita Ryan (New York: Norton, 1973).

faithful in some startling directions. The Fourth Crusade, 1202–1204, is a much-studied example: the Christian forces, with inadequate resources to reach their goal of Jerusalem, were seduced by the great wealth of the Eastern Orthodox capital of Constantinople. Sacking the city and plundering its churches, the crusaders carried back with them relics and treasures. Just a few years later, in the Albigensian Crusade, Christian forces from northern France attacked and killed Christians in the South of France accused of heresies.

The speech by Pope Urban II that first aroused the crusading spirit was remembered and written down years later by a number of different witnesses. None was more actively involved in the aftermath than Fulcher of Chartres, a cleric who went with the crusaders to Antioch and Jerusalem, and later became the canon of the rebuilt Church of the Holy Sepulchre in Jerusalem. He spent many years in the crusader states and wrote a full account of the First Crusade and its results up until the date that he presumably died, in 1127.

[Call to Arms by Pope Urban II, 27 November 1095]

III

When these and many other matters were satisfactorily settled, all those present, clergy and people alike, spontaneously gave thanks to God for the words of the Lord Pope Urban and promised him faithfully that his decrees would be well kept. But the pope added at once that another tribulation not less but greater than that already mentioned, even of the worst nature, was besetting Christianity from another part of the world.

He said, "Since, oh sons of God, you have promised Him to keep peace among yourselves and to faithfully sustain the rights of Holy Church more sincerely than before, there still remains for you, newly aroused by Godly correction, an urgent task which belongs to both you and God, in which you can show the strength of your good will. For you must hasten to carry aid to your brethren dwelling in the East, who need your help for which they have often entreated.

"For the Turks, a Persian people, have attacked them, as many of you already know, and have advanced as far into Roman territory as that part of the Mediterranean which is called the Arm of St. George. They have seized more and more of the lands of the Christians, have already defeated them in seven times as many battles, killed or captured many people, have destroyed churches, and have devastated the kingdom of God. If you allow them to continue much longer they will conquer God's faithful people much more extensively.

"Wherefore with earnest prayer I, not I, but God exhorts you as heralds of Christ to repeatedly urge men of all ranks whatsoever, knights as well as foot-soldiers, rich and poor, to hasten to exterminate this vile race from our lands and to aid the Christian inhabitants in time.

"I address those present; I proclaim it to those absent; moreover Christ commands it. For all those going thither there will be remission of sins if they come to the end of this fettered life while either marching by land or crossing by sea, or in fighting the pagans. This I grant to all who go, through the power vested in me by God.

"Oh what a disgrace if a race so despicable, degenerate, and enslaved by demons should thus overcome a people endowed with faith in Almighty God and resplendent in the name of Christ! Oh what reproaches will be charged against you by the Lord Himself if you have not helped those who are counted like yourselves of the Christian faith!

"Let those," he said, "who are accustomed to wantonly wage private war against the faithful march upon the infidels in a war which should be begun now and be finished in victory. Let those who have long been robbers now be soldiers of Christ. Let those who once fought against brothers and relatives now rightfully fight against barbarians. Let those who have been hirelings for a few pieces of silver now attain an eternal reward. Let those who have been exhausting themselves to the detriment of body and soul now labor for a double glory. Yea on the one hand will be the sad and the poor, on the other the joyous and the wealthy; here the enemies of the Lord, there His friends.

"Let nothing delay those who are going to go. Let them settle their affairs, collect money, and when winter has ended and spring has come, zealously undertake the journey under the guidance of the Lord."

Peter Abelard (1079–1142)

The History of My Misfortunes

The story of Abelard and Heloise is among the best-known of medieval love stories, and it has moved people since the time the lovers were still living. Abelard was a brilliant and contentious student who went from teacher to teacher and town to town, finally establishing himself in Paris as a popular teacher.

Abelard's immersion in philosophy and his commitment to logic and the study of language led him to conclusions that often ran counter to the teachings of the church. For much of his life, even ignoring the sensational affair with Heloise, he was the center of controversy, facing charges of heresy, and escaping from attempts on his life. Abelard was never one to back down, and during his career he published tract after tract that offended clerics in authority.

The flames of notoriety were fanned by Abelard and Heloise themselves. The story of Abelard's castration would have spread among his many rivals and his students in any event. But Abelard wrote an account of his life which made clear the contempt he felt for other thinkers and described the passion of his love. Near the ends of their lives, Abelard and Heloise jointly published their correspondence, usually called the Letters of Abelard and Heloise. *After spending all the later years of their lives in various nunneries and monasteries, they can today be found buried together in the cemetery of Père-Lachaise in Paris.*

[The University of Paris and Heloise]

While these things were happening, it became needful for me again to repair to my old home, by reason of my dear mother, Lucia, for after the conversion of my father, Berengarius, to the monastic life, she so ordered her affairs as to do likewise. When all this had been completed, I returned to France, above all in order that I might study theology, since now my oft-mentioned teacher, William, was active in the episcopate of Châlons. In this field of learning Anselm of Laon, who was his teacher therein, had for long years enjoyed the greatest renown.

This translation by Henry Adams Bellows was first published by the Free Press in 1922.

I sought out, therefore, this same venerable man, whose fame, in truth, was more the result of long-established custom than of the potency of his own talent or intellect. If any one came to him impelled by doubt on any subject, he went away more doubtful still. He was wonderful, indeed, in the eyes of these who only listened to him, but those who asked him questions perforce held him as nought. He had a miraculous flow of words, but they were contemptible in meaning and quite void of reason. When he kindled a fire, he filled his house with smoke and illumined it not at all. He was a tree which seemed noble to those who gazed upon its leaves from afar, but to those who came nearer and examined it more closely was revealed its barrenness. . . .

It was not long before I made this discovery, and stretched myself lazily in the shade of that same tree. I went to his lectures less and less often, a thing which some among his eminent followers took sorely to heart, because they interpreted it as a mark of contempt for so illustrious a teacher. Thenceforth they secretly sought to influence him against me, and by their vile insinuations made me hated of him. . . .

In truth at [my] first lecture . . . only a few were present, for it seemed quite absurd to all of them that I, hitherto so inexperienced in discussing the Scriptures, should attempt the thing so hastily. However, this lecture gave such satisfaction to all those who heard it that they spread its praises abroad with notable enthusiasm, and thus compelled me to continue my interpretation of the sacred text. When word of this was bruited about, those who had stayed away from the first lecture came eagerly, some to the second and more to the third, and all of them were eager to write down the glosses which I had begun on the first day, so as to have them from the very beginning.

Now this venerable man of whom I have spoken was acutely smitten with envy, and straightway incited, as I have already mentioned, by the insinuations of sundry persons, began to persecute me for my lecturing on the Scriptures no less bitterly than my former master, William, had done for my work in philosophy. At that time there were in this old man's school two who were considered far to excel all the others: Alberic of Rheims and Lotulphe the Lombard. The better opinion these two held of themselves, the more they were incensed against me. Chiefly at their suggestion, as it afterwards transpired, yonder venerable coward had the impudence to forbid me to carry on any further in his school the work of preparing glosses which I had thus begun. The pretext he alleged was that if by chance in the course of this work I should write anything containing blunders—as was likely enough in view of my lack of training—the thing might be imputed to him. When this came to the ears of his scholars, they were filled with indignation at so undisguised a manifestation of spite, the like of which had never been directed against any one before. The more obvious this rancour became, the more it redounded to my honour, and his persecution did nought save to make me more famous.

And so, after a few days, I returned to Paris, and there for several years I peacefully directed the school which formerly had been destined for me, nay, even offered to me, but from which I had been driven out. At the very outset of my work there, I set about completing the glosses on Ezekiel which I had begun at Laon. These proved so satisfactory to all who read them that they came to believe me no less adept in lecturing on theology than I had proved myself to be in the field of philosophy. Thus my school was notably increased in size by reason of my lectures on subjects of both these kinds, and the amount of financial profit as well as glory which it brought me cannot be concealed from you, for the matter was widely talked of. But prosperity always puffs up the foolish, and worldly comfort enervates the soul, rendering it an easy prey to carnal temptations. Thus I, who by this time had come to regard myself as the only philosopher remaining in the whole world, and had ceased to fear any further disturbance of my peace, began to loosen the rein on my desires, although hitherto I had always lived in the utmost continence. And the greater progress I made in my lecturing on philosophy or theology, the more I departed alike from the practice of the philosophers and the spirit of the divines in the uncleanness of my life. For it is well known, methinks, that philosophers, and still more those who have devoted their lives to arousing the love of sacred study, have been strong above all else in the beauty of chastity.

Thus did it come to pass that while I was utterly absorbed in pride and sensuality, divine grace, the cure for both diseases, was forced upon me, even though I, forsooth, would fain have shunned it. First was I punished for my sensuality, and then for my pride. For my sensuality I lost those things whereby I practiced it; for my pride, engendered in me by my knowledge of letters—and it is even as the Apostle said: "Knowledge puffeth itself up" (i Cor. viii, i)—I knew the humiliation of seeing burned the very book in which I most gloried. And now it is my desire that you should know the stories of these two happenings, understanding them more truly from learning the very facts than from hearing what is spoken of them, and in the order in which they came about. Because I had ever held in abhorrence the foulness of prostitutes, because I had diligently kept myself from all excesses and from association with the women of noble birth who attended the school, because I knew so little of the common talk of ordinary people, perverse and subtly flattering chance gave birth to an occasion for casting me lightly down from the heights of my own exaltation. Nay, in such case not even divine goodness could redeem one who, having been so proud, was brought to such shame, were it not for the blessed gift of grace.

Now there dwelt in that same city of Paris a certain young girl named Heloise, the niece of a canon who was called Fulbert. Her uncle's love for her was equalled only by his desire that she should have the best education which he could possibly procure for her. Of no mean beauty, she stood out above all by reason of her abundant knowledge of letters. Now this virtue is rare among women, and for that very reason it doubly graced the maiden, and made her the most worthy of renown in the entire kingdom. It was this young girl whom I, after carefully considering all those qualities which are wont to attract lovers, determined to unite with myself in the bonds of love, and indeed the thing seemed to me very easy to be done. So distinguished was my name, and I possessed such advantages of youth and comeliness, that no matter what woman I might favour with my love, I dreaded rejection of none. Then, too, I believed that I could win the maiden's consent all the more easily by reason of her knowledge of letters and her zeal therefor; so, even if we were parted, we might yet be together in thought with the aid of written messages. Perchance, too, we might be able to write more boldly than we could speak, and thus at all times could we live in joyous intimacy.

Thus, utterly aflame with my passion for this maiden, I sought to discover means whereby I might have daily and familiar speech with her, thereby the more easily to win her consent. For this purpose I persuaded the girl's uncle, with the aid of some of his friends, to take me into his household—for he dwelt hard by my school—in return for the payment of a small sum. My pretext for this was that the care of my own household was a serious handicap to my studies, and likewise burdened me with an expense far greater than I could afford. Now, he was a man keen in avarice, and likewise he was most desirous for his niece that her study of letters should ever go forward, so, for these two reasons, I easily won his consent to the fulfillment of my wish, for he was fairly agape for my money, and at the same time believed that his niece would vastly benefit by my teaching. More even than this, by his own earnest entreaties he fell in with my desires beyond anything I had dared to hope, opening the way for my love; for he entrusted her wholly to my guidance, begging me to give her instruction whensoever I might be free from the duties of my school, no matter whether by day or by night, and to punish her sternly if ever I should find her negligent of her tasks. In all this the man's simplicity was nothing short of astounding to me; I should not have been more smitten with wonder if he had entrusted a tender lamb to the care of a ravenous wolf. When he had thus given her into my charge, not alone to be taught but even to be disciplined, what had he done save to give free scope to my desires, and to offer me every opportunity, even if I had not sought it, to bend her to my will with threats and blows if I failed to do so with caresses? There were, however, two things which particularly served to allay any foul suspicion: his own love for his niece, and my former reputation for continence.

Why should I say more? We were united first in the dwelling that sheltered our love, and then in the hearts that burned with it. Under the pretext of study we spent our hours in the happiness of love, and learning held out to us the secret opportunities that our passion craved. Our speech was more of love than of the books which lay open before us; our kisses far outnumbered our reasoned words. Our hands sought less the book than each other's bosoms; love drew our eyes together far more than the lesson drew them to the pages of our text. In order that there might be no suspicion, there were, indeed, sometimes blows, but love gave them, not anger; they were the marks, not of wrath, but of a tenderness surpassing the most fragrant balm in sweetness. What followed? No degree in love's progress was left untried by our passion, and if love itself could imagine any wonder as yet unknown, we discovered it. And our inexperience of such delights made us all the more ardent in our pursuit of them, so that our thirst for one another was still unquenched.

In measure as this passionate rapture absorbed me more and more, I devoted ever less time to philosophy and to the work of the school. Indeed it became loathsome to me to go to the school or to linger there; the labour, moreover, was very burdensome, since my nights were vigils of love and my days of study. My lecturing became utterly careless and lukewarm; I did nothing because of inspiration, but everything merely as a matter of habit. I had become nothing more than a reciter of my former discoveries, and though I still wrote poems, they dealt with love, not with the secrets of philosophy. Of these songs you yourself well know how some have become widely known and have been sung in many lands, chiefly, methinks, by those who delighted in the things of this world. As for the sorrow, the groans, the lamentations of my students when they perceived the preoccupation, nay, rather the chaos, of my mind, it is hard even to imagine them.

A thing so manifest could deceive only a few, no one, methinks, save him whose shame it chiefly bespoke, the girl's uncle, Fulbert. The truth was often enough hinted to him, and by many persons, but he could not believe it, partly, as I have said, by reason of his boundless love for his niece, and partly because of the well-known continence of my previous life. Indeed we do not easily suspect shame in those whom we most cherish, nor can there be the blot of foul suspicion on devoted love. Of this St. Jerome in his epistle to Sabinianus (Epist. 48) says: "We are wont to be the last to know the evils of our own households, and to be ignorant of the sins of our children and our wives, though our neighbours sing them aloud." But no matter how slow a matter may be in disclosing itself, it is sure to come forth at last, nor is it easy to hide from one what is known to all. So, after the lapse of several months, did it happen with us. Oh, how great was the uncle's grief when he learned the truth, and how bitter was the sorrow of the lovers when we were forced to part! With what shame was I overwhelmed, with what contrition smitten because of the blow which had fallen on her I loved, and what a tempest of misery burst over her by reason of my disgrace! Each grieved most, not for himself, but for the other. Each sought to allay, not his own sufferings, but those of the one he loved. The very sundering of our bodies served but to link our souls closer together; the plentitude of the love which was denied to us inflamed us more than ever. Once the first wildness of shame had passed, it left us more shameless than before, and as shame died within us the cause of it seemed to us ever more desirable. And so it chanced with us as, in the stories that the poets tell, it once happened with Mars and Venus when they were caught together.

It was not long after this that Heloise found that she was pregnant, and of this she wrote to me in the utmost exultation, at the same time asking me to consider what had best be done. Accordingly, on a night when her uncle was absent, we carried out the plan we had determined on, and I stole her secretly away from her uncle's house, sending her without delay to my own country. She remained there with my sister until she gave birth to a son, whom she named Astrolabe. Meanwhile her uncle, after his return, was almost mad with grief; only one who had then seen him could rightly guess the burning agony of his sorrow and the bitterness of his shame. What steps to take against me, or what snares to set for me, he did not know. If he should kill me or do me some bodily hurt, he feared greatly lest his dear-loved niece should be made to suffer for it among my kinsfolk. He had no power to seize me and imprison me somewhere against my will, though I make no doubt he would have done so quickly enough had he been able or dared, for I had taken measures to guard against any such attempt.

At length, however, in pity for his boundless grief, and bitterly blaming myself for the suffering which my love had brought upon him through the baseness of the deception I had practiced, I went to him to entreat his forgiveness, promising to make any amends that he himself might decree. I pointed out that what had happened could not seem incredible to any one who had ever felt the power of love, or who remembered how, from the very beginning of the human race, women had cast down even the noblest men to utter ruin. And in order to make amends even beyond his extremest hope, I offered to marry her whom I had seduced, provided only the thing could be kept secret, so that I might suffer no loss of reputation thereby. To this he gladly assented, pledging his own faith and that of his kindred, and sealing with kisses the pact which I had sought of him—and all this that he might the more easily betray me.

Forthwith I repaired to my own country, and brought back thence my mistress, that I might make her my wife. She, however, most violently disapproved of this, and for two chief reasons: the danger thereof, and the disgrace which it would bring upon me. She swore that her uncle would never be appeased by such satisfaction as this, as, indeed, afterwards proved only too true. She asked how she could ever glory in me if she should make me thus inglorious, and should shame herself along with me. What penalties, she said, would the world rightly demand of her if she should rob it of so shining a light! What curses would follow such a loss to the Church, what tears among the philosophers would result from such a marriage! How unfitting, how lamentable it would be for me, whom nature had made for the whole world, to devote myself to one woman solely, and to subject myself to such humiliation! She vehemently rejected this marriage, which she felt would be in every way ignominious and burdensome to me. . . .

Her final argument was that it would be dangerous for me to take her back to Paris, and that it would be far sweeter for her to be called my mistress than to be known as my wife; nay, too, that this would be more honourable for me as well. In such case, she said, love alone would hold me to her, and the strength of the marriage chain would not constrain us. Even if we should by chance be parted from time to time, the joy of our meetings would be all the sweeter by reason of its rarity. But when she found that she could not convince me or dissuade me from my folly by these and like arguments, and because she could not bear to offend me, with grievous sighs and tears she made an end of her resistance, saying: "Then there is no more left but this, that in our doom the sorrow yet to come shall be no less than the love we two have already known." Nor in this, as now the whole world knows, did she lack the spirit of prophecy.

So, after our little son was born, we left him in my sister's care, and secretly returned to Paris. A few days later, in the early morning, having kept our nocturnal vigil of prayer unknown to all in a certain church, we were united there in the benediction of wedlock, her uncle and a few friends of his and mine being present. We departed forthwith stealthily and by separate ways, nor thereafter did we see each other save rarely and in private, thus striving our utmost to conceal what we had done. But her uncle and those of his household, seeking solace for their disgrace, began to divulge the story of our marriage, and thereby to violate the pledge they had given me on this point. Heloise, on the contrary, denounced her own kin and swore that they were speaking the most absolute lies. Her uncle, aroused to fury thereby, visited her repeatedly with punishments. No sooner had I learned this than I sent her to a convent of nuns at Argenteuil, not far from Paris, where she herself had been brought up and educated as a young girl. I had them make ready for her all the garments of a nun, suitable for the life of a convent, excepting only the veil, and these I bade her put on.

When her uncle and his kinsmen heard of this, they were convinced that now I had completely played them false and had rid myself forever of Heloise by forcing her to become a nun. Violently incensed, they laid a plot against me, and one night, while I, all unsuspecting, was asleep in a secret room in my lodgings, they broke in with the help of one of my servants, whom they had bribed. There they had vengeance on me with a most cruel and most shameful punishment, such as astounded the whole world, for they cut off those parts of my body with which I had done that which was the cause of their sorrow. This done, straightway they fled, but two of them were captured, and suffered the loss of their eyes and their genital organs. One of these two was the aforesaid servant, who, even while he was still in my service, had been led by his avarice to betray me.

When morning came the whole city was assembled before my dwelling. It is difficult, nay, impossible, for words of mine to describe the amazement which bewildered them, the lamentations they uttered, the uproar with which they harassed me, or the grief with which they increased my own suffering. Chiefly the clerics, and above all my scholars, tortured me with their intolerable lamentations and outcries, so that I suffered more intensely from their compassion than from the pain of my wound. In truth I felt the disgrace more than the hurt to my body, and was more afflicted with shame than with pain. My incessant thought was of the renown in which I had so much delighted, now brought low, nay, utterly blotted out, so swiftly by an evil chance. I saw, too, how justly God had punished me in that very part of my body whereby I had sinned. I perceived that there was indeed justice in my betrayal by him whom I had myself already betrayed; and then I thought how eagerly my rivals would seize upon this manifestation of justice, how this disgrace would bring bitter and enduring grief to my kindred and my friends, and how the tale of this amazing outrage would spread to the very ends of the earth. What path lay open to me thereafter? How could I ever again hold up my head among men, when every finger should be pointed at me in scorn, every tongue speak my blistering shame, and when I should be a monstrous spectacle to all eyes? I was overwhelmed by the remembrance that, according to the dread letter of the law, God holds eunuchs in such abomination that men thus maimed are forbidden to enter a church, even as the unclean and filthy; nay, even beasts in such plight were not acceptable as sacrifices. Thus in Leviticus (xxii, 24) is it said: "Ye shall not offer unto the Lord that which hath its stones bruised, or crushed, or broken, or cut." And in Deuteronomy (xxiii, i), "He that is wounded in the stones, or hath his privy member cut off, shall not enter into the congregation of the Lord."

I must confess that in my misery it was the overwhelming sense of my disgrace rather than any ardour for conversion to the religious life that drove me to seek the seclusion of the monastic cloister. Heloise had already, at my bidding, taken the veil and entered a convent. Thus it was that we both put on the sacred garb, I in the abbey of St. Denis, and she in the convent of Argenteuil, of which I have already spoken.

Heloise (c.1100–c.1163)

Personal Letters

Heloise's name will forever be bound up with Abelard's (see the previous selection). We know nothing about her background and parentage except what we can learn from Abelard's description of her in his History of My Calamities *and from her own correspondence. By reputation she was lively, intelligent, and independent, qualities that shine through her letters. She was fortunate that her guardian, Fulbert, sought for her an education that would have been unusual for a young woman in her day. And she was fortunate that he chose as tutor the greatest teacher of the day, Abelard, although their passionate affair and disastrous marriage became a real-life counterpart to the tragic story of Tristan and Iseult that was popular at the same time. The published correspondence started when, after a period in the abbey without word from Abelard, Heloise received a copy of his "letter to a friend," that is, his account of his misfortunes. Hurt at her own isolation, and chafing with the knowledge that her religious vocation was a sham, she wrote to him of her grievance. The correspondence continued, focusing first on the deep wounds left by their notorious affair, their hasty and deceptive marriage, and his castration. In her third letter, Heloise described the difficulty of breaking away from fantasies which afflicted her: "Everything we did and also the times and places are stamped on my heart along with your image, so that I live through it all again with you." In his response Abelard confessed that his love was actually "unbridled lust" and that "as yours was the weaker nature I often forced you to consent with threats and blows." Arguing that their punishment had been just, he then urged her to turn truly to Christ through a devotion to the vows of her order. Heloise replied to Abelard as a transformed person, a sign of her strength and resolution: from that point on, their correspondence dealt importantly with theological questions, the rigors of monastic life, and the practicalities of monastic administration, in what have come to be called "the letters of direction." Already an Abbess, Heloise proved an able administrator and spiritual guide: during her lifetime her abbey founded six daughter houses. Heloise remained ever devoted to an ideal, an "ethic of intention," that she expressed in her first letter (below): "It is not the deed but the intention of the doer which makes the crime, and justice should weigh not what was done but the spirit in which it is done."*

Heloise's letter is translated by Betty Radice and collected in *The Letters of Abelard and Heloise* (Baltimore: Penguin, 1974).

Letter 1. Heloise to Abelard

Not long ago, my beloved, by chance someone brought me the letter of consolation you had sent to a friend. I saw at once from the superscription that it was yours, and was all the more eager to read it since the writer is so dear to my heart. I hoped for renewal of strength, at least from the writer's words which would picture for me the reality I have lost. But nearly every line of this letter was filled, I remember, with gall and wormwood, as it told the pitiful story of our entry into religion and the cross of unending suffering which you, my only love, continue to bear.

In that letter you did indeed carry out the promise you made your friend at the beginning, that he would think his own troubles insignificant or nothing, in comparison with your own. . . .

No one, I think, could read or hear it dry-eyed; my own sorrows are renewed by the detail in which you have told it, and redoubled because you say your perils are still increasing. All of us here are driven to despair of your life, and every day we await in fear and trembling the final word of your death. And so in the name of Christ, who is still giving you some protection for his service, we beseech you to write as often as you think fit to us who are his handmaids and yours, with news of the perils in which you are still storm-tossed. We are all that are left you, so at least you should let us share your sorrow or your joy.

It is always some consolation in sorrow to feel that it is shared, and any burden laid on several is carried more lightly or removed. And if this storm has quietened down for a while; you must be all the more prompt to send us a letter which will be the more gladly received. But whatever you write about will bring us no small relief in the mere proof that you have us in mind. Letters from absent friends are welcome indeed, . . .

Thank God that here at least is a way of restoring your presence to us which no malice can prevent, nor any obstacle hinder; then do not, I beseech you, allow any negligence to hold you back.

You wrote your friend a long letter of consolation, prompted no doubt by his misfortunes, but really telling of your own. The detailed account you gave of these may have been intended for his comfort, but it also greatly increased our own feeling of desolation; in your desire to heal his wounds you have dealt us fresh wounds of grief as well as re-opening the old. I beg you, then, as you set about tending the wounds which others have dealt, heal the wounds you have yourself inflicted. You have done your duty to a friend and comrade, discharged your debt to friendship and comradeship, but it is a greater debt which binds you in obligation to us who can properly be called not friends so much as dearest friends, not comrades but daughters, or any other conceivable name more tender and holy. How great the debt by which you have bound yourself to us needs neither proof nor witness, were it in any doubt; if the whole world kept silent, the facts themselves would cry out. For you after God are the sole founder of this place, the sole builder of this oratory, the sole creator of this community. You have built nothing here upon another man's foundation. Everything here is your own creation. This was a wilderness open to wild beasts and brigands, a place which had known no home nor habitation of men. In the very lairs of wild beasts and lurking-places of robbers, where the name of God was never heard, you built a sanctuary to God and dedicated a shrine in the name of the Holy Spirit. To build it you drew nothing from the riches of kings and princes, though their wealth was great and could have been yours for the asking: whatever was done, the credit was to be yours alone. Clerks and scholars came flocking here, eager for your teaching, and ministered to all your needs; and even those who had lived on the benefices of the Church and knew only how to receive offerings, not to make them, whose hands were held out to take but not to give, became pressing in their lavish offers of assistance.

And so it is yours, truly your own, this new plantation for God's purpose, but it is sown with plants which are still very tender and need watering if they are to thrive. Through its feminine nature this plantation would be weak and frail even if it were not new; and so it needs a more careful and regular cultivation, according to the words of the Apostle: 'I planted the seed and Apollos watered it; but God made it grow.' . . . You devote your care to another's vineyard; think what you owe to your own. You teach and admonish rebels to no purpose, and in vain you throw the pearls of your divine eloquence to the pigs. While you spend so much on the stubborn, consider what you owe to the obedient; you are so generous to your enemies but should reflect on how you are indebted to your daughters. Apart from everything else, consider the close tie by which you have bound yourself to me, and repay the debt you owe a whole community of women dedicated to God by discharging it the more dutifully to her who is yours alone.

Your superior wisdom knows better than our humble learning of the many serious treatises which the holy Fathers compiled for the instruction or exhortation or even the consolation of holy women, and of the care with which these were composed. And so in the precarious early days of our conversion long ago I was not a little surprised and troubled by your forgetfulness, when neither reverence for God nor our mutual love nor the example of the holy Fathers made you think of trying to comfort me, wavering and exhausted as I was by prolonged grief, either by word when I was with you or by letter when we had parted. Yet you must know that you are bound to me by an obligation which is all the greater for the further close tie of the marriage sacrament uniting us, and are the deeper in my debt because of the love I have always borne you, as everyone knows, a love which is beyond all bounds.

You know, beloved, as the whole world knows, how much I have lost in you, how at one wretched stroke of fortune that supreme act of flagrant treachery robbed me of my very self in robbing me of you; and how my sorrow for my loss is nothing compared with what I feel for the manner in which I lost you. Surely the greater the cause for grief the greater the need for the help of consolation, and this no one can bring but you; you are the sole cause of my sorrow, and you alone can grant me the grace of consolation. You alone have the power to make me sad, to bring me happiness or comfort; you alone have so great a debt to repay me, particularly now when I have carried out all your orders so implicitly that when I was powerless to oppose you in anything, I found strength at your command to destroy myself. I did more, strange to say—my love rose to such heights of madness that it robbed itself of what it most desired beyond hope of recovery, when immediately at your bidding I changed my clothing along with my mind, in order to prove you the sole possessor of my body and my will alike. God knows I never sought anything in you except yourself; I wanted simply you, nothing of yours. I looked for no marriage-bond, no marriage portion, and it was not my own pleasures and wishes I sought to gratify, as you well know, but yours. The name of wife may seem more sacred or more binding, but sweeter for me will always be the word mistress, or, if you will permit me, that of concubine or whore. I believed that the more I humbled myself on your account, the more gratitude I should win from you, and also the less damage I should do to the brightness of your reputation.

You yourself on your own account did not altogether forget this in the letter of consolation I have spoken of which you wrote to a friend; there you thought fit to set out some of the reasons I gave in trying to dissuade you from binding us together in an ill-starred marriage. But you kept silent about most of my arguments for preferring love to wedlock and freedom to chains. God is my witness that if Augustus, Emperor of the whole world, thought fit to honour me with marriage and conferred all the earth on me to possess for ever, it would be dearer and more honourable to me to be called not his Empress but your whore.

For a man's worth does not rest on his wealth or power; these depend on fortune, but worth on his merits. And a woman should realize that if she marries a rich man more readily than a poor one, and desires her husband more for his possessions than for himself, she is offering herself for sale. Certainly any woman who comes to marry through desires of this kind deserves wages, not gratitude, for clearly her mind is on the man's property, not himself, and she would be ready to prostitute herself to a richer man, if she could. . . .

It is a holy error and a blessed delusion between man and wife, when perfect love can keep the ties of marriage unbroken not so much through bodily continence as chastity of spirit. But what error permitted other women, plain truth permitted me, and what they thought of their husbands, the world in general believed, or rather, knew to be true of yourself; so that my love for you was the more genuine for being further removed from error. What king or philosopher could match your fame? What district, town or village did not long to see you? When you appeared in public, who did not hurry to catch a glimpse of you, or crane his neck and strain his eyes to follow your departure? Every wife, every young girl desired you in absence and was on fire in your presence; queens and great ladies envied me my joys and my bed.

You had besides, I admit, two special gifts whereby to win at once the heart of any woman—your gifts for composing verse and song, in which we know other philosophers have rarely been successful. This was for you no more than a diversion, a recreation from the labours of your philosophic work, but you left many love-songs and verses which won wide popularity for the charm of their words and tunes and kept your name continually on everyone's lips., The beauty of the airs ensured that even the unlettered did not forget you; more than anything this made women sigh for love of you. And as most of these songs told of our love, they soon made me widely known and roused the envy of many women against me. For your manhood was adorned by every grace of mind and body, and among the women who envied me then, could there be one now who does not feel compelled by my misfortune to sympathize with my loss of such joys? Who is there who was once my enemy, whether man or woman, who is not moved now by the compassion which is my due? Wholly guilty though I am, I am also, as you know, wholly innocent. It is not the deed but the intention of the doer which makes the crime, and justice should weigh not what was done but the spirit in which it is done. What my intention towards you has always been, you alone who have known it can judge. I submit all to your scrutiny, yield to your testimony in all things.

Tell me one thing, if you can. Why, after our entry into religion, which was your decision alone, have I been so neglected and forgotten by you that I have neither a word from you when you are here to give me strength nor the consolation of a letter in absence? I Tell me, I say, if you can—or I will tell you what I think and indeed the world suspects. It was desire, not affection which bound you to me, the flame of lust rather than love. So when the end came to what you desired, any show of feeling you used to make went with it. This is not merely my own opinion, beloved, it is everyone's. There is nothing personal or private about it; it is the general view which is widely held. I only wish that it were mine alone, and that the love you professed could find someone to defend it and so comfort me in my grief for a while. I wish I could think of some explanation which would excuse you and somehow cover up the way you hold me cheap.

I beg you then to listen to what I ask—you will see that it is a small favour which you can easily grant. While I am denied your presence, give me at least through your words—of which you have enough and to spare—some sweet semblance of yourself. It is no use my hoping for generosity in deeds if you are grudging in words. Up to now I had thought I deserved much of you, seeing that I carried out everything for your sake and continue up to the present moment in complete obedience to you. It was not any sense of vocation which brought me as a young girl to accept the austerities of the cloister, but your bidding alone, and if I deserve no gratitude from you, you may judge for yourself how my labours are in vain. I can expect no reward for this from God, for it is certain that I have done nothing as yet for love of him. When you hurried towards God I followed you, indeed, I went first to take the veil-perhaps you were thinking how Lot's wife turned back, when you made me put on the religious habit and take my vows before you gave yourself to God. Your lack of trust in me over this one thing, I confess, overwhelmed me with grief and shame. I would have had no hesitation, God knows, in following you or going ahead at your bidding to the flames of Hell. My heart was not in me but with you, and now, even more, if it is not with you it is nowhere; truly, without you it cannot exist. See that it fares well with you, I beg, as it will if it finds you kind, if you give grace in return for grace, small for great, words for deeds. If only your love had less confidence in me, my dear, so that you would be more concerned on my behalf! But as it is, the more I have made you feel secure in me, the more I have to bear with your neglect.

Remember, I implore you, what I have done, and think how much you owe me. While I enjoyed with you the pleasures of the flesh, many were uncertain whether I was prompted by love or lust; but now the end is proof of the beginning. I have finally denied myself every pleasure in obedience to your will, kept nothing for myself except to prove that now, even more, I am yours. Consider then your injustice, if when I deserve more you give me less, or rather, nothing at all, especially when it is a small thing I ask of you and one you could so easily grant. And so, in the name of God to whom you have dedicated yourself, I beg you to restore your presence to me in the way you can-by writing me some word of comfort, so that in this at least I may find increased strength and readiness to serve God. When in the past you sought me out for sinful pleasures your letters came to me thick and fast, and your many songs put your Heloise on everyone's lips, so that every street and house echoed with my name. Is it not far better now to summon me to God than it was then to satisfy our lust? I beg you, think what you owe me, give ear to my pleas, and I will finish a long letter with a brief ending: farewell, my only love.

Usama ibn Munqidh (1095–1188)

THE BOOK OF CONTEMPLATION

*There are a number of medieval accounts of life during the Crusades, including the Old French chronicles by Villehardouin (*The Conquest of Constantinople*) and Jean, Lord of Joinville (*The Life of Saint Louis*). None is more appealing, however, than a view from across the battle lines, in the writings of the Muslim nobleman Usama ibn Munqidh. His book,* Kitab al-I'tibar, *is not so much a history of the early Crusades as an engaging and humane memoir drawing on his own experiences and on those of his older relatives. He was well positioned to reflect on the conflicts that dominated his region and his era; his greatest insights, however, lie in his descriptions of the European crusaders, whom he calls* Franks, *and on the contrasts he perceives in this great clash of cultures.*

Born and raised in one of the emirates of Syria, Usama was exiled as a young man when his family was viewed by his clan's Sultan as aspiring rivals. Exile thrust Usama into various Muslim courts as a warrior and as a diplomat. He was in Jerusalem in 1138 to negotiate common cause between the Muslim governor of Damascus and the French Christian King of Jerusalem against the expansionist emir of Aleppo and Mosul. During the brief periods of peace that followed, Usama spent time among the Franks in Jerusalem, and this experience fueled his amused and fair-minded observations on the strange habits and backward customs of the European "enemies" in the following excerpts.

In 1157, when he was in Damascus, his home provinces were rocked by severe earthquakes that killed nearly all of his extended and influential family, putting an end to Usama's high ambitions. He spent some time at the court of the increasingly powerful Saladin, the Kurdish Sultan of Syria and Egypt who was to lead the Muslim resistance in the Third Crusade, but differences with Saladin forced him into retirement until his death. His retirement, though unsought, allowed him the leisure to reflect on his experiences and to write (or dictate) his memoirs, which are formally a reflection on the governance of Fate.

These selections are from a new translation by Paul M. Cobb (London: Penguin Books, 2008).

THE 'WONDERS' OF THE FRANKISH RACE

Glory be to the Creator, the Maker! Indeed, when a person relates matters concerning the Franks, he *should* give glory to God and sanctify Him! For he will see them to be mere beasts possessing no other virtues but courage and fighting, just as beasts have only the virtues of strength and the ability to carry loads. I shall now relate something of their ways and the wonders of their intelligence.

THE FRANKS' LACK OF INTELLIGENCE: AN INVITATION TO VISIT EUROPE

In the army of King Fulk, son of Fulk, there was a respected Frankish knight who had come from their country just to go on pilgrimage and then return home. He grew to like my company and he became my constant companion, calling me 'my brother'. Between us there were ties of amity and sociability. When he resolved to take to the sea back to his country, he said to me:

'My brother, I am leaving for my country. I want you to send your son (my son, who was with me, was fourteen years old) with me to my country, where he can observe the knights and acquire reason and chivalry. When he returns, he will be like a truly rational man.'

And so there fell upon my ears words that would never come from a truly rational head! For even if my son were taken captive, his captivity would not be as long as any voyage he might take to the land of the Franks.

So I said, 'By your life, I was hoping for this very thing. But the only thing that has prevented me from doing so is the fact that his grandmother adores him and almost did not allow him to come here with me until she had exacted an oath from me that I would return him to her.'

'Your mother,' he asked, 'she is still alive?'

'Yes,' I replied.

'Then do not disobey her,' he said.

THE MARVELS OF FRANKISH MEDICINE

Here is an example of the marvellous nature of their medicine. The lord of al-Munaytira wrote to my uncle to request that he send him a physician to treat some of his companions who were ill. So my uncle sent him a native Christian physician called Thabit. He was barely gone ten days when he returned to Shayzar. So we said to him, 'My, you healed your patients so quickly!' He explained:

> They brought before me a knight in whose leg an abscess had formed and a woman who was stricken with a dryness of humours. So I made a small poultice for the knight and the abscess opened up and he was healed. For the woman, I prescribed a special diet and increased the wetness of her humours. Then a Frankish physician came to them and said, 'This fellow don't know how to treat them.' He then said to the knight, 'Which would you like better: living with one leg or dying with both?' 'Living with one leg,' replied the knight. The physician then said, 'Bring me a strong knight

and a sharp axe.' A knight appeared with an axe—indeed, I was just there—and the physician laid the leg of the patient on a block of wood and said to the knight with the axe, 'Strike his leg with the axe and cut it off with one blow.' So he struck him—I'm telling you I watched him do it—with one blow, but it didn't chop the leg all the way off. So he struck him a second time, but the marrow flowed out of the leg and he died instantly.

He then examined the woman and said, 'This woman, there is a demon inside her head that has possessed her. Shave off her hair.' So they shaved her head. The woman then returned to eating their usual diet—garlic and mustard. As a result, her dryness of humours increased. So the physician said, 'That demon has entered further into her head.' So he took a razor and made a cut in her head in the shape of a cross. He then peeled back the skin so that the skull was exposed and rubbed it with salt. The woman died instantaneously. So I asked them, 'Do you need anything else from me?' 'No,' they said. And so I left, having learned about their medicine things I had never known before.

Now, I have observed in their medicine a case exactly the opposite of this. Their king named as treasurer one of their knights, called Bernard (may God curse him), one of the most accursed and filthy Franks around. A horse kicked him in his leg and his lower leg started to fester and open up in fourteen different places. Every time these wounds would close in one place, another would open somewhere else. I prayed that he would just perish. But then a Frankish physician came and removed all the ointments that were on him and had him washed with strong vinegar. The wounds closed up and he was well and up again, like the very devil.

Here is another wondrous example of their medicine. We had at Shayzar an artisan called Abu al-Fath, who had a son on whose neck scrofula sores had formed. Every time one would close in one place, another would open up in another place. Once Abu al-Fath went to Antioch on an errand and his son accompanied him. A Frankish man noticed him and asked him about the boy. 'He is my son,' Abu al-Fath said.

The Frank said to him, 'Do you swear to me by your religion that, if I prescribe for you some medicine that will cure your boy, you will not charge money from anyone else whom you yourself treat with it?'

Our man swore to that effect. The Frank then said, 'Take him some uncrushed leaves of glasswort, burn them, then soak the ashes in olive oil and strong vinegar. Treat him with this until it eats up the pustules in the affected area. Then take some fire-softened lead and soak it in butter. Then treat the boy with this and he will get well.'

So our man treated the boy as he was told and the boy got well. The wounds closed up and he returned to his previous state of health. I have myself treated people afflicted by this ailment with this remedy, and it was beneficial and removed all of their complaints.

Newly Arrived Franks are the Roughest

Anyone who is recently arrived from the Frankish lands is rougher in character than those who have become acclimated and have frequented the company of Muslims. Here is an instance of their rough character (may God abominate them!):

Whenever I went to visit the holy sites in Jerusalem, I would go in and make my way up to the al-Aqsa Mosque, beside which stood a small mosque that the Franks had converted into a church. When I went into the al-Aqsa Mosque—where the Templars, who are my friends, were—they would clear out that little mosque so that I could pray in it. One day, I went into the little mosque, recited the opening formula 'God is great!' and stood up in prayer. At this, one of the Franks rushed at me and grabbed me and turned my face towards the east, saying, 'Pray like *this*!'

A group of Templars hurried towards him, took hold of the Frank and took him away from me. I then returned to my prayers. The Frank, that very same one, took advantage of their inattention and returned, rushing upon me and turning my face to the east, saying, 'Pray like *this*!'

So the Templars came in again, grabbed him and threw him out. They apologized to me, saying, 'This man is a stranger, just arrived from the Frankish lands sometime in the past few days. He has never before seen anyone who did not pray towards the east.'

'I think I've prayed quite enough,' I said and left. I used to marvel at that devil, the change of his expression, the way he trembled and what he must have made of seeing someone praying towards Mecca.

When God was Young

I saw one of the Franks come up to the amir Mu'in al-Din (may God have mercy upon him) while he was in the Dome of the Rock, and say, 'Would you like to see God when He was young?'

'Why yes,' Mu'in al-Din replied.

So this Frank walked in front of us until he brought us to an icon of Mary and the Messiah (Peace be upon him) when he was a child, sitting in her lap. 'This is God when He was young,' he said.

May God be exalted far beyond what the infidels say!

Franks have no Honour or Propriety

The Franks possess nothing in the way of regard for honour or propriety. One of them might be walking along with his wife and run into another man. This other man might then take his wife to one side and chat with her, while the husband just stands there waiting for her to finish her conversation. And if she takes too long, he'll just leave her alone with her conversation partner and walk away!

Here is an example that I myself witnessed. Whenever I went to Nablus, I used to stay at the home of a man called Mu'izz, whose home was the lodging-house for Muslims. The house had windows that opened onto the road and, across from it on the other side of the road, there was a house belonging to a Frankish man who sold wine for the merchants. He would take some wine in a bottle and go around advertising it, saying, 'So-and-So the merchant has just opened a cask of this wine. Whoever wishes to buy some can find it at such-and-such a place.' And the fee he charged for making that announcement was the wine in the bottle. So one day, he came back home and discovered a man in bed with his wife. The Frank said to the man, 'What business brings you here to my wife?'

'I got tired,' the man replied, 'so I came in to rest.'

'But how did you get into my bed?' asked the Frank.

'I found a bed that was all made up, so I went to sleep in it,' he replied.

'While my wife was sleeping there with you?' the Frank pursued.

'Well, it's her bed,' the man offered. 'Who am I to keep her out of it?'

'By the truth of my religion,' the Frank said, 'if you do this again, we'll have an argument, you and I!'

And that was all the disapproval he would muster and the extent of his sense of propriety!

Here is another example. We had with us a bath-keeper called Salim, who was originally an inhabitant of Ma'arra, and who served in the bath-house of my father (may God have mercy upon him). He told me:

> I once opened a bath-house in Ma'arra to earn my living. Once, one of their knights came in. Now, they don't take to people wearing a towel about their waist in the bath, so this knight stretched out his hand, pulled off my towel from my waist and threw it down. He looked at me—I had recently shaved my pubic hair—and said, 'Salim!' Then he moved in closer to me. He then stretched his hand over my groin, saying, 'Salim! Good! By the truth of my religion, do that to me too!'
>
> He then lay down on his back: he had it thick as a beard down in that place! So I shaved him and he passed his hand over it and, finding it smooth to the touch, said, 'Salim, by the truth of your religion, do it to Madame!'—*madame* in their language means 'the lady', meaning his wife. He then told one of his attendants, 'Tell Madame to come here.'
>
> The attendant went and brought her and showed her in. She lay down on her back and the knight said, 'Do her like you did me!' So I shaved her hair there as her husband stood watching me. He then thanked me and paid me my due for the service.

Now, consider this great contradiction! They have no sense of propriety or honour, yet they have immense courage. Yet what is courage but a product of honour and disdain for ill repute?

Here is an example close to that one. I once went to the baths in the city of Tyre and took a seat in a secluded room there. While I was there, one of my attendants in the bath said to me, 'There are women here with us!' When I went outside, I sat down on the benches and, sure enough, the woman who was in the bath had come out and was standing with her father directly across from me, having put her garments on again. But I couldn't be sure if she was a woman. So I said to one of my companions, 'By God, go have a look at this one—is she a woman?' What I meant was for him to go and ask about her. But instead he went—as I watched—and lifted her hem and pulled it up. At this, her father turned to me and explained, 'This is my daughter. Her mother died, and so she has no one who will wash her hair. I brought her into the bath with me so that I might wash her hair.'

'That's a kind thing you're doing,' I assured him. 'This will bring you heavenly reward.'

ANOTHER EXAMPLE OF THEIR MEDICINE

Another example of their wondrous medicine was related to us by William de Bures, lord of Tiberias and a man with some standing among the Franks. It happened that he travelled with the amir Mu'in al-Din (may God have mercy upon him) from Acre to Tiberias, and I accompanied him. On the way, he related to us the following story:

> In our land there was a highly esteemed knight who took ill and was on the point of death. We went to one of our notable priests and asked him, 'Will you come with us and have a look at Sir So-and-So?' 'Yes,' he replied and walked back with us. We were certain now that if only he would lay his hands upon him, he would recover. When the priest saw the knight he said, 'Bring me some wax.' So we brought him a bit of wax, which he softened and shaped like a knuckle-bone. Then he inserted one in each nostril and the knight died. 'He's dead!' we remarked. 'Yes,' the priest replied. 'He was in great pain, so I closed up his nose so that he could die and find relief.'

EXAMPLES OF FRANKISH JURISPRUDENCE

I was an eyewitness one day in Nablus when two men came forward to fight a duel. The reason behind it was that some Muslim bandits took one of the villages of Nablus by surprise, and one of the peasants there was accused of complicity. They said, 'He guided the bandits to the village!' So he fled.

But the king sent men to arrest the peasant's sons, so the man came back before the king and said, 'Grant me justice. I challenge to a duel the man who said that I guided the bandits to the village.'

The king said to the lord of the village, its fief-holder, 'Bring before me the man whom he has challenged.'

So the lord went off to his village, where a blacksmith lived, and took him, telling him, 'You will fight in a duel.' This was the fief-holder's way of making sure that none of his peasants would be killed and his farming ruined as a result.

I saw that blacksmith. He was a strong young man, but lacking resolve: he would walk a bit, then sit down and order something to drink. Whereas the other man, who had demanded the duel, was an old man but strong-willed: he would shout taunts as if he had no fears about the duel. Then the *vicomte* came—he is the governor of the town—and gave each one of the duellists a staff and a shield and arranged the people around them in a circle.

The two men met. The old man would press the blacksmith back until he pushed him away as far as the circle of people, then he would return to the centre. They continued exchanging blows until the two of them stood there looking like pillars spattered with blood. The whole affair was going on too long and the *vicomte* began to urge them to hurry, saying, 'Be quick about it!'

The blacksmith benefited from the fact that he was used to swinging a hammer, but the old man was worn out. The blacksmith hit him and he collapsed, his staff falling underneath his back. The blacksmith then crouched on top of him and tried to stick his fingers in the old man's eyes, but couldn't do it because of all the blood. So he stood up and beat the man's head in with his staff until he had killed him. In a flash, they tied a rope round the old man's neck, dragged him off and strung him up. The blacksmith's lord now came and bestowed his own mantle upon him, let him mount behind him on his horse and rode away with him.

And that was but a taste of their jurisprudence and their legal procedure, may God curse them!

On one occasion, I went with the amir Mu'in al-Din (may God have mercy upon him) to Jerusalem, and we stopped at Nablus. While there, a blind man—a young man wearing fine clothes, a Muslim—came out to the amir with some fruit and asked him for permission to be admitted into his service in Damascus. The amir did so. I asked about him and I was told that his mother had been married to a Frank, whom she had killed. Her son used to attempt various ruses on their pilgrims, and he and his mother used to work together to kill them. They finally brought charges against him for that and made him subject to the legal procedure of the Franks, to wit:

They set up a huge cask and filled it with water and stretched a plank of wood across it. Then they bound the arms of the accused, tied a rope around his shoulders and threw him into the cask. If he were innocent, then he would sink in the water and they would then pull him up by that rope so he wouldn't die in the water; if he were guilty, then he would not sink in the water. That man tried eagerly to sink into the water when they threw him in, but he couldn't do it. So he had to submit to their judgment—may God curse them—and they did some work on his eyes.

The man later arrived in Damascus, so the amir Mu'in al-Din (may God have mercy upon him) assigned him a stipend to meet all his needs and said to one of his attendants, 'Take him to Burhan al-Din ibn al-Balkhi (may God have mercy upon him) and tell him to order someone to teach the Qur'an and some jurisprudence to this man.'

At this the blind man said, 'Victory and mastery be yours! This wasn't what I was thinking!'

'Then what were you thinking I would do?' asked the amir.

'That you would give me a horse, a mule and weapons, and make a horseman out of me!' the man answered.

The amir then said, 'I never thought that a blind man would join the ranks of our cavalry.'

Franks that are Acclimatized are Better

Among the Franks there are some who have become acclimatized and frequent the company of Muslims. They are much better than those recently arrived from their lands, but they are the exception and should not be considered representative.

Here is an example. I sent one of my men to Antioch on an errand. At the time, Chief Tadrus ibn al-Saffi was there, and his word had great influence in Antioch; there was a mutual bond of friendship between us. One day he said to my man, 'A Frankish friend of mine has invited me to his home. You should come along so you can observe their ways.' My man told me:

> I went along with him and we came to the home of one of the old knights who came out in one of the first expeditions of the Franks. He was since

removed from the stipend-registry and dismissed from service, but he had some property in Antioch off which he lived. He presented a very fine table, with food that was extremely clean and delicious. But seeing me holding back from eating, he said, 'Eat and be of good cheer! For I don't eat Frankish food: I have Egyptian cooking-women and never eat anything except what they cook. And pork never enters my house.' So I ate, though guardedly, and we left.

After passing through the market, a Frankish woman suddenly hung onto me while babbling at me in their language—I didn't understand what she was saying. Then a group of Franks began to gather around me and I was certain that I was going to perish. But suddenly, who should turn up but that knight, who saw me and approached. He came and said to that woman, 'What's the matter with you and this Muslim?'

'This man killed my brother 'Urs.' This 'Urs was a knight in Apamea whom someone from the army of Hama had killed.

The knight shouted at her and said, 'This man is a *bourgeois* (i.e., a merchant), who neither fights nor attends battle.' And he yelled at the assembled crowd and they dispersed. He then took me by the hand and went away. Thus, the effect of that meal was my deliverance from death.

Brave Men may Hold Unusual Fears

One of the wonders of the human heart is that a man may face certain death and embark upon every danger without his heart quailing from it, and yet he may take fright from something that even boys and women do not fear.

I have seen my uncle, Sultan (may God have mercy upon him)—who was one of the most courageous members of his household, having taken famous stands in battle and struck renowned spear-thrusts—suddenly, upon seeing a mouse, change the expression on his face, become overcome by shudders at the mere sight of it, and take himself away from the place where he saw it.

Among his attendants was a courageous fellow whose name was Sunduq, known for his bravery and audacity. He was so afraid of snakes that he would practically lose his mind. My father (may God have mercy upon him) said to him as he was standing before my uncle, 'Sunduq, you're a good man, known for your bravery. Aren't you ashamed to be so afraid of snakes?'

'My lord,' he replied, 'what's so surprising about that? In Homs there is a brave man, a hero's hero, who is scared to death of mice,' meaning his master.

And so my uncle (may God have mercy upon him) cursed at him, 'May God abominate you, you dirty so-and-so!'

I also knew a *mamluk* belonging to my father (may God have mercy upon him), called Lu'lu'. A good man, stalwart fellow. One night I went out from Shayzar, taking with me a large number of mules and other beasts, which I hoped to use to carry some wood that I had cut up in the mountains for a water-wheel that belonged to me. We left the lands surrounding Shayzar, thinking that daybreak was approaching, but we arrived at a village called Dubays before even passing half the night.

So I said, 'Let's set up camp. We shouldn't go into the mountains at night.'

Once we had dismounted and settled in, we heard the neighing of horses.

'The Franks!' we said. So we mounted up in the dark, and I told myself that I would put my spear through one of them and take his horse while they were trying to rustle the animals and capture the men who were tending them.

I said to Lu'lu' and three of the attendants, 'Go ahead and find out what all that neighing is about.'

They went on ahead at full gallop and met some others, lots of people in quite a crowd. Lu'lu' was the first to reach them and said, 'Let's hear it! Or else I'll kill you one and all'—he being an excellent archer.

But they recognized his voice and said, 'Chamberlain Lu'lu'?'

'Yes,' he replied. And what do you know, but they were the army of Hama! They were under the command of the amir Sayf al-Din Sawar (may God have mercy upon him), and had made a raid on the lands of the Franks and were on their way back home. Such was this man's audacity against that crowd. Yet if he should see a snake in his house, he would run out fleeing, saying to his wife, 'The snake's all yours!' And she would have to get up and kill it.

The Devil is in the Details

The warrior, even if he is lion-hearted, can be ruined and reduced to impotence by the most trifling impediment, as happened to me before Homs. I rode out, but my horse was killed and I was struck by fifty swords—all through the execution of the divine will and, on top of it, through the sloppiness of my groom in arranging the reins of my bridle. He attached the reins to the rings without sliding them all the way through. So when I pulled on the reins, hoping to escape from the enemy, the reins came undone from the rings and there happened to me what happened.

One day, the alarm was sounded at Shayzar, from the south. We suited up and prepared ourselves. But it was a false alarm. My father and uncle (may God have mercy upon the two of them) went away but I stayed behind. The alarm was then sounded from the north, from the direction of the Franks. I galloped on my horse towards the sound of the alarm and saw our men crossing the ford, some riding on the shoulders of the others, shouting, 'The Franks!'

I crossed the ford and told the men, 'Don't worry, I stand between you and the enemy!' I then galloped up to Rabiyat al-Qaramita and there were the enemy cavalry, advancing in a large body, preceded by a horseman wearing a mail hauberk and a helmet. He was already close to me. So I made straight for him, taking the opportunity to attack some of his comrades after him. He stood ready to receive me. But the moment I spurred my horse on towards him, my stirrup snapped. And there was no way for me to avoid meeting him. So I confronted him without a stirrup. When we got so close to one another that there was nothing to do but thrust our spears about, the horseman greeted me and offered his services to me, for it was none other than Commander 'Umar, the uncle of Commander Zayn al-Din Isma'il. He had gone out with the army of Hama to the territory of Kafartab, where the Franks made a sortie against them. So they returned to Shayzar in flight, led by the amir Sawar (may God have mercy upon him).

Thus, the best course for the warrior to follow is to inspect the tack on his horse frequently. For even the smallest and most insignificant of things can lead to injury and destruction—all that dependent upon the course of fate and destiny.

Hildegard of Bingen (1098–1179)

Hildegard recently celebrated her 900th birthday, and a great party it continues to be. New CD's of her music are issued monthly, some dressed up electronically, some marketed as New Age. Web sites tell about her life, offer translations of her poetry, and allow fans to download images of her music in the original notation. There are also testimonials from people whose lives she has changed. Every year San Francisco plays host to a weekend-long celebration of her work, through readings, music performances, and displays of images. Part of her popularity comes from feminist interest in a truly remarkable woman living in an age of great men. Another part results from a new interest in things medieval, associated with albums of Gregorian Chant showing up on the pop charts. Another part simply arises from familiarity, now that people have more opportunity to view, read, and listen to the artistic works of a woman who was, after all, a phenomenon in her own time.

Hildegard entered a Benedictine monastery when she was only 8 and became abbess in that monastery before she was forty. A few years later she began writing down the visions that first troubled her and later brought her fame and attention. In 1151 she published Scivias *("Know the Ways"), a collection of prophecies, music, and illuminations prepared under her supervision. The following year she fought a long battle to move her nuns to a female monastery at Rupertsberg, near Bingen. For the next 28 years her reputation and her political power grew, as kings, popes, and nobles sought her advice.*

More than 100 letters to and from Hildegard survive, dealing with all aspects of public and private life. Three books record her visions and prophecies. Her manuscript paintings (many produced under her supervision), music and song texts, The Play of the Virtues *(a liturgical play with music)—all of these attest to Hildegard's creative ability and her talent for accomplishing great things. She is a striking example of a person who successfully united the active life with the contemplative life.*

Reprinted from *Scivias*, translated by Bruce Hozeski (Bear and Company, 1986).

Scivias

"Protestificatio"

In the year 1141 of the incarnation of Jesus Christ, the Word of God, when I was forty-two years and seven months old, a burning light coming from heaven poured into my mind. Like a flame which does not burn but rather enkindles, it inflamed my heart and my breast, just as the sun warms something with its rays. And I was able to understand books suddenly, the psaltery clearly, the evangelists and the volumes of the Old and New Testament, but I did not have the interpretation of the words of their texts nor the division of their syllables nor the knowledge of their grammar. Previously though, I had felt within myself the gift of secret mysteries and wondrous visions from the time I was a little girl, certainly from the time I was five years old right up to the present time. I revealed my gift to no one except to a select few and some religious who were living in my area, and I concealed my gift continuously in quiet silence until God wished it to be manifest by God's own grace. I truly saw those visions; I did not perceive them in dreams, nor while sleeping, nor in a frenzy, nor with the human eyes or with the external ears of a person, nor in remote places; but I received those visions according to the will of God while I was awake and alert with a clear mind, with the innermost eyes and ears of a person, and in open places. There may be a reason why I received those visions in this manner, but it is difficult for a human person to understand why. But after I had passed through the turning point of young womanhood, when I had arrived at the beginning of the age of perfect fortitude, I again heard a heavenly voice speaking to me:

> *I, the living light and the obscured illumination, appointed the person whom I wished, and I drove out the person whom I wished, wondrously according to what pleased me, with great wonders across the boundary of ancient people, who have seen many secrets in me; indeed I struck people down on earth, so that they might not lift themselves up in any exaltation of their own minds. The world also had no joy in it nor playfulness nor practice in those things which belong to the world, because I restrained it from stubborn daring, having fear and quaking in its own labors. People indeed suffered pain in their hearts and in the veins of their flesh, having bound together soul and senses, and sustaining the many passions of the body so that diverse peace of mind was not concealed in them, but they judged themselves blameworthy in all their motives. For I surrounded the fissures of their hearts, lest their minds might raise themselves up through pride or through glory; but that they might have in all these things fear and sorrow rather than delight and wantonness. Whence they searched through my love in their own souls, where they came upon the one who hastened the way of salvation. And the one came upon those people and loved them, acknowledging that they had been faithful and similar to the one in some part of that labor which they had done for me. And holding themselves together with that one, they strained in all these things with heavenly zeal, so that my hidden miracles might be revealed. And the same people did not place*

> *themselves above that one, but when they came to that one with an ascent of humility and with the intention of good will, the one bent over them with warm protection. You therefore, o person, who receive these things not in the turmoil of deceit, but in the purity of simplicity, who receive these things straight for the manifestation of the things concealed, write what you see and hear.*

Although I saw and heard these things, I nevertheless refused to write them because of doubt and evil opinion and because of the diversity of other people's words, not so much out of stubbornness, but out of humility, until I became sick, pressed down by the scourge of God. I was sick for a long time with many different illnesses. Eventually, with the testimony of a certain noble man and a young woman of good wishes, I started to write what I had searched out and come upon secretly. As soon as I did that, I became healthy with a received strength, and knowing—as I said—the profoundness of the narration of books, I was able to bring my work to completion with difficulty, taking ten years. . . .

LETTERS
[TO BERNARD OF CLAIRVAUX, 1147]

Most praiseworthy Father Bernard, through God's power you stand wonderfully in highest honor. You are formidable against the indecent foolishness of this world. Full of lofty zeal and in ardent love for God's Son, you capture men with the banner of the holy cross so that they will wage war in the Christian army against the wrath of the pagans. I beseech you, father, by the living God, hear me in what I ask you.

I am very concerned about this vision which opens before me in spirit as a mystery. I have never seen it with the outer eyes of the flesh. I am wretched and more than wretched in my existence as a woman. And yet, already as a child, I saw great things of wonder which my tongue could never have given expression to, if God's spirit hadn't taught me to believe.

Gentle father, you are so secure, answer me in your goodness, me, your unworthy servant girl, who from childhood has never, not even for one single hour, lived in security. In your fatherly love and wisdom search in your soul, since you are taught by the Holy Spirit, and from your heart give some comfort to your servant girl.

I know in Latin text the meaning of the interpretation of the psalms, the gospels, and the other books which are shown to me through this vision. It stirs my heart and soul like a burning flame and teaches me the depth of interpretation. And yet this vision doesn't teach me writings in the German language; these I don't know. I can simply read them but have no ability to analyze them. Please answer me: what do you make of all of this? I am a person who received no schooling about external matters. It is only within, in my soul, that I have been trained. And that is why I speak in such doubt. But I take consolation from all that I have heard of your wisdom and fatherly love. I have not talked about this to anyone else, because, as I hear it said, there is so much divisiveness among people. There is just one person with whom I have shared

The letters here are from *Hildegard of Bingen's Book of Divine Works,* translated by Matthew Fox (Santa Fe: Bear, 1987).

this, a monk [Volmar] whom I have tested and whom I have found reliable in his cloistered way of life. I have revealed all of my secrets to him and he has consoled me with the assurance that they are sublime and awe-inspiring.

I beg you, father, for God's sake, that you comfort me. Then I will be secure. More than two years ago, I saw you in my vision as a person who can look at the sun and not be afraid, a very bold man. And I cried because I blushed at my faint-heartedness.

Gentle father, mildest of men, I rest in your soul so that through your word you can show me, if you wish, whether I should say these things openly or guard them in silence. For this vision causes me a lot of concern about the extent to which I should talk about what I have seen and heard. For a time, when I was silent about these things, I was confined to my bed with serious illnesses, so intense that I was unable to sit up. This is why I complain to you in such sadness: I will be so easily crushed by the falling wooden beams in the winepress of my nature, that heavy wood growing from the root which sprang up in Adam through Satan's influence and cast him out into a world where there was no fatherland.

But now I lift myself up and hasten to you. I say to you: you will not be crushed. On the contrary, you constantly straighten the wooden beam and hold it upright; in your soul you are a conqueror. But it's not only yourself that you hold upright; you raise the world up towards its salvation. You are the eagle who gazes at the sun.

I ask you by the radiant clarity of the Divine and by the marvelous Word and by sweet tear-gifted repentance, the Spirit of truth, and by the holy sound which echoes through the whole creation: by him, the Word, from whom the world has come to be. By the majesty of the Divine, who in sweet greening power sent the Word into the womb of the Virgin, from whom he took flesh, as the honey is built up around the honeycomb.

And may this sound, the power of the Divine, strike your heart and elevate your soul, so that you do not grow stiffly indifferent through the words of this woman [Hildegard], since you yourself seek out everything with God or with human beings or with any mystery until you press so far forward through the opening of your soul that you discern all of these things in God. Farewell, live well in your soul and be a strong warrior for God. Amen.

[To Pope Anastasius IV, 1153]

O shining bulwark, peak of guiding power in the lovely city prepared as Christ's bride, hear him, whose life is without beginning and never dissipates into fatigue.

O man, the eye of your discernment weakens; you are becoming weary, too tired to restrain the arrogant boastfulness of people to whom you have trusted your heart. Why do you not call these shipwrecked people back? They can be rescued from serious danger only through your help. And why do you not cut out the roots of the evil which chokes out the good, useful, fine-tasting, sweet-smelling plants? You are neglecting justice, the King's daughter, the heavenly bride, the woman who was entrusted to you. And you are even tolerant that this princess be hurled to the ground. Her crown and jewelled raiments are torn to pieces through the moral crudeness of men who bark like dogs and make stupid sounds like chickens which sometimes begin to cackle in the middle of the night. They are hypocrites. With their words they make a show of illusory peace; but within, in their hearts, they grind their teeth, like a dog who wags its tail at a recognized friend but bites with his sharp teeth an experienced warrior who fights for the King's house. Why do you tolerate the evil ways of people who in the darkness of foolishness draw everything harmful to themselves? They are like hens who make noise during the night and terrify themselves. People who act like this aren't rooted in goodness.

Listen then, O man, to him who loves exceedingly sharp discrimination. For he has put in place a strong instrument of uprightness, one that should do battle with evil. But that is precisely what you aren't doing when you don't dig out by the root that evil which suffocates the good. And you tolerate even more than that, allowing the evil to raise itself up proudly. And why? Because of your fear of the evil men who lay snares in nocturnal ambush and love the gold of death more than the beautiful King's daughter, justice.

But all the works made by God radiate the brightest light. Listen, O man. Before the world came to be, God spoke in divine inwardness the Word: "O my Son!" And the world came to be because it picked up the sound that went forth from God. The various kinds of creatures still lay hidden in darkness. As it is written, when God said: "Let it be!" the various types of creatures came forth. So it was through the Word of the Father and for the sake of the Word that all creatures were fashioned through God's will.

God sees and knows everything beforehand. But evil, on the other hand, through itself can neither by its rising or falling do anything or create anything or cause anything—for it is nothing. Evil should be valued only as the deceptive product of wishes and rebellious fantasies. For human beings do evil when they deal deceptively and rebelliously.

God sent the divine Son into the world so that through him the Devil, who had produced evil in its entirety and seduced humanity, might be conquered and thereby the human race, given over to corruption through that evil, might be saved. Therefore God abhors the perverted works of indecency, murder, theft, rebellion, tyranny, and hypocrisy of the godless. For God has crushed all of these under foot through the divine Son, who has totally scattered the plunder of the hellish tyrants.

Therefore, O man, you who sit on the papal throne, you despise God when you don't hurl from yourself the evil but, even worse, embrace it and kiss it by silently tolerating corrupt men. The whole Earth is in confusion on account of the ever recurring false teaching whereby human beings love what God has brought to nothing. And you, O Rome, are like one in the throes of death. You will be so shaken that the strength of your feet, the feet on which you now stand, will disappear. For you don't love the King's daughter, justice, with glowing love but as in a delirium of sleep so that you push her away from you. And that is why she also will flee from you, unless you call her back. Nevertheless, the high mountains will still offer the strength of their help to you; they will raise you up and support you with the strong branches of their high trees, so that you don't completely collapse in your dignity, namely in the dignity of your marriage to Christ. So there still remain for you a few blades of your beauty, until the snow of manifold sarcasm comes and blows out much foolishness. Protect yourself that you don't fall, since you open the doors to the ways of the pagans.

Therefore, hear him who lives and who cannot be pushed out of the way. Already the world is full of aberration; later it will be in sadness, and then in such a horrible state that it will not matter to people if they are killed. But from the heart comes healing, when the red sky of morning becomes visible, like the light of the first sunrise. Words cannot express the new longings and enthusiasm that follow.

But he who is great without limit has in our time touched a small tent so that it might behold wonders, fashion unknown letters, and let an unknown language be heard. And it was said to this little tent: "What you express in the language announced to you from above will not be in the ordinary human forces of expression, for that was not given to you. But let him who has the file eagerly smooth this speech so that it receives the right sound for human ears."

And you, O man, who have been placed as the visible shepherd, rise up and hasten quickly to justice, so that you will not be criticized by the great Doctor for not having cleansed your flock from dirt and for not having anointed them with oil. But if the will knows nothing about these things that have passed and the man does not cling to these cravings, he will not incur heavy judgment. But the guilt of this ignorance will be washed away through acts of penance.

And so, O man, stand upon the right way and God will rescue you. God will lead you back to the fold of blessing and election and you will live forever.

[To the Monks of Zwiefalten]

The clear-shining brightness speaks: *The strong light of the Godhead knows and recognizes all things even to their last details. Who rests on this insight and who grasps it, if not that person who sees with sapphire-blue eyes that God who is over all is so changeless in divine justice that God lets no injustice stand, for injustice can find no rest in God!*

God the Father had such delight in himself that he called forth the whole creation through the divine Word. And then the divine creation pleased God, too, and every creature that God lovingly touched, God took in divine arms. O what great delight you have in your work!

God the Father is changeless in justice and spares the unjust only because they pray to the divine Son for forgiveness. For God looks at the divine Word made flesh and is reminded that it is through the Word that all creatures were made. God's saints, too, in a similar way touch God through their pleas with their clear voices, like shining clouds on a gentle mist over the water.

Listen, therefore, you who break out in your evil deeds! You were called "Mountain of the Lord" because you should imitate the Son of God through your cloistered behavior. So why do you transgress the motherly inner realm of love and modesty, like those who on Horeb disciplined their bodies according to the Law but then went astray on another path? Or like sentinels at the gate, who call up the guard with loud voice and thereby insidiously clear a way into the city. Your spirits are like storm-pregnant clouds—first they give themselves over to slothful anger, but then they turn about and give themselves in high spirits to bestial filth. And thus you neglect the sacrifice you are called to make and say: "We don't have the will to oppose our own natures, for we cannot gird the loins of our bodies since we're born from Adam." For even though your life in the cloister puts you in the palace of the Divine, you don't want to tame the fire in your loins. You were rescued from the stall of the ass and placed by the highest Lord in the exalted service of honor in the festivals of the holy Church. Why then are you not ashamed to run back again like dummies to the stall of the ass? Alas, in this you are like Balaam who, rabid with wounds and burning scars, took his repose in the land of the shadow of death. (cf. Numbers 31:8 & 16; II Peter 2:16; Revelation 2:14) Don't, therefore, abandon the holy mountain in scandalous adultery. Woe to the disgrace of the prostitute who is cast forth abroad! For those who fail against the holy institution go to ruin.

So take hold of the discipline [of the Lord] so that you don't wander from the ways of justice, as though you had no law and as though the sun didn't shine over the blessed censer, so that the Lord isn't angered and that you don't go to ruin far from the right way. For ruin is what lies under your feet because of your transgressions. O awesome offering deserving of every honor, to which neither the unbelief of idols nor the burden of mortal wounds clings.

Alas, what pain over this misery! For God will throw you down with all your grumbling just like the Ninevites, unless you hasten quickly to the olive tree of salvation in Christ. A sweet fragrance streams forth from this tree and it allows the blossoms of the just fulfillment of the law to sprout. Why are you so twisted in your lies that you don't realize your blindness? For you are blind, because you have not kept earnestly in mind the guilt in which you were born through Adam's fall. But you have embraced that guilt with laughter and jokes, as though it didn't exist for you. Avoid this so that your salvation may quickly come. Use your eyes and walk on the paths of justice.

[TO ELISABETH OF SCHÖNAU]

. . . I am but a poor creature and fragile vessel; yet what I speak to you comes not from me but from the clear light. Human beings are vessels God had made and filled with the Spirit so that the divine work might come to perfection in them. For God does not do things the way we humans do. It was through the divine Word of command alone that everything came into existence perfect. The grasses, the woods, the trees came forth. The sun too and the moon and the stars went to their appointed places to perform their service. The waters sent out fish and birds. Cattle too and wild beasts arose. All of these creatures—each according to the assignment given it by God—came into being to serve human beings with all of creation.

It was only humans themselves who did not know their Creator. For although God bestowed great knowledge on humans, they raised themselves up in their hearts and turned away from God. It had been God's intention that all of the divine works should be brought to completion in humankind. And yet the old trickster deceived those first human beings and in a flattering whisper infected them with the virus of disobedience, so that they strove for more than they were supposed to. Alas, all the elements got entangled in the confusion of light and darkness, just as humankind did through its transgression of God's command.

But God endowed certain persons with insight so that humankind should not completely fall into derision. Abel was good; Cain a murderer. And many saw God in a mysterious light, while others committed very serious sins until that time came in which the Word of God shone forth, as it is written: "You are the fairest of the sons of men." (Psalm 45:2) Then the sun of justice arose and it made humans shine with good works in faith and deed, just as it is when the redness of morning first appears in the sky and then the other hours of the day follow till the night breaks in.

How the world changes, O daughter Elisabeth: The world no longer has the driving force from which the green of virtues blossoms, neither in the early morning nor in the first, the third, nor especially in the sixth hour of the day. It is truly necessary in our time that God choose certain people so that the divine instruments are not idle.

Listen, then, my troubled daughter: The whispering of the ambitious serpent sometimes seeks to wear down precisely those people our God instructed through divine inspiration. For when the old snake spots a gem of special worth, he hisses, raising himself up, and says: "What is that?" And then he torments with many afflictions the heart that longs to fly above the clouds (as the old serpent himself once did), as though human beings were gods.

And now I want you to listen further to me. Those who long to bring God's words to completion must always remember that, because they are human, they are vessels of clay and so should continually focus on what they are and what they will be. They should leave heavenly things to the One who is heavenly, for they are themselves exiles who do not recognize what is heavenly. They only announce the mysteries like a trumpet which indeed allows the sound but is not itself the source that produces the note. For someone else is blowing into the trumpet and causing the note to be produced.

They should put on the armor of faith, being mild, gentle, poor, and despised. This was the condition of that Lamb whose trumpet notes sound in them from the childlike intuition of their behavior. But God always disciplines those who blow God's trumpets and God sees to it that the earthen vessel does not break but pleases the Divine.

O daughter, may God make you a mirror of life! But even I who suffer from a heart of little courage and am again and again disturbed and crippled by fear, even I sometimes sound with a weak note from the trumpet of the living light. And may God help me to persevere in divine service!

[To Wibert of Gembloux, 1175]

. . . The words which I speak are not my own nor those of any human being, but what I say comes from the vision which I received from above.

O true servant of God, if it had pleased God to raise not only my soul but my body as well to a prophetic vision, still that could not cause the fear to diminish from my spirit and my heart. For I know that I am a human being, even though I have been cloistered from my childhood. There have been many who were wise and whose lives were so filled with wonders that they proclaimed a great number of mysteries. And yet, from a vain pursuit of glory, they ascribed these things to themselves, and thus came to their downfall. But those, on the other hand, who in their spiritual advancement derived their wisdom from God and regarded themselves as nothing—they became pillars of heaven. This is what happened in the case of St. Paul who, although he excelled the other apostles in preaching, regarded himself as nothing. The same is true of the evangelist John who was filled with tender humility, and because of this was able to obtain so much from the divine spring.

How would it be understood if a poor creature like myself were not to recognize this gift? God works where God wills, for the honor of the divine name and not for the honor of earth-bound mortals. But I am continuously filled with fear and trembling. For I do not recognize in myself security through any kind of personal ability. And yet I raise my hands aloft to God, that I might be held by God, just like a feather which has no weight from its own strength and lets itself be carried by the wind.

I cannot fully understand the things I see, not as long as I remain in bondage to the body and the invisible soul. For in both cases we human beings suffer from want.

I also saw in my vision that the first book of my visions should be called Scivias, because it would proclaim the way of the living light and not derive from any other teaching.

From my childhood days, when my limbs, nerves, and veins were not yet strong, the gift of this vision brought joy to my soul; and this has remained true up to this very time when I am a woman of more than 70 years. And as God wants, my soul climbs in this vision high above, even to the height of the firmament. But I do not see these things with my external eyes nor do I hear them with my external ears. I do not perceive them through the thoughts of my heart or through the mediation of my five senses. I see them much more in my soul alone, with my physical eyes open, in such a way that I never experience the unconsciousness of ecstasy, but I see all of this awake, whether by day or night.

The light which I see is not bound by space. It is much, much more light-filled than a cloud that carries the sun in itself. There is nothing in it to recognize of height, length, or breadth. It was described to me as the "shadow of the living light." And just as the sun, the moon, and the stars are reflected in water, so writings, talks, powers, and certain actions of people are illuminated for me in this light.

I was often severely hindered by sickness and involved with heavy sufferings that threatened to bring me to death's door. And yet God has always made me alive again, even to this day.

I keep for a long time in memory all the things I see and learn in the vision, because as soon as I see or hear it, it enters my memory. I simultaneously see, hear, and understand. In an instant I learn what I know through the vision. But whatever I do not see in the vision, I have no knowledge of, for I am without formal education and was only instructed to read simple letters. And I write what I see and hear in the vision and I don't add any other words. I communicate the plain Latin words just as I hear them in the vision. For I do not become educated in my vision so that I can write like the philosophers. The words in the vision do not sound like words from a human mouth, but they are like flaming lightning and like a cloud moving in the pure ether. I am not able to perceive the shape of this light, just as I cannot look with unprotected eyes at the disk of the sun.

It is in this light that I sometimes see, though not often, another light that I call "the living light." When and how I see this, I cannot say. But as long as I see this "living light" all sadness and anxiety are taken away from me. The result is that I feel like a simple young girl and not like an old lady.

[During these experiences] I do not know myself, either in body or soul. And I consider myself as nothing. I reach out to the living God and turn everything over to the Divine that God, who has neither beginning nor end, can preserve me from evil in every situation. And that is why I ask you to pray for me too, since you have requested this reply from me. And ask all of those to pray for me, too, who, like you, desire to hear these words in good faith. Pray that I may persevere in God's service.

But I want to say something to you, too, O son of God, for you seek God in faith and are filled with desire for the Divine. God wants to save you. Pay attention to the eagle who with his two wings flies towards the clouds. If he lost his wings, he would fall down to the Earth and not be able to raise himself up again, no matter how eagerly he sought to lift himself up in flight. Human beings also fly with two wings; the right wing is the knowledge of good and the left wing is the knowledge of evil. The knowledge of evil serves the good, insofar as the good is sharpened and highlighted through the knowledge of evil; and so through this knowledge human beings become wise in all things.

O true son of God, may God raise the wings of your knowledge so that you can fly the right paths. Thus when sin hankers after you and touches you—for you are born such that you cannot exist without sin—you will be able not to satisfy it through action. Then you will have a good flight. The heavenly choir sings the praises of God for people who conduct themselves in this way and they praise such people. For though they are created out of ashes, they love God so much that, for God's sake, they are able completely to despise themselves. So persevere in this battle, strong warrior, so that you may enter into the heavenly harmony where God will say to you: you belong to the children of Israel. For in the zeal of your desire for heaven, you have kept your eyes on the mountain peak, past all the craggy clefts. And may all of those names you included in your letter to me be so guided by the Holy Spirit that they will be inscribed in the book of life.

Songs

When Hildegard was a girl the Rhineland was electrified at the discovery in 1106 of a mass grave containing many bones outside of Cologne. This discovery seemed to support an old legend about Ursula, a fifth-century British princess who, not wanting to marry a pagan prince, received her father's permission to postpone the wedding until she and her handmaids could complete a pilgrimage to Rome. (She actually intended to remain a virgin dedicated to God.) In earlier versions of the legend Ursula was accompanied by five, eight, even eleven virgin companions. By the tenth century, Ursula was said to travel with 11,000 virgins for three years, until, while returning from Rome to Britain, she was stopped in Cologne and urged to marry the chief of a tribe of Huns. When she refused, she and all of her followers were martyred. Hildegard's younger contemporary, the visionary Elisabeth of Schönau, claimed to have received visions about the bones and in 1157 wrote a book about the revelations, adding details to the accepted story. (Elisabeth herself had visited Hildegard once and written to her three times, troubled about her visions. Hildegard's letter of reassurance is reproduced above.) In light of these events, the Feast of St. Ursula became very popular in the Rhineland and Hildegard wrote the music for several services in her honor. Here songs are chosen from the services of Matins, of Lauds, and of Vespers.

The songs are translated for this collection by the editor.

"Spiritui Sancto" (Matins)

All honor be to the holy spirit,
who in the mind of the virgin Ursula
gathered a virginal flock, like doves;
because of this, like Abraham, she left her fatherland.

And, indeed, because of the lamb's embrace, she freed herself
from betrothal to a man.

For this most chaste and golden army
with maidenly, flowing hair
crossed the sea:
O who had ever heard of such a thing?

And, indeed, because of the lamb's embrace,
she freed herself from betrothal to a man.

Glory to the father and to the son
and to the holy spirit.

And, indeed, because of the lamb's embrace,
she freed herself from betrothal to a man.

"O Ecclesia" (Lauds)

O Ecclesia, your eyes are like sapphire,
your ears like Mount Bethel,
your nose like a mountain of myrrh and incense,
and your mouth like the sound of many waters.

In a vision of true faith
Ursula loved the son of God,
gave up both man and this world,
and looked into the sun
and called to a most handsome youth, saying:

With great desire I have desired to come to you,
to sit with you at the heavenly wedding,
running to you through strange ways
just as the clouds float through air
that is pure as sapphire.

And after Ursula had spoken in this way
a report ran among all the people,
and they said: this is the innocence and ignorance
of a girl who doesn't understand what she is saying.

And they mocked her in a great symphony,
until a fiery burden fell upon her.
Then they all recognized
that contempt for the world is like Mount Bethel.

And they all noticed also
the sweetest odor of myrrh and incense,
because contempt for the world
rises above everything else.

Then the devil inspired his allies
to put these most noble women to death.
And all the elements heard this deed cry out,
and before the throne of God they said:

Woe! The ruby blood of an innocent lamb
has been poured out for her betrothal.
Let all the heavens listen
and in a great symphony praise the lamb of God,
because the throat of the ancient serpent
has choked on these pearls
formed from the word of God.

"Cum vox sanguinis" (Vespers)

When the voice of blood
of Ursula and her innocent company
resounds before the throne of God,
an ancient prophecy comes
from the root of Mamre
in a true revelation of the Trinity
and it says:

This blood touches us,
now let us all rejoice.

And after that comes the congregation of the lamb,
for the sake of the ram caught among the thorns,
and it says:

Praise be in Jerusalem,
because of the redness of this blood.

Then comes the sacrifice of the calf
as ancient law laid out,
a sacrifice of praise in colorful garments,
which veiled God's face from Moses,

showing only his back.
Here are the priests who show God through their words
and are not able to see him perfectly,
and they say:

O most noble throng,
this virgin who on earth is called Ursula
in heaven is named Columba [Dove],
because she gathered around her an innocent throng.

O Ecclesia, you are to be praised for this multitude:
like the un-burning bush which Moses saw
and which God had planted in the first root
of the man whom he had formed of clay,
this great throng signifies that they would live
without sexual union with men.

They cried out with the clearest voice,
in purest gold, topaz,
and sapphire wrapped in gold.
Now let all the heavens rejoice,
and all peoples be adorned with these. Amen.

Marie de France (fl. late 12th century)

Lais

Marie is the earliest known French woman poet. We know virtually nothing about her. She presumably was called "of France" because she was not *there, but in England, attached to the French speaking court of Henry II. Her audience, then, would have been a group of Anglo-Norman nobles and ladies. Although she wrote a collection of fables in the style of Aesop and a work called "St. Patrick's Purgatory," she is best known for her wonderful collection of twelve Breton lais. These lais are narrative poems in the form of short romances about love, sometimes unhappy or treacherous love, with elements of magic and the supernatural. Her lais are remarkable for their psychological realism, and she seems strikingly honest, too, in divulging her desire to make a name for herself as a writer but having to search for the right form and subject matter.*

Prologue

Those to whom God has given the gift of comely speech, should not hide their light beneath a bushel, but should willingly show it abroad. If a great truth is proclaimed in the ears of men, it brings forth fruit a hundred-fold; but when the sweetness of the telling is praised of many, flowers mingle with the fruit upon the branch.

According to the witness of Priscian, it was the custom of ancient writers to express obscurely some portions of their books, so that those who came after might study with greater diligence to find the thought within their words. The philosophers knew this well, and were the more unwearied in labour, the more subtle in distinctions, so that the truth might make them free. They were persuaded that he who would keep himself unspotted from the world should search for knowledge, that he might understand. To set evil from me, and to put away my grief, I purposed to commence a book. I considered within myself what fair story in the Latin or Romance I could turn into the common tongue. But I found that all the stories had been written, and scarcely it seemed the worth my doing, what so many had already done. Then I called to mind those Lays I had so often heard. I doubted nothing—for well I know—that our fathers fashioned them, that men should bear in remembrance the

Marie's Old French poetry is here translated into English prose by Eugene Mason, *French Mediaeval Romances* (London: Dent, 1911).

deeds of those who have gone before. Many a one, on many a day, the minstrel has chanted to my ear. I would not that they should perish, forgotten, by the roadside. In my turn, therefore, I have made them a song, rhymed as well as I am able, and often has their shaping kept me sleepless in my bed.

In your honour, most noble and courteous King, to whom joy is a handmaid, and in whose heart all gracious things are rooted, I have brought together these Lays, and told my tales in seemly rhyme. Ere they speak for me, let me speak with my own mouth, and say,

"Sire, I offer you these verses. If you are pleased to receive them, the fairer happiness will be mine, and the more lightly I shall go all the days of my life. Do not deem that I think more highly of myself than I ought to think, since I presume to proffer this, my gift." Hearken now to the commencement of the matter.

THE WERE-WOLF

Amongst the tales I tell you once again, I would not forget the Lay of the Were-Wolf. Such beasts as he are known in every land. Bisclavaret he is named in Brittany; whilst the Norman calls him Garwal.

It is a certain thing, and within the knowledge of all, that many a christened man has suffered this change, and ran wild in the woods, as a Were-Wolf. The Were-Wolf is a fearsome beast. He lurks within the thick forest, mad and horrible to see. All the evil that he may, he does. He goeth to and fro, about the solitary place, seeking man, in order to devour him. Hearken, now, to the adventure of the Were-Wolf, that I have to tell.

In Brittany there dwelt a baron who was marvelously esteemed of all his fellows. He was a stout knight, and a comely, and a man of office and repute. Right private was he to the mind of his lord, and dear to the counsel of his neighbours. This baron was wedded to a very worthy dame, right fair to see, and sweet of semblance. All his love was set on her, and all her love was given again to him. One only grief had this lady. For three whole days in every week her lord was absent from her side. She knew not where he went, nor on what errand. Neither did any of his house know the business which called him forth.

On a day when this lord was come again to his house, altogether joyous and content, the lady took him to task, right sweetly, in this fashion,

"Husband," said she, "and fair, sweet friend, I have a certain thing to pray of you. Right willingly would I receive this gift, but I fear to anger you in the asking. It is better for me to have an empty hand, than to gain hard words."

When the lord heard this matter, he took the lady in his arms, very tenderly, and kissed her.

"Wife," he answered, "ask what you will. What would you have, for it is yours already?"

"By my faith," said the lady, "soon shall I be whole. Husband, right long and wearisome are the days you spend away from your home. I rise from my bed in the morning, sick at heart, I know not why. So fearful am I, lest you do aught to your loss, that I may not find any comfort. Very quickly shall I die for reason of my dread. Tell me now, where you go, and on what business! How may the knowledge of one who loves so closely, bring you to harm?"

"Wife," made answer the lord, "nothing but evil can come if I tell you this secret. For the mercy of God do not require it of me. If you but knew, you would withdraw yourself from my love, and I should be lost indeed."

When the lady heard this, she was persuaded that her baron sought to put her by with jesting words. Therefore she prayed and required him the more urgently, with tender looks and speech, till he was overborne, and told her all the story, hiding naught.

"Wife, I become Bisclavaret. I enter in the forest, and live on prey and roots, within the thickest of the wood."

After she had learned his secret, she prayed and entreated the more as to whether he ran in his raiment, or went spoiled of vesture.

"Wife," said he, "I go naked as a beast."

"Tell me, for hope of grace, what you do with your clothing?"

"Fair wife, that will I never. If I should lose my raiment, or even be marked as I quit my vesture, then a Were-Wolf I must go for all the days of my life. Never again should I become man, save in that hour my clothing were given back to me. For this reason never will I show my lair."

"Husband," replied the lady to him, "I love you better than all the world. The less cause have you for doubting my faith, or hiding any tittle from me. What savour is here of friendship? How have I made forfeit of your love; for what sin do you mistrust my honour? Open now your heart, and tell what is good to be known."

So at the end, outwearied and overborne by her importunity, he could no longer refrain, but told her all.

"Wife," said he, "within this wood, a little from the path, there is a hidden way, and at the end thereof an ancient chapel, where oftentimes I have bewailed my lot. Near by is a great hollow stone, concealed by a bush, and there is the secret place where I hide my raiment, till I would return to my own home."

On hearing this marvel the lady became sanguine of visage, because of her exceeding fear. She dared no longer to lie at his side, and turned over in her mind, this way and that, how best she could get her from him. Now there was a certain knight of those parts, who, for a great while, had sought and required this lady for her love. This knight had spent long years in her service, but little enough had he got thereby, not even fair words or a promise. To him the dame wrote a letter, and meeting, made her purpose plain.

"Fair friend," said she, "be happy. That which you have coveted so long a time, I will grant without delay. Never again will I deny your suit. My heart, and all I have to give, are yours, so take me now as love and dame."

Right sweetly the knight thanked her for her grace, and pledged her faith and fealty. When she had confirmed him by an oath, then she told him all this business of her lord—why he went, and what he became, and of his ravening within the wood. So she showed him of the chapel, and of the hollow stone, and of how to spoil the Were-Wolf of his vesture. Thus, by the kiss of his wife, was Bisclavaret betrayed. Often enough had he ravished his prey in desolate places, but from this journey he never returned. His kinsfolk and acquaintance came together to ask of his tidings, when this absence was noised abroad. Many a man, on many a day, searched the woodland, but none might find him, nor learn where Bisclavaret was gone.

The lady was wedded to the knight who had cherished her for so long a space. More than a year had passed since Bisclavaret disappeared. Then it chanced that the

King would hunt in that self-same wood where the Were-Wolf lurked. When the hounds were unleashed they ran this way and that, and swiftly came upon his scent. At the view the huntsman winded on his horn, and the whole pack were at his heels. They followed him from morn to eve, till he was torn and bleeding, and was all adread lest they should pull him down. Now the King was very close to the quarry, and when Bisclavaret looked upon his master, he ran to him for pity and for grace. He took the stirrup within his paws, and fawned upon the prince's foot. The King was very fearful at this sight, but presently he called his courtiers to his aid.

"Lords," cried he, "hasten hither, and see this marvellous thing. Here is a beast who has the sense of man. He abases himself before his foe, and cries for mercy, although he cannot speak. Beat off the hounds, and let no man do him harm. We will hunt no more to-day, but return to our own place, with the wonderful quarry we have taken."

The King turned him about, and rode to his hall, Bisclavaret following at his side. Very near to his master the Were-Wolf went, like any dog, and had no care to seek again the wood. When the King brought him safely to his own castle, he rejoiced greatly, for the beast was fair and strong, no mightier had any man seen. Much pride had the King in his marvelous beast. He held him so dear, that he bade all those who wished for his love, to cross the Wolf in naught, neither to strike him with a rod, but ever to see that he was richly fed and kennelled warm. This commandment the Court observed willingly. So all the day the wolf sported with the lords, and at night he lay within the chamber of the King. There was not a man who did not make much of the beast, so frank was he and debonair. None had reason to do him wrong, for ever was he about his master, and for his part did evil to none. Every day were these two companions together, and all perceived that the King loved him as his friend.

Hearken now to that which chanced.

The King held a high Court, and bade his great vassals and barons, and all the lords of his venery to the feast. Never was there a goodlier feast, nor one set forth with sweeter show and pomp. Amongst those who were bidden, came that same knight who had the wife of Bisclavaret for dame. He came to the castle, richly gowned, with a fair company, but little he deemed whom he would find so near. Bisclavaret marked his foe the moment he stood within the hall. He ran towards him, and seized him with his fangs, in the King's very presence, and to the view of all. Doubtless he would have done him mischief, had not the King called and chidden him, and threatened him with a rod. Once, and twice, again, the Wolf set upon the knight in the very light of day. All men marvelled at his malice, for sweet and serviceable was the beast, and to that hour had shown hatred of none. With one consent the household deemed that this deed was done with full reason, and that the Wolf had suffered at the knight's hand some bitter wrong. Right wary of his foe was the knight until the feast had ended, and all the barons had taken farewell of their lord, and departed, each to his own house. With these, amongst the very first, went that lord whom Bisclavaret so fiercely had assailed. Small was the wonder that he was glad to go.

No long while after this adventure it came to pass that the courteous King would hunt in that forest where Bisclavaret was found. With the prince came his wolf, and a fair company. Now at nightfall the King abode within a certain lodge of that country, and this was known of that dame who before was the wife of Bisclavaret. In the morning the lady clothed her in her most dainty apparel, and hastened to the lodge, since she desired to speak with the King, and to offer him a rich present. When the lady entered in the chamber, neither man nor leash might restrain the fury of the Wolf. He became as a mad dog in his hatred and malice. Breaking from his bonds he sprang at the lady's face, and bit the nose from her visage. From every side men ran to the succour of the dame. They beat off the wolf from his prey, and for a little would have cut him in pieces with their swords. But a certain wise counsellor said to the King,

"Sire, hearken now to me. This beast is always with you, and there is not one of us all who has not known him for long. He goes in and out amongst us, nor has molested any man, neither done wrong or felony to any, save only to this dame, one only time as we have seen. He has done evil to this lady, and to that knight, who is now the husband of the dame. Sire, she was once the wife of that lord who was so close and private to your heart, but who went, and none might find where he had gone. Now, therefore, put the dame in a sure place, and question her straitly, so that she may tell—if perchance she knows thereof—for what reason this Beast holds her in such mortal hate. For many a strange deed has chanced, as well we know, in this marvellous land of Brittany."

The King listened to these words, and deemed the counsel good. He laid hands upon the knight, and put the dame in surety in another place. He caused them to be questioned right straitly, so that their torment was very grievous. At the end, partly because of her distress, and partly by reason of her exceeding fear, the lady's lips were loosed, and she told her tale. She showed them of the betrayal of her lord, and how his raiment was stolen from the hollow stone. Since then she knew not where he went, nor what had befallen him, for he had never come again to his own land. Only, in her heart, well she deemed and was persuaded, that Bisclavaret was he.

Straightway the King demanded the vesture of his baron, whether this were to the wish of the lady, or whether it were against her wish. When the raiment was brought him, he caused it to be spread before Bisclavaret, but the Wolf made as though he had not seen. Then that cunning and crafty counsellor took the King apart, that he might give him a fresh rede.

"Sire," said he, "you do not wisely, nor well, to set this raiment before Bisclavaret, in the sight of all. In shame and much tribulation must he lay aside the beast, and again become man. Carry your wolf within your most secret chamber, and put his vestment therein. Then close the door upon him, and leave him alone for a space. So we shall see presently whether the ravening beast may indeed return to human shape."

The King carried the Wolf to his chamber, and shut the doors upon him fast. He delayed for a brief while, and taking two lords of his fellowship with him, came again to the room. Entering therein, all three, softly together, they found the knight asleep in the King's bed, like a little child. The King ran swiftly to the bed and taking his friend in his arms, embraced and kissed him fondly, above a hundred times. When the man's speech returned once more, he told him of his adventure. Then the King restored to his friend the fief that was stolen from him, and gave such rich gifts, moreover, as I cannot tell. As for the wife who had betrayed Bisclavaret, he bade her avoid his country, and chased her from the realm. So she went forth, she and her second lord together, to seek a more abiding city, and were no more seen.

The adventure that you have heard is no vain fable. Verily and indeed it chanced as I have said. The Lay of the Were-Wolf, truly, was written that it should ever be borne in mind.

Andreas Capellanus (fl. late 12th century)

The Art of Courtly Love

Andrew the Chaplain's De arte honeste amandi *is usually translated as* The Art of Courtly Love, *even though the term "courtly love" was an invention of the nineteenth century. It characterizes a kind of romantic love which idealizes passion and worship of the beloved, or, as some might say, makes a virtue out of sexual frustration. Andreas's work was part of the revolution in style that occurred in the twelfth century—a move away from literary works that were martial, heroic, and male-centered and toward works that were more intimate and at least pretended to notice the place and attitudes of women, even if this attention, for noble women at least, was itself stifling.*

Important in this development were the court circles that grew up around Eleanor of Aquitaine, the wife of King Louis VII of France (and later of King Henry II of England), and their two daughters, Alix and especially Marie, the Countess of Champagne. Eleanor was the granddaughter of the first troubadour, William IX of Aquitaine, the first known secular love poet of the later Middle Ages. She and her daughters took under their patronage troubadours who sang about courtly love and poets who revived the Celtic stories about Merlin and King Arthur. Andreas describes Eleanor's and Marie's courts as true love courts, in the legal sense: in one case about adulterous love, Andreas tells us, Marie handed down the decision that love can only exist outside of marriage and not within marriage. Andreas wrote his treatise about 1182 at the court of Champagne for Marie, Eleanor's daughter; Marie also commissioned the first romance about the adulterous affair of Lancelot and Guinevere, The Knight of the Cart, *by Chrétien de Troyes.*

The Art of Courtly Love *is a handbook of love addressed in Latin to a young cleric named Walter. The first two-thirds offer a series of highly stylized sample dialogues in which male speakers of varying social ranks try to win to their sides (and their beds) women of varying social ranks. These dialogues amount to a kind of rhetorical handbook in matching the style and the nature of the arguments to the ranks of the speakers, male and female. Finally, indeed, all language breaks down as Andreas considers the more general cases of love of clergy and of nuns, of love got for money, and the love of peasants and prostitutes. If Walter is unfortunate enough to fall in love with a peasant, for instance, Andreas advises: "puff*

"The Rules of Love" are translated for this collection by the editor. The other selection is taken from *The Art of Courtly Love* by Andreas Capellanus, translated by John Jay Parry (New York: Columbia University Press, 1941).

them up with lots of praise and then, when you find a convenient place, do not hesitate to take what you seek and to embrace them by force. . . . a little compulsion [is] a convenient cure for their shyness." That section of the work ends with Andreas's summary of the rules that characterize and guide this kind of secular, passionate love.

In Book III, called "The Rejection of Love," Andreas does a sudden and complete about-face, rejecting as folly all the kinds of love he has just explored in such compelling detail. He suggests instead that only the love of God is truly important. Much of this last part of the work is devoted to a detailed, virulent, and entirely conventional, medieval attack upon women for bringing about men's downfall—following in the footsteps of Eve in the Garden of Eden—and for their vanity, drunkenness, wantonness, and greed: ". . . not only is every woman by nature a miser, but she is also envious and a slanderer of other women, greedy, a slave to her belly, inconstant, fickle in her speech, disobedient and impatient of restraint, spotted with the sin of pride and desirous of vainglory, a liar, a drunkard, a babbler, no keeper of secrets, too much given to wantonness, prone to every evil, and never loving any man in her heart" (trans. John Jay Parry; Columbia University Press, 1941).

The ultimate meaning of this work may be enigmatic, but the passionate love it maps has become in the West what we feel as romantic love. We may no longer believe in "rules of love," but we have been schooled in a surprising number of these ideas about lovers' behavior by countless poems, novels, operas, and films.

[Decisions in the Court of Love]

The Letter Sent to the Countess of Champagne

I. To the illustrious and wise woman M., Countess of Champagne, the noble woman A. and Count G. send greeting and whatever in the world is more pleasing. . . .

"Now on a certain day, as we sat under the shade of a pine tree of marvellous height and great breadth of spread, devoted wholly to love's idleness and striving to investigate Love's mandates in a good-tempered and spirited debate, we began to discern a twofold doubt, and we wearied ourselves with laborious arguments as to whether true love can find any place between husband and wife and whether jealousy flourishing between two lovers ought to be approved of. After we had argued the matter back and forth and each of us seemed to bolster up his position with reasonable arguments, neither one would give in to the other or agree with the arguments he brought forward. We ask you to settle this dispute, and we have sent you both sides of the question in detail, so that after you have carefully examined the truth of it our disagreement may be brought to a satisfactory end and settled by a fair decision. For knowing clearly and in manifest truth that you have a great abundance of wisdom and that you would not want to deprive anyone of justice, we believe that we will in no wise be deprived of it; we most urgently implore Your Excellency's decision, and we desire with all our hearts, begging you most humbly by our present address, that you will give continued attention to our case and that Your Prudence will render a fair decision in the matter without making any delay in giving the verdict."

The Letter sent back by the Countess of Champagne

"To the prudent and noble woman A. and the illustrious and famous Count G., M., Countess of Champagne, sends greeting.

"Since we are bound to hear the just petitions of everybody, and since it is not seemly to deny our help to those who ask what is proper, especially when those who go wrong on questions of love ask to be set right by our decision—which is what the tenor of your letter indicates—we have tried diligently and carefully to carry this out without any extended delay.

"Now your letter has shown that this is the doubt that has arisen between you: whether love can have any place between husband and wife and whether between lovers jealousy is blameworthy; in both questions each of you falls back on his own opinion and opposes that of the other, and you want us to give our opinion which side properly should get the decision. We have therefore examined carefully the statements of both sides and have in very truth inquired into the matter by every possible means, and we wish to end the case with this decision. We declare and we hold as firmly established that love cannot exert its powers between two people who are married to each other. For lovers give each other everything freely, under no compulsion of necessity, but married people are in duty bound to give in to each other's desires and deny themselves to each other in nothing. Besides, how does it increase a husband's honor if after the manner of lovers he enjoys the embraces of his wife, since the worth of character of neither can be increased thereby, and they seem to have nothing more than they already had a right to? And we say the same thing for still another reason, which is that a precept of love tells us that no woman, even if she is married, can be crowned with the reward of the King of Love unless she is seen to be enlisted in the service of Love himself outside the bonds of wedlock. But another rule of Love teaches that no one can be in love with two men. Rightly, therefore, Love cannot acknowledge any rights of his between husband and wife. But there is still another argument that seems to stand in the way of this, which is that between them there can be no true jealousy, and without it true love may not exist, according to the rule of Love himself, which says, 'He who is not jealous cannot love.'

"Therefore let this our verdict, pronounced with great moderation and supported by the opinion of a great many ladies, be to you firm and indubitable truth.

"The first day of May, in the year 1174, the seventh of the indiction."

II. Again. Another man, although he was enjoying the embraces of a most excellent love, asked her for permission to obtain the embraces of a different woman. Having received this he went away and refrained longer than usual from the solaces of the first lady. But after a month had elapsed he came back to the first one and said that he had never received any solaces from the other lady, nor had he wished to receive them, but he had merely wanted to test the constancy of his loved one. This woman refused him her love on the ground that he was unworthy, saying that for him to ask and receive such permission was reason enough for her to deprive him of her love. But the opinion of Queen Eleanor, who was consulted on the matter, seems to be just the opposite of this woman's. She said, "We know that it comes from the nature of love that those who are in love often falsely pretend that they desire new embraces, that they may the better test the faith and constancy of their co-lover. Therefore a woman sins against the nature of love itself if she keeps back her embraces from her lover on this account or forbids him her love, unless she has clear evidence that he has been unfaithful to her."

III. There were two men who were equal in birth and life and morals and everything else except that one happened to have more property than the other, so that many wondered which was preferable as a lover. From this case came the dictum of the Countess of Champagne, who said, "It would not be right for one to prefer a vulgar rich man to a noble and handsome poor one. Indeed a handsome poor man may well be preferred to a rich nobleman if both are seeking the love of a rich woman, since it is more worthy for a woman who is blessed with an abundance of property to accept a needy lover than one who has great wealth. Nothing should be more grievous to all good men than to see worth overshadowed by poverty or suffering from the lack of anything. It is right, therefore, for men to praise a wealthy woman who disregards money and seeks a needy lover whom she can help with her wealth, for nothing seems so praiseworthy in a lover of either sex as to relieve the necessities of the loved one so far as may be. But if the woman herself is in need, she is more ready to accept the rich lover; for if both lovers are oppressed by poverty there is little doubt that their love will be of short duration. Poverty brings a great feeling of shame to all honorable men and gives them many an anxious thought and is even a great disturber of quiet sleep; so as a result it commonly puts love to flight.

XVI. Another problem of this kind was brought before them. A certain knight was suing for a woman's love, and he did not have frequent opportunities of speaking to her, so with the woman's consent he chose a go-between for this purpose, that with his help each of them might the more easily know the other's wishes and in greater secrecy make known his own and that the love between them might forever be managed in even greater secrecy. This go-between accepted the office of legate, but broke faith with his confederate, took upon himself the name of lover, and commenced to look out for himself. The lady in the case had the bad taste to assent to his fraud, and finally she consummated love with him and fulfilled all his wishes. But the knight was wrought up over the fraud and told the whole course of the affair to the Countess of Champagne, asking that the culprit be tried by her decision and that of the other ladies. Even the wrongdoer praised the Countess's verdict. She summoned sixty ladies to her assistance and settled the matter with this decision: "Let that crafty lover who has found a woman suited to his deserts, one who wasn't ashamed to accept so great a villain, enjoy his evilly acquired love if he wants to, and let her enjoy the kind of lover she deserves. But let both be forever deprived of the love of any other person, and let neither be invited hence-forward to gatherings of ladies or courts of knights, because he has acted contrary to the honesty of the order of knighthood and she, contrary to the decency of ladies, has disgracefully assented to the love of a go-between."

XVII. Again. A certain knight was in love with a woman who had given her love to another man, but he got from her this much hope of her love—that if it should ever happen that she lost the love of her beloved, then without a doubt her love would go to this man. A little while after this the woman married her lover. The other knight then demanded that she give him the fruit of the hope she had granted him, but this she absolutely refused to do, saying that she had not lost the love of her lover. In this affair the Queen gave her decision as follows: "We dare not oppose the opinion of the Countess of Champagne, who ruled that love can exert no power between husband and wife. Therefore we recommend that the lady should grant the love she has promised."

XVIII. A certain knight shamefully divulged the intimacies and the secrets of his love. All those who were serving in the camp of Love demanded that this offense should be most severely punished, lest if so serious a transgression went unavenged, the example might give occasion to others to do likewise. A court of ladies was therefore assembled in Gascony, and they decided unanimously that forever after he should be deprived of all hope of love and that in every court of ladies or of knights he should be an object of contempt and abuse to all. And if any woman should dare to violate this rule of the ladies, for example by giving him her love, she should be subject to the same punishment, and should henceforth be an enemy of all honest women.

XIX. Another decision very properly belongs with these. A certain knight asked for the love of a certain lady, and she absolutely refused to love him. The knight sent her some rather handsome presents, and these she accepted with eager face and greedy heart; she did not, however, grow any more yielding in the matter of love, but gave him a flat refusal. The knight complained that the woman, by accepting appropriate gifts, had given him a hope of love, which she was trying to take away from him without a cause. To those facts the Queen responded in this fashion. "Let a woman either decline gifts which are offered her with a view to love, or let her pay for them with her love, or let her suffer in patience being classed with the prostitutes."

XX. The Queen was also asked which was preferable: the love of a young man or of one advanced in years. She answered this question with wonderful subtlety by saying, "We distinguish between a good and a better love by the man's knowledge and his character and his praiseworthy manners, not by his age. But as regards that natural instinct of passion, young men are usually more eager to gratify it with older women than with young ones of their own age; those who are older prefer to receive the embraces and kisses of young women rather than of the older ones. But on the other hand a woman whether young or somewhat older likes the embraces and solaces of young men better than those of older ones. The explanation of this fact seems to be a physiological one."

[The Rules of Love]

1. Marriage is not a good excuse for not loving.
2. The person who is not jealous cannot love.
3. No one can be bound by two loves.
4. Love is known to be always increasing or decreasing.
5. What a lover takes from an unwilling partner is bitter.
6. A male usually does not love until he reaches puberty.
7. When a lover dies, the survivor is required to remain without a partner for two years.
8. No one should be deprived of love except for the strongest reason.
9. No one can love unless he is compelled by Love's persuasion.
10. Love is always an exile from the home of avarice.
11. One should not love a woman whom one would be ashamed to seek to marry.
12. A true lover does not desire the embraces of any but his beloved.
13. Love rarely survives being made public.
14. A love easily achieved will be regarded with contempt; love achieved with difficulty will be valued.
15. Every lover turns pale when he is near his beloved.
16. When a lover suddenly sees his beloved, his heart pounds.
17. A new love drives out an old one.
18. Good character alone makes a man worthy of love.
19. If love diminishes, it quickly fades and rarely regains strength.
20. One in love is always fearful.
21. True jealousy always causes the feeling of love to grow.
22. When one begins to suspect his beloved, jealousy and the feeling of love both grow.
23. One who is vexed by the thought of love sleeps and eats very little.
24. Every act of a lover ends in thoughts of his beloved.
25. A true lover regards as good only what he thinks will please his beloved.
26. Love can deny nothing to love.
27. A lover can never have enough of the solaces of his beloved.
28. The slightest presumption causes a lover to harbor sinister suspicions about his beloved.
29. One who is vexed by excessive passion is usually not in love.
30. A true lover is constantly and without intermission preoccupied by thoughts of his beloved.
31. Nothing prevents one woman from being loved by two men, or one man by two women.

Chrétien de Troyes (fl. late 12th c.)

Chrétien came presumably from the French town of Troyes. He is one of a group of northern French poets who drew inspiration from the new twelfth-century movement of singers and poets from the South of France known as troubadours. *These poets made love and longing the subjects of their songs. Chrétien coupled this new interest in love with the martial material in the older verse epics (like the* Song of Roland*) and created extended verse romances, in rhyming couplets. The new heroism, linking prowess on the battlefield with exemplary behavior in the chamber, came to be known as* chivalry, *and the romances show knights being tested according to wildly conflicting chivalric codes. Discovering a new courtly audience for these elaborate stories, and patrons to feed him, Chrétien created the first Arthurian romances, perhaps drawing on French or Breton sources that have not been discovered. Chrétien's* Knight of the Cart, *for instance, first introduces into literature the character of Lancelot, a knight whose loyalty to King Arthur is supplanted by his passionate love and worship of Queen Guinevere.*

Chrétien's romances give only a few clues about his life. Chrétien claims in his story of Lancelot to be writing at the command of Marie, the Countess of Champagne, the daughter of Eleanor of Aquitaine. If this is so, Chrétien sought patronage in the same courts that sustained Andreas Capellanus (see the preceding reading).

[The Town of Dire Adventure]
from *The Knight with the Lion (Yvain)*

The courtly world can be seen clearly reflected in The Knight with the Lion, *the story of Yvain, the knight from Arthur's court who wins a wife and promptly leaves her in search of adventure. The challenges that Yvain faces invariably win him kingdoms and brides. Because his larger quest is to reclaim his estranged wife and her kingdom, he must deflect with courtliness these offers of marriage and property. Nowhere is this more difficult than*

The translation is by William Kibler, in Chrétien's *Arthurian Romances* (Penguin, 1991).

in the charmed town of Dire Adventure. There Yvain discovers, strangely, a kind of medieval sweat shop, in which the women are forced by magic into poverty and labor. As in most Arthurian romances, Chrétien offers us an exploration of conflicting codes and a reflection on medieval social orders.

So she galloped through the mire as fast as over the smooth and level road, until she caught sight of the knight in company with his lion.

She rejoiced and said: 'God help me! Now I see the knight I've hunted so long; I've followed and tracked him well. But if I hunt him and return empty-handed, what good will it be to catch up with him? Little or nothing, to be sure. Yet if he does not return with me, then all my efforts will have been wasted.'

As she spoke these words, she hurried on so fast her palfrey was in a lather. When she caught up with the knight, she hailed him, and he replied at once: 'May God be with you, fair one, and keep you from cares and woe.'

'And you, too, sir, for I hope that you will be able to help me!' Then she came up beside him and said: 'My lord, long have I sought you. Word of your great prowess has kept me on a very weary search through many lands yet I've continued my search, thank God, until finally I have caught up with you. And if I have suffered any hardship it doesn't matter to me, nor do I complain or remember it; all my limbs are lightened, for the pain was lifted from me as soon as I encountered you. I do not have need of you: someone who is better than I, a nobler and worthier woman, sends me to you. And if you disappoint her hopes, then your reputation has betrayed her: for no one else will help her. With your aid the maiden, who has been disinherited by her sister, expects to win her suit completely. She doesn't want anyone else to intervene; she cannot be convinced that anyone else could help her. You can truly rest assured that if you triumph in this cause you will have redeemed the landless girl's inheritance and added to your own glory. She herself was seeking you to defend her inheritance, because of the good she expected from you; and she would have let no one come in her place had she not been detained by an illness that forced her to bed. Now tell me, if you please, whether you dare to come or will remain idle here.'

'No,' he said, 'no one gains a reputation by idleness, and I'll not fail to act but will gladly follow you, my sweet friend, wherever you please. And if she on whose behalf you seek my help has great need of me, don't despair: I'll do everything in my power for her. Now may God grant me the courage and grace that will enable me, with His good help, to defend her rights.'

So the two of them rode along talking until they approached the town of Dire Adventure. They did not wish to pass it by because the day was growing late. They drew near to this town, and the people who saw them coming all said to the knight: 'Beware, sir, beware! You were directed to this place of lodging to cause you shame and suffering; an abbot would swear this to you.'

'Ah!' he said, 'foolish, vulgar people, full of every wickedness and lacking every good quality, why have you accosted me like this?'

'Why? You'll know it well enough if you ride on just a little further! But you'll never know anything until you have stayed in this high fortress.'

Immediately my lord Yvain headed towards the keep, while all the people cried out in loud voices: 'Hey! Hey! Wretch, where are you going? If ever in your life you've encountered anyone who's shamed and vilified you, in there where you're headed they'll do much worse by you than you could ever tell!'

'Dishonourable and unkind people,' said my lord Yvain as he heard them, 'meddlesome and foolish people, why do you assail me? Why attack me? What do you ask of me? What do you want of me that you growl so after me?'

'Friend, do not get angry,' said a lady somewhat advanced in years, who was very courteous and sensible, 'for indeed they mean no harm by what they say and are only warning you not to go to take lodging up there, if you would but heed their words. They dare not to tell you why, but they warn and rebuff you because they want to scare you away. Custom ordains that they do this to everyone who approaches, to keep them from entering there. And the custom in this town is such that we dare not offer lodging in our homes, under any circumstances, to any gentleman who comes from outside. Now it is up to you alone: no one is standing in your way. If you wish, you can ride up there, but I would advise you to turn around.'

'My lady,' said he, 'I believe it would be to my honour and benefit to accept your advice; but if I did, I don't know where else I could find lodging for this night.'

'Upon my word,' said she, 'I'll say no more, for this is none of my business. Go wherever you wish. However, I would be very happy to see you come back out without having suffered too great shame within. But this could never happen!'

'My lady,' he replied, 'may God bless you for your words of warning! But my innocent heart draws me there, and I shall do what my heart desires.'

Immediately he headed for the gate, with his lion and the maiden. The porter called him aside and said: 'Come quickly, come, for you have arrived at a place where you will be held fast; and cursed be your arrival.'

Thus the porter called to him and urged him to hasten and come up, but in a very rude way. And my lord Yvain, without reply, passed in front of him and discovered a large hall, lofty and new. Before it was a meadow enclosed with huge, round, pointed staves; and by peering between the staves he could make out up to three hundred maidens doing various kinds of needlework. Each one sewed as best she could with threads of gold and silk; but they were so poor that many among them wore their hair loose and went ungirded. Their dresses were worn through at the breasts and elbows, and their shifts were filthy at the collar, their necks were gaunt and their faces pale from the hunger and the deprivation they had known. He observed them, and as they caught sight of him they lowered their heads and wept; and for a long while they remained there without doing anything, because they felt so miserable that they could not raise their eyes from the ground.

After my lord Yvain had watched them for a while, he turned around and headed straight for the gate; but the porter sprang up before him and shouted: 'It is no use, you can't escape now, good master. You'd like to be outside again now, but, by my head, you can't do it: before you escape you'll have suffered so much shame that you couldn't suffer more. It wasn't at all clever of you to enter here, for there's no question of leaving.'

'Nor do I want to, good brother!' he said. 'But tell me, on the soul of your father: the damsels that I saw in this meadow, who were weaving cloths of silk and orphrey, where do they come from? Their needlework pleases me, but I was very distressed to see that their faces and bodies are so thin and pale and sad. I'm sure that they would be quite beautiful and attractive, if they had what they desired.'

'I will never tell you,' he said; 'find someone else to answer that question.'

'So I shall, since there's no better way.'

Then he searched until he found the door to the meadow in which the damsels were working. He arrived in front of them and greeted them all, and he saw teardrops trickling down from their eyes as they wept.

He said to them: 'May it please God to lift from your hearts this sadness, whose origin I do not know, and turn it into joy.'

'May God, whom you've invoked, hear your prayer!' one maiden answered him. 'Who we are and from what land will not be hidden from you; I believe this is what you wish to ask.'

'I've come for no other reason,' he said.

'Sir, it happened long ago that the king of the Isle of Maidens went seeking new ventures through courts and countries. Like a true fool, he continued until he fell into this peril. He came here in an evil hour, for we who are held captive here now must bear shame and suffering without ever having deserved it. And rest assured that you yourself can expect great shame here if they refuse your ransom. At any rate, it happened that my lord came to this town, inhabited by two sons of the Devil (and don't think this is made up, for they were born of a woman and a demon!). And these two were about to do battle with the king, which was a most wretched thing, for he was not yet eighteen. They could easily have run him through like a tender lamb, so the terrified king saved himself as best he could: he swore that he would send here each year, as long as he lived, thirty maidens from his land; he was released for this payment. And it was decreed by oath that this tribute was to last as long as the two demons prevailed, unless some knight could vanquish them in battle, and then he would no longer have to pay this tribute and we would be free from shame, grief, and misery. Never again will anything please us. But I'm babbling on like a child when I speak of freedom, for we can never escape this place; we shall weave silk cloth all our days, yet never be better dressed than now.

'We shall remain poor and naked for ever and shall always be hungry and thirsty; no matter how hard we try, we'll never have anything better to eat. Our bread supply is very meagre: little in the morning and less at night, for by the work of our hands we'll never have more to live on than fourpence in the pound; and with this we cannot buy sufficient food and clothing. For though our labour is worth twenty shillings a week, we have barely enough to live on. And you can be sure that there's not one of us whose work doesn't bring in twenty shillings or more, and that's enough to make a duke wealthy! Yet here we are in poverty, while he for whom we labour grows rich from our work. We stay awake much of the night and all day long to earn his profit, for he has threatened us with torture if we rest; therefore we dare not rest. But what more should I tell you? We are so ashamed and ill-treated that I cannot tell you the fifth of it. And we are racked with sorrow whenever we see young knights and gentlemen die in combat with the two demons. They pay most dearly for their lodgings, as you must do tomorrow: for alone and unaided you must, whether you wish to or not, do battle and lose your reputation against these two incarnate devils.'

'May God, our true spiritual King, protect me,' said my lord Yvain, 'and restore you to honour and joy, if it be His will! Now I must go and see what welcome will be shown to me by those within.'

'Go now, sir. May He who gives and bestows all gifts watch over you!'

Yvain continued until he reached the main hall, without having encountered anyone, good or evil, to speak with them. After passing through the manor, they emerged into an orchard. They never had to inquire or worry about stabling their horses; why should they, since those who thought they would win them stabled them well? But I think they were overconfident, for their owner was still in perfect health. The horses had oats and hay, and fresh litter up to their bellies.

Then my lord Yvain entered the orchard, followed by his retinue. He saw a wealthy man lying there, propped up on his elbow on a silken cloth; and a maiden was reading to him from a romance (I don't know what it was about). And to listen to the romance, a woman too had sat down there. She was the maid's mother, and the gentleman was her father. It gave them pleasure to watch and listen to her, for she was their only child. She was not more than sixteen, but was so beautiful and elegant that the god of Love would have sought to serve her, had he seen her, and would never have let her love anyone but himself alone. To serve her he would have taken on human flesh, abandoned his divinity, and struck his own body with the dart whose wound never heals unless an unfaithful doctor tends it. It is not right for anyone to be healed unless he encounters unfaithfulness, for he who is healed in any other way does not love truly. I could tell you so much about these wounds that it would take all day, if you were pleased to hear it, but there are those who would be quick to say I speak of idle tales, for people no longer fall in love, nor do they love as once they did, nor even want to hear love spoken of.

So listen now to how, with what hospitality and good cheer, my lord Yvain was given lodging. All those who were in the orchard sprang to their feet to greet him, and as soon as they saw him they addressed him with these words: 'This way, good sir, and may you and all with you be called blessed in every way that God can bring about or decree!'

I do not know whether they were feigning, but they welcomed him jubilantly and acted as if they were very pleased to lodge him comfortably. The daughter of the lord herself served and paid him great respect, as one should to a noble guest: not only did she remove all his armour, but with her own hands she washed his neck and face and forehead. Her father wished him to be paid every due respect, just as she did. She brought forth a pleated shirt and white breeches from her wardrobe; with needle and thread she laced up his sleeves as she clothed him. May God grant that this attention and service should not come at too dear a cost. To wear over his shirt she offered him a new surcoat, and over his shoulders she placed an unworn mantle of fur-trimmed scarlet. She was so diligent in serving him that he was embarrassed and troubled, but the maiden was so courteous, so guileless, so well-mannered, that she still did not feel she was doing enough; for she knew well that her mother wanted her guest to lack nothing that she could do to honour him.

That evening he was served so many courses at dinner that there were far too many: just carrying in the many courses tired the serving-men. That night they paid him every honour and put him comfortably to bed; the lion slept at his feet as was its custom. Once he was in his bed, no one went near him again. In the morning, when God, by whose command all is done, had relit His light throughout the world as early as was fitting, my lord Yvain arose at once, and he and the maiden went to a nearby chapel to hear Mass, which was speedily said for them in honour of the Holy Spirit.

After Mass, when my lord Yvain felt it was time to leave and that nothing would prevent it, he heard baleful news: it was not to be as he chose. When he said, 'Sir, if it please you, I should like your leave to depart,' the lord of the manor replied, 'Friend, there is a reason I cannot yet give you my leave: in this town a wicked and devilish custom prevails that I am compelled to uphold. Shortly I shall summon here before you two tall and powerful men of mine, against whom, right or wrong, you must take up arms. If you can hold your own against them and defeat and kill them both, my daughter desires you for her spouse, and this town and everything that goes with it awaits you.'

'Sir,' replied Yvain, 'I want none of your wealth. May God grant me no share here, and may your daughter remain with you. In her the Emperor of Germany would find a good match, were he to win her, for she is beautiful and well-bred.'

'Enough, dear guest!' said the lord. 'I don't have to listen to your refusal, for you cannot escape. The knight who can defeat the two demons who are about to attack you must take my town, wed my daughter, and rule over all my lands. The combat cannot be averted or postponed for any reason. But I am convinced that cowardice makes you refuse my daughter's hand: in this way you hope to avoid the combat altogether. Yet you cannot fail to fight, because no knight who has slept here can possibly escape. This is a custom and fixed payment that will last for a long time to come, because my daughter will not be wed until I see them dead or vanquished.'

'Then I must fight them, though it's against my will; but I would very gladly pass this by, I assure you! So now, though it pains me, I'll do battle, since it cannot be avoided.'

Immediately the two black and hideous demon's sons came forth. Each had a spiked club of cornel wood, which had been covered with copper and wound with brass. They were in armour from their shoulders to their knees, but their heads and faces were left unarmed, and their stocky legs were likewise left uncovered. Armed like this they came, holding over their heads round shields, strong and light for fighting.

The lion began to bristle as soon as it saw them, for it well knew and could see by the arms they carried that they had come to fight its master. The hair on its back stood up and its mane bristled; it shook with rage in its eagerness to fight and struck the earth with its tail, for it was determined to rescue its master before they killed him.

When they saw the lion, they said: 'Vassal, take your lion away from here! It is threatening us. Either you must admit defeat, or else I swear you must put it somewhere where it cannot undertake to help you or harm us. You must have your sport with us alone, for the lion would be glad to help you if it could.'

'If you are afraid of it, take it away yourselves,' said my lord Yvain, 'for I would be quite pleased and satisfied if it did harm you if it could, and I am grateful to have its help.'

'Upon our oath,' they said, 'this cannot be, for you must have no help from it! Do the best you can alone, with no help from any other. You must face the two of us alone; if the lion were to join you and attack us, then you wouldn't be alone: it would be two against two. So I swear to you, you must take your lion away from here, though you may soon regret it.'

'Where do you want it to go?' he asked. 'Where would it please you for me to put it?'

'Lock it in there,' they said, showing him a little room.

'It shall be done as you wish.'

Then he took it and locked it in. At once the people went to fetch Yvain's armour and helped him don it. Next they led out his horse and handed it to him, and he mounted. The two champions charged Yvain to shame and injure him, for they were unafraid of the lion that was now locked within the room. With their maces they struck him such blows that his shield and helmet afforded him little protection, for when they hit his helmet they bludgeoned and knocked it awry, and his shield shattered and dissolved like ice; they made such holes in it that you could put your fist right through. Both of them were greatly to be feared. And how did he handle the two demons? Sparked by shame and fear, he defended himself with all his strength; he exerted himself and strove to land mighty and powerful blows. He was not sparing in his gifts to them, for he doubled their own generosity.

Now the lion, still locked within the room, had a sad and troubled heart, for it recalled the great kindness shown it by this noble man who now stood in dire need of its aid and service. The lion would return it in full measure and copiously repay his kindness; its payment would not be discounted if it could get out of that room. It searched in every direction, but could find no escape. It heard clearly the blows of the fierce and lethal battle and began to moan so much that it was beside itself with rage. It searched until it discovered that the threshold was rotten near the ground; it scratched until it could squeeze under just up to its haunches. My lord Yvain was by this time hard pressed and bathed in sweat, having found the two louts to be strong, cruel, and persistent. He had suffered many a blow and returned them as best he could, but he had not succeeded in wounding them at all, for they were too skilled in swordplay, and their shields could not be dented by any sword, no matter how sharp or well-tempered.

So my lord Yvain had every reason to fear for his life; but he was able to hold his own until the lion clawed beneath the threshold enough to work itself completely free. If now the fiends are not defeated then they will never be, because the lion will allow them no respite as long as it knows them to be alive. It pounces upon one and throws him to the ground like a log. Now the fiends fear for their lives, and there is not a man there whose heart does not rejoice. The demon who was dashed to the earth by the lion will never rise again if he is not rescued by the other. His companion ran over to bring him aid and to save himself, so the lion would not charge him once it had killed the demon it had already thrown to the ground. Indeed he was much more afraid of the lion than of its master.

Once the demon turned his back Yvain, who could now see his bare neck exposed, would be a fool to let him live any longer, for he was fortunate to get such an opportunity. The fiend offered him his exposed neck and head, and Yvain struck him such a blow that he severed head from trunk so swiftly that he never knew it. Then Yvain quickly dismounted to rescue the demon held down by the lion, for he intended to release and spare him. But to no avail: the lion in its wrath had so wounded him in its attack that he was hideously disfigured and was by now so far gone that no doctor could arrive in time to save him: When Yvain drove back the lion, he saw that it had ripped the demon's shoulder from its place. Yvain had no more reason to fear him, for his club had fallen to the ground and he lay there like a corpse, without moving or twitching.

But he was still able to speak and said with what little strength he had: 'Please call off your lion, good sir, so he'll harm me no more; from this moment on you may do with me whatever you wish. Only a man without pity would refuse to show mercy to another who's begged and pleaded for it. I will defend myself no longer; since I'll never rise from here by my own strength, I place myself in your power.'

'Say then,' said Yvain, 'whether you acknowledge that you are vanquished and defeated?'

'Sir,' he said, 'it is obvious: I am vanquished in spite of myself, and I acknowledge that I'm defeated.'

'Then you have no need to fear either myself or my lion.'

Immediately all the people ran up and gathered around Yvain. Both the lord and lady embraced the knight in their great joy and spoke to him of their daughter, saying: 'Now you will be lord and master over us all, and our daughter will be your lady, for we shall give her to you to be your wife.'

'And I,' he replied, 'return her to you. Let whoever wants her have her! I don't want her, but I am not saying this out of disdain: don't be upset if I don't take her, for I cannot and must not do so. However, if you please, release to me the captives you are holding; you are well aware that it is time for them to be set free.'

'What you say is true,' the lord answered, 'and I release them to you, for there is no longer anything to prevent it. But you would be wise also to accept my daughter with all my possessions, for she is beautiful, rich, and sensible. You will never make a better marriage than this one!'

'Sir,' said Yvain, 'you are unaware of my difficulties and my duties, and I don't dare explain them to you; but rest assured that, although I refuse what no one would refuse who was able to devote his heart and mind to a fair and lovely maiden, I would gladly take her if I could or should take her or any other. Yet I cannot—and this is the truth—so leave me in peace because this other damsel who came here with me awaits me now. She has kept me company, and I wish now to go with her, no matter what the future may bring me.'

'You wish to leave, good sir? But how? Unless it meets with my approval and I order it, my gate will never be opened for you; you will remain my prisoner here instead. You are mistaken and arrogant when you disdain my daughter, whom I have begged you to accept.'

'Disdain, sir? Indeed not, upon my soul; but I cannot marry any woman nor remain here, whatever the penalty. I must follow the damsel who is leading me, for it cannot be otherwise. But, if it please you, with my right hand I will swear, and you must believe me, that if I am able I will return just as you see me here now and take your daughter's hand at whatever time you think appropriate.'

'Cursed be anyone,' he said, 'who would require an oath or pledge or promise! If my daughter pleases you, you'll return soon enough; no oath or vow, I believe, would make you come back sooner. Go now, for I absolve you of all pledges and promises. If you are detained by rain and wind, or by nothing at all, it doesn't matter to me! I will never hold my daughter so cheap that I would force her upon you. Now go about your business, for it makes no difference to me whether you return or stay away.'

Immediately my lord Yvain turned away and remained no longer in the town. He took away with him the captives who had been released; although the lord delivered them poorly and shabbily garbed to him, it seemed to them now that they were rich. Two by two they all left the town, walking before my lord Yvain; I don't believe they would have expressed any more joy for this world's Creator, had He come from heaven to earth, than they showed for Yvain. All these people who had insulted him before in every way they could imagine now came to beg his forgiveness; they walked beside him pleading for mercy, but he insisted he didn't understand: 'I don't know what you're talking about,' he said, 'so I bear no grudge against you, for I cannot remember that you ever said anything that would have hurt me.'

Everyone rejoiced at what they heard, and praised him greatly for his courtliness. When they had accompanied him a long while, they all commended him to God and begged his leave. The damsels, too, took their leave and as they did so they all bowed low before him, praying that God would grant him happiness and health and let him fulfil his desires wherever he might go.

And he, who was troubled by the delay, asked God to watch over them: 'Go,' he said, 'and may God bring you safe and happy into your own lands.'

They went on their way at once, rejoicing greatly on their departure.

And my lord Yvain immediately set off in the opposite direction.

[Perceval in the Castle of the Fisher King] from *The Story of the Grail (Perceval)*

The Holy Grail makes its first appearance in Chrétien's The Story of the Grail, *left unfinished when the poet died in the 1190s. Nobody knows where Chrétien found his story. He claims in his prologue to have been given a book called* The Story of the Grail *by Count Philip of Flanders, the cousin of Marie of Champagne, with orders to "put into rhyme the greatest story that has ever been told in royal court." Wherever he first heard the tale, if it isn't his own creation, he loosed on the western world an enigmatic symbol that has fueled hundreds of poems, novels, operas, and films that explore the many possible meanings of the Grail. The story is actually about the young Perceval, raised by his mother in the wilds of Wales so that he has no contact with the chivalry that killed her husband and other sons. When Perceval becomes entranced by some of Arthur's passing knights, he abandons his mother (who collapses at their parting) and seeks experience and adventure. Among his adventures (playing mainly on his inordinate strength and his rustic naiveté) is his chance encounter with a mysterious Fisher King in whose castle Perceval sees a Grail procession but fails to ask about its meaning.*

The passage included here introduces Chrétien's gral *into the story for the first time, and it is interesting to note what is* not *there. Although it is associated with ethereal light, the Grail is only "a grail," with no suggestion that it is the cup or chalice of later tradition. When a hermit who is actually Perceval's uncle later explains the experience to him, he says that the grail delivers sustenance to a wounded king; but "do not imagine he is served pike or lamprey or salmon," for the grail delivers a single communion wafer. So Chrétien's* gral *is something like a fish platter. Within a few years, Chrétien's unfinished story attracted four different continuations, and in other new versions the grail quickly became,*

The translation is by William Kibler, in Chrétien's *Arthurian Romances* (London: Penguin Books, 1991).

in turn, a philosopher's stone sent from heaven, a cup used by Jesus at the Last Supper, a dish used to capture some of his blood while on the cross, and a communion chalice in which the bread and wine visibly become the body and blood of Christ. Before long, even Perceval was not good enough to be the Grail knight, and the perfect Galahad was invented to undertake the Grail Quest.

The mysteries of the Grail have never ceased, but two works particularly have spurred international revivals of interest in Grail traditions. The first was Richard Wagner's opera Parsifal, *first performed in 1882 at his Festspielhaus in Bayreuth. In this influential work the bleeding spear is nearly as important as the Grail, which is a chalice carried in procession during communal liturgies. The deep spiritual associations Wagner invested in his Grail, partly through the music itself, as well as the later "adoption" of this music drama and its notion of the Grail's power by Hitler and the Nazis, contributed to its almost religious status in the twentieth century.*

Second was Dan Brown's Da Vinci Code *(2003), a best-selling thriller that exposed to popular consciousness a number of recent (and not so recent) conspiracy theories: that the Grail represents the bloodline of Jesus preserved in western Europe, that the Grail is actually the bones or remains of Mary Magdalene (Jesus's wife!), that the Grail is a secret preserved in documents smuggled by the Templars out of the Temple in Jerusalem during the Crusades, and so on. The great variety of these theories and interpretations simply proves the suggestive power of Chrétien's imaginative invention of "the greatest story that has ever been told in royal court."*

So he rode along the bank until he neared a large boulder sitting in the water and blocking his path. Then he caught sight of a boat drifting down-river with two men in it. He stopped and waited, thinking they would eventually come as far as where he was. But they both stopped in midstream and stayed perfectly still, for they were anchored fast. The man in front was fishing with a line, baiting his hook with a little fish, somewhat larger than a minnow.

The knight, not knowing what to do or how to cross, greeted them and inquired: 'Tell me, my lords, if there is a ford or bridge across this river.'

And the one who was fishing replied: 'Not at all, brother, upon my word; nor is there a boat, I assure you, larger than the one we're in, which would not hold five men. There's no way to get a horse across, for there's no ferry, bridge, or ford for twenty leagues upstream or down.'

'Then tell me, in God's name, where I can find lodgings.'

And he replied: 'You'll need that and more, I believe. I'll give you lodging tonight. Go up through that cleft cut into the rock, and when you reach the top you'll see in a valley before you a house where I live, near the river and woods.'

The young knight climbed until he reached the top of the hill; and when he was at the top he looked all around him and saw only sky and earth, and said: 'What have I come for? Deceit and trickery! May God bring shame today on him who sent me here. He sent me on a wild goose chase when he told me I'd see a house when I came up here! Fisherman, you did me great dishonour when you told me this, if you said it out of malice!'

Then, in a valley before him, he caught sight of the top of a tower. From there to Beirut you could not find a finer or better situated one. It was square in construction, of dark stone, with two turrets flanking it. The hall was in front of the keep, and the galleries in front of the hall. The youth headed down in that direction, exclaiming now that the man who had sent him there had guided him well. And so he praised the fisherman and no longer called him deceitful, disloyal, or lying, since now he had found lodgings. He rode towards the gate, before which he discovered a lowered drawbridge. He crossed over the bridge and four squires hastened towards him: two of them helped him remove his armour, the third took charge of his horse and gave it hay and oats, while the fourth robed him in a fresh, new mantle of scarlet. Then they took him towards the galleries, which I assure you were more splendid than any that could be sought out or seen from here to Limoges. The youth waited in the galleries until the lord of the castle sent two squires there to summon him, and he accompanied them into the great hall, which was square in shape—as long as it was wide.

In the middle of the hall he saw a handsome nobleman with greying hair seated upon a bed. His head was covered by a cap of sable—black as mulberry, with a purple peak—and his robe was of the same material. He was leaning on his elbow before a very large fire of dry logs, blazing brightly between four columns. Four hundred men could easily sit around that fire, and each would have a comfortable spot. A tall, thick, broad, brass chimney was supported by those strong columns. The two squires who were escorting his guest came before their lord, flanking him on either side.

When the lord saw him approaching he greeted him at once, saying: 'Friend, don't be offended if I don't rise to greet you, for it is not easy for me to do so.'

'In God's name, sire,' he replied, 'say no more, for I am not at all offended, as God gives me health and happiness.'

To do his guest honour, the gentleman rose as much as he was able, and said: 'Friend, come over here and don't be frightened of me; sit down confidently at my side, for so I command you.' The youth sat down beside him and the nobleman continued: 'Friend, where did you come from today?'

'Sire,' he said, 'this morning I left Biaurepaire, so the place is called.'

'So help me God,' said the nobleman, 'you've ridden a great distance today. You must have set off this morning before the watchman sounded the dawn.'

'No,' said the youth, 'I assure you that the hour of prime had already been sounded.'

As they were conversing in this way, a squire entered by the door. He was carrying a sword hanging by straps from his neck; he handed it to the noble lord, who unsheathed it halfway so that it could clearly be seen where it had been made, for it was engraved upon the blade. He also saw that it was made of such good steel that it could not be broken except in one singularly perilous circumstance known only to him who had forged and tempered it.

The squire who had brought it said: 'Sire, your niece, the beautiful maiden with the blonde tresses, sent you this gift; you can never have beheld a finer sword, in its length and weight, than this one here. You may bestow it upon whomsoever you choose; but my lady would be most pleased if it were given to someone who would use it well, for the man who forged it made only three and he will die before being able to make another sword after this one.'

Immediately, the lord invested the stranger among them with the sword by placing its straps, a great treasure in themselves, over his shoulders. The sword's pommel was of gold, the finest in Arabia or Greece; its scabbard was the work of a Venetian goldsmith. The lord gave it to him in all its splendour and said: 'Good brother, this sword was ordained and destined for you, and I am eager for you to have it. Put it on now and draw it.'

He thanked him and strapped it on loosely, then drew it shining from its scabbard; after he had held it for a moment he replaced it in its scabbard. I assure you it was magnificent at his side and even better in his grip, and it was obvious that in time of need he would wield it bravely. Behind him he saw squires standing around the blazing fire: he caught sight of the one in charge of his armour and handed him the sword to keep. Then he sat down again beside the lord, who paid him every honour. Within that hall the light from the burning candles was as bright as could be found in any castle.

As they were speaking of one thing and another, a squire came forth from a chamber carrying a white lance by the middle of its shaft; he passed between the fire and those seated upon the bed. Everyone in the hall saw the white lance with its white point from whose tip there issued a drop of blood, and this red drop flowed down to the squire's hand. The youth who had come there that night observed this marvel but refrained from asking how it came about, for he recalled the admonishment given by the gentleman who had knighted him, who taught and instructed him not to talk too much; he was afraid that if he asked they would consider him uncouth, and therefore he did not ask.

Then two other squires entered holding in their hands candelabra of pure gold, crafted with enamel inlays. The young men carrying the candelabra were extremely handsome. In each of the candelabra there were at least ten candles burning. A maiden accompanying the two young men was carrying a grail with her two hands; she was beautiful, noble, and richly attired. After she had entered the hall carrying the grail the room was so brightly illumined that the candles lost their brilliance like stars and the moon when the sun rises. After her came another maiden, carrying a silver carving platter. The grail, which was introduced first, was of fine pure gold. Set in the grail were precious stones of many kinds, the best and costliest to be found in earth or sea: the grail's stones were finer than any others in the world, without any doubt. The grail passed by like the lance; they passed in front of the bed and into another chamber. The young knight watched them pass by but did not dare ask who was served from the grail, for in his heart he always held the wise gentleman's advice. Yet I fear that this may be to his misfortune, for I have heard it said that at times it is just as wrong to keep too silent as to talk too much. Whether for good or for ill he did not ask or inquire anything of them.

The lord of the castle ordered his squire to bring water and to prepare the tablecloths. Those whose duty it was did these things as they were accustomed. The lord and his young guest washed their hands in warm water, and two squires carried in a broad ivory table: as the story relates, it was entirely made of a single piece. They held it a moment before their lord and the youth, until two other squires came bearing two trestles. The wood of the supports had two excellent qualities: the trestles would last for ever since they were of ebony, a wood that no one need fear would ever rot or burn, for ebony will do neither. The table was placed upon these supports, with the tablecloth over it. What could I say about the cloth? No pope, cardinal, or papal legate ever ate off one so white.

The first course was a haunch of venison cooked in its fat with hot pepper. They were not short of clear, strong wine, which could be drunk easily from golden goblets. Before them a squire carved the haunch of peppered venison, which he had brought within his reach upon its silver carving platter, and he placed the pieces before them on whole loaves of flat bread. Meanwhile the grail passed again in front of them, and again the youth did not ask who was served from the grail. He held back because the gentleman had so gently admonished him not to talk too much, and he kept this warning constantly to heart. But he kept more silent than he should have, because with each course that was served he saw the grail pass by completely uncovered before him. But he did not learn who was served from it, though he wanted to know; he said to himself that he would be sure to ask one of the court squires before he left there, but would wait until he was taking leave of the lord and all the rest of his household in the morning. So the question was put off, and he set his mind to drinking and eating. The wine and food were delicious and agreeable, and were served at table in generous portions. The meal was excellent and good: the nobleman was served that evening with food fit for a king, count or emperor, and the young knight with him.

After the meal the two stayed a long while in conversation. As squires were preparing the beds, baskets of all the finest fruits were served them: dates, figs and nutmeg, cloves and pomegranates, and electuaries for dessert, with Alexandrian gingerbread, pliris and arcoticum, resontif and stomaticum. Afterwards they drank many a drink, sweet wine without honey or pepper, good mulberry wine, and clear syrup.

The youth was astonished by all this, for he had never experienced anything like it; and the nobleman said to him: 'Friend, now it is time for bed. Don't be offended if I leave you and go into my own chambers to sleep; and whenever you are ready you may lie down out here. I have no strength in my body and will have to be carried.'

Four strong and nimble servants promptly came out from a chamber, seized by its four corners the coverlet that was spread over the bed on which the nobleman was lying, and carried it to where they were ordered. Other squires remained with the youth to serve him, and saw to his every need. When he requested, they removed his shoes and clothing and bedded him down in fine, white, linen sheets.

And he slept until morning, when dawn had broken and the household was awake. But he saw no one there when he looked around and so he had to get up alone, although it bothered him to do so. Seeing he had no choice he arose, for there was nothing else to do, and pulled on his shoes without help; then he went to don his armour, which he found at the head of the dais, where it had been left for him. After having armed himself fully, he approached the doors of chambers he had observed open the night before; but his steps were wasted, for he found them tightly closed. He shouted and knocked for a long while: no one opened them or gave a word in reply. After having shouted a long while, he tried the door to the great hall; finding it open, he went down the steps, where he discovered his horse saddled and saw his lance and shield leaning against the wall. He mounted and rode all around, but he found none of the servants and saw no squire or serving boy. So he went straight to the gate and found the drawbridge lowered; it had been left like that so that nothing might prevent him from traversing it unimpeded whenever he came there. When he found the bridge lowered, he thought that perhaps the squires had gone into the forest to check the traps and snares. He made up his mind to set off at once in pursuit, to see whether any of them would explain to him why the lance bled (if it were possible for him to know) and tell him to where the grail was carried.

Then he rode off through the gate, but before he had crossed the bridge he felt it drawing up under the hooves of his horse; but the horse made a great leap, and if he had not done so both horse and rider would have come to grief. The youth turned around to see what had happened and saw that the drawbridge had been raised; he shouted out, but no one answered.

'Say there,' he said, 'whoever raised the bridge, speak to me! Where are you that I can't see you? Come forward where I can see you and ask you about something I want to know.'

But he made a fool of himself shouting like this, for no one would reply. Then he headed for the forest and found a path on which he discovered fresh hoofprints of horses that recently had passed by.

'This makes me think,' he said to himself, 'that those I'm seeking passed this way.'

He rode swiftly through the forest following the tracks as far as they went, until he saw by chance beneath an oak tree a maiden crying, weeping, and lamenting, as though she were a woman in great distress. 'Wretched me!' she exclaimed. 'I was born in an evil hour! Cursed be the hour I was begotten and the day I was born, for I've never before been made so miserable by anything! So help me God, I shouldn't have to hold my dead lover in my arms; it would have been far better if he were alive and I were dead! Why did Death, which tortures me, take his soul instead of mine? When I behold lying dead the one I most love what is life to me? With him dead, indeed I have no interest in my life or body. So come, Death, and take my soul and let it be a servant and companion to his, if he'll deign to accept it.'

Her grief was caused by a knight she held in her arms, whose head had been cut off. The youth, after catching sight of her, rode right up to where she sat. As he came before her he greeted her and she, with head still lowered and without ceasing her lament, returned his salutation.

And the youth asked her: 'My lady, who has slain this knight lying in your lap?'

'Good sir,' said the maiden, 'a knight killed him just this morning. But your appearing here is truly remarkable: as God is my witness, they say that one could ride for twenty-five leagues in the direction from which you have come without finding a good, honest, and proper lodging place. Yet your horse's belly is so full and his coat so shining that he couldn't appear more satisfied or his coat smoother had he been washed and combed and given a bed of hay and oats. And it appears to me that you yourself have had a comfortable and restful night.'

'Upon my word,' he said, 'I was as comfortable as I could possibly be, and it's only right that it should show. If you were to shout out loudly from this spot, it could easily be heard at the place where I slept last night. You must not know this country well or have travelled through all of it, for without a doubt I had the best lodgings I've ever enjoyed.'

'Ah, my lord! Did you sleep then in the castle of the noble Fisher King?'

'Maiden, by our Lord and Saviour, I don't know if he is a fisherman or a king, but he is most noble and courteous. All I can tell you is that late last night I came upon two men, sitting in a boat rowing slowly along. One of the men was rowing while the other was fishing with a hook, and this latter showed me the way to his house last night and gave me lodging.'

And the maiden said: 'Good sir, I can assure you that he is a king, but he was wounded and maimed in the course of a battle so that he can no longer manage on his own, for he was struck by a javelin through both thighs and is still in so much pain that he cannot ride a horse. Whenever he wants to relax or to go out to enjoy himself, he has himself put in a boat and goes fishing with a hook: this is why he's called the Fisher King. And he relaxes in this way because he cannot tolerate the pain of any other diversion: he cannot hunt for flesh or fowl, but he has hunters, archers, and gamesmen who hunt his forests for him. That is why he likes to stay in this hidden retreat, for there's no retreat in the world more suited to his needs, and he has had a mansion built that is worthy of a noble king.'

'My lady,' he said, 'what you say is true, upon my word, for I was in awe last night as soon as I was brought before him. I kept back a little distance from him, and he told me to be seated beside him and not to consider him too proud for not rising to greet me, since he didn't have the means or strength. And I went to sit beside him.'

'Indeed he did you a great honour by having you sit beside him. And as you were sitting beside him, tell me whether you saw the lance with the tip that bleeds, though it has neither blood nor veins.'

'Yes, upon my word, I did see it!'

'And did you ask why it bled?'

'I never spoke a word.'

'So help me God, let me tell you then that you have done ill. And did you see the grail?'

'Quite clearly.'

'Who carried it?'

'A maiden.'

'Where did she come from?'

'From a chamber.'

'And where did she go?'

'She entered another chamber.'

'Did anyone precede the grail?'

'Yes.'

'Who?'

'Only two squires.'

'And what were they holding in their hands?'

'Candelabra full of candles.'

'And who came after the grail?'

'Another maiden.'

'What was she holding?'

'A small silver carving platter.'

'Did you ask the people where they were going in this manner?'

'No question came from my mouth.'

'So help me God, now it's even worse! What is your name, friend?'

And the youth, who did not know his name, guessed and said he was called Perceval the Welshman. But although he did not know if that were true or not, he spoke the truth without knowing it. And when the damsel heard him, she stood up before him and said as in anger: 'Your name is changed, fair friend!'

'To what?'

'Perceval the wretched! Ah, unlucky Perceval, how unfortunate you were when you failed to ask all this, because you would have brought great succour to the good king who is maimed: he would have totally regained the use of his limbs and ruled his lands, and much good would have come of it! But understand this now: much suffering will befall you and others. And understand, too, that it came upon you because you sinned against your mother, who has died of grief on your account. I know you better than you do me, for you do not know who I am. I was raised with you for many years in your mother's house; I am your first cousin and you are mine. Your failure to have asked what is done with the grail and where it is carried is just as painful to me as your mother's death or the death of this knight whom I loved and held dear, who called me his dearest friend and loved me like a good and faithful knight.'

'Ah, cousin,' said Perceval, 'if what you say is true, tell me how you know it.'

'I know it,' said the damsel, 'as truly as one who saw her buried in the ground.'

'May God in His goodness have mercy on her soul!' said Perceval.

The Saga of the Volsungs

The Saga of the Volsungs *is an Icelandic tale based on a much older body of Norse and Germanic legends, stories, and myths. The nameless author of the saga wrote it down in the thirteenth century, probably between 1200 and 1270. At about the same time, around 1200, a writer in Germany composed a more courtly—and now better known—epic,* The Nibelungenlied, *drawing on the same body of materials. The Icelandic version is altogether more primitive, cutting closer in its first half to the related mythical poems in the Viking age* Elder Edda.

This first half, from which the selection here is drawn, tells of the memorable hero Sigurd the Dragon-Slayer, who gained the Rhinegold, refashioned the broken sword, slew the dragon Fafnir and drank its blood, and is finally entangled in a bloody web of deceit, rivalry, murder, and revenge. This tale, rediscovered in the nineteenth century, was translated into modern German in 1815; it became the basis for Richard Wagner's cycle of four operas, Der Ring des Nibelungs, *which in spite of the title and the hero's name (Siegfried) owes most of its inspiration to the* Volsunga Saga *and not to the* Nibelungenlied. *In 1870 the saga was translated into English by William Morris, a member of the influential artists and craftsmen of the Pre-Raphaelite Brotherhood. Morris also composed his own poems based on the stories and characters. Morris's works in turn influenced J. R. R. Tolkien, who in 1914 used some prize money to purchase Morris's translation of the* Volsunga Saga. *Tolkien's world of Hobbits, Elves, Dwarves, and cursed Rings draws vibrant energy from the Scandinavian saga.*

The last half of the saga is less mythological and bases most of its characters on historical persons and events of the great period of migrations in the fourth and fifth centuries—the Huns, the Goths, and the Burgundians. In fact, Atli, in whose court the final slaughter in the work takes place, is actually Attila the Hun, remembered by students more as a name to conjure with than as a shaper of the European heritage.

The translation is an old classic by Eirikr Magnusson and William Morris (London: Norroena Society, 1907).

[Sigurd and the Dragon]
Regin's Tale of His Brothers, and of the Gold Called Andvari's Hoard

"Thus the tale begins," said Regin. "Hreidmar was my father's name, a mighty man and a wealthy: and his first son was named Fafnir, his second Otter, and I was the third, and the least of them all both of prowess and good conditions, but I was cunning to work in iron, and silver and gold, whereof I could make matters that availed somewhat. Other skill my brother Otter followed, and had another nature withal, for he was a great fisher, and above other men herein; in that he had the likeness of an otter by day, and dwelt ever in the river, and bare fish to bank in his mouth, and his prey would he ever bring to our father, and that availed him much; for the most part he kept him in his otter-gear, and then he would come home, and eat alone, and slumbering, for on the dry land he might see naught. But Fafnir was by far the greatest and grimmest, and would have all things about called his.

"Now," says Regin, "there was a dwarf called Andvari, who ever abode in that force, which was called Andvari's force, in the likeness of a pike, and got meat for himself, for many fish there were in the force; now Otter, my brother, was ever wont to enter into the force, and bring fish aland, and lay them one by one on the bank. And so it befell that Odin, Loki, and Hœnir, as they went their ways, came to Andvari's force, and Otter had taken a salmon, and ate it slumbering upon the river bank; then Loki took a stone and cast it at Otter, so that he gat his death thereby; the gods were well content with their prey, and fell to flaying off the otter's skin; and in the evening they came to Hreidmar's house, and showed him what they had taken: thereupon he laid hands on them, and doomed them to such ransom, as that they should fill the otter skin with gold, and cover it over without with red gold; so they sent Loki to gather gold together for them; he came to Ran, and got her net, and went therewith to Andvari's force, and cast the net before the pike, and the pike ran into the net and was taken. Then said Loki—

"'What fish of all fishes,
 Swims strong in the flood,
But hath learnt little wit to beware?
 Thine head must thou buy,
 From abiding in hell,
And find me the wan waters flame.'

He answered—

"'Andvari folk call me,
 Call Oinn my father,
Over many a force have I fared;
 For a Norn of ill-luck,
 This life on me lay
Through wet ways ever to wade.'

"So Loki beheld the gold of Andvari, and when he had given up the gold, he had but one ring left, and that also Loki took from him; then the dwarf went into a hollow of the rocks, and cried out, that that gold-ring, yea and all the gold withal, should be the bane of every man who should own it thereafter.

"Now the gods rode with the treasure to Hreidmar, and fulfilled the otter-skin, and set it on its feet, and they must cover it over utterly with gold: but when this was done then Hreidmar came forth, and beheld yet one of the muzzle hairs, and bade them cover that withal; then Odin drew the ring, Andvari's loom, from his hand, and covered up the hair therewith; then sang Loki—

"'Gold enow, gold enow,
A great weregild, thou hast,
That my head in good hap I may hold;
But thou and thy son
Are naught fated to thrive,
The bane shall it be of you both.'

"Thereafter," says Regin, "Fafnir slew his father and murdered him, nor got I aught of the treasure, and so evil he grew, that he fell to lying abroad, and begrudged any share in the wealth to any man, and so became the worst of all worms, and ever now lies brooding upon that treasure: but for me, I went to the king and became his master-smith; and thus is the tale told of how I lost the heritage of my father, and the weregild for my brother."

So spake Regin; but since that time gold is called Ottergild, and for no other cause than this.

But Sigurd answered, "Much hast thou lost, and exceeding evil have thy kinsmen been! but now, make a sword by thy craft, such a sword as that none can be made like unto it; so that I may do great deeds therewith, if my heart avail thereto, and thou wouldst have me slay this mighty dragon."

Regin says, "Trust me well herein; and with that same sword shalt thou slay Fafnir."

OF THE WELDING TOGETHER OF THE SHARDS OF THE SWORD GRAM

So Regin makes a sword, and gives it into Sigurd's hands. He took the sword, and said—

"Behold thy smithying, Regin!" and therewith smote it into the anvil, and the sword brake; so he cast down the brand, and bade him forge a better.

Then Regin forged another sword, and brought it to Sigurd, who looked thereon.

Then said Regin, "Belike thou art well content therewith, hard master though thou be in smithying."

So Sigurd proved the sword, and brake it even as the first; then he said to Regin—

"Ah, art thou, mayhappen, a traitor and a liar like to those former kin of thine?"

Therewith he went to his mother, and she welcomed him in seemly wise, and they talked and drank together.

Then spake Sigurd, "Have I heard aright, that King Sigmund gave thee the good sword Gram in two pieces?"

"True enough," she said.

So Sigurd said, "Deliver them into my hands, for I would have them."

She said he looked like to win great fame, and gave him the sword. Therewith went Sigurd to Regin, and bade him make a good sword thereof as he best might; Regin grew wroth thereat, but went into the smithy with the pieces of the sword, thinking well meanwhile that Sigurd pushed his head far enow into the matter of smithying. So he made a sword, and as he bore it forth from the forge, it seemed to the smiths as though fire burned along the edges thereof. Now he bade Sigurd take the sword, and said he knew not how to make a sword if this one failed. Then Sigurd smote it into the anvil, and cleft it down to the stock thereof, and neither burst the sword nor brake it. Then he praised the sword much, and thereafter went to the river with a lock of wool, and threw it up against the stream, and it fell asunder when it met the sword. Then was Sigurd glad, and went home.

But Regis said, "Now whereas I have made the sword for thee, belike thou wilt hold to thy troth given, and wilt go meet Fafnir?"

"Surely will I hold thereto," said Sigurd, "yet first must I avenge my father."

Now Sigurd the older he grew, the more he grew in the love of all men, so that every child loved him well.

The Prophecy of Grifir

There was a man hight Grifir (Gripir), who was Sigurd's mother's brother, and a little after the forging of the sword Sigurd went to Grifir, because he was a man who knew things to come, and what was fated to men: of him Sigurd asked diligently how his life should go; but Grifir was long or he spake, yet at the last, by reason of Sigurd's exceeding great prayers, he told him all his life and the fate thereof, even as afterwards came to pass. So when Grifir had told him all even as he would, he went back home; and a little after he and Regin met.

Then said Regin, "Go thou and slay Fafnir, even as thou has given thy word."

Sigurd said, "That work shall be wrought; but another is first to be done, the avenging of Sigmund the king and the other of my kinsmen who fell in that their last fight."

Of Sigurd's Avenging of Sigmund His Father

Now Sigurd went to the kings, and spake thus—

"Here have I abode a space with you, and I owe you thanks and reward, for great love and many gifts and all due honour; but now will I away from the land and go meet the sons of Hunding, and do them to wit that the Volsungs are not all dead; and your might would I have to strengthen me therein."

So the kings said they would give him all things soever that he desired, and therewith was a great army got ready, and all things wrought in the most heedful wise, ships and all war-gear, so that his journey might be of the stateliest: but Sigurd himself steered the dragon-keel which was the greatest and noblest; richly wrought were their sails, and glorious to look on.

So they sail and have wind at will; but when a few days were overpast, there arose a great storm on the sea, and the waves were to behold even as the foam of men's blood; but Sigurd bade take in no sail, howsoever they might be riven, but rather to lay on higher than heretofore. But as they sailed past the rocks of a ness, a certain man hailed the ships, and asked who was captain over that navy; then was it told him that the chief and lord was Sigurd, the son of Sigmund, the most famed of all the young men who now are.

Then said the man, "Naught but one thing, certes, do all say of him, that none among the sons of kings may be likened unto him; now fain were I that ye would shorten sail on some of the ships, and take me aboard."

Then they asked him of his name, and he sang—

Hnikar I hight,
When gladdened Huginn,
And went to battle,
Bright son of Volsung;
Now may ye call
The carl on the cliff top,
Feng or Fjolnir:
Fain would I with you.

They made for land therewith, and took that man aboard.

Then the storm abated, and on they fared till they came aland in the realm of Hunding's sons, and then Fjolnir vanished away.

Then they let loose fire and sword, and slew men and burnt their abodes, and did waste all before them: a great company of folk fled before the face of them to Lyngi the King, and tell him that men of war are in the land, and are faring with such rage and fury that the like has never been heard of; and that the sons of King Hunding had no great forecast in that they said they would never fear the Volsungs more, for here was come Sigurd, the son of Sigmund, as captain over this army.

So King Lyngi let send the war-message all throughout his realm, and has no will to flee, but summons to him all such as would give him aid. So he came against Sigurd with a great army, he and his brothers with him, and an exceeding fierce fight befell; many a spear and many an arrow might men see there raised aloft, axes hard driven, shields cleft and byrnies torn, helmets were shivered, skulls split atwain, and many a man felled to the cold earth.

And now when the fight has long dured in such wise, Sigurd goes forth before the banners, and has the good sword Gram in his hand, and smites down both men and horses, and goes through the thickest of the throng with both arms red with blood to the shoulder; and folk shrank aback before him wheresoever he went, nor would either helm or byrny hold before him, and no man deemed he had ever seen his like. So a long while the battle lasted, and many a man was slain, and furious was the onset; till at last it befell, even as seldom comes to hand, when a land army falls on, that, do whatso they might, naught was brought about; but so many men fell of the sons of Hunding that the tale of them may not be told; and now whenas Sigurd was among the foremost, came the sons of Hunding against him, and Sigurd smote therewith at Lyngi the king, and clave him down both helm and head, and mail-clad body, and thereafter he smote Hjorward his brother atwain, and then slew all the other sons of Hunding who were yet alive, and the more part of their folk withal.

Now home goes Sigurd with fair victory won, and plenteous wealth and great honour, which he had gotten to him in this journey, and feasts were made for him against he came back to the realm.

But when Sigurd had been at home but a little, came Regin to talk with him, and said—

"Belike thou wilt now have good will to bow down Fafnir's crest according to thy word plighted, since thou hast thus revenged thy father and the others of thy kin."

Sigurd answered, "That will we hold to, even as we have promised, nor did it ever fall from our memory."

Of the Slaying of the Worm Fafnir

Now Sigurd and Regin ride up the heath along that same way wherein Fafnir was wont to creep when he fared to the water; and folk say that thirty fathoms was the height of that cliff along which he lay when he drank of the water below. Then Sigurd spake:

"How sayedst thou, Regin, that this dragon was no greater than other lingworms; methinks the track of him is marvellous great?"

Then said Regin, "Make thee a hole, and sit down therein, and whenas the worm comes to the water, smite him into the heart, and so do him to death, and win for thee great fame thereby."

But Sigurd said, "What will betide me if I be before the blood of the worm?"

Says Regin, "Of what avail to counsel thee if thou art still afraid of everything? Little are thou like thy kin in stoutness of heart."

Then Sigurd rides right over the heath; but Regin gets him gone, sore afraid.

But Sigurd fell to digging him a pit, and whiles he was at that work, there came to him an old man with a long beard, and asked what he wrought there, and he told him.

Then answered the old man and said, "Thou doest after sorry counsel: rather dig thee many pits, and let the blood run therein; but sit thee down in one thereof, and so thrust the worm's heart through."

And therewithal he vanished away; but Sigurd made the pits even as it was shown to him.

Now crept the worm down to his place of watering, and the earth shook all about him, and he snorted forth fire and venom on all the way before him as he went; but Sigurd neither trembled nor was afraid at the roaring of him. So whenas the worm crept over the pits, Sigurd thrust his sword under his left shoulder, so that it sank in up to the hilt; then up leapt Sigurd from the pit and drew the sword back again unto him, and therewith was his arm all bloody, up to the very shoulder.

Now when that mighty worm was ware that he had his death-wound, then he lashed out head and tail, so that all things soever that were before him were broken to pieces.

So wheneas Fafnir had his death-wound, he asked "Who art thou? and who is thy father? and what thy kin, that thou wert so hardy as to bear weapons against me?"

Sigurd answered, "Unknown to men is my kin. I am called a noble beast: neither father have I nor mother, and all alone have I fared hither."

Said Fafnir, "Whereas thou has neither father nor mother, of what wonder wert thou born then? But now, though thou tellest me not thy name on this my death-day, yet thou knowest verily that thou liest unto me."

He answered, "Sigurd am I called, and my father was Sigmund."

Says Fafnir, "Who egged thee on to this deed, and why wouldst thou be driven to it? Hast thou never heard how that all folk were afraid of me, and of the awe of my countenance? But an eager father thou hadst, O bright-eyed swain!"

Sigurd answered, "A hardy heart urged me on hereto; and a strong hand and this sharp sword, which well thou knowest now, stood me in stead in the doing of the deed; *Seldom hath hardy eld a faint-heart youth*."

Fafnir said, "Well, I wot that hadst thou waxed amid thy kind, thou mightest have good skill to slay folk in thine anger; but more of a marvel is it, that thou, a bondsman taken in war, shouldst have the heart to set on me, *for few among bondsmen have heart for the fight*."

Said Sigurd, "Wilt thou then cast it in my teeth that I am far away from my kin? Albeit I was a bondsman, yet was I never shackled. God wot thou hast found me free enow."

Fafnir answered, "In angry wise dost thou take my speech; but hearken, for that same gold which I have owned shall be thy bane too."

Quoth Sigurd, "Fain would we keep all our wealth till that day of days; yet shall each man die once for all."

Said Fafnir, "Few things wilt thou do after my counsel; but take heed that thou shalt be drowned if thou farest unwarily over the sea; so abide thou rather on the dry land, for the coming of the calm tide."

Then said Sigurd, "Speak, Fafnir, and say, if thou art so exceeding wise, who are the Norns who rule the lot of all mothers' sons."

Fafnir answers, "Many there be and wide apart; for some are the kin of the Æsir, and some are of Elfin kin, and some there are who are daughters of Dvalin."

Said Sigurd, "How namest thou the holm whereon Surt and the Æsir mix and mingle the water of the sword?"

"Unshapen is that holm hight," said Fafnir.

And yet again he said, "Regin, my brother, has brought about my end, and it gladdens my heart that thine too he bringeth about; for thus will things be according to his will."

And once again he spake, "A countenance of terror I bore up before all folk, after that I brooded over the heritage of my brother, and on every side did I spout out poison, so that none durst come anigh me, and of no weapon was I afraid, nor ever had I so many men before me, as that I deemed myself not stronger than all; for all men were sore afraid of me."

Sigurd answered and said, "Few may have victory by means of that same countenance of terror, for whoso comes amongst many shall one day find that no one man is by so far the mightiest of all."

Then says Fafnir, "Such counsel I give thee, that thou take thy horse and ride away at thy speediest, for ofttimes it falls out so, that he who gets a death-wound avenges himself none the less."

Sigurd answered, "Such as thy redes are I will nowise do after them; nay, I will ride now to thy lair and take to me that great treasure of thy kin."

"Ride there then," said Fafnir, "and thou shalt find gold enow to suffice thee for all thy life-days; yet shall that gold be thy bane, and the bane of every one soever who owns it."

Then up stood Sigurd, and said, "Home would I ride and lose all that wealth, if I deemed that by the losing thereof I should never die; but every brave and true man will fain have his hand on wealth till that last day; but thou, Fafnir, wallow in the death-pain till Death and Hell have thee."

And therewithal Fafnir died.

Of the Slaying of Regin, Son of Hreidmar

Thereafter came Regin to Sigurd, and said, "Hail, lord and master, a noble victory hast thou won in the slaying of Fafnir, whereas none durst heretofore abide in the path of him; and now shall this deed of fame be of renown while the world stands fast."

Then stood Regin staring on the earth a long while, and presently thereafter spake from heavy mood: "Mine own brother hast thou slain, and scarce may I be called sackless of the deed."

Then Sigurd took his sword Gram and dried it on the earth, and spake to Regin—

"Afar thou faredst when I wrought this deed and tried this sharp sword with the hand and the might of me; with all the might and main of a dragon must I strive, while thou wert laid alow in the heather-bush, wotting not if it were earth or heaven."

Said Regin, "Long might this worm have lain in his lair, if the sharp sword I forged with my hand had not been good at need to thee; had that not been, neither thou nor any man would have prevailed against him as at this time."

Sigurd answers, "Whenas men meet foes in fight, better is stout heart than sharp sword."

Then said Regin, exceeding heavily, "Thou hast slain my brother, and scarce may I be sackless of the deed."

Therewith Sigurd cut out the heart of the worm with the sword called Ridil; but Regin drank of Fafnir's blood, and spake, "Grant me a boon, and do a thing little for thee to do. Bear the heart to the fire, and roast it, and give me thereof to eat."

Then Sigurd went his ways and roasted it on a rod; and when the blood bubbled out he laid his finger thereon to essay it, if it were fully done; and then he set his finger in his mouth, and lo, when the heart-blood of the worm touched his tongue, straightway he knew the voice of all fowls, and heard withal how the wood-peckers chattered in the brake beside him—

"There sittest thou, Sigurd, roasting Fafnir's heart for another, that thou shouldest eat thine ownself, and then thou shouldest become the wisest of all men."

And another spake: "There lies Regin, minded to beguile the man who trusts in him."

But yet again said the third, "Let him smite the head from off him then, and be only lord of all that gold."

And once more the fourth spake and said, "Ah, the wiser were he if he followed after that good counsel, and rode thereafter to Fafnir's lair, and took to him that mighty treasure that lieth there, and then rode over Hindfell, whereas sleeps Brynhild; for there would he get great wisdom. Ah, wise he were, if he did after your redes, and bethought him of his own weal; *for where wolf's ears are, wolf's teeth are near.*"

Then cried the fifth: "Yea, yea, not so wise is he as I deem him, if he spareth him, whose brother he hath slain already."

At last spake the sixth: "Handy and good rede to slay him, and be lord of the treasure!"

Then said Sigurd, "The time is unborn wherein Regin shall be my bane; nay, rather one road shall both these brothers fare."

And therewith he drew his sword Gram and struck off Regin's head.

Then heard Sigurd the wood-peckers a-singing, even as the song says.

Then Sigurd ate some deal of Fafnir's heart, and the remnant he kept. Then he leapt on his horse and rode along the trail of the worm Fafnir, and so right unto his abiding-place; and he found it open, and beheld all the doors and the gear of them that they were wrought of iron; yea, and all the beams of the house; and it was dug down deep into the earth: there found Sigurd gold exceeding plenteous, and the sword Rotti; and thence he took the Helm of Awe, and the Gold Byrny, and many things fair and good. So much gold he found there, that he thought verily that scarce might two horses, or three belike, bear it thence. So he took all the gold and laid it in two great chests, and set them on the horse Grani, and took the reins of him, but nowise will he stir, neither will he abide smiting. Then Sigurd knows the mind of the horse, and leaps on the back of him, and smites and spurs into him, and off the horse goes even as if he were unladen.

MAGNA CARTA (1215)

One of the central political documents of the Middle Ages is the "Great Charter," by which King John of England submitted to the demands of his hostile barons. The charter was, in fact, a practical and focused contract aimed at addressing the grievances of the land barons, grievances that had been building for many years and that exposed a nearly continuous difficulty in the feudal system. From the time of the Norman Conquest (1066) English nobility (transplanted Normans, after all) had large holdings in the north of France. John's father, King Henry II, had married Eleanor of Aquitaine and gained for England lands in western France that were greater than those held by the French king (Eleanor's first husband). In addition, these Plantagenet kings were, for practical purposes, French at heart. When John's brother Richard became King Richard I ("the Lion-Hearted") at age 32, he had been in England only twice and, during his reign as king, spent only a few months in England. Instead, while he was off fighting against Saladin in the Third Crusade, he supported his adventures by taxing his feudal barons severely, as they thought. In addition, the barons had to end his imprisonment at the hands of the Holy Roman Emperor by paying a huge ransom (see Richard's song among the Medieval Lyrics *in this collection). So, when Richard was followed in kingship by his less popular brother John, the landed barons of England were already resentful. In conflicts with the Pope, John managed to be excommunicated and have the entire realm barred from worship and the sacraments. Struggles with the French, begun under Richard, yielded the loss of Normandy, and the barons, in open revolt against the crown, forced John to agree to a set of remedies.*

Although the clauses of the Magna Carta *are addressed to particular thirteenth-century grievances, embedded in the language (Latin in the original copies disbursed throughout the realm) are principles that became the basis of English freedoms later enshrined in the American Constitution and the Bill of Rights. Central to these is chapter 39, which requires that each accused person be tried according to the "law of the land," which became in the next century the important notion of "due process of the law" (as in the Fifth and Fourteenth Amendments to our Constitution). Other chapters require that*

The translation from Latin from which these selections are taken is by William Sharp McKechnie (rev. 1914), from *Source Problems in English History*, ed. Albert Beebe White and Wallace Notestein. New York: Harper and Brothers, 1915.

courts be held in specific places, that local crimes be tried locally, that the punishments should fit the crimes, that accusations must be substantiated to be acted upon, that an accused person shall not be cut off from his means of living—all of these abiding principles in our constitutional law. And, whatever it may have meant in the thirteenth century, the leveling language of equality throughout, as in the final clause ("the men in our kingdom have and hold all the aforesaid liberties, rights, and concessions, well and peaceably, freely and quietly, fully and wholly, for themselves and their heirs*"), certainly seeped, however slowly, into the western consciousness, underpinning the declarations of human rights of later centuries.*

John, by the grace of God, king of England, lord of Ireland, duke of Normandy and Aquitaine, and count of Anjou, to the archbishops, bishops, abbots, earls, barons, justiciars, foresters, sheriffs, stewards, servants, and to all his bailiffs and liege subjects, greeting. Know that, having regard to God and for the salvation of our soul, and those of all our ancestors and heirs, and unto the honor of God and the advancement of holy church, and for the reform of our realm, by advice of our venerable fathers, Stephen archbishop of Canterbury, primate of all England and cardinal of the holy Roman Church, Henry archbishop of Dublin, . . . and others, our liegemen.

1. In the first place we have granted to God, and by this our present charter confirmed for us and our heirs for ever that the English church shall be free, and shall have her rights entire, and her liberties inviolate; and we will that it be thus observed; which is apparent from this that the freedom of elections, which is reckoned most important and very essential to the English church, we, of our pure and unconstrained will, did grant, and did by our charter confirm and did obtain the ratification of the same from our lord, Pope Innocent III., before the quarrel arose between us and our barons: and this we will observe, and our will is that it be observed in good faith by our heirs for ever. We have also granted to all freemen of our kingdom, for us and our heirs for ever, all the underwritten liberties, to be had and held by them and their heirs, of us and our heirs for ever.

2. If any of our earls or barons, or others holding of us in chief by military service shall have died, and at the time of his death his heir shall be of full age and owe "relief" he shall have his inheritance on payment of the ancient relief, namely the heir or heirs of an earl, £100 for a whole earl's barony; the heir or heirs of a baron, £100 for a whole barony; the heir or heirs of a knight, 100*s.* at most for a whole knight's fee; and whoever owes less let him give less, according to the ancient custom of fiefs.

7. A widow, after the death of her husband, shall forthwith and without difficulty have her marriage portion and inheritance; nor shall she give anything for her dower, or for her marriage portion, or for the inheritance which her husband and she held on the day of the death of that husband; and she may remain in the house of her husband for forty days after his death, within which time her dower shall be assigned to her.

8. No widow shall be compelled to marry, so long as she prefers to live without a husband; provided always that she gives security not to marry without our consent, if she holds of us, or without the consent of the lord of whom she holds, if she holds of another.

9. Neither we nor our bailiffs shall seize any land or rent for any debt, so long as the chattels of the debtor are sufficient to repay the debt; nor shall the sureties of the debtor be distrained so long as the principal debtor is able to satisfy the debt; and if the principal debtor shall fail to pay the debt, having nothing wherewith to pay it, then the sureties shall answer for the debt; and let them have the lands and rents of the debtor, if they desire them, until they are indemnified for the debt which they have paid for him, unless the principal debtor can show proof that he is discharged thereof as against the said sureties.

10. If one who has borrowed from the Jews any sum, great or small, die before that loan can be repaid, the debt shall not bear interest while the heir is under age, of whomsoever he may hold; and if the debt fall into our hands, we will not take anything except the principal sum contained in the bond.

11. And if any one die indebted to the Jews, his wife shall have her dower and pay nothing of that debt; and if any children of the deceased are left under age, necessaries shall be provided for them in keeping with the holding of the deceased; and out of the residue the debt shall be paid, reserving, however, service due to feudal lords; in like manner let it be done touching debts due to others than Jews.

12. No scutage ["knight's fee"] nor aid shall be imposed on our kingdom, unless by common counsel of our kingdom, except for ransoming our person, for making our eldest son a knight, and for once marrying our eldest daughter; and for these there shall not be levied more than a reasonable aid. In like manner it shall be done concerning aids from the city of London.

13. And the city of London shall have all its ancient liberties and free customs, as well by land as by water; furthermore, we decree and grant that all other cities, boroughs, towns, and ports shall have all their liberties and free customs.

17. Common pleas shall not follow our court, but shall be held in some fixed place.

20. A freeman shall not be amerced ["fined"] for a slight offense, except in accordance with the degree of the offense; and for a grave offense he shall be amerced in accordance with the gravity of the offense, yet saving always his "contenement"; and a merchant in the same way, saving his "merchandise"; and a villein shall be amerced in the same way, saving his "wainage"—if they have fallen into our mercy: and none of the aforesaid amercements shall be imposed except by the oath of honest men of the neighborhood.

21. Earls and barons shall not be amerced except through their peers, and only in accordance with the degree of the offense.

28. No constable or other bailiff of ours shall take corn or other provisions from any one without immediately tendering money therefor, unless he can have postponement thereof by permission of the seller.

29. No constable shall compel any knight to give money in lieu of castle-guard, when he is willing to perform it in his own person, or (if he cannot do it from any reasonable cause) then by another responsible man. Further, if we have led or sent him upon military service, he shall be relieved from guard in proportion to the time during which he has been on service because of us.

30. No sheriff or bailiff of ours, or other person, shall take the horses or carts of any freeman for transport duty, against the will of the said freeman.

31. Neither we nor our bailiffs shall take, for our castles or for any other work of ours, wood which is not ours, against the will of the owner of that wood.

35. Let there be one measure of wine throughout our whole realm; and one measure of ale; and one measure of corn, to wit, "the London quarter"; and one width of cloth (whether dyed, or russet, or "halberget"), to wit, two ells within the selvages; of weights also let it be as of measures.

38. No bailiff for the future shall, upon his own unsupported complaint, put any one to his "law," without credible witnesses brought for this purpose.

39. No freeman shall be taken or imprisoned or disseised ["dispossessed"] or exiled or in any way destroyed, nor will we go upon him nor send upon him, except by the lawful judgment of his peers or by the law of the land.

40. To no one will we sell, to no one will we refuse or delay, right or justice.

42. It shall be lawful in future for any one (excepting always those imprisoned or outlawed in accordance with the law of the kingdom, and natives of any country at war with us, and merchants, who shall be treated as is above provided) to leave our kingdom and to return, safe and secure by land and water, except for a short period in time of war, on grounds of public policy—reserving always the allegiance due to us.

45. We will appoint as justices, constables, sheriffs, or bailiffs only such as know the law of the realm and mean to observe it well.

46. All barons who have founded abbeys, concerning which they hold charters from the kings of England, or of which they have long-continued possession, shall have the wardship of them, when vacant, as they ought to have.

52. If any one has been dispossessed or removed by us, without the legal judgment of his peers, from his lands, castles, franchises, or from his right, we will immediately restore them to him; and if a dispute arise over this, then let it be decided by the five-and-twenty barons of whom mention is made below in the clause for securing the peace. Moreover, for all those possessions, from which any one has, without the lawful judgment of his peers, been disseised or removed, by our father, King Henry, or by our brother, King Richard, and which we retain in our hand (or which are possessed by others, to whom we are bound to warrant them) we shall have respite until the usual term of crusaders; excepting those things about which a plea has been raised, or an inquest made by our order, before our taking of the cross; but as soon as we return from our expedition (or if perchance we desist from the expedition) we will immediately grant full justice therein.

54. No one shall be arrested or imprisoned upon the appeal of a woman, for the death of any other than her husband.

61. Since, moreover, for God and the amendment of our kingdom and for the better allaying of the quarrel that has arisen between us and our barons, we have granted all these concessions, desirous that they should enjoy them in complete and firm endurance for ever, we give and grant to them the underwritten security, namely, that the barons choose five-and-twenty barons of the kingdom, whomsoever they will, who shall be bound with all their might, to observe and hold, and cause to be observed, the peace and liberties we have granted and confirmed to them by this our present Charter, so that if we, or our justiciar, or our bailiffs or any one of our officers, shall in anything be at fault toward any one, or shall have broken any one of the articles of the peace or of this security, and the offense be notified to four barons of the

foresaid five-and-twenty, the said four barons shall repair to us (or our justiciar, if we are out of the realm) and, laying the transgression before us, petition to have that transgression redressed without delay. And if we shall not have corrected the transgression (or, in the event of our being out of the realm, if our justiciar shall not have corrected it) within forty days, reckoning from the time it has been intimated to us (or to our justiciar, if we should be out of the realm), the four barons aforesaid shall refer that matter to the rest of the five-and-twenty barons, and those five-and-twenty barons shall, together with the community of the whole land, distrain and distress us in all possible ways, namely, by seizing our castles, lands, possessions, and in any other way they can, until redress has been obtained as they deem fit, saving harmless our own person, and the persons of our queen and children; and when redress has been obtained, they shall resume their old relations toward us. And let whoever in the country desires it, swear to obey the orders of the said five-and-twenty barons for the execution of all the aforesaid matters, and along with them, to molest us to the utmost of his power; and we publicly and freely grant leave to every one who wishes to swear, and we shall never forbid any one to swear. All those, moreover, in the land who of themselves and of their own accord are unwilling to swear to the twenty-five to help them in constraining and molesting us, we shall by our command compel the same to swear to the effect foresaid. . . .

62. And all the ill-will, hatreds, and bitterness that have arisen between us and our men, clergy and lay, from the date of the quarrel, we have completely remitted and pardoned to every one. Moreover, all trespasses occasioned by the said quarrel, from Easter in the sixteenth year of our reign till the restoration of peace, we have fully remitted to all, both clergy and laymen, and completely forgiven, as far as pertains to us. . . .

63. Wherefore it is our will, and we firmly enjoin, that the English Church be free, and that the men in our kingdom have and hold all the aforesaid liberties, rights, and concessions, well and peaceably, freely and quietly, fully and wholly, for themselves and their heirs, of us and our heirs, in all respects and in all places for ever, as is aforesaid. An oath, moreover, has been taken, as well on our part as on the part of the barons, that all these conditions aforesaid shall be kept in good faith and without evil intent. Given under our hand—the above-named and many others being witnesses—in the meadow which is called Runnymede, between Windsor and Staines, on the fifteenth day of June, in the seventeenth year of our reign.

Guillaume de Lorris (fl. 1225–1230) and Jean de Meun (d. 1305)

The Romance of the Rose

Along with Boethius's Consolation of Philosophy, *the* Roman de la Rose *commanded the best-seller lists of the late Middle Ages. It survives in several hundred manuscripts and was known by important later writers. Geoffrey Chaucer, in his poem* The Legend of Good Women, *shows himself assigned as penance to write about "good" women by the God of Love because "Thow hast translated the Romauns of the Rose, / That is an heresye ageyns my lawe." The poem is certainly among the masterpieces exploring the meaning of "courtly love," both as a code for living and as a stylish game of language.*

Like Andreas Capellanus's Art of Courtly Love, *the* Romance of the Rose *is one of those strange works that seems to contradict itself, taking away with one hand what it gave with the other. The first part of the* Romance, *some 4,000 lines written about 1230 by Guillaume de Lorris, is an elaborate and stylized allegorical description of a seduction. The lover ("Amans") enters the Garden of Pleasure, spies a delightful rosebush reflected in the Spring of Narcissus, and sets about trying to pluck the rose flower, hindered or encouraged by a host of allegorical characters representing physical and psychological forces. The poem takes the action, if it can be called that, right up to the point of "deflowering" without quite "going all the way," and it is possible that Guillaume considered the poem completed where he left it.*

Nevertheless, many readers considered it unfinished and, in medieval fashion, the poem soon found a conclusion. About 1275 the cleric Jean de Meun, himself a translator of Boethius, added an ending: nearly 18,000 lines worth of verse that finally show the lover penetrating the defenses of the object of his desire, now transformed allegorically into a fortified tower that must be besieged. Along the way, Jean explores love from every angle, offering an encyclopedic elaboration of clerical attitudes toward women, sex, friendship, and desire, as well as a survey of science and cosmology, psychology, and human nature. He does this through long speeches delivered by his main characters, particularly Reason (whose speech is nearly as long as the whole of Guillaume's original poem), Nature, and Genius (Nature's confessor). Reason, on the one hand, and Nature and Genius, on the other, engage in an extensive and encyclopedic debate about sexuality and marriage,

This translation of the Old French verse into modern English prose is by Frances Horgan (New York: Oxford World's Classics, 1994).

spiced up with contributions from the cynical and worldly-wise Old Woman (the source of Chaucer's Wife of Bath).

As with the Art of Courtly Love, *the perspective of the poem is decidedly masculine, and Jean de Meun, particularly, relishes trading in all the medieval stereotypes about women. So widely read and influential was the poem that by 1400 a debate raged about the poem's moral stance. The writer Christine de Pizan (1365-c.1430) joined an exchange of letters about the poem, attacking Jean de Meun's "excessive, violent, and totally unfounded criticism, denigration, and defamation of women, insofar as he claims that they are guilty of many a terrible vice and that their behavior is perverse in every conceivable way." If women are as weak and inconstant as "some clerks would have us believe," she says in another letter, "why don't women quickly succumb . . . without the need for all this skill and ingenuity in conquering them?" (trans. Karen Pratt and cited in* Woman Defamed and Woman Defended, *ed. Alcuin Blamires; Oxford: Clarendon Press, 1992: pp. 286-287, 282)*

Guillaume de Lorris: [The Garden of Pleasure]

Some say that there is nothing in dreams but lies and fables; however, one may have dreams which are not in the least deceitful, but which later become clear. In support of this fact, I can cite an author named Macrobius, who did not consider that dreams deceived, but wrote of the vision that came to King Scipio. Whoever thinks or says that it is foolish or stupid to believe that a dream may come true, let him think me mad if he likes; for my part I am confident that a dream may signify the good and ill that may befall people, for many people dream many things secretly, at night, which are later seen openly.

In my twentieth year, at the time when Love claims his tribute from young men, 21
I lay down one night, as usual, and fell fast asleep. As I slept, I had a most beautiful and pleasing dream, but there was nothing in the dream that has not come true, exactly as the dream told it. Now I should like to recount that dream in verse, the better to delight your hearts, for Love begs and commands me to do so. And if any man or woman should ask what I wish this romance, which I now begin, to be called, it is the *Romance of the Rose*, in which the whole art of love is contained. The matter is fair and new; God grant that she for whom I have undertaken it may receive it with pleasure. She it is who is so precious and so worthy of being loved that she ought to be called Rose.

It seemed to me that it was May, five years ago or more; I dreamed that it was 45
May, the season of love and joy, when everything rejoices, for one sees neither bush nor hedge that would not deck itself for May in a covering of new leaves. The woods, which are dry all winter long, regain their greenness; the very earth glories in the dew that waters it, and forgets the poverty in which it has spent the whole winter; this is the time when the earth becomes so proud that it desires a new dress, and is able to make a dress so lovely that there are a hundred pairs of colours in it. The grass, and the flowers, which are white and blue and many different colours, these are the dress that I am describing, and in which the earth takes pride. The birds, silent during the

cold, harsh, and bitter weather, are so happy in the mild May weather, and their singing shows the joy in their hearts to be so great that they cannot help but sing. It is then that the nightingale strives to sing and make his noise, and the parrot and lark are glad and joyful; it is then that young men must seek love and merriment in the fair, mild weather. The man who does not love in May, when he hears the birds on the branches singing their sweet and touching songs, is hard of heart indeed. I dreamed one night that it was that delightful season, when everything is excited by love, and as I slept, it seemed to me that it was already broad daylight. I rose from my bed at once, put on my shoes and washed my hands, then took a silver needle from its dainty and charming case and began to thread it. I felt like going out of the town to hear the sound of birds singing among the bushes in this new season. Lacing up my sleeves, I set off alone, rejoicing and listening to the birds, who were singing with all their might because the gardens were coming into flower. . . .

When I had gone a little further, I saw a large and extensive garden, entirely surrounded by a high, crenellated wall, which was decorated on the outside with paintings and carved with many rich inscriptions.

. . . I could not possibly recount all the beauties and charms of the garden. I wandered to right and to left until I had seen the whole garden and explored all its features. And all this time the God of Love followed me, watching like the hunter, who waits until the animal is in a good position before loosing his arrow. I reached a most delightful spot, rather out of the way, where I came across a spring beneath a pine-tree. Never since Charlemagne or Pepin had such a handsome pine been seen, and it had grown so high that it was the tallest tree in the garden. Nature by her great skill had sent the water gushing from a marble stone beneath the pine, and had written in small letters around the upper edge of the stone that fair Narcissus had died there. Narcissus was a young man whom Love caught in his snares, and so tormented him and made him weep and groan that he must needs die. For Echo, a noble lady, had loved him more than any living thing, and was so distressed on his account that she said that she would die if he did not give her his love. But he was so haughty, so proud of his own beauty that he would not grant her his love in spite of her requests and prayers. When she heard him refuse her, her grief and anger were so great and she held him in such contempt that she died at once. But just before she died she asked and prayed God that hardhearted Narcissus, whom she had found so unwilling a lover, should one day be tortured and tormented by just such a love as hers, for which he could expect no cure; thus he who so basely refused loyal lovers might understand and realize how much they suffered. Since that prayer was reasonable, God granted it, for one day when Narcissus was returning from hunting, he happened to seek the shade of the pine by the clear, pure spring. He had followed the hunt uphill and down, and had endured such hardship that he was thirsty, for the heat was fierce and he was breathless with weariness. When he came to the spring shaded by the branches of the pine-tree he decided to drink there, and lay face down on the ground above the spring to drink from it. And so it was that he saw in the bright, clean water his own face, his nose and his mouth, and he was at once astounded, for his reflection had so deceived him that he imagined it to be the face of a wonderfully handsome youth. And then Love had his revenge for the proud, arrogant way in which Narcissus had treated him. He had his just reward then, for he lingered so long at the spring that he fell in love with his own reflection and finally died, and that is the end of the story.

For when he saw that he could not accomplish his desire, a desire which had so inexorably taken possession of him that he could in no way whatsoever be consoled, he swooned away for grief and soon died. And so he received his reward and his just deserts from the maiden whom he had earlier refused.

You ladies who behave badly to your lovers, learn from this example, for if you leave them to die, God will repay you. When I had discovered from the inscription that this was most certainly the spring of fair Narcissus, I withdrew a little, not daring to look into it, and began to feel afraid, remembering how badly Narcissus had fared. But I reflected that I could safely approach the spring without fear of ill fortune, and that it was foolish of me to retreat. I drew near to the spring and, on reaching it, bent down to see the running water and the gravel, brighter than fine silver, that seethed in its depths. All that can be said of the spring is that there was none so beautiful in all the world. The water is always cool and fresh, and gushes out day and night in great waves through two channels, bright and deep. Because of the water, the dense grass all around grows thick and strong, and cannot die in winter, just as the water cannot dry up or cease to flow. Down at the bottom of the spring were two crystals, which I gazed at most attentively. And I shall tell you something that will, I think, seem marvellous to you when you hear it. When the all-seeing sun sends down its rays into the spring, and light descends into its depths, more than a hundred colours appear in the crystal, which turns blue and yellow and red in the sunlight. The crystal is so marvellous and has such power that the whole place, with its trees and flowers and everything adorning the garden, is revealed there in due order. To help you understand the phenomenon I shall give you an illustration. Just as things placed in front of a mirror are reflected in it, and their appearance and colour are seen quite plainly, exactly so, I assure you, does the crystal truly disclose the whole of the garden to him who gazes into the water. For whichever side he is on, he can always see half of the garden, and by turning he is at once able to see the remainder. And so there is nothing so small, so secret, or so hidden that it is not displayed there, as if it were etched in the crystal.

This is the perilous mirror where proud Narcissus looked at his face and his 1569
bright eyes, and afterwards lay stretched out in death. Whoever looks at himself in this mirror can have no help or remedy against seeing something which promptly causes him to fall in love. This mirror has caused the deaths of many valiant men, for the wisest, the bravest, and the most experienced are all caught and ensnared here. Here new and violent feelings spring up in men, and their hearts are changed; here sense and moderation are of no use, and there is only the total will to love; here no one knows what to do, for Cupid, Venus' son, sowed here the seed of Love which covers the whole spring; here he set his nets and snares to trap young men and maidens, for Love wants no other birds. Because of the seed that was sown here, this spring was rightly called the Spring of Love, and many have spoken of it in many places, in books and romances. But you will never hear a better exposition of the truth of the matter, once I have explained the mystery.

I was happy then to linger, admiring the spring and the crystals which revealed 1601
to me a thousand things around me. But it was an evil hour when I looked at my reflection. Alas, how often I have since sighed about it! The mirror deceived me, and if I had known in advance what force and power it had, I would never have approached it, for at once I fell into the trap that has captured and betrayed many men.

1613 I perceived in the mirror, among a thousand other things, rose-bushes laden with roses in a secluded place completely enclosed by a hedge. Immediately I was seized with such desire that not for Pavia or Paris would I have failed to go to the place where I saw the greatest number of them. Possessed by this madness, as many others have been, I at once approached the rose-bushes, and I assure you that when I drew near, the sweet scent of the roses penetrated my very entrails and I was all but filled with their fragrance. If I had not imagined that I would be attacked or insulted, I would have plucked at least one and held it in my hand, savouring its scent. But I was afraid that I might repent my action, since it could easily have displeased the lord of the garden.

1635 There were roses in profusion, the most beautiful in all the world. There were buds, some tiny and closed up and others slightly larger, and some much larger ones which were coming into flower and were on the point of bursting. These buds are attractive, for wide-open roses have completely faded after a day, whereas buds stay fresh for at least two or three days. The buds pleased me greatly, for none finer grew anywhere. The man who could pluck one should cherish it greatly, and if I could have made a garland of them, there is nothing I would have loved so well. From among these buds I chose one so beautiful that when I had observed it carefully, all the others seemed worthless in comparison. It shone with colour, the purest vermilion that Nature could provide, and Nature's masterly hand had arranged its four pairs of leaves, one after the other. Its stem was as straight as a reed, and the bud was set on top in such a way that it neither bent nor drooped. The area around it was filled with its perfume, and the sweet scent that rose from it pervaded the whole place. When I became aware of this scent, I had no wish to depart, but drew nearer and would have plucked it had I dared stretch out my hands. But sharp, pointed thistles forced me to draw back, while barbed, keen-edged thorns and prickly nettles and brambles prevented me from advancing, for I was afraid of hurting myself.

1679 The God of Love, whose constant endeavour had been to watch and follow me with drawn bow, had stopped beneath a fig-tree; and when he observed that I had chosen that bud, which pleased me better than any of the others, he at once took an arrow. When the string was in the nock, he drew the bow, which was wonderfully strong, back to his ear, and loosed his arrow at me in such a way and with such force that the point entered my eye and penetrated my heart. Then I was seized with a chill which has often made me shiver since, even when wearing a warm, fur-lined cloak. When I had been thus shot, I immediately fell backwards. My heart was false and failed me and I lay for a long time in a swoon. When I recovered consciousness and came to my senses I was very weak and therefore imagined that I had lost a lot of blood. But the point that pierced me drew no blood at all, and the wound was quite dry. Then I took hold of the arrow with both hands and began to pull hard, sighing a great deal as I pulled. I pulled so hard that I drew out the flighted shaft, but the barbed point, which was named Beauty was so fixed in my heart that it could not be torn out; it remains there still, and yet the wound has never bled.

1719 I was in great trouble and torment, unable, on account of this double danger, to do or say anything or to find a physician for my wound, for no medicine could be expected from herb or root; instead my heart drew me towards the rose-bud, and desired nothing else. If I had had it in my possession, it would have given me back my life; the mere sight and scent of it brought me considerable relief from pain. . . .

On coming to my senses, I moaned and sighed, for my pain was growing worse 1829
and I had no hope of cure or relief. I would rather have been dead than alive, for in the end, I thought, I would become a martyr to Love, there was no other way out. Meanwhile he took another arrow, which he prized greatly and which I hold to be most wounding: it was Fair Seeming, which does not permit a lover to repent of serving Love, whatever he may feel. It is sharp and piercing and keen as a steel razor, but Love had thoroughly anointed its tip with precious ointment so that it would not hurt me too much, for Love did not want me to die, but rather to find relief through the application of the ointment, which was full of comfort. Love has made it with his own hands to comfort true lovers, and to soothe my hurts he shot this arrow at me, and made a great wound in my heart. The ointment spread through my wounds and gave me back my heart, which had failed me completely. I would have been dead and in a bad way had it not been for that sweet ointment. I quickly drew out the shaft, but the point, newly sharpened, remained within. Five arrowheads [Beauty, Simplicity, Courtesy, Company, Fair Seeming] were thus embedded and it will scarcely be possible to remove them. The ointment was very good for my wounds, yet the wound hurt me so much that the pain made me change colour. It is the strange property of this arrow to be both sweet and bitter. I felt and realized that it helped me, but it also hurt me; the point was painful although the unction brought relief. On the one hand it soothed, on the other it made me smart, and thus it both helped and harmed. Straightaway Love came towards me with rapid steps, crying as he came: 'Vassal, you are captured, there is no way to escape or defend yourself. Yield, and do not resist. The more willingly you surrender, the sooner you will find mercy. It is foolish to behave arrogantly towards one whom you should flatter and beseech. You cannot struggle against me, and I wish you to learn that wickedness and pride will avail you nothing. Surrender, since I wish it, peacefully and with good grace.'

Immediately I replied: 'In God's name, I give myself up willingly, and will never defend myself against you. . . .

'I have heard so much good of you that I wish to place my heart and body entirely at your service, for nothing can hurt me if I do your will. I will also, I think, receive at some time the mercy that I hope for, and under these conditions I surrender.'

Thereupon I joined my hands and became his liegeman, and you may be sure 1953
that I was very proud when his mouth kissed mine: it was this that gave me the greatest joy. Then he asked me for sureties: 'My friend,' he said, 'I have received the homage of many men who have since disappointed me. These false traitors have often deceived me, and I have heard many complaints about them, but they shall know how much they have grieved me. If I can get them into my power, I will make them pay dearly. Now because I love you, I wish to be so certain of you and bind you to me so closely that you are unable to be false to your promise and agreement, or to commit any wrong act. It would be a crime for you to cheat, for you seem to me to be fair-minded.'

'Sir,' I said, 'now hear me. I do not know why you are asking me for pledges and securities. You know for certain that you have so stolen and taken my heart that, even if it wished to, it could do nothing for me unless you permitted it. My heart is yours and not my own, for it must do your will, for good or ill, and no one can take it from you. You have set a guard about it which guards it very diligently and if, in spite of all this, you fear anything, make a key for it and take it with you; it will serve instead of sureties.'

'By my head,' replied Love, 'that is not unreasonable, and I accept. He who commands the heart has sufficient power over the body, and would be unreasonable if he asked for more.' Then he took from his purse a beautifully made little key of purest gold. 'With this', he said, 'I will lock your heart, and I ask no other guarantee. My jewels are under this key, and I promise you on my soul that it is mistress of my jewel-case and thus has very great power.' Then he touched my side and locked my heart so gently that I could scarcely feel the key.

'Sir,' I said, 'by God's grace, give me your commandments before you depart from here. I am encouraged to perform them, but I would perhaps soon go astray if I did not know [them].'

Anyone who wishes to make Love his master must be courteous and free from pride, elegant and light-hearted and esteemed for his generosity.

2221 'Next I will give you a penance; it is that day and night, without backsliding, you should fix your thoughts on love. Think of it always and unceasingly, and remember the sweet hour whose joy remains with you. In order that you might be a true lover, it is my wish and my command that your whole heart may be set in a single place, and that it should not be divided, but whole and entire, without deceit, for I do not like sharing. Whoever divides his heart between many places leaves a poor part of it everywhere, but I have no fear for him who sets his whole heart in one place, and I therefore wish you to do so. But take care that you do not lend it, for if you had lent it, I would consider that you had behaved unworthily. By giving it freely and absolutely you will win greater merit, for when something is lent, the favour is soon returned and the debt discharged, whereas the reward for something given as a gift must be great. Therefore give it absolutely and graciously, for something given with a good grace should be greatly cherished, whereas I do not give a fig for a gift unwillingly given.

2253 'When you have given your heart as I have exhorted you, things will befall you that are hard and painful for lovers. Often, when you remember your love, you will perforce have to leave the company of other people, lest they notice the pain that torments you. You will withdraw by yourself, apart from the rest, and then you will sigh and lament and tremble and suffer many other pains. You will endure many sorts of distress, being sometimes hot and sometimes cold, sometimes flushed and sometimes pale; no quartan or quotidian fever was ever so bad. Before you leave that place, you will have experienced fully all the pains of love. Another time it will happen that you lose yourself in your thoughts and remain for a long time like a dumb image, still and motionless, without moving foot or hand, finger or eye, and without speaking. At last you will come to your senses, quivering with agitation as you do so, like a man afraid, and you will sigh from the depths of your heart; know, then, that this is the behaviour of those who have experienced those pains which so terrify you now.

JEAN DE MEUN: [THE ADVICE OF REASON]

As I thus bewailed the great sufferings that I endured, and knew not where to seek a healer for my frantic grief, I saw the fair and charming Reason, who had come down from her tower on hearing my lamentations, coming straight towards me once again.

'Fair friend,' said lovely Reason, 'How is this case progressing? Are you now 4199
weary of loving? Have you not suffered enough? What do you think now of the torments of love? Are they too sweet or too bitter? Can you now choose from among them the happy medium that will be sufficient to support you? Was it a good lord you served who thus captured and enslaved you and torments you incessantly? It was an unhappy day for you when you did him homage, and you were foolish to get involved. Doubtless you did not know what lord you were dealing with, for if you had known him well you would never have become his man, or if you had done, you would not have served him for a single summer, or even for a day or an hour. On the contrary, I believe that you would without delay have renounced the homage you did him and would never have loved *par amour*. Have you any knowledge of him?'

'Yes, lady.'

'You do not.'

'Yes I do.'

'How, by your soul?'

'From the fact that he said to me: "You should be very glad that you have so good a master and so renowned a lord." '

'Have you any other knowledge of him?'

'No, except that he gave me his commandments and then fled away more swiftly than an eagle, while I remained in trouble.'

'That is poor knowledge indeed. But I want you to know him now, for you have 4232
drunk so deeply of his bitterness that you are quite warped. No unhappy, miserable wretch could bear a greater burden. It is good to know one's lord, and if you knew this one well you could easily escape from the duress in which you languish.'

'In truth, lady, since he is my lord and I his liegeman, heart and soul, my heart would be very glad to hear and learn more about him, if there were anyone to teach it.'

'By my head, I am glad to teach you, since your heart wants to hear. Now I shall soberly demonstrate to you something that is not demonstrable, and you will soon know without knowledge and understand without understanding that which cannot be known or demonstrated or understood. This is in order that any man who fixes his heart on love should know more about it, although his suffering will not be lessened as a result unless he wishes to flee from love. Then I shall have untied for you the knot that you will always find tied. Now pay close attention, for this is the description of love.

'Love is hostile peace and loving hatred, disloyal loyalty and loyal disloyalty; it is 4263
confident fear and desperate hope, demented reason and reasonable madness. It is the sweet danger of drowning and a heavy burden that is easy to handle; it is perilous Charybdis, disagreeable and gracious at the same time; it is a most healthful sickness and a most sickly health; a hunger abundantly satisfied and a covetous affluence, a thirst that is always drunk, an intoxication drunk with thirst. It is a false delight, a joyful sorrow and an unhappy joy, a sweet torment and an unkind sweetness, a taste

at once pleasant and distasteful; it is a sin touched by pardon and a pardon tainted by sin, a most joyful suffering and a merciful cruelty. It is an ever-shifting game, a state which is very firm but also very changeable, an infirm strength and a strong infirmity that sets everything in motion through its efforts, a foolish sense and a wise folly, a sad and joyful prosperity; it is laughter that sobs and weeps, repose that toils unceasingly, a hell that soothes and a heaven that tortures, a prison that offers relief to prisoners, a cold and wintry spring-time. It is a moth that refuses nothing and consumes purple and homespun alike, for lovemaking is no better in fine clothes than in homespun. No one has been found who is so highly born, so wise, of such proven strength or courage, or so virtuous in other respects that Love has not conquered him. The whole world treads that path, for he is the god who leads everyone astray except those excommunicated by Genius because their evil ways are an offence against Nature. I am not concerned with these, however, but I do not want people to love in such a way, to be so maddened by Love that in the end they admit themselves to be unhappy and sorrowful wretches. But if you really want to avoid being hurt by Love and to be cured of this madness, you cannot drink a better draught than the thought of fleeing from him. This is the only way you can be happy: if you follow him, he will follow you, and if you flee him he will flee away.'

4329 When I had listened carefully to Reason, who had exerted herself in vain, I said: 'Lady, for my part I declare that I know no better than before how to detach myself from Love. There are so many contradictions in this lesson that I can learn nothing from it.

'Although I can recite it by heart, since my heart has forgotten none of it, and can understand it well enough to give a public lecture on the subject, to me alone it means nothing. But since you have described love to me, both praising and condemning it to such an extent, I would beg you to define it in such a way that I can better remember it, for I have never heard a definition of it.'

'Gladly, now pay attention. Love, if my judgement is correct, is a mental illness afflicting two persons of opposite sex in close proximity who are both free agents. It comes upon people through a burning desire, born of disordered perception, to embrace and to kiss and to seek carnal gratification. A lover is concerned with nothing else but is filled with this ardent delight. He attaches no importance to procreation, but strives only for pleasure. There are people of such a kind that they do not care for this love; nevertheless, they pretend to be true lovers while disdaining to love *par amour*, and they make fools of ladies, promising them their bodies and souls and swearing false and deceitful oaths to those whom they are able to deceive, until they have had their pleasure. But these are the least deceived, for it is always better, fair master, to deceive than to be deceived, especially in this war in which they cannot seek a compromise. But I know well, and this is no conjecture, that anyone who lies with a woman should wish to the best of his ability to perpetuate his divine essence and to preserve himself in a creature like himself (for all men are subject to decay), so that the succession of generations should not fail. For since fathers and mothers pass away, Nature wants their children to spring up to continue this work, so that one is replaced by another. Therefore Nature made the work pleasurable, desiring that it should be so delightful that the workmen should not take to their heels or hate it, for there are many who would never perform this task unless they were attracted by pleasure.

'Thus Nature used her ingenuity. You should know that no one can love as he 4391
ought or with the right intentions if he desires only delight. Do you know what he does, the man who seeks delight? He surrenders, a wretched and foolish slave, to the prince of all the vices. . . .

'Now since our discourse on love has led us to Fortune, I should like to tell you 4807
of a most wondrous thing, the like of which I do not believe you will ever have heard. I do not know if you will be able to believe it, but it is true nevertheless and found in books. It is that people benefit and profit more from Fortune when she is perverse and unfavourable than when she is gentle and gracious. And if this seems doubtful to you, it can be proved by argument, for when Fortune is gracious and gentle, she lies to people and deceives them into madness, suckling them like a mother who does not appear to be harsh. She pretends to be true to them when she gives them her jewels, which are honours and wealth, dignities and high offices, and, placing them on her wheel, she promises them stability where all is changeable, and feeds them all with vainglory in their worldly prosperity. Then they imagine themselves to be so exalted and their state to be so secure that they could never fall from it. When she has established them in this condition, she makes them believe that they have so many friends that they can neither count them all nor be free of them, for they are always coming and going around them, making lords of them and promising to serve them; indeed they are ready to lose the shirts on their backs and to spill their blood in order to protect and defend them, and they are prepared to follow and obey them all the days of their lives. Those who hear such words glory in them and believe them as they would the Gospel, but it is all flattery and deception, as they would later discover if they had lost all their goods with no prospect of recovery. Then they would see their friends in action, for if out of one hundred ostensible friends, whether companions or relatives, they were left with one, then they should praise God for it. When this Fortune whom I have described makes her home with men, she confuses their understanding and nurtures them in ignorance.

'But when she is unfavourable and perverse, topples them from their high estates 4863
and with a turn of her wheel tumbles them from the summit down into the mud; when, like a cruel stepmother, she sticks a painful plaster to their hearts, moistened not with vinegar but with thin and wretched poverty, then she shows that she is sincere and that no one should trust Fortune's favour, for it is utterly unreliable. When men have lost their wealth, she makes them know and understand the kind of love felt for them by their former friends, for friends bestowed upon them by good fortune are so dazed by misfortune that they all become enemies and not one, not even half a one, remains. They all run away and disown them as soon as they see that they are poor, nor do they stop there, but criticize and slander them everywhere they go, and call them wretched fools. Even those whom they most helped when they were men of high estate go around cheerfully swearing that they are well aware of their folly; they find not a single one to aid them. But their true friends remain to them, those whose hearts are so noble that they do not love for the sake of wealth or with any expectation of gain. These aid and defend them, for Fortune has no stake in them. A friend loves for ever. A man is not cut off from his friend's love, not even if he draws his sword upon him, except in the circumstances that I will now describe: such love is lost by pride and anger, by reproaches, by the disclosure of secrets that ought to be concealed, and by the painful wound of venomous detraction. In these

circumstances a friend would take flight; nothing else could harm the friendship. But such friends are worth a great deal if but a single one is found among a thousand. And since no wealth can compare with the value of a friend or attain such heights that the worth of a friend would not be greater, then a friend on the road is always worth more than money in one's belt. And when Fortune falls unfavourably on men, this adversity makes them all see so clearly that they discover their friends and prove by experiment that they are worth more than any wealth the world could offer them. Thus adversity is of more use to them than prosperity, for from prosperity comes ignorance and from adversity knowledge.

4931 'As for the poor man who has thus proved which friends are true and which false and now knows them and can distinguish between them, when he was as rich as he could desire and everyone offered him their hearts and bodies and everything they had for ever, what would he not then have paid for the knowledge he has now? He would have been less deceived if he had realized it then. Thus the misfortune that he now receives, in turning him from a fool into a wise man, brings him greater profit than the wealth that deceives.

'Wealth does not enrich the man who locks it up in treasure; a simple competence allows a man to live richly, for a man not worth two loaves may be wealthier and more comfortable than one who has a hundred barrels of grain, and I can tell you why. The latter may perhaps be a merchant whose heart is so wretched that he has suffered great torments before amassing his pile, and continues to fret about increasing and multiplying it, for he will never have enough, however much he manages to acquire. But the other, who relies only on having enough to live on for the day, is satisfied with what he earns and lives on his income. He imagines that he lacks for nothing and although he has not a halfpenny, he sees that he will earn enough to eat when the need arises, and to buy shoes and suitable clothes. Or if he happens to fall ill and finds his food tasteless, he reflects that in any case he will not need to eat in order to get off this unpleasant path and out of danger, or that a little nourishment will be sufficient come what may, or again that he will be taken to the *hôtel-Dieu*, where he will be well looked after. Perhaps he does not think that he will ever get into such a state, or if he believes that it might happen to him, he thinks that he will have saved up enough before he falls ill to deal with the situation when it arises. If he cares nothing about saving against the time when cold or heat or hunger might cause his death, perhaps he comforts himself with the thought that the sooner he dies, the sooner he will go to heaven, for he believes that God will grant him paradise when he leaves this present exile. (Pythagoras himself tells you, if you have read that book of his that we call *Golden Verses* on account of its honoured sayings: "When you have left the body, you will mount freely into the blessedness of the upper air, leaving humanity behind and living in pure deity." He is a wretched and stupid fool who believes that this is his country: your country is not on earth, as you can learn from the clerks who explain Boethius' *Consolation* and the thoughts contained in it. If someone were to translate this book for the laity, he would do them a great service.)

5011 'Or again he may be such a man as can live on his income, not coveting other men's goods but believing himself to be free from poverty, for, as your masters say, no one is wretched who does not believe himself to be so, whether he be king, knight, or pauper. Many poor men . . . do not give a fig for treasure, but spend all their earnings and savings in the tavern and then go back to carry their loads, but with joy, not lamentations. They earn their bread honestly, disdaining theft and robbery, then they go back to drink from the barrel and live as they should. All such are abundantly wealthy if they believe that they have enough: indeed, as the good God knows, they are wealthier than if they were usurers, for usurers, I can tell you, can never be rich but are so mean and covetous that they are always in poverty and penury.

'And so it is true, no matter who does not like it, that no merchant lives in com- 5041
fort, for such a war rages in his heart that he burns alive to acquire more goods and will never have enough. He is afraid of losing what he has acquired and chases after what remains to be gained. . . .

Now I have no wish to forbid anyone to occupy himself with love, but only with the love that is harmful. Though I may forbid drunkenness, I do not wish to forbid drinking; such counsel would not be worth a grain of pepper. Though I may ban extravagant generosity, men would think me mad if I ordered them to be avaricious, for both the one and the other are great vices. I do not use such arguments.'

'Indeed you do.'

'That simply is not true. I will not flatter you; you have not examined the old books in order to defeat me, and you are not a good logician. This is not a lecture on love, but I have never said that men should hate anything. It is possible to find a middle way; it is the love that I so love and esteem and that I have taught you in order that you might put it into practice.

'There is another, natural, kind of love, which Nature created in the animals and 5733
that enables them to produce their young, and to suckle and rear them. If you wish me to define for you the love of which I speak, it is a natural and properly motivated inclination to wish to preserve one's fellow creatures, either by engendering them or by seeing to their rearing. Men and beasts are equally well fitted for this love, which, however profitable it may be, carries with it no praise or blame or merit, and those who love thus deserve neither blame nor praise. In truth, Nature pledges them to it by force, and it does not involve any victory over vice, but if they did not practise it, they would most certainly deserve blame. When a man eats, what praise is due to him for that? Whereas if he forswore eating he would certainly deserve to be abused. But I know very well that you are not concerned with this love, and therefore I do not insist upon it. You have embarked upon a far more foolish enterprise in the love that you have undertaken, and you would be better off abandoning it if you wish to seek what is good for you.

'Nevertheless, I have no wish for you to remain without a sweetheart. If it please 5765
you, fix your thoughts on me. Am I not a beautiful and noble lady, fit to serve any worthy man, were he emperor of Rome? I would like to become your beloved, and if you will be true to me, do you know what my love will be worth to you? So much that you will never lack anything you need, whatever misfortune may befall you. Then you will find yourself to be so great a lord that you never heard tell of a greater. I shall do whatever you want; no wish of yours can be too extreme, provided only that you carry out my works, nor is it fitting that you act otherwise. And you will have the advantage that your beloved is of such high lineage that none can compare with her, being the daughter of God, the lord and father who thus made and shaped me. Gaze on this form and see yourself in my bright face. No high-born maiden was ever so free to love as I am, for I have my father's permission to take a lover and to be loved, and he says that I shall not be blamed for it. You need not fear blame either, for you will be

in my father's keeping and he will nurture both of us together. Do I say well? Answer, how does that seem to you? Does the god who drives you to this folly reward his people so well? Does he prepare such good wages for the madmen who pay him homage? For God's sake take care not to refuse me. Maidens who are not accustomed to beg are very sad and abashed when men refuse them, as you yourself can demonstrate through the example of Echo, without seeking other proofs.'

5809 'Now tell me, not in Latin but in French, what you want me to do for you.'

'Allow me to be your servant, and be yourself my loyal friend. You shall leave the god who has brought you to this, and not give so much as a fig for the whole of Fortune's wheel. You shall be like Socrates, who was so firm and strong that he was neither happy in prosperity nor sad in adversity. He put everything in one balance, both good and evil fortune, and gave them equal weight, so that they caused him neither joy nor sorrow, for he was never happy nor sad about anything, whatever it was. He it was, as Solinus says, who, according to Apollo's answer, was judged the wisest man in the world; he it was whose expression, whatever befell him, always stayed the same, and was found unchanged even by those who killed him with hemlock because he denied that there were many gods and trusted in one, and preached that men should avoid swearing by many gods. Heraclitus and Diogenes were also of such a spirit that they were never saddened, not even by poverty or distress. Firm in their purpose, they endured every misfortune that befell them. This is the only way for you to behave: serve me in no other way. Take care not to be cast down by Fortune, whatever blows and torments she may administer, for there is no good or strong fighter who will not do battle with Fortune when she strives to defeat and overcome him. We should not allow ourselves to be taken, but should defend ourselves vigorously, for she knows so little of fighting that anyone who fights with her, be it in a palace or on a dunghill, can overcome her in the first round. No man of courage will have any fear of her, for no one who was aware of the limits of her strength and knew himself to be without fear could be tripped up by her, unless he threw himself voluntarily to the ground. It is also most shameful to see a man who is perfectly well able to defend himself allowing himself to be taken off and hanged, and you would be wrong to want to pity him, for there is no greater slackness. Take care, then, that you place no value on her honours or services; leave her to turn her wheel, as she does continually and ceaselessly, sitting in the centre like one who is blind. Some she blinds with riches, honours, and dignities, while to others she gives poverty, and when it pleases her, she takes everything back. So it is very foolish to feel sorrow or joy about anything, given that you can prevent yourself from doing so, and you certainly can prevent yourself, provided the will is there. Moreover, it is also clear that you are making Fortune into a goddess and raising her to the heavens, which you ought not to do, for it is neither right nor reasonable that she should dwell in paradise. She is not so blessed; instead her dwelling is very perilous.

Statutes of Gregory IX for the University of Paris in 1231

Gregory IX, pope from 1227 to 1241, was an expert in canon law and theology and a staunch defender of papal prerogatives and powers. A stern and often angry man, he engaged in political struggles with secular nobles who seemed to act on their own authority in violation of his. As with other popes in the twelfth and thirteenth centuries, he supported the crusades and worried about heresy in southern France and northern Italy. In 1231, the year of these university statutes, he established the papal Inquisition as a way to root out heresy. Under later popes, the Inquisition became a tool against alchemy, witchcraft, and sorcery.

Gregory's interest in the University of Paris arose early. As a young man, Ugo di Segni, he studied theology there and discovered his skills in diplomacy. The late twelfth and early thirteenth centuries were a time of ferment in the church. St. Dominic and St. Francis, both friends of Ugo, founded their orders of mendicant friars then. And the University of Paris was founded about the time Gregory was born, shortly before 1170. Before that time—in the time of Abelard, for instance—the schools were attached to the Cathedral of Notre-Dame. The chancellor at Notre-Dame had the power to license a master of arts degree, which meant that students in schools at Notre-Dame could themselves become teachers, that is, be recognized as a master instead of an apprentice ("bachelor"). In the early thirteenth century, Paris had three superior faculties, each headed by a dean—theology, canon law, and medicine—and one inferior (this is a title, not a judgment!) faculty, headed by a rector—the arts. In addition, the students and faculties were organized into four "nations," each headed by a proctor—French, Picard, Norman, and English.

The first university was that at Bologna, specializing in law. The University of Paris, famous for theology, was the first university in northern Europe, and it was the model for a similar university in England, at Oxford. Armed with a charter granted by pope, king, or emperor, and a caveat against teaching heresy or atheism, teachers and students essentially formed corporations and ruled themselves, with the students paying the teachers. Teachers had to be popular, therefore, or students would wander off to other universities. Sometimes the students even started their own, as in the case of Cambridge, which was started by some students unhappy with their experience at Oxford.

This translation is by D. C. Munro in *University of Pennsylvania Translations and Reprints* (Philadelphia, 1897).

Removed from the world in the "ivory towers" of their colleges, students became accustomed to living by rules that were different from those in the surrounding towns. Reports of drunkenness and fighting were common, and occasionally brawls occurred between students and townspeople. On the Feast of St. Scholastica (the sister of St. Benedict) in Oxford in 1355, for example, a fight broke out in an Oxford tavern which quickly erupted into the streets and escalated into a pitched battle between "town and gown." In the end, 63 students were killed and many more left the university in fear. As self-governing entities, universities established principles of conduct, like these for the University of Paris.

Gregory, the bishop, servant of the servants of God, to his beloved sons, all the masters and students of Paris—greeting and apostolic benediction.

Paris, the mother of sciences, like another Cariath Sepher, a city of letters, stands forth illustrious, great indeed, but concerning herself she causes greater things to be desired, full of favor for the teachers and students. There, as in a special factory of wisdom, she has silver as the beginnings of her veins, and of gold is the spot in which according to law they flow together; from which the prudent mystics of eloquence fabricate golden necklaces inlaid with silver, and making collars ornamented with precious stones of inestimable value, adorn and decorate the spouse of Christ. There the iron is raised from the earth, because when the earthly fragility is solidified by strength, the breastplate of faith, the sword of the spirit, and the other weapons of the Christian soldier, powerful against the brazen powers, are formed from it. And the stone melted by heat, is turned into brass, because the hearts of stone, enkindled by the fervor of the Holy Ghost, at times glow, burn and become sonorous, and by preaching herald the praises of Christ.

Accordingly, it is undoubtedly very displeasing to God and men that any one in the aforesaid city should strive in any way to disturb so illustrious grace, or should not oppose himself openly and with all his strength to any who do so. Wherefore, since we have diligently investigated the questions referred to us concerning a dissension which, through the instigation of the devil, has arisen there and greatly disturbed the university, we have decided, by the advice of our brethren, that these should be set at rest rather by precautionary measures, than by a judicial sentence.

Therefore, concerning the condition of the students and schools, we have decided that the following should be observed: each chancellor, appointed hereafter at Paris, at the time of his installation, in the presence of the bishop, or at the command of the latter in the chapter at Paris—two masters of the students having been summoned for this purpose and present in behalf of the university—shall swear that, in good faith, according to his conscience, he will not receive as professors of theology and canon law any but suitable men, at a suitable place and time, according to the condition of the city and the honor and glory of those branches of learning; and he will reject all who are unworthy without respect to persons or nations. Before licensing anyone, during three months, dating from the time when the license is requested, the chancellor shall make diligent inquiries of all the masters of theology present in the city, and of all other honest and learned men through whom the truth can be ascertained, concerning the life, knowledge, capacity, purpose, prospects and other qualities needful in such persons; and after the inquiries, in good faith and according to his conscience, he shall grant or deny the license to the candidate, as shall seem fitting and expedient. The masters of theology and canon law, when they begin to lecture, shall take a public oath that they will give true testimony on the above points. The chancellor shall also swear, that, he will in no way reveal the advice of the masters, to their injury; the liberty and privileges being maintained in their full vigor for the canons at Paris, as they were in the beginning. Moreover, the chancellor shall promise to examine in good faith the masters in medicine and arts and in the other branches, to admit only the worthy and to reject the unworthy.

In other matters, because confusion easily creeps in where there is no order, we grant to you the right of making constitutions and ordinances regulating the manner and time of lectures and disputations, the costume to be worn, the burial of the dead; and also concerning the bachelors, who are to lecture and at what hours, and on what they are to lecture; and concerning the prices of the lodgings or the interdiction of the same; and concerning a fit punishment for those who violate your constitutions or ordinances, by exclusion from your society. And if, perchance, the assessment of the lodgings is taken from you, or anything else is lacking, or an injury or outrageous damage, such as death or the mutilation of a limb, is inflicted on one of you; unless through a suitable admonition satisfaction is rendered within fifteen days, you may suspend your lectures until you have received full satisfaction. And if it happens that any one of you is unlawfully imprisoned, unless the injury ceases on a remonstrance from you, you may, if you judge it expedient, suspend your lectures immediately.

We command, moreover, that the bishop of Paris shall so chastise the excesses of the guilty, that the honor of the students shall be preserved and evil deeds shall not remain unpunished. But in no way shall the innocent be seized on account of the guilty; nay rather, if a probable suspicion arises against anyone, he shall be detained honorably and on giving suitable bail he shall be freed, without any exactions from the jailors. But if, perchance, such a crime has been committed that imprisonment is necessary, the bishop shall detain the criminal in his prison. The chancellor is forbidden to keep him in his prison. We also forbid holding a student for a debt contracted by another, since this is interdicted by canonical and legitimate sanctions. Neither the bishop, nor his official, nor the chancellor shall exact a pecuniary penalty for removing an excommunication or any other censure of any kind. Nor shall the chancellor demand from the masters who are licensed an oath, or obedience, or any pledge; nor shall he receive any emolument or promise for granting a license, but be content with the above-mentioned oath.

Also, the vacation in summer is not to exceed one month, and the bachelors, if they wish, can continue their lectures in vacation time. Moreover, we prohibit more expressly the students from carrying weapons in the city, and the university from protecting those who disturb the peace and study. And those who call themselves students but do not frequent the schools, or acknowledge any master, are in no way to enjoy the liberties of the students.

Moreover, we order that the masters in arts shall always read one lecture on Priscian, and one book after the other in the regular courses. Those books on natural philosophy which for a certain reason were prohibited in a provincial council, are not to be used at Paris until they have been examined and purged of all suspicion of error. The masters and students in theology shall strive to exercise themselves laudably in the branch which they profess; they shall not show themselves philosophers, but they shall strive to become God's learned. And they shall not speak in the language of the people, confounding the sacred language with the profane. In the schools they shall dispute only on such questions as can be determined by theological books and the writings of the holy fathers.

Also, about the property of the scholars who die intestate or do not commit the arrangement of their affairs to others, we have determined to arrange thus: namely, that the bishop and one of the masters, whom the university shall appoint for this purpose, shall receive all the property of the defunct, and placing it in a suitable and safe spot, shall fix a certain date, before which his death can be announced in his native country, and those who ought to succeed to his property can come to Paris or send a suitable messenger. And if they come or send, the goods shall be restored to them, with the security which shall have been given. If no one appears, then the bishop and masters shall expend the property for the soul of the departed, as seems expedient; unless, perchance, the heirs shall have been prevented from coming by some good reason. In that case, the distribution shall be deferred to a fitting time.

Truly, because the masters and students, who harassed by damages and injuries, have taken a mutual oath to depart from Paris and have broken up the school, have seemed to be waging a contest not so much for their own benefit as for the common good; we consulting the needs and advantage of the whole church, wish and command that after the privileges have been granted to the masters and students by our most dearly beloved son in Christ, the illustrious King of the French, and amends have been paid by the malefactors, they shall study at Paris and shall not be marked by any infamy or irregularity on account of their staying away or return.

It is not lawful for any man whatever to infringe this deed of our provision, constitution, concession, prohibition and inhibition or to act contrary to it, from rash presumption. If anyone, however, should dare to attempt this, let him know that he incurs the wrath of almighty God and of the blessed Peter and Paul, his apostles.

Given at the Lateran, on the Ides of April [April 13], in the fifth year of our pontificate.

Thomas Aquinas (c.1225–1274)

Summa Theologica

Thomas Aquinas came from a wealthy land-owning family who wanted their son to become an abbot of a monastery. They placed him as a young boy in the famous abbey at Monte Cassino near their home. When the emperor closed the abbey and expelled the monks, Thomas decided against the monastic life in favor of the newest order of mendicant friars, the Dominicans, founded 30 years before. Monks made vows of personal poverty, but lived in the luxury of religious communities that had accumulated great wealth over the years. The fraternal orders, beginning with St. Francis, who founded the Franciscans in 1209, were devoted to poverty, both individually and as a brotherhood. They sustained themselves by becoming expert street preachers and teachers. To Aquinas, the dedication to learning that characterized the order founded by St. Dominic must have felt like a new freedom. When he was sent by his order to the Dominican house at the University of Paris, he was put in contact with revolutionary old ideas. (To keep this from happening, his family had him abducted on his way to Paris, and held him prisoner for a year before releasing him in 1245.)

The ideas that were shaking up Paris were Aristotle's, available in Latin translations for the first time by way of Muslim Spain (Aristotle's works had been preserved among Arabic scholars). Christian theology, cast in Platonic terms for more than a thousand years, suddenly faced the challenge of Aristotle's scientific rationalism. In the course of earning a bachelor's degree, a "license to teach," and a master's degree (1256), Thomas studied theology and the new science. After a sojourn in Italy, he returned to Paris to find the view growing among intellectuals that scientific investigation based on reason might lead to truths that contradicted those asserted by faith. He began to lecture and write, taking the position that reason could operate within the faith, so that theology itself could be organized on a rational basis. Beginning with a few simple truths revealed by God, the entire edifice of Christian belief could be constructed by means of the question and answer method then popular in the university. In terms of Aristotle's causes, the final cause, which set all in motion, was God, the summum bonum *"highest good," or happiness.*

In 1272, Thomas was sent to Naples to found a Dominican school in the University of Naples. At that time his ideas, which were laid out in two large treatises, were being

Reprinted from *Summa Theologica*, translated by the Father of the English Dominican Province, (1947), by permission of Benziger Publishing Company.

attacked as part of the general religious reaction against radical scientific rationalism. After his death, however, his logical constructions were seen as ways of preserving doctrinal clarity, and even in the last century renewal movements within Roman Catholicism were grounded in his teachings. He became a saint in 1323. His philosophy, in which revelations of God's truth become the basis of an orderly examination of the human and natural worlds, came to be called scholasticism *or* Thomism.

On the Existence of God
Question 2: The Existence of God (in Three Articles)
Third Article

Whether God Exists?

We proceed thus to the Third Article:—

Objection 1. It seems that God does not exist; because if one of two contraries be infinite, the other would be altogether destroyed. But the word "God" means that He is infinite goodness. If, therefore, God existed, there would be no evil discoverable; but there is evil in the world. Therefore God does not exist.

Obj. 2. Further, it is superfluous to suppose that what can be accounted for by a few principles has been produced by many. But it seems that everything we see in the world can be accounted for by other principles, supposing God did not exist. For all natural things can be reduced to one principle, which is nature; and all voluntary things can be reduced to one principle, which is human reason, or will. Therefore there is no need to suppose God's existence.

On the contrary, It is said in the person of God: *I am Who am* (Exod. iii. 14).

I answer that, The existence of God can be proved in five ways.

The first and more manifest way is the argument from motion. It is certain, and evident to our senses, that in the world some things are in motion. Now whatever is in motion is put in motion by another, for nothing can be in motion except it is in potentiality to that towards which it is in motion; whereas a thing moves inasmuch as it is in act. For motion is nothing else than the reduction of something from potentiality to actuality. But nothing can be reduced from potentiality to actuality, except by something in a state of actuality. Thus that which is actually hot, as fire, makes wood, which is potentially hot, to be actually hot, and thereby moves and changes it. Now it is not possible that the same thing should be at once in actuality and potentiality in the same respect, but only in different respects. For what is actually hot cannot simultaneously be potentially hot; but it is simultaneously potentially cold. It is therefore impossible that in the same respect and in the same way a thing should be both mover and moved, i.e., that it should move itself. Therefore, whatever is in motion must be put in motion by another. If that by which it is put in motion be itself put in motion, then this also must needs be put in motion by another, and that by another again. But this cannot go on to infinity, because then there would be no first mover, and, consequently, no other mover; seeing that subsequent movers move only inasmuch as they are put in motion by the first mover; as the staff moves only because it is put in motion by the hand. Therefore it is necessary to arrive at a first mover, put in motion by no other; and this everyone understands to be God.

The second way is from the nature of the efficient cause. In the world of sense we find there is an order of efficient causes. There is no case known (neither is it, indeed, possible) in which a thing is found to be the efficient cause of itself; for so it would be prior to itself, which is impossible. Now in efficient causes it is not possible to go on to infinity, because in all efficient causes following in order, the first is the cause of the intermediate cause, and the intermediate is the cause of the ultimate cause, whether the intermediate cause be several, or one only. Now to take away the cause is to take away the effect. Therefore if there be no first cause among efficient causes, there will be no ultimate, nor any intermediate cause. But if in efficient causes it is possible to go on to infinity, there will be no first efficient cause, neither will there be an ultimate effect, nor any intermediate efficient causes; all of which is plainly false. Therefore it is necessary to admit a first efficient cause, to which everyone gives the name of God.

The third way is taken from possibility and necessity, and runs thus. We find in nature things that are possible to be and not to be, since they are found to be generated, and to corrupt, and consequently, they are possible to be and not to be. But it is impossible for these always to exist, for that which is possible not to be at some time is not. Therefore, if everything is possible not to be, then at one time there could have been nothing in existence. Now if this were true, even now there would be nothing in existence, because that which does not exist only begins to exist by something already existing. Therefore, if at one time nothing was in existence, it would have been impossible for anything to have begun to exist; and thus even now nothing would be in existence—which is absurd. Therefore, not all beings are merely possible, but there must exist something the existence of which is necessary. But every necessary thing either has its necessity caused by another, or not. Now it is impossible to go on to infinity in necessary things which have their necessity caused by another, as has been already proved in regard to efficient causes. Therefore we cannot but postulate the existence of some being having of itself its own necessity, and not receiving it from another, but rather causing in others their necessity. This all men speak of as God.

The fourth way is taken from the gradation to be found in things. Among beings there are some more and some less good, true, noble, and the like. But "more" and "less" are predicated of different things, according as they resemble in their different ways something which is the maximum, as a thing is said to be hotter according as it more nearly resembles that which is hottest; so that there is something which is truest, something best, something noblest, and, consequently, something which is uttermost being; for those things that are greatest in truth are greatest in being, as it is written in *Metaph.* ii. Now the maximum in any genus is the cause of all in that genus; as fire, which is the maximum of heat, is the cause of all hot things. Therefore there must also be something which is to all beings the cause of their being, goodness, and every other perfection; and this we call God.

The fifth way is taken from the governance of the world. We see that things which lack intelligence, such as natural bodies, act for an end, and this is evident from their acting always, or nearly always, in the same way, so as to obtain the best result. Hence it is plain that not fortuitously, but designedly, do they achieve their end. Now whatever lacks intelligence cannot move towards an end, unless it be directed by some being endowed with knowledge and intelligence; as the arrow is shot to its mark by the archer. Therefore some intelligent being exists by whom all natural things are directed to their end; and this being we call God.

Reply Obj. 1. As Augustine says (*Enchir.* xi): *Since God is the highest good, He would not allow any evil to exist in His works, unless His omnipotence and goodness were such as to bring good even out of evil.* This is part of the infinite goodness of God, that He should allow evil to exist, and out of it produce good.

Reply Obj. 2. Since nature works for a determinate end under the direction of a higher agent, whatever is done by nature must needs be traced back to God, as to its first cause. So also whatever is done voluntarily must also be traced back to some higher cause other than human reason or will, since these can change and fail; for all things that are changeable and capable of defect must be traced back to an immovable and self-necessary first principle, as was shown in the body of the *Article*.

Jacobus de Voragine (c.1229–1298)

THE GOLDEN LEGEND

The Legenda Aurea *was the main source of popular information about the saints and religious festivals in the late Middle Ages. It was organized around the calendar of saints' days and festivals, beginning with Advent, and it included accounts of miracles that occurred during the lifetime of its author, who became the Archbishop of Genoa and was himself beatified in 1816. It was among the first books to be printed in Europe (about 1469), a sure sign of its continued popularity, and it was widely translated from its original Latin language.*

Jacobus was a Dominican, one of the orders of friars dedicated to preaching and enforcing right conduct. His collection may have been a helpful handbook of the kinds of stories that enlivened sermons or served as examples of exemplary conduct. The saints' lives were notoriously fanciful and inaccurate—from a modern historical perspective. The heroes and heroines of these stories often faced horrific tortures, sometimes upheld by amazing miracles, sometimes succumbing with steadfast faith. Women were frequently threatened with marriage when they wished to remain virgins, or with unsuitable mates when they wished to marry Christians. The visual imagery of the stories often found its way into stained glass windows and paintings, so that certain objects became emblematic of the saints associated with them, like the wheel on which Saint Catherine was to have been tortured, the gridiron on which Saint Laurence was cooked, or the ship transporting St. Ursula and her eleven thousand virgins. The saint's life became a popular literary genre in the Middle Ages, fueling retellings of the life stories of popular saints as well as the invention of fictions about "new" heroes and heroines whose virtues matched the steadfastness of true saints. In the Canterbury Tales, *for instance, Chaucer's Second Nun retells the story of Saint Cecilia and the Physician tells of the virgin martyr Virginia, while the Man of Law imitates a saint's life in his allegorical story of Constance.*

The stories of these martyrs follow a traditional pattern, imitating the life of Christ and showing the triumph of faith in death. Beyond the martyrs (like St. Ursula, who was important to Hildegard of Bingen, composer of songs in her honor), there are saints who held important positions in the church—St. Dominic, the founder of Jacobus's order, for

These selections from the *Golden Legend* are translated by Christopher Stace (London: Penguin Books, 1998).

instance. Alongside surely fictional tales about nearly unknown figures, Jacobus included detailed accounts of the lives of apostles, evangelists, and other biblical figures. Often these stories preserved traditions that had little or no basis in the New Testament. Mary Magdalene, for instance, is said to be the Mary of Bethany (sister of Martha and Lazarus) from John's gospel, and also the woman sinner in Luke's gospel (7:37). Besides being fabulously wealthy, sometime after the crucifixion she goes to southern France and lives as a desert hermit for thirty years. All of these traditions are unsupported interpretations of the scant evidence in the Bible, and even Jacobus acknowledges having heard different versions of Mary's story. The controversy about Mary continues, however: in 1969 the Roman Catholic Church declared that Mary should no longer be viewed as a prostitute (the Eastern Orthodox Church never considered her a sinner), and Dan Brown's 2003 Da Vinci Code *brought new life to old and new "traditions" about cults of Mary Magdalene in the South of France.*

ST MARY MAGDALENE—22 JULY

Mary Magdalene is so called because of her connection with the town of Magdalum. She was born of most noble parents who were indeed of royal descent. Her father's name was Syrus, and her mother was called Eucharia. Together with her brother Lazarus and sister Martha she owned Magdalum, a fortified town two miles from Genezareth, Bethany, near Jerusalem, and a large part of Jerusalem itself. But they divided up their inheritance in such a way that Mary kept Magdalum (hence her name Magdalene), Lazarus the family property in Jerusalem, and Martha, Bethany. Mary Magdalene gave herself up entirely to the pleasures of the flesh, while Lazarus devoted much of his time to soldiering, and the prudent Martha was active in managing her sister's and brother's estates, and attending to the needs of her men-at-arms, her servants and the poor. But after Christ's ascension they sold everything they possessed and laid the proceeds at the feet of the apostles.

Since Mary Magdalene was enormously wealthy, and pleasure is the boon companion of affluence, she was as notorious for her abandonment to fleshly pleasures as she was celebrated for her beauty and riches. So much so, in fact, that people soon forgot her real name and referred to her as 'the sinner'. But when Christ was travelling about the country preaching, Mary, inspired by the will of God, hurried to the house of Simon the leper, where she had heard that he was a guest. Being a sinner, she did not dare to be seen among decent people, so she held back and sat at the Lord's feet, washed them with her tears, dried them with her hair, and anointed them with precious ointment (because of the intense heat of the sun the inhabitants of that region often anointed themselves and took baths). And just as Simon the Pharisee was thinking to himself that, if Jesus was a true prophet, he would never allow himself to be touched by a sinful woman, the Lord reproached him for his presumption, and forgave the woman all her sins. It was this Magdalene on whom the Lord conferred such great blessings, and to whom he showed so many signs of his love. For he cast seven demons out of her, set her all on fire with love for him, made her one of his most intimate associates, was a guest at her house, let her provide for him on his travels, and lovingly defended her on many occasions. He took her part against the Pharisee, who said she was unclean; against her sister, who said she was idle; and against Judas, who said she was wasteful. If he saw Mary in tears, he could not hold back his own. Out of love for her he raised her brother to life again, when he had been dead four days; out of love for her he freed her sister Martha from the flux of blood which she had suffered for seven years; and in recognition of her merits he gave Martilla, Martha's maid, the honour of uttering those sweet and glorious words: 'Blessed is the womb that bore you!' For, according to Ambrose, the woman with the flux of blood was indeed Martha, and the woman who uttered these words was her maid. 'It was she [Mary Magdalene], I say, who washed the Lord's feet with her tears, dried them with her hair, and anointed them with ointment. It was she who in the time of grace did solemn penance, who chose the best part, who sat at the Lord's feet and listened to his word, who anointed his head, who stood by the cross at the Lord's passion, who prepared the unguents and anointed his body; she who, when the disciples left the sepulchre, would not go away; and it was she to whom Christ first appeared when he had risen, thus making her an apostle to the apostles.'

Then, fourteen years after the passion and ascension of the Lord, long after the Jews had killed Stephen and expelled the rest of the disciples from Judaean territory, the disciples went off to spread the word of the Lord in the various regions inhabited by the Gentiles. At that time blessed Maximinus, one of the Lord's seventy-two disciples, was with the apostles, and it was to his care that St Peter had entrusted Mary Magdalene. When the disciples went their separate ways, the blessed Maximinus, Mary Magdalene, her brother Lazarus, her sister Martha, Martha's maid Martilla and the blessed Cedonius, who had been blind from his birth but was cured by the Lord, together with many other Christians, were put on board ship by unbelievers and set adrift on the sea without a pilot so that they should all be drowned. But by God's will they reached Marseilles. There they found nobody prepared to take them in, so they sheltered under the portico of a shrine where the people of that region worshipped. When the blessed Mary Magdalene saw the people streaming to the shrine to sacrifice to the idols, she got up, quite calmly, and, with a serene expression on her face and with measured words, began to turn them from their idol worship, and with great single-mindedness to preach the Gospel of Christ. Everyone there admired her for her beauty, for her eloquence, and for her sweet manner of speaking. And it is no wonder that the lips which had pressed kisses so loving and so tender on our Lord's feet should breathe the perfume of the word of God more copiously than others.

Later the prince who ruled that region arrived there with his wife to offer sacrifice to the gods and to pray for a child. Magdalene preached Christ to him and persuaded him not to offer sacrifice. A few days later she appeared to his wife in a vision: 'Why, when you are so very rich,' she asked, 'do you allow God's faithful servants to die of hunger and cold?' She also added the threat that, if she did not persuade her husband to relieve the misery of the faithful, she would incur the wrath of Almighty God. But the lady was frightened to tell her husband about the vision. The following night Magdalene appeared to her again with the same message, but still she said nothing to her husband. The third time, in the silence of the dead of night, Magdalene appeared to both of them, trembling with rage, her face so afire with anger that it seemed that the whole house was ablaze! 'Asleep, tyrant?' she said. 'Are you asleep, you son of Satan, with that viper, your wife, who refused to give you my message? Can you rest, you enemy of the cross of Christ, when your fat belly is stuffed full of all sorts of food, and you let the holy ones of God die of hunger and thirst? Can you lie here in your palace, covered with bedclothes of silk, and see them desolate, without a roof over their heads, and ignore them? No, no! You shall not get away with this, you monster! You know you should help them, and you shall not go unpunished for your procrastination!' With these words she vanished. When the wife awoke she was breathless and trembling, her husband, too, was similarly troubled. 'My lord,' she said, 'have you had the same dream I had?' 'Yes,' he replied. 'I cannot believe it, and it fills me with dread. What are we going to do?' 'It would be better,' his wife said, 'to do as she says, rather than incur the wrath of this God of hers whom she preaches.' So they gave the Christians shelter and looked after their needs.

One day when Mary Magdalene was preaching, the prince asked her: 'Do you think you can defend the faith you preach?' She replied: 'I am more than ready to defend it! My faith is strengthened daily by the miracles and preaching of my master Peter, who governs the Church in Rome.' The prince and his wife then declared to her: 'We are ready to do anything you say if you can get this God whom you preach to grant us a son.' 'He will not deny you this,' Magdalene assured them. Then blessed Mary prayed to the Lord to deign to grant them a son, and the Lord heard her prayers, and the prince's wife conceived. After this the prince was seized with a desire to go to Peter in Rome to see if what Magdalene preached about Christ was the truth. 'What is this?' demanded his wife. 'Are you planning to go without me? Oh no! God forbid! If you go, I go, too: if you come back, I come back with you. Where you stay, I stay!' 'Madam, it cannot be,' her husband told her. 'You are pregnant and the perils of the sea are numberless. You would be running too great a risk. Stay at home and take care of things here.' But she insisted and, using all her feminine guile, she threw herself at his feet in floods of tears, and finally had her way. So Mary made the sign of the cross upon their shoulders to stop the Ancient Enemy harming them on their voyage. Then, loading a ship with a plentiful supply of all the things they needed, they left the rest of their possessions in the safe-keeping of Mary Magdalene and set sail.

They were only a day and a night into their voyage when a gale blew up, the sea began to swell and, as the huge waves pounded them and broke over the ship, everyone on board began to fear for their lives, and especially the prince's pregnant wife, whose health was in a delicate state. Suddenly she was gripped by the pangs of labour; and, racked with pain and in the most pitiful circumstances, she died as she gave birth to a son. The tiny baby felt about him, seeking the comfort of his mother's breasts and uttering the most pathetic cries. Ah! The bitter irony of it! The child is born alive, and in the same moment becomes his mother's murderer, when it is he who should be dead, since he has no one to feed him and keep him alive! What will the pilgrim do, now he sees his wife lying dead and his child whimpering pitifully as he searches for his mother's breast? The prince was beside himself with grief. 'Luckless man!' he cried to himself. 'What will you do now? You longed to have a son, and now you have lost both your son and the mother that bore him!' Meanwhile the sailors were shouting: 'Throw the body overboard before we all go down together. As long as it stays on board, this storm will never let up.' They grabbed the body and were about to throw it into the sea, but the pilgrim pleaded with them. 'No!' he cried. 'Please! If you will not spare me or the mother, at least take pity on the weeping of a poor little child. Wait just a moment. Perhaps she has just fainted with pain—perhaps she may start breathing again.' Then, out of the blue, not far ahead a hilly coastline hove into view, and it occurred to the prince that the best he could do would be to put his dead wife and the baby ashore—anything rather than throw them overboard as food for the monsters of the deep! He offered the sailors bribes, pleaded with them to put in there, and, finally, with great difficulty, got them to agree. Once ashore, however, he was unable to dig a grave, because the ground was too hard, so he picked a sheltered part of the hillside, spread his cloak on the ground, and put the corpse upon it, laying the child at his mother's breast. 'O Mary Magdalene,' he mused tearfully, 'when you landed at Marseilles it was to my utter ruin. Why did I ever take your advice, luckless wretch that I am, and come on this journey? Is this what you prayed for—that my wife might conceive only to die in labour? For conceive she did, and has died in childbirth: my son was conceived only to die, because there is no one to nurse him. Yes, that is all your prayers have brought me! I put my whole life in your hands, and now I put myself in the hands of your God. If he has the power, let him remember the soul of my wife, and, in answer to your prayer, have pity on my son and let him live!' He then wrapped his cloak about his dead wife and the child, and went back on board ship.

When he reached Rome, Peter came to meet him and, seeing the sign of the cross on his shoulder, asked him who he was and where he came from. He told Peter the whole story and Peter replied: 'Peace be with you! You have done well to come here, and the advice you took was good. Do not grieve too much if your wife sleeps and your little child is at rest with her, for the Lord has power to give gifts to whomever he wishes, to take away what he has given, to restore what he has taken away, and to turn your grief to joy.' Peter then took him off to Jerusalem and showed him all the places in which Christ had preached and performed miracles, and also the place where he suffered and the place where he ascended into heaven. For two years Peter instructed him fully in the faith, and then his disciple boarded ship in order to return home again. In the course of his voyage, by God's will, the ship passed close by the same hilly coastline where he had left the body of his wife and his baby son, and, by bribing the crew and pleading with them, he persuaded them to put in there.

Now the little boy had been preserved and kept free from harm by Mary Magdalene, and used often to go down to the seashore and play with the pebbles and shingle there, as children will. As the ship's boat was putting in, the pilgrim saw the small child playing his usual games with the pebbles on the shore and was unable to believe his eyes. He sprang from the boat, but the child, who had never seen anything like a man before, was terrified and ran back to the familiar comfort of his mother's bosom, and hid himself with her under the cloak. The pilgrim followed, determined to discover the truth of the matter, and found the child, a bonny boy, suckling at his mother's breast. He took him in his arms and cried: 'O blessed Mary Magdalene, how happy I would be, how perfectly everything would have turned out for me, if only my wife could come back to life and return home with me! Indeed I know, yes I know and believe without any doubt, that you, who have given me this child and nursed him for two years upon this rock, will be able, by your prayers, to restore his mother to life.' As he finished speaking, his wife began to breathe again. As if waking from sleep, she said: 'Great is your merit, blessed Mary Magdalene, and great the glory you have won! When I suffered the pangs of labour, you served me as midwife, you attended to my every need like a loyal handmaid.' When he heard her speak, the pilgrim exclaimed in astonishment: 'My dearest wife, are you really alive?' 'I am indeed!' she replied. 'I have just come back from the pilgrimage from which you yourself are returning. Just as blessed Peter took you to Jerusalem and showed you all the places in which Christ suffered and died and was buried, and many other places, so I, with blessed Mary Magdalene as my guide and companion, was with you, and I have committed to memory everything I saw.' She then began to describe all the places in which Christ had suffered and all the marvels that she had seen, and her account was accurate in every detail. Overcome with joy at recovering his wife and son, the pilgrim boarded ship again and soon enough they put in at Marseilles. When they entered the city, they found Mary Magdalene among her disciples, preaching. In tears they threw themselves at her feet, told her all that had happened to them, and then received holy baptism at the hands of Maximinus. Subsequently the Christians destroyed all the temples of the idols in the city of Marseilles and built churches to Christ, and they unanimously elected blessed Lazarus as bishop of the city. In due course divine providence took them to the city of Aix, and by many miracles they led the people there to believe in Christ, and blessed Maximinus was ordained bishop of Aix.

In the meantime blessed Mary Magdalene, wishing to devote herself to heavenly contemplation, withdrew to a barren wilderness where she remained in anonymity for thirty years in a place prepared for her by the hands of angels. In this wilderness there was no water, and there were no trees or grass, nor any comforts of any kind, so that it was clear that our Redeemer had meant to feed her not with earthly foods, but with the sweets of heaven alone. Each day at the seven canonical hours she was lifted in the air by angels and actually heard, with her bodily organs of hearing, the glorious harmonies of the celestial chorus. So, filled day by day with this exquisite heavenly fare, when she was brought back to her cave, she had not the slightest need for bodily nourishment.

Now there was a priest who desired to live a solitary life and made himself a cell some twelve furlongs from Mary's cave. One day the Lord opened the eyes of this priest, and he saw quite clearly, with his own eyes, how the angels came down to the place where blessed Mary lived, lifted her in the air, and an hour later returned her to the same place, singing the praises of God. The priest, eager to know if this wonderful vision was a true one, commended himself in prayer to his Creator, and then, with courageous determination, hurried off to Mary's cave. But when he was only a stone's throw away from the place, his legs began to give way, he was gripped with terror, and he started to gasp for breath. If he took a step back, his legs and feet behaved normally; but every time he turned and tried to get closer to the cave, his body was instantly paralysed and his brain benumbed, and he could not move an inch. Then the man of God knew for a certainty that there was some heavenly mystery afoot which was beyond the reach of human experience. So, invoking the name of his Saviour, he cried out: 'I adjure you, in the Lord's name, if you are a human or any rational creature, you who live in that cave, answer me and tell me truly who you are!' When he had repeated this three times, blessed Mary Magdalene answered: 'Come closer, and you will learn the truth about everything your heart desires to know.' The trembling priest had gone half-way towards the cave when she said to him: 'Do you remember the story in the Gospel about Mary, the notorious sinner, who washed the Saviour's feet with her tears, dried them with her hair, and won forgiveness for her sins?' 'I do,' the priest replied. 'And more than thirty years have gone by since Holy Church has believed the story and acknowledged it as fact.' 'I am that woman,' she told him. 'For the space of thirty years I have lived here, unknown to anyone. As you were allowed to see yesterday, each day I am carried aloft by the hands of angels, and seven times every day I have been accorded the privilege of hearing with my own ears the joyous rapture of the heavenly hosts. Now, because it has been revealed to me by the Lord that I am soon to depart from this world, I beg you to go to Maximinus and be sure to give him this message: next year, on the day of the Lord's resurrection, at the hour when he rises to go to matins, he is to go into his church alone, and there he will find me, attended by bands of angels.'

The priest thought he must be hearing the voice of an angel, but he could not see anyone. So he hurried off to Maximinus and told him all that had happened. St Maximinus was overcome with joy and gave heartfelt thanks to the Saviour. On Easter Day, at the appointed hour, he entered his church alone, and saw Mary Magdalene standing in the midst of the choir of angels who had brought her. She was raised several feet above the floor and thronged by angels, with her arms outstretched in prayer to God. Maximinus hesitated to approach her, but she turned to him and said: 'Come closer, father. Do not run from your daughter!' So he went up to her, and, as we read in the writings of Maximinus himself, the saint's visage was so radiant from her continuous daily vision of the angels that one could more easily have looked into the rays of the sun than into her face. Maximinus summoned all the clergy, including the aforementioned priest, and Mary Magdalene wept copiously as she received our Lord's body and blood from the hands of the bishop. Then she prostrated herself before the foot of the altar, and at once her most holy soul passed to the Lord. After her death a perfume of such sweetness flooded the church that for seven days everyone who entered the place was aware of it. Maximinus gave her most holy body honourable burial, embalming it with aromatic spices, and ordered that when he died, he should be buried next to her.

Hegesippus—or according to some sources, Josephus—is in general agreement with this version of the events. He says in one of his treatises that Mary Magdalene, after the Lord's ascension, burnt with such love for Christ, and was so weary of the world, that she wanted never to set eyes on any human being again. Then, after she went to Aix, she withdrew into the desert and lived there for thirty years unknown to anyone. There, as he asserts, she was carried up to heaven by angels every day at the seven canonical hours. But he adds that the priest who visited Mary found her enclosed in her cell. She asked him for something to wear and he gave her a garment, which she put on, and then went with him into the church. There, after receiving communion, she lifted her hands in prayer before the altar and peacefully passed away . . .

ST DOMINIC—4 AUGUST

Dominic, the celebrated founding father of the Order of Preachers, was born in Spain in the village of Calaruega in the diocese of Osma. His father's name was Felix, his mother's Johanna. Before his birth his mother dreamt that she was carrying a little dog in her womb, which held a blazing torch in its mouth, and that when the dog issued from her womb, it set fire to the entire fabric of the world. And when Dominic was baptized, the woman who lifted him from the sacred font saw upon his forehead a brilliant star that lit up the whole universe.

While still a small child and under the care of a nurse, Dominic was often caught leaving his bed at night to sleep on the bare earth. For his education he was sent to Palentia, and such was his passion for learning that for ten years he never tasted wine. When a terrible famine ravaged the city, he sold his furniture and books and gave the proceeds to the poor. His reputation spread, and the bishop of Osma made him a canon regular in his church. Not long after this, since his life was universally judged to be a mirror of perfection, the canons elected him as their sub-prior. Day and night Dominic gave himself up to reading and prayer, begging God unceasingly to deign to give him grace to devote himself entirely to the salvation of his neighbour. He was assiduous in his study of the *Discourses of the Fathers* and soon progressed to a high degree of perfection.

He went with his bishop to Toulouse, but discovered that his host there had been corrupted by the perversion of heresy. Dominic turned him back to the true faith of Christ, and presented him to the Lord as a token of the first-fruits of the harvest to come.

We read in the *Deeds of the Count of Montfort* that one day, after preaching against the heretics, Dominic made a copy of all his most important arguments and gave the document to one of the heretics so that he could ponder his objections at length. That night, when the heretics gathered round a fire, this man brought out and showed them the document he had been given. His friends said that he should throw it on to the fire; if it burnt, their faith ('heresy', they should have said) would be proved true; if it refused to burn, they would preach the true faith of the Roman Church. So it was thrown on to the fire, and after a short while it suddenly leapt unmarked from the flames. They were all dumbfounded, but one of them, who was more hard-headed than the rest, said: 'Throw it in again. If we try it a second time, we shall be that much more sure of the truth.' In it went a second time, and a second time it leapt out untouched. Again, the sceptic told them: 'Throw it in a third time. Then we shall know for certain: there will be no doubt.' In it went a third time, and again it leapt out untouched, without a mark on it. But still the heretics persisted in their disbelief and bound each other on the strictest of oaths not to reveal what had happened to anyone. But there was a soldier present who had some leanings towards our faith, and he later made the miracle common knowledge. This all happened at Montréal, and something similar is said to have taken place around that time at Fanjeaux, when a solemn disputation with the heretics was in progress.

When the bishop of Osma died, most of St Dominic's companions returned to their homes, but the saint stayed on with a small remnant and resolutely preached the word of God against the heretics. The enemies of the truth mocked him, spitting at him, throwing mud and all sorts of filth at him, and tying wisps of straw on his back to make fun of him. They even threatened to kill him, but he answered them fearlessly: 'I am not worthy of the glory of martyrdom. I have not merited such a death.' Accordingly, when he was passing a place where they lay in wait for him, not only was he unafraid, but he was clearly in the best of spirits, singing to himself as he walked along. Astonished at this, they said to him: 'Have you no fear of death at all?' 'None,' he replied: 'I would have begged you not to kill me quickly, with a few swift blows, but little by little, lopping off my limbs one by one, holding up to my eyes the bits you had cut off, then tearing out my eyes, and leaving my half-dead, mutilated body to wallow in a pool of its own blood—or to kill me in any other way you please.'

He once came across a man who, because of his extreme poverty, had joined the ranks of the heretics. So Dominic resolved to sell himself, so that, with the money he raised, he could relieve the man's distress, and at the same time deliver him from the error into which it had driven him. And he would have gone through with his plan, had not God in his mercy provided otherwise for the pauper.

On another occasion a woman came to him weeping bitterly and told him her brother was a prisoner of the Saracens, and she had no idea how she could secure his freedom. Dominic was moved to deep compassion, and offered to sell himself in order to redeem the prisoner. But God would not permit this, for he foresaw that the saint had a far more important role to play in the redemption of numberless spiritual captives.

When in the neighbourhood of Toulouse, Dominic was a guest in the house of some ladies who had been led into error by the heretics' outward display of piety. So, deciding to use a hair of the dog that bit them, Dominic and his companion fasted the whole of Lent on bread and cold water, keeping vigil during the nights, and, when sleep became a necessity, resting their tired limbs on a bare board. In this way he brought the ladies once again to recognize the truth.

Soon after this he began to think about the establishment of a religious order, whose mission it would be to journey the length and breadth of the world preaching and defending the Catholic faith against the heretics. After he had remained in the region of Toulouse for ten years, that is from the death of the bishop of Osma up to the time of the Lateran Council, he went to Rome with Fulk, bishop of Toulouse, and attended the general council. There he asked the pontiff, Pope Innocent, to recognize for himself and his successors the foundation of an order which would be called, and would in fact be, the Order of Preachers. For some time the pope proved difficult, but then one night he had a dream in which he saw the Lateran Church suddenly threatening to collapse in ruins. But as he looked on in horror, St Dominic came running from the opposite direction, put his shoulders against the building, and kept the whole structure from falling. Upon waking, the pope understood the significance of his vision, and gladly granted the man of God's petition, advising him to return to his brethren and choose one of the already approved Rules, then to come back and receive formal approval. So Dominic rejoined his brethren and told them what the supreme pontiff had said. Now the brethren were sixteen in number, and, after invoking the Holy Spirit, they unanimously chose the Rule of St Augustine, the great doctor and preacher, for preachers they would be called, and preachers they would be. In addition they adopted certain stricter practices which they resolved to observe as constitutions. But meanwhile Pope Innocent had died and Honorius had been raised to the supreme pontificate, so it was from Honorius, in the year of our Lord 1216, that Dominic obtained confirmation of his Order.

Dominic was praying in the church of St Peter in Rome for the increase of his Order, when in a vision he saw those glorious princes of the apostles, Peter and Paul, coming towards him. Peter seemed to hand him a staff and Paul a book, then they said to him: 'Go forth and preach, for that is your God-appointed task.' Then, in an instant, he seemed to see his sons spread throughout the whole world, walking two by two and preaching the word of God to all the people. Accordingly he returned to Toulouse and sent his brethren out, some to Spain, some to Paris, and others to Bologna. He himself went back to Rome.

Before the establishment of the Order of Preachers, a certain monk had an ecstatic vision of the Blessed Virgin: she was kneeling with her hands joined, praying to her son for the human race. Several times Christ refused to listen to his loving mother, then finally, since she persisted, he said: 'Mother, what more can I do, or ought I to do for them? I have sent them patriarchs and prophets, and they did little to better themselves. I went to them myself, then I sent them my apostles, and they killed us all. I sent them my martyrs and confessors and doctors, and they would not listen to them. But since it is not right for me to refuse you anything, I will give them my preachers to enlighten them and purify them. And if they do not mend their ways, I shall visit them myself, in wrath!'

Another monk had a similar vision around the same time; it was when twelve abbots of the Cistercian Order were sent to Toulouse to denounce the heretics. In this vision, when the Son gave the above answer to his mother's prayer, she replied: 'Dear son, you must not deal with them as their evil deserves, but as your grace and compassion require.' Then, won over by her pleading, he replied: 'In answer to your prayers I shall grant them one more mercy: I shall send them my preachers to admonish them and teach them, and if they do not mend their ways, I will spare them no longer.'

A friar minor, who had for a long time been a companion of St Francis, told the following story to several friars of the Order of Preachers: when blessed Dominic was at Rome to persuade the pope to confirm his Order, he had a vision one night in which he saw Christ, upraised in the air, holding in his hand three spears which he brandished menacingly above the world. His mother hurried to his side, and asked what he meant to do. 'The whole world is beset by three vices,' he told her, 'pride, lust and greed. So I will use these three spears to destroy it.' The Virgin fell at his knees and said: 'My dearest son, have pity and temper your justice with mercy!' Christ replied: 'Do you not see what wrongs they do me?' 'Restrain your wrath, my son,' Mary said, 'and wait a while. For I have a faithful servant, a tireless champion who will travel the whole world and conquer it and place it beneath your sway. And I will give him another servant to help him, one who will fight faithfully by his side.' Her son replied: 'Very well. You have appeased me and I grant your request. But I would like to see whom you have chosen for such an important mission.' Thereupon she presented St Dominic to Christ. 'This is a strong and valiant warrior indeed,' he said to her. 'He will be sure to do all you have said.' Then she brought St Francis before him, and Christ commended him as warmly as he had St Dominic. Dominic, during this vision, looked closely at his new ally, and next day, when he came upon him in church, though he had never met him in the flesh, he needed no introduction: he knew him immediately from his vision of the night before. He ran up to him, threw his arms around him, and kissed him affectionately. 'You are my companion,' he cried. 'You will run the same course, side by side with me. Let us stand together and no enemy will prevail against us!' Dominic then told Francis in detail of the vision he had had. From that moment they were one heart and soul in the Lord, and made a rule that their followers should live in the same spirit of friendship for ever.

The Eleven Thousand Virgins—21 October

The following is an account of the glorious martyrdom of the eleven thousand virgins. In Britain lived a most Christian king named Nothus (or Maurus) who had a daughter called Ursula. Ursula was exceptionally virtuous, wise and beautiful, and her fame swiftly spread far and wide. The king of Anglia, whose power was immense, and who had subjected many nations and brought them beneath his sway, came to hear of Ursula's renown, and declared that his happiness would be complete if she were married to his only son. The young man himself also passionately desired this union. So they dispatched an official embassy to the girl's father, and the ambassadors made him generous promises and paid him elaborate compliments, but also added the direst threats about what might happen if they returned empty-handed to their master. Now King Nothus was in a terrible dilemma, firstly because he thought it would be improper of him to hand over a girl who was such a devout Christian to a worshipper of idols; secondly because he knew that she would never agree to such a marriage; and thirdly because he was absolutely terrified of the savage reprisals the pagan king might exact. Ursula, however, inspired by God, persuaded her father to agree to the king's proposal, but only on the following conditions: that the king and her father were to grant her ten, carefully selected, virgins as companions, and then assign to her and each of her ten virgin companions one thousand other virgins; that a fleet of triremes should be assembled for her use; that she should be allowed a space of three years in which to fulfil her vow of virginity; and that her betrothed should be baptized and, during the three years, instructed in the faith. Ursula was acting shrewdly in all this: she hoped that, since her conditions were so difficult to meet, her suitor might have second thoughts about the marriage; or else that she might be presented with an opportunity to dedicate all the virgins, as well as herself, to God. But the young man accepted the conditions willingly, and compelled his father to agree. He was baptized forthwith, and ordered that everything Ursula had demanded be done with all possible speed. Ursula's father also gave orders that his daughter, whom he loved dearly, should take with her as many soldiers as she and her company needed for their assistance and protection.

Then the virgins flooded in from all sides, and people came running from far and wide to witness this great spectacle. Many bishops came to join the virgins on their pilgrimage, among them Pantalus, bishop of Basle, who led them to Rome, came back with them, and with them suffered martyrdom. St Gerasina, the queen of Sicily, came, too. (She had married a cruel beast of a man, but had made him as gentle as a lamb.) Gerasina was the sister of Bishop Maurisius and of Daria, St Ursula's mother. Ursula's father had written a letter to his sister-in-law telling her of Ursula's secret plan, and, inspired by God, she at once left her kingdom in the hands of one of her sons and set sail for Britain with her four daughters, Babilla, Juliana, Victoria and Aurea, and her little son Adrian, who, because of his love for his sisters, had insisted on joining the pilgrimage. At the invitation of Queen Gerasina virgins gathered there from many different lands, and she remained their leader until finally sharing in their martyrdom. When Ursula's demands had been met, and the virgins were finally assembled and the ships and provisions were ready, the queen revealed the secret to her comrades, who unanimously swore loyalty to this unique crusade. Then, running to and fro busily, they began their preparations. Sometimes, as if they were already at war, they staged a simulated flight; they practised all kinds of ploys, trying out every manoeuvre they could think of, and leaving nothing to chance. Sometimes they came back from their exercises at midday, sometimes only just before darkness fell. Princes and noblemen streamed to see the great spectacle and were all filled with admiration and joy.

Finally, after Ursula had converted all the virgins to the faith, they set sail, and in the space of one day, sped by a favourable wind, they reached the Gallic port of Tyella, and from there went on to Cologne. In that city an angel of the Lord appeared to Ursula and told her that they would all return to Cologne, every one of them, and there receive the crown of martyrdom. Then, acting at the angel's behest, they set off for Rome and put in at the city of Basle, where they left the fleet and went on to Rome on foot. Pope Cyriacus was delighted at their arrival (he was himself of British origin, and found many blood relatives among the virgins), and so he and his entire clergy welcomed them with every possible honour. That same night it was divinely revealed to the pope that he would win the palm of martyrdom at their side. But he kept this to himself, and meanwhile baptized many of the virgins who had not yet received the sacrament.

Cyriacus, the nineteenth pope after Peter, had ruled the Church now for one year and eleven weeks, and, seeing that the time was ripe, he summoned his court and informed them of his intention; then, in the presence of them all, he resigned his office and all its privileges. Everyone protested at this, especially the cardinals, who thought he was mad to relinquish the glory of the pontificate in order to chase off after some silly women. But he absolutely refused to listen, and appointed a holy man named Ametos as pope in his place. And it was because he resigned from the apostolic see against the wishes of his clergy that the said clergy removed his name from the register of popes, and, from that time on, the sacred band of virgins lost all the support they had enjoyed within the Roman curia.

Now there were in the Roman army two villainous commanders named Maximus and Africanus, who, seeing this vast gathering of virgins and the great numbers of men and women that flocked to join them, were afraid that because of them the Christian religion might become too widespread. So they investigated the route the virgins were taking, and sent messengers to their kinsman Julius, who was a chief of the Hunnish people, asking him to lead his army against them, since they were Christians, and to massacre them when they reached Cologne. Cyriacus duly left Rome with this noble company of virgins. He was followed by Vincent, a cardinal priest, and James, who had left his native Britain for Antioch, where he had held the office of archbishop for seven years. James had been on a visit to the pope, and had already left Rome when he heard of the arrival of the virgins, so he hurried back to share in their crusade and in their martyrdom. Maurisius, bishop of the city of Levicana, who was the uncle of Babilla and Juliana, and Follarius, bishop of Lucca, and Sulpicius, bishop of Ravenna, were all in Rome at the time and they, too, joined the virgins on their march.

Ethereus, Ursula's betrothed, had remained in Britain, and subsequently, through the message of an angel, was commanded by the Lord to urge his mother to become a Christian. (Ethereus's father had been converted, but had died in the same year, and his son had succeeded to the kingdom.) Now when the holy virgins were returning from Rome with the above-mentioned bishops, Ethereus was prompted by the Lord to go and meet his bride-to-be, and to win the palm of martyrdom with her at Cologne. In obedience to God's commands he had his mother baptized, then, taking her, his little sister Florence (who was already a Christian) and Bishop Clement, he went off to meet the virgins and to share their martyrdom. Marculus, bishop of Greece, and his niece Constantia, the daughter of Dorotheus, king of Constantinople, also went. (Constantia had been pledged in marriage to the young son of a king, but, when he died before their wedding, she had vowed her virginity to the Lord.) They had been urged by a vision to go to Rome, and there they, too, joined the army of virgins to share their martyrdom.

So all the virgins, together with the bishops already mentioned, travelled back to Cologne, where they found the city under siege by the Huns. As soon as the barbarians saw them they rushed at them with terrifying yells, and, like wolves savaging a flock of sheep, put all of them to the sword. They slaughtered every one of them, until at last they came to blessed Ursula. But their chief was so captivated by her extraordinary beauty that he tried to console her for the death of her virgin band, and promised to make her his wife. Ursula contemptuously spurned his offer, and the Hun, realizing that she despised him, let fly an arrow at her, transfixed her and so accomplished her martyrdom.

One of the virgins, a girl named Cordula, had hidden herself on board ship that night in terror, but next day she gave herself up of her own volition to be killed, and so she, too, won her crown of martyrdom. But because she had not suffered with the rest, her feast was never celebrated, until, long afterwards, she appeared to an anchorite and instructed her to see that her own feast should be remembered on the day following that of the other virgins. The martyrdom of these virgins took place in AD 238 . . .

Pope Boniface VIII (1235–1303)

UNAM SANCTAM

Benedetto Gaetani was born in 1235 to an Italian noble family. Late in his life, in 1294, he was invested as Pope Boniface VIII and immediately became embroiled in controversies with the European kings. In 1295 Edward I of England and Philip IV of France, in order to pay for ongoing wars, sought money from clergy in their countries. Boniface responded by issuing a bull forbidding the taxation of the clergy by secular authorities. The kings, in turn, declared the clergy outlaws and stopped the transfer of any money to Rome. Boniface backed down for a time, but the issue returned in broader terms when Philip accused a bishop of treason. Both Philip and Boniface claimed the case for trial in their own courts. In the papal bull Unam Sanctam *(1302) Boniface set forth sweeping claims of papal supremacy. Asserting the unity of the church and the necessity of belonging to the church to achieve salvation, Boniface then requires absolute submission to the pope in order to belong to the church and achieve salvation. In response to Boniface's claim that spiritual authority is greater than secular authority, Philip plotted to abduct Boniface and bring him to France. In 1303, Boniface was attacked in his residence. Although the abduction was not successful, the injuries caused his death a month later.*

We are compelled, our faith urging us, to believe and to hold—and we do firmly believe and simply confess—that there is one holy catholic and apostolic church, outside of which there is neither salvation nor remission of sins; her Spouse proclaiming it in the canticles: "My dove, my undefiled is but one, she is the choice one of her that bare her"; which represents one mystic body, of which body the head is Christ; but of Christ, God. In this church there is one Lord, one faith and one baptism. There was one ark of Noah, indeed, at the time of the flood, symbolizing one church; and this being finished in one cubit had, namely, one Noah as helmsman and commander. And, with the exception of this ark, all things existing upon the earth were, as we read, destroyed. This church, moreover, we venerate as the only one, the Lord saying through His prophet: "Deliver my soul from the sword, my darling from the power of the dog." He prayed at the same time for His soul—that is, for Himself the Head—and for His body—which body, namely, he called the one and only church on account of the unity of the faith promised, of the sacraments, and of the love of

The translation by E. F. Henderson (London: 1896) is printed from Norton Downs' *Basic Documents in Medieval History* (Princeton: Van Nostrand, 1959).

the church. She is that seamless garment of the Lord which was not cut but which fell by lot. Therefore of this one and only church there is one body and one head—not two heads as if it were a monster:—Christ, namely, and the vicar of Christ, St. Peter, and the successor of Peter. For the Lord Himself said to Peter, Feed my sheep. My sheep, He said, using a general term, and not designating these or those particular sheep; from which it is plain that He committed to Him all His sheep. If, then, the Greeks or others say that they were not committed to the care of Peter and his successors, they necessarily confess that they are not of the sheep of Christ; for the Lord says, in John, that there is one fold, one shepherd and one only. We are told by the word of the gospel that in this His fold there are two swords,—a spiritual, namely, and a temporal. For when the apostles said "Behold here are two swords"—when, namely, the apostles were speaking in the church—the Lord did not reply that this was too much, but enough. Surely he who denies that the temporal sword is in the power of Peter wrongly interprets the word of the Lord when He says: "Put up thy sword in its scabbard." Both swords, the spiritual and the material, therefore, are in the power of the church; the one, indeed, to be wielded for the church, the other by the church; the one by the hand of the priest, the other by the hand of kings and knights, but at the will and sufferance of the priest. One sword, moreover, ought to be under the other, and the temporal authority to be subjected to the spiritual. For when the apostle says "there is no power but of God, and the powers that are of God are ordained," they would not be ordained unless sword were under sword and the lesser one, as it were, were led by the other to great deeds. For according to St. Dionysius the law of divinity is to lead the lowest through the intermediate to the highest things. Not therefore, according to the law of the universe, are all things reduced to order equally and immediately; but the lowest through the intermediate, the intermediate through the higher. But that the spiritual exceeds any earthly power in dignity and nobility we ought the more openly to confess the more spiritual things excel temporal ones. This also is made plain to our eyes from the giving of tithes, and the benediction and the sanctification; from the acceptation of this same power, from the control over those same things. For, the truth bearing witness, the spiritual power has to establish the earthly power, and to judge it if it be not good. Thus concerning the church and the ecclesiastical power is verified the prophecy of Jeremiah: "See, I have this day set thee over the nations and over the kingdoms," and the other things which follow. Therefore if the earthly power err it shall 'be judged by the spiritual power; but if the lesser spiritual power err, by the greater. But if the greatest, it can be judged by God alone, not by man, the apostle bearing witness. A spiritual man judges all things, but he himself is judged by no one. This authority, moreover, even though it is given to man and exercised through man, is not human but rather divine, being given by divine lips to Peter and founded on a rock for him and his successors through Christ himself whom he has confessed; the Lord himself saying to Peter: "Whatsoever thou shalt bind," etc. Whoever, therefore, resists this power thus ordained by God, resists the ordination of God, unless he makes believe, like the Manichean, that there are two beginnings. This we consider false and heretical, since by the testimony of Moses, not "in the beginnings," but "in the beginning" God created the Heavens and the earth. Indeed we declare, announce and define, that it is altogether necessary to salvation for every human creature to be subject to, the Roman pontiff. The Lateran, Nov. 14, in our 8th year. As a perpetual memorial of this matter.

Medieval Lyric Poetry

Carmina Burana

Perhaps the best-known manuscript of medieval songs was found at the Benedictine monastery of Benediktbeuern, Bavaria, in 1803. The collection includes songs that celebrate spring, drinking, love, and learning in rhymed Latin (and occasionally German) lyrics that are sometimes serious, often satirical, always clever. The songs were presumably the products of the revelries of itinerant students and scholars who gathered in taverns in university towns. Although the original music for the Carmina Burana *has been recorded several times, many of the songs are familiar today mainly through the great rhythmic setting for chorus, orchestra, and dancers by Carl Orff (1895-1982), the Munich composer, conductor, and theorist who was interested in musical education that involved rhythm and movement. The two songs given here are also high points in Orff's* Carmina Burana *(1937), and the translations attempt the difficult task of miming the rhythm of Orff's setting of the colloquial Latin.*

"O Fortuna"

O how Fortune,
inopportune,
apes the moon's inconstancy:
waxing, waning,
losing, gaining,
life treats us detestably:
first oppressing
then caressing
shifts us like pawns in her play:
destitution,
restitution,
mixes and melts them away.

Reprinted from *Selections from the Carmina Burana*, translated by David Parlett (Penguin, 1986).

Fate, as vicious
as capricious,
whirling your merry-go-round:
evil doings,
worthless wooings,
crumble away to the ground:
darkly stealing,
unrevealing,
working against me you go:
for your measure
of foul pleasure
I bare my back to your blow.

Noble actions,
true transactions,
no longer fall to my lot:
powers to make me
then to break me
all play their part in your plot:
now seize your time—
waste no more time,
pluck these poor strings and let go:
since the strongest
fall the longest
let the world share in my woe.

"In Taberna Quando Sumus"

In the tavern when we're drinking,
though the ground be cold and stinking,
down we go and join the action
with the dice and gaming faction.
what goes on inside the salon
where it's strictly cash per gallon
if you'd like to know, sir, well you
shut your mouth and I shall tell you.

Some are drinking, some are playing,
some their vulgar side displaying:
most of those who like to gamble
wind up naked in the scramble;
some emerge attired in new things,
some in bits and bobs and shoestrings:
no one thinks he'll kick the bucket
dicing for a beery ducat.

First to those who pay for wallowing,
then we layabouts toast the following:
next we drink to all held captive,
thirdly drink to those still active,
fourthly drink to the Christian-hearted,
fifthly drink to the dear departed,
sixthly to our free-and-easy sisters,
seventhly to all out-of-work enlisters.

Eighthly drink to friars deconverted,
ninthly, monks from monast'ries diverted,
tenthly, sailors of the oceans,
eleventhly, louts who cause commotions,
twelfthly, those who wear the penitential,
thirteenth, and whose journey is essential—
to this fat pope, to that thin king—
who the hell cares why they're drinking!

Drinking tinker, drinking tailor,
drinking soldier, drinking sailor,
drinking rich man, drinking poor man,
drinking beggarman, thief and lawman,
drinking servant, drinking master,
drinking mistress, drinking pastor,
drinking doctor, drinking layman,
drinking drunkard, drinking drayman:

Drinking rude man, drinking proper,
drinking tiddler, drinking whopper,
drinking scholar, drinking gypsy,
drinking drunk or maudlin tipsy,
drinking father, drinking mother,
drinking sister, drinking brother,
drinking husbands, wives and lovers
and a hundred thousand others—

Half a million pounds would never
pay for all we drink together:
for we drink beyond all measure,
purely for the sake of pleasure:
thus you see us, poor and shoddy,
criticized by everybody—
God grant that they be confounded
when at last the trump is sounded!

KING RICHARD I (1157–1199)

Richard Coeur-de-Lion (reigned 1189–1199) was the son of England's King Henry II and Eleanor of Aquitaine, whose first husband was the king of France. A sometime crusader, Richard was captured in Austria and held for an enormous ransom. This song, in the style of the troubadour music that was all the rage in France in the late twelfth century, is a musical curse upon Richard's friends for letting him rot so long in prison. Although the Robin Hood legends make him heroic next to his brother, the evil King John, he was a weak and absent king. In fact, his mother ruled during his absences, she saw to the gathering of the ransom, and she traveled to Austria to accompany him home.

"JA NULS HOMS PRIS NE DIRA SA RAISON"

1. A man imprisoned can never speak his mind
As cleverly as those who do not suffer,
But through his song he can some comfort find.
I have a host of friends, poor the gifts they offer.
Shame on them if this ransoming should trail
Into a second year in jail!

2. This they know well, my barons and my men,
English, Norman, Gascon, and Poitevin,
What I'd leave of my property in prison!
O I'm not saying this to cast derision,
But still I'm here in jail!

3. Here is a truth I know that can be told:
Dead men and prisoners have neither parents nor friends,
No one to offer up their silver and gold.
It matters to me, but much more to my men.
For after my death, they'll be bitterly assailed
Because I'm so long in jail!

4. No wonder if I have a grieving heart
When I see my land torn by its lord asunder:
If he'll recall the pact in which we took part
And remember the pledges we vowed we'd both live under,
Truly within the year, without a fail,
I'd be out of jail!

This translation is by James J. Wilhelm in *Lyrics of the Middle Ages* (New York: Garland, 1990).

5. This they know, the Angevins and Tourains,
Those bachelors there who are strong and own a lot,
While I'm encumbered here in another's hands;
They loved me lots, but now they don't love a jot;
Over the plains I don't see a piece of mail
Although I'm still in jail!

6. I've loved and I love still my companions true,
The men of Cahiu and the men of Porcherain,
But tell me, song, if they still love me too,
For never to them was I double-faced or vain:
They're villains if my lands they now assail—
Since I am here in jail!

CONTESSA DE DIA

In twelfth-century France a new way of talking about love swept the country, beginning in the south with the troubadours, *and then spreading northward and into Germany. So popular was the intimate, personal style cultivated by these singers—as if, like today's country-and-western singers, they were giving heartfelt expression to the joys and torments of their own experience—that we know the names of some 400 troubadours and the melodies of almost 300 songs have survived. The melodies were monophonic and could be sung without accompaniment or could be adapted to a variety of styles, some of them borrowed from Arabic music. Four songs have come down from the Contessa de Dia, about whom we know very little. In this song she tells of her resentment at losing her lover to another woman.*

"A CHANTAR M'ER DE SO Q'IEU NO VOLRIA"

I must sing of things I would rather not sing.
So much rancor have I against the man whose sweet friend I am.
For I love him more than anything.
Pity and courtesy are worth nothing to him.
Neither are my beauty or my merit or my good sense.
I'm as trapped and betrayed
as I might have deserved to be, if I hadn't the least charm.

But this consoles me—that I have committed no injury
against you, dear friend, through any fault of mine.
I love you more than Seguin loved valor.
It gives me pleasure to vanquish you in loving—
since you, dearest friend, are the most valiant of men.

This song is translated by Marcelle Thiébaux in the *Writings of Medieval Women:* 2nd Ed. (New York: Garland, 1994).

You treat me proudly in words and looks,
while showing gentleness to all the others.

I marvel at your arrogant presence
confronting me; for I have good reason to grieve.
It's unjust that another love tears you from me.
Whatever she may say—however she may welcome you—
remember the beginning
of our love. Please God that I'm not at fault
for this parting of ours!

Both the great prowess that lodges in your heart,
and your striking pride make me unhappy.
For I don't know of any woman, near or far,
who wouldn't be drawn to you—if she were ready for love.
But you, dear friend, are so knowing, that you ought to
recognize the truest woman.
Remember the verses we exchanged at our parting.

My merit, my high rank, should count for something,
and my beauty, and my faithful heart above all.
And so I'm sending you—there to your great house—
this song that serves as my messenger.
I want to know, best and dearest of noble friends,
why you show yourself so fierce, so savage to me.
I don't know if it's arrogance or ill will.

Messenger, I wish you to tell him this besides:
that lofty pride damages many a man.

WALTHER VON DER VOGELWEIDE (C.1170–C.1230)

As is the case with so many courtly singers of the Middle Ages, very little is known of the life of Walther von der Vogelweide except what he hints at in his songs. He was probably of the nobility, but the name Vogelweide (= not the usual castle or town, but "a field where birds are caught") suggests that he was not of the highest rank. Very likely he travelled from court to court in Austria (where he was born) and Germany, where his political poems suggest he became linked with the movement for freedom from papal power, and where he settled near the end of his life near Würzburg. Some 200 poems by Walther survive, about half of them dealing with the popular theme of love. He is recognized today as the greatest of the German minnesingers *(*minne *= Middle High German for "love"), and "Under der Linden," his best-known song, is admired as a delicate evocation of nature and desire. It is a simple lyric, with the distinction of imagining a young girl as its speaker.*

"UNDER DER LINDEN"

1. Under the linden
On the heath
Where a bed for two was massed,
There you could see
Piled up neat
Pluckings of flowers and of grass.
At the edge of the copse within a vale—
Tandaradei—
Sweetly sang the nightingale.

2. I went secretly
To a meadow shady
Where my sweetheart had gone before.
He did greet me:
"Pretty lady!"—
Then made me happy forevermore.
Did he kiss? Ach, a thousandfold!—
Tandaradei—
See, my mouth still holds the mold!

3. Heaped up there
With royal pride
Was a bedstead he formed of flowers.
A laugh you'd hear
From deep inside
If a stranger ventured into our bower.
From the roses he could tell—
Tandaradei—
Exactly where my head fell.

This translation by James J. Wilhelm is taken from *Medieval Song* (New York: Dutton, 1971).

4. God forbid
That our rendezvous
Be known, for it would bring us shame.
What we did,
Just we two,
We've sworn to hide in each other's name.
O yes—and that little bird—
Tandaradei—
He said he would keep his word.

Dante Alighieri (1265–c. 1321) *Three Sonnets from* La Vita Nuova

Dante is considered by many to be the greatest writer of the Middle Ages. His masterpiece, the Divine Comedy, *traces his visionary journey through Hell, Purgatory, and Heaven, guided first by the spirit of the Roman poet Virgil, then, in Heaven, by his "beloved," Beatrice Portinari. In the fiction of the poem, the heavenly spirit of the dead Beatrice has recognized that Dante has "lost his way" and is in danger of forfeiting his eternal salvation. The vision she sends—vividly portraying the afterlife reserved for souls in the medieval Church's elaborate hierarchy of sins, punishments, and rewards—is intended to recall him to the path of Christian truth.*

If the Divina Commedia *represents Dante's idea of Beatrice's abiding love for him, his earlier treatise,* La Vita Nuova *(= The New Life), describes his love for Beatrice. On its face, the book is actually an analysis of the shorter poetry—twenty-five sonnets, five canzoni, and a ballad—for which he had gained a reputation. The poems are arranged around an account of the events which led to their composition, in the order in which they were written, lending the book the quality of a literary autobiography. Central to its conception was Dante's realization that his love for Beatrice could form the entire motivation and inspiration for his art. By Dante's account—perhaps less factually true than artistically real—he fell in love with Beatrice when he first met her: he was nine and she was eight! According to Dante's account, they didn't speak again until he was eighteen and he soon formed the resolution that all his art from that time forward would be in her honor. His was a rarefied version of "courtly love," for in fact, both Beatrice and Dante married others and lived entirely separate lives. Only a few years later, when she was just twenty-four, Beatrice died and became in Dante's imagination the kind of angelic spirit who manifests the highest form of love in the* Paradiso.

The achievement of Dante, for Italians, is partly his "creation" of the Italian language, the transformation of his Tuscan dialect into what he described as a courtly language that superseded the many dialects that fragmented communication in Italy. In poetry, he was part of a movement called dolce stil nuovo *(= "sweet new style"), which had as its main theme the intense reflection on love and the noble or gentle heart, first showcased in the poetry of Guido Guinizelli, the "wise man" that Dante pays tribute to in "Sonnet 10" below. The beatification of Beatrice into a heavenly inspiration is captured in*

This translation from Dante's Italian by Barbara Reynolds is taken from *La Vita Nuova* (Penguin Classics, 1969).

the twenty-fifth sonnet, near the end. At the end of La Vita Nuova, *just after this sonnet, Dante says: "I hope to compose concerning her what has never been written in rhyme of any woman"—a hope fulfilled in the* Divine Comedy*!*

[SONNET 10]

Love and the noble heart are but one thing,
Even as the wise man tells us in his rhyme,
The one without the other venturing
As well as reason from a reasoning mind.
Nature, disposed to love, creates Love king
Making the heart a dwelling-place for him
Wherein he lies quiescent, slumbering
Sometimes a little, now a longer time.
Then beauty in a virtuous woman's face
Pleases the eyes, striking the heart so deep
A yearning for the pleasing thing may rise.
Sometimes so long it lingers in that place
Love's spirit is awakened from his sleep.
By a worthy man a woman's moved likewise.

[SONNET 15]

So deeply to be reverenced, so fair,
My lady is when she her smile bestows,
All sound of speaking falters to a close
And eyes which would behold her do not dare.
Of praises sung of her she is aware,
Yet clad in sweet humility she goes.
A thing from Heaven sent, to all she shows
A miracle in which the world may share.
Her beauty entering the beholder's eye
Brings sweetness to the heart, all sweets above:
None comprehends who does not know this state;
And from her lips there seems to emanate
A gentle spirit, full of tender love,
Which to the soul enraptured whispers: "Sigh!"

[SONNET 25]

Beyond the widest of the circling spheres
A sigh which leaves my heart aspires to move.
A new celestial influence which Love
Bestows on it by virtue of his tears
Impels it ever upwards. As it nears

Its goal of longing in the realms above
The pilgrim spirit sees a vision of
A soul in glory whom the host reveres.
Gazing at her, it speaks of what it sees
In subtle words I do not comprehend
Within my heart forlorn which bids it tell.
That noble one is named, I apprehend,
For frequently it mentions Beatrice;
This much, beloved ladies, I know well.

English Songs

"Sumer is icumen in"

This well-known thirteenth-century song, from British Museum MS Harley 978, f. 11v (modernized here by the editor), is the first known example of a canon *(rota, or "round"), and it is also important in the development of* gymel. *A round (like "Row, row, row your boat") was called a canon because a single line of music could be elaborated into a complex piece simply through rules. In the* Sumer-*canon, four voices sing through the whole song, the second, third, and fourth singers each beginning when the previous voice has finished the first line. A fifth and sixth voice sing the two* pes *("foot") lines continuously beneath the melody. The result is a six-part full harmony based on major thirds (*gymel*), the pleasant harmony that is considered natural today but in the Middle Ages was admired only in England. In Europe, medieval harmony was based on Pythagorean ideas that favored the fourth (C-F), fifth (C-G), and octave (C-C)—intervals that sound "hollow" or "medieval" today. In the fifteenth century, parallel thirds (C-E) came to be accepted as non-dissonant throughout Western music, under the influence of English music.*

Sumer is icumen in—	*Spring has come*
lhude sing, cuccu!	*loudly*
Groweth sed and bloweth med	*meadow*
and springth the wde nu.	*woods*
Sing, cuccu!	
Awe bleteth after lomb,	*ewe bleats*
lhouth after calve cu;	*lows, cow*
bulluc sterteth, bucke verteth—	*bull leaps, farts*
murye sing, cuccu!	
Cuccu, cuccu!	
Wel singes thu, cuccu;	
ne swik thu naver nu.	*Cease, never*

pes
Sing, cuccu, nu! Sing, cuccu!
Sing, cuccu! Sing, cuccu, nu!

"Myrie it is"

This Middle English song, from Bodleian Library MS Rawlinson G.22, f. 1v (modernized here by the editor), is, along with the Sumer-canon *above, one of only 33 English songs before 1400 which survive with their music intact. It is much more common in medieval Europe for words to have been written down without any notation of the music: people either just "knew" the melody ("to be sung to the tune of* Greensleeves*") or they didn't know how to read or write musical notation but wanted to remember the words. This short poem, sung to a wonderful dance melody that doesn't quite match the stark ending of the text, is typical of English lyrics that allow several possible interpretations.*

Myrie it is while sumer ilast	
with fugheles song;	*bird's*
oc nu neheth windes blast	*but, draws near*
and weder strong.	*weather*
Ei, ei! what this niht is long!	*Alas! how long this night is!*
And ich, with wel michel wrong,	*very great*
soregh and murn and fast.	*sorrow*

"Ubi Sunt Qui Ante Nos Fuerunt"

Although this lyric is in Middle English, it is customarily assigned as a title the Latin phrase Ubi sunt qui ante nos fuerunt, *for the first line of the poem ("Where are they who lived before us") is an exact translation of this phrase associated with medieval Latin poems celebrating the "good old days" or lamenting the transitoriness of the pleasures of life. For instance, the Latin line begins the second stanza in the well-known—even today—student tavern song,* Gaudeamus igitur *("Let us rejoice while we are young"). In fact, this theme in poetry—"where are they now"—is usually called the* ubi sunt *motif, and it has its own characteristic images. In the Old English poetry of the Anglo-Saxons, for instance, this motif is often expressed in the image of a hawk flying through an abandoned hall. "Were beth they" is not, however, simply a nostalgic lament for the warmth of court and companions. Instead it condemns the courtly pleasures so attractive to the "rich ladies in their bower" with the startling punch line: "in a twinkling of an eye/ Their souls were lost." The poem is, then, a Christian attack upon the vanities of the world, and is closely related to the similar medieval motifs of* contemptus mundi *("contempt for the world") and* memento mori *("reminder of death").*

Were beth they biforen us weren,	
Houndes laden and havekes beren,	*led, hawks, carried*
And hadden feld and wode?	*woods*
The riche levedies in hoere bour,	
That wereden gold in hoere tressour,	*wore, headdress*
With hoere brightte rode?	*face*
Eten and drounken, and maden hem glad;	*(they) ate, made themselves merry*
Hoere lif was al with gamen ilad;	*games, led (i.e., "spent")*
Men kneleden hem biforen;	*knelt*

They beren hem wel swathe heye; — *carried themselves very high*
And, in a twincling of on eye,
  Hoere soules weren forloren.

Were is that lawing and that song — *laughing*
That trayling and that proude yong, — *parading, gait*
  Tho hauekes and tho houndes?
Al that joye is went away,
That wele is comen to "Weylaway!"— — *weal, woe*
  To manie harde stoundes. — *times*

Hoere paradis they nomen here, — *took*
And nou they lien in helle ifere; — *together*
  The fuir hit brennes hevere. — *fire, burns ever*
Long is ay, and long is o, — *alas, oh*
Long is wy, and long is wo; — *why, woe*
  Thennes ne cometh they nevere. — *thence*

This poem from *MS Digby 86* in Oxford's Bodleian Library has been regularized and glossed for this collection by the editor.

Geoffrey Chaucer (c.1343–1400) "Chaucers Wordes Unto Adam, His Owne Scriveyn"

In this lyric poem the English poet Geoffrey Chaucer (c.1343–1400) complains about the bad job his scribe does in copying his works. Because Chaucer must rub and scrape the parchment to make corrections, he curses the scribe to the same fate, rubbing and scraping the dandruff on his head. The text, from Trinity College Cambridge MS R.3.20, is modernized by the editor.

In July, 2004, the world of Chaucerian scholarship was rocked when a scholar from Maine, after she had studied the signatures of more than 200 scribes on many official documents, announced that she had discovered the identity of Chaucer's scribe. He was Adam Pinkhurst, son of a Surrey landowner. The discovery is important not simply for revealing the butt of Chaucer's anger in this short poem, but because Pinkhurst, as the "writer" of the two earliest and most authoritative manuscripts of Chaucer's Canterbury Tales, *put together from scattered fragments after Chaucer's death, is in effect the first editor of Chaucer's masterpiece.*

Adam scriveyn, if ever it thee befalle — *scribe*
Boece or Troylus for to wryten newe, — *Boethius' Consolation,*
Under thy long lokkes thou most have the scalle, — *Troilus & Criseyde*
But after my makyng thow wryte more trewe; — *scales on the scalp*
So ofte adaye I mot thy werk renewe, — *writing (poems)*
It to correcte and eke to rubbe and scrape, — *also*
And al is thorugh thy negligence and rape.

Richard Rolle (1290–1349)

Mysticism is broadly understood to have as its goals release from worldly entanglements and the experience of union with a spiritual reality or with God. Eastern religions (Hinduism, Buddhism, Taoism) are often characterized as having a strong core of mysticism, and the same is true of sufi *Islam. Less well known is the significant tradition of Christian mysticism during the Middle Ages. Christians who felt a mystical calling were often nurtured in the monastic or fraternal orders, because those orders had been created to provide a communal release from the gritty necessities of living in the world. Hildegard of Bingen, for instance, was a Benedictine, Meister Eckhart a Dominican, and Teresa of Ávila a Carmelite. There were other individuals for whom even communal worship would have impeded their sense of Christian vocation, and they often flourished in varying degrees of isolation. Anchorites and anchoresses lived lives of prayer and meditation walled up in enclosed cells on the sides of churches. Hermits, like Richard Rolle of Hampole, usually lived in a cave or a cell, traditionally in the desert, in the forest, or on someone's "back eighty." In his Latin treatise,* The Fire of Love, *Richard Rolle says that "hermits rightly have one controlling motive: they live loving God and their neighbour; they despise worldly approval; they flee, so far as they may, from the face of man; they hold all men more worthy than themselves; they give their minds continually to devotion; they hate idleness; they withstand manfully the pleasures of the flesh; they taste and seek ardently heavenly things; they leave earthly things on one side without coveting them; and they find their delight in the sweetness of prayer" (trans. Clifton Wolters; Penguin Classics, 1972: p. 83).*

Richard Rolle was educated at the University of Oxford, but began a life of wandering in hermit's clothing when he was not yet twenty. Later in his life, he settled in an isolated hermit's cell in Hampole, near a Cistercian nunnery. He wrote religious treatises in English and in Latin, translated parts of the Bible, and (like many other mystics) found his solitude tried by the intrusions of people seeking counsel, by followers, and by disciples. Most of his English works were written for the education of groups of women and nuns,

These selections have been translated by the editor for this collection from the Middle English texts found in *Yorkshire Writers: Richard Rolle,* Vol 1 (1895): "Ego dormio" from *MS Cambridge Dd V.64,* and the "Passion Meditation" from *MS Cambridge L1 I.8.*

and he became particularly influential among a group of fourteenth-century English mystics, including Walter Hilton (The Scale of Perfection), *Dame Julian of Norwich* (Revelations of Divine Love), *and the writer of the* Cloud of Unknowing. *Margery Kempe, whose autobiography is excerpted in this volume, also believed her "shewings" to be mystical experiences in this strong English tradition.*

The mystical experience, being beyond language, is notoriously difficult to describe. In The Fire of Love, *Rolle describes his own mystical union with God as the perfect expression of love: "I have found that to love Christ above all else will involve three things: warmth and song and sweetness. . . . let me press forward with all my strength so that my love becomes more fervent, my song more fluent, and my experience of love's sweetness all the fuller" (88-89). This experience for Rolle comes about through prayer and meditation, motivated by an intense love. In his instructional letter addressed to a young nun,* "Ego dormio et cor meum vigilat" *(="I sleep but my heart is awake"), he describes this love and suggests meditation on the name of Jesus. Among his writings are several such meditations, including extended meditations on the Passion (crucifixion) of Christ. These meditations are surprisingly vivid in their detail, adding to the biblical accounts the sensual cues of one who in his imagination is present as the events unfold. While the fourteenth century is often described as being saturated with the imagery of death and suffering, these striking images in Rolle work (as was sometimes said of Mel Gibson's controversial 2004 film,* The Passion of the Christ*) more specifically to create a strong identification with the human Jesus, a first step in the ascent toward participation in the love of God.*

---

from "*Ego dormio et cor meum vigilat*"

Perfect spiritual life is to despise the world and desire the joy of heaven, and destroy through God's grace all wicked desires of the flesh. It is to forget the solace and the affection of your family, and love them only for God—whether they die or live, or be poor or rich, healthy or sick, or in woe or well-being, to give thanks always to God and bless him for all his works. For his judgments are so secret that no creature can comprehend them. Oftentimes people gain their desires and their wants in this world, but hell in the other; others have pain and persecution and anguish in this life, but gain heaven for their reward. Therefore, if your friends are always at their ease with health and wealth in this world, you and they both should have the more fear that they will lose heaven's joy without end. If they are in penance and sickness, or if they live rightly, they may trust to come into bliss. Therefore in this degree of love you shall be filled with the grace of the Holy Spirit so that you shall not feel any sorrow nor tears except for spiritual things, such as for your sins and other men's, or for the love of Jesus Christ, in thinking of his Passion. And I want you to have it much in mind for it will kindle your heart to count as nothing all the goods of this world, and the joy they bring, and to desire burningly the light of heaven, with angels and saints.

And when your heart is wholly ordained to the service of God, and all worldly thoughts put out, then you will want to steal off alone to think on Christ and to be constantly praying. For through good thoughts and holy prayers, your heart will burn with the love of Jesus Christ, and then you will feel sweetness and spiritual joy both in praying and in meditation. And when you are alone, give your attention to saying the psalms in the Psalter, and the "Our Father," and the Ave Maria. And do not concern yourself to say many, but rather only to say them well, with all the devotion that you can, lifting up your thoughts to heaven. It is better to say seven psalms with the desire of Christ's love, having your heart in your praying, than to say seven hundred thousand, letting your heart wander to the vanities of bodily things. What good hopes can come from it, if you let your tongue blabber on the book while your heart runs about to different places in the world? Therefore set your thought on Christ and he will attract it to him, and protect you from the venom of worldly business.

And I pray you, as you yearn to become God's lover, that you love his name JESUS and meditate on it in your heart, so that you never forget it, wherever you are. And truly I say to you that you will find much joy and comfort therein: and for the love with which you love Jesus so tenderly and so specially, you shall be filled full of grace on earth and become Christ's dear servant in heaven. For nothing pleases God so much as the true love of this name Jesus. If you love it right and lastingly, and never stop for anything that men may do or say, you shall be received into a higher life than you can imagine. His goodness is so great, that when we inwardly ask him for one, he will give five: so well paid is he when we set our hearts to love him.

In this degree of love you will surely overcome your enemies: the world, the devil, and the flesh. But nevertheless you will always have to do battle while you live; until you die it is necessary for you to take care to stand, so that you don't fall into delights, nor into evil thoughts, nor into evil words, nor into evil deeds. Therefore, always treasure your desire to love Christ truly. Your flesh you will overcome by saving your virginity for God's love only; or, if you are no longer a virgin, through chaste living and self-control in thought and deed, and through careful abstinence.

from "*Meditations on the Passion*"

Dear Lord Jesus, mercy, who are the fountain of mercy, why will my heart not burst and cleave in two? How can it ever last, when it runs in my heart how woeful you were when they removed your tunic? When the false Herod commanded that it be taken off of you, it clung fast to the blood from that harsh scourging of the flesh of your body, so that your blessed skin was cruelly beaten and ripped; your robe clung to it and was dried to it. Your flesh was so tender, so weak and so sore, but they pulled it off your body piteously and roughly, without regard for your agony, and the stripping ripped off pieces of dried blood and torn skin. Then was your weak body, precious Lord, all ruefully raw and bleeding; the steam rose from your body and reeked all around—one can imagine the dew-drops that formed from it.

Ah, Lord, I see your red blood run down your cheeks in streams after each stroke, in front and behind. The skin of your head has been ripped by your crown, each thorn piercing through to the skull. Alas that I shall live to see my gracious Lord, who never did any harm, suffering so meekly, and so shamefully treated! The lamenting and the groaning, the sorrow and the sighing, the pity of his countenance—I would it were my death! The Crown of all bliss, who crowns all the blessed and is King of all kings and Lord of all lords, is himself crowned with thorns by these hellhounds, who despised and befouled the worship of heaven. . . .

Ah, Lord, your sorrow, why was it not my death? Now they lead you forth naked as a worm, the tormenters and armed knights all about you. The press of the people was exceedingly strong; they pushed and harried you so shamefully; they spurned you with their feet as if you were a dog. I see in my mind how pitifully you go, your body is so bloody, so raw and so scabbed, the crown is so sharp that sits on your head. Your hair, matted with blood, moves in the wind; your lovely face so pale and so bruised with buffeting and with beating, with spitting and with squirting, the blood flowed down so that I shudder at the sight. So loathsome and so ugly have the Jews made you that you look more like a leper than a clean man. So heavy, so high, and so hard is the cross that they tied so tightly to your bare back.

Ah, Lord, the groaning that you made, so painfully and so heavily it pressed on your bone. Your body is so weak, so feeble and so weary, what with your great fasting before you were taken, and all night kept awake without any rest, with beating and with buffeting so far overtaken, that you go all stooped over, and grim is your expression. The flesh where the cross sits is all raw, the wounds and blisters are black and blue; the pain of that burden sits so sorely on you that each foot that you go stings you to the heart. Thus in this groaning and in this much pain you go out of Jerusalem to your death. . . .

Ah, Lord, the sorrow that pierces your heart when you cast your eyes on your mother. You saw her following after you among the great press of people; as a woman besides herself she wrung her hands, weeping and sighing, her arms flailing above her, the tears from her eyes falling at her feet. She fell in a dead swoon more than once, for sorrow at the pains that smite her heart. The grief that she felt and the great sorrow added even more to all your other pains. And when she knew that *that* was so, then she felt even worse, and you also for her weeping: so was your grief, each for the other, increased many times with heaping sorrows.

Jacob von Königshofen (1346–1420)

CHRONICLE

Jacob von Königshofen was an archivist, and his Chronicle *contains an account that reminds us that the twentieth century doesn't have a monopoly on atrocities. In fact, before the Nazi Holocaust in the middle of the last century, the worst cases of wholesale slaughter probably occurred in the Middle Ages, the favorite victims being heretical Christians in southern France and Jews.*

In earlier times, Christian doctrine labeled as usury the collection of any interest on loans. Christians were therefore forbidden to lend money at interest, and Jews became the principal moneylenders, especially on the scale needed to finance the wars of the nobility. It often became convenient for a king, when his debts were particularly large, to find an excuse to banish the Jews, and cancel any debts owed them. Because of the loss of property, the Jews early on learned not to have their own money tied up in real estate, preferring easily portable valuables like jewelry and precious metals.

The same prejudices which justified the confiscation of property often inflamed more dangerous passions. Jews, conveniently remembered from the gospel accounts as the people who had killed Christ, were resented by some Christians. The rumors spread that Passover rituals required the blood of Christian children, or that water supplies were poisoned by Jews to cause outbreaks of disease and plague. In these cases, unruly mobs committed atrocities like that in Strasbourg on St. Valentine's Day in 1349, during the Black Death. The Strasbourg historian F. Closener was probably an eyewitness to the terrible events, and his account was incorporated by Königshofen into his Chronicle.

[THE CREMATION OF THE STRASBOURG JEWRY]

In the year 1349 there occurred the greatest epidemic that ever happened. Death went from one end of the earth to the other, on that side and this side of the sea, and it was greater among the Saracens than among the Christians. In some lands everyone died so that no one was left. Ships were also found on the sea laden with wares; the

This document is taken from *The Jew in the Medieval World: A Source Book: 315–1791,* by Jacob R. Marcus (Jewish Publication Society, 1938; rpt. Atheneum, 1969).

crew had all died and no one guided the ship. The bishop of Marseilles and priests and monks and more than half of all the people there died with them. In other kingdoms and cities so many people perished that it would be horrible to describe. The pope at Avignon stopped all sessions of court, locked himself in a room, allowed no one to approach him and had a fire burning before him all the time. [This last was probably intended as some sort of disinfectant.] And from what this epidemic came, all wise teachers and physicians could only say that it was God's will. And as the plague was now here, so was it in other places, and lasted more than a whole year. This epidemic also came to Strasbourg in the summer of the above-mentioned year, and it is estimated that about sixteen thousand people died.

In the matter of this plague the Jews throughout the world were reviled and accused in all lands of having caused it through poison which they are said to have put into the water and the wells—that is what they were accused of—and for this reason the Jews were burnt all the way from the Mediterranean into Germany, but not in Avignon, for the pope protected them there.

Nevertheless they tortured a number of Jews in Berne and Zofingen [Switzerland] who then admitted that they had put poison into many wells, and they also found the poison in the wells. Thereupon they burnt the Jews in many towns and wrote of this affair to Strasbourg, Freiburg, and Basel in order that they too should burn their Jews. But the leaders in these three cities in whose hands the government lay did not believe anything ought to be done to the Jews. However in Basel the citizens marched to the city hall and compelled the council to take an oath that they would burn the Jews, and that they would allow no Jew to enter the city for the next two hundred years. Thereupon the Jews were arrested in all these places and a conference was arranged to meet at Benfeld [Alsace, February 8, 1349]. The bishop of Strasbourg [Berthold II], all the feudal lords of Alsace, and representatives of the three above-mentioned cities came there. The deputies of the city of Strasbourg were asked what they were going to do with their Jews. They answered and said that they knew no evil of them. Then they asked the Strasbourgers why they had closed the wells and put away the buckets, and there was a great indignation and clamour against the deputies from Strasbourg. So finally the bishop and the lords and the Imperial Cities agreed to do away with the Jews. The result was that they were burnt in many cities, and wherever they were expelled they were caught by the peasants and stabbed to death or drowned. . . .

[The town-council of Strasbourg which wanted to save the Jews was deposed on the 9th/10th of February, and the new council gave in to the mob, who then arrested the Jews on Friday, the 13th.]

On Saturday—that was St. Valentine's Day—they burnt the Jews on a wooden platform in their cemetery. There were about two thousand people of them. Those who wanted to baptize themselves were spared. [Some say that about a thousand accepted baptism.] Many small children were taken out of the fire and baptized against the will of their fathers and mothers. And everything that was owed to the Jews was cancelled, and the Jews had to surrender all pledges and notes that they had taken for debts. The council, however, took the cash that the Jews possessed and divided it among the working-men proportionately. The money was indeed the thing that killed the Jews. If they had been poor and if the feudal lords had not been in debt to them, they would not have been burnt. After this wealth was divided among the artisans some gave their share to the cathedral or to the Church on the advice of their confessors.

Thus were the Jews burnt at Strasbourg, and in the same year in all the cities of the Rhine, whether Free Cities or Imperial Cities or cities belonging to the lords. In some towns they burnt the Jews after a trial, in others, without a trial. In some cities the Jews themselves set fire to their houses and cremated themselves.

It was decided in Strasbourg that no Jew should enter the city for a hundred years, but before twenty years had passed, the council and magistrates agreed that they ought to admit the Jews again into the city for twenty years. And so the Jews came back again to Strasbourg in the year 1368 after the birth of our Lord.

Giovanni Boccaccio (1313–1375)

THE DECAMERON

In spite of his literary bent, Boccaccio's early years were spent in business in Naples, where he also studied canon law. Because of his family's implication in a bankruptcy, he returned to his family home in Florence and began more seriously pursuing his literary interests, troubled by poverty and financial reverses. His early poems (some written in Naples) exploited the romance themes of chivalry and love. Several of them, in fact, are well known to English readers because they were translated, or transformed, by the English poet Geoffrey Chaucer (1343–1400)—Boccaccio's Teseida *became Chaucer's* Knight's Tale, *Boccaccio's* Il Filostrato *became Chaucer's* Troilus and Criseyde, *which in turn became Shakespeare's play* Troilus and Cressida.

The Black Death, which struck Florence when Boccaccio was there in 1348, became the occasion for his masterpiece, The Decameron. *It is a collection of 100 tales told by a group of 7 young ladies and 3 young men from Florence, who decide to flee to one of their villas outside the city when the plague is at its height. To pass the time, they devise a tale-telling game: every day each of them will tell a tale, the theme for each day being set by the presiding ruler for that day. After ten days, each of them would have chosen the theme for a day, and each would have told ten tales, a hundred in all. Framed thus, Boccaccio's collection provides a remarkable view of medieval preoccupations, expressed through tales of love, treachery, nobility, lust, piety, and idealism. Some of the tales were so scurrilous—like the "Tale of Alibech," naturally included here—that they were excluded from English versions of* The Decameron *until well into the twentieth century. In addition, Boccaccio's introductory account of the plague in Florence is a remarkable social document, providing a unique view of one of the most devastating calamities in human history.*

AUTHOR'S INTRODUCTION [THE PLAGUE IN FLORENCE]

Most gracious ladies, knowing that you are all by nature pitiful, I know that in your judgment this work will seem to have a painful and sad origin. For it brings to mind

Reprinted from *Tales from the Decameron of Giovanni Boccaccio*, translated by Richard Aldington (Garden City Publishing Company, 1930).

the unhappy recollection of that late dreadful plague, so pernicious to all who saw or heard of it. But I would not have this frighten you from reading further, as though you were to pass through nothing but sighs and tears in your reading. This dreary opening will be like climbing a steep mountain side to a most beautiful and delightful valley, which appears the more pleasant in proportion to the difficulty of the ascent. The end of happiness is pain, and in like manner misery ends in unexpected happiness.

This brief fatigue (I say brief, because it occupies only a few words) is quickly followed by pleasantness and delight, as I promised you above; which, if I had not promised, you would not expect perhaps from this opening. Indeed, if I could have taken you by any other way than this, which I know to be rough, I would gladly have done so; but since I cannot otherwise tell you how the tales you are about to read came to be told, I am forced by necessity to write in this manner.

In the year 1348 after the fruitful incarnation of the Son of God, that most beautiful of Italian cities, noble Florence, was attacked by deadly plague. It started in the East either through the influence of the heavenly bodies or because God's just anger with our wicked deeds sent it as a punishment to mortal men; and in a few years killed an innumerable quantity of people. Ceaselessly passing from place to place, it extended its miserable length over the West. Against this plague all human wisdom and foresight were vain. Orders had been given to cleanse the city of filth, the entry of any sick person was forbidden, much advice was given for keeping healthy; at the same time humble supplications were made to God by pious persons in processions and otherwise. And yet, in the beginning of the spring of the year mentioned, its horrible results began to appear, and in a miraculous manner. The symptoms were not the same as in the East, where a gush of blood from the nose was the plain sight of inevitable death; but it began both in men and women with certain swellings in the groin and under the armpit. They grew to the size of a small apple or an egg, more or less, and were vulgarly called tumours. In a short space of time these tumours spread from the two parts named all over the body. Soon after this the symptoms changed and black or purple spots appeared on the arms and thighs or any other part of the body, sometimes a few large ones, sometimes many little ones. These spots were a certain sign of death, just as the original tumour had been and still remained.

No doctor's advice, no medicine could overcome or alleviate this disease. An enormous number of ignorant men and women set up as doctors in addition to those who were trained. Either the disease was such that no treatment was possible or the doctors were so ignorant that they did not know what caused it, and consequently could not administer the proper remedy. In any case very few recovered; most people died within about three days of the appearance of the tumours described above, most of them without any fever or other symptoms.

The violence of this disease was such that the sick communicated it to the healthy who came near them, just as a fire catches anything dry or oily near it. And it even went further. To speak to or go near the sick brought infection and common death to the living; and moreover, to touch the clothes or anything else the sick had touched or worn gave the disease to the person touching.

What I am about to tell now is a marvelous thing to hear; and if I and others had not seen it with our own eyes I would not dare to write it, however much I was willing to believe and whatever the good faith of the person from whom I heard it. So violent was the malignancy of this plague that it was communicated, not only from one man to another, but from garments of the sick or dead man to animals of another species, which caught the disease in that way and very quickly died of it. One day among other occasions I saw with my own eyes (as I said just now) the rags left lying in the street of a poor man who had died of the plague; two pigs came along, and as their habit is, turned the clothes over with their snouts and then munched at them, with the result that they both fell dead almost at once on the rags, as if they had been poisoned.

For these and similar or greater occurrences, such fear and fanciful notions took possession of the living that almost all of them adopted the same cruel policy, which was entirely to avoid the sick and everything belonging to them. By so doing, each one thought he would secure his own safety.

Some thought that moderate living and the avoidance of all superfluity would preserve them from the epidemic. They formed small communities, living entirely separate from everybody else. They shut themselves up in houses where there were no sick, eating the finest food and drinking the best wine very temperately, avoiding all excess, allowing no news or discussion of death and sickness, and passing the time in music and suchlike pleasures. Others thought just the opposite. They thought the sure cure for the plague was to drink and be merry, to go about singing and amusing themselves, satisfying every appetite they could, laughing and jesting at what happened. They put their words into practice, spent day and night going from tavern to tavern, drinking immoderately, or went into other people's houses, doing only those things which pleased them. This they could easily do because everyone felt doomed and had abandoned his property, so that most houses became common property and any stranger who went in made use of them as if he had owned them. And with all this bestial behaviour, they avoided the sick as much as possible.

In this suffering and misery of our city, the authority of human and divine laws almost disappeared, for, like other men, the ministers and the executors of the laws were all dead or sick or shut up with their families, so that no duties were carried out. Every man was therefore able to do as he pleased.

Many others adopted a course of life midway between the two just described. They did not restrict their victuals so much as the former, nor allow themselves to be drunken and dissolute like the latter, but satisfied their appetites moderately. They did not shut themselves up, but went about, carrying flowers or scented herbs or perfumes in their hands, in the belief that it was an excellent thing to comfort their brain with such odours; for the whole air was infected with the smell of dead bodies, of sick persons and medicines.

Others again held a still more cruel opinion, which they thought would keep them safe. They said that the only medicine against the plaguestricken was to go right away from them. Men and women, convinced of this and caring about nothing but themselves, abandoned their own city, their own houses, their dwellings, their relatives, their property, and went abroad or at least to the country round Florence, as if God's wrath in punishing men's wickedness with this plague would not follow them but strike only those who remained within the walls of the city, or as if they thought nobody in the city would remain alive and that its last hour had come.

Not everyone who adopted any of these various opinions died, nor did all escape. Some when they were still healthy had set the example of avoiding the sick, and, falling ill themselves, died untended.

One citizen avoided another, hardly any neighbour troubled about others, relatives never or hardly ever visited each other. Moreover, such terror was struck into the hearts of men and women by this calamity, that brother abandoned brother, and the uncle his nephew, and the sister her brother, and very often the wife her husband. What is even worse and nearly incredible is that fathers and mothers refused to see and tend their children, as if they had not been theirs.

Thus, a multitude of sick men and women were left without any care except from the charity of friends (but these were few), or the greed of servants, though not many of these could be had even for high wages. Moreover, most of them were coarse-minded men and women, who did little more than bring the sick what they asked for or watch over them when they were dying. And very often these servants lost their lives and their earnings. Since the sick were thus abandoned by neighbours, relatives and friends, while servants were scarce, a habit sprang up which had never been heard of before. Beautiful and noble women, when they fell sick, did not scruple to take a young or old man-servant, whoever he might be, and with no sort of shame, expose every part of their bodies to these men as if they had been women, for they were compelled by the necessity of their sickness to do so. This, perhaps, was a cause of looser morals in those women who survived.

In this way many people died who might have been saved if they had been looked after. Owing to the lack of attendants for the sick and the violence of the plague, such a multitude of people in the city died day and night that it was stupefying to hear of, let alone to see. From sheer necessity, then, several ancient customs were quite altered among the survivors.

The custom had been (as we still see it today), that women relatives and neighbours should gather at the house of the deceased, and there lament with the family. At the same time the men would gather at the door with the male neighbours and other citizens. Then came the clergy, few or many according to the dead person's rank; the coffin was placed on the shoulders of his friends and carried with funeral pomp of lighted candles and dirges to the church which the deceased had chosen before dying. But as the fury of the plague increased, this custom wholly or nearly disappeared, and new customs arose. Thus, people died, not only without having a number of women near them, but without a single witness. Very few indeed were honoured with the piteous laments and bitter tears of their relatives, who, on the contrary, spent their time in mirth, feasting and jesting. Even the women abandoned womanly pity and adopted this custom for their own safety. Few were they whose bodies were accompanied to church by more than ten or a dozen neighbours. Nor were these grave and honourable citizens but grave-diggers from the lowest of the people who got themselves called sextons, and performed the task for money. They took up the bier and hurried it off, not to the church chosen by the deceased but to the church nearest, preceded by four or six of the clergy with few candles and often none at all. With the aid of the grave-diggers, the clergy huddled the bodies away in any grave they could find, without giving themselves the trouble of a long or solemn burial service.

The plight of the lower and most of the middle classes was even more pitiful to behold. Most of them remained in their houses, either through poverty or in hopes of safety, and fell sick by thousands. Since they received no care and attention, almost all of them died. Many ended their lives in the streets both at night and during the day;

and many others who died in their houses were only known to be dead because the neighbours smelled their decaying bodies. Dead bodies filled every corner. Most of them were treated in the same manner by the survivors, who were more concerned to get rid of their rotting bodies than moved by charity towards the dead. With the aid of porters, if they could get them, they carried the bodies out of the houses and laid them at the doors, where every morning quantities of the dead might be seen. They then were laid on biers, or, as these were often lacking, on tables.

Often a single bier carried two or three bodies, and it happened frequently that a husband and wife, two or three brothers, or father and son were taken off on the same bier. It frequently happened that two priests, each carrying a cross, would go out followed by three or four biers carried by porters; and where the priests thought there was one person to bury, there would be six or eight, and often, even more. Nor were these dead honoured by tears and lighted candles and mourners, for things had reached such a pass that people cared no more for dead men than we care for dead goats. Thus it plainly appeared that what the wise had not learned to endure with patience through the few calamities of ordinary life, became a matter of indifference even to the most ignorant people through the greatness of this misfortune.

Such was the multitude of corpses brought to the churches every day and almost every hour that there was not enough consecrated ground to give them burial, especially since they wanted to bury each person in the family grave, according to the old custom. Although the cemeteries were full they were forced to dig huge trenches, where they buried the bodies by hundreds. Here they stowed them away like bales in the hold of a ship and covered them with a little earth, until the whole trench was full.

Not to pry any further into all the details of the miseries which afflicted our city, I shall add that the surrounding country was spared nothing of what befell Florence. The villages on a smaller scale were like the city; in the fields and isolated farms the poor wretched peasants and their families were without doctors and any assistance, and perished in the highways, in their fields and houses, night and day, more like beasts than men. Just as the townsmen became dissolute and indifferent to their work and property, so the peasants, when they saw that death was upon them, entirely neglected the future fruits of their past labours both from the earth and from cattle, and thought only of enjoying what they had. Thus it happened that cows, asses, sheep, goats, pigs, fowls and even dogs, those faithful companions of man, left the farms and wandered at their will through the fields, where the wheat crops stood abandoned, unreaped and ungarnered. Many of these animals seemed endowed with reason, for, after they had pastured all day, they returned to the farms for the night of their own free will, without being driven.

Returning from the country to the city, it may be said that such was the cruelty of Heaven, and perhaps in part of men, that between March and July more than one hundred thousand persons died within the walls of Florence, what between the violence of the plague and the abandonment in which the sick were left by the cowardice of the healthy. And before the plague it was not thought that the whole city held so many people.

Oh, what great palaces, how many fair houses and noble dwellings, once filled with attendants and nobles and ladies, were emptied to the meanest servant! How many famous names and vast possessions and renowned estates were left without an heir! How many gallant men and fair ladies and handsome youths, whom Galen, Hippocrates and AEsculapius themselves would have said were in perfect health, at noon dined with their relatives and friends, and at night supped with their ancestors in the next world!

THIRD DAY, TENTH TALE [ALIBECH AND RUSTICO]

Most gracious ladies, perhaps you have never heard how the devil is put into hell; and so, without departing far from the theme upon which you have all spoken today, I shall tell you about it. Perhaps when you have learned it, you also will be able to save your souls, and you may also discover that although love prefers to dwell in gay palaces and lovely rooms rather than in poor huts, yet he sometimes makes his power felt among thick woods and rugged mountains and desert caves. Whereby we may well perceive that all us are subject to his power.

Now, to come to my story—in the city of Capsa in Barbery there lived a very rich man who possessed among other children a pretty and charming daughter, named Alibech. She was not a Christian, but she heard many Christians in her native town crying up the Christian Faith and service to God, and one day she asked one of them how a person could most effectively serve God. The reply was that those best serve God who fly furthest from the things of this world, like the hermits who had departed to the solitudes of the Thebaid Desert.

The girl was about fourteen and very simple minded. Urged by a mere childish enthusiasm and not by a well ordered desire, she secretly set out next morning quite alone, without saying a word to anyone, to find the Thebaid Desert. Her enthusiasm lasted several days and enabled her with great fatigue to reach those solitudes. In the distance she saw a little hut with a holy man standing at its entrance. He was amazed to see her there, and asked her what she was seeking. She replied that by God's inspiration she was seeking to serve Him, and begged the hermit to show her the right way to do so. But the holy man saw she was young and pretty, and feared that if he kept her with him he might be tempted of the devil. So he praised her good intentions, gave her some roots and wild apples to eat and some water to drink, and said:

"Daughter, not far from here dwells a holy man who is a far greater master of what you are seeking than I am; go to him."

And so he put her on the way. When she reached him, she was received with much the same words, and passing further on came to the cell of a young hermit named Rustico, to whom she made the same request as to the others. To test his spiritual strength, Rustico did not send her away, but took her into his cell. And when night came, he made her a bed of palm leaves and told her to sleep there.

Almost immediately after this, temptation began the struggle with his spiritual strength, and the hermit found that he had greatly over-estimated his powers of resistance. After a few assaults of the demon he shrugged his shoulders and surrendered. Putting aside holy thoughts and prayers and macerations, he began to think of her beauty and youth, and then pondered how he should proceed with her so that she should not perceive that he obtained what he wanted from her like a dissolute man. First of all he sounded her by certain questions, and discovered that she had never lain with a man and appeared to be very simple minded. He then saw how he could bring her to his desire under pretext of serving God. He began by eloquently showing how the devil is the enemy of the Lord God, and then gave her to understand that the service most pleasing to God it to put the devil back into hell, to which the Lord God has condemned him. The girl asked how this was done, and Rustico replied:

"You shall soon know. Do what you see me do."

He then threw off the few clothes he had and remained stark naked, and the girl imitated him. He kneeled down as if to pray and made her kneel exactly opposite him. As he gazed at her beauty, Rustico's desire became so great that the resurrection of the flesh occurred. Alibech looked at it with amazement, and said:

"Rustico, what is that thing I see sticking out in front of you which I haven't got?"

"My daughter," said Rustico, "that is the devil I spoke of. Do you see? He gives me so much trouble at this moment I can scarcely endure him."

Said the girl:

"Praised be God! I see I am better off than you are, since I haven't such a devil."

"You speak truly," said Rustico, "but instead of this devil you have something else which I haven't."

"What's that?" said Alibech.

"You've got hell," replied Rustico, "and I believe God sent you here for the salvation of my soul, because this devil gives me great trouble, and if you will take pity upon me and let me put him into hell, you will give me the greatest comfort and at the same time will serve God and please Him, since, as you say, you came here for that purpose."

In all good faith the girl replied: "Father, since I have hell in me, let it be whenever you please."

Said Rustico: "Blessings upon you, my daughter. Let us put him in now so that he will afterwards depart from me."

So saying, he took the girl on one of their beds, and showed her how to lie so as to imprison the thing accursed of God. The girl had never before put any devil into her hell and at first felt a little pain, and exclaimed to Rustico:

"O father! This devil must certainly be wicked and the enemy of God, for even when he is put back into hell he hurts it."

"Daughter," said Rustico, "it will not always be so."

To prevent this from happening, Rustico put it into hell six times, before he got off the bed, and so purged the devil's pride that he was glad to rest a little. Thereafter, he returned often and the obedient girl was always glad to take him in; and then the game began to give her pleasure, and she said to Rustico:

"I see that the good men of Capsa spoke the truth when they told me how sweet a thing is the service of God. I certainly do not remember that I ever did anything which gave me so much delight and pleasure as I get from putting the devil into hell. I think that everyone is a fool who does anything but serve God."

Thus it happened that she would often go to Rustico, and say:

"Father, I came here to serve God and not to remain in idleness. Let us put the devil in hell."

And once as they were doing it, she said:

"Rustico, I don't know why the devil ever goes out of hell. If he liked to remain there as much as hell likes to receive and hold him, he would never leave it."

The girl's frequent invitations to Rustico and their mutual pleasures in the service of God so took the stuffing out of his doublet that he now felt chilly where another man would have been in a sweat. So he told the girl that the devil must not be chastened or put into hell except when pride makes him lift his head. "And we," he said, "have so quelled his rage that he prays God to be left in peace." And in this way he silenced the girl for a time. But when she found that Rustico no longer asked her to put the devil in hell, she said one day:

"Rustico, your devil may be chastened and give you no more trouble, but my hell is not. You should therefore quench the raging of my hell with your devil, as I helped you to quell the pride of your devil with my hell."

Rustico, who lived on nothing but roots and water, made a poor response to this invitation. He told her that many devils would be needed to soothe her hell, but that he would do what he could. In this way he satisfied her hell a few times, but so seldom that it was like throwing a bean in a lion's mouth. And the girl, who thought they were not serving God as much as she wanted, kept murmuring.

Now, while there was this debate between the excess of desire in Alibech's hell and the lack of potency in Rustico's devil, a fire broke out in Capsa, and burned Alibech's father with all his children and servants. So Alibech became heir to all his property. A young man named Neerbale, who had spent all his money in riotous living, heard that she was still alive and set out to find her, which he succeeded in doing before the Court took over her father's property as that of a man who had died without heirs. To Rustico's great relief, but against her will, Neerbale brought her back to Capsa and married her, and together they inherited her large patrimony. But before Neerbale had lain with her, certain ladies one day asked her how she had served God in the desert. She replied that her service was to put the devil in hell, and that Neerbale had committed a great sin by taking her away from such service. The ladies asked:

"And how do you put the devil in hell?"

Partly in words and partly in gestures, the girl told them. At this they laughed so much that they are still laughing, and said:

"Be not cast down, my child, they know how to do that here, and Neerbale will serve the Lord God with you in that way."

As they told it up and down the city, it passed into a proverb that the service most pleasing to God is to put the devil into hell. And this proverb crossed the seas and remains until this day.

Therefore, young ladies, when you seek God's favour, learn to put the devil in hell, because this is most pleasing to God and to all parties concerned, and much good may come of it.

FIFTH DAY, NINTH TALE [FEDERIGO'S GENEROSITY]

In the past there was in Florence a young man named Federigo, the son of Messer Filippo Alberighi, renowned above all other young gentlemen of Tuscany for his prowess in arms and his courtesy. Now, as most often happens to gentlemen, he fell in love with a lady named Monna Giovanna, in her time held to be one of the gayest and most beautiful women ever known in Florence. To win her love, he went to jousts and tourneys, made and gave feasts, and spent his money without stint. But she, no less chaste than beautiful, cared nothing for the things he did for her nor for him who did them.

Now as Federigo was spending far beyond his means and getting nothing in, as easily happens, his wealth failed and he remained poor with nothing but a little farm, on whose produce he lived very penuriously, and one falcon which was among the best in the world. More in love than ever, but thinking he would never be able to live in the town any more as he desired, he went to Campi where his farm was. There he spent his time hawking, asked nothing of anybody, and patiently endured his poverty.

Now while Federigo was in this extremity it happened one day that Monna Giovanna's husband fell ill, and seeing death come upon him, made his will. He was a very rich man and left his estate to a son who was already growing up. And then, since he had greatly loved Monna Giovanna, he made her his heir in case his son should die without legitimate children; and so died.

Monna Giovanna was now a widow, and as is customary with our women, she went with her son to spend the year in the country house she had near Federigo's farm. Now the boy happened to strike up a friendship with Federigo, and delighted in dogs and hawks. He often saw Federigo's falcon fly, and took such great delight in it that he very much wanted to have it, but did not dare ask for it, since he saw how much Federigo prized it.

While matters were in this state, the boy fell ill. His mother was very much grieved, as he was her only child and she loved him extremely. She spent the day beside him, trying to help him, and often asked him if there was anything he wanted, begging him to say so, for if it were possible to have it, she would try to get it for him. After she had many times made this offer, the boy said:

"Mother, if you can get me Federigo's falcon, I think I should soon be better."

The lady paused a little at this, and began to think what she should do. She knew that Federigo had loved her for a long time, and yet had never had one glance from her, and she said to herself:

"How can I send or go ask for this falcon, which is, from what I hear, the best that ever flew, and moreover his support in life? How can I be so thoughtless as to take this away from a gentleman who has no other pleasure left in life?"

Although she knew she was certain to have the bird for the asking, she remained in embarrassed thought, not knowing what to say, and did not answer her son. But at length love for her child got the upper hand and she determined that to please him in whatever way it might be, she would not send, but go herself for it and bring it back to him. So she replied:

"Be comforted, my child, and try to get better somehow. I promise you that tomorrow morning I will go for it, and bring it to you."

The child was so delighted that he became a little better that same day. And on the morrow the lady took another woman to accompany her, and as if walking for exercise went to Federigo's cottage, and asked for him. Since it was not the weather for it, he had not been hawking for some days, and was in his garden employed in certain work there. When he heard that Monna Giovanna was asking for him at the door, he was greatly astonished, and ran there happily. When she saw him coming, she got up to greet him with womanly charm, and when Federigo had courteously saluted her, she said:

"How do you do, Federigo? I have come here to make amends for the damage you have suffered through me by loving me more than was needed. And in token of this, I intend to dine today familiarly with you and my companion here."

"Madonna," replied Federigo humbly, "I do not remember ever to have suffered any damage through you, but received so much good that if I was ever worth anything it was owing to your worth and the love I bore it. Your generous visit to me is so precious to me that I could spend again all that I have spent; but you have come to a poor host."

So saying, he modestly took her into his house, and from there to his garden. Since there was nobody else to remain in her company, he said:

"Madonna, since there is nobody else, this good woman, the wife of this workman, will keep you company, while I go to set the table."

Now, although his poverty was extreme, he had never before realised what necessity he had fallen into by his foolish extravagance in spending his wealth. But he repented of it that morning when he could find nothing with which to do honour to the lady, for love of whom he had entertained vast numbers of men in the past. In his anguish he cursed himself and his fortune and ran up and down like a man out his senses, unable to find money or anything to pawn. The hour was late and his desire to honour the lady extreme, yet he would not apply to anyone else, even to his own workman; when suddenly his eye fell upon his falcon, perched on a bar in the sitting room. Having no one to whom he could appeal, he took the bird, and finding it plump, decided it would be food worth such a lady. So, without further thought, he wrung its neck, made his little maid servant quickly pluck and prepare it, and put it on a spit to roast. He spread the table with the whitest napery, of which he had some left, and returned to the lady in the garden with a cheerful face, saying that the meal he had been able to prepare for her was ready.

The lady and her companion arose and went to table, and there together with Federigo, who served it with the greatest devotion, they ate the good falcon, not knowing what it was. They left the table and spent some time in cheerful conversation, and the lady, thinking the time had now come to say what she had come for, spoke fairly to Federigo as follows:

"Federigo, do you remember your former life and my chastity, which no doubt you considered harshness and cruelty, I have no doubt that you will be surprised at my presumption when you hear what I have come here for chiefly. But if you had children, through whom you could know the power of parental love, I am certain that you would to some extent excuse me."

"But, as you have no child, I have one, and I cannot escape the common laws of mothers. Compelled by their power, I have come to ask you—against my will, and against all good manners and duty—for a gift, which I know is something especially dear to you, and reasonably so, because I know your straitened fortune has left you no other pleasure, no other recreation, no other consolation. This gift is your falcon, which has so fascinated my child that if I do not take it to him, I am afraid his present illness will grow so much worse that I may lose him. Therefore I beg you, not by the love you bear me (which holds you to nothing), but by your own nobleness, which has shown itself so much greater in all courteous usage than is wont in other men, that you will be pleased to give it to me, so that through this gift I may be able to say that I have saved my child's life, and thus be ever under an obligation to you."

When Federigo heard the lady's request and knew that he could not serve her, because he had given her the bird to eat, he began to weep in her presence, for he could not speak a word. The lady at first thought that his grief came from having to part with his good falcon, rather than from anything else, and she was almost on the point of retraction. But she remained firm and waited for Federigo's reply after his lamentation. And he said:

"Madonna, ever since it has pleased God that I should set my love upon you, I have felt that Fortune has been contrary to me in many things, and have grieved for it. But they are all light in comparison with what she has done to me now, and I shall never be at peace with her again when I reflect that you came to my poor house, which you never deigned to visit when I was rich, and asked me for a little gift, and Fortune has so acted that I cannot give it to you. Why this cannot be, I will briefly tell you.

"When I heard that you in your graciousness desired to dine with me and I thought of your excellence and your worthiness, I thought it right and fitting to honour you with the best food I could obtain; so, remembering the falcon you ask me for and its value, I thought it a meal worthy of you, and today you had it roasted on the dish and set forth as best I could. But now I see that you wanted the bird in another form, it is such a grief to me that I cannot serve you that I think I shall never be at peace again."

And after saying this, he showed her the feathers and the feet and the beak of the bird in proof. When the lady heard and saw all this, she first blamed him for having killed such a falcon to make a meal for a woman; and then she inwardly commended his greatness of soul which no poverty could or would be able to abate. But, having lost all hope of obtaining the falcon, and thus perhaps the health of her son, she departed sadly and returned to the child. Now, either from disappointment at not having the falcon or because his sickness must inevitably have led to it, the child died not many days later, to the mother's extreme grief.

Although she spent some time in tears and bitterness, yet, since she had been left very rich and was still young, her brothers often urged her to marry again. She did not want to do so, but as they kept on pressing her, she remembered the worthiness of Federigo and his last act of generosity, in killing such a falcon to do her honour.

"I will gladly submit to marriage when you please," she said to her brothers, "but if you want me to take a husband, I will take no man but Federigo degli Alberighi."

At this her brothers laughed at her, saying:

"Why, what are you talking about, you fool? Why do you want a man who hasn't a penny in the world?"

But she replied:

"Brothers, I know it is as you say, but I would rather have a man who needs money than money which needs a man."

Seeing her determination, the brothers, who knew Federigo's good qualities, did as she wanted, and gave her with all her wealth to him, in spite of his poverty. Federigo, finding that he had such a woman, whom he loved so much, with all her wealth to boot, as his wife, was more prudent with his money in the future, and ended his days happily with her.

Sixth Day, Seventh Tale [Madonna Filippa's Defense]

Most worthy ladies, it is always a good thing to know how to speak well, but I think it is best of all when it is called for by necessity. This was well done by a lady, of whom I intend to tell you, for she not only provided merriment and laughter to those who heard her, but saved herself from the snare of a shameful death, as you shall hear.

In Prato there was once a law, no less blameworthy than harsh, which without any distinction condemned to be burned alive any woman whose husband found her in adultery with a lover, just like a woman who lay with any other man for money.

While this law was in force a beautiful woman, named Madonna Filippa, who was very much in love, was found one night in her room by her husband, Rinaldo de' Pugliesi, in the arms of Lazzarino de' Guazzagliotri, a noble and handsome young man of that country, whom she loved beyond her own self. Rinaldo was exceedingly angry when he saw this, and could scarcely refrain from rushing at them and killing them. And if he had not feared the consequences to himself in following his anger, he would have done so.

He restrained himself from this, but could not refrain from claiming from the law of Prato what was forbidden him to take himself—his wife's life. He produced sufficient evidence, and the next day he brought the accusation against his wife and had her cited before the court, without consulting anyone.

The lady was a great-hearted woman, as usually happens with women who are really in love; and although she was advised against it by her numerous friends and relatives, she determined to appear before the Court and rather die bravely confessing her fault than to live in exile by basely fleeing, and thus showing herself unworthy of such a lover as the man in whose arms she had lain the night before. She appeared before the judge accompanied by many men and women, who urged her to deny the fault; and asked him in a clear voice and with firm countenance what he wanted of her.

The judge looked at her, saw she was beautiful and accomplished, and, as her speech showed, a woman of high spirit. He felt compassion for her, suspecting that she would make the confession which, for his honour's sake, would force him to condemn her to death. But, since he could not avoid putting the question to her, he said:

"Madonna, as you see, here is Rinaldo your husband, and he lays a plaint against you that he has found you in adultery with another man. And therefore he demands that in accordance with the law I punish you for it by death. But this I cannot do unless you confess it, and so beware of what you say in answer, and tell me if your husband's accusation is true."

The lady, without the slightest fear, replied in a pleasant voice:

"Messer, it is true that Rinaldo is my husband, and that last night he found me in the arms of Lazzarino, wherein I have often lain, through the deep and perfect love I have for him. Nor shall I ever deny it. But I am certain you know that the laws should be equal for both sexes and made with the consent of those who are to obey them. That is not so in this case, for it only touches us poor women, who are yet able to satisfy many more than men can; moreover, no woman gave her consent or was even consulted when this law was passed. And so it may reasonably be called an inequitable law.

"If, to the harm of my body and your own soul, you choose to carry out this law, it is for you to do so. But before you proceed to judgment, I ask one little favour of you—ask my husband whether or not I have not always wholly yielded him my body whenever and howsoever often he asked it."

Rinaldo, without awaiting the judge's question, immediately replied that beyond all doubt she had always yielded to his pleasure whenever he required it.

"Then," said the lady swiftly, "I ask you, Messer Judge, if he has always had from me what he needed and pleased, what should and shall I do with what remains over? Should I throw it to the dogs? Is it not far better to give it to a gentleman who loves me beyond himself than to let it spoil or go to waste?"

This case concerning so well known a lady had attracted to the Court almost all the inhabitants of Prato. When they heard this amusing question they laughed heartily, and then almost with one voice shouted that the lady was right and spoke well. Before they separated, with the judge's consent they modified this cruel law, and limited it only to those women who were unfaithful to their husbands for money.

So Rinaldo departed in confusion, and the lady returned home free and happy and in triumph, like one escaped from the flames.

Tenth Day, Tenth Tale [The Story of Griselda]

A long time ago the eldest son of the Marquess of Saluzzo was a young man named Gualtieri. He was wifeless and childless, spent his time hunting and hawking, and never thought about marrying or having children, wherein he was probably very wise. This displeased his subjects, who several times begged him to take a wife, so that he might not die without an heir and leave them without a ruler, offering to find him a wife born of such a father and mother as would give him good hopes of her and content him. To which Gualtieri replied:

"My friends, you urge me to do something I was determined never to do, seeing how hard it is to find a woman of suitable character, and how many of the opposite sort there are, and how wretched is the life of a man who takes a wife unsuitable to him. It is foolishness of you to think you can judge a girl by the characters of her father and mother (from which you argue that you can find me one to please me), for I do not see how you can really know the fathers' or mothers' secrets. And even if you did know them, daughters are often quite different from their fathers and mothers."

"But you want me to take these chains, and I am content to do so. If it turns out badly I want to have no one to complain of but myself, and so I shall choose for myself. And I tell you that if you do not honour the wife I choose as your lady you will find out to your cost how serious a thing it is to have compelled me by your entreaties to take a wife against my will."

They replied that they were content, if only he would take a wife.

For some time Gualtieri had been pleased by the character of a poor girl in a hamlet near his house. He thought her beautiful, and that he might live comfortably enough with her. So he decided that he would marry her without seeking any further, and, having sent for her father, who was a very poor man, arranged to marry her. Having done this, Gualtieri called together all his friends from the surrounding country, and said:

"My friends, it has pleased you to desire that I should marry, and I am ready to do so, more to please you than from any desire I have of taking a wife. You know you promised me that you would honour anyone I chose as your lady. The time has now come for me to keep my promise to you and you to keep yours to me. I have found a girl after my heart quite near here; I intend to marry her and to bring her home in a few days. So take thought to make a handsome marriage feast and how you can honourably receive her, so that I may consider myself content with your promise as you may be with mine."

The good men cheerfully replied that they were glad of it, and that they would consider her their lady and honour her as their lady in all things. After which, they all set about preparing a great and handsome wedding feast, and so did Gualtieri. He prepared a great and fine banquet, and invited many friends and relatives and noblemen and others. Moreover, he had rich and beautiful dresses cut and fitted on a girl, who seemed to him about the same build as the girl he proposed to marry. And he also purchased girdles and rings and a rich and beautiful crown, and everything necessary to a bride.

When the day appointed for the wedding arrived, Gualtieri about the middle of Terce mounted his horse, and so did those who had come to honour him. Everything being arranged, he said:

"Gentlemen, it is time to go for the bride."

Setting out with all his company he came to the hamlet and the house of the girl's father, where he found her drawing water in great haste, so that she could go with the other women to see Gualtieri's bride. And when Gualtieri saw her, he called her by her name, Griselda, and asked where her father was. She blushed and said:

"He is in the house, my lord."

Gualtieri dismounted, told everyone to wait for him, and entered the poor little house where he found the girl's father (who was named Giannucole), and said to him:

"I have come to marry Griselda, but first I want to ask her a few things in your presence."

He then asked her whether, if he married her, she would try to please him, and never be angry at anything he said or did, and if she would be obedient, and several other things, to all of which she said "Yes." Gualtieri then took her by the hand and led her forth. In the presence of all his company he had her stripped naked, and then clothes he had prepared were brought, and she was immediately dressed and shod, and he had a crown put on her hair, all unkempt as it was. Everyone marvelled at this, and he said:

"Gentlemen, I intend to take this girl as my wife, if she will take me as her husband."

He then turned to her, as she stood blushing and irresolute, and said:

"Griselda, will you take me as your husband?"

"Yes, my lord," she replied.

"And I will take you as my wife," said he.

Then in the presence of them all he pledged his faith to her; and they set her on a palfrey and honourably conducted her to his house. The wedding feast was great and handsome, and the rejoicing no less than if he had married the daughter of the King of France.

The girl seemed to have changed her soul and manners with her clothes. As I said, she was beautiful of face and body, and she became so agreeable, so pleasant, so well-behaved that she seemed like the daughter of a nobleman, and not Giannucole's child and a cattle herder; which surprised everyone who had known her before. Moreover, she was so obedient and so ready to serve her husband that he felt himself to be the happiest and best matched man in the world. And she was so gracious and kindly to her husband's subjects that there was not one of them but loved her and gladly honoured her, while all prayed for her good and her prosperity and advancement. Whereas they had said that Gualtieri had showed little wisdom in marrying her, they now said that he was the wisest and shrewdest man in the world, because no one else would have known the lofty virtue hidden under her poor clothes and village garb.

In short, before long she acted so well that not only in the marquisate but everywhere people were talking of her virtues and good actions; and whatever had been said against her husband for having married her was now turned to the opposite. She had not long been with Gualtieri when she became pregnant, and in due time gave birth to a daughter, at which Gualtieri rejoiced greatly.

Soon after this the idea came to him to test her patience with a long trial and intolerable things. He said unkind things to her, seemed to be angry, and said that his subjects were most discontented with her on account of her low birth, and especially when they saw that she bore children. He said they were very angry at the birth of a daughter and did nothing but murmur. When the lady heard these words, she did not change countenance or cheerfulness, but said to him:

"My lord, you may do with me what you think most to your honour and satisfaction. I shall be content, for I know that I am less than they and unworthy of the honour to which you have raised me by your courtesy."

Gualtieri liked this reply and saw that no pride had risen up in her from the honour done her by him and others.

Soon after, he informed his wife in general terms that his subjects could not endure the daughter she had borne. He then gave orders to one of his servants whom he sent to her. The man, with a dolorous visage, said:

"Madonna, if I am to avoid death I must do what my lord bids me. He tells me I am to take your daughter and . . ."

He said no more, but the lady, hearing these words and seeing the servant's face, and remembering what had been said to her, guessed that he had been ordered to kill the child. She went straight to the cradle, kissed and blessed the child, and although she felt great anguish in her heart, put the child in the servant's arms without changing her countenance, and said:

"Do what my lord and yours has ordered you to do. But do not leave her for the birds and animals to devour her body, unless you were ordered to do so."

The servant took the child and told Gualtieri what the lady had said. He marvelled at her constancy, and sent the servant with the child to a relative at Bologna, begging her to bring her up and educate her carefully, but without ever saying whose daughter she was.

After this the lady again became pregnant, and in due time brought forth a male child, which delighted Gualtieri. But what he had already done was not enough for him. He pierced the lady with a worse wound, and one day said to her in pretended anger:

"Since you have borne this male child, I cannot live at peace with my subjects, who complain bitterly that a grandson of Giannucole must be their lord after me. If I am not to be driven out, I fear I must do now as I did before, and in the end abandon you and take another wife."

The lady listened to him patiently, and her only reply was:

"My lord, content yourself and do what is pleasing to you. Do not think about me, for nothing pleases me except as it pleases you."

Not many days afterwards Gualtieri sent for his son in the same way that he had sent for his daughter, and while pretending in the same ways to kill the child, sent it to be brought up in Bologna, as he had sent the girl. And his wife said no more and looked no worse than she had done about the daughter. Gualtieri marvelled at this and said to himself that no other woman could have done what she did; and if he had not seen that she loved her children while she had them, he would have thought she did it to get rid of them whereas he saw it was from obedience to him.

His subjects thought he had killed his children and blamed him severely and thought him a cruel man, while they felt great pity for his wife. And when the women condoled with her on the death of her children, she never said anything except that it was not her wish but the wish of him who begot them.

Several years after his daughter's birth, Gualtieri thought the time had come for the last test of his wife's patience. He kept saying that he could no longer endure to have Griselda as his wife, that he knew he had acted childishly and wrongly when he married her, that he therefore meant to solicit the Pope for dispensation to marry another woman and abandon Griselda; for all of which he was reproved by many good men. But his only reply was that it was fitting this should be done.

Hearing of these things, the lady felt she must expect to return to her father's house and perhaps watch cattle as she had done in the past, and see another woman take the man she loved; at which she grieved deeply. But she prepared herself to endure this with a firm countenance, as she had endured the other wrongs of Fortune.

Not long afterwards Gualtieri received forged letters from Rome, which he showed to his subjects, pretending that the Pope by these letters gave him a dispensation to take another wife and leave Griselda. So, calling her before him, he said to her in the presence of many of his subjects:

"Wife, the Pope has granted me a dispensation to leave you and to take another wife. Now, since my ancestors were great gentlemen and lords of this country while yours were always labourers, I intend that you shall no longer be my wife, but return to Giannucole's house with the dowry you brought me, while I shall bring home another wife I have found more suitable for me."

At these words the lady could only restrain her tears by a great effort, beyond that of women's nature, and replied:

"My lord, I always knew that my lowly rank was in no wise suitable to your nobility; and the rank I have had with you I always recognized as coming from God and you, and never looked upon it as given to me, but only lent. You are pleased to take it back, and it must and does please me to return it to you. Here is the ring with which you wedded me; take it. You tell me to take the dowry I brought you; to do this there is no need for you to pay anything nor shall I need a purse or a sumpter horse, for I have not forgotten that I came to you naked. If you think it right that the body which has borne your children should be seen by everyone, I will go away naked. But in exchange for my virginity, which I brought here, and cannot carry away, I beg you will at least be pleased to let me take away one shift over and above my dowry."

Gualtieri, who was nearer to tears then anyone else present, managed to keep his countenance stern, and said:

"You shall have a shift."

Those who were present urged him to give her a dress, so that she who had been his wife for thirteen years should not be seen to leave his house so poorly and insultingly as it would be for her to leave it in a shift. But their entreaties were vain. So the lady, clad only in her shift, unshod and with nothing on her head, commended him to God, left his house, and returned to her father accompanied by the tears and lamentation of all who saw her.

Giannucole (who had never believed it was true that Gualtieri would keep his daughter as a wife and had always expected this event), had kept the clothes she had taken off the morning when Gualtieri married her. So she took them and put them on, and devoted herself to drudgery in her father's house, enduring the assaults of hostile Fortune with a brave spirit.

After Gualtieri had done this, he told his subjects that he was to marry the daughter of one of the Counts of Panago. He therefore made great preparations for the wedding, and sent for Griselda to come to him; and when she came, he said:

"I am bringing home the lady I have just married, and I intend to do her honour at her arrival. You know there is not a woman in the house who can prepare the rooms and do many other things needed for such a feast. You know everything connected with the house better than anyone, so you must arrange everything that is to be done, and invite all the women you think fit and receive them as if you were mistress of the house. Then, when the marriage feast is over, you can return home."

These words were a dagger in Griselda's heart, for she had not been able to dispense with the love she felt for him as she had her good fortune, but she said:

"My lord, I am ready."

So, in her coarse peasant dress, she entered the house she had left a little before in her shift, and had the rooms cleaned and arranged, put out hangings and carpets in the halls, looked to the kitchen, and set her hand to everything as if she had been a scullery wench of the house. And she never paused until everything was ready and properly arranged.

After this she invited all the ladies of the surrounding country in Gualtieri's name, and then awaited the feast. On the wedding day, dressed in her poor clothes, she received all the ladies with a cheerful visage and a womanly manner.

Gualtieri had had his children carefully brought up in Bologna by his relative, who was married into the family of the Counts of Panago. The daughter was now twelve years old, the most beautiful thing ever seen, and the boy was seven. He sent for her and asked her to come to Saluzzo with his son and daughter, to bring an honourable company with her, and to tell everyone that she was bringing the girl as his wife, and never to let anyone know that the girl was anything else. Her husband did what the Marquess asked, and set out. In a few days he reached Saluzzo about dinner time, with the girl and boy and his noble company; and all the peasants of the country were there to see Gualtieri's new wife.

The girl was received by the ladies and taken to the hall where the tables were spread, and Griselda went cheerfully to meet her, saying:

"Lady, you are welcome."

The ladies had begged Gualtieri, but in vain, to allow Griselda to stay in her room or to lend her one of her own dresses, so that she might not have to meet strangers in such a guise. They all sat down to table and began the meal. Every man looked at the girl and said that Gualtieri had made a good exchange, and Griselda above all praised her and her little brother.

Gualtieri now felt that he had tested his wife's patience as far as he desired. He saw that the strangeness of all this did not alter her and he was certain it was not the result of stupidity, for he knew her to be an intelligent woman. He thought it now time to take her from the bitterness which he felt she must be hiding behind a smiling face. So he called her to him, and in everyone's presence said to her smilingly:

"What do you think of my new wife?"

"My lord," replied Griselda, "I see nothing but good in her. If she is as virtuous as she is beautiful, as I well believe, I have no doubt that you will live with her the happiest lord in the world. But I beg you as earnestly as I can not to give her the wounds you gave the other woman who was your wife. I think she could hardly endure them, because she is younger and because she has been brought up delicately, whereas the other laboured continually from her childhood."

Gualtieri saw that she really believed he was to marry the other, and yet spoke nothing but good of her. He made her sit down beside him, and said:

"Griselda, it is now time that you should reap the reward of your long patience, and that those who have thought me cruel and wicked and brutal should know that what I have done was directed towards a pre-determined end, which was to teach you to be a wife, then how to choose and keep a wife, and to procure me perpetual peace for so long as I live with you. When I came and took you to wife, I greatly feared that this would not happen to me; and so, to test you, I have given you the trials and sufferings you know. I have never perceived that you thwarted my wishes by word or deed, and I think that in you I have the comfort I desire. I mean to give you back now what I deprived you of for a long time, and to heal the wounds I gave you with the greatest delight. Therefore, with a glad spirit, take her whom you think to be my wife and her brother as your children and mine. They are the children whom you and many others have long thought that I had cruelly murdered. And I am your husband, who loves you above all things, believing I can boast that no man exists who can so rejoice in his wife as I in you."

He then embraced and kissed her. She was weeping with happiness. They both arose and went to where their daughter was sitting, quite stupefied by what she had heard, and tenderly embraced her and her brother, thus undeceiving them and many of those present.

The ladies arose merrily from the table and went with Griselda to her room. With better hopes they took off her old clothes and dressed her in one of her noble robes, and brought her back to the hall a lady, which she had looked even in her rags.

They rejoiced over their children, and everyone was glad at what had happened. The feasting and merrymaking were prolonged for several days, and Gualtieri was held to be a wise man, although they thought the testing of his wife harsh and intolerable. But above all they esteemed the virtue of Griselda.

The Count of Panago soon afterwards returned to Bologna. Gualtieri took Giannucole away from his labour and installed him as his father-in-law, so that he ended his days honourably and in great content. He afterwards married off his daughter to a nobleman of great wealth and distinction, and lived long and happily with Griselda, always honouring her as much as he could.

What more is to be said, save that divine souls are sometimes rained down from Heaven into poor houses, while in royal palaces are born those who are better fitted to herd swine than to rule over men? Who but Griselda could have endured with a face not only tearless but cheerful, the stern and unheard-of tests imposed on her by Gualtieri? It would perhaps not have been such a bad thing if he had chosen one of those women who, if she had been driven out of her home in a shift, would have let another man so shake her fur that a new dress would have come from it.

Geoffrey Chaucer (c.1343–1400)

From *The Canterbury Tales*

"She advocates dirty books!—Chaucer! Rabelais! Balzac!" That's how the doyennes of River City, Iowa, launch the worst attack they can imagine upon Marion the Librarian in Meredith Willson's celebrated musical The Music Man. *Chaucer's place at the head of this short list of scurrilous writers betrays his paradoxical position. Once called "the Father of English Poetry," he has also mostly been read in expurgated or cleaned up versions, and sometimes translated into niceness. And because he wrote in Middle English and in poetry—both difficult languages these days—he is perhaps more often worshipped than read. Yet for those who take the trouble to read him, his poetry provides an unforgettable picture of what life felt like in the late fourteenth century.*

The fourteenth was, to borrow the adjective from the subtitle of Barbara Tuchman's bestselling A Distant Mirror, *a calamitous century, beginning and ending with the deposition and murder of a king. Most of the century was clouded by a continuous war with France, a war which brought death, taxation, and political turmoil. And at mid-century, when Chaucer was a young boy, the Black Death killed more than a third of the population of the country in two years.*

The world into which Chaucer was born was very much an urban world. London, a thriving metropolis of about 50,000, was England's commercial, social, and religious power. At the center of these circles of influence was the royal court, with palaces at the Tower in London and at Westminster down the road southwest of the city. Through Chaucer's half of the century only two kings reigned, Edward III and his grandson Richard II. Both were capable and treacherous. Edward, who fancied himself a King Arthur presiding over a reborn Round Table, pursued an endless French war and at the end of a fifty-year reign seemed fully under the spell of his mistress Alice Perrers. Richard, though in many ways politically astute, was finally unable to extricate himself from the conflicting rivalries of his powerful uncles and the other nobles.

Because of the concentration of royal power in London, the great dukes and bishops, wherever their lands might be, also had London palaces. As if to keep a sacred eye on things temporal, all the orders of monks, nuns, and friars were blessed with extensive holdings in

This modern verse translation of Chaucer's Middle English verse original is by Joseph Glaser in *The Canterbury Tales in Modern English* (Indianapolis: Hackett, 2005).

and around the city. Towering over dozens of parish churches in the city was the great cathedral, St. Paul's, with its school and great bevy of clerics.

London was a circumscribed city, with walls built on the old Roman boundaries established centuries earlier. There were gates through the walls on three sides, so that the city could be closed up at curfew each night. The fourth boundary of the city was the river Thames, a single bridge with its own gate serving as the entrance of the city from the south bank, the village of Southwark. It was here across the river that the Bishop of Winchester had his estates and prison (the "Clink"), where Shakespeare's Globe would one day be built, and where the Tabard Inn could put up pilgrims bound for an early departure to Canterbury.

The cathedral in Canterbury, some sixty miles to the southeast of London, housed the shrine of Thomas Becket, who had been martyred by thugs of Henry II back in 1170. Over the years a thriving pilgrimage trade developed, bringing people "from every shires ende of Engelond to Caunterbury, the hooly blisful martir for to seke." It is through Chaucer's extraordinary description of one such imaginary pilgrimage that we get a rich picture of late-medieval social and religious preoccupations.

The Canterbury Tales *is a collection of stories told by some thirty pilgrims (including Chaucer himself) during a fictional three- or four-day ride to Becket's shrine at Canterbury. Like modern disaster movies (and the medieval Ship of Fools), the pilgrims represent a revealing cross-section of the middle strata of fourteenth-century society, tossed together in an unlikely combination. From the high end of medieval society—"those who fight"—Chaucer includes only a knight, leaving untouched in this satirical picture all those titled representatives of the nobility who may have been his primary audience. At the low end, representing landless peasants or "those who work," Chaucer includes a virtuous plowman, who doesn't tell a tale. The many clerics ("those who pray")—priests, nuns, monks, friars, pardoners, summoners, students—were an everyday presence in Chaucer's world and they play a heavy role in Chaucer's work, as they do in medieval satirical literature. A third of his pilgrims are clerics, but only one of them, a poor parish priest, can be said to have integrity or a true vocation, except perhaps the bookish Clerk of Oxenford, who like Chaucer "wolde gladly lerne and gladly teche."*

But it was abundantly clear to Chaucer that the old feudal model of these "three estates" didn't begin to describe the bustle of London life. He includes a fourth group, the merchants, tradesmen, guildsmen, lawyers, physicians, managers, and arrangers who make up the greatly expanding middle class. Chaucer's Wife of Bath, for instance, is both independent and independently wealthy, a successful participant in the cloth trade and in "gold digging." It is from this commercial class that Chaucer's own family came, and it is as a successful representative of this class that we meet him in historical records, for Chaucer lived at a time when an Englishman would not have dreamed of making his way by writing poetry.

There are 493 documentary records of Chaucer's life, so we actually know a great deal of specific information about him. These records trace the career of a government functionary and businessman, one who worked for and traveled on behalf of kings and dukes, and one who lived in a society at least as litigious as our own. Official documents show why and when he was paid, how he was outfitted for court occasions, and who the courtiers, officials, and businessmen were that he counted as friends. In one mysterious case, for instance, Chaucer was granted immunity in 1380 from prosecution on a rape charge. When Cecily Champain signed her release, standing in as witnesses for Chaucer were the chamberlain of the king's household, a collector of the Wool Custom who was a former mayor of London, the admiral of the northern fleet, a poet from the king's household, and a neighbor who was of the Grocer's Company.

Chaucer was born in 1343 or a few years before. His father, John, was in the wine trade and the family lived in the Vintry, the London ward along the Thames just west of the Tower where ships with wine from the continent unloaded their stocks. It seems likely that as a young boy, Chaucer would have attended the cathedral school at St. Paul's. As a boy of about 14, he became a page to the Countess of Ulster, who was married to Prince Lionel, the second son of Edward III. Two years later, on campaign as a squire in France, he was captured near Reims and held for ransom—the main reason for going to war in the Middle Ages. The next year (1360) his ransom was paid with a contribution from the king himself.

Around 1366, when his father died, Chaucer became even more closely tied to the royal family. He married a lady-in-waiting to the Queen and became an Esquire of the Royal Household. Perhaps because of his language skills (he knew Latin, Italian, French, and maybe Spanish), he took part in royal negotiations on extensive trips to Spain, France, and Italy. At the same time, he became attached to another brother of the King—John of Gaunt, the Duke of Lancaster and one of the richest and most powerful men in England. Chaucer's wife became part of the Lancaster household, even as her sister, Katherine Swynford, became Gaunt's mistress (later, third wife). Because of these connections, both Chaucer and his wife received several annuities-for-life, including one from the king to Geoffrey in 1374 of a pitcher of wine each day for life.

In 1374, Chaucer moved into quarters above Aldgate, in the city wall on the east side of the city, and became the Controller of the King's Custom for the wool trade. King Edward III died in 1377, but his son and heir Edward the Black Prince had died the year before; the throne went to the Black Prince's son, Richard, a boy of ten. Chaucer had already made trips to the continent to help arrange a marriage for Richard, and this task was resumed, resulting in Richard's engagement to Anne of Bohemia in 1381.

1381 also saw the crisis of the Peasants' Revolt. Storming London, slaughtering Flemish cloth workers, killing the Archbishop of Canterbury, burning the Savoy Palace of John of Gaunt, the rebellious peasants confronted the fourteen-year-old king in a field outside Aldgate, a stone's throw from Chaucer's apartment. With great equanimity, Richard agreed to all their demands, sent them home, then had their leaders arrested and executed. This bold stroke won the young king support for a while, but the contention for power was stirring behind Richard's throne between two of his uncles John of Gaunt, the Duke of Lancaster, and Thomas of Woodstock, the Duke of Gloucester.

Always associated with the ascendant Lancastrians, Chaucer took up residence in Greenwich, became justice of the peace in Kent, and was elected knight of the shire, enabling him to sit as a member of the "Wonderful Parliament" of 1386. As Gloucester's party increasingly gained control of the king, however, Chaucer's fortunes changed: he gave up his positions with the Customs and his gatehouse over Aldgate, he sold out his annuities before they could be stripped away, and then his wife died. Finally, the "Merciless Parliament" of 1388 sentenced and executed a number of Chaucer's friends, including the poet Thomas Usk and the king's tutor, Simon Burley.

In 1389 the King declared himself fit to rule without the guidance of his uncles, and he appointed Chaucer Clerk of the King's Works, in charge of building and repairing certain royal properties, including the palace at Westminster and the Tower of London. Chaucer kept this position for less than two years, resigning it after he was robbed of public funds twice in the same day, and then assaulted again by the same robbers. He became instead the deputy forester of North Petherton, a quieter position, and a position assumed by his son Thomas Chaucer in later years.

In 1399, Chaucer's longtime friend John of Gaunt died, even while Gaunt's son Henry Bolingbroke seized the throne from Richard and became Henry IV. Chaucer meanwhile moved into a cottage in the garden of Westminster Abbey and, having fallen on hard times, wrote the short poem "Complaint to His Purse," urging the new king to renew his annuities. In February of 1400 King Richard II was murdered and Chaucer's annuities were renewed and increased. In October of that year, Chaucer died and was buried in Westminster Abbey. Around his tomb, beginning in the Renaissance, the "Poet's Corner" came into being.

But it wasn't the Poet's Corner when Chaucer was buried there. The records which allow us to sketch out his life so fully never mention his poetry; in fact the official records give no clue that Chaucer was even a poet. We have, it seems, a civil servant and man about court who moonlighted as a court entertainer. He certainly wrote poetry for special occasions. The Book of the Duchess *is a poem honoring at her death the wife of John of Gaunt, presumably about the time Chaucer's sister-in-law became Gaunt's mistress.* The Legend of Good Women *says that it was written at the command of Queen Anne, wife of King Richard II.*

It is easy to imagine the tales of Canterbury being read or recited at court as an ongoing entertainment, the courtiers laughing at the foibles of Chaucer's double cast of characters—the pilgrims and the people in their stories. The court would laugh as well at Chaucer's self-portrait, especially since we guess that he himself most often read his poetry aloud to his friends, as one famous manuscript illumination shows him doing.

His poems show him in his own name as a fat, bookish man with insomnia who prefers reading to almost all other pleasures. He is wide-eyed, reticent, and a novice in the art of love. In The House of Fame, an eagle (borrowed from Dante's Purgatorio*) accuses him of having no experience and writing about love only from old books. Even in* The Canterbury Tales, *the pilgrim Geffrey Chaucer, who recounts the journey for us, is easily "taken in" by his own characters, like the sentimental Prioress or the virile Monk. When his turn to tell a tale comes up, his attempt in verse is so bad ("thy drasty rymyng is nat worth a tord," he is told) that he alone among the pilgrims must start over, this time telling a tale in prose.*

Chaucer's friends must truly have enjoyed his play with characters like the Wife of Bath. When a friend was considering marriage, for instance, Chaucer even recommended in a verse letter that he consult the words of the Wife of Bath, who seems to have taken on a life of her own. And for good reason: she is both an example of the vices and stereotypes that writers like Andreas Capellanus or Jean de Meun charged against women, even while she uses arguments that sound remarkably modern in their indictment of the patriarchal tradition of art and power:

By God, if wommen hadde writen stories,
As clerkes han withinne hire oratories,
They wolde han writen of men moore wikkednesse
Than al the mark of Adam may redresse. (699-702)

Part of the fun of reading Chaucer, as with Shakespeare, is sifting through the multiplicity of angles and reflections that give the works their expansive sense of human nature fully drawn. It is Chaucer's remarkable achievement, as Elizabethan poet Edmund Spenser said of him, "that in that mistie time he could see so clearly."

[from *The Wife of Bath's Prologue*]

My life gives me authority,
Enough and more, it seems to me,
To speak of all the woe in marriage,
For since I was twelve years of age,
By God, who's evermore alive,
Of wedded husbands, I've had five
(If they were all legitimate),
And each a man of worth and weight.
But someone said, upon that heading,
As Christ attended just one wedding—
At Cana, it was, in Galilee—
That fact alone should prove to me
That I should marry only once.
Then there's that text where Christ confronts
Beside a well, as God and man,
A neighborly Samaritan:
"You've married five," he said, "but stay.
I say the man with you today
Is not your husband." So he said,
But who knows what went through his head?
No one can explain his grounds
For placing five men out of bounds.
How many husbands might she marry?
Now I don't wish to be contrary,
But no one has defined that number.
Priests may reproach, condemn, encumber,
But I know well, without a lie,
God bade us wax and multiply.
That gentle text I understand!
This too: that when I take a man,
Sirs, *I* become his chief concern
Not his relations, though they burn.
These rules define the wedded state,
And not how many men you mate.
Bigamy, octogamy—
To me such terms are value free.
How many wives had Solomon?
Why, hundreds when the count was done.
I wish it were permitted me
To taste love half as oft as he!
Ah, what a gift he had for wives!
No living man could match his drives.
God knows, and why should we forget,
That king had many a merry fit
With each of them while yet alive!

So I praise God I've had my five.
Then too, I always picked the best
For manly wares and all the rest.
As many schools improve a clerk,
And widespread practice in his work
Corrects a craftsman, all agree,
Five husbands have perfected me.
Welcome the sixth when he appears!
I won't live chaste through all my years,
But when my spouse is dead and gone,
I'll wed another man anon.
Saint Paul himself says I am free
To wed a man who pleases me.
He sanctions marriage, though he's stern.
Far better that we wed than burn!
Though folks may call it villainy,
Lamech invented bigamy.
Abraham was a holy man,
And Jacob too, I understand,
Yet each of them had several wives
Like other men of holy lives.
Who has ever heard or read
That God forbid mankind to wed?
Why, no one, or it's news to me.
Did he require virginity?
Of course he never did, nor could.
Where Paul discusses maidenhood,
He says it is a blessed state
When women live without a mate.
That's all he says, and though it's true,
It's not a law—a good thing too.
Say God commanded chastity:
No one could wed by his decree.
With no seeds sown in marriage then,
He'd lose all virgins—and all men!
Paul couldn't bar, despite his bent,
What God ordained. No, he was sent
To make the virgin life a goal
For those already chaste of soul.
　But that's not all of us, you know.
God designates: And rightly so.
Saint Paul himself was always chaste,
Abstemious in every taste.
He wished the same for every man
But never issued that command.
Thus I have leave to wed again.
No single man should think it sin

Or bigamy, once my mate's dead,
To take me up and share my bed.
Though Paul held women bad to touch,
Reclining on a couch or such
(That put the fire to the flax,
And you've seen how that mixture acts!),
He only termed virginity
A better choice than frailty;
He calls us merely frail, you see,
Who moderate our chastity.
  I grant his point. Virginity
Surpasses sexuality.
Virgins are clean, body and soul;
We wives must play a lesser role.
But even in a lord's household
Not every dish is made of gold.
Some are wood, and yet they serve.
God calls us just as we deserve.
Each person has a gift, we're told:
Some formed to give and some, withhold.
  Virginity's a great perfection.
A life is crowned by that election,
But Christ, who is perfection's fount,
Knew well not everyone would want
To sell his all and feed the poor,
Though he himself did that and more.
Only the best of us should try.
Only the best, my lords, not I.
No, I'll bestow my flowers in life
On husbands, as befits a wife.
  Just tell me your interpretation
Of members shaped for generation.
Why were the sexes made that way?
Sure, nature didn't go astray.
It's only half an explanation
To say they're simply for purgation,
Or to pretend that such details
Just set us females off from males.
That's simpleminded as you know;
Our whole lives say it isn't so.
Though clerks may blame me, on my oath,
I say we have these tools for both:
For daily tasks and as a way
Of getting children, if we may.
Why else would this old saw be true,
"A man must pay his wife her due"?
By "man must pay" what could be meant

But serve her with his instrument?
No, those parts have a dual causation—
For purging and for procreation.
  Of course I don't say everyone
Must use his gear as I have done,
That is to say, engendering.
For chastity's a noble thing.
Christ was a maid shaped as a man,
And ever since the world began,
Saints have lived in chastity.
I'll not decry virginity.
Virgins are bread of finest wheat,
Wives, barley bread, more coarse and sweet.
Yet barley loaves of God's creation,
Fed Jesus and his congregation.
So just as God's hand molded us
I'll live my life in open trust
And use my wifely instrument
Without restraint, as it was sent.
If I'm standoffish, give me sorrow!
My man shall have it night and morrow,
Whenever he comes to pay his debt.
My husband, sirs, must be my thrall,
A man to answer every call,
And tire his flesh, while I'm his wife.
For I have power throughout my life
To rule his body, and not he.
That's what Paul's teaching means to me.
He bid our husbands love us well.
Lords, I agree, as you can tell! . . .
  Now, sirs, I will tell my tale.
As truly as I relish ale,
Of those five husband that I had,
Three were good, and two were bad.
The three good men were rich and old
And scarcely able to uphold
The contract binding them to me—
You take my meaning, as I see.
I swear I'm laughing even yet
At how I made them heave and sweat.
Their antics gave me little pleasure
Once I controlled their land and treasure.
With that I ceased my diligence,
My wifely love and reverence.
They loved me so, by God above,
That I thought nothing of their love.
A woman's work is never done

To capture love when she has none.
But once I had them in my hand,
Their bodies, purses, and their land,
Why should I care if they were pleased?
I was the one to be appeased. . . .
I governed them with such dispatch
That they were happy just to catch
My smile with gay things from the fair.
But my compliant moods were rare,
For I could sting them piteously.
Now listen close and follow me,
All wives who want to understand
The fittest way to treat a man.
Men can't rival, though they try,
A woman's gift to swear and lie.
(Of course I don't mean proper wives,
But those perniciously advised.)
An able wife who knows her good
Can make men trust her as they should,
Believe her maid and not the town.
Here's what I said to beat them down:
"Sir, only dotards talk that way.
Why is our neighbor's wife so gay?
She's honored over all the rest.
I sit at home and poorly dressed.
What are you up to over there?
Are you so fond? Is she so fair?
What do you whisper to our maid?
A common lecher and his jade!
But let me have a passing friend
In innocence, why you contend
I've lost my virtue at his house.
You drag home drunken as a mouse,
And preach to me upon your bench!
'A man just digs an endless trench,'
You say, 'to wed a needy wife.
And if she's rich, of gentle life,
Why, she repays his loving folly
By being proud or melancholy.
And if she's fair, then he must dread
Some gigolo will turn her head.'
You say our virtue's soon untied
When it's assailed from every side. . . .
"You say that now your daily duty,
Is coining tributes to my beauty.
You say I make you scan my face
And call me fair and praise my grace,

And make a feast to mark my birthday,
And work to keep me fresh and gay,
And give my old nurse help and aid,
And cultivate my chambermaid,
And kowtow to my father's kin—
Ach, what a sink of lies and sin!
"Yet Jenkin drives you to despair,
The apprentice with the golden hair—
Shining, crisped, upon his crown—
Because he squires me up and down.
I'd spurn him if you died tomorrow!
But tell me why, to my great sorrow,
You hide your treasure chest and key,
When half your goods belong to me.
Would you hoard money from your wife?
No, you shall not, upon my life!
You can't contrive by force or stealth
To rule my body and my wealth.
One will elude you, curse your eyes,
For all your prying and your spies.
You'll never lock *me* in your chest!
Just say, 'Dear, do as you think best.
I'll not attend to tales or malice;
I love and trust you, dearest Alice!'
No woman will be kept in charge.
We must be free and roam at large.
"A man as learned as men may be,
The astrologer Don Ptolemy,
Put this down in his *Almagest*:
'Of all wise men, that one is best,
Who doesn't care who rules the world.'
Ptolemy's saying, when uncurled,
Means 'Have enough, and never care
However well your friends may fare.'
That is, old fool, for all your spite,
You get your fill of me each night.
Only a miser blind to shame
Would grudge to share his lantern's flame.
No sharing hurts his light, indeed.
Enough is plenty. More is greed. . . .
"You say a woman's love is hell,
A desert land without a well,
An unrestrained and raging fire
That burns its fuel and then desires
To spread as far as one can see.
You say as worms consume a tree
So does a wife consume a man—

A truth all husbands understand. . . ."
  Friends, that's the way I dealt with strife,
I made those old men rue their life.
I damned their drinking and caprice.
I called on Jenkin and my niece,
To swear their charges were untrue.
Ah, Lord, the grief I put them through!
All innocent, as God is kind,
But, like a horse, I bit and whined.
Though guilty, I got off by squawking.
I cowed them with torrential talking.
The first in line is first to grind.
I started first and nagged them blind.
They'd confess (I'd growl and glower!)
Offenses quite beyond their power.
I'd damn their lust—and plump their egos—
When illness made them rasp and doze.
  (How they managed to suppose
That I was jealous, heaven knows.)
I swore I only walked at night
To keep their fancy girls in sight.
That pretext won me hours of mirth.
We wives are fitted out at birth
For such deceiving. God supplies
Us arts to make men doubt their eyes.
Why, even now it makes me proud:
I beat them all, as I've allowed,
With tricks or force or loud complaints,
Or murmurs that would try a saint.
Their luck was even worse in bed.
I scolded so, they went in dread.
I'd leave the bed itself in pride
If they so much as touched my side
Before they had rewarded me.
Then I'd endure their nicety.
No doubt you understand this tale.
Prepare to pay; it's all for sale.
No empty hand can lure a hawk;
For money, though, I'd never balk.
I'd even feign an appetite,
Though bacon's far from my delight.
And thus, my lords, I'd scold and mope,
For though they sat beside the pope
They'd get no peace at their own board.
In short, I paid them word for word.
I swear by God omnipotent,
I'll say in my last testament,

I gave back every word I owed.
I made my tongue so sharp a goad
They had to yield—I'd never cease—
Or give up any hope of peace.
They snapped and snarled, you understand,
But knew I had the upper hand.
Then I would say, "Dear, don't be silly,
Do what I say like our sheep, Willy.
Come, husband, let me kiss your cheek.
A good man should be mild and meek,
Wrapped in patience like a robe.
I've heard you say you honor Job;
So bear with us, the ones you preach to.
If not, depend on me to teach you
How sweet peace is compared to strife.
Now, you or I must rule our life.
As men are mild, disposed to thought,
Give way to me, dear, as you ought.
Why must you always grouch and groan?
Perhaps you want my crotch alone?
Have it! Take it! Every bit!
By God, I'm glad you relish it;
If I should sell my sweet *belle chose*
I'd walk as fresh as any rose.
But, no, I keep it for your tooth.
Your fears are groundless. That's the truth."
Three husbands sank beneath such lore;
Now let me speak of number four:
Ah, that one was a reveler;
That is to say, he had a paramour—
And I was young and ripe for play,
Bold and stubborn as a jay.
How I could dance! I wasn't frail.
I'd outsing any nightingale
When I had drunk a draught of wine.
Metellius, the Roman swine,
Beat his poor wife to death for toping.
Ha! I'd have cured his interloping!
He never could bar *me* from wine!
Still, drinking leads to Venus' shrine,
For just as sure as cold breeds hail,
A liquorish mouth has a lecherous tail.
A drunken woman has no defense—
Ask lechers their experience!
But, Christ, when I look back and see
My youth and strength and jollity,
It tickles me, and well it should.

Even now it does me good.
I had the world once in my time.
But age dims everything with grime.
I've lost my beauty and my pith.
So what? The Devil go therewith!
The flour is gone now, sad to tell,
But I still have the bran to sell.
I'll still be genial and jocund.
Now let me speak of my fourth husband.
  Although it gave me great despite,
Some strumpet was his chief delight.
But I got even, to his cost.
I hung him on the selfsame cross,
Not by adultery as such,
But making people think as much.
I fried the man in his own grease.
His fancies seldom gave him peace.
God sent me for his purgatory,
For which I hope his soul's in glory.
He sang for woe and hung his jaw.
I was the shoe that rubbed him raw.
God alone knows how I wrung him,
Thwarted him, deceived him, stung him! . . .
  Now of the fifth one let me tell.
I pray his soul is not in hell!
He was the sharpest one, God knows!
Why, even now I feel his blows
And will until my dying day,
But in our bed he was so gay,
And wheedled with so fine a grace
To pleasure me in his embrace
That though he beat on every bone,
He held my heart, and he alone.
I loved him best of all, for he
Withheld his love to punish me.
We women harbor, I'll not lie,
A strange and wayward fantasy:
Whatever we can't have at will,
We clamor for it, good or ill.
Forbid a thing, and we pursue it.
Approve of it, and we won't do it.
Some men act scornful to entice us
And thus inflate their asking prices.
Too cheap a conquest lacks appeal.
At least that's how most women feel.
  My fifth man, then, God bless his spirit,
Was not a tycoon—nowhere near it.

No, he was once a clerk at Oxford,
And later he returned to board
With my best friend in all our town—
God save her soul!—my Alison.
She knew my heart and secrets too
Far better than our priest could do.
I'd tell her anything at all.
If my poor man pissed on a wall
Or did a thing that meant his life,
To her (and to one other wife,
And to my niece, whom I loved then)
I'd detail where and how and when.
I blabbed so often, by my head,
My husband's face was always red.
He knew no man of average sense
Would trust me with his confidence.
   It happened that one time in Lent—
A season I as much as spent
With Alison to flirt and play
And gad abroad from March to May—
That Jenkin, Alison, and I
Walked out into the fields nearby. . . .
   Across the fields we tripped along, 569
Caught up in foolish play and song.
We blushed and mooned and flirted so
That I at last let Jenkin know
He was the man, and only he,
I'd wed if I were ever free.
For I'm the sort, sirs, understand,
Who's never caught without a plan
In love or in my other interests.
There's no heart in a mouse's breast
That has but one poor hole to hide him.
He's dead if that one hole's denied him.
   I claimed he had enchanted me
(My mother's brand of subtlety)
And said I dreamed of him all night—
He slew me as I lay upright
And all the bedclothes swam in blood,
But I took comfort in that flood,
For blood betokens gold, I thought.
A pack of lies, for I dreamed naught,
But spoke as Mother said I should.
Her love advice was always good.
   But tell me, sirs, . . . what was I saying?
It's here, by God. My tale again!
   When Husband Four was on his bier,

I moaned and groaned with sorry cheer,
As good wives must, for that's our place.
Yet I took care to hide my face.
Because I'd found another man,
My tears held back, as dry as sand.
   Men bore the corpse to church next day
With neighbors sighing "Welladay!"
Jenkin himself was in the crowd
Behind the bier, and I allowed,
I'd never seen another pair
Of legs and feet so clean and fair.
I gave him all my heart to hold.
Now he was twenty winters old,
And I was forty; that's the truth.
I always had a young colt's tooth.
I had gap teeth, and that was fine.
Who else should wear Dame Venus' sign?
By God, I was a lusty one,
Fair and rich, excelled by none,
And truly all my husbands said
My *queynt* was fit for any bed.
From birth the working of my stars
Was ruled by Venus and by Mars.
As Venus made me lecherous,
Mars made me bold and treacherous.
Born in the Bull when Mars was there,
Supplied with love and pluck to spare,
I followed every inclination
Thrust on me by my constellation.
That's why I never could withhold
My Venus box when well cajoled.
Yet I have Mars' mark on my face
And in another secret place.
As God may witness my confession,
I never used the least discretion,
But chose my men by appetite.
Short or tall or dark or light,
I never cared, if someone loved me,
How poor he was, or what degree.
   What can I say? A few weeks later,
This pretty Jenkin, no one greater,
Married me with pomp and pleasure.
I gave him all my land and treasure,
All the gains I'd won before,
And afterward repented sore.
I'd ask for things. He wouldn't hear.
He cuffed me so upon the ear

(I ripped a leaf out of his book),
My ear went dead where I was struck.
But I was cross-grained as a cat
And talked him down in every spat.
I vowed I'd roam just as before,
No matter how he scowled and swore.
He paid me back, for he would quarry
His book for every hurtful story— . . .
But I'd not give an inch, I promise.
   Now let me tell, by holy Thomas,
The reason I ripped out the page,
For which he struck me in his rage.
He had some works that night and day
He'd read aloud to my dismay:
Valerius and Theophrastus
(Both hated women and harassed us);
Another clerk of ancient Rome,
That cardinal now called Saint Jerome,
Who wrote a tract against Jovinian;
Crisippus and Tertulian;
Trotula, too; and Heloise
(Yes, she affronted Church decrees);
The Parables of Solomon;
And Ovid's *Art*— no more, I'm done.
All these were bound in one great book,
And all the time he could he took,
Each time he had the least vacation
From other worldly occupation,
To read to me of wicked wives.
For he knew more bad women's lives
Than there are names in Holy Writ.
No clerk will willingly admit
That any good is found in wives,
Except in some saints' pious lives.
They slander us. You know they do.
Who paints the lion, tell me, who?
By God, if women wrote these tales,
As clerks do, or some other males,
We'd hear more of men's wickedness
Than all their gender could redress.
Scholars are ruled by Mercury.
That god and Venus don't agree.
He favors scholarship and reason.
She loves excess in any season.
That's why his star sign hovers low
When hers puts on its greatest show.
Thus Mercury is on the lees

When Venus rules the sky in Pisces,
And Venus falls as he is raised,
And women leave most clerks unfazed.
When clerks are old and cannot do
Dame Venus' labor worth a shoe,
They all endeavor to disparage
The female sex along with marriage.
   But, as I said, it was my luck
To lose my hearing for a book!
Once Jenkin sat beside his fire
Reading like a country squire,
Of Eve, who for her appetite
Caused all of us to share the blight
For which the Son of God was slain
And bought us with his blood again.
Of course, it was a she who thus
Loosed sin and death on all of us. . . .
   Concerning later wives, he read
How some had killed their men in bed
And frolicked with a paramour,
Their husbands dead upon the floor.
Some drove nails through their men's brains
And watched the blood drip from their veins,
Or else put poison in their drink.
He spoke more harm than you can think. . . .
How my rage grew with each new libel.
   I saw he'd never quit his bible,
His bale of lies, his book of sages,
So I reached out and snatched three pages
Clean from the book, beneath his nose.
I hit him too, you may suppose,
So he fell backward in the fire.
Up he jumped—his rage was dire—
And punched me roundly in the head.
Lord! I collapsed and acted dead.
Now when he saw how still I lay,
He made as if to run away,
But I began to stir instead.
"You've killed me now, false thief," I said,
"Robbed and murdered, what a crime!
But come and kiss me one last time."
   He ventured near and knelt beside me,
And said, "No matter what betides me,
I'll never buffet you again.
You pushed till I was half insane.
Forgive me, dear, that's all I seek."
By God, I clubbed him on the cheek!

And said, "There, thief, accept your pay!
I'm dead. I have no more to say."
But, still, at length with care and tact
We found our roles and made a pact.
He put the bridle in my hand,
The government of house and land,
And of his tongue and his behavior.
We burnt his book, as God's my savior.
And when I gathered in to me
All the rule and sovereignty,
And when he said, "My own true wife,
Do as you will throughout your life:
Preserve your name and my possessions"—
We had no more head-knocking sessions.
As God's my hope, I was as kind
As any wife you'll ever find,
And true to him, and he to me.
I pray great God in majesty
May bathe his soul in heaven's glory.
And now, sirs, I will tell my story.

The Wife of Bath's Tale

Once in good King Arthur's days,
Which Britons now revere and praise,
Fairies filled our pleasant land.
The elf-queen and her gay command
Danced on many a vernal mead—
Or most men think they did, indeed—
Many hundred years ago.
But now they're gone, as all men know. . . .
   This Arthur I alluded to
Retained a lusty bachelor
Who went one day along a shore
And happened, riding on his own,
To meet a maid, like him, alone.
He threw her down, with little said,
And robbed her of her maidenhead.
This villain's work raised such a pother
That soon it reached the court and Arthur,
Who damned the boorish knight to die.
His head must roll—nowhere to fly!
Perhaps that's what the statutes said.
The queen had other plans instead
And asked her husband for the knight,
To punish him as she thought right.
The courteous king gave up the man

To live or die at her command.
She thanked the king for what he gave,
Then pondered how to treat the knave.
"See here," she told him, "how your tricks,
Have put you in this wretched fix.
Your life is forfeit, sir; it's mine.
I send you on a quest to find
What one thing women most desire.
Fail me, and your fate is dire.
I won't demand your answer now.
No, I'll have mercy and allow
The coming year for you to try
To find the single best reply.
Come swear to this, and vow to be
Back here in time to answer me."
  The man was in a sorry plight.
His queen was well within her right.
He had no reason to protest,
And so he undertook the quest.
He prayed that God would save his neck,
But feared he'd have a pointless trek.
  He left the court and took his way
In hope someone he met might say
What every woman most preferred.
But nothing that he ever heard
Convinced him that his trial was passed.
Each one he asked belied the last.
Some said that women lived for wealth.
Some said honor; some said health.
Some lust in bed; some, clothes and goods;
Some said frequent widowhoods.
Some said that our hearts are eased
When we are humored, praised, and pleased.
That's close to true, it seems to me,
For women thrive on flattery.
A sycophant who comes on call
Delights most women, great or small.
Some said we never rest until
We're free to do just as we will,
And no man dares dispraise our habits,
But says we live like pious abbots.
That covers most of us indeed,
For when men pay unseemly heed
To our shortcomings, we will bite.
Try if you will. You'll find I'm right.
For be what women may within,
We won't admit the smallest sin.

Still others said our favorite treat
Is being held to be discreet,
Trustworthy in affairs as well,
Aware of things we'll never tell.
Sirs, that thought's hardly worth a flea.
No woman honors privacy. . . .
Back now to our oafish knight.
For all his wandering day and night,
He couldn't find what women wanted.
Conflicting answers had him daunted.
He must go home; the time was nigh.
The queen awaited his reply.
But on the way he chanced to ride
Beside a forest where he spied
About two dozen lovely maids
Dancing in the woodland glades.
He made toward the girls to ask
If they could help him with his task.
But when they saw him riding there,
They vanished lightly into air,
And on the green, sirs, by my life,
There sat an ancient, loathsome wife.
A fouler sight you'll never see.
She scrambled up beside his knee
And cackled, "Sir, there's no path here.
But what explains your sorry cheer?
Tell me, young man, what you need.
Old heads like mine are wise indeed."
"Dearest mother," said the knight,
"I have to learn before tonight
What women want. I need advice.
If you can say, just name your price."
"Ah, that I could," she said, "but shan't
Unless you swear to me you'll grant
The next request I send your way,
And you will hear it, lad, today."
"Done, mother," said the knight, "I swear."
"Then," she said, "You're in my care.
Your life is safe, as you will see.
The queen herself must side with me.
The proudest wife who wears a gown
Cannot deny my answer's sound.
They can't dispute what I will say.
Let's go and face the court today.
She whispered something in his ear,
And said, "That's all it is, my dear."
They rode to court, not far away,

The knight relieved to keep his day.
He had his answer pat, he said.
Full many a wife and many a maid,
Full many a widow (for they're wise)
Sat with the queen in her assize.
They gathered there for his response,
While he affected nonchalance.
   It soon grew quiet in the court.
The knight stood by with his retort—
The thing that women love the best—
Observing silence like the rest.
The high queen beckoned, and he spoke,
Standing stoutly, like an oak.
   "My lady, most of all," said he,
"You women value sovereignty:
To rule your husband or your love
To do your will. By God above,
That's your wish, although you kill me.
I'm at your mercy, as you see."
In all the court, no wife or maid
Could disapprove of what he said.
They all agreed he'd won his life,
And on that cue up spoke the wife
Whom he had met upon the green.
"Mercy," she said, "My lady! Queen!
Before you leave, grant me my right.
I taught that answer to this knight,
And in return at my behest
He said he'd grant my next request.
He vowed to do it if he could.
And now, sir, make your promise good:
Take me to you as your wife.
For as you know, I saved your life.
Is that not so? What do you say?"
   But all he said was "Welladay!
I know as well as you I promised,
But, for God's love, change your request.
Take all my goods, but let me go!"
   "I won't," she said, "by Scorpio,
For though I'm old and foul and poor,
Not for all the gold and ore
Beneath the earth or here above
Will I forbear to be your love."
   "My love!" he said. "No, my damnation!
No other man of my relations
Has ever tasted such disgrace!"
But nothing worked. This was his case:

He was well caught; now he must wed
And take that old wife to his bed.
Well, some might think it mean of me
That I neglect, as you will see,
To tell the joy and rich array
That dignified their feast that day.
But here's my answer, short and plain:
There was no joy that day, just pain
And heaviness and gnawing sorrow.
They wed in secret on the morrow.
The knight hid all day like an owl.
His life was ruined. She was so foul.
Still greater woe welled in his head
That night when she was in his bed.
He writhed and wallowed to and fro.
His wife lay sweetly smiling though,
And said, "Now, benedicity,
Is this the way a knight should be?
Is this the law of Arthur's house?
Are his knights so fastidious?
I am your own, your loving wife,
The lady, sir, who saved your life.
I'm sure I never did you wrong.
So, sweetheart, why hold back so long?
You're like a man who's lost his wit.
If I'm to blame, why, out with it,
And I'll amend things right away."
"Amend?" he said, "and how, I pray?
By God, I'll never be consoled,
You are so loathly and so old!
You're low born, too. No family.
What else could you expect from me?
The heart will burst within my breast!"
"And this," she said, "prompts your unrest?"
"It does," he said, "and so it should."
"Well," she said, "my dear, I could
Correct all this within three days
If you adopted kinder ways.
"But do you think that gentleness
Is just old money, more or less,
And that's what makes you gentlemen?
Bah! That conceit's not worth a hen!
The virtuous man who works each day,
In town, alone, in every way,
To do what gentle deeds he can,
Sir, he's the world's true gentleman.
A Christian's goodness comes from Christ,

And not rich elders, duly priced.
Though they may leave their wealth and fees,
And old, deep-rooted family trees,
They can't pass on their virtuous lives,
The reason that their fame survives,
And their true value, if we know it.
"Just listen to the princely poet,
Dante, who has this to say,
At least his thinking runs this way:
'Men seldom rise by human virtue;
Success falls under God's purview.
To him we owe our gentleness.
And all true men will say no less.'
Goods, sir, are all that we inherit,
And goods may work against our merit.
"You shouldn't have to learn from me
If virtue flourished naturally
In families, right down the line,
You'd never see a large decline
From goodness and true gentleness.
Each child would match his parents' best. . . .
"True gentleness is not a guise,
Nor does it come with wealth and lands;
Rich men may shirk its stern demands.
It's not a fire that always burns.
No, every generation learns
A lord's son may do villainy.
A man who claims nobility
Because he's from a noble house,
Whose forebears honored all their vows,
And yet won't do a gentle deed
Or pay his own best models heed,
Why, he's not gentle, duke or earl—
He's just a rich but common churl.
Think of this: the glowing fame
Of your august and ancient name,
Owes not a blessed thing to you.
Now, God may make you gentle too,
But that rides on his will and grace.
It's not a perquisite of place. . . .
"You charge me next with poverty.
Well, Christ, who ransomed you and me,
Chose to live among the poor;
And every Christian heretofore
Has known that Jesus, Heaven's king,
Would hardly choose a vicious thing. . . .
Poverty can be the prod

That makes man know himself and God.
Then too it is a looking glass
Through which you see false friends, alas.
You're right. I'm poor. That much is true.
But, sir, I'm quite as good as you.
"Then too, you jeer because I'm old.
The soundest books and thinkers hold
That old age should be reverenced—
Certainly not gibed against.
Old folks deserve one's veneration.
This holds for every time or nation.
"You say I'm foul. My lord, that's true.
Why then, don't fear I'll cuckold you,
For wrinkles and senility
Are sovereign guards to chastity.
Yet I'll take pity on your plight
And cater to your appetite.
"Sir, you may have me as you please:
Foul and old at all degrees,
But yet a true and humble wife,
A trusted stay throughout your life;
Or young and fair and doubtless wild,
So you must fear you'll be beguiled,
And likely will be when I roam
Or when you think I'm safe at home.
Now which arrangement suits you best?"
The knight looked harried and oppressed.
Consternation made him say:
"You tell me, lady; I'll obey.
I'll gladly follow your direction.
Choose yourself upon reflection
What's advantageous for us both.
I won't object, upon my oath.
What you think best will do for me."
"Ah," she said, "full mastery!
I hold the reins, no second guessing?"
"Indeed," he said, "and with my blessing."
"Kiss me," she said, "and don't be loath,
For from today I will be both—
That is to say, both good and fair.
For may I die in black despair
If I don't stay as good and true
As any wife you ever knew.
And if I'm not as fair of feature
This selfsame night as any creature
Between the farthest east and west,
Why, kill me, dear, at my behest.

Draw the curtain, now, and see."
He looked at her, and verily
She was so young and beauteous,
He clasped her in a glad caress.
He seemed to hear the heavens chime,
He kissed her face a thousand times,
And she complied with every measure
That might increase his joy and pleasure.
They lived in joy throughout their lives.
Now, sirs, may Jesus send all wives
Meek husbands who are fresh in bed
And strength to rule them when we wed.
And may Our Lord cut off men's lives
Who won't be governed by their wives.
And old and angry married skinflints . . .
God curse them all with boils and squints!

Heere endeth the Wyves Tale of Bathe.

Margery Kempe (c.1373–aft.1439)

The Book of Margery Kempe

Margery Kempe lived in a time when the mystical impulses in Christianity were particularly strong in England, energized by the accounts of visions and meditations of hermits and anchorites writing in Middle English. Margery was first remembered, in fact, because in the early sixteenth century passages from the book she wrote were published as the Treatyse of Contemplacyon, *in an edition of 500 copies. Only one of these printed copies survived and, where Margery was known at all, it was as an English mystic. In 1934 a scholar was shown a manuscript in a private collection and she recognized it as the original source for the published passages in the* Treatyse. *She saw also that Margery had written something entirely other than a mystical handbook: she had in fact written the first autobiography in English.*

This book is remarkable partly because Margery Kempe was not an aristocrat, but a thoroughly middle-class woman, and illiterate to boot. The daughter of John Burnham, sometime mayor of Lynn in Norfolk, she married John Kempe of Lynn when she was about twenty years old and had fourteen children. During this same time she also started several businesses, all enterprises that failed. When she was about thirty-five, she had a visionary experience that seemed to her to be calling her to a new kind of life. Finally, after a five-year struggle, she persuaded her husband to give up sexual relations so that she could live chastely within her marriage. Then, when she was about forty, she began a series of pilgrimages to holy sites, and these travels to York, Canterbury, London, Rome, Jerusalem, Santiago de Compostela, Germany, and Norway form the basis of her narrative.

These journeys were punctuated by Margery's very public episodes of praying, crying, and shouting, to the evident embarrassment and annoyance of those around her. Because she sensed this hostility, she sought vindication for her calling from religious authorities. In the nearby city of Norwich, for instance, she visited the famous Julian of Norwich, author of Revelations of Divine Love, *seeking authentication of her own visionary experience (much as Hildegard of Bingen and Elisabeth of Schönau did in earlier selections in this collection). Sometimes the hostility toward her felt by male authorities became dangerous,*

These selections from Margery Kempe's *Book* are translated for this collection by the editor. Where possible the flavor of the idiosyncratic Middle English is kept, while spelling and punctuation are modernized and archaic words transformed into modern idiom.

as when she was arrested and charged with Lollardy, the crime of following the heretical beliefs of Oxford theologian and reformer John Wyclif. Sometime during these years, a scribe began writing down Margery's dictated account of her life and journeys, which she tells in the third person, calling herself "this creature." When the scribe died, Margery enlisted a priest to revise the completed portion (89 chapters) and add ten additional chapters about the journeys to Germany and Norway. We don't know when or how Margery Kempe died; the last record of her dates from 1439 in Lynn.

[The birth of her first child, her first vision, and her failure at business]

1. When this creature was twenty years of age and somewhat more, she was married to a worshipful burgess and was with child within a short time, as nature would have it. And after she had conceived she was labored with great attacks of sickness till the child was born, and then, because of the labor she had in childing and because of the sickness going before, she despaired of her life, believing she might not live. And then she sent for her priest, for she had a thing in her conscience which she had never showed before that time in all her life. For she was ever hindered by her enemy, the Devil, evermore saying to her while she was in good health she needed no confession but to do penance by herself alone, and all should be forgiven, for God is merciful enough. And therefore this creature often did great penance in fasting bread and water and other deeds of alms with devout prayers, except that she would not show it in confession. And when she was at any time sick or diseased, the Devil said in her mind that she should be damned for she was not pardoned for that fault. Wherefore after her child was born she, not trusting her life, sent for her priest, as was said before, in full will to be pardoned for all her lifetime as near as she could. And, when she came to the point for to say that thing which she had so long concealed, her confessor was a little too hasty and began sharply to reprove her before she had fully said her intent, and so she would not say more for anything he might do.

And anon for the dread she had of damnation on the one side and his sharp reproving on the other side, this creature went out of her mind and was awfully vexed and labored with spirits for a half year eight weeks and odd days. And in this time she saw, as she thought, devils open their mouths all inflamed with burning flames of fire as they should've swallowed her in, sometime ramping at her, sometime threatening her, sometime pulling her and hauling her both night and day during the foresaid time. And also the devils cried upon her with great threats and bade her that she should forsake her Christendom, her faith, and deny her God, his Mother, and all the saints in Heaven, her good works and all good virtues, her father, her mother, and all her friends. And so she did. She slandered her husband, her friends, and her own self; she spoke many a reproving word and many an ill-tempered word; she knew no virtue nor goodness; she desired all wickedness; just as the spirits tempted her to say and do so she said and did. She would've killed herself many a time at their stirrings and been damned with them in Hell. And in witness thereof she bit her own hand so violently that it was seen all her life after. And also she tore the skin on her body near her heart with her nails grievously, for she had no other instruments, and worse she would've done except that she was bound and kept with strength both day and night so that she might not have her will.

And when she had long been labored in this and many other temptations so that men thought she should never've escaped or lived, then one time as she lay alone and her keepers were away from her, our merciful Lord Christ Jesu, ever to be trusted (worshiped be his name), never forsaking his servant in time of need, appeared to his creature, which had forsaken him, in the likeness of a man, most seemly, most beauteous, and most amiable that ever might be seen with man's eye, clad in a mantle of purple silk, sitting upon her bed's side, looking upon her with so blessed a cheer that she was strengthened in all her spirits, said to her these words: "Daughter, why hast thou forsaken me, and I forsook never thee?" And anon as he had said these words she saw truly how the air opened as bright as any lightning, and he rose up into the air, not right hastily and quickly, but fair and easily so that she might well behold him in the air till it was closed again.

And anon the creature was settled in her wits and in her reason as well as ever she was before, and prayed her husband as soon as he came to her that she might have the keys of the buttery to take her meat and drink as she had done before. Her maids and her keepers counseled him that he should deliver no keys to her, for they said she would only give away such goods as there were, for she knew not what she said, as they thought. Nevertheless, her husband, ever having tenderness and compassion for her, commanded that they should deliver to her the keys. And she took her meat and drink as her bodily strength would serve her, and she knew her friends and her servants and all others that came to her to see how our Lord Jesu Christ had worked his grace in her, so blessed must he be who is ever near in tribulation. When men think he is far from them, he is full near by his grace. Since then this creature did all other occupations as befell for her to do wisely and seriously enough, except that she knew not truly the ecstasy of our Lord.

2. And when this creature was thus graciously come again to her mind, she thought she was bound to God and that she would be his servant. Nevertheless, she would not leave her pride nor the pompous array that she had worn before, neither for her husband's nor for any other man's counsel. And yet she knew full well that men said of her great villainy, for she wore gold pipes on her head [a fashionable headdress] and her hoods with the tippets were dagged [decorated with points and cuts]. Her cloaks also were dagged and laid with various colors between the dags so that it should be the more conspicuous to men's sight and she herself the more worshiped. And when her husband would urge her to leave her pride she answered shrewdly and shortly and said that she came from worthy kindred—he did not seem the type to've wedded her—for her father was sometime mayor of the town N and afterward he was alderman of the high Guild of the Trinity [a parish fraternity] in N. And therefore she would preserve the honor of her kindred whatever any man said. She was greatly envious of her neighbors that they should be arrayed as well as she. All her desire was to be worshiped by the people. She would not be wary of anyone's chastening nor be content with the goods that God had sent her, as her husband was, but ever desired more and more.

And then, out of pure covetousness and to maintain her pride, she began to brew and was one of the greatest brewers in the town N for three years or four till she lost many goods, for she had no experience with it. For though she had never such good servants and cunning in brewing, yet it would never be successful with them. For when the ale was as fair standing under barm [the yeast] as any man might see, suddenly the barm would fall down so that all the ale was lost every brewing after the other, so that her servants were ashamed and would not dwell with her. Then this creature remembered how God had punished her before and she could not be wary, and now again by losing her goods, and so she left and brewed no more. And then she asked for her husband's mercy because she would not follow his counsel before, and she said that her pride was the cause of all her punishing and she would amend what she had done wrong with good will. . . .

[Margery and Her Husband Reach a Settlement]

11. It befell on a Friday on Midsummer Eve in right hot weather, as this creature was coming from the direction of York bearing a bottle of beer in her hand and her husband a cake in his bosom, he asked his wife this question: "Margery, if there came a man with a sword and he would smite off my head unless I should commune naturally [i.e. have sexual intercourse] with you as I have done before, say me truth of your conscience—for you say you will not lie—whether you would allow my head to be smitten off or else suffer me to meddle [i.e. have sexual intercourse] with you again as I did sometime?" "Alas, sir," she said, "why do you bring this matter up and have we been chaste this eight weeks?" "Because I want to know the truth of your heart." And then she said with great sorrow, "In truth, I would rather see you slain than that we should turn again to our uncleanness." And he said again, "You are no good wife."

And then she asked her husband why he had not meddled with her for eight weeks before, since she lay with him every night in his bed. And he said he was made so afraid when he would've touched her that he dared no more do it. "Now, good sir, amend you and ask God's mercy, for I told you nearly three years ago that you should be slain suddenly, and now this is the third year, and yet I hope I shall have my desire. Good sir, I pray you grant me what I shall ask, and I shall pray for you that you shall be saved through the mercy of our Lord Jesu Christ, and you shall have more reward in Heaven than if you wore a hair shirt or a mail jacket [next to your skin]. I pray you, allow me to make a vow of chastity in whatever bishop's hand that God chooses." "Nay," he said, "that will I not grant you, for now I may use you without deadly sin but then I might not do so." Then she said again, "If it be the will of the Holy Ghost to fulfill what I have said, I pray God you might consent to it; and if it be not the will of the Holy Ghost, I pray God you never consent to it."

Then they went forth toward Bridlington in right hot weather, the foresaid creature having great sorrow and great dread for her chastity. And as they came by a cross, her husband set him down under the cross, calling his wife to him and saying these words to her, "Margery, grant me my desire, and I shall grant you your desire. My first desire is that we shall still lie together in one bed as we have done before; the second that you shall pay my debts before you go to Jerusalem; and the third that you shall eat and drink with me on Fridays as you used to do." "Nay sir," she said, "to break the Friday fast I will never grant you while I live." "Well, he said, "then shall I meddle with you again."

She prayed him that he would give her leave to make her prayers, and he granted it well. Then she knelt down beside a cross in the field and prayed in this manner with great abundance of tears, "Lord God, thou knowest all things; thou knowest what sorrow I have had to be chaste in my body for thee all these three years, and now might I have my will but I dare not for love of thee. For if I would break that manner of fasting which thou commandest me to keep on Fridays without meat or drink, I should now have my desire. But, blessed Lord, thou knowest I will not act contrary to thy will, and much now is my sorrow unless I find comfort in thee. Now, blessed Jesu, make thy will known to me, unworthy, that I may follow thereafter and fulfil it with all my might." And then our Lord Jesu Christ with great sweetness spoke to this creature, commanding her to go again to her husband and pray him to grant her what she desired, "And he shall have what he desireth. For, my dear worthy daughter, this was the reason that I bade thee fast so thou shouldest the sooner obtain and get thy desire, and now it is granted thee. I will no longer thou fast, therefore I bid thee in the name of Jesu eat and drink as thy husband doth."

Then this creature thanked our Lord Jesu Christ of his grace and his goodness, afterward rose up and went to her husband saying unto him, "Sir, if it please you, you shall grant me my desire and you shall have your desire. Grant me that you shall not come into my bed, and I grant you to repay your debts before I go to Jerusalem. And make my body free to God so that you never make no challenge to me to ask no marriage debt after this day while you live, and I shall eat and drink on Fridays at your bidding." Then said her husband again to her, "As free may your body be to God as it has been to me." This creature thanked God greatly, joyful that she had her desire, praying her husband that they should say three Our Fathers in the worship of the Trinity for the great grace that he had granted them. And so they did, kneeling under a cross, and afterward they ate and drank together in great gladness of spirit. This was on a Friday on Midsummer Eve.

[Pilgrimage to Jerusalem]

28. . . . And so they went forth into the Holy Land until they could see Jerusalem. And when this creature saw Jerusalem, riding on an ass, she thanked God with all her heart, praying him for his mercy that just as he had brought her to see this earthly city Jerusalem, he would grant her grace to see the blissful city Jerusalem above, the city of Heaven. Our Lord Jesu Christ, answering her thought, granted her to have her desire. Then for the joy that she had and the sweetness that she felt in the dalliance of our Lord, she was at the point of falling off her ass, for she could not bear the sweetness and grace that God wrought in her soul. Two German pilgrims went to her and kept her from falling, of which one was a priest. And he put spices in her mouth to comfort her, thinking she had been sick. And so they helped her forth to Jerusalem. And when she arrived there, she said, "Sirs, I pray you be not displeased though I weep sore in this holy place where our Lord Jesu Christ was alive and dead."

Then they went to the Temple in Jerusalem, and they were let in one day at evensong time and they remained there until the next day at evensong time. Then the friars lifted up a cross and led the pilgrims about from one place to another where our Lord had suffered his pains and his passions, every man and woman bearing a wax candle in their hand. And the friars always as they went about told them what our Lord had suffered in every place. And the foresaid creature wept and sobbed as plenteously as if she had seen our Lord with her bodily eye suffering his Passion at that time. Before her in her soul she saw him truly by contemplation, and that caused her to have compassion. And when they came up onto the Mount of Calvary she fell down so that she might not stand nor kneel, but wallowed and wrested with her body, spreading her arms abroad, and cried with a loud voice as though her heart should've burst asunder, for in the city of her soul she saw truly and freshly how our Lord was crucified. Before her face she heard and saw in her ghostly sight the mourning of our Lady, of St. John and of Mary Magdalene, and of many others who loved our Lord. And she had such great compassion and such great pain to see our Lord's pain that she could not keep herself from crying and roaring, even if she would've died because of it.

And this was the first cry that ever she cried in any contemplation. And this manner of crying endured many years after this time for aught that any man might do, and therefore she suffered much scorn and much reproof. The crying was so loud and so wonderful that it made people astonished unless they had heard it before or else they knew the cause of the crying. And she had them so often that they made her right weak in her bodily strength, and especially if she heard of our Lord's Passion. And sometime when she saw the Crucifix, or if she saw that a man had a wound or a beast, whichever it were, or if a man beat a child in front of her or struck a horse or another beast with a whip, if she either saw it or heard it, she thought she saw our Lord being beaten or wounded just as she saw in the man or in the beast, as well in the field as in the town, and by herself alone as well as among the people. First when she had her cryings at Jerusalem, she had them often, and in Rome also. And when she came home into England, at first it happened but seldom, as it were once in a month, then once in a week, afterward daily, and once she had fourteen in one day, and another day she had seven, and so as God would visit her, sometime in the church, sometime in the street, sometime in the chamber, sometime in the field when God would send them, for she never knew the time nor the hour when they should come. And they never came without great sweetness of devotion and high contemplation. And as soon as she perceived that she would cry, she would keep it in as much as she might so that people should not've heard it for annoying of them. For some said it was a wicked spirit that vexed her; some said it was a sickness; some said she had drunk too much wine; some cursed her; some wished she had been in the harbor; some wished she had been in the sea in a bottomless boat; and so each man as he thought. Other ghostly men loved her and favored her all the more. Some great clerks said that even our Lady never cried so, nor no saint in Heaven, but they knew full little what she felt, nor would they not believe but that she might've abstained from crying if she had wanted to.

[Examination before Henry Bowet, the Archbishop of York]

52. . . . On the next day she was brought into the Archbishop's chapel, and there came many of the Archbishop's servants, despising her, calling her "Lollard" and "heretic," and swearing many a horrible oath that she should be burnt. And she, through the strength of Jesu, said again to them, "Sirs, I fear you shall be burnt in hell without end unless you correct your oath-swearing, for you keep not the commandments of God. I would not swear as you do for all the goods in this world." Then they went away as if they were ashamed. She then, making her prayer in her mind, asked grace so to conduct herself that day as was most pleasing to God and profitable to her own soul and a good example to her fellow Christians. Our Lord, answering her, said it should be right well.

At last the said Archbishop came into the chapel with his clerks, and sharply he said to her, "Why do you wear white? Are you a maiden?" She, kneeling on her knees before him, said, "Nay, sir, I am no maiden; I am a wife." He commanded his servants to fetch a pair of fetters and said she should be fettered, for she was a false heretic. And then she said, "I am no heretic, nor shall you prove me one." The Archbishop went away and left her standing alone. Then she made her prayers to our Lord God Almighty to help her and comfort her against all her enemies, ghostly and bodily, for a long while, and her flesh trembled and quaked awfully so that she wanted to put her hands under her clothes so that it might not be seen. Afterward the Archbishop took his seat, and his clerks also, each of them in his degree, many people being present. And in the time that the people were gathering together and the Archbishop taking his seat, the said creature stood all behind, making her prayers for help and comfort against her enemies with high devotion so long that she melted all into tears. And at the last she cried loudly, so that the Archbishop and his clerks and many people were greatly surprised at her, for they had not heard such crying before.

When her crying had passed, she came before the Archbishop and fell down on her knees, the Archbishop saying full roughly to her, "Why do you weep so, woman?" She, answering, said, "Sir, you shall wish someday that you had wept as much as I." And then anon, after the Archbishop put to her the Articles of Faith, to which God gave her grace to answer well and truly and readily without any great study so that he might not blame her, then he said to the clerks, "She knows her faith well enough. What shall I do with her?" The clerks said, "We know well that she knows the Articles of Faith, but we will not suffer her to dwell among us, for the people have great faith in her dalliance, and perhaps she might pervert some of them." Then the Archbishop said to her, "I am told bad things about you; I hear tell that you are a right wicked woman." And she said again, "Sir, so I hear said that you are a wicked man. And if you are as wicked as men say, you shall never come to heaven unless you mend your ways while you are here." Then he said full roughly, "Why, you, what do men say of me?" She answered, "Other men, sir, can tell you well enough." Then said a great clerk with a fur hood, "Peace, you speak of yourself and let him be."

Afterward the Archbishop said to her, "Lay your hand on the book here before me and swear that you shall go out of my diocese as soon as you may." "Nay, sir," she said, "I pray you, give me leave to go again into York to take my leave of my friends." Then he gave her leave for one day or two. . . . Then the Archbishop said to her, "You shall swear that you shall not teach nor challenge the people in my diocese." "Nay, sir, I shall not swear," she said, "for I shall speak of God and reprove them that swear great oaths wherever I go until the time that the pope and holy church ordain that no man shall be so hardy as to speak of God, for God Almighty forbids not, sir, that we shall speak of him. And also the gospel makes mention that, when the woman had heard our Lord preach, she came before him with a loud voice and said, 'Blessed be the womb that bore you and the tits that gave you suck.' Then our Lord said again to her, 'Indeed so are they blessed that hear the word of God and keep it.' And therefore, sir, it seems to me that the gospel gives me leave to speak of God." "Ah sir," said the clerks, "here we know well that she has a devil within her, for she speaks of the gospel." Immediately a great clerk brought forth a book and laid Saint Paul for his part against her that no woman should preach [1 Corinthians 14:34–35]. She, answering that, said, "I preach not, sir, I come in no pulpit. I use only communication and good words, and that will I do while I live." . . .

And then afterward the Archbishop said, "Where shall I get a man who might lead this woman away from me?" . . . Then a good sober man of the Archbishop's household asked his lord what he would give him if he should lead her. The Archbishop offered him five shillings and the man asked for a noble. The Archbishop, answering, said, "I will not spend so much on her body." "Yes, good sir," said the said creature, "our Lord shall reward you right well again." Then the Archbishop said to the man, "See, here is five shillings, and lead her fast out of this country."